# TRIAL ADVOCACY

ASPEN COURSEBOOK SERIES

# TRIAL ADVOCACY
## Planning, Analysis, and Strategy

**Fourth Edition**

MARILYN J. BERGER
*Professor Emeritus of Law*
*Seattle University School of Law*

JOHN B. MITCHELL
*Professor of Law*
*Seattle University School of Law*

RONALD H. CLARK
*Distinguished Practitioner in Residence*
*Seattle University School of Law*

Wolters Kluwer
Law & Business

To contact Customer Service, e-mail customer.service@wolterskluwer.com, call
1-800-234-1660, fax 1-800-901-9075, or mail correspondence to:
Wolters Kluwer Law & Business
Attn: Order Department
PO Box 990
Frederick, MD 21705

Printed in the United States of America.
5 6 7 8 9 0
ISBN 978-1-4548-4153-1

**Library of Congress Cataloging-in-Publication Data**
Berger, Marilyn J., author.
Trial advocacy : planning, analysis, and strategy / Marilyn J. Berger, Professor Emeritus
of Law, Seattle University School of Law; John B. Mitchell, Professor of Law, Seattle
University School of Law; Ronald H. Clark, Distinguished Practitioner in Residence,
Seattle University School of Law. — Fourth Edition.
    pages cm. — (Aspen coursebook series)
Includes bibliographical references and index.
ISBN 978-1-4548-4153-1 (alk. paper)
1. Trial practice—United States. I. Mitchell, John B. (John Barry), 1944- author.
II. Clark, Ronald H., author. III. Title.
KF8915.B45 2015
347.73'7—dc23

                                                                    2014021676

# About Wolters Kluwer Law & Business

Wolters Kluwer Law & Business is a leading global provider of intelligent information and digital solutions for legal and business professionals in key specialty areas, and respected educational resources for professors and law students. Wolters Kluwer Law & Business connects legal and business professionals as well as those in the education market with timely, specialized authoritative content and information-enabled solutions to support success through productivity, accuracy and mobility.

Serving customers worldwide, Wolters Kluwer Law & Business products include those under the Aspen Publishers, CCH, Kluwer Law International, Loislaw, ftwilliam.com and MediRegs family of products.

**CCH** products have been a trusted resource since 1913, and are highly regarded resources for legal, securities, antitrust and trade regulation, government contracting, banking, pension, payroll, employment and labor, and healthcare reimbursement and compliance professionals.

**Aspen Publishers** products provide essential information to attorneys, business professionals and law students. Written by preeminent authorities, the product line offers analytical and practical information in a range of specialty practice areas from securities law and intellectual property to mergers and acquisitions and pension/benefits. Aspen's trusted legal education resources provide professors and students with high-quality, up-to-date and effective resources for successful instruction and study in all areas of the law.

**Kluwer Law International** products provide the global business community with reliable international legal information in English. Legal practitioners, corporate counsel and business executives around the world rely on Kluwer Law journals, looseleafs, books, and electronic products for comprehensive information in many areas of international legal practice.

**Loislaw** is a comprehensive online legal research product providing legal content to law firm practitioners of various specializations. Loislaw provides attorneys with the ability to quickly and efficiently find the necessary legal information they need, when and where they need it, by facilitating access to primary law as well as state-specific law, records, forms and treatises.

**ftwilliam.com** offers employee benefits professionals the highest quality plan documents (retirement, welfare and non-qualified) and government forms (5500/PBGC, 1099 and IRS) software at highly competitive prices.

**MediRegs** products provide integrated health care compliance content and software solutions for professionals in healthcare, higher education and life sciences, including professionals in accounting, law and consulting.

Wolters Kluwer Law & Business, a division of Wolters Kluwer, is headquartered in New York. Wolters Kluwer is a market-leading global information services company focused on professionals.

This book is rededicated to our families.

To Albert J. and Dorian S.
—Marilyn J. Berger

To Eva, David, Sarah and Tyler.
—John B. Mitchell

To Nancy, Brady, Soojin, Malachi, Riley, Clancy, Kara,
Beatrice, Samuel, Colby, and Darren.
—Ronald H. Clark

And to Laurie Wells, our administrative assistant and a member of our extended family.

# Summary of Contents

# Contents

CHAPTER 4

# JURY SELECTION
## Two-Way Exchange

CHAPTER 5

# OPENING STATEMENT
## Storytelling

CHAPTER 10
# CROSS-EXAMINATION
## Concession Seeking

CHAPTER 11

# EXPERTS
## Yours and Theirs

Marilyn J. Berger, John B. Mitchell, and Ronald H. Clark

# Acknowledgments

The cover of this book indicates that it is the work of three authors. Yet there were truly so many other individuals—in so many capacities—who were essential to this book. Their combined contributions are visible to us on every page. We do more than thank them; we share credit with them for this work.

Charlotte Anderson, copy center coordinator and business office accounts auditor.
Authors of *The Appellate Prosecutor*.
Mimy Bailey, attorney at law.
William S. Bill Bailey, attorney.
Daniel Baker, attorney at law.
Dorian S. Berger, attorney.
Mike Bitando, general manager of the Garage billiards hall and bowling.
The Honorable Judge Timothy Bradshaw, King County Superior Court.
Brady Clark, professor of linguistics, Northwestern University.
Clancy Clark, M.D.
Colby Clark, graphics designer.
Nancy Clark, artist and editor.
Abra Conitz, law clerk, Seattle University School of Law, class of 2015.
Fred DeKay, adjunct professor of law, Seattle University School of Law.
Sean P. Dowell, law clerk, Seattle University School of Law, class of 2015.
Anne Enquist, associate director of legal writing, Seattle University School of Law.
The faculty of the University of Montana Law School's Advanced Trial Advocacy Program.
Justin Farmer, attorney at law.
Kerry Fitz-Gerald, associate librarian, Seattle University School of Law.
Tyler Fox, movie editor.
Steve Fury, attorney at law.
Captain Tag Gleason, Seattle Police Department, Violent Crimes Section.
Nancy Harrop, coordinator of secretarial support and legal assistant, Seattle University School of Law.
Monica Hartsock, attorney at law.
Daniel Jackson, and Carol Jackson, with Katie, Briana, Ryan, and Sean Jackson.
Sarah Johnson, attorney at law.
The Honorable Judge Ronald Kessler, King County Superior Court.
The Honorable Judge Robert S. Lasnik, Chief Judge, the United States District Court, Western District of Washington.
Law students at Seattle University School of Law.

Gretchen Ludwig, director of the Garage movie and the Freck Point trial movie, both on website.

The Honorable Judge Terrance Lukens, JAMS (Judicial Arbitration Mediation Services).

The Honorable Judge Dean Lum, King County Superior Court; adjunct professor of law, at Seattle University School of Law.

Jason MacLeod, DVD editor, Seattle University School of Law, class of 2012.

Deborah Maenhout, actor, the Freck Point trial movie.

Dr. Norman Mar, Ph.D.

Lisa Marchese, attorney at law.

Terry McAdam, Forensic Supervisor, Washington State crime laboratory and actor.

Hannalore B. Merritt.

Rebecca Miller, officer, Seattle Police Department, East Precinct.

Melissa (Missy) Mordy, attorney at law.

The Honorable Judge Dean Morgan.

Theodore Myhre, lecturer, University of Washington School of Law.

National College of District Attorneys faculty.

The Honorable Judge Jack Nevin, Pierce County Superior Court; adjunct professor of Law, Seattle University School of Law.

Laurel Oates, professor of law and director of legal writing, Seattle University School of Law.

Kyle C. Olive, attorney at law.

Rex Prout, assistant chief of enforcement and education, Washington State Liquor Control Board.

Ryan Rautio, attorney at law.

Kristin Richardson, senior deputy, King County Prosecutor's Office.

Ann Rule, true crime author.

Nora Santos, legal administrative assistant, Seattle University School of Law.

Vonda M. Sargent, attorney.

Richard Sherwin, professor of law and director, New York Law School's Visual Persuasion Project.

Craig Sims, Chief, Criminal Division, Seattle City Attorney's Office.

John Jay Syverson, photographer, OnPoint Productions, Seattle.

Travis Ronald Tillman, law clerk, Seattle University School of Law, class of 2010.

Melinda Tilton, Department of Communications and Theater, Montana State University, Billings.

The Honorable Judge Karen Townsend, Judge Missoula County District Court and Director of the University of Montana Law School's Advanced Trial Advocacy Program and the faculty of the Advanced Trial Advocacy Program.

Kyle Tretheway, attorney at law.

The Honorable Judge Michael Trickey, King County Superior Court.

Kirk Van Scoyoc, actor.

Justin Walsh, attorney at law.

Laurie Wells, legal administrative assistant, Seattle University School of Law.

The Honorable Matt Williams, King County Superior Court; adjunct professor of Law, Seattle University School of Law.

Ric Wyant, forensic scientist, Firearm/Toolmark Section, Crime Laboratory Division; firearms examiner for the Washington State Patrol Crime Laboratory.

A special thank you for the assistance we were provided at Seattle University School of Law: Dean Annette C. Clark, Associate Dean for Finance and Administration Richard Bird, Kristin Cheney, Associate Dean for Library and Educational Technology, Stephanie Zimmerman, Director of Instructional Technology, and J. Barratt Godfrey, multimedia specialist.

And finally, thanks to our friends and professional colleagues at Aspen Publishers: Carol McGeehan, Publisher; Steve Errick, former managing director; Dana Wilson, our managing editor, John Devins, former managing editor; Christine Hannan, Managing Editor; Carmen Corral-Reid, Assistant Editorial Director; Michael A. Gregory, Director of New Markets; and Lisa Wehrle, Manuscript Editor.

# TRIAL ADVOCACY

# CHAPTER 1

# THE TRIAL TOOLBOX
## The Book, the Case Files, Trial Movie, and Website

*"I'll always be a trial lawyer. No higher calling has come my way. I do not know when the next case will come or if I'll be able to resist."*

> —**Morris Dees** with **Steve Fiffer**, in *A Season for Justice: The Life and Times of Civil Rights Leader Morris Dees* (Scribner 1991)

*"They're certainly entitled to think that, and they're entitled to full respect for their opinions . . . but before I can live with other folks I've got to live with myself. The one thing that doesn't abide by majority rule is a person's conscience."*

> —**Atticus Finch**, in Harper Lee's *To Kill a Mockingbird,* 120 (40th ann. ed., HarperCollins Publishers 1999) (1960)

## I.  TRIAL ADVOCACY TODAY

The world of today's lawyer is inhabited by computer graphics, digitally stored documents, DNA leading to convictions and exonerations, cases turning on the contents of a supposedly deleted e-mail retrieved by an expert from a hard drive. In place of boxes of tabbed and magic-marker-highlighted documents, attorneys instantly access one of a thousand records indexed on the database of a laptop computer. Science, technology, and experts of all stripes fill today's courtrooms.

Frequently, cases are not being resolved in a courtroom in which opposing counsel sit nervously awaiting the decision of 12 citizens. Increasingly, cases are being arbitrated or mediated—often as a requirement of a prior written contractual agreement or as required by court rules or statutes. Many others are resolved as negotiated settlements. Pretrial litigation, including advocacy in an alternate dispute resolution situation and negotiation, are examined in depth in Berger, Mitchell, and Clark's *Pretrial Advocacy: Planning, Analysis, and Strategy, Fourth Edition.* However, many of the trial skills and strategies are applicable to alternative dispute resolution.

Today's lawyer must be fluent with technology for case organization and courtroom presentation, as well as with alternative forms of dispute resolution. But despite these new tools, trials and trial lawyers remain very much the same as they have throughout the history of the legal profession.

*Trial Advocacy: Planning, Analysis, and Strategy* provides you with the experience and approach to thinking, planning, and performing as a practicing lawyer. The book presents a wide range of practice situations and fosters the kinds of analytic processes and skills needed to perform trial work. On the accompanying website, detailed and realistic practice assignments replicate the trial lawyer's world.

This introduction to the book and website provides a basic understanding of how each tool is structured and intended to be used.

## II.  TRIAL ADVOCACY BOOK

*Trial Advocacy: Planning, Analysis, and Strategy, Fourth Edition,* is divided into 14 chapters. Each chapter covers a separate trial subject area—persuasion, jury selection, opening statement, objections, exhibits, direct examination, and so on. Each chapter presents a theoretical and practical approach to the particular skill that is the subject of that chapter, provides illustrations of practice as applied to hypothetical situations, and offers a series of practical and strategic pointers in the subject area. The illustrations that we provide are not meant to be exhaustive, but are intended to illustrate the point in question. Each chapter also comes with a checklist of skills dealt with in the chapter.

Where possible, the text also includes references to outside sources that may assist you.

## III.  ASSIGNMENTS AND CASE FILES: WEBSITE

*Assignments and Case Files:* Along with *Trial Advocacy: Planning, Analysis, and Strategy,* you receive 79 performance role-play assignments and case files that may be used for either professional development CLE sessions or a law school trial advocacy course. The performance assignments are based on a multifaceted fact pattern that manifests itself in two fictitious cases—a criminal case, *State v. Hard,* and a civil case, *Summers v. Hard.* You will find the assignments, case files, and a factual summary of the fact pattern for the case files on the website *http://www.aspenlawschool.com/books/berger_trialad4e.* Students, please contact your professor for the password to access the materials on the website. The case files contain the criminal and civil case files for, respectively, *State v. Hard* and *Summers v. Hard.* These materials include diagrams, documents, expert reports, jury instructions, pleadings, research memoranda, statutes, and witness statements. These materials are to be used to perform the role-play assignments.

The materials on the website allow you to print individual documents or the entire case file.

*The Actors' Guide:* To make the various role-playing simulations in the skills practice assignments as realistic as possible, the *Actors' Guide* (provided to your instructor) contains information for distribution to the role players. Background materials detailing the witness's personal history, the instructions for how the witness is to behave and respond, and information on an expert's field will be provided to the person playing the witness.

## IV.  TRIAL DEMONSTRATION AND CRIME SCENE
## MOVIES: WEBSITE

A trial demonstration movie accompanies this text. The movie presents experienced lawyers demonstrating trial advocacy skills in the *Freck Point* case, a hypothetical wrongful death case. The *Freck Point* case is inspired by real cases, including one that is the subject of a true crime thriller, *A Rose for Her Grave* (True Crime Files) by Ann Rule. These demonstrations provide you with the experience of seeing a trial conducted from beginning to end. Also on the website is a movie of a detective-guided crime-scene tour that takes you to the Garage tavern where the fictitious *State v. Hard* and *Summers v. Hard* cases all began. You may view the trial demonstration movie on the website *http://www .aspenlawschool.com/books/berger_trialad4e.*

3

## V. WEBSITE: CASE FILES, ASSIGNMENTS, AND SUPPLEMENTARY MATERIALS

The book's accompanying website, *http://www.aspenlawschool.com/books/berger_trialad4e,* besides containing the case files and advocacy skills practice assignments, displays an array of supplementary materials. These include chapters on trial motion practice, articles on pretrial and trial practice, exemplary pleadings, and links to other valuable websites.

# PERSUASION PRINCIPLES

"**Sincere** *(adj.) . . . without deceit, pretense or hypocrisy; truthful; straightforward; honest. . . .*"
— *Webster's New World College Dictionary,*
4th ed. (Merriam-Webster 2007)

*"Be sure of it; give me the ocular proof."*
—**William Shakespeare** (1564-1616),
in *Othello* (c. 1604)

## I.  PERSUASION PRINCIPLES

Advocacy work is communication. Experts in communication describe the communication process as having four components: message, messenger, media, and receiver. Translating this into a practice setting, the communication components are as follows.

- The *message* is the case theory and theme.
- The *messenger* is the lawyer who creates the case theory and theme for communicating.
- The *media* is how the message is transmitted (opening statement, witness testimony, exhibits, or trial visuals).
- The *receiver* is the jury or the judge.

In this chapter, we introduce you to three persuasion principles. These principles are also applicable to alternative dispute resolution (mediation, arbitration, and negotiation). These three principles are also expressed in communication process terms:

1. Developing a persuasive message,
2. Being a persuasive messenger, and
3. Making use of persuasive media.

While we provide you with an introduction to the persuasion principles here and in the next chapter, these principles permeate this book. In the next chapter, Case Theory and Theme Development, you will learn how to formulate the message that will compel the jury or judge to decide in your client's favor. In this chapter, you learn how to be a persuasive messenger—a convincing communicator in trial. Also in this chapter, we show you how, through persuasive media, you can create a dynamic presentation of your story, your argument, and yourself.

## II.  PERSUASIVE MESSENGER: THE LAWYER

What is the most important characteristic of a persuasive lawyer? Is it eloquence? Some of the most eloquent lawyers fail to connect with a jury because they speak over the jurors' heads by using technical or other unfamiliar words. Is it the lawyer who makes the most logical arguments? Most lawyers have had the experience of making what, in their view at least, was the most logical of all arguments on an issue, only to have the argument fail to convince the court or jury. Is it good looks that sway the jury? Some highly successful lawyers would never win an attractiveness contest.

The traits that above all else make a lawyer a great communicator are a sincere belief in the case and an ability to project sincerity. That is, counsel who can project a sincere belief in the cause for which the lawyer is advocating will be a persuasive communicator. While, under Rule of Professional Conduct 3.4, trial counsel may never express personal opinions about the credibility of witnesses or about the justness of a cause, no rule exists or ever would be fashioned to prohibit counsel from projecting sincerity to a jury.

A lawyer who projects sincerity is a person who conveys the impression to the jury that she is fully prepared, has examined the case from all sides, and communicates the facts and inferences firmly based on the evidence. A sincere lawyer is one whom jurors believe is a seeker of truth whom they can trust. A sincere lawyer is a person who would not mislead. To envision how you want to be perceived by the jurors and how to conduct yourself during trial, ask yourself: "What type of lawyer would I trust if I were on the jury, and how would that lawyer behave?"

Here is a nine-point checklist that contains tips to help you project sincerity to the jury. When you are preparing for trial or any other type of hearing, use this checklist as a refresher so that you will be a great communicator in trial.

---

### CHECKLIST

**Persuasive Messenger: Projecting Sincerity**

☐ 1. Be sincere.
☐ 2. Deliver on promises.
☐ 3. Admit weaknesses.
☐ 4. Be civil.
☐ 5. Be open.
☐ 6. Sell with plain language and integrity.
☐ 7. Be yourself.
☐ 8. Meet judicial expectations.
☐ 9. Maintain a good reputation.

---

## A. Projecting Sincerity: Nine Points

### 1. Be Sincere

Persuasion starts with you. To persuade, you must be persuaded. To project sincerity, you must be sincere. Conversely, if you do not believe in your case and what you are doing, your body and your voice will betray you no matter how you try to mask them. Allen and Barbara Pease state in their book, *The Definitive Book of Body Language* 27 (Bantam 2004), that you cannot fake body language:

The general answer to this question ("Can you fake body language?") is no, because of the lack of congruence that is likely to occur between the main gestures, the body's microsignals, and the spoken word. For example, open palms are associated with honesty, but when the faker holds his palms out and smiles at you as he tells a lie, his microgestures give him away. His pupils may contract, one eyebrow may lift, or the corner of his mouth may twitch, and these signals contradict the Open-Palm gesture and the sincere smile. The result is that the receivers, especially women, tend not to believe what they hear.

## 2. Deliver on Promises

To be trustworthy, you must deliver on your promises. A lawyer should never overpromise the jury and risk coming up with an empty or partially fulfilled promise. A lawyer's word is the lawyer's bond. The most common danger zone for making promises is opening statement, when you tell the jurors what you expect to prove. If you fail to fulfill your promise by not proving what you said you would, opposing counsel normally will remind the jury of your promise and how you broke it. It is wise to underpromise in opening to avoid this breach of sincerity.

## 3. Admit Weaknesses

If your case has a weakness, such as a missing piece of evidence, admit the weakness fully and as soon as possible. Your willingness to divulge weaknesses buttresses your image as a sincere seeker of truth. It shows that you have examined the case from all angles and are freely admitting the existence of blemishes. You have nothing to conceal. You may be able to reveal the deficiency during jury selection and ask the prospective jurors about whether it would affect their judgment. By not revealing the problem, you risk opposing counsel doing so and inferring or arguing that you intentionally concealed the problem from the jurors.

On the other hand, the case may have a weakness that is founded in inadmissible evidence—for instance, a witness has a prior conviction that is inadmissible under Federal Rules of Evidence 609, or the client took remedial measures that are inadmissible under Federal Rules of Evidence 407. In that case, you should move in limine to exclude any mention of the case weakness.

## 4. Be Civil

Jurors see everything that takes place in the courtroom. They see how you are received and perceived by others. If you are a person who is treated with respect and courtesy by others in the courtroom, it is all the more likely that the jurors will believe that you are a person of integrity who should be respected, listened to, and trusted.

If you are civil to others, it is more likely they will return that civility. Civility is different from ethical behavior, which is moral conduct. Civility consists of being courteous and respectful of others. Lawyers are normally civil to both the judge and jury, and that civility should also be extended to three very important people in the courtroom, the lower bench—the court reporter, court clerk, and bailiff. The lower bench may be in chambers speaking to the judge, sometimes sharing their thoughts about counsel. Courtesies toward the court reporter include speaking at a rate that does not outrun the court reporter, providing the reporter with the spellings of your witnesses' names, and making sure to get verbal responses (not nods and the like) from witnesses. Premarking exhibits for the court clerk and other acts of courtesy and professionalism are beneficial.

Be civil to opposing counsel. Seems simple, right? However, we predict that a time will come when you will not be able to tolerate opposing counsel. You will wish that the earth would open and swallow her. At that point in time, be strong, and remain professional and courteous. It will all eventually pass. And your civility in the face of opposing counsel's misbehavior will be appreciated. A lawyer can be an aggressive advocate while behaving in a civil manner.

The American Board of Trial Advocates promulgated *Principles of Civility, Integrity, and Professionalism*, which govern courtroom conduct as follows:

---

## Principles of Civility, Integrity, and Professionalism

**When in Court I Will:**

1. Always uphold the dignity of the court and never be disrespectful.
2. Never publicly criticize a judge for his or her rulings or a jury for the court's verdict. Criticism should be reserved for appellate court briefs.
3. Be punctual and prepared for all court appearances, and, if unavoidably delayed, notify the court and counsel as soon as possible.
4. Never engage in conduct that brings disorder or disruption to the courtroom.
5. Advise clients and witnesses of the proper courtroom conduct expected and required.
6. Never misrepresent or misquote facts or authorities.
7. Verify the availability of clients and witnesses, if possible, before dates for hearings or trials are scheduled, or immediately thereafter. Promptly notify the court and counsel if their attendance cannot be ensured.
8. Be respectful and courteous to court marshals or bailiffs, clerks, reporters, secretaries, and law clerks.

---

To encourage civility, many state and local bar associations have also embraced creeds of civility, such as the Washington State Bar Association's Creed of Professionalism, adopted in 2001 (*http://www.wsba.org/Legal-Community/ Committees-Boards-and-Other-Groups/Professionalism-Committee*).

### 5. Be Open

Besides waiting, bench conferences are at the top of the list of things that jurors dislike about jury service. Put yourself in their place. The lawyers go to the side bar on the far side of the courtroom away from the jury box and confer secretly with the judge. Could anything be more blatantly designed to exclude the people who have been told that they have been chosen to "well and truly try the case"? The fact that jurors dislike this procedure should enlighten trial lawyers to be as open and candid as possible.

Steps that lawyers can take both to be and appear open in the way they conduct their trial work include taking care of as many problematic areas of admissibility of evidence by motions in limine; requesting side bars only when necessary; keeping counsel table as clear of clutter as possible; making understandable objections so jurors do not conclude that the lawyers are trying to conceal information by objecting (discussed in Chapter 5); and so on.

### 6. Sell with Plain Language and Integrity

Trial work involves selling yourself and your case. This means that you need to be a person whom the jury can understand and relate to, which further means that you should rid yourself of habits that impede clear communication, such as speaking in legalese. Lawyers should shed legalese and speak to the jurors in everyday language that they can understand.

Successful salespeople persevere in pursuit of a cause. They believe in the products, and this gives them the confidence, energy, and dedication to convince others of the product's value. For the lawyer, the product is not a car or a can of soup; it's a client's cause. When a successful lawyer is in court, it is the lawyer's court (yes, the judge presides), where that lawyer is at home and has a particular purpose—to win for the client. An exception to this tenet is the prosecutor, the people's lawyer in a criminal case. This lawyer, who is the representative of the people, is called by different titles depending on the jurisdiction, such as prosecuting attorney, solicitor, commonwealth attorney, county attorney, state's attorney, district attorney, attorney general, city attorney, or United States attorney for federal cases. In this text, we refer to that trial attorney by the generic term *prosecutor*. The prosecutor, as the people's representative, has a unique set of responsibilities in trial. The prosecutor's job is not just to win—or convict. Rather, it is to do justice.

Determination and perseverance in pursuit of a cause are essential qualities because going to trial is tough business. Criminal defense lawyer Roy Black, in *Black's Law* (Simon & Schuster 2000), paints this picture:

> I worked on my summation. I figured I could get through the last day just on adrenaline. Being in trial is like fighting all night in the foxhole and then looking up in the morning and seeing the enemy charging with bayonets. I don't care how tired you are—you're going to keep going. I worked sprawled in a chair, making notes and constantly rearranging the outline of my remarks.

While we stress the importance of persistence in pursuit of winning or, for the prosecutor, doing justice, prevailing is worth it only if you, as an officer of the court, behave ethically and maintain your integrity.

### 7. Be Yourself

Jurors can detect a phony, so be yourself. However, if you see an approach, a demeanor, an argument, or another skill or strategy that is effective, adopt it; but do so only if it comports with your personality and approach. Again, our advice is to be yourself.

### 8. Meet Judicial Expectations

Before entering the courtroom, a lawyer should become familiar with what the judge in that courtroom expects of counsel. Failure to comply with the court's practices, procedures, or customs can result in the judge's rebuke and damage counsel's credibility and standing with the judge and the jury.

Determining what the bench expects of counsel can be a challenge, because practices, procedures, and customs vary from courthouse to courthouse, and from courtroom to courtroom within the same courthouse. If possible, you should scout the judge to determine what is expected of you. Speak with lawyers who have appeared there, court personnel or others in the know, or best of all, watch the judge in action. Check the Internet to see if the judge has posted information online about what the court requires of counsel. Many judges use the Internet to put counsel on notice of what is required. On the website for this book, *http://www.aspenlawschool.com/books/berger_trialad4e*, you will find links to judicial websites where you can examine requirements for particular courts. If you are unable to ascertain your judge's predilections prior to trial, you are usually safe if you abide by the most rigorous standard of conduct.

Throughout this book we highlight situations where judges are likely to have preferences for how counsel should perform, and we examine what they are likely to be. This includes how judges would like attorneys to conduct themselves during bench trials.

The following are judicial expectations for the fundamentals of trial practice and decorum:

---

#### Judicial Expectations: Trial Fundamentals

- **Professional Responsibility:** It is a given that the judge expects that counsel will comply with the rules of professional conduct. This book explains those rules and ethical pitfalls for counsel during each stage of trial, from jury selection through closing argument.
- **Time Management:** Judges expect counsel to be on time for each court appearance. Make it a practice to arrive early. Absent some unforeseen occurrence, such as a car accident on the way to the courthouse, you must notify the court in advance if you need to be excused or will be late. The court's time is the most important, taking priority over other matters. Also, during trial, do not waste the court's time.

*continued* ▶

- **Stand Up:**  Rise when you address the court, question a witness, or object.
- **Stand Back:**  Do not invade the space of a witness, court personnel, or the jury. Stand at a courteous distance. Exceptions exist when, for instance, you hand an exhibit to a witness or publish an exhibit to the jury. If required by court custom, stay at the lectern. If the court requires that permission be granted before approaching a witness or the bar (for example, to make an argument on a motion), or if counsel is more comfortable asking for permission, request and receive it before moving ahead. In some courts, this is required, or is required only the first time counsel wishes to approach. In other courts, counsel can roam the courtroom at will.
- **Courtesy:**  Show courtesy and respect for everyone in the courtroom, including the lower bench—the clerk, court reporter, and bailiff. This includes addressing witnesses and others by their surnames and titles, such as Mr. Jones or Dr. Smith. When speaking with a young child, the first name is appropriate.
- **Avoid Distractions:**  Do not bring food, beverages, chewing gum, or a cell phone/smartphone (unless silenced) into the courtroom. Refrain from distracting behavior, such as making facial expressions or distracting noises when opposing counsel is examining a witness. Counsel should advise associates and witnesses of this etiquette.
- **Technology:**  Make arrangements for the use of technology in the courtroom outside of court time, and have it ready when court convenes. Do not install any technology or courtroom equipment without the express permission of the judge.

## 9. Maintain a Good Reputation

Courthouses, big or small, are like small communities. In that small courthouse community, everyone knows who the lawyers are and what their reputations are. When you are assigned to a court for trial, the judge and court personnel know who you are even if you have never stepped into that courtroom.

A good reputation is extremely valuable to a lawyer. When a lawyer has a first-rate reputation, the judge will listen carefully to counsel's arguments and will treat counsel with respect. This treatment will radiate to the jury and enhance the lawyer's image as a sincere advocate. The good reputation is very much like a life preserver. When the sea gets rough, as it does in trial, a good reputation will buoy the lawyer up and away from harm.

Most lawyers must believe in what they are doing to be able to project sincerity to the jury. Therefore, above all else, remember to be sincere. Armed with that sincerity, you will project it and be a formidable advocate.

## B. Inspirational Role Model

Reverend Martin Luther King Jr., in *Stride Toward Freedom* (Harper 1958), wrote about his struggles to organize the civil rights movement and his inspirational role model:

As the days unfolded, however, the inspiration of Mahatma Gandhi began to exert its influence. I had come to see early that the Christian doctrine of love operating through the Gandhian method of non violence was one of the most potent weapons available.

James M. Washington, ed., *A Testament of Hope: The Essential Writings and Speeches of Martin Luther King Jr.* 447 (HarperCollins 1986).

Inspirational role models can be guiding forces demonstrating how to be a superior communicator in trial as well as how to conduct yourself as a lawyer. Inspirational role models abound, such as David Boies, trial lawyer in *Bush v. Gore* and the Proposition 8 case; Gloria Allred, trial advocate for women's rights; and Kathryn Ruemmler, prosecutor in the Enron case and, later, White House Counsel. You can and are most likely to find your inspirational role model practicing in your town or in your firm. This will be someone who has integrity and who is a persuasive lawyer. Once you have found that person, you can pattern your behavior after that inspirational role model.

We want to go back in history and suggest a lawyer for your consideration as an inspirational role model. He built his practice from nothing, and over the 23 years he was in practice he tried more cases in the highest court of his state than any other trial lawyer. While you may remember him with a full beard, Abraham Lincoln was clean shaven when he was trying cases. This picture of the lawyer Lincoln was taken in New York shortly before his Cooper Union speech, which helped propel him to national prominence.

Bearing in mind that sincerity matters above all else when it comes to communication, the following account of Lincoln's Cooper Union address is instructive:

When Lincoln rose to speak, I was greatly disappointed. He was tall, tall, oh, so tall, and so angular and awkward that I had for an instant a feeling of pity for so ungainly a man. . . . His clothes were black and ill-fitting, badly wrinkled—as if they had been jammed carelessly into a small trunk. His bushy head, with the stiff black hair thrown back, was balanced on a long and lean head-stalk, and when he raised his hands in opening gesture, I noticed that they were very large. He began in a low tone of voice—as if he were used to speaking out-doors and was afraid of speaking too loud.

He said, "Mr. Cheerman," instead of "Mr. Chairman," and employed many other words with an old-fashioned pronunciation. I said to myself, "Old fellow, you won't do; it is all very well for the Wild West, but this will never go down in New York." But pretty soon he began to get into the subject; he straightened up, made regular and graceful gestures; his face lighted as with an inward fire; the whole man was transfigured.

I forgot the clothing, his personal appearance, and his individual peculiarities. Presently, forgetting myself; I was on my feet with the rest . . . cheering the wonderful man. In the closing parts of his argument you could hear the gentle sizzling of the gas burners.

Harold Holzer, *Lincoln at Cooper Union: The Speech that Made Abraham Lincoln President* (Simon & Schuster 2006).

Lincoln's sincerity and conviction came across in his Cooper Union address and swayed the audience. Public speaking research suggests that two things emerge as the most powerful in persuasion: sincerity and conviction of the speaker. And this explains why Lincoln had this effect on his audience. Lincoln's skill as an advocate emanated from his integrity and the firmness of his beliefs. Lincoln can be an inspirational role model for any lawyer who aspires to be an excellent communicator in trial—one who is sincere about the cause and able to project that sincerity to the audience.

## III.  PERSUASIVE MEDIA

Make your story, your argument, and yourself dynamic. The goals of utilizing persuasive media are to present the story and argument in a way that engages the jurors and convinces them. This can be accomplished by using three types of media effectively:

1. The nonverbal medium (lawyer appearance and body language),
2. Visual media, and
3. The verbal medium (persuasive language).

### A.  Nonverbal Media: Lawyer Appearance

Amazingly, 60 to 80 percent of communication is nonverbal in nature. *See* Allan & Barbara Pease, *The Definitive Book of Body Language* 10 (Bantam 2004). In trial, the lawyer is the means by which the case theory is conveyed to the jury. Of course, the lawyer is not the only medium. The witnesses and the exhibits also communicate. Nevertheless, the lawyer is a constant throughout the trial, questioning prospective jurors during jury selection, making an opening statement, conducting direct and cross-examinations, and delivering closing argument. Additionally, in many cases other supporting legal personnel are present: associates, paralegal staff, and investigators, for instance. For these reasons, we want to discuss your appearance. How you dress, stand, gesture, and so on can favorably influence the jury.

### Dress

We begin with how you should dress for court. Generally, you want a neat and professional appearance, one that does not include distracting clothes or accessories. For men, the traditional trial uniform is a dark suit (navy blue, charcoal gray), white or blue shirt, tame tie, shined shoes, and dark socks. Reasonable variations can be worn. Indeed, counsel may decide that lighter tones are more consistent with the lawyer's case, approach, and geographic locale, under the theory that a relaxed and laughing jury is not going to convict. For women lawyers, dress is slightly more challenging. For example, if the jurors in the jurisdiction are likely to be older, some suggest that a dress may be more appropriate than slacks. The goal for female lawyers, as with their male counterparts, is to neither offend nor distract jurors. Hale Starr and Mark McCormick's *Jury Selection* 432-433 (3d ed., Aspen 2001) offers an extensive discussion of proper attire for women trial lawyers.

### Eye Contact
#### *Importance of Eye Contact*

People do believe the adage "she couldn't look me in the eye." A fundamental tenet of communication is to make eye contact, because through eye contact the listener makes a connection with the speaker. Numerous opportunities exist to make eye contact. When the jurors move into the jury box and are waiting to be told to take their seats, strive to make eye contact. During jury selection, look the prospective jurors in the eye when you talk to them. The same goes for opening statement, closing argument, and other opportunities to address the jurors. The lawyer's goal should be to make meaningful eye contact with each juror. The normal inclination is to look into the eyes of those jurors you feel most comfortable with and to avoid the eyes of those you feel ill at ease with; fight against this tendency and look into every juror's eyes. It matters.

#### *The Eye Magnet: Notes*

A major obstacle to achieving eye contact is your notes. Notes are like a magnet, attracting your eyes to the page to the exclusion of everything else. The more detailed the notes, the greater the attraction. Make it your goal to deliver opening statement and closing argument without notes. This is not an impossible goal, because by the time you go to trial, you will be well acquainted with the participants in the lawsuit and will have mastered the facts and arguments. One technique that can assist you is to use visuals, such as a computer slideshow. People will praise you for speaking without notes, even though the notes are right there on the visual.

We suggest that you write your opening and closing in their entirety. After you have written the statements, reduce them to cue idea notes that will jog your memory. Otherwise, you risk looking down at notes too often and reading, which disconnects you from your listeners. Reading from notes separates you personally and emotionally from the jurors; you become less of a living, breathing person they must respond to, and instead become someone merely playing the role of an attorney. Using a keyword outline allows you to engage the jury. If you absolutely need notes nearby, use techniques such as highlighting keywords or using a large font so that you need only glance at them.

### Staging and Stance

#### Staging

To effectively communicate with the jury, you want to position yourself and others supporting your case in the best spots in the courtroom. The best spot varies depending on the activity. As an example, for opening statement, when you want the jury's complete attention, the ideal location is in front of the jury at a comfortable distance back from the jurors so that you are not invading their space.

Court custom and culture and courtroom design dictate how you can stage people and things in the courtroom. In federal and some state courts, you are required to stand behind a podium, and the placement of courtroom technology may require that you and your witnesses be in certain locations in the courtroom. Some courts may require you to be seated at counsel table when questioning witnesses, while others will permit you to move about at will. Recognizing these factors, throughout this book we present ideal staging for you to consider and modify based on the courtroom and customs where you are trying the case.

#### Stance

If you are a pacer, compelled to wander back and forth in front of the jurors as you address them, we have some advice for you: Don't do it. You want the jurors' complete attention; your pacing is distracting. If your wandering is a result of nervousness, consult the end of this section, which covers coping with nerves. This does not mean that you must remain static; you can move. But when you move about the courtroom, do it with a purpose in mind. For example, to maintain the jury's interest, you can move to another place when you change subjects during closing argument, or to an easel to draw their attention to a diagram that you wish to discuss.

### Body Language

Your body language can communicate your emotions and thoughts. You want to appear open and amiable toward the jury. You do not want to have body language that suggests you are hiding something. For example, the fig-leaf or folded-arms posture should be avoided. Open posture and open hand gestures communicate sincerity and openness.

### Coping with Nerves

As professional golfer Hale Irwin put it, "If you're not just a little bit nervous before a match, you probably don't have the expectations of yourself that you should have." Trial work entails what surveys have concluded is the greatest fear that people have—public speaking. Even the most experienced lawyers become nervous. Nervousness is natural; it proves you are alive, that you are aware of the seriousness of the matter to your client and your resulting responsibilities, and that any case can be won and any case can be lost. Nervousness also provides you with a force that can be redirected into giving energy to your presentation. Following are some pointers on how to manage nervousness.

## Managing Nervousness

Here are some techniques for combating nervousness.

- **Believe in Yourself:** Recognize that it is natural for you to feel nervous. Others are nervous too. You, just like others, can do it. You have successfully navigated through law school courses and are ready to enter the profession as a trial lawyer. Trial work is hard work. But trial work is also rewarding and enjoyable. You have the good fortune to represent your client and to do good work. Take full advantage of these opportunities.
- **Prepare:** Being thoroughly prepared on the facts and law will help you overcome nervousness. You can overcome stage fright by being a master of what you are discussing.
- **Rehearse:** How do you get to perform in Carnegie Hall? The Hollywood Bowl? The Grand Ole Opry? Practice, practice, practice. The same is true for coping with nervousness. Practice is a critical part of your preparation. For instance, deliver your opening statement to anyone who will listen: colleagues, family, friends, a focus group. Ask them how you might improve it. Remember that actors do not just walk on stage; they rehearse again and again.
- **Concentrate on the Message:** The more you can forget about yourself, the more at ease you will be, and you will be a better communicator. Look back at the account of Lincoln's Cooper Union address. Once he got into his subject, he loosened up and got his message across. Visualize moving the message from your mind to the minds and hearts of the jurors. Watch their eyes to see if they are receiving your message and understanding it. When you realize that the story is the thing and that you are just the messenger, you will cease to be so worried and nervous about yourself.
- **Speak to Your Audience:** Recognize that your audience, the jury, is normally attentive and receptive (except perhaps for juror number six, who just fell asleep again). They have been selected to serve on the jury and instructed that they are the finders of fact who are to decide the case. In this role, they want to hear what you have to say about the case. Besides, when will you ever get a captive audience that can't get up and walk out if they don't like what you say?

*continued* ▶

- **Redirect Nervousness:** Nervousness can be a positive force. Redirect it into energy that you can inject into your trial work and engage the jury. Think of the nervousness as providing an opportunity to challenge your extra energy and make it appear to the jury as energy and commitment.
- **Breathe Deeply:**  To slow down your heart rate and calm yourself, breathe deeply from your diaphragm. When you inhale, your stomach will enlarge. Hold your breath for a few seconds, and then breathe out with your stomach moving in.

## B.  The Visual Media

Technological advancements bring cases visually alive in the courtroom. Trial lawyers now can persuade jurors by using a chart showing a timeline, images projected on a large screen, reconstruction of an event (for example, an automobile accident or a product failure), or a digital slideshow that aids the advocate's telling of the story. Creative use of visuals is successful advocacy. Today's lawyers are taking full advantage of visual media. William S. Bailey and Robert Bailey, in *Show the Story: The Power of Visual Advocacy* (Trial Guides 2011), take a comprehensive look at effective trial advocacy with visuals and the various forms of technology now available, as well as provide advice and direction on the proper foundations for these exhibits.

Visuals are critical to trial persuasion. Besides this introduction, which briefly introduces you to the importance of visuals, we reference trial visuals throughout this book, and in particular in Chapter 8, where we specifically address the use of visuals in trial.

### Why Use Visuals?

Visuals dynamically present the story and the argument. They enable the lawyer to emphasize the important aspects of the case theory.

### Visuals to Emphasize Case Theory

#### The George Zimmerman Case

An example is the high-profile Florida murder trial of George Zimmerman, for fatally shooting 17-year-old Trayvon Martin. Zimmerman claimed self-defense, and in closing argument defense counsel utilized a computer-generated animated video to depict the defense's version of how the events leading up to and including the shooting took place. *https://www.youtube.com/watch?v=b-VeqBTb0rc.*

There are at least six reasons why lawyers use visuals, and they relate to trial persuasion.

1. **Perception and Retention:** Studies show that we retain less than 15 percent of what we hear, but we remember over 80 percent of what we

see and hear. Consequently, witness testimony is much more likely to be remembered when it is accompanied by visuals.

2. **How Jurors Learn:**  Today's jurors receive news and entertainment over the Internet and television. The Millennial generation, the generation of rising adults with birthdates in the early 1980s to the early 2000s, compose over 40 percent of the jury pool nationally. They grew up with television delivery in short bursts, interspersed pictures, and videos. Technology permeates our lives. Most jurors own a computer or have access to one at work. They have tablets and smartphones. They are receptive and accustomed to computer information. It is how they learn.

3. **The Technology Exists:**  Why employ visuals? Answer: Because you can. Technology allows lawyers to create and display visuals faster and in ways that were only dreamed about a few years ago. In a movie on this book's accompanying website, you can examine some of the possibilities of today's technology.

4. **Repetition and Highlighting:**  A lawyer is able to repeat and highlight information with visuals. For example, the lawyer elicits testimony from the witness about an event. Then, the lawyer introduces into evidence a diagram of the location where the event took place and goes back over the event, having the witness use the diagram to show where certain acts occurred.

5. **Time Saver:**  For a lawyer who tries a particular type of case over and over, a software program like PowerPoint can conserve time. Rather than remaking a visual for each trial, the lawyer can develop a visual in PowerPoint (for instance, a chart with the elements of negligence on it) and then copy it into a new presentation for the next trial. This is a time saver and works well (provided the lawyer remembers to change the names and dates on the chart for the new case).

6. **Successful Advocacy:**  Visuals dynamically present the story and the argument. They enable the lawyer to emphasize the important aspects of the case theory. See the discussion on page 18, of the computer-generated video used in the high-profile Florida trial of George Zimmerman.

### High-, Medium-, Low-, and No-Tech
*Choosing Media*

Visuals come in a wide variety, ranging from a no-tech courtroom demonstration to a high-tech computer-generated animation of an airplane crash. We do not suggest that a high-tech presentation is necessarily more effective than a low-tech or no-tech presentation. Holding a deceased child's photograph cradled in your hands as you walk slowly beside the jury box while pausing long enough so each juror can get a good look could leave an even more lasting impression than displaying the child's picture on a large screen. The important point is that the lawyer should select the visual medium that is most compelling under the particular set of circumstances.

Restraint should be exercised so that the high-tech approach is not overused. A presentation overloaded with technology may interfere with jury communication rather than facilitate it. See Chapter 8, chart at page 265.

*The Options*

Computer software enables you to select from several methods for displaying visuals. For a discussion of the array of options, see Chapter 8, Introducing Exhibits, pages 265-270.

## C.  Verbal Media: Persuasive Language

Few lawyers will have the powerful delivery style of Martin Luther King Jr. But consider another characteristic of Dr. King's speeches. The following is an excerpt from Dr. King's "I Have a Dream" speech. Note the persuasive language he chose.

### Pick Persuasive Language

**Excerpt from Martin Luther King Jr.'s "I Have a Dream" Speech**

Let us not wallow in the valley of despair, I say to you today, my friends.

And so even though we face the difficulties of today and tomorrow, I still have a dream. It is a dream deeply rooted in the American dream.

I have a dream that one day this nation will rise up and live out the true meaning of its creed: "We hold these truths to be self-evident, that all men are created equal."

> I have a dream that one day on the red hills of Georgia, the sons of former slaves and the sons of former slave owners will be able to sit down together at the table of brotherhood.
>
> I have a dream that one day even the state of Mississippi, a state sweltering with the heat of injustice, sweltering with the heat of oppression, will be transformed into an oasis of freedom and justice.
>
> I have a dream that my four little children will one day live in a nation where they will not be judged by the color of their skin but by the content of their character.
>
> I have a *dream* today!

While a lawyer may never be able to master a delivery style that is as dynamic as Dr. King's, the lawyer can do what Dr. King did so well—carefully select and craft the language of the speech. Your opening statements and closing arguments are speeches. So, the maxim for the last medium you can employ to make your story, argument, and yourself dynamic is this: Pick persuasive language.

Vivid, persuasive language comes in many forms. Select impact words with connotations. Visual imagery (word pictures that present essential details) gives the listener the sense of seeing the object, person, or event described.

### Powerful Language

You want to choose powerful language that will connect with the jurors and move them to render a verdict for your client. Repetition, rhetorical questions, and analogies are particularly powerful language tools for a trial lawyer. *Repetition* can be used in a variety of ways throughout the trial to drive the idea home—to etch ideas into memory. *Rhetorical questions* invite jurors to participate with you in thinking; more specifically, rhetorical questions introduce an idea, make an accusation, or issue a challenge. *Analogies*, especially with a human touch, provide a convincing, concrete form of inductive reasoning. Equally important as selecting persuasive language is the culling of dull, sterile, and technical language.

You will want to avail yourself of figurative language, figures of arrangement, and silence.

### *Figurative Language*

Figurative language is a means of expressing ideas in vivid ways. A trial lawyer can take full advantage of figures of speech such as the following.

- Simile: "When he walked into that bar, he was not Bill Ross, he was like a machine, moving without thinking."
- Metaphor: "When the defendant was made chief compliance officer for the Jones Investment Firm, that company in effect left the fox to guard the henhouse."

- **Understatement:** "To say the least, leaving a three-year-old child alone without food in a freezing apartment for four days does not comport with our concept of good parenting."
- **Irony:** "The producer was going to give the starring role to the defendant anyway; he didn't even need to murder his rival to get that 'role of a lifetime.'"
- **Analogy:** "It's illegal to drive past a stop sign without braking your car. Dr. Blossom blew a stop sign in his care of Victoria Russell."

### *Figures of Arrangement*

Figures of arrangement include the following.

- **Alliteration:** "And after he completed psychologically belittling and breaking her, he proceeded to brutally beat her, leaving her bloody and battered."
- **Word Repetition:** "She lied to the board of trustees, lied to the employees, lied to the stockholders, and seems even to have lied to herself about what she did."
- **Tricolon:** The rule of three—"Ours is the age of substitutes: Instead of language, we have jargon; instead of principles, slogans; instead of genuine ideas, bright ideas." From Eric Bentley, *The Dramatic Event* (Horizon Press 1954).
- **Parallelism:** "The victim tried to conceal herself in one of the nearby apartments, but all the doors were locked. She tried to hide outside, but there was no cover except some low-lying bushes. Finally, she tried to run, but she could not run fast enough."
- **Antithesis:** "A parent is someone who would give his life to protect his child from harm, to make that child safe. How far from this is the defendant, a father who would sexually molest his ten-year-old daughter?"

### *Silence*

One of a lawyer's valuable instruments is courtroom silence. To drive home a point to the jury, be silent; let the idea sink in. If the witness gives that priceless answer on cross, do not rush on to the next question. Pause and let the silence underline the answer.

## IV. ETHICAL CONSIDERATIONS

How you behave toward others can positively influence the jury and judge. Civility both inside and outside the courtroom can go a long way toward creating a favorable image for yourself and for lawyers. While the ABA Model Rules of Professional Conduct do not mandate civility, the Preamble sets civility and a positive image as goals for lawyers:

Many of a lawyer's professional responsibilities are prescribed in the Rules of Professional Conduct, as well as substantive and procedural law. However, a lawyer is also guided by personal conscience and the approbation of professional peers. A lawyer should strive to attain the highest level of skill, to improve the law and the legal profession and to exemplify the legal profession's ideals of public service.

This statement of aspirational goals in the Preamble is intended to inspire lawyers to strive for the highest possible degree of ethical conduct; our conscience and desire for the respect of our peers should inform many of our decisions as lawyers.

## CHECKLIST: PERSUASION

### Premier Persuasion Principles

- ☐ Develop a persuasive message—see Chapter 3, Case Theory and Theme Development.
- ☐ Be a persuasive messenger—the successful communicator in trial.
- ☐ Use persuasive media to make your story, argument, and self dynamic in trial.

### Persuasive Messenger

- ☐ To be a great communicator in trial, be sincere and project sincerity.
- ☐ Nine points to project sincerity:
  - Be sincere.
  - Deliver on promises.
  - Admit weaknesses.
  - Be civil.
  - Be open.
  - Sell with plain language and integrity.
  - Be yourself.
  - Meet judicial expectations.
  - Maintain a good reputation.
- ☐ To be a great communicator, have an inspirational role model.

### Meet Judicial Expectations: Trial Fundamentals

Fundamentals of trial decorum and performance:

- ☐ Adhere to the rules of professional conduct;
- ☐ Be on time for court appearances;
- ☐ Stand when objecting, addressing the court, or questioning unless disabled or another court custom is followed;
- ☐ Maintain a respectful distance from jurors, court personnel, and jurors;
- ☐ Show courtesy and respect to all;
- ☐ Avoid distracting behavior; and
- ☐ Make arrangements for courtroom technology prior to court time.

*continued* ▶

**Persuasive Media**

To make your story, your argument, and yourself dynamic, use persuasive media, as follows.

☐ Nonverbal media—lawyer appearance:
  - Dress professionally; do not let your appearance become a distraction or issue in the case.
  - Maintain eye contact.
  - Position your witnesses and yourself for greatest impact on the jury.
  - Avoid distracting behavior, such as pacing.
  - Manage nervousness.
☐ Visual media—take full advantage of trial visuals and trial technology.
☐ Verbal media—pick persuasive language. Select powerful language that will persuade the jury.

# CHAPTER 3

# CASE THEORY AND THEME DEVELOPMENT

*"The theory of the case is a product of the advocate. It is the basic concept around which everything revolves."*

—**James McElhaney**, *McElhaney's Trial Notebook* (4th ed., ABA 2005)

*"A theory is the more impressive the greater is the simplicity of its premises, the more different are the kinds of things it relates and the more extended the range of its applicability."*

—**Albert Einstein** (1879-1955), quoted in John E.J. Schmitz, *The Second Law of Life: Energy, Technology, and the Future of Earth As We Know It* 84 (William Andrew Publishing 2007)

*"We have, as human beings, a storytelling problem. We're a bit too quick to come up with the explanations for things we don't really have an explanation for."*

—**Malcolm Gladwell**, *Blink: The Power of Thinking Without Thinking* (Back Bay Books 2007)

## I. CASE THEORY

The case theory is the *message* that the lawyer communicates to the jury. Beyond that, the case theory provides a structure that serves as the organizing principle for all of your pretrial and trial endeavors. It guides every activity, from interviewing, pleadings, discovery, and pretrial motions to jury selection, witness examinations, and opening statement and closing argument. It is the core concept that runs throughout your work as a lawyer.

This chapter examines how to develop a case theory in the context of both criminal and civil cases. You will learn how to develop a case theory both as plaintiff and defense counsel. We explain how to formulate a case theme that encapsulates the case theory into a memorable statement for the jury.

This chapter also introduces you to two cases: the *Freck Point* case and the *Hill Moveit* case. Both of these cases will be revisited throughout this book to illustrate planning, analysis, and strategies in civil and criminal cases. The *Freck Point* case is the case used in the trial demonstration movie that is located on the book's website, *http://www.aspenlawschool.com/books/berger_trialad4e*. The trial demonstration movie shows experienced lawyers engaging in the various aspects of trial work, from jury selection through closing argument.

Most important, this chapter explains the case theory—the legal and factual theory that is the backbone for all the trial components. As you progress through a case, you will encounter these principles as applied in the body of the trial: jury selection, opening statement, direct and cross-examination, and closing argument. So, throughout the forthcoming chapters we refer to the case theory development in this chapter. Similarly, keep in mind that case theories are also applicable to alternative dispute resolution (mediation, arbitration, and negotiation).

## II. DEVELOPING THE CASE THEORY

### A. Case Theory Components

The case theory has two interdependent components: the *legal theory* and the *factual theory*. While, for clarity, the legal and factual theories are discussed separately, the two concepts are interrelated, linked through law, information, and the client's objectives.

**Case Theory**

| Legal Theory | + | Factual Theory |
|---|---|---|

The legal theory is a legal framework developed by a lawyer from interpretation, analysis, and expansion of legal rules and standards found in cases, statutes, and regulations. It is a framework from which the lawyer posits that if the facts exist as alleged and under applicable legal burdens, the client is legally entitled to the relief sought. Thus, even though the legal theory is based on the law, one cannot say that it is the law. It is one attorney's interpretation of law. In practice, some legal theories will be beyond dispute (for instance, negligence in an automobile accident), while others may encounter quite vigorous opposition (for instance, strict liability of handgun manufacturers to those injured by the intentional use of those weapons).

The factual theory is the party's story justifying relief under the legal theory, and is based on all of the evidence as well as logical inferences that are drawn from that evidence. In criminal cases, the defense may rely on a pure reasonable doubt defense—not put on any evidence, and rest after the prosecution's case-in-chief. In this situation, the defense story is really a commentary on the deficiencies in the prosecution's factual theory.

### B. Relationship Between the Legal and Factual Theory

When selecting and developing a case theory, recognize that the legal and factual theories are interrelated. They are linked by the client's objectives, the law, and available information. Tentative case theories start to develop when you possess even minimal information. These hypotheses, à la Sherlock Holmes, arise at an early stage, perhaps even before talking to the client or other witnesses, and are subsequently sifted through as you learn more of your client's objectives, acquire more information, and understand more of the law's applicability to the client's case. Early theorizing is possible because, in each situation, there are generally finite legal theories available, and under each legal theory there is a somewhat foreseeable spectrum of facts that will strengthen or weaken the supporting factual theory.

### Client's Objectives

After identifying the client's objectives (such as to be acquitted of the crime, obtain damages, avoid damages, get an injunction), you research the law to find authority for a legal theory that can achieve these objectives. Imagine you are representing a client accused of burglary. An acquittal is your client's initial objective and, therefore, the initial focus of your case strategy. Research reveals that the legal theories available to achieve this objective include a mental defense, lack of intent, and misidentification. Therefore, the objective of acquittal can be reached by using more than one legal theory.

### Evidence

Your legal theory, in turn, leads you to seek evidence from which you can develop a factual theory to support your legal theory. In a burglary case, assume three possible legal theories—mental defense, lack of intent, and misidentification. You, as defense counsel, would look for information that the defendant has a history of mental problems, was intoxicated at the time of the offense, or thought he was entering his own home; or that eyewitnesses were biased or had perceptual problems; and so on.

The information you obtain will then limit the available legal theories. If the defendant in the burglary was caught by police in the home, a reasonable doubt based on misidentification will not be a viable legal theory. Limiting the available legal theories may then alter the client's objectives, bringing you back full circle. Additionally, if no viable legal theories remain after analysis of the available evidence in the burglary case, the client's objectives may have to be changed from acquittal to a satisfactory plea bargain.

## III.  PLAINTIFF'S CASE THEORY

### A.  Legal Theory

The specific development of the legal theory varies according to whether you are the attorney for the plaintiff or for the defendant. The principal difference between civil and criminal legal theories is the legal source of the theory. Civil legal theories of both plaintiff and defendant may be founded on common law cases, statutory enactments, administrative regulations, and so on. For most prosecutors in a criminal case, however, there are no common law crimes, only statute-based crimes, limiting the legal theories to those found in the statutes.

A criminal defendant, on the other hand, may base a legal theory on a creative interpretation of a range of legal sources, much like her civil counterpart. The advocate must also consider the possibility of multiple or backup theories, which we discuss later in this chapter.

### Civil Plaintiff

For the civil plaintiff, the legal theory corresponds to the claim for relief—damages for negligence, slander, or breach of contract, or the right to possession of land through adverse possession, for example. The civil plaintiff's legal theory asserts that the plaintiff can, under the burden of proof, establish every element of the civil claim. Thus, to propose a legal theory of negligence is to assert that counsel can prove, by a preponderance of the evidence, that (1) the defendant had a duty of care to the plaintiff, (2) the defendant committed an act that breached that duty, and (3) as a proximate result of that breach, (4) the plaintiff suffered compensable harm.

### The Prosecutor

For the prosecutor, the representative of the people and the plaintiff in a criminal case, the legal theory corresponds to the statutory definition, including any interpretation by the courts, of the particular crime involved—burglary, second degree theft, arson, conspiracy to import a controlled substance. The prosecutor's legal theory asserts that the prosecution can establish within the required burden of persuasion every element of a statutory offense. Accordingly, to propose the legal theory of burglary is to allege that the prosecutor can prove, beyond a reasonable doubt, that (1) the defendant (2) entered a dwelling (3) that belonged to another (4) at nighttime (5) with the intent to commit a crime.

### Start with Jury Instructions

A helpful starting point for identifying plaintiff's legal theory—what plaintiff's attorney must prove at trial—is the jurisdiction's pattern jury instructions. Those pattern instructions lay out the elements of either a civil claim or criminal charge, which were discussed in the previous two sections, as well as other aspects of the law applicable to the case. Pattern jury instructions are the products of a jury instructions committee composed of lawyers, judges, and academics, and those pattern instructions are intended to provide uniform and accurate statements of the law. Trial judges give deference to those pattern instructions. Rather than waiting until late in trial preparation to pull together jury instructions, one of the first things counsel should do during trial preparation is to develop a tentative set of proposed jury instructions.

## B.  Selecting the Legal Theory

The potential legal theories for a particular circumstance (an automobile accident, a failed business, a violent death) may be numerous. How then does counsel for plaintiff choose a legal theory? This requires a two-step process.

### Identifying Potential Legal Theories

For the first step in this process, after considering pattern jury instructions, case law, periodicals, discussions with fellow attorneys, and so on, counsel for the plaintiff will attempt to conceive of all the potential legal theories, based on accepted statements of existing law and plausible arguments for expansion and modification of that law, that the available information suggests. When initially developing a legal theory, the lawyer also considers potential information that reasonably may be found during subsequent fact gathering.

---

#### Step 1: Identifying Potential Plaintiff Legal Theories

##### The *Injured Pedestrian* Case

Imagine you represent plaintiff Jay Solomon, a pedestrian who was hit by a car while crossing the street in a crosswalk.

Through your own knowledge and research, you could immediately think of several possible legal theories:

- Intentional tort,
- Negligent operation of the car,
- Negligent maintenance of the car (worn brakes),
- Negligent repair of the car by some third party, and
- Defective manufacture of the car.

Which of these potential theories, however, should you choose as your initial legal theory?

---

### Assessing Strengths and Weaknesses

In the second step of this process for choosing the preferable legal theory, counsel for the plaintiff answers the question of which theory is preferred by assessing the strengths and weaknesses of each potential legal theory

1. in the abstract,
2. in relation to other potential theories, and
3. in conjunction with the available and potential evidence in the case.

Think again about the *Injured Pedestrian* case.

---

#### Step 2: Assessing Strengths and Weaknesses

##### The *Injured Pedestrian* Case

In this second step, plaintiff's counsel simultaneously considers the legal theory in three ways:

1. **Assessing the Legal Theory in the Abstract:** Look at the potential legal theories (intentional tort, negligent operation) in the abstract. Are any so novel as to invite

a likely defense attack on their legal propriety? Intentional tort, negligent operation of the car, negligent maintenance of the car (worn brakes), negligent repair of the car by some third party, and defective manufacture of the car. It does not seem so in this case.

2. **Assessing the Legal Theory in Relation to Other Potential Theories:** Consider the practical advantages and disadvantages of each of these potential legal theories in comparison with each available theory. A theory of product liability–defective manufacture may require far more expensive and complex expert testimony than a theory of negligent repair. A theory of intentional tort will require establishing a much greater level of culpability on the part of the defendant than is required for a theory of negligent maintenance. A theory of negligent operation may only require obtaining the evidence of a single neutral eyewitness, or even the evidence of your own client, while a theory of defective manufacture may require gaining court-ordered access to thousands of pages of corporate documents. On the other hand, if the defendant-driver is uninsured and indigent, the manufacturer may be the only source for damages.

3. **Assessing the Legal Theory in Conjunction with the Available and Potential Evidence in the Case:** At the same time, you may assess the legal theory in conjunction with available and potential evidence. Assume that through interviewing, investigation, and discovery you obtain information indicating that the brakes are fine and that the car is mechanically perfect. This evidence would eliminate defective manufacture, negligent repair, and negligent maintenance as viable legal theories. Also assume that several witnesses claim to have seen the defendant-driver talking on a cell phone and drinking a latte at the time he drove through the crosswalk, hitting your client. That information would greatly weaken any theory of intentional tort, but would support negligence as a good tentative legal theory.

## Criminal Case: Selecting a Legal Theory

To again illustrate how to select a legal theory, this time in a criminal case, assume that you are the prosecutor assigned to what has been described at this juncture as the *Freck Point Murder* case. The case involves a death in the Freck Point neighborhood in Ruston, State of Major.

### The *Freck Point Murder* Case

Assume you are the prosecutor in the *Freck Point Murder* case. You have reviewed the police report, spoken at length with the investigating detective, interviewed witnesses, and examined the physical evidence. In brief, the investigation shows:

On Sunday morning, October 16th of last year, at 1:10 A.M., Samuel L. Griffith, 55 years old, called the Ruston Police Department. He stated that his house had been burgled and his wife had been stabbed to death. Eight minutes later, when the police arrived at Griffith's mansion in the Freck Point neighborhood of Ruston, they

*continued* ▶

encountered Mr. Griffith barefoot and dressed in shorts and T-shirt, standing at the front door. In the upstairs bedroom, police found Sondra Griffith, 51, lying on the bed. She had multiple stab wounds and blood was everywhere—on her, the ceiling, the bed, the carpet, and the walls. Mr. Griffith said that his wife's wedding ring was missing from her finger. The drawers on the dresser and the bedside table were open. A jewelry box on the dresser was open, and jewelry was missing.

Samuel Griffith said that he and his wife, Sondra, spent the evening together in their home in Freck Point. After dinner, they watched a DVD of an old movie, *A Place in the Sun*.

Following the movie, the two changed into bathrobes and went out to their hot tub in the gazebo. The gazebo was situated some 30 yards behind the house and separated from the house by a tall hedge. There they sat and drank wine until midnight, when Mrs. Griffith said that she was going to bed. Mr. Griffith stayed by the pool reading a book.

He said that when he came in through the back door, around 1:00 A.M., he saw the front door open and heard a sound upstairs. He ran up the stairs where he saw a tall man—6 feet 2 inches tall—knife in hand, run from their bedroom. The man shoved him aside, ran down the stairs and out the front door.

When the police arrived, a bloody bathrobe was located in the bathroom. Sam Griffith said he had been wearing a robe because he and his wife had been in the hot tub in the backyard. A forensic expert later concluded that Sam Griffith's robe and slippers had castoff blood spatter patterns, indicating that he was in his wife's presence when she was stabbed. The police found a bloody knife in bushes three blocks away from the Griffiths' home, and it matched a set of knives in the Griffiths' kitchen. Near where the knife was found, police also located a Sprite can. DNA testing of the Sprite can showed blood that came from Sondra Griffith and saliva that came from Sam Griffith. Griffith had told the police that he had not chased after the intruder and that he remained at the house until the police arrived.

It appeared that the Griffiths were prosperous. Sam, a Marine Corps veteran, has had some success as a writer of popular mysteries. Sondra was a high-paid executive with Shepard Pharmaceuticals Corporation. However, the investigation disclosed that Sondra was in jeopardy of losing her job, and the couple had $190,000 in credit lines in 15 accounts. Worse, they were spending $125,000 per year more than their income. Sam Griffith's royalties from mysteries were minimal. Sondra was insured for $2 million through Shepard Pharmaceuticals.

Sam Griffith was having an affair with Roberta Dicer, who was 33 and their former maid.

Mr. Griffith was previously married to his first wife Marian for nine years; they had a son, Matthew, who was eight years old, and a daughter, Molly, who was 13 years old on the day their mother died. Marian Griffith also had a daughter from a previous marriage, Kathleen Brenneman, whom the Griffiths later adopted when Sondra's first husband died in a car accident. Shortly after the murder of Sondra Griffith, who was Sam Griffith's second wife, the Jamner County Prosecutor's office requested that the investigation into the death of Sam's first wife, Marian Griffith, be reopened.

### RUSTON POLICE DEPARTMENT
### CASE SUMMARY

**Suspect: Samuel L. Griffith**                                  **Case No. 65943**
**Victim: Marian Griffith**

The Jamner County Prosecutor's office requested that an investigation into the death of Marian Griffith, Sam Griffith's first wife, be reopened. The Jamner Prosecutor's office contacted the Mal Police Department because Marian Griffith died in Mal, Oregon. The reason for additional investigation of that death is that suspect Samuel Griffith's second wife, Sondra, was murdered in Ruston. Both Mal and Ruston Police Department homicide detectives worked in cooperation with the Richland County district attorney in Mal, Oregon.

#### The History of the Investigation of Marian Griffith's Death

Twenty-five years ago, suspect Samuel Griffith married Marian Earl in Mal, Oregon. Marian had a daughter, Kathleen Brenneman, by a prior marriage. The Griffiths later adopted Kathleen. Together, Sam and Marian had two children—son, Matthew, and daughter, Molly. During their marriage, Sam worked as a journalist with the *Mal Gazette*, a daily newspaper.

On August 20, 16 years ago, Sam and Marian Griffith were staying at the Gun Lodge at Priest Lake, Oregon. Their children were away with relatives. According to suspect Griffith's statement at the time to Mal Police Department, that afternoon he and Marian decided to take their inflatable Sevylor raft out on the lake for a row and swim because Marian thought it would be romantic. They set off at around 5:00 P.M. from the Gun Lodge dock. They paddled over to Portage Bay, which is just around a point from the Lodge.

Again, according to the suspect at the time, Sam Griffith, after they arrived in Portage Bay, they were swimming near the raft. Marian developed a leg cramp and was clinging to the raft. Then the wake from a speedboat 25 yards away caused the raft to overturn. He heard Marian cough. Sam said that he righted the raft and pulled his wife into it. Marian was not conscious, and he attempted CPR but got no response from her. Sam said he then rowed her to shore, which took around ten minutes. By the time they reached shore, Marian was dead.

At the time Marian Griffith died, she was insured for $250,000 and was unemployed. For over a year, the Griffiths had been facing bankruptcy. As her beneficiary, the suspect collected on the policy. Oregon's Medical Examiner found no marks on Marian's body and classified the death as a "possible accident" and that Marian died from asphyxia due to drowning.

The Mal Police Department case file revealed that the detectives, during the week after Marian Griffith's death, went to the lake with the seized raft. Two lifeguards, who were the same size as the suspect and Marian, got in the water and attempted to reenact what the suspect had described. Several boats were run by the raft to create the largest waves they could, but the raft never capsized. This reenactment was videotaped, and the tape is still with the case file.

*continued* ▶

> ### Present Investigation
>
> Reopening the Marian Griffith case, the Oregon autopsy report along with the Mal Police Report and autopsy photographs have been reviewed by Dr. Rheanna Rule, the Jamner County pathologist. Dr. Rule concluded that Marian Griffith could have been deliberately drowned without any marks being inflicted on her body.
>
> In cooperation with the Ruston Police Department investigation, the Mal Police Department canvassed cabins in the Portage Bay area and located a new witness, Alexandra Torres. She recalled the rafting incident because of the news about the drowning near the Gun Lodge. At the time of the incident, the police never contacted her. Ms. Torres had been sitting on her cabin porch that faces Portage Bay. She was reading and watching a couple in the raft 150 yards away as they paddled into the Bay and paddled around. There was some boat traffic. She saw the couple get in the water and swim around, but she never saw the raft turn over. Ms. Torres watched as Sam slowly rowed toward Gun Lodge.
>
> Charges were never filed against Sam Griffith in Oregon, and the State of Major has no jurisdiction over the case.
>
> *Michael Doerty*
> Detective, Ruston Police Department

Shortly after Sondra Griffith's murder, her daughter by a former marriage, Kathleen Brenneman, stepped forward.

> ### The *Freck Point Wrongful Death* Case
>
> After the death of Sondra Griffith, Kathleen Brenneman, Sondra's and Sam's adopted daughter, learned that her mother was insured for $2 million and contacted a lawyer. The lawyer determined that under Sondra's life insurance policy, her husband, Samuel Griffith, was the primary beneficiary. But under the State of Major's slayer statute, Kathleen would inherit if Sam was found to have killed his wife. Kathleen contemplated filing a wrongful death suit alleging that Samuel Griffith caused her mother's death.

As the prosecutor, your first obligation is to decide what criminal charges, if any, should be filed against the suspect, Samuel L. Griffith. When you do so, you are selecting your legal theory of the case. Suppose that you, as the prosecutor, make the filing decision rather than submitting it to a grand jury. You apply the same two-step process described on pages 29-31 that can be used whenever you select a legal theory.

### Step 1: Identify Potential Legal Theories

In a homicide case, the potential legal theories range from murder in the first degree with aggravating factors, a charge that would allow for the imposition of the death penalty, down to involuntary manslaughter. In this case, the significant question is whether any of the legal theories apply because of problems with proving that Samuel Griffith committed the crime. Before you would file charges, you would need to be satisfied that sufficient evidence exists to prove that he was the killer. We will reserve an analysis of that issue until we later discuss factual and persuasive sufficiency of the legal theory.

### Step 2: Assessing the Strengths and Weaknesses

The next step is to use the three analytical considerations to determine which legal theory or theories should be chosen.

*1. Assessing the Legal Theory in the Abstract:* Assuming that the evidence is sufficient to prove that Samuel Griffith killed his wife Sondra, most of the legal theories from manslaughter to aggravated first degree murder seem invulnerable to a defense challenge that the legal theory is improperly charged.

However, when you review the statutory list of aggravating factors (multiple victims, murdering a witness or a law enforcement officer, and so on) that would elevate a premeditated murder in the first degree charge to aggravated murder and a possible death penalty, you find that only one aggravating factor might apply—murder in the first degree committed in the course of or furtherance of a robbery.

Also, you consider charging felony murder in the first degree based on a first degree robbery theory. The murder statute states that a person commits first degree murder if the person "commits or attempts to commit the crime of robbery in either the first or second degree . . . and in the course of or in furtherance of such crime, or in immediate flight therefrom, he or she, or another participant, causes the death of a person other than one of the participants."

While at the crime scene you note that Sondra Griffith's wedding ring and other jewelry are missing. While that seems to provide sufficient evidence for an allegation that she was killed during a robbery, that allegation would be in conflict with a case theory that her husband killed her and staged the robbery.

*2. Assessing the Legal Theory in Relation to Other Potential Theories:* This requires evaluating the advantages and disadvantages of each potential legal theory against each available factual theory. As the prosecutor, your objective is to identify the crime that most accurately labels the defendant's conduct, because your overall responsibility as a prosecutor is to do justice. If the defendant is convicted of the appropriate crime, the proportionate sentence will apply.

You examine the facts to determine whether there is sufficient evidence to prove that Sam Griffith committed murder in the first degree on a premeditated murder legal theory. The murder statute states, "all murder which is premeditated by any kind of willful, deliberate, and premeditated killing is murder of the first degree." The word *premeditated* under the case law means "considered beforehand." Setting aside the main issue of whether Sam Griffith stabbed his wife, the evidence seems sufficient for a jury to be justified in concluding that the murder was premeditated. The perpetrator stabbed her multiple times, indicating that he considered the killing beforehand, although the defense could argue that this is consistent with sudden rage and passion. The jewelry was set up to look like a robbery; and perhaps most significant, the killer took a knife from the kitchen and brought the knife upstairs to the bedroom. If that killer is Sam Griffith, that single act of obtaining the knife and walking upstairs will satisfy any requirement of having "considered beforehand."

Now compare murder in the first degree with murder in the second degree, which does not require the proof of premeditation—just that the defendant killed the victim and intended to do so. Manslaughter charges require even lesser mental states—recklessness and criminal negligence. While the manner in which Sondra was killed suggests that the killer was more than merely reckless, murder in the second degree could describe the conduct, but not as accurately as first degree murder. Also, a major factor leaning toward filing first degree murder is that these crimes are, by state law, considered lesser included crimes that the jury can consider if they do not find the defendant guilty of murder in the first degree.

Let's revisit the robbery-murder theory and consider it in the context of the other legal theories. Again, the circumstantial evidence at the scene tends to show that Mrs. Griffith was killed during a robbery. Her wedding ring is gone from her hand along with the jewelry from the jewelry box on the dresser, and the open dresser and bedside table drawers would suggest robbery. However, if you charged Samuel Griffith on a robbery-murder theory, that charge would be inconsistent with your factual and legal theories that Sam Griffith premeditated the killing of his wife and staged the robbery scene. So, you could settle on a charge of first degree murder on a premeditation theory.

*3. Assessing the Legal Theory in Conjunction with the Available and Potential Evidence in the Case:* As you conduct the preceding assessments of the legal theory, you are always mindful of assessing the legal theory within the context of evaluating whether there is sufficient evidence to support the legal theory. The ABA Model Rule of Professional Conduct 3.8 provides that "the prosecutor in a criminal case shall: (a) refrain from prosecuting a charge that the prosecutor knows is not supported by probable cause." This is a low evidentiary standard requiring only that the prosecutor have a reasonable belief that a crime was committed and that the defendant committed the crime. Prosecutors have developed other higher evidentiary standards. For instance, a higher evidentiary standard for filing charges requires that the evidence will prove the defendant guilty beyond a reasonable doubt. Another prosecutorial standard requires that sufficient evidence exists so a reasonable jury would be justified in convicting, taking into consideration potential defenses. This filing standard requires less than the reasonable doubt standard. In the *Freck Point* case, the prosecutor would apply the probable cause test required by the Rules of Professional Conduct and any evidentiary standard that the prosecutor's office applies in making a filing decision when examining the two major issues in the case: (1) whether the defendant murdered his wife, and (2) if he did, whether he premeditated the killing or stabbed his wife multiple times in the heat of passion.

## C.  Factual Theory

The factual theory is more than an accumulation of relevant information. It is constructed from the mass of evidence you have, or have reasonable belief you might subsequently obtain, to support your legal theory. While the case theory is made up of two components—the legal and factual theories—the factual theory can be conceptualized as also having two subparts. The factual theory must be both (1) *factually sufficient* to support the legal theory, and (2) *factually persuasive*. It can be viewed as follows:

**Case Theory**

#### Factually Sufficient

As the plaintiff's counsel or prosecutor, your factual theory must be factually sufficient to support your legal theory. During the trial you must get sufficient evidence admitted to legally entitle your client to have the jury deliberate on her case. In other words, when you state at the conclusion of the prosecution's case that the "State rests," if the defense moves to dismiss your case, the judge will deny the motion, ruling that you have established a prima facie case and that it should be up to the jury to decide whether it has been proven beyond a reasonable doubt. The *factual sufficiency* component of your case theory will have been satisfied.

For example, in the *Freck Point Murder* case, if the defendant is charged with premeditated first degree murder, as the prosecutor you will have proved enough facts to establish a prima facie case that on October 16 of last year, defendant Griffith considered beforehand taking his wife's life and that he then killed her in Jamner County, Major.

#### Persuasive

As the prosecutor, you have a story with a plot, and it is factually sufficient to support your legal theory of premeditated first degree murder: Samuel Griffith stabbed his wife and got blood spatter on his robe. He staged a robbery to make it look like she had been killed by an intruder. This is factually sufficient to support your legal theory of premeditated murder in the first degree. Most lawyers understand the concept that they must produce sufficient evidence to support their legal theories.

However, it is also necessary to prove a factually persuasive case. You want to persuade the jury to want to render the verdict that you are seeking. For instance, in the *Freck Point* case, the prosecutor should go further and tell a persuasive story that will compel the jury to want to find the defendant guilty beyond a reasonable doubt. To create a persuasive story requires attention to at least these five key essentials: (1) human values and needs, (2) human story, (3) believable and understandable story, (4) quantity of evidence, and (5) quality of evidence.

### 1. Human Values and Needs

To be persuasive, the factual story should be about human values that the jurors share. These are values that are common in the community, such as honesty, fair treatment, safety, family, and so on. Having a factual story that radiates human values is critical to swaying a jury.

The history of Dr. Jack Kevorkian's trials provides a striking illustration of the importance of human values to a jury. Dr. Kevorkian was prosecuted repeatedly for assisting suicides. Prosecutors presented evidence that was factually sufficient to support the murder charges and successfully defeated motions to dismiss for insufficient evidence. But factual sufficiency was not enough. Three times Dr. Kevorkian was acquitted, and on another occasion the court granted a mistrial when the jury deadlocked. In each case, the defense told a story about human suffering that cried out for mercy, and that story with human values at its core was compelling. It was not until Dr. Kevorkian went on national television, helping a man commit suicide and goading prosecutors to charge him, that he was eventually convicted.

One of the values that we all care about is the fulfillment of human needs. We all require food, sleep, love, freedom, belonging, safety, and other human needs. The plaintiff is usually telling a story of deprivation of human needs, such as safety, financial security, or love. In this regard, Abraham Maslow's theory regarding human needs is helpful. Professor Maslow, who was the chair of the psychology department at Brandeis University, created a pyramid of human needs. He theorized that each person has these needs. A person, Maslow also believed, cannot fulfill higher-level needs such as esteem or self-actualization if he does not consistently have his lower-level needs met. Jurors can relate to the deprivation of these human needs. Therefore, trial lawyers should focus on these fundamental needs when crafting the story. Abraham H. Maslow, *Motivation and Personality* (Abraham H. Maslow ed., Harper Collins Publishers 1987) (1954).

**MASLOW'S PYRAMID**

## Human Values and Needs

### The *Freck Point Murder* Case

In the *Freck Point Murder* case, the prosecutor can emphasize the value of personal safety and a human life in closing argument:

> "Ladies and gentlemen, this case is about the taking of a human life. That man, Samuel Griffith—the person the victim most trusted in the place she felt safest, her own bedroom—coldly stabbed his wife six times as part of his scheme to collect on her life insurance."

### 2. Human Story

Trial work is storytelling. Whether plaintiff, prosecutor, or defense counsel, the attorney crafts the trial evidence or lack of evidence into a story to tell the jurors. The story must be brought alive or the jury just won't care. To accomplish this, counsel will want to tell a story about a real human being, someone the jury can care about. To this end, the plaintiff will want to elicit from witnesses at trial as much human background information as the law allows.

## Human Story

### The *Freck Point Murder* Case

In the *Freck Point Murder* trial, the prosecutor will want to prove as much background information as possible about Sondra Griffith. During the prosecution's case-in-chief, the prosecutor would elicit testimony about who she was, and get a photograph of her admitted into evidence. This testimony could cover her education, her life before meeting the defendant, Sondra's adopted daughter Kathleen, her successful work career, the whirlwind courtship, and her marriage to Samuel Griffith. The goal is to paint a picture of Sondra as a living, breathing human being, not a one-dimensional stick figure.

### 3. Believable and Understandable Story

Like any story, the trial story must be believable. A believable story for the jury is one that comports both with common experience and common sense. Failing to tell a believable story leaves an opening for jurors to frame the story instead of you, and it might not be favorable to your case.

The problem is that life, as the attorney's case may present, will not always appear to make sense within the context of the jurors' existing belief systems. The jurors may conclude that the story presented at trial fails to comport with their experiences or beliefs in human behavior and the way life works. At times this will be because the story presented is unworthy of belief; for example, look at some of the beliefs that have been held or discarded over the past 50 years. Belief: A rape victim will attempt to escape if given a chance. However, there are instances when a rape victim did not try to escape when she had the opportunity. Belief: An abused child will report the abuse. However, there are countless cases where children abused by an authority figure (stepfather, priest, teacher) did not report the abuse. Belief: A domestic violence victim will call the police, leave the batterer, or at least tell someone about the beatings. Again, there are scores of cases where a defendant shot her partner whom she claims abused her for years, although she never called the police or left the abuser.

In the *Freck Point Murder* case, as the prosecutor, you have a story that at first may not make sense to the jurors. If Samuel Griffith planned the murder, jurors might conclude it makes no sense that he would be at home, call 911, and not create an alibi. Even though the evidence shows that he had a different plan than their preferred script for committing a murder and getting away with it, you do not want the jury to reach the conclusion he didn't commit the murder because there is a better way to plan a murder. This is when your story is critical to the success of the case.

It is when the potential conflict between reality and juror preconceptions exists that getting the full story before the jury is so important. By full story, we mean the story that accounts for or explains human behavior and events that may not otherwise make sense to the jurors. This may involve having the rape victim explain her fear of injury that prevented her from trying to escape. It may involve calling an expert to explain child abuse syndrome and the fact that it is common for a child *not* to confide in an adult. It also may involve supporting the defendant's self-defense claim in the murder case by calling an expert in battered woman syndrome to explain the cycle of violence.

Another critical point is that the jury must understand the story. Trials are complex in three ways. First, the story involves numerous events and/or players. Second, the story is complex because the subject matter involves technical information—scientific methodologies. Third, the story involves both of the first two complexities. To present a complex story that will be digestible by the jurors, counsel can use experts to translate and explain technical information. Trial visuals, such as charts and computer slideshow presentations (PowerPoint), are valuable tools to communicate complex information, and may be used to make the information accessible to the jurors.

### 4. *Quantity of Evidence*

Even if there is sufficient evidence to defeat a motion for judgment as a matter of law (directed verdict), or to prevent the case from being dismissed at the close of the plaintiff's case, it still may not be enough to convince a jury. While the judge will review the evidence in the light most favorable to the plaintiff when deciding these motions, the jury weighs the evidence under a higher burden of proof—a preponderance of the evidence in a civil case and beyond a reasonable doubt in a criminal case. When applying those burdens, the fact finder is not bound to see facts in favor of either side, though in a criminal case they begin with the presumption that the defendant is not guilty.

## Quantity of Evidence

### The *Freck Point Murder* Case

Suppose that defendant Griffith filed a motion to dismiss. The prosecution can offer testimony describing the crime scene on the night of the murder and the defendant's presence. Expert testimony demonstrated that the blood spatter patterns on defendant Griffith's robe showed he was present and in close proximity to his wife when she was stabbed. The trial judge would deny a defense motion to dismiss on the basis of insufficient evidence to prove the defendant committed the crime. The judge would rule that by viewing blood spatter evidence in a light most favorable to the prosecution, the prosecution established a prima facie case on the issue of who stabbed the victim. The judge would most likely state that the jury should weigh expert's testimony and decide whether the prosecution proved that Samuel Griffith was the murderer beyond a reasonable doubt. This evidence submitted by the prosecutor defeated the motion to dismiss.

To persuade the jury, the prosecutor would not rely merely on this evidence. Rather, the prosecutor would offer a quantity of evidence to convince the jury beyond a reasonable doubt that Samuel Griffith murdered his wife Sondra. That evidence, among other things, would include the insurance money he would receive on her death, the DNA evidence of saliva on the Sprite can splattered with the victim's blood, the fact that he left the home (contrary to what he told the police), that he was in the vicinity of where the knife was found, that he delayed before calling the police, and so on.

### 5. Quality of Evidence

The evidence you have to support your story must be believable—that is, it must be of sufficient quality. Thus, establishing the believability of your witness and the witness's testimony is essential.

Also, as previously mentioned, the story itself must be believable. It must appear coherent and comport with the jury's common sense and everyday experience with human nature. In short, it must make sense. If the prosecution's story does not make sense, the jury is likely to translate the lack of quality into reasonable doubt. If a civil plaintiff's story does not make sense, the jury is likely to give credence to the alternative factual theory that supports the defense. Here, we focus more narrowly on the witness testimony, rather than the overarching trial story of the plaintiff or defendant. Evidence offered by each witness must make sense to the jurors; otherwise, the jury could find a weakness leading to a reasonable doubt.

## Quality of Evidence

### The *Freck Point Murder* Case

In the *Freck Point Murder* case, the blood spatter expert put the defendant in close proximity of his wife Sondra at the time of the stabbing. Therefore, the quality of the expert as a witness and of the witness's testimony is essential to a conviction. To persuade the jury, the expert must appear to be a well-qualified, credible, unbiased witness.

## D.  Case Assessment

Next, you need a methodology for identifying and assessing positive and negative factors, particularly in regard to the ingredients of a persuasive story that support and undermine your case. The methodology we suggest is a case assessment exercise to detect those strengths and weaknesses.

The case assessment is a brainstorming exercise in which you draw a line down the middle of a sheet of paper. On the left side, record the strengths of the case; on the right side, list the weaknesses. The best time to engage in a case assessment is when you first review the case file, for that is when you will view the evidence as a juror would for the first time. Repeat the case assessment exercise later, after you have accumulated more evidence. Also, involve as many other people in the brainstorming session as you can. In this way, you gain their impressions of the case as well. Like any brainstorming session, there is no necessary order to what you list. Judgment on the worthiness of the listed items is withheld during the brainstorming session to avoid stifling the flow of ideas. It is important to think in terms of the five key essentials of a persuasive story that are covered above: (1) human values and needs, (2) human story, (3) believable and understandable story, (4) quantity of evidence, and (5) quality of evidence.

To illustrate how case assessment works, we use the *Freck Point Murder* case. The prosecutor's brainstorming session could produce, among other items, the following lists of strengths and weaknesses about the prosecution's case.

### CASE ASSESSMENT CHART

| Strengths | Weaknesses |
| --- | --- |
| • Loss of human life—Sondra Griffith. <br> • Victim is defendant's wife of 12 years. <br> • Domestic violence. | • Defendant's wife killed. <br> • Appear to be loving couple. <br> • No prior domestic abuse known. <br> • Circumstantial evidence only—no witness except the defendant. |

| Strengths | Weaknesses |
|---|---|
| • Brutal stabbing.<br>• Victim is a sympathetic businesswoman and mother of Kathleen Brenneman.<br>• Motive—life insurance.<br>• Defendant was in serious financial difficulty.<br>• Defendant's wife was in jeopardy of losing her job.<br>• Blood spatter on defendant's bathrobe and slippers show he was in close proximity of wife when stabbed.<br>• Defendant was having an affair.<br>• Defendant's saliva and victim's blood on Sprite can near where the knife was found.<br>• Defendant said he didn't leave the house.<br>• Knife goes with the Griffiths' set of knives.<br>• Evidence that the defendant walked around the bedroom in bare feet. | • Defendant called 911.<br>• Defendant said there was an intruder who killed his wife.<br>• Home invasion.<br>• Defendant is a respected member of the community and a writer of some renown.<br>• Sondra was employed and making $185,000 per year.<br>• They had some financial holdings, including equity in the house, rental properties, and so on.<br>• Defendant was working on a new mystery novel, which he thought would sell well.<br>• Defense likely to employ a blood spatter expert who disagrees with the state's blood spatter expert.<br>• Jewelry and ring are missing.<br>• No gloves found—forensics indicate gloves were worn. |

The results of the case assessment brainstorming are a wealth of information for the development of your persuasive factual theory. For instance, the values that the prosecutor could stress that the jury can relate to and be deeply moved by, in addition to the loss of Sondra's life, include the abhorrence of greed, domestic violence, and brutal killing. The human story to be told is one about Sondra. The strengths of the circumstantial case also become readily apparent.

This case assessment has also disclosed case weaknesses, such as circumstantial evidence, a concept the prosecutor can discuss during jury selection and opening statement. The assessment also revealed parts of the prosecution's story that do not seem to make common sense—the missing gloves and jewelry. All of that will, if possible, have to be explained.

## IV. DEFENDANT'S CASE THEORY

### A. Types of Theories

Potential theories available to a civil or criminal defendant are more varied than those available to the plaintiff or prosecutor. Plaintiff's case theory, both the legal theory and the factual theory, is an attack on the defendant. The plaintiff, through the case theory, is accusing the defendant of breaching a contract, causing harm through negligence, murdering someone, violating a lease, manufacturing hazardous products, and so on. The defendant can respond to this attack in three ways: (1) strike at weaknesses in the plaintiff's case theory in an attempt to blunt or end the plaintiff's attack, (2) launch a separate counterattack, and/or (3) decide that negotiation is the most viable alternative.

### 1. Attacking Weaknesses in the Plaintiff's Case Theory

Defense legal theories that strike at weaknesses in the plaintiff's case theory concentrate their attack in one or more of four directions:

- *Legality* of the plaintiff's case theory (there is no such legal theory);
- *Factual sufficiency* of the plaintiff's case theory (such a legal theory exists, but the party's factual allegations are insufficient as a matter of law to raise the legal theory);
- *Persuasive sufficiency* of the plaintiff's case (though such a legal theory exists and sufficient facts have been presented to avoid summary judgment motions and motions for a judgment as a matter of law, the jury should not be persuaded given the applicable burden of persuasion); and/or
- *Procedural aspects* of the plaintiff's case theory (the party is barred because of some procedural rule, such as a statute of limitations or lack of personal jurisdiction).

### 2. Affirmative Defense and Other Attacks

Defense legal theories exist that do not specifically attack the plaintiff's legal or factual theories, but rather are independent claims in defense. These are *affirmative defenses*. Even if the plaintiff's legal theory cannot be attacked, the defendant should not be liable, or defendant's liability should be mitigated, due to some affirmative grounds such as fraud, self-defense, and accord and satisfaction.

Defense legal theories based on attacks on persuasive sufficiency and on affirmative defenses provide the principal focus for defense trial strategies in this book. Yet attacks based on legality, factual sufficiency, and procedural concerns (such as motion to dismiss or motion for summary judgment) also constitute legal theories, although some might not initially think of them as such. This may be because these theories are generally directed to the court, which, rather than the jury, will make any factual findings under the theories that are required.

### 3. Start with Jury Instructions

Just as pattern jury instructions serve as a starting point for identifying and planning plaintiff's legal theory, they also often can serve as the common sense touchstone for determining defenses—the defense legal theory. Instructions setting out what the plaintiff must prove to prevail inform the defense as to what elements the defense can attack for insufficient proof. Also, the jury instructions set out the elements of an affirmative defense—what the defense attorney must prove at trial. Because jury instructions state the defense's legal theory of insufficient evidence or an affirmative defense, defense counsel, just like plaintiff's counsel, should assemble jury instructions early in trial preparation.

### 4. Negotiation and Settlement

The defendant can decide that negotiation is the best alternative. However, even if the case strategy centers on obtaining some form of settlement, an attorney wants to develop the best possible case theory and prepare for trial, because that preparation will provide the most leverage in terms of making the adversary consider the evidence and risk of trial, and will best enable the lawyer to be an able advocate during negotiation.

## B. Legal Insufficiency

A defense legal theory that attacks the legality of plaintiff's case theory focuses on the validity of plaintiff's claim under existing law. This type of attack takes the position that, as a matter of law, plaintiff's legal theory should not be recognized as one for which the court will provide a remedy. In this type of attack, plaintiff has raised all the elements of her claim, but the defense argues that the claim itself is not recognized as law.

These types of defense legal theories are developed by analyzing plaintiff's legal theory within the context of relevant substantive law. This analysis, of course, is not a neutral inquiry, but takes place from an ends-means perspective. Defense counsel begins with the position that a claim for relief is not stated because current law (statutes, regulations, cases) does not recognize the claim as presented by plaintiff. Counsel then scrutinizes plaintiff's claim and the existing law in an attempt to develop a plausible argument to sustain that position. Naturally, there may not be a plausible argument for this position, and defense counsel then will have to focus on other lines of attack.

To illustrate this and other theories, consider the *Hill Moveit Personal Injury* case. This case is set out as plaintiff's case and defendant's case.

---

### The *Hill Moveit Personal Injury* Case
#### Plaintiff's Case

On Saturday, September 8, two years ago and just after midnight, Darcy Rutherford, 36 years old, just concluded her shift at the Korner Restaurant and Lounge, where she worked as a bartender. Before leaving work, fellow employee Millie Steadman

*continued* ▶

---

saw her drink a glass of pinot noir. Darcy was driving home on Highway 57 in Ruston, Major. She was following an SUV driven by Stan Luby. Luby's vehicle was pulling an uncovered utility trailer with a label on its side reading "Hill Moveit."

Suddenly, an entertainment center tumbled out of the Hill Moveit utility trailer. A piece of the furniture smashed through the windshield of Darcy Rutherford's car, and the full force of the furniture and windshield glass struck her head and upper body. Ms. Rutherford was rushed to Ruston Medical Center (RMC), where on arrival she was nearly dead. But she did not die. According to medical staff at RMC, she had the most serious medical injuries from which anyone had ever recovered.

Darcy Rutherford filed suit against Hill Moveit International Corporation, Stanley Luby, and Fergun GasPump, the company that leased the Hill Moveit trailer to Luby, and plead the following claims:

- Against Hill Moveit: Under the State of Major's Product Liability Act (MPLA), claim for strict liability for unsafe construction and design because of the trailer's open construction and lack of tie-downs, failure to provide adequate warnings with the product, failure to provide adequate warnings after manufacture about the dangers of carrying a load in the trailer, not utilizing tie-downs, as well as negligent failure to warn;
- Against Fergun GasPump: The same claims for product liability and failure to warn, as well as negligent lease of chattel; and
- Against Stanley Luby: A claim for negligent use of the trailer that he rented.

The complaint seeks general damages for permanent injuries and disability, and for pain and loss of enjoyment of life; special damages include loss of earnings and capacity to earn, as well as expenses for care and medical treatment. The complaint requests that judgment for damages be joint and several against the three defendants.

---

### The *Hill Moveit Personal Injury* Case
### Defendant's Case

The defense raised as defenses the plaintiff's intoxication at the time of the accident, making her negligent per se and barring recovery, and plaintiff's comparative fault by following the trailer too closely. The last two defenses would have significant consequences if the defense prevails for, under the State of Major law, joint and several liability can apply only where the plaintiff is fault free. So, if the jury were to decide that Darcy Rutherford contributed to the accident by being intoxicated or following too closely behind the trailer pulled by Stanley Luby's car, each defendant would have to pay only its portion of the verdict.

The intoxication and following-too-closely defenses have been developed during discovery and pretrial preparation. Plaintiff's discovery included Darcy Rutherford's medical records from Ruston Medical Center, which included testing for alcohol in her blood. From the testing done at the Medical Center, a defense consulting toxicologist concluded that her blood alcohol level was between .06 and .10. The legal limit in the State of Major is .08. The defense expert contends that this test is valid and that Darcy Rutherford was impaired at the time she was injured, while the plaintiff's expert opines that the test was unreliable and inaccurate.

Also, the defense hired an accident reconstruction expert, Dr. Riley, who reviewed the evidence and concluded that Ms. Rutherford's vehicle was following too closely behind the trailer. According to Dr. Riley, the damage pattern on plaintiff's SUV when compared with the entertainment center's construction shows that the furniture piece was upside down when the SUV hit it. The base of the entertainment center was above the hood when Ms. Rutherford drove into it. It is that base that went through the windshield. The entertainment center was intact when it fell out of the trailer, and the plaintiff's vehicle hit it before the furniture could tumble and break apart. As he put it, "If she had been two seconds back—which is the Major Department of Transportation's rule—the accident would not have occurred because she would not have hit the furniture."

[Note: The plaintiff's collision reconstruction expert, Janet Strait, claims that "it's impossible for a reasonably prudent collision reconstruction expert to determine what happened, because no evidence exists that can be scientifically analyzed."]

Based on this evidence, the defense alleges in its amended answer to the complaint the plaintiff's negligence for following too closely and negligence per se for her intoxication. The thrust of the defense is this.

- She was intoxicated.
- She followed too closely behind the trailer.
- She was (therefore) incapable of evading the furniture as it fell off the trailer.

The attack on a legal theory's insufficiency asserts that no such legal theory exists. Assume that the plaintiff had alleged negligence per se based on a statute requiring secured loads. The negligence per se allegation in the complaint would be subject to dismissal if the State of Major had no specific statutory prohibition against unsecured loads. It is not hard to imagine that general statutes covering the topic of trailers would not be a sufficient basis for a negligence per se claim. Incidentally, the *Hill Moveit* case so captured the public's and media's attention that the State of Major, at the urging of the Jamner County Prosecutor, enacted a statute making it a gross misdemeanor if a person, with criminal negligence, fails to secure all or part of a load being driven on a public highway and the unsecured load causes substantial bodily harm to another person.

## C. Factual Insufficiency

Attacks on the factual sufficiency of plaintiff's case theory center on the lack of a sufficient quantum of evidence to submit the case to a jury—that is, plaintiff has failed to prove a prima facie case. We have already discussed this from the perspective of the plaintiff developing a case theory resistant to such an attack. A factual sufficiency attack takes the position that even if such a legal theory exists, plaintiff's factual allegations are insufficient as a matter of law to permit a reasonable fact finder to find one or more elements of the claim. For example, a claim is factually insufficient when there is no evidence of any consideration in a breach of contract suit, or when the only evidence in a robbery case is that the defendant was seen within a block of the victim's home because of a successful motion suppressing the victim's identification of the defendant.

These defense attacks on factual sufficiency are developed by assessing plaintiff's factual theory in the context of plaintiff's legal theory. To illustrate how an attack on factual sufficiency operates, assume that you represent Fergun GasPump, the gas station that rented the trailer to Stanley Luby. You begin to analyze plaintiff's claim by researching the pertinent substantive law—the statutes constituting the State of Major's Product Liability Act (MPLA). For plaintiff's causes of action to apply, GasPump must constitute either a manufacturer or otherwise be subject to manufacturer liability under the Revised Code of Major §§7.27.030-7.27.080. You determine that GasPump does not meet the statutory definition of a manufacturer because there is insufficient factual evidence to prove that it ever did, in the language of RCM §7.27.030(1), "design, produce, make, fabricate, construct or remanufacture the relevant product or any component part. . . ." For that reason, GasPump should not be found to be a "manufacturer" under the statute. Plaintiff also has alleged that GasPump is subject to the MPLA because its leasing activities are so vast that it should be held accountable for the acts of Hill Moveit. However, plaintiff has insufficient evidence to make a prima facie case for this proposition. Under this analysis, plaintiff's legal theory is deficient, and the court should grant a partial summary judgment dismissing causes of action against GasPump brought under MPLA.

Now that we have discussed legal and factual insufficiency, these categories need further comment. While factual insufficiency has been categorized as "factual" for purposes of organization, one could also reasonably have classified it under "legality," as it refers to factual insufficiency as a matter of law. Like most attempts at categorization, alternative schemes are thus plausible. In fact, defense legal theories could also have been divided according to the decision maker that is given the institutional role of assessing the particular defense legal theory. The defense legal theories under this alternative would be divided into those decided by

- the court (procedural attacks such as venue and lack of personal jurisdiction, failure to state a claim, and legally insufficient information to allow claim to be considered by the trier of fact);
- the fact finder after the court has determined that there is a prima facie case (affirmative defenses and procedural attacks such as the statute of limitations); and
- the fact finder without an initial determination by the court (defense based on persuading the fact finder that plaintiff has not carried its burden as to one or more elements of its legal theory).

The categorization employed in these materials, however, was chosen because it facilitates discussing the development of the various defense legal theories.

## D. Persuasive Insufficiency

An attack on the persuasive sufficiency of plaintiff's case theory focuses on plaintiff's inability to convince a jury of the plaintiff's position. This type of attack takes the position that even if plaintiff's allegations are sufficient to be submitted to the jury, the jury should find that the plaintiff has failed to carry its burden of proving one or more elements of the civil claim by a preponderance of the evidence, or the prosecution failed to prove a crime beyond a reasonable doubt. For instance, in a civil case, the persuasiveness of expert testimony regarding the cause of the plaintiff's disability might lead a jury to find that there is not proximate causation between the car accident and physical injuries. Or, in a criminal case, credibility problems with an eyewitness to an assault might raise reasonable doubt in the jurors' minds.

### Combating the Persuasiveness

Defense counsel can undermine the persuasiveness of the plaintiff's case in three ways: (1) seek to preclude the plaintiff's evidence; (2) present a competing story; and (3) focus on deficiencies in quantity, quality, and plausibility.

### 1. Preclude Plaintiff's Evidence

Defense counsel can seek to keep out plaintiff's evidence. For example, in the *Hill Moveit* case, the defense could move to bifurcate the issues of liability and damages so the jury would first resolve the issue of liability based on evidence relating only to that liability. If the motion is successful, the jury would not receive the damages evidence before reaching a verdict on liability. Only if the jury finds liability would the jury then hear evidence relating to damages. The arguments in favor of bifurcation include the following:

- **Liability and Damages Issues Are Separate:** The evidence regarding liability relates to the accident on September 8 and is not interwoven with the expert and other testimony regarding Darcy Rutherford's injuries, treatment, and care, and therefore the issues can be tried separately.
- **Judicial Economy:** Bifurcation would save court time and resources, because if the defendants are not found liable, then there would be no need to expend additional court time addressing damages. Even if the defendants were found liable, and the defendant was found to have contributed to the accident, the parties would then have a basis for further negotiation during a break before the damages phase.
- **Undue Prejudice:** The issues relating to liability can be heard by the jurors without being informed of the extensive damages' evidence that could unnecessarily prejudice them on the liability issue.

A more common way to exclude plaintiff's evidence is for the defense to make pretrial motions in limine to exclude plaintiff's evidence. For example, defense counsel in the *Freck Point Murder* case could move to exclude Sondra Griffith's autopsy photographs on the grounds that their probative value is substantially outweighed by the unfair prejudice. Fed. R. Evid. 403. In Chapter 6, we use a defense motion in limine to exclude propensity evidence of the death of Mr. Griffith's first wife, Marian, as an illustration of motions advocacy, pages 206-212.

### 2. Present a Competing Human Story with Values

Defense counsel can attempt to blunt the persuasiveness of the plaintiff's case by presenting a human story that competes with and nullifies the plaintiff's persuasive story. For example, in the *Freck Point Murder* case, defense counsel could seek to humanize the defendant and stress the value of a loving relationship with his wife, Sondra, and the loss the defendant has suffered because an intruder invaded their home and brutally murdered her.

### 3. Focus on Deficiencies in Quantity, Quality, and Plausibility

Jurors use stories to filter and sort information. In making their decision, jurors compare the stories presented to them with what they understand to be common experience and common sense. They will reject stories that don't make sense to them.

Jurors are also receptive to arguments regarding the quantity and quality of the plaintiff's proof. They fully understand that their job includes determining whether the plaintiff has met the burden of persuasion, deciding such things as whether plaintiff's witnesses are credible. Therefore, defense counsel will scrutinize the plaintiff's story to detect flaws in it.

One approach to detect deficiencies in quantity, quality, and plausibility in the plaintiff's case is to first visualize a set of facts that would constitute the perfect case for the plaintiff. Once that perfect case is constructed, defense counsel compares and contrasts it with the actual facts of the case. With this analysis, the deficiencies in the plaintiff's case are revealed, and a defense story and argument can be built from the lack of evidence.

### Implausible Story

#### The *Freck Point Murder* Case

Assume you are defense counsel in the *Freck Point Murder* case. The ideal prosecution case on identity would be one where Sondra's jewelry, wedding ring, and the gloves worn by the killer were all recovered and linked to defendant Samuel Griffith. You, as defense counsel, can compare these with the facts of the prosecution's case and argue that the prosecution has not offered a sufficient quantity of evidence to prove Samuel Griffith guilty beyond a reasonable doubt:

> "It makes no sense. If Samuel Griffith had murdered his own wife, the police would have found some evidence to show that he took his wife's jewelry and

ring, and that he possessed gloves. We know from the criminalist that the killer wore gloves—no prints were found on the knife or on the jewelry box. Within eight minutes of the 911 call, the police arrived. Sam was searched, and he didn't have gloves or jewelry. Additionally, the police thoroughly searched the Griffith home and the neighborhood, and neither jewelry nor gloves were recovered. It makes no sense that Sam killed his wife and then drove miles away to hide the evidence. He didn't have time. And there is no blood in his car. Where are the gloves and jewelry? We know where from the evidence—the intruder ran off with them in the night."

## E. Procedural Insufficiency

Defense legal theories that strike at procedural aspects of plaintiff's case theory encompass procedural considerations such as the failure to obtain personal or subject matter jurisdiction, lack of venue, or the expiration of a statute of limitations.

These legal theories are developed by comparing a list of available procedural bars (derived from the interpretation of cases, statutes, court rules, and so on, as well as any unique, creative analysis that adds to the list in a particular case) with all information in the case relevant to these procedural postures. Subsequent information, the significance of which is appreciated because you have the list of procedural bars and their corresponding elements in mind, may add possible procedural grounds as the case progresses.

## F. Affirmative Defense

### The Defense Case Theory

Defense legal theories are not restricted specifically to attacking plaintiff's legal or factual theory. The defense may raise an independent claim that, if successful, will preclude or mitigate plaintiff's right to relief. When asserting this claim, known as an affirmative defense, defense counsel is taking the position that even if plaintiff has established all the elements of his theory, the defendant has a legal defense based on case law or statute (for example, fraud in the inducement, latches, or insanity). Some affirmative defenses attack the propriety of plaintiff's behavior, accusing the plaintiff, say, of delay or fraud, much as plaintiff's legal theory attacks the defendant. Other affirmative defenses merely assert that the defendant has done no wrong, claiming privilege or insanity. In criminal law, while some authorities reserve the use of the term *affirmative defense* to those defenses that carry a burden of proof, the term when used here does not carry that implication.

As independent claims for relief, seeking to deny or mitigate plaintiff's claim, affirmative defenses are composed of elements, just as plaintiff's legal theories are. For example, in setting forth an affirmative defense of self-defense in using deadly force, a defendant is asserting that under the applicable burden of proof (which may be on the defense or prosecution depending on jurisdiction), these elements exist: (1) Defendant reasonably feared she was threatened, (2) with death or great bodily injury, (3) the threat was imminent, and (4) the amount of force used in defense was necessary.

### 1. Available Defenses

In developing an affirmative defense, you must first determine the affirmative defenses theoretically possible in the case. This requires examining plaintiff's legal theory. Every legal theory carries with it a number of accepted affirmative defenses found in cases, statutes, or court rules, as well as the possibility of new affirmative defenses that evolve from creative analysis of case trends. These new or creative affirmative defenses are also likely to arise through inductive thinking: Information in a case can provide a brainstorm for a new affirmative defense theory. You will then seek supporting and analogous authority to uphold the theory.

### 2. Available Evidence

Consider the evidence that is, and reasonably may be, available in the case. Try to match this evidence, and the inferences from the evidence, with the required elements of each potential affirmative defense. When appropriate, also consider each affirmative defense in the abstract and in conjunction with other affirmative defenses.

---

## Affirmative Defenses

### The *Hill Moveit Personal Injury* Case

#### Available Affirmative Defenses

As Hill Moveit's lawyer, your research of State of Major law revealed these potential affirmative defenses to product liability: substantial alteration of the trailer after it left your client's possession; abnormal and unforeseen use of the trailer; plaintiff's intoxication at the time of the accident, making her negligent per se and barring recovery provided the plaintiff was more than 50 percent at fault; and plaintiff's comparative fault by following the trailer too closely. The last two defenses, plaintiff's intoxication and following the trailer too closely, would have significant consequences if the defense prevails because under the State of Major law, joint and several liability applies only where the plaintiff is fault free. If the jury was to decide that Darcy Rutherford contributed to the accident by being intoxicated or following too closely behind the trailer pulled by Stanley Luby's car, each defendant would have to pay only his or her portion of the verdict.

#### Available Evidence

The intoxication and following-too-closely defenses have been developed during discovery and pretrial preparation. Plaintiff's discovery included Darcy Rutherford's medical records from Reston Medical Center that showed that her blood alcohol level was between .06 and .10. The limit in the State of Major is .08. Also, the defense hired an accident reconstruction expert who reviewed the evidence and concluded that Ms. Rutherford's vehicle was following too closely behind the trailer. Based on this evidence, the defense alleges in its amended answer to the complaint the plaintiff's negligence for following too closely and negligence per se for her intoxication. The thrust of the defenses is that she was intoxicated and was following too closely, and therefore was incapable of evading the furniture as it fell off the trailer.

### Plaintiff's Attacks on Defense Case Theory

It should not be surprising that the process for selecting an affirmative defense is analogous to the process of selecting the plaintiff's legal theory. Likewise, plaintiff's attacks on a defense case theory founded on an affirmative defense parallels the types of attacks a defendant generally can make against a plaintiff's legal theory.

For instance, how can plaintiff Rutherford respond to the affirmative defenses of negligence based on intoxication and following too closely? Here are a few illustrations:

- Factual Insufficiency: Concerning the intoxication affirmative defense, plaintiff could attack the proximate cause element. In other words, even if it is assumed that Rutherford was intoxicated, no evidence exists that her impairment was a proximate cause of the accident; therefore, she could not have been negligent.
- Combating the Persuasiveness by Excluding Evidence: Plaintiff could make a motion in limine to exclude the hospital blood test results as unreliable, and to exclude the accident reconstruction expert's testimony because the expert lacks the necessary qualifications to render an opinion.

## V. MULTIPLE LEGAL THEORIES

There are three situations in which a party might consider more than one legal theory in a case: evidence gathering, strategic sequence, and alternatives.

### A. Evidence Gathering

First, counsel may pursue several tentative legal theories during the evidence-gathering phase, which usually, but not always, takes place at a relatively early stage. As facts are uncovered, these multiple tentative theories generally are eliminated or abandoned because of lack of evidence to support them, inconsistency, or strategic concerns. Counsel will usually try to reduce the number of legal theories as quickly as is feasible because the evidence-gathering process itself is far more efficient if guided by a single legal theory.

## B.  Strategic Sequence

Second, multiple legal theories may be used in strategic sequence. A defendant in a breach of contract case may begin by alleging a procedural bar, then, failing in that, move to dismiss for failure to state a claim for relief, and finally end up arguing the case on the basis that the plaintiff's witnesses attesting to the element of consideration are too biased to be believed. This use of multiple theories illustrates the concept of the backup theory. This concept reflects the necessity of an attorney planning for every conceivable contingency and alternative throughout the representation of a client.

## C.  Alternatives

Third, a party may present the fact finder or adversary in negotiation with alternative legal theories. The plaintiff in a contract dispute may allege both a breach of contract and fraud. A prosecutor may charge the same defendant with theft and burglary. At some point, however, the factual theories (stories) underlying the alternative legal theories may become so divergent, or even inconsistent, that a choice must be made prior to negotiation or trial.

## VI.  CASE THEME

First-rate case themes are a lawyer's treasure. The theme captures the case theory and distills it so that it will be memorable and sway the jury. It is the bridge between the factual theory and the jury's human experience and understanding. The theme can be a word, a phrase, an analogy, or another device that vividly describes the case. The theme can be repeated and become the structural glue holding the case together throughout the various stages of trial from opening through closing. The task of crafting a case theme is a challenging one. It requires a firm grasp of the case and its significance.

### Theme: "The Ultimate Betrayal of Trust"

#### The *Freck Point Murder* Case

Marriage is the ultimate example of placing your trust in another person. You trust the person to be on your side, to never betray you, to be loyal and faithful, and to try to protect you from the cruelties of the outside world. How did Samuel Griffin demonstrate his love for his wife, Sondra? Far from just failing to protect Sondra, he repeatedly stabbed and savagely murdered her. And for what? To get money to maintain his lifestyle.

## A.  Attributes of a Good Theme

### Crafting a Case Theme

Good case themes are constructed with three characteristics in mind: The theme should (1) be memorable, (2) express values, and (3) match the case and fact finder.

### 1.  Memorable and the Moral Imperative

Your goal is to formulate or find a theme that captures the essence of your case theory in a way that convinces the jurors and is easily remembered. Think in terms of an advertising slogan that catches attention and holds it. The perfect theme is one that expresses a moral imperative; it is one that will drive the jury to want to render a verdict for your client. Your theme can be reiterated and expanded during the trial. For example, in a sexual assault case, the prosecution's theme could be: "Rape is a secretive crime." In jury selection, the prosecutor could state, "Ms. Enquist, you understand that rape is a secretive crime. It doesn't happen in a room like this with 40-some people watching. It can happen in an alley, a car on a dark road, in an empty house with only two people present. Would you, if you become a juror in this case, require the state to produce multiple eyewitnesses to what happened before you could find the defendant guilty of rape?" The prosecutor's questioning would then continue to probe whether the prospective jurors would be able to convict based on the testimony of the victim alone if they were convinced beyond a reasonable doubt that the defendant committed the sexual assault. In opening statement, the prosecutor could begin with "rape is a secretive crime," and describe how the victim was raped when there were no witnesses present.

### 2.  Express Values

In developing your case theory, you used the case assessment brainstorming exercise to identify strengths and weaknesses in the case. On the strengths side of the ledger, you listed values that would be important to the jury. Applying the case assessment approach to the rape case, the prosecutor would probably have listed on the strengths side: "vulnerable victim alone" and "personal safety," among others. On the weaknesses side, the prosecutor would list "no other witnesses." As it often happens, a strength can also be a weakness. Here, "being alone" is on both sides of the ledger. "Rape is a secretive crime" is a theme that rings true to the situation in recognizing the reality that there are no other witnesses to the sex assault and also communicates a value that every juror can relate to, because everyone has at some time been alone and vulnerable.

### 3.  Match the Case and the Fact Finder

A significant theme can be reused provided it fits the case. The jury will not know that it's a pre-owned theme. For example, "profits before people," and "this case is about corporate responsibility," are plaintiff themes that can be recycled, just as the defense "scapegoat" theme is worthy of replay in the right case. However, take care to make sure that the theme is tailored to the case. An ill-fitting theme can make a bad impression on the fact finder. Also, the theme should be designed for the audience. A "rape is a secretive crime" theme would be ill suited to a bench trial before a judge seasoned in sexual assault trials.

## B.  Detecting the Theme

The theme is there; you just have to detect it.

One technique for detecting a theme for your case is to brainstorm the possibilities by completing this sentence: "This case is about . . . ." Make a list and then refine the themes. Here is a list of some memorable themes that complete the sentence "This case is about . . ."

- taking risks without regard for the consequences.
- profits over people.
- police and a prosecutor rushing to judgment.
- protecting the weak and vulnerable.
- being accountable.
- power and control.
- breaking promises.
- police brutality.
- dishonesty.
- scapegoating.
- betraying a trust.
- a powerboat owner ignoring the manufacturer's warnings.
- keeping promises.

Chapter 5 on opening statements has more examples of themes with case examples.

## VII.  TENTATIVE CLOSING ARGUMENT

Using a tentative closing argument helps shape the case theory. The closing argument is the embodiment of your case theory, so begin at the end and work backwards by having a vision of your closing argument. The tentative outline of your argument will pull together the legal and factual theories, because the essence of a good closing is the trial lawyer making suggestions to the jury about how they should apply the law to the facts during jury deliberations. We will return several times to the concept that the best way to craft parts of trial is to apply this technique of employing a closing argument outline. For example, a trial lawyer will design a witness's direct examination by thinking ahead to how the trial lawyer wants to discuss the witness's testimony and credibility in closing.

## VIII.  TEST DRIVE

So, you have formulated the case theory and theme, which here we treat as one vehicle. Now it is time to test drive it. Will it accomplish what you want, or is it in need of adjustment or a total overhaul before trial? To get a sense of how jurors will respond to it, you can test it on a variety of people—colleagues, friends, family. A simulated trial before a focus group can provide you with constructive information about how the jury will react. A trial simulation can also provide you with input concerning witness effectiveness, the value of particular trial visuals, and your own trial performance.

The focus group of jurors should be unfamiliar with the case, qualified for jury duty, and as diverse as possible. If possible, they should be paid a minimal fee for service. The focus group can be recruited by advertising, through community groups, and so on. As part of their service, the focus group jurors can hear the truncated case, deliberate (which can be recorded), and answer questionnaires about what they observed. For instance, the questionnaire can ask about the credibility of a witness, what fact was most important, missing evidence, advice for the attorneys, and so on. This feedback can reassure you that your legal and factual theories and your theme are coming across clearly, or can point out deficiencies that can be rectified before trial.

## IX.  CASE THEORY AS A COMPREHENSIVE GUIDE

The case theory serves as an all-embracing guide for your trial, through each part of the trial:

- Case Theory and Theme Development:  Trial preparation is the process of preparing the legal and factual components of the case theory (getting the law and facts ready for trial, where you will present them to support your case theory and undercut the other side's).
- Trial Motions Advocacy:  Motions, which are structured by a motion theory analogous to a case theory, are commonly used to obtain information helpful to your case theory or to keep out evidence helpful to your opponent.
- Objections:  A major judgment factor in determining whether to object is whether the evidence the questioner is trying to elicit will help or hurt the lawyer's case theory.
- Jury Selection:  In the exchange with prospective jurors, you determine whether they are likely to be receptive to your case theory and, especially, how they react to case weaknesses. To the extent permitted by the court, you begin to advocate for the case theory.
- Opening Statement:  In opening statement, you relate the persuasive factual story component of your case theory to the jury.

- **Direct Examination:** Direct examinations are the building blocks that construct the sufficient and persuasive factual story that you have promised the jury in opening statement.
- **Cross-Examination:** The primary purpose of cross-examination is to gain concessions that bolster the case theory. Only secondarily should cross be used to impeach the witness.
- **Jury Instructions:** Jury instructions are expressions of the trial lawyer's legal theory component of the case theory.
- **Closing Argument:** In closing argument, the trial lawyer persuades the jury of the case theory. The lawyer argues how the jury is to apply the law (counsel's legal theory) to the facts (counsel's factual theory), and thereby reach the desired verdict.

## X.  ETHICAL CONSIDERATIONS

All of the advice we have offered in this chapter about putting together a persuasive story is premised on these propositions: Facts do not change, and you should never hide them. Facts are facts. It is not only proper, but we believe it is also critical that you detect facts that will make your case persuasive. On the other hand, some witnesses are malleable. It is unethical to coach a witness into a false or misleading story that may be more persuasive; to prevent the other side from having access to a witness; or to alter, destroy, or conceal evidence. ABA Model Rule of Professional Conduct 3.4 states, in part:

> A lawyer shall not:
>
>    (a) unlawfully obstruct another party's access to evidence or unlawfully alter, destroy or conceal a document or other material having potential evidentiary value. A lawyer shall not counsel or assist another person to do any such act;
>    (b) falsify evidence, counsel or assist a witness to testify falsely, or offer an inducement to a witness that is prohibited by law;

For instance, assume that in the *Hill Moveit* case, plaintiff made proper requests for production of Hill Moveit International Corporation's internal e-mails relating to utility trailer safety. If Hill counsel suggested to company executives that they should delete all harmful electronic communication about dangers of open trailers and the need to warn customers, counsel would violate Model Rule of Professional Conduct 3.4(a).

Or, in the *Freck Point Murder* case, the prosecution's case would be more persuasive if the testimony of the investigating officers was consistent. Suppose the prosecutor interviewed two homicide detectives who were in the Griffith bedroom on the night of the murder. Although one detective said that the victim's jewelry box was open, the other said that the box was closed. It would be a violation of Model Rule of Professional Conduct 3.4(b) for the prosecutor to point out the discrepancy to the two detectives and advise them that they should "get together and get the facts straight." The prosecutor should not coach or lead the witnesses into a story that is not true to the witness's recall.

---

## CHECKLIST: CASE THEORY AND THEME DEVELOPMENT

### Developing a Case Theory

*Guide to Trial Activities*

The case theory is a comprehensive guide to all aspects of trial and ADR proceedings.

- ☐ *Trial Preparation:* Prepare the law and facts for trial, where you will present them to support your case theory and undercut the other side's.
- ☐ *Trial Motions Advocacy:* Motions commonly obtain information helpful to your case theory or keep out evidence helpful to your opponent.
- ☐ *Objections:* Objections are designed to exclude evidence harmful to the case theory.
- ☐ *Jury Selection:* In the exchange with prospective jurors, you determine whether they are likely to be receptive to your case theory.
- ☐ *Opening Statement:* Opening statement relates the persuasive factual story component of the case theory to the jury.
- ☐ *Direct Examination:* Direct examinations construct the sufficient and persuasive factual story that you have promised the jury in opening statement.
- ☐ *Cross-Examination:* The primary purpose of cross-examination is to gain concessions that bolster the case theory. Only secondarily should cross be used to impeach the witness.
- ☐ *Jury Instructions:* Jury instructions are expressions of the lawyer's legal theory component of the case theory.
- ☐ *Closing Argument:* In closing argument, the lawyer persuades the jury of the case theory. The lawyer argues how the jury is to apply the law (counsel's legal theory) to the facts (counsel's factual theory), and thereby reach the desired verdict.

*Ethical Considerations*

Witnesses should not be coached to give false or misleading evidence, nor should evidence be misused or destroyed.

### Developing Plaintiff's Case Theory

*Legal Theory*

- ☐ *Civil Plaintiff:* Assert that each element of the claim and damages can be proven by a preponderance of the evidence.
- ☐ *Prosecution Legal Theory:* Alleges that every element of the crime can be proven beyond a reasonable doubt.
- ☐ *Selecting a Legal Theory:* Apply a two-step process in selecting a legal theory.
  1. Research to identify all possible legal theories that may apply to the case.
  2. Assess the strengths and weaknesses of each potential legal theory considering the legal theory

*continued* ▶

☐ in the abstract,

☐ in relation to other potential theories, and

☐ in conjunction with the available and potential evidence in the case.

### Factual Theory

☐ Appreciate that a good factual theory is both *factually sufficient* (it is sufficient to support the plaintiff's legal theory) and *factually persuasive* (it will convince the fact finder—jury or, in a bench trial, the judge—to render the verdict that the plaintiff is seeking).

### Factual Sufficiency

☐ Identify all the elements of the civil complaint or criminal charge.

☐ Present sufficient evidence on each element to establish a prima facie case.

### Persuasive Story

☐ A persuasive story is a factual story that will convince the fact finder. It contains the following six essential elements.

1. It is about *human values* (for example, family, freedom, or fairness) that the jurors believe in.

2. It is about the loss of *human needs* (for example, safety or love).

3. It is about *human beings* who are brought to life by the evidence and who the jurors can care about.

4. It is *believable* and *understandable* in that it is clear and comports with stories that the jurors are familiar with. It makes sense to the jurors.

5. It is supported by a sufficient *quantity* of evidence so that the elements are proven in accordance with the burden of proof.

6. It is supported by a sufficient *quality* of evidence (such as credible witnesses who support the story).

## Developing Defendant's Case Theory

### Three Types of Defense Case Theories

☐ Attack the weaknesses in the plaintiff's case theory by
- attacking its *legality*,
- attacking its *factual* sufficiency,
- attacking its *persuasive* sufficiency, or
- attacking its *procedural* sufficiency.

☐ Raise an affirmative defense.

☐ Negotiate.

### Legal Sufficiency of Plaintiff's Case Theory

☐ Show that the plaintiff's legal theory is not valid under existing law (it's unconstitutional).

☐ Note that a fine line exists between legal and factual insufficiency.

### Factual Sufficiency of Plaintiff's Case Theory

☐ Assert to the court that the plaintiff has not proven one or more elements with sufficient evidence to establish a prima facie case, so the case should not be submitted to the jury.

*Persuasive Sufficiency of Plaintiff's Case*

☐ Blunt or terminate the plaintiff's attempt to tell a human story about human values by

  • excluding as much as possible of the plaintiff's evidence from which that story could be told (motion in limine to exclude evidence);
  • telling a competing human story with human values;
  • attacking deficiencies in quality, quantity, and plausibility of the plaintiff's case by using the perfect plaintiff's case approach; and/or
  • asserting to the jury that the plaintiff has not proven one or more elements of the complaint by a preponderance of the evidence in a civil case or beyond a reasonable doubt in a criminal case.

*Procedural Insufficiency*

Attack the procedural aspects of the plaintiff's case theory (the statute of limitations has passed, improper venue, and so on).

*Affirmative Defense*

Raise an independent claim or an affirmative defense that will either mitigate or preclude a plaintiff's verdict.

## Case Theory Standards for Plaintiff and Defendant

*Case Assessment*

Use the case assessment brainstorming exercise to identify case strengths and weaknesses, particularly the values that will appeal to the jury.

*Multiple Legal Theories*

There are three situations in which a party may want to offer more than one legal theory:

☐ During the early *evidence-gathering* stage, before the focus has narrowed to a limited number of legal theories;

☐ When the theories are used in *strategic sequence* (move to dismiss for insufficient evidence and, failing that, argue that the plaintiff has not met the burden of proof); and

☐ When *alternate* theories exist (prosecutor charges murder in the first degree but argues the lesser included crime of murder in the second degree).

*Developing a Case Theme*

Have a theme that meets these requirements:

☐ Is short—a phrase, sentence, or analogy;
☐ Captures the essence of the case theory;
☐ Is memorable;
☐ Conveys values that the jury cares about; and
☐ Is suitable to the case and the fact finder.

# CHAPTER 4

# JURY SELECTION
## Two-Way Exchange

> *"I'm no idealist to believe firmly in the integrity of our courts and in the jury system—that is no ideal to me, it is a living, working reality."*
>
> —**Atticus Finch**, in Harper Lee's *To Kill a Mockingbird* 234 (40th ann. ed., HarperCollins Publishers 1999) (1960)

> *"The jury consist of twelve persons chosen to decide who has the better lawyer."*
>
> —**Robert Frost** (1874-1963), quoted in *Oxford Dictionary of American Legal Quotations* 226 (Fred R. Shapiro, ed., Oxford University Press 1993)

## I. CONCEPTUAL FRAMEWORK

There is truth to what Frost wrote about jurors deciding who has the better lawyer. Jury selection is a two-way exchange. While you are evaluating the prospective jurors to determine whether they should sit on the jury, those prospective jurors are evaluating you. Jury selection is when the prospective jurors first meet you. Are you making a good first impression? Are you someone they trust? Are you someone they feel comfortable with?

When done properly, the opportunity to question the prospective jurors is an opportunity for a conversation, not a lawyer's chance to deliver a monologue. This is the only time that you will be able to hear from them until after jury deliberations. This two-way exchange is crucial to a successfully conducted jury selection. To that end, this chapter will provide an approach for conducting jury selection, developing the content of your questions, and employing trial advocacy skills to present yourself, information, and questions during jury selection.

### A. Rules, Procedures, and Terminology

Jury selection is circumscribed by rules and procedures. The extent of attorney participation in jury selection varies from jurisdiction to jurisdiction and even from courtroom to courtroom within the same courthouse. We provide an approach to jury selection that is designed for a court that allows full attorney participation in questioning the jury panel. Also, we suggest strategies and techniques for jurisdictions, such as federal court, where the judge predominantly conducts jury selection and the lawyer's role is limited. These rules and procedures are derived from case law, statutes, rules, and the customs and usage of the particular venue and judge. These rules encompass processes for selecting people from the community who eventually become the qualified pool, which is reduced to the jury panel, and from the jury panel, the petit jury selected for the case.

### Waiver of Jury

If a jury demand must be filed in a civil case, and it is not done before the deadline, you may have effectively waived a jury. In a criminal case, a defendant must knowingly and voluntarily waive the right to a jury trial. In many jurisdictions, the criminal defendant's waiver, while necessary due to the constitutionally guaranteed right to a jury trial, is not sufficient; the prosecution must also agree if the case is to be tried as a bench trial.

### Jury or Bench Trial

If you are assigned to a judge whom you believe will be preferable to a jury as a fact finder, you may decide to forgo a jury for a bench trial.

Assuming that your client can waive a jury in favor of a bench trial, is that wise? Stereotypical answers to this question include: In a criminal case, a jury is best for the defendant because it only takes one to hang a jury; in a civil case, a jury is better for the plaintiff because it is more likely that it can be swayed to render a generous damages award. But broad generalizations are not a sound basis for deciding whether to waive a jury. If possible, counsel should investigate both the potential jurors and the judge. You may be able to afford a jury consultant to study and report on potential jurors' attitudes. Or you can use focus groups that review the facts and law of your case and enable the consultant to forecast how the jurors are likely to view the case. By contacting lawyers who have tried cases before the judge, reviewing the judge's record in reported cases, and researching the judge's background, counsel may be able to determine the judge's inclinations in a case like the one you have for trial.

### Jury Pool

The court randomly summons citizens to jury service using a system that draws names, for instance, from voter registrations or drivers' licenses. Those citizens are further screened and may be required to complete a juror questionnaire. Then the court jury commissioner can determine whether they are statutorily qualified based on age, jurisdiction, prior felony convictions, and so on. Those selected become the jury pool. The length of jury service depends on the jurisdiction. The procedure may require two days of service unless seated on a jury, in which case service lasts until conclusion of the case; in other jurisdictions service may be for a longer period, during which time a person may be called to appear in court.

### Jury Panel and the Jury

From the jury pool, a jury panel (also called "venire") of a number of prospective jurors (for instance, 40) is chosen and sent to a courtroom. To understand the elimination process, envision a courtroom. Seated in the courtroom is the panel, some sitting in the jury box, some in the spectators' section. The clerk randomly selects the prospective jurors to sit in the jury box, up to the number of jurors required for the type of case. The judge will swear the panel of prospective jurors under oath to answer truthfully during voir dire. Then the judge and lawyers question members of the panel. The attorneys will exercise challenges (described later in this chapter) and whittle down the panel to the number of jurors who will hear the case. Once the attorneys have exercised their challenges and accepted the jury as constituted, the jury is sworn under oath a second time, this time to well and truly try the case. The number of jurors is determined by court rule or statute, though limited by federal constitutional law as to the minimum number of jurors in a criminal case. The number depends on the type of case: for instance, 6 jurors for a misdemeanor, but 12 plus alternate jurors for a felony. While for civil trials in the federal court, "[a] jury must begin with at least 6 and no more than 12 members, and each juror must participate in the verdict unless excused under Rule 47(c). . . . Unless the parties stipulate otherwise, the verdict must be unanimous and be returned by a jury of at least 6 members." Fed. R. Civ. P. 48.

### Challenges

Challenges are the procedural mechanisms through which a prospective juror is disqualified from hearing the case. Attorneys may make three types of challenges:

- Challenge to the panel or pool,
- Challenge for cause, and
- Peremptory challenge.

#### Challenge to the Panel or Pool

A challenge to the pool or panel (also called "challenge to the array") is generally made by motion before jury selection begins. Grounds for this type of challenge include, but are not limited to, defects in the system for selecting the pool on constitutional grounds. Generally, the challenge will assert that some cognizable class (women, Hispanics, or African Americans, for example) is substantially underrepresented in the pool due to the selection process. Challenges to the panel or pool are uncommon.

### Challenge for Cause

Challenges for cause are made during voir dire. Challenges for cause are unlimited in number, but require specific showings for their exercise. There are three types of for-cause challenges:

- Not qualified,
- Implied bias, and
- Actual bias.

*Not Qualified:* Challenges can be made for lack of juror qualifications, such as when a person is under the required age, has a prior unpardoned felony conviction, or falls into some other disqualifying status as enumerated by statute. This type of challenge is also referred to as a "principle challenge." Generally, the jury commissioner has already removed persons failing to meet these standards, and they never join the panel in court.

*Implied Bias:* Challenges for implied bias (also called "for favor") are usually enumerated in statute. The grounds for this challenge involve the juror's relationship to a particular case or its parties or witnesses (the juror's brother is the plaintiff or a witness, or the plaintiff in a suit for damages owes the juror money).

*Actual Bias:* The reasons supporting challenges for actual bias are not enumerated in statute, although there may be some case law regarding these potential situations; for example, exposure to pretrial publicity. Rather, the existence of actual bias is judged against a general standard: The juror cannot be fair to one or more parties in the case. The topics that could bear on this type of challenge are almost limitless because they are specific to each case. Challenges for actual bias exercised by the attorneys, or the gentler exercise of this challenge where the judge excuses a juror, present the primary type of challenges for cause in jury selection.

### Peremptory Challenge

Peremptory challenges do not need to be justified by the attorney making the challenge and result in the removal of a juror. These challenges are granted automatically, provided they do not run afoul of the Constitution by being based solely on the race or gender of the prospective juror and thereby constitute impermissible discrimination. Thus, when an attorney exercises a peremptory challenge, the prospective juror must be excused from the case. However, peremptory challenges are limited in number. For example, there are typically six peremptory challenges allowed in a felony case. In civil cases, the number of peremptories is set by statute or court rule and can vary according to the number of parties. Rules also provide for an increase in the number of challenges depending on the number of parties in criminal cases.

## B. Procedures and Practices for Questioning

Procedures and practices for jury selection vary from jurisdiction to jurisdiction, and sometimes from judge to judge within the same courthouse. Judicial expectations of counsel during jury selection are probably the most varied of all areas of courtroom procedures and practices. The following are matters about which counsel will want to determine the court's preferences:

### Judicial Expectations

#### Jury Selection

**Who Conducts Voir Dire:** In state and local courts, the common practice is for the judge to make introductory remarks, and then to ask general questions of the panel and leave it to counsel to ask follow-up questions. Once the judge has finished, counsel is given an opportunity to inquire of the prospective jurors. The practice in federal courts and some state and local courts is for the judge to conduct all of the questioning of the panel. Under both approaches, the judge usually will allow counsel to submit written questions for the court to consider asking during the judge's questioning of the panel.

**Types of Questions:** What one judge allows counsel to ask prospective jurors, another judge may find inappropriate. For instance, one judge may permit counsel to ask hypothetical questions, while another won't permit it. Judge Timothy Bradshaw of the King County Superior Court in Washington State has this list of expectations:

> The sole purpose of voir dire is to elicit information that will enable the parties to make an informed exercise of peremptory challenges and challenges for cause. Questions are governed by the following general rules.
>
> * Questions must be reasonable.
> * Proper questions are probative of and germane to the particular ground of possible disqualification disclosed by responses to the judge's questions.
> * Inquiry is proper as to employment, business, experience or feelings and beliefs of any juror where the juror's special knowledge, sympathy, or bias could reasonably affect his or her ability to be impartial.
> * Questions should not be designed to trick the juror.
> * Questions that anticipate instructions on the law (other than burden of proof) are improper.
> * Asking a juror to speculate on his or her verdict if certain facts are proved is improper.

When counsel knows what questions are considered improper, counsel can avoid asking them and also prepare to object if opposing counsel violates any of the judge's rules.

> **Facts of the Case:** Some judges permit counsel to give a thumbnail sketch of the case facts for the jurors. Others won't. The court may permit counsel to prepare a summary of the case that the judge can read to the jury during the court's opening remarks in voir dire.

In the rest of this section we examine practices and procedures in greater depth.

## Questioning Procedure

### Federal or Court-Run Model

The court-run model, in which only the judge asks questions during jury selection, and attorneys are only permitted to submit questions to the judge, predominates in the federal justice system. Federal Rule of Civil Procedure 47(a), regarding questioning prospective jurors, states:

> The court may permit the parties or their attorneys to examine prospective jurors or may itself do so. If the court examines the jurors, it must permit the parties or their attorneys to make any further inquiry it considers proper, or must itself ask any of their additional questions it considers proper.

The Federal Rule of Criminal Procedure counterpart, Rule 24(a), and most states' rules have similar provisions.

### Judge-Run or Attorney-Run Model

In the judge-run model, the judge conducts most of the questioning. The lawyer's role is limited to suggesting questions for the judge to ask, or perhaps to ask a limited number of follow-up questions after making a specific request to the judge.

In other courts, the attorney-run model prevails. Here the attorneys do most of the questioning, with the judge's role limited to asking general questions at the beginning of voir dire ("Please raise your jury numbers if you have ever served on a jury."), leaving the attorneys to do any follow-up with any prospective jurors who responded affirmatively to the judge's questions.

## Types of Questions

Typically, two types of questions are used in jury selection: general questions and specific questions.

### General Questions

General questions are usually designed and structured to eliminate persons for legal cause (challenge for cause). Legal cause is established by statutes or rules that define persons who are not qualified to be a juror and should be excused from the venire. Thus, general questions concern the juror's fairness, impartiality, and whether the individual satisfies the legal qualifications for a juror. Although it varies in each jurisdiction, the range of topics for general questions is determined by the requirements of the legal cause statutes and case law. Topics include:

- Prior knowledge about the case;
- Acquaintance with the lawyers, judge, parties, or witnesses in the case;
- Involvement in a similar incident; or
- Any reason why a juror believes he or she may not be able to be impartial.

In some jurisdictions, the questions may concern factors within the particular case that could lead to a challenge for legal cause. For instance, in a case involving a particular drug used for atrial fibrillation, a question might be: "Does anyone take medication for a heart condition?"

General questions are addressed to the panel as a whole, and not to individual prospective jurors, which is why they are called general questions. The questioning process may be conducted solely by the judge, by the attorneys, or by the judge and attorneys together. For instance, the process of shared questioning could begin with the judge starting the jury selection with general questions. After the judge concludes, the judge would allow the attorneys to ask general questions, and then, when general questions have been exhausted, the judge would permit counsel to ask specific questions.

When general questions are asked, the judge may tell jurors that they should raise their hand if they have an affirmative answer to a question. If a juror responds affirmatively to the judge's or an attorney's general questions, the judge may inquire further or ask the attorneys to inquire further. Alternately, the judge may not permit further inquiry and ask the attorneys to note the juror and question that particular juror later. General questions are discussed in more detail later in the section on challenge for cause questions.

### Specific Questions

*Procedure:*  Specific questions ordinarily follow the general questions. Or, the judge may permit the attorneys to intersperse general questions with specific questions. Specific questions, if allowed, are addressed to individual prospective jurors. These questions are also referred to as individual questions. Specific questions may be asked by the judge, the attorneys, or a combination of judge questioning followed by attorney questioning of individual prospective jurors.

The jury selection process may provide the plaintiff's lawyer the first opportunity to question the prospective jurors, followed by the defense's turn; however, the court may also allow the defense the first opportunity. The court may dictate time limits and rotations. For instance, each side may be given two opportunities to question for a half-hour each with a rotation as follows: plaintiff's counsel, defense counsel, plaintiff's counsel, and defense counsel. This approach is most common in the "struck" jury method. Under this method, 40 prospective jurors, for instance, are seated in the jury box and spectator area in the courtroom. Counsel then takes turns questioning all jurors in the panel, making challenges for cause as they proceed, and using peremptories at the end to select the final jury. (The number of jurors in the panel varies, but one system bases this number on adding the number of jurors needed to hear the case (12), plus two alternate jurors (alternates are needed in longer cases in which one or more jurors could be excused for some reason before the end of trial), plus the number of peremptory challenges allotted both sides (12 or 6 per side), plus an estimate of the other prospective jurors that may be excused by the court, such as for hardship or for other cause.)

Another jury selection procedure involves the parties questioning each separate juror sitting in the jury box one at a time, passing each juror for cause before proceeding to the next prospective juror. When both sides complete questioning, one side (usually alternating plaintiff and then defendant, plaintiff and so on) will then begin with peremptory challenges and may remove one of the 12. The challenged juror is then replaced with someone sitting in the panel. The process then renews with both sides questioning the new juror, passing for cause or challenging for cause the newly seated juror, exercising peremptories until a jury is chosen.

*Types of Specific Questions:* The primary purpose for specific questions is to gain information to decide whether grounds exist to exercise challenges for cause or peremptory challenges. The types of questions permitted by judges vary greatly. This is in large part due to the particular judge's philosophy, or sometimes the law of the jurisdiction, about jury selection. Some judges have restrictive views and believe in allowing only questions on which to base challenges for cause. They barely tolerate questions that may indoctrinate the prospective jurors. Other judges disagree and allow full latitude of questioning. Likewise, in one court, you may inquire about a prospective juror's attitude toward a particular legal principle, while in another court the judge could rule the same inquiry an invasion of the court's province to instruct the jury on the law. Some judges permit extensive questioning about jurors' personal habits, relationships, views on political matters, and so on. Other judges abhor such practices, believing that type of inquiry to be an invasion of the juror's privacy. By understanding the judge's viewpoint, you can formulate questions that will be permissible and avoid those that will be impermissible. Specific questions are discussed further at pages 97-100.

## C. Exercising Challenges

Methods for exercising challenges vary from jurisdiction to jurisdiction, and you need to learn the jury selection procedures for your jurisdiction and the particular court.

### Exercising a Challenge for Cause

A prospective juror may indicate by her responses a basis recognized as legal cause for the juror to be excused from jury service, such as stating emphatically that she cannot be fair and impartial, cannot serve because of a clear conflict of interest, or cannot serve because of the length of the trial or hardship. After some inquiry into the basis and insistence of the prospective juror's indication of inability to fairly serve on the jury, the judge may excuse the juror for legal cause. Most challenges for cause, however, are made by the attorneys as the result of information obtained in voir dire. Counsel states, "Challenge for cause." Opposing counsel, under court procedure, would then be allowed to ask questions through which they likely will try to rehabilitate the person, such as: "Will you be able to set aside your personal feelings that because he is a doctor, the defendant's testimony is more likely to be truthful, and follow the court's instructions on credibility?" Following this, the court would rule on the challenge—allowing or disallowing it. If the challenge is granted, the juror is excused to return to the jury pool room. If the court asks counsel whether there is any challenge for cause and counsel does not wish to exercise a challenge, counsel can state, "Your Honor, pass for cause."

### Exercising a Peremptory Challenge

Most courts do not proceed with peremptory challenges until after the challenges for cause and the voir dire questioning are completed. Methods for exercising peremptory challenges vary. Under one procedure, each party, beginning with the plaintiff, alternates its peremptory challenges against prospective jurors in the jury box. The empty seat is filled with a prospective juror from the spectator seats. The process continues until both sides have exercised the number of peremptories they wish and have accepted the panel: "The plaintiff accepts the panel as presently constituted." Another approach is for the parties to receive a list of all of the prospective jurors and then strike (strike method) lines through the names of the prospective jurors against whom they wish to exercise peremptories. The clerk then calls the first 12 unstruck jurors to be seated as the trial jury.

## II.  PLANNING JURY SELECTION

### A.  Being Organized

Ideally, jury selection resembles a conversation between you and the jurors. To this end, you want to appear confident, organized, and engaged in that conversation. You want to eliminate barriers to communication, such as excessive note taking and fumbling through papers. A jury selection binder, an agenda for jury selection, jury seating and challenges charts, and a case summary sheet can be used to organize information and minimize impediments to the communication.

### Jury Selection Binder

A separate trial binder for jury selection serves as a ready source for legal authority, notes, and jury selection tools. It helps keep you organized during the jury selection process, which can increase your confidence and favorably impress the jurors with your organization and professionalism. The following is a list of items that you may place in your binder. The last two items can remain in the binder and be reused at different trials.

## Jury Selection Binder

- Agenda for jury selection;
- Jury selection notes of questions grouped by subject areas;
- Jury seating chart;
- Challenges chart;
- Case summary sheet;
- Good juror and bad juror profiles;
- A list of witnesses with names, addresses, and occupations (so the jurors can be questioned, and so the list can be presented to the judge to inquire whether the jurors are acquainted with any of the witnesses);
- Information from any pretrial investigation (a jury questionnaire);
- Law relevant to jury selection (statutes and court rules on challenges for cause and peremptory challenges); and
- A list of objections that may be made during jury selection.

### Jury Selection Agenda and Notes

You can use a jury selection agenda, jury seating chart, and your notes for questioning prospective jurors. We discuss these notes further at pages 74-77. The jury selection agenda contains introductory remarks, general questions on a handful of issues, specific questions, and concluding questions and remarks, if any. Your notes for questioning prospective jurors should constitute an outline of the question areas, and should be in large, readable print so they are visible at a distance. In that way, you will need to only glance at your notes while maintaining eye contact with the jurors.

### Jury Seating Chart

Jury selection moves relatively rapidly; consequently, it is essential to have a system for note taking. A jury seating chart, which shows the placement of the jurors in their chairs (see below), helps organize the information you obtain prior to and during jury selection. In the jury chart that follows, the numbers represent where the jurors sit when the jury is ultimately selected; for example, juror number one is in the first row in the far left-hand seat in the jury box. You can modify this seating chart to your courtroom situation. The chart can be expanded to include both the jury box and the spectator seats in the courtroom where the other prospective jurors sit, because you will need to include notes regarding them as well. As the juror is seated, the person's name is recorded in the box. Prospective jurors may move to different seats in the courtroom; for instance, when a juror is excused from the jury box and replaced by a prospective juror from the spectator seats. Because they move, it is common practice to write on yellow sticky notes in the boxes. If the prospective juror moves to another seat, the sticky note is moved on the chart to the new box.

Your jurisdiction may give each prospective juror a card with a number on it. So, jurors in the box and those in the spectator seats all have juror numbers. This is for convenience in note taking and making a record. For instance, when the judge asks all the jurors a general question, the jurors respond by holding up their cards with their numbers on them so that the numbers can be read into the record and the attorneys can take note of who responded to the question and how they answered. These notes enable you to ask follow-up questions to their responses.

**JURY SEATING CHART**

| Row 2 | 7 | 8 | 9 | 10 | 11 | 12 | Alternate 1 |
|---|---|---|---|---|---|---|---|
| | | | | | | | |
| Row 1 | 1 | 2 | 3 | 4 | 5 | 6 | Alternate 2 |
| | | | | | | | |

This jury seating chart provides a place to systematically catalog responses by jurors as well as your impressions of the prospective jurors. A series of abbreviations will help you include as much information as you need. For instance, you could use the letter *C* to designate prior jury service on a civil case and *CR* to designate prior service on a criminal case. You can adopt a coding system for rating prospective jurors, such as one to ten (one representing the worst possible juror and ten the best possible from the prospective of your case) so you can later refer to the ratings when you decide how to exercise your peremptory challenges.

### Challenges Chart

You should also make a challenges chart, which can be written either on a separate piece of paper or on the jury selection chart. On the challenges chart, you record the challenges for cause made by you and opposing counsel and how the court ruled, the prospective jurors whom the judge excused, and your and opposing counsel's peremptory challenges. This chart will give you a ready reference when you need to know how many peremptories you and opposing counsel have left. It will also indicate (if a question arises) what happened with regard to a particular prospective juror when considering an appeal based on an improperly excused juror or a challenge that was improperly denied.

### CHALLENGES FOR CAUSE / EXCUSED BY JUDGE

| Excused by Judge | Exercised by Plaintiff | | Exercised by Defendant | |
|---|---|---|---|---|
| | Granted | Denied | Granted | Denied |
| | | | | |

### PEREMPTORY CHALLENGES

| Exercised by Plaintiff | Exercised by Defendant |
|---|---|
| | |

#### Jury Selection Applications

In the future, the paper chart with sticky notes likely will be replaced by an application for a tablet that not only records juror information but also analyzes that information and ranks jurors. Computer applications have been developed for jury selection, including: iJuror (*https://itunes.apple.com/us/app/ijuror/id372486285?mt=8*), JuryPad (*https://itunes.apple.com/us/app/jurypad/id580845085?mt=8*), JuryTracker (*https://itunes.apple.com/us/app/jurytracker/id408560814?mt=8*), and Jury Duty (*https://itunes.apple.com/us/app/jury-duty/id414359607?mt=8*). However, the software is still in its infancy and may not satisfy your needs. For instance, an app may not facilitate the recording of juror information and the movement of those notes in a manner that is easier than working with sticky notes. Nevertheless, in the near future you may integrate an app into your practice that will make your jury selection tasks easier.

### Case Summary Sheet

A case summary sheet with basic information about the case is extremely important during jury selection. This safety net will be there to jog your memory if you forget some basic case fact in the midst of all you must concentrate on in jury selection. It can happen.

| CASE SUMMARY |
| --- |
| CASE CAPTION: |
| CLIENT'S NAME: |
| OTHER PARTIES' NAME(S): |
| CLAIMS WITH DATES: |
| TIME(S) & LOCATION(S): |
| THUMBNAIL CASE DESCRIPTION: |

### Assistance

If you are the trial attorney or the lead trial attorney with co-counsel, it is ultimately your decision how to exercise challenges. Having a person assist you during jury selection is highly beneficial because having an assistant to take some of the workload allows you to connect with the prospective jurors more freely. While we refer to an assistant here, the help could come from more than one person. The assistance could come from co-counsel, the client, a jury consultant, an investigator, a paralegal, a more junior associate sitting with you at counsel table as a so-called second chair, or someone else.

The assistance may include

- taking notes of juror responses and other matters, such as notes for the jury seating and challenges charts, which allows you to focus on prospective jurors; and
- assessing the prospective jurors to determine whether to challenge them.

The assistance rendered depends on the skills of the helper. Co-counsel may do the note taking, collaborate with you about exercising challenges, and share the voir dire. A jury consultant can both offer suggestions regarding questioning and assess the prospective jurors (providing you with an expert's perspective). A client, an investigator, a junior associate, or a paralegal may be able to provide valuable reactions to prospective jurors and/or serve as a note taker. The assistant's communication with you during jury selection should be inconspicuous, such as during recesses or by notes, so that it does not distract the jurors from your discussion with them.

## B.  Jury Consultant

Do you need a jury consultant for your client? Consultants can perform a variety of services from pretrial planning (such as survey research, participation in the case assessment, and trial communication advice) through actual jury selection at trial (assisting in jury selection and evaluating witnesses). Budget constraints, however, may prohibit hiring a consultant because these services can be extraordinarily costly.

## C.  Obtaining Information About Jurors

You will need to collect and evaluate information about prospective jurors to identify those who will be likely to render an unfavorable verdict to your client. This information-gathering process has two stages. The first phase occurs before the actual jury selection begins; the second phase takes place during jury selection. Here we examine information that may be available before jury selection.

### Jury Pool List

A list of the pool of jurors may be available from the jury commissioner or court clerk's office. The jury pool list might contain information about the juror's age, gender, address, occupation, and so on. The trial lawyer and/or assistant can investigate prospective jurors, if only with an Internet name search. Under no circumstances should the investigator contact the prospective juror. This information concerning members of the pool is helpful because it permits you to formulate a tentative strategy as to the range of potential jurors available. If you receive the information in advance of trial, you can use it to formulate questions suited for the potential jurors and their mix of ages, occupations, and other personal factors.

### Juror Information Form

The jury commissioner or court may direct that prospective jurors complete an individual juror information form, also called a juror questionnaire or juror qualification form. This information form may be routinely provided to the attorneys at the time of jury selection, or you may need to request the questionnaires from the jury commissioner or court. If forms are provided, you should study them closely to determine the basics about the juror, such as education, employment, prior jury service, and so on. This can be used during voir dire: "Mr. Jensen, I understand from your jury information form that you served on a jury before. What was the nature of the case?"

### Community Attitude Studies

You might, if economics permit, engage a survey firm to study a sample of the population from which prospective jurors will be drawn. The goal of such a study is to identify characteristics of the best and worst juror so that good and bad juror profiles can be designed (discussed in the next section). Studies of community attitudes also can serve as support for such things as a change of venue motion, a challenge to the jury pool or panel, or a motion for additional time for voir dire.

### Jury Indoctrination

You should learn what prospective jurors have been told about the justice system. This is important so you can avoid repeating information they have already received and instead build on the information they have. You may gain this knowledge by becoming acquainted with the court's instructional process for new jurors. For example, in many jurisdictions, jurors are given a handbook. Be sure you read it. Similarly, if a movie is shown to the jury panel, you should watch it to learn what new jurors are told about what will happen in the courtroom. In this way, you will not repeat the obvious during your discussion with them and will know something about their expectations.

### Track Record of Jury Service

You may be able to determine an individual juror's prior jury service by consulting with colleagues or by tracking individual juror performance in other cases. Some professional organizations—prosecutors, defense counsel, plaintiff's lawyers, defense insurance counsel—maintain jury books that record jurors' prior service. A juror book may show that the individual prospective juror sat on another case, indicate the nature of the case, and record the verdict. While the book might not always indicate how the juror voted (such as a hung jury), it can provide valuable information to help you evaluate how the juror might vote in your case based on the verdict in the juror's prior case. The law varies regarding whether and on what showing, if at all, you may be able to obtain an institutional party's jury book. Usually, however, juror books are considered to be work product and are not accessible to attorneys outside the firm that created them without making a specific showing of extreme need. Of course, the mental impressions of the attorneys creating the jury book are absolutely barred as attorney work product regardless of any showing. Fed. R. Civ. P. 26(b)(3).

### Special Juror Questionnaires

Another technique for learning more about prospective jurors before jury selection begins is to request, or file a motion requesting, that the judge have jurors fill out a special juror questionnaire. Jury questionnaires vary according to the particular case and issues. You can prepare this questionnaire yourself or do so with opposing counsel. A jury consultant or other specialist can also help to design the questionnaire. This questionnaire supplements any juror information form that is routinely required by the court. Before the questionnaire is proposed to the judge, it is best that the parties reach an agreement as to the format and questions in order to conserve court time. Otherwise, the judge will have to spend time deciding on the number of questions and content, and might choose the path of least resistance by denying its use altogether. Once approved by the judge, the questionnaire is given to prospective jurors when they are called for the case. They complete the questionnaires and return them to the court; the completed questionnaires are then copied and given to counsel for review before commencing with jury selection. During this review, counsel can concentrate on identifying prospective jurors who may be subject to a challenge for cause, appear to fit the bad juror profile, be excused for hardship, and/or should be asked follow-up questions on sensitive areas.

Such special juror questionnaires can be particularly helpful when inquiry into sensitive areas is appropriate—for example, inquiring in a child abuse case whether the juror was abused as a child. If the juror's response in the questionnaire indicates that further inquiry into a sensitive area is called for, the court may hold individual juror voir dire outside the presence of other prospective jurors. Because this procedure elicits more information about prospective jurors than could possibly be gained during the time usually allotted for jury selection, the attorneys are better informed. The *Freck Point Murder* case illustrates other situations where consideration could be given to employing a juror questionnaire.

## Juror Questionnaire

### The *Freck Point Murder* Case

#### Pretrial Publicity

Because Samuel Griffith is a well-known author, and because the manner of his wife's death was so tragic and movie-like, the *Freck Point Murder* case has received intense media coverage, including a number of front-page newspaper stories and a great deal of radio and television airtime. One front-page article is reproduced in this chapter at page 124.

As defense counsel, you made a motion to change venue, which was denied, but the judge said that he might revisit his decision depending on what prospective jurors say they know about the case and whether they can fairly and impartially hear the case. You are concerned about Assistant Prosecutor Michael Gonnif's pretrial statements, which you believe were both highly prejudicial and unethical. While you want to learn what prospective jurors recall about the media coverage, you are concerned that during jury selection a prospective juror may blurt out prejudicial information gained through the media and contaminate the rest of the jurors. The use of a questionnaire would avoid this risk. Also, if you questioned each juror about what he or she had learned through the media, the voir dire would be repetitive and boring. A questionnaire could ask these questions.

*continued* ▶

- Have you heard or read of a case referred to as the *Freck Point Murder* case?
- What have you heard or read?
- Are you aware of any evidence or information that would make you believe that the defendant is guilty?

### Domestic Violence

As defense counsel, you also are concerned that the prosecutor may adopt a domestic violence theme for the case, which she will begin to establish in voir dire. You may want to know whether any prospective jurors have been abused by a domestic partner. Recognizing that this can be a sensitive area that may call for individual voir dire of a prospective juror outside the presence of other jurors, you could design questions along these lines.

- What is your opinion of persons who commit domestic violence?
- Have you, a member of your family, or a close friend ever been subject to verbal or physical abuse from a domestic partner or family member?

For another example of a juror questionnaire (and an elaborate one, too), visit this book's website, *http://www.aspenlawschool.com/books/berger_trialad4e*, under "trial bonus material," to read the questionnaire used in the 2008 O.J. Simpson robbery case.

## D.  Designing Juror Profiles

A juror profile is a description of the characteristics of a mythical juror. As part of the jury selection planning process, you want to think about whom you want on the jury—the Good Juror: someone who would look favorably on you, your client, your witnesses, and your case theory. More important, you want to think about the type of juror that you don't want on the jury—the Bad Juror—for it is that person whom you want to be able to identify during jury selection and challenge.

These profiles can be helpful in at least three ways. First, they will give you some sense of the type of person you are looking for and the type of person you don't want on the jury. The process of developing a juror profile forces trial counsel to sit back and think about the characteristics of jurors that the lawyer wants and doesn't want. Second, a profile can guide information seeking. For example, if your profile includes a high level of education as a desirable attribute, you will ask about a juror's education or take note of a juror's answer should the other attorney or judge ask about the juror's education before you do. Third, a juror profile can provide a point of reference against which to evaluate the mass of juror information that will be elicited: How well does this juror line up with what I've been looking for?

How, then, do you create a profile? This process requires you to be creative, insightful, and open to exercising your judgment. That is why some attorneys scoff at this process as crystal-ball gazing; others do not believe they have the competence to create a profile. You will have to judge from your own experience.

Depending on the importance of the case, as well as time and economic constraints, you may consider employing a jury consultant, psychologist, or other expert specializing in jury selection to aid you.

### The Good Juror Profile

Here we discuss creating the profile of the juror you want—someone who will look favorably on you, your client, your witnesses, and your case theory, and render a verdict accordingly. For this section, imagine the *Blue Moon News Robbery* criminal case.

---

### The *Blue Moon News Robbery* Case

Blue Moon News is a popular newspaper and magazine shop. It is open 24 hours a day. At about 11:30 P.M. on January 15 of this year, the elderly clerk, Mr. Gardner Newman, noticed a man, about 5 feet 7 inches tall, who had been browsing at the magazine rack, approach the counter. The convenience store was dimly lit. No one else was in the store. The man had his baseball hat pulled down, laid the magazine he was carrying on the counter, put his hand into his coat pocket, pulled out what appeared to be a revolver, and demanded cash from the register. Newman handed over the money, and the man fled on foot. A partial print on the magazine matched the fingerprint of a 23-year-old defendant, Mike Ryan, who has a lengthy juvenile criminal history for shoplifting and a robbery. The defendant is from a low-income background and used to work at a tire dealership. Newman identified the defendant's picture in a photomontage as that of the robber. He initially described the robber to the police as 6 feet tall.

The defense filed a notice of alibi, stating that Greg Lewis Delaney would be called to testify. Detective Malcomb interviewed Delaney. Delaney told the detective that on January 15 he had a party at his apartment complex, which is approximately four miles from Blue Moon News, and that "Mike was at my party from 10:00 P.M. until the end at 3:00 A.M., at least I think so." According to Delaney, 40 to 50 people attended the party, and "most everybody was drinking." Delaney and the defendant worked together at Tire Universe, a tire dealership, for two years until the defendant was laid off on December 15 of last year. After the party, Delaney did not hear from the defendant for about two months until the defendant called to ask Delaney to testify for him.

---

Assume that economic constraints prohibit you from hiring a jury consultant, or that the case is not of such magnitude to warrant such an effort. You will try to create a juror profile yourself. We suggest that you develop the profile in two steps.

- First, consider juror identification with you, your client, your witnesses, and the facts of the case. You will be searching for shared or similar life experiences or interests that coincide with the situation described in the case.
- Second, consider the pivotal issues in your case.

*Juror Identification: Step 1*

To illustrate this first step in the process of creating a juror profile, imagine the *Blue Moon News Robbery* criminal case.

---

### Good Juror Profile

#### The *Blue Moon News Robbery* Case

Start with trying to have the juror identify with the client and the situation.

##### Prosecutor's Good Juror Profile

While the prosecutor represents the state, the victim will be treated as the client for purposes of this analysis. A superficial application of this first step may leave the prosecutor with a list of the following characteristics for a favored juror:

- A person with a stake in the community, who therefore will probably enforce the law against robbery;
- A mature adult who may identify with the elderly victim; and
- A business person who is preferably a sole proprietor, because the business person might share the same feelings as the victim in the case.

##### Defense Counsel's Good Juror Profile

By contrast, having made an equivalent analysis like the prosecutor's, defense counsel's profile of the mythical defense juror might have these characteristics:

- A person from a lower-income economic background who may identify with the defendant and the alibi witness; and
- A person without significant ties to or stake in the community, who may not care about crime rate in the area.

---

This process is a rudimentary one that depends on socioeconomic stereotyping; it therefore may be inaccurate when applied to specific individuals. But it provides an initial framework for doing a job that many think is pure guesswork—making serious judgments about total strangers in an extremely brief period of time, and doing so when equipped only with minimal information.

Next, trial counsel must refine their ideas about juror profiles. The prosecutor must consider, for instance, that not every mature adult will identify with the victim; the potential juror has attributes in addition to age. A mature juror may have had friends who were prosecuted or may have developed a view of the legal system as one indifferent to fairness or truth, where the government, through design or indifference, often railroads the innocent. Likewise, defense counsel's lower-income prospective juror has attributes in addition to economic status. She may also have views that do not fit neatly into the defense profile. While the juror perhaps identifies generally with the defendant's economic group, the juror may not do so with an accused robber. Rather, the juror may be a person who has worked hard to survive, has never stolen a penny, and believes criminals prey on those in the juror's neighborhood.

In fact, creating a juror profile can prove even more complicated. The juror whom defense counsel wants may depend on the chosen trial strategy. If the defendant will be testifying, defense counsel may want jurors who can empathize with the defendant and his background, particularly if behavior that would be associated with a consciousness of guilt in one social group—for example, failing to immediately tell police the names of your alibi witness while protesting innocence when arrested—may not be in another. If defense counsel intends, however, to keep the defendant from testifying and to raise a reasonable doubt as to the element of identity, counsel may seek an entirely different type of juror. In fact, defense counsel may want one who, superficially at least, may even seem pro-prosecution. Because of the case theory, defense counsel may want a person who can make clear, tough decisions, perhaps a professional or an executive type who can question whether the prosecutor has proved the case beyond a reasonable doubt. Some criminal defense attorneys begin the case with the strategy to raise reasonable doubt and seek a hung jury. Hence, defense counsel would not call any witnesses. For this strategy, the defense attorney might look for two jurors with strong personalities who would tend to disagree with the majority. Of course, if they do agree with the majority, the defendant should be prepared for sentencing!

### Pivotal Issues: Step 2

Now let's move to the second step: weighing the pivotal issues in the case. In the *Blue Moon News Robbery* case, the question of the accuracy of the store clerk's identification will be pivotal. The prosecution wants a juror who trusts identifications; the defense wants the opposite. Looking at the profiles so far, what bearing does the misidentification issue have on your analysis? In the prosecutor's view, a mature adult juror may tend to trust the store owner's perceptions: "People don't realize how capable we people are; these young folks think we're all senile." On the other hand, a mature adult juror may have had experiences that lead him or her to believe otherwise. Again, here and elsewhere, you need to exercise caution when relying on stereotypes. The profiles nevertheless can be useful as rough guides and points of reference, especially if you cannot obtain any other information about a potential juror.

### Bad Juror Profile

A profile of the type of juror you do not want is also of practical use to guide you in determining how to exercise your challenges for cause and peremptory challenges. The juror you do not want will have the characteristics of a person who would be adverse to you, your client, your witnesses, or your case theory. This profile generally will closely correspond to opposing counsel's ideal juror. To create this bad juror profile, consider the same two steps that you used to develop your good juror, but now do so from the perspective of your opponent's client, witnesses, case issues, and case theory.

To illustrate, we use the *Hill Moveit Personal Injury* case, which was first introduced in Chapter 3. Recall that Darcy Rutherford was driving home just after midnight from her work as a bartender. She was following an SUV driven by Stan Luby. The SUV was pulling a Hill Moveit trailer. Suddenly, an entertainment center tumbled out of the trailer. The furniture smashed through the windshield of Rutherford's car, injuring her severely. See pages 45-47.

## Bad Juror Profile

### The *Hill Moveit Personal Injury* Case

Defendant's Bad Juror Profile

Jurors you would like to strike from the jury would be those who would sympathize with plaintiff because they have similar life experiences as plaintiff or plaintiff's witnesses or sympathize with people with these life experiences. Therefore, given your initial superficial application of the first step, the type of juror you may wish to strike would have some of the following characteristics:

- Someone who harbors animosity against corporations,
- A working woman who would identify with the plaintiff, and
- A person who likely would have difficulty making hard decisions and who is sympathetic by nature.

Now take a careful look at the list again. Remember that there is no magic formula you can use. Other attorneys contemplating the same fact situation and the parties in the case might decide that working women are not likely to relate and be sympathetic to the plaintiff because the blood alcohol evidence indicates she had been drinking and was perhaps legally intoxicated at the time of the accident. Legal intoxication is .08 in the State of Major. This, in fact, leads to the second step: looking at the list in the context of pivotal issues. Defense counsel wants people who will make decisions more with their heads than their hearts. First, the defendant wants a person who will decide the liability question uninfluenced by the plaintiff's injuries. Second, defense would rather have a person who will dispassionately scrutinize the damages question rather than being guided unreflectively by sympathy for the plaintiff. Is this all guessing? Guessing is surely involved, but it's guessing with a foundation, guessing supported by research, reasons, and caution.

## E. Objections and Motions

### Preparation

Before jury selection begins, you can plan to make and meet objections during voir dire. This preparation to make and meet objections is discussed in greater detail in Chapter 6. In your jurisdiction, there will be a body of law that you can research regarding the types of questions and conduct that are acceptable and objectionable in jury selection. Also, judges have their own approaches to jury selection, and you should consult with the court personnel, such as the clerk or bailiff, to learn about the judge's proclivities.

In terms of objections you might make, it is helpful to be familiar with your adversary's style and approach to voir dire. Consult with attorneys who have tried cases with or against opposing counsel, or better yet, watch the person in trial. This will help you anticipate opposing counsel's tactics and plan how you will contend with her at trial. Think about making a motion in limine regarding opposing counsel's anticipated behavior in lieu of waiting until jury selection to object. The advantage of the motion is that it will be ruled on outside the jury's presence and shield the jurors from opposing counsel's conduct if the motion is granted. For example, you might make a motion in limine if you expect opposing counsel is likely to argue the case, quoting from jury instructions. In this situation, if it would be in line with how the judge normally conducts voir dire, you could move to have the judge prohibit counsel from referring to jury instructions.

## Jury Selection Objections

These are commonly made objections in jury selection:

- Has already been asked,
- Anticipates instructions on the law that have not been given,
- Asks the juror to speculate on the verdict if certain facts are proven and that attempts to get the juror's commitment to a verdict,
- Is unfair and embarrassing to the juror,
- Is unnecessarily probing,
- Is an argument of the case,
- Poses an improper hypothetical question,
- Asks for a verdict from a previous trial, and
- Has no bearing on a challenge for cause (this objection is valid only if the sole legal purpose of voir dire in the particular jurisdiction is to seek information bearing on the exercise a challenge for cause).

### Batson

*Batson v. Kentucky*, 476 U.S. 79, was decided in 1986 by the U.S. Supreme Court and refined in *Snyder v. Louisiana*, 128 S. Ct. 1203 (2008) and *Felkner v. Jackson*, 131 S. Ct. 1305 (2011). In essence, its holding was that in a criminal case neither side may exercise a peremptory challenge based on the prospective juror's race or gender. The *Batson* doctrine was extended to civil cases in 1991. *Edmonson v. Leesville Concrete*, 500 U.S. 614 (1991). The Supreme Court in *Batson* created a three-point process:

> ### The *Batson* Three-Point Process
>
> - The party objecting to the peremptory challenge must make a prima facie showing that it was exercised based on race or gender.
> - If the court finds that a prima facie showing was made, the burden shifts to the party that wanted to exercise the peremptory challenge to state a comprehensible race- or gender-neutral explanation that is not discriminatory.
> - The court decides whether the objecting party met its burden of proving purposeful discrimination, considering whether the reason given by the party wanting to exercise the challenge overcomes the discrimination claim.

Since the *Batson* decision, courts have ruled on numerous *Batson*-type challenges. It is worthwhile to check these decisions for examples of successful *Batson* motions.

## III.  MODEL APPROACH FOR JURY SELECTION

### A.  Setting Objectives

From a justice system perspective, the purpose of the jury selection process is to seat a fair and impartial jury. However, from the point of view of an attorney engaged in the process, the purpose of jury selection is to select a jury that can be fair in considering the attorney's case theory. Achieving this goal is vital. If you fail, you have lost the case before it begins.

While you might desire jurors biased in your favor, opposing counsel is not likely to let that happen. Rather, opposing counsel will try to remove all jurors favorable to you, as you will try to remove those favorable to the other side. Therefore, you must direct your attention to making certain that the jurors will view the presentation of your case theory on its merits, without the extraneous distortion that will result from any personal biases against you, your client, your witnesses, or your case. You are entitled to a fair shot, not a rigged game. If you have thoroughly prepared your meritorious case, a fair shot is all you need.

With this realistic view in mind, a lawyer can view jury selection as having these four objectives:

- First, to make a favorable impression on the prospective jurors, including putting them at ease so that they will speak freely and reveal pertinent information;
- Second, to evaluate the prospective jurors and decide against whom to exercise challenges for cause;
- Third, to gather information from each juror that can be used in deciding whether to exercise a peremptory challenge; and

- Fourth, to persuade the prospective jurors to be receptive to the attorney's case theory. This last one can be viewed as educating the jury and is an important goal, provided, as with the rest, it is allowed.

As we examine jury selection in this chapter, you will see how to accomplish these objectives.

> Watch the Jury Selection scenes in the *Freck Point* trial demonstration movie to see plaintiffs' and defense counsel interact with the jurors during voir dire. See the movie on the website *http://www.aspenlawschool.com/books/berger_trialad4e.*

## B.  A Positive Relationship

If at the end of jury selection the prospective jurors trust you, and see you as someone they'd like to go out to dinner with, you have really done your job. Watch good trial lawyers work; they achieve this sort of rapport with jurors. With experience, so can you. Because jury selection is your first opportunity to make an impression on the jury, your job is to make a favorable one. You want to sell yourself so the prospective jurors are receptive to your case theory and not antagonized by you. Here, we give you some philosophical as well as concrete advice as to how you can create a positive relationship with the jurors.

### Your Image

To understand what type of lawyer a juror ordinarily will relate to, ask yourself what type of person you would pay the most attention to if you were sitting in the courtroom as a prospective juror. You would probably be amenable to a person who appears to be relaxed, pleasant, professional, and honest, as well as fair, truth seeking, sincere, well organized, and polite. Therefore, these are the characteristics you want to project during jury selection and display throughout the trial. At the same time, you must be yourself—avoid constructing a facade that could become transparent as the trial progresses. Review the advice in Chapter 2 on persuasion strategies, particularly the advice on how to project sincerity to the jury, pages 7-12, 13-14. It is during jury selection that you first want to make the strong impression that you are a sincere person whom jurors can rely on and feel comfortable with.

### A Good Conversation

Good verbal and nonverbal skills will help you accomplish two of your objectives in jury selection:

- To make a favorable impression and develop a positive relationship, and
- To make them comfortable so they will speak freely.

With these skills, you can stimulate a good conversation with the prospective jurors.

*Verbal Skills*

Good verbal skills not only make a favorable impression but also generate a flowing exchange with the prospective jurors. To have a good dialogue means that you need to decide on an agenda for your segment of jury selection and how to frame your jury selection questions. This is a matter of preparation. Here we concentrate on the fundamentals of communicating in jury selection by offering some pointers that should guide you in framing questions. Later in this chapter we will go deeper into framing particular questions.

## Verbal Skills for Jury Selection

### Practical Considerations in Framing Jury Selection Questions

- **Easily Understood:**  Questions should be easily understood by prospective jurors. That means avoiding compound questions: "If a male supervisor invited his female employee on a date *and* made sexual remarks to her, would you consider that to be sexual harassment?"
- **Negative Phrases:** Questions that include negative phrases are difficult to understand: "If the supervisor invited the employee to dinner, you wouldn't consider that to be sexual harassment, would you?"
- **Common Words:** Questions should be couched in simple sentences, omitting unnecessary legal jargon and unfamiliar words with which some jurors have little or no experience.
- **Nonrepetitive:** Questions should be varied, particularly those on the same subject, to avoid repetition and a loss of interest.

*Connecting with Jurors*

Address your questions and comments to your audience. When asking a general question to the panel, speak to the group. However, if you are asking a specific question of a particular person, look the person in the eye and speak directly as you would in any conversation. Should you call the prospective juror by name? It has been said that each person's favorite word is his or her own name, so as a rule begin your question with the person's last name—that is, unless you might mispronounce it. If you're not sure of the name's pronunciation, courteously ask the person how the name is pronounced. Some trial lawyers with keen minds are able to remember prospective jurors' names and are able to jump around, asking questions using their names. With practice, you too may be able to do this. If not, use your jury seating chart to locate the person's name before you begin questioning.

### Something in Common

Some trial lawyers insert asides about themselves into the questioning process. These remarks are designed to create an atmosphere in which the prospective jurors feel at ease, to give the jurors a favorable impression of the lawyer, and to demonstrate that the lawyer doesn't take him or herself too seriously. We all tend to communicate better with people with whom we have something in common or find likeable. The aside, for instance, may be self-deprecating, may refer to the lawyer's children being the same age as the juror's, may mention that the lawyer has also served on a jury, or be some other statement that makes the lawyer more human and connected to the prospective jurors. However, carried too far or used in front of a judge who does not tolerate tangential comments, these remarks are objectionably irrelevant and improper.

### Helping Hand

Place yourself in the juror's position. What is the juror thinking and feeling during jury selection? This may not be too difficult a task—just place yourself back to your first month as a law student, or in another new, fairly intimidating situation. Many are apprehensive about what is about to happen. Most prospective jurors are unfamiliar with the personnel, the court procedures, or their roles, even if they have read a juror handbook or viewed a movie about what to expect. The more you can familiarize the jury with the case, the process, the participants, and participants' roles, the more they will be at ease and positively disposed toward you and your client.

### Conversational Tone

Your manner in asking the questions should be conversational. Your tone of voice should be informal but still polite, just as you would use in speaking to an acquaintance or a coworker. Use everyday words, not slang, legalese, or overly formal word choices. Speak loudly enough so that prospective jurors can hear you, and modulate your voice to avoid a monotone.

### Appearance and Nonverbal Behavior

Your appearance and nonverbal behavior in the courtroom assist in projecting your desired image and in generating a conversation with the prospective jurors. You should be well groomed and wear courtroom attire so your appearance does not distract from your interaction with the jurors.

### Active Listening

Your best jury selection performances are those where the prospective jurors do most of the talking. When you get them to talk on pertinent subjects, you can listen carefully for information that will assist you in determining how to exercise your challenges.

Being a good listener shows that you are interested in what the prospective jurors have to say. When a juror speaks, look the person in the eye and resist the urge to interrupt. Probing follow-up questions tell the jurors that you are listening to them and are interested in their responses. To be able to ask those follow-up questions requires active listening, where you are fully listening and not merely thinking about the next thing you will say. The more you are involved with what they are saying, the more that they will be at ease with you and willing to speak out.

### *Manage the Discussion*

You want to have as many prospective jurors speak as possible so you can evaluate them. The ones you will worry about most as the trial progresses are those who were seated on the jury but hardly spoke during voir dire. You will run across prospective jurors who will dominate the jury selection discussion if you let them, and thus prevent others from joining the conversation. The technique that you can use to move the conversation to others is known as the bouncing-ball method. You, as the moderator of the discussion, politely take the ball from the incessant talker, Mr. Blab, and bounce it to another: "Thank you, Mr. Blab. Juror number three, Ms. Kearney, what do you think about this question?" It sounds a bit like a Socratic law school class, because it is. Also, you want to engage those prospective jurors who are reticent to talk. To involve them, you can ask them easy questions in a friendly manner to draw them out.

### *Remain Nonjudgmental*

Throughout your discussion with the prospective jurors, you want to appear nonjudgmental both verbally and physically. In this way, you encourage the prospective jurors to speak freely. If you visibly or verbally register what appears to be a negative reaction to a response, it is likely to hamper the free flow of information from that person and other like-minded persons in the panel. Mentally note the unfavorable response from the person and welcome the information, because it will help you decide how to exercise your challenges.

## C.  Jury Selection Agenda

A jury selection agenda is a valuable organizational tool that can aid you in conducting an effective jury selection. During trial preparation, this agenda can be prepared and then placed in your jury selection binder. The agenda has these components:

- Introductory comments to the jury panel,
- General questions for half a dozen areas,
- Specific questions, and
- Concluding questions and remarks.

In the next section, we describe how to prepare opening and closing remarks for your agenda with illustrations. We cover how to draft jury selection questions and provide examples.

## D.  Introductory and Concluding Remarks

### Introductory Remarks

If you are in a jurisdiction where attorneys are allowed to actively participate in jury selection, generally you will be permitted to make some introductory remarks. Introductory remarks provide an opportunity to introduce yourself and your client to the jury. Design your comments so that you put the prospective jurors at ease. Explain the jury selection process so they know what to expect. This will allay any fears or possible embarrassment they may have regarding their interrogation. The remarks should be delivered in as conversational a manner as possible.

Think about how you can best present yourself and your client's cause in your introduction. You usually can include a succinct statement of the case, your name, whom you represent, and the purpose of your questions. One caution is in order: You must avoid argument.

Your introductory remarks should be scripted, memorized, and rehearsed. They should be rehearsed until they can be delivered in a confident and conversational manner. This is an important minute or two in front of your future jurors because this is when they first meet you; you need to make a favorable impression.

The following introductory remarks illustrate a nonargumentative description of a case (assuming that this is permitted by your judge). Of course, trial counsel must modify the introductory remarks to fit the court's practices and to avoid unnecessary repetition of what the judge and opposing counsel have covered.

## Jury Selection

### Introductory Remarks
### The *Hill Moveit Personal Injury* Case

#### Introductions and a Word or Two About the Case

"Good morning, members of the jury. My name is Rebecca Cunningham. I represent Darcy Rutherford, the plaintiff in this case, who is sitting on your left at counsel table. Ms. Rutherford was driving on Highway 57 when a piece of furniture tumbled out of an open utility trailer. The furniture smashed through her windshield and hit her. Darcy nearly died at the hospital, and as you can see, she was left blinded, disfigured, and permanently disabled. Twelve people need to decide who's responsible."

#### Explanation of the Process and Urging Prospective Jurors to Speak Freely

"As Judge Coffey has just explained to you, jury selection is a process intended to select a fair and impartial jury for this case. A fair and impartial jury is one that can decide this case based on the factual evidence and the law. The purpose of the questions the judge and counsel ask is to understand what you think about various issues that relate to this case. We do not intend to embarrass you or to pry into your personal lives. We need to know your true feelings on the issues in this case to ensure that the purpose of jury selection—finding the jurors who are collectively right to hear this case—is achieved."

*continued* ▶

"If you are selected to hear this case, the formality of trial will require that you be separated from the lawyers, the witnesses, and the judge throughout the trial. It is not until jury deliberations that you will be able to discuss the evidence and the law with other jurors. And it is only now that we can talk with you. Now you have an opportunity to express your thoughts and feelings to us. We hope you feel free to tell us how you feel about matters that may come up during the trial or how you might view the case. Only if you express yourself in that open way can a jury suitable to hear this case be chosen."

Agenda

"Just a word or two about my agenda. I will be mixing questions addressed to individual jurors with general questions to all of you. I will attempt to speak to as many of you as possible. If there is something that you believe might be important for us to hear, please raise your hand. If your own answer to a question I ask a prospective juror would be markedly different from that of other prospective jurors, please let us know by raising your hand."

"Because of time restraints I probably will be prevented from speaking with many of you at length. For that, I apologize in advance."

---

Opening remarks can be inventive, seize the jurors' attention, and get them interested in talking. For example, defense counsel, following the plaintiff's voir dire, could begin: "Ever see a coin with only one side? Or a person with only one side, for that matter? I want to talk to you about this case, and ask only that you have an open mind to the proposition that there is another side to this case."

### Concluding Questions and Remarks and Accepting the Jury
You can prepare your concluding questions so you end on a high note.

---

**Jury Selection**

### Concluding Questions and Remarks
### The *Hill Moveit Personal Injury* Case

Plaintiff's counsel representing Darcy Rutherford might use a concluding question such as, "Ms. Brand, can you assure me that if the preponderance of evidence proves each element of Ms. Rutherford's claim, you will return a verdict for plaintiff?" Or plaintiff's counsel might ask, "If you were plaintiff in this case, would you be satisfied to have a juror like yourself on the case? If you would not be satisfied, kindly raise your hand."

As defense counsel, you might conclude, "Can you promise that you will keep an open mind and wait until the defendant's case is presented?" or, "My last question: Is there any reason at all that makes you feel that you do not want to serve on this case? If so, could you raise your hand?"

Once questioning is concluded, it is time for the final steps in jury selection. Eventually, you will reach that point where you have no jurors you wish to challenge for cause, and have either decided to not exercise any more peremptory challenges or have exhausted your challenges. When the judge signals that it is your turn, stand, look each juror in the eye, and confidently show that you are satisfied with the jury, and state, "Your Honor, we accept the jury as presently constituted."

## IV. JURY SELECTION QUESTIONS

Successful jury selection requires that you plan the subject areas that you want to explore and the specific content of the questions that you wish to ask in these areas. You must also keep in mind that when you are actually performing jury selection, you will need to speak extemporaneously as the situation unfolds, have a conversation with the jurors, and pose follow-up questions.

Framing questions for jury selection should be designed to accomplish objectives. In this section, as we explore how to frame questions, we examine such objectives as making a positive impression, getting the jurors to speak freely so you can obtain information that can be used in deciding whether to exercise a challenge, and persuading the prospective jurors to be receptive to the attorney's case theory.

### A. Gathering Information

Jury selection questions should be designed to accomplish your ultimate objective—seating jurors who can decide the case in your client's favor. You already should have obtained information about the jury panel (perhaps including individual juror questionnaires) before voir dire began, but that information will be superficial. You will need to obtain more specific information during jury selection to help you decide whether to challenge a prospective juror. That is the primary function of voir dire questions. The information you obtain will enable you to compare the particular juror you are questioning with your ideal juror, to determine the type of juror you do not want, and to help you decide whether to exercise a challenge for cause or expend a peremptory challenge. In the case of a challenge for cause, the information you elicit will also form your factual record for what will in effect be a legal argument that the juror cannot, as a matter of law, fairly sit on the jury.

### B. Framing Questions

Questions may be framed in two ways: as open-ended and closed-ended questions. Learning when to ask these different types of questions is an essential advocacy skill that is necessary when conducting interviews, taking depositions in a civil case, conducting direct examination, and especially during jury selection. You should ask open-ended questions to encourage the prospective jurors to talk. This will allow you an opportunity to listen and evaluate.

An open-ended question generates the prospective juror's narrative response. For example, if a prospective juror has grown children, you might use an open-ended question such as, "Could you tell us what your children are doing now?" To get jurors conversing with you in a narrative form, ask journalist-type questions: who, what, when, where, and why.

A closed-ended question calls for a yes or no response: "Is your oldest son employed?"

The best jury selections are where the prospective jurors do most of the talking. For instance, consider the *Hill Moveit Personal Injury* case.

## Obtaining Juror Information

### Open-Ended Questions
### The *Hill Moveit Personal Injury* Case

Plaintiff's counsel wants to explore how a juror might consider a major issue in the case—that the plaintiff was affected by alcohol. Counsel asks a prospective juror, Mr. Rankin, the following open-ended question:

Q:  What do you think about people who drink and drive?
A:  I do not approve of alcoholic beverages. A drunk driver killed my wife and two babies—just drove right into their lane.

While such a response would be damaging to the plaintiff's case, defense counsel may decide nevertheless to ask the question, feeling it is beneficial to discover this information, and then rely on his or her ability to ask follow-up questions to cure the damage.

In contrast, when you are planning a challenge for cause or when you are just trying to commit jurors to basic propositions, you want to use closed-ended (cross-examination-like) questions.

## Obtaining Juror Information

### Closed-Ended Questions
### The *Hill Moveit Personal Injury* Case

Closed-ended questions are designed to obtain a limited amount of information. They restrict the information and curtail the juror's ability to communicate. To illustrate, consider this question posed by plaintiff's attorney:

*Q:* Mr. Rankin, the evidence will show that plaintiff Darcy Rutherford consumed alcohol prior to being injured when furniture fell off the trailer. Do you agree with the proposition that merely the fact Ms. Rutherford had something to drink doesn't change defendant's corporate responsibility to manufacture safe trailers and to warn users of dangers?

The following are words and phrases that you may find useful in drafting your jury selection questions. Some are open-ended questions, while others are closed-ended questions.

## Structuring Questions for Jury Selection

### Key Words and Phrases

- The evidence may show that . . . How do you feel about this?
- Are you opposed to . . . ?
- Are you willing . . . ?
- Can you decide . . . ?
- Can you listen to all the evidence?
- Could you decide the case fairly on the evidence?
- Could you nevertheless be fair and impartial and put out of your mind . . . ?
- Could you resolve this case solely on the basis of the testimony and the exhibits admitted?
- Did anything ever occur . . . ?
- Do you believe . . . ?
- Do you feel . . . ?
- Do you know any reason why you could not be fair?
- Do you think that . . . ?
- Do you understand . . . ?
- Have you ever (studied medicine, been in a car accident) . . . ?
- Have you heard the expression . . . ? How do you feel about that expression?
- How do you feel about that?
- If the court instructs you . . . would you be able to apply . . . ?
- If the evidence proves . . . could you . . . ?
- Just because . . .
- Some people would say . . . How do you feel about that?
- Tell me about that . . .
- What do you think about the proposition . . . ?
- Will you avoid . . . ?
- Will you be able to set aside your feelings in this case?
- Will you consider all . . . ?
- Would the fact that . . . be considered improper by you?
- Would the fact that . . . mean you would . . . (make you . . .)?
- Would the mere fact that . . . ?

*continued* ▶

- Would you accept what the court tells you, even though you might believe the law should be different?
- Would you be able to find . . . if you were told . . . ?
- Would you be prejudiced . . . because . . . ?
- Would you be reluctant to . . . ?
- Would you penalize someone for . . . ?

## C.  Challenge for Cause Questions

The grounds for challenges for cause are enumerated in statutes, court rules, and case law (see pages 66-67). To construct questions that seek information relevant to a challenge for cause, begin by referring to the statutes, court rules, or case law that specify the bases that make up for-cause challenges. Make a list of these grounds, organizing the list according to the three categories of challenges that provide the legal basis for challenges for cause: juror qualifications, implied bias, and actual bias. This list will then yield the subject areas for composing your challenge for cause questions.

### Method for Drafting Challenge for Cause Questions
*Implied Bias*

To illustrate how to draft these questions designed to elicit evidence to support a challenge for cause, imagine that in your jurisdiction §4.0 of the Code of Civil Procedure provides that implied bias includes "close acquaintance with the attorneys or witnesses." "Close acquaintance" is a legal standard that will not be fulfilled by every contact. There may or may not be case law further defining "close acquaintance." If there is, it is likely to state something like the following: "an acquaintance such as would tend to render a juror partial to one or the other side on its account."

Thus, you can develop questions that will probe into the nature of any contact to elicit information bearing on the question of whether the contact does constitute "close acquaintance" such that one can infer implied bias from the contact. You might create something like the following questions chart in preparing the content of your jury selection questions in this area.

**QUESTIONS CHART**

| *Statutory Basis* | *Subject Area* | *General Questions* | *Specific Questions* |
| --- | --- | --- | --- |
| §4.0 | Close acquaintance | Contact with whom? Plaintiff? Counsel? Law firm? Key witnesses? | Nature of contact (if any)? Circumstances? Impression? Friendship? Extent? |

In many jurisdictions, the jury commissioner or judge at trial will probably inquire as to juror qualifications and grounds for implied bias. If the grounds exist, an automatic challenge will be granted. In a situation such as the one above in which the issue of close acquaintance is involved, most of your questions will be directed at obtaining sufficient information to determine whether a challenge for cause for implied bias should be made.

---

### Jury Selection: Challenge for Cause Questions

#### Implied Bias: Acquaintance

**Judge:**

"The attorneys will be addressing general questions to all potential jurors in the courtroom, both those seated in the jury box and those in the spectator area of the courtroom, the panel. Please listen carefully and raise your hand if you would answer the question 'yes.' Counsel, you may begin."

**Counsel:**

*Q:* Do any of you know plaintiff's attorney in this case?

*Q:* Do any of you know defendant's attorney in this case?

*Q:* Would your acquaintance with the person involved in this case cause you to begin the trial with bias or prejudice one way or another?

*Q:* Do you know of any reason why you could not try this case fairly and impartially?

Assume that juror one raises her hand in answer to the question "Do any of you know defendant's attorney in this case?" Her affirmative answer indicates that counsel needs to inquire further with specific questions. Counsel could review the chart and, addressing juror one, determine the nature of her acquaintance with defendant's attorney. That done, the judge may believe that counsel has established a sufficient basis for a challenge for cause and excuse the juror:

> "Ms. Schlore, thank you for your candor. I would like to thank and excuse you for the reasons indicated. Please report back to jury room 305."

---

### Actual Bias

Now let's turn to developing challenge for cause questions for *actual bias*—a juror's inability to be fair and impartial because of strong feelings about your case. To develop such questions, we suggest using your case theory and the bad juror profile (see pages 84-85) to identify factors that could cause a juror to be unable to be impartial in your case.

To illustrate, suppose you are defense counsel in the *Landlord-Tenant* case. One significant factor in your case is that the plaintiff is a tenant. You believe that jurors who are tenants or sympathize with tenants could, based on their own experience, harbor a bias against your client, the landlord. Your specific questions can be about whether jurors were or are tenants, their experience as tenants, their feelings toward landlords, and so on. As always, the questions in your chart are just tentative first questions; you must then listen to the answer and ask appropriate follow-up questions. The follow-up questions will likely provide your most important avenue to information during jury selection.

---

## Jury Selection: Challenge for Cause

### Actual Bias Questions
### The *Landlord-Tenant* Case

The following questions are designed by defendant landlord's attorney to identify if a prospective juror was actually biased:

#### General Questions to the Panel

Q:  Please indicate if you were ever a tenant.
(Two jurors answer yes by raising their hands.)

#### Specific Questions to One Juror

Q:  Ms. Markov, are you a tenant now?
A:  No. I live in a house in the east side of town, a nice residential neighborhood.
Q:  How long have you lived there?
A:  Two years.
Q:  Is that the first home you have owned?
A:  Yes. (Pause.) I am enjoying living in a house. I previously lived in the Eastbrook Apartments.
Q:  You are enjoying home ownership. Can you compare it to your experience in Eastbrook?
A:  I had an awful landlord, Mr. Odell, who refused to repair anything until you threatened him. I endured that for 14 years. Never again.

#### Follow-Up Questions

Q:  Would you say you harbor bad feelings toward Mr. Odell?
Q:  Would it be a correct statement to say that when you heard that you might be a juror in a landlord-tenant case concerning repairs that you had an opinion as to whom you would be more willing to believe?
Q:  Because of your own experience, might you tend to empathize with the plaintiff in this case?
Q:  Do you think it's possible that you might find yourself not being able to clearly separate the plaintiff's case from your own experience?
Q:  Because of your previous experience, you would have to hear some really overwhelming evidence to accept the landlord's defense, correct?
Q:  In fact, you believe that the landlord has to present evidence that will overwhelmingly convince you before you render a defense verdict, correct?
Q:  So it is fair to state that you cannot be fair and impartial in this case?

---

If Ms. Markov were to concede that she could not be fair and impartial in the *Landlord-Tenant* case, you would challenge her for cause under the applicable method, stating, "Your Honor, challenge for cause." Plaintiff's counsel would be given an opportunity to question Ms. Markov, and then the judge would rule on your challenge (excuse the juror or deny the challenge).

### Questions to Rehabilitate: Meeting a Challenge for Cause

Now suppose you are plaintiff's counsel. Strategically, you want jurors who were or are tenants on the jury. Imagine that defense counsel has challenged Ms. Markov for cause, and the judge has permitted you to question her further. From what you have heard so far, you believe Ms. Markov appears to be someone who would be sympathetic to your case because she once was a tenant who had problems with her landlord. You do not want her excused for cause.

Your strategy is to use your questions to rehabilitate her by establishing that she is not actually biased and therefore should not be excused for legal cause. If you are able to rehabilitate her so that the court will deny the challenge, defense counsel will most likely feel compelled to exercise one of a limited number of peremptory challenges against her. Another possibility is that your line of inquiry may convince the defense that the prospective juror is not so bad, and defense counsel may withdraw the challenge for cause.

---

### Jury Selection: Challenge for Cause

#### Rehabilitation Questions
#### The *Landlord-Tenant* Case

As plaintiff's counsel, you might ask to rehabilitate Ms. Markov (a juror you would like to keep on the jury), who has been challenged for cause due to her actual bias:

Q: Do you accept the proposition of law that the plaintiff has to prove her case by a preponderance of the evidence?

A: Yes.

Q: If the court instructs you that you must decide this case only on the evidence before you, can you put aside any feelings you might have based on your personal experience with a landlord?

A: Yes.

Q: You can be fair and impartial to both plaintiff and defendant in this case?

A: Yes.

---

### General Questions

As has been discussed, the judge begins jury selection by asking the panel of prospective jurors a series of general questions. The judge may have the jurors answer by raising their hands and identifying themselves by name or number for the record so counsel can take note of them and ask follow-up questions later. These general questions are usually directed at uncovering grounds for challenges for cause. After the judge has exhausted his general questions, the judge may ask if counsel has any general questions for the panel.

To be able to take advantage of the court's offer to ask general questions, trial counsel should prepare a list of pertinent general questions for the panel. The method used for formulating these questions is the one outlined at pages 87-88. The following sampler of general questions may be useful in drafting the questions.

---

## Jury Selection: Challenge for Cause

### General Questions for the Jury
### The *Landlord-Tenant* Case

The judge may state: "Anyone who would answer 'yes' or 'probably' to any of the questions addressed generally to all of the prospective jurors, please raise your hand until the judge and the lawyers have made a note of the response. At this time I will ask all of you a few questions touching on your qualifications to sit on this jury. Please do not relate any specific thing you may have seen or heard concerning the case."

Q:   "Have you heard of this case before?"

Q:   "Has anyone ever expressed to you an opinion concerning this case?"

Q:   "Do you know either the plaintiff or the defendant or any of the lawyers involved?" (If any so indicate, the judge should inquire further to ascertain the extent of the acquaintance or permit the lawyers to conduct such inquiry.)

Q:   "Do you know any of these persons [give names of prospective witnesses] who might be called as witnesses?"

Q:   "Might such acquaintance influence your consideration of this case?"

Q:   "Has any prospective juror had any personal experience with a similar or related type of case or incident?"

Q:   "Might this influence your consideration of the case?"

Q:   "Has anyone had a close friend or relative who has had experience with a similar or related type of case or incident?"

Q:   "Might this influence your consideration of the case?"

Q:   "Is anyone related to any person connected in any way with courts or the administration of justice, including law enforcement?"

Q:   "Might this influence your consideration of the case?"

Q:   "After the evidence has been presented, I will instruct you on the law that applies to this case. If you disagree with that law, will you have difficulty following it?"

Q:   "Is there anything about this case that might cause you to begin this trial with any feelings or concerns either one way or the other?"

Q:   "Do you know of any reason why you might not be able to try this case impartially?"

Q:   The judge might estimate the length of the trial and then say, "Does anyone have any reason whatever why you should not sit on this case?"

These questions are adapted with permission from Washington Practice Series, Volume 6A, Washington Pattern Jury Instructions, Civil, pages 675-676. Copyright © 2012 by Thomson Reuters.

## D.  Case Theory and Theme Questions

When trial attorneys are permitted to actively and freely participate in jury selection, they can use the occasion both to educate the jury about their case theories and themes and to persuade the prospective jurors to be receptive to them. In other jurisdictions, trial attorneys are either bystanders to the judges' voir dire, or the attorneys may participate but the courts prohibit questioning to indoctrinate the jurors. Here, we explore the use of jury selection to advance the case theory and theme.

To illustrate how to advance the case theory and theme, imagine that you represent a defendant accused of assisting in a bank robbery as the getaway driver. The legal defense focuses on raising a reasonable doubt about the element in the prosecution's legal theory that requires that the defendant know the conduct of the person he is accused of aiding. In other words, you will try to raise a reasonable doubt that, while he sat in the car, the defendant knew that his friend was committing a bank robbery.

### Advancing The Case Theory: Jury Questions

#### The *Bank Robbery* Case

You want to raise a doubt about whether the defendant knew about the robbery, and you are concerned that some jurors will believe

- it would be impossible not to know such a thing;
- if you hang around someone like the codefendant, you get what you deserve; or
- some combination of the two.

Thus, in jury selection, you might ask beginning questions to open a conversation.

*Q:*  Do you believe it is possible to be with someone who does something very wrong, but not be aware of what he or she is doing?

*Q:*  Do you agree with the phrase "you're known by the company you keep"?

*Q:*  Does that mean that if you choose to hang around with bad people, you should be punished for whatever they do, regardless of your involvement beyond choosing to be with them?

These questions educate the jury about your case theory. Every question by defense counsel is aimed at beginning a conversation that could elicit information on bias regarding your case theory, which is the crux of your defense to aiding and abetting.

Certain approaches to questioning, while consistent with the use of voir dire questions to elicit information uncovering prospective juror bias, can also result in advancing the case theory and theme. We now will discuss three such approaches to questioning:

- Integrating your case theory within questions,
- Posing questions that reveal weaknesses or problems in your case, and
- Framing questions that counter opposing counsel's efforts to indoctrinate the jury.

### Case-Specific Questions

Case-specific questions may be employed to educate and persuade the prospective jurors regarding the significant aspects of your case theory while at the same time seeking to uncover actual bias. Those factors in the case theory could be a witness, a piece of evidence, or a principle of law. In this section, we describe how your questions can be phrased and organized to advance your factual theory, while at the same time using jury selection to expose prospective juror bias. Also, throughout the book, you will learn how to integrate your case theory and theme into every stage of trial. Jury selection is the first stage to conduct that integration in your trial.

#### *Integrating Theory and Theme into Stages of Trial*

To convince the jury of the merits of your case, you must use repetition and sound persuasive concepts. Discuss your case theory by referencing the key factors and central theme in jury selection, opening statement, witness examination, and closing argument. The more they hear your side of the case and can relate to it, the greater chance that jurors will remember it and be persuaded by it. For example, consider the *Hill Moveit Personal Injury* case.

---

### Jury Questions Advancing the Case Theory and Theme

#### The *Hill Moveit Personal Injury* Case

##### Theme: Corporate Responsibility

Imagine that plaintiff's counsel adopted "corporate responsibility" as the descriptive theme. Plaintiff's counsel could attempt to introduce both the theme and the concept in jury selection with these questions.

Q: Ms. Erlich, do you think that a company has the obligation for manufacturing a product that is safe for use?

Q: What do you think about the idea that a company must warn users of its product concerning potential dangers in the use of the product?

Q: You hear a lot in newspapers, radio, and television about something called "corporate responsibility." What does that phrase mean to you?

Q: Some people say that a corporation's only responsibility is to make all the money it can. How do you feel about that?

##### Legal Theory

Product liability is one of the plaintiff's legal theories, and plaintiff's counsel can use voir dire to introduce and educate prospective jurors about this legal theory.

Q: One way that defendant Hill Moveit International Corporation can be found liable is called "strict liability." Under product liability law, a manufacturer can

---

be held strictly liable. In other words, if a manufacturer creates an unsafe product or fails to provide adequate warnings that the product could be unsafe, then the manufacturer will be held responsible for harm done. Do any of you have a quarrel with this concept of strict liability?

**Defense counsel:**

"Objection. Counsel is anticipating the court's instructions, and is also not fully stating the law."

**Judge:**

"I'll allow it."

Once the concept of corporate responsibility has been introduced in jury selection, the theory and theme can be reiterated and expanded on in later stages of trial. In opening statement, plaintiff's counsel might begin by saying, "This case is about corporate accountability." During direct and cross-examination, counsel can return to the importance of product safety and the need to provide adequate warnings to consumers. In closing, plaintiff's counsel could finish with the theme:

Recall that during jury selection you were asked whether a company has an obligation to manufacture a product safe for use and to warn of all potential dangers. Each of you replied that a corporation had these responsibilities. Well, you have now heard the evidence, and it proves conclusively that Hill Moveit International Corporation neither produced a safe trailer nor warned users of the dangers. Darcy suffered the consequences of this defendant's failure to fulfill its corporate responsibility.

### Damages Questions

Besides advancing the case theory and theme, parties in a civil case will want to question jurors concerning damages. These questions can be employed to probe for bias and to condition the prospective jurors to be receptive to the party's position on damages. For instance, in the *Hill Moveit* case, plaintiff's counsel will want to determine the jurors' attitudes toward damages and introduce them to what may be argued in closing argument regarding compensation.

## Questions

### Jury Damages
### The *Hill Moveit Personal Injury* Case

**Plaintiff's counsel:**

*Q:* If defendants are found liable, we are going to ask you for an award of damages. Does anyone feel this is just not right—that it's nothing more than blood money?

*Q:* I'm not asking you to prejudge this case. But how do you feel about someone coming to court and asking for money for injury done to them?

*continued* ▶

> *Q:* If you find the defendants liable, and after you have heard evidence about damages—medical, loss of earnings, pain and suffering, ongoing care—you conclude that it would take a substantial amount of money to compensate Darcy, would you have any difficulty awarding her that compensation?
>
> *Q:* Is there anything—an experience, a belief, anything in your background—that would prevent you from awarding the full measure of compensation that the law provides for?
>
> *Q:* Is there a dollar ceiling limit that you already have in your mind beyond which you feel that you could not award money to a plaintiff in a lawsuit?
>
> *Q:* Do you have a preconceived notion that $20 million is just too high no matter what the evidence regarding damages might show in this or any case? In other words, does anyone think that $20 million is just too much money to award in a lawsuit?

### *Storytelling and the Factual Theory*

Another technique for incorporating the case theory into jury selection questions is really an organizational tool. Questions aimed at eliciting information relevant to bias are organized so they narrate all or part of your factual story.

To illustrate, suppose you are plaintiff's attorney in the *Sexual Harassment* case. See pages 105-106. Your factual theory can be set forth as a narrative, a story. You want to tell the jurors that the plaintiff, Cindy Kwon, a female employee, was the victim of sexual harassment and discrimination by her male supervisor. The defendant supervisor made sexual jokes and remarks, and invited the plaintiff to dinner and a movie. She rebuffed and rejected these social and sexual overtures. In retaliation, the defendant supervisor failed to promote her.

You, as plaintiff's counsel, want to blunt the defense position that plaintiff invited the sexual encounters partly by placing herself in a workforce dominated by males, and that, further, her poor performance on the job, not the encounters, is the reason she has not been promoted, received a raise, and so on. Your factual theory is persuasive because it tells a human story and involves values that jurors likely share—fair treatment. You can list the main points that constitute your narrative story and then develop a sequence of questions in such a way that they narrate your factual story:

| *Topics in Story* | *Questions* |
|---|---|
| Women suffer sexual harassment. | Can women suffer sexual harassment in the workplace? Why do you think so? |

| Topics in Story | Questions |
|---|---|
| Women in the workplace experience sexual jokes by male supervisors. | What do you think about the proposition that women who work in a predominantly male work environment are inviting sexual encounters?<br><br>Do you think that they can't be harassed because they are really seeking male attention? |
| Refusal by female of invitation to dinner; retaliation by supervisor failure to promote. | Do you think it's possible that a female's refusal of a supervisor's social invitation could really lead that supervisor to refuse to promote her? |

### Counteracting Opposing Counsel's Efforts to Advance Theory, Theme, and Damages

#### Objecting

Two methods may be used to meet opposing counsel's attempts to indoctrinate the jury. First, you can object to questions on the grounds opposing counsel is asking questions that are inappropriate for jury selection: Counsel is arguing the case, anticipating instructions on the law, inappropriately asking the jurors to promise how they would vote based on a hypothetical set of facts, or asking highly sensitive or embarrassing questions. This approach can be successful in courts that have a restrictive view of the purpose of voir dire.

#### Countering

A second approach, which we have illustrated in prior sections, is to anticipate questions that opposing counsel might ask to advance that party's theme and theory. Then plan questions that educate the jurors and use the method described in the preceding section to persuade the jury of your theory and theme.

One way to anticipate opposing counsel is to figuratively step into the shoes of opposing counsel and ask yourself, "What legal and factual points that are particularly important would I ask during voir dire if I were opposing counsel?" Of course, it will be easier to predict if you know how opposing counsel usually approaches jury selection. It would be ideal if you could watch opposing counsel select a jury or, better yet, have previously tried a case against opposing counsel.

Once you have anticipated opposing counsel's areas of inquiry, you can then develop your questions to counteract opposing counsel's strategy. For example, suppose you are plaintiff's counsel in the *Sexual Harassment* case (discussed on page 104). You believe defense counsel might discuss areas that will educate the jurors to defendant's view of compensatory damages. A few possibilities that you anticipate the defense might stress include: that injuries were minimal injuries, that sympathy with the plaintiff should not influence the jurors, and that the fact the defendant is a corporation should not be held against the defendant. As expected, during jury selection, defense counsel asks the following:

---

### Jury Questions

#### Anticipating the Adversary's Questions by Advancing a Theory and Theme
#### The *Sexual Harassment* Case

As plaintiff's counsel, you anticipate defense counsel may ask questions such as:

Q: Sympathy hasn't anything to do with this lawsuit; do you agree?

Q: The defendant is a corporation made up of people. Does the mere fact that the defendant is a company mean you should punish the company?

Q: If a person has just minimal injuries, would you be able to award minimal damages?

---

### Jury Questions

#### Countering Your Adversary and Advancing Your Theory and Theme
#### The *Sexual Harassment* Case

As plaintiff's counsel, having anticipated defense lines of inquiry with the jury, you are prepared to counteract them. When proper, you may object when the questions are asked. (See page 105.) If the judge sustains your objections, you will have cured the problem. However, if the objections are overruled, or if you decide not to object because you want to be free to educate the jury on behalf of your own client, you could ask prospective jurors questions embodying your own theory concerning compensatory damages:

Q: Regardless of your sympathies, if plaintiff Cindy Kwon proves to you that she was not promoted because she failed to cooperate sexually with her supervisor, will you be able to return a verdict in her favor?

Q: Do you believe that the value of an injured person's emotional injuries can be as great or greater than the financial loss that person has suffered?

Q: If Ms. Kwon proves to you that she suffered substantial injuries—emotional and physical—would you award the amount shown by the evidence?

Q: Could you award those damages even if the damage sums seem large to you?

Q: Just because defendant is a company does not mean that it doesn't have to pay for the damage it inflicts; would you agree?

Q: Do you believe that a company is less obligated to fully compensate a party whom it has injured than an individual who has caused similar harm?

---

## E. Case Weaknesses Questions

As part of the process of developing the case theory, you conducted an exercise to identify and assess case strengths and weaknesses with the case assessment brainstorming sessions (pages 42-43). Ideally, you will have noted these strengths and weaknesses when you first read through the file. This initial encounter with the case is where you gain your first and often your best impressions. Later, you will brainstorm to better identify the positives that you want to emphasize in your presentation and the negatives that you must reckon with during the trial.

Generic case weaknesses include the following:

- Type of clients (corporate);
- Witness problems (prior felony conviction, speech impediments, physical impairments, occupation);
- Harshness of penalties (capital litigation);
- Type of offense or defense (child molestation, rape, self-defense, diminished capacity);
- The principles of law involved (right to remain silent);
- Behavior involved (alcohol, drugs); or
- Specific case weaknesses (gruesome photographic exhibits or amount of damages).

We offer these categories for purposes of analysis; in actuality, distinctions between them are often blurred. Generally, case weaknesses should be revealed and dealt with during jury selection for at least four reasons.

- First, if you recognized the vulnerabilities during case preparation, they are unlikely to escape opposing counsel's attention. If you do not divulge the weaknesses to the jury, opposing counsel will probably expose them at some point during the trial, and you run the risk of appearing to have attempted to conceal them.
- Second, if you reveal your own case weaknesses, you will appear candid and fair.
- Third, by exposing areas of vulnerability and putting them in the best light, you may be able to blunt their impact.
- Fourth (and most important), these weaknesses and problems are perhaps the most significant areas to probe for biases that will affect a prospective juror's ability to consider your case theory. At the same time, they will aid you in obtaining the necessary information to determine whether to exercise a challenge.

### Juror Beliefs and Expectations

Prospective jurors report to jury duty with beliefs and expectations. These beliefs and expectations have been generated by their background, culture, and environment. The media has influenced how many think about the justice system and its participants. For example, media coverage of litigation, including the McDonald's scalding coffee case (*http://www.lectlaw.com/files/cur78.htm*) and the threadbare lawsuit in which the plaintiff was awarded what seemed a seriously disproportionate sum for a claim that the cleaners lost his pants (*http://www.cbsnews.com/stories/2007/06/25/national/main2974217.shtml*), have given rise to the public perception that there are too many lawsuits. Entertainment programs, such as the television *CSI* series, have created expectations that the prosecution should be able to produce forensic evidence that was readily detected at the scene, and that the analysis of that trace evidence should produce not only the identification of the perpetrator, but also the person's full biography. The impact of this television show on prospective jurors has been referred to as the "*CSI* Effect" (*http://www.nij.gov/journals/259/csi-effect.htm*). The expectations and beliefs discussed here are case weaknesses, even though their causes are extrinsic to the case itself.

To be successful, trial lawyers must recognize the beliefs and expectations that may influence the jurors' judgments and determine how to contend with them. It is unrealistic to expect that an attorney can change a prospective juror's beliefs during jury selection. Rather, a trial lawyer can seek to distinguish the prospective juror's beliefs and expectations from the case to be tried. For instance, to contend with the preconceived notion about frivolous litigation, plaintiff's counsel can bring it to the surface by inquiring, "This is a lawsuit, and we've all heard 'there are too many lawsuits.' Do you think there are too many?" Inevitably prospective jurors will mention specific frivolous suits, ones that have garnered media attention. Once the concern is raised, plaintiff's counsel can guide the discussion to recognize that valid lawsuits do exist and then inquire, "If the evidence in this case proves that the defendant was at fault, will you hold the defendant responsible?" Or the prosecutor, in an effort to fight the *CSI* Effect, can ask questions to get the prospective jurors to acknowledge that the television show is entertainment, that it does not replicate real-life criminal investigations. Then the prosecutor can seek a commitment from the prospective jurors that they would not require the prosecution to produce forensic evidence like that portrayed on the television show. In both examples, the trial lawyer should not seek to change prospective juror beliefs. Rather, counsel should try to distinguish beliefs from the case at hand.

### Formulating Questions

To illustrate how to develop questions that deal with a weakness, imagine you are plaintiff's counsel in the *Sexual Harassment* case. The defense will present evidence that plaintiff asked her supervisor to join her for lunch on several occasions and twice suggested drinks after work. Plaintiff will admit this, but will contend that she never discussed anything but business with her supervisor. The defense theory is that Ms. Kwon encouraged her supervisor to ask her for a date and is now using that as an excuse for the real reason for not being promoted— her failure to perform in her job. This problem involves a specific case concern amplified by certain attitudes toward sex discrimination in the workplace. As plaintiff's attorney, you want to prepare the jurors for the evidence concerning your client's invitations to her supervisor.

## Jury Questions

### Questions Addressing Case Weaknesses
### The *Sexual Harassment* Case

As plaintiff's counsel, you might ask the following questions to reveal a case weakness and obtain information about prospective juror reactions to the weakness:

#### Questions

Q: What do you think about the saying that if a woman wants to, she can stop sexual advances from being made by a male supervisor or employer?

Q: What do you think about the proposition that it is illegal for a supervisor to sexually harass a female employee?

Q: Do you believe that if a woman asks a male work supervisor out to lunch or for a drink after work to discuss work, she has encouraged sexual advances? Why do you think so?

#### Obtaining a Commitment

You may also want to extract a commitment from the juror to "put aside your feelings and promise me to decide this case on the law and the evidence presented." You can then refer to that commitment in your closing argument.

You could ask:

Q: If the judge instructs you that it is against the law for a supervisor to sexually harass a female employee, will you be able to apply that rule of law?

Q: Can you fully accept this proposition of law and apply it to Ms. Kwon's case?

Q: If Ms. Kwon proves her case by a preponderance of the evidence, will you apply the rule of law and find that Ms. Kwon was sexually harassed?

## F. Personal Questions

The purpose of directing personal questions to a juror is to elicit information to determine whether the prospective juror shares the attributes of the type of juror you do not want sitting on your case. Also, the questions can be designed to influence the prospective jurors regarding decision making in the justice system. Here you can refer to the bad juror profile that you have developed, as discussed on pages 83-84. Begin with the list of concrete characteristics that you identified for the bad juror profile (employment, types of community involvement, associates, experience, and so on). Then, brainstorm questions that will gather information about the extent to which a specific juror possesses these characteristics and, inferentially, meets your profile. The information you gather through specific questions will enable you to decide whether to exercise a peremptory challenge against the prospective juror. Again, appreciate how inexact this process is. You are inferring a profile from characteristics and inferring bias from the profile.

To illustrate, suppose that you are defense counsel in the *Hill Moveit Personal Injury* case. As you may recall from your prior analysis at page 84, the profile of the type of juror you do not want for the defense is one who would identify with the plaintiff, dislikes corporations, would have trouble making hard decisions (finding the defendant not at fault), and would sympathize with the plaintiff's plight. Because not everyone who shares these characteristics will be anti-defense, it is essential to craft questions that will uncover the true attitudes of the potential juror.

---

### Jury Questions

#### Personal Matters
#### The *Hill Moveit Personal Injury* Case

Let's examine the type of questions you could ask to uncover a juror's anti-defense attitudes or a juror's willingness to sympathize with the plaintiff's problems and injuries. These questions are unlikely to lead to a challenge for cause, though you never know.

**Defense counsel:**

*Q:* Now, here is a personal question for each one of you, and it has to do with how you make hard decisions. Some are made with the brain and others with the heart. In this case, you will decide whether to award damages to Darcy Rutherford. She has suffered greatly; she has been damaged. About this there is no question. But there is a question about whether Hill Moveit caused that damage. Is there anyone who, because of sympathy for her, would feel guilty if you didn't award her damages? Please raise your hand if you would feel uncomfortable not awarding her damages.

*Q:* Is there any one of you who would say to me, "I don't care what the evidence shows, she's been blinded, disfigured, and disabled"?

*Q:* The judge will instruct you that you are not to be swayed by sympathy or sidetracked by prejudice in reaching your decision on liability. Can you do this?

*Q:* Can you assure us that if you become jurors in this case you will decide this case based on the evidence and not be swayed by sympathy for the plaintiff?

---

## G.  Trial Questions

The jurors' understanding of their duties as fact finders in the trial can be critical to the jurors' adoption of your case theory. We categorize questions that deal with burden of proof, witness credibility, expert witness testimony, computation of damages, and so on as trial questions. These trial questions can uncover information useful in determining whether to exercise a challenge, and can also educate the jurors about their role in the decision-making process.

There are two steps to observe in developing this type of question.

- First, you should determine whether you need to ask these questions. Consult a list of the actual functions jurors will perform in your trial. You can do this by reviewing your proposed jury instructions.
- Second, review your case theory to determine the effect of these trial duties on your case.

If, after such a review, you decide that jurors' awareness of their trial duties will not be important to a favorable outcome for your client, or you believe the judge has adequately covered this issue, you might concentrate on the other types of juror questions and avoid the trial questions. This advice is particularly important if you have time constraints in jury selection.

## Jury Questions

### Burden of Proof
### The *Hill Moveit Personal Injury* Case

Suppose you are plaintiff's counsel in the *Hill Moveit* case. You want to discuss the plaintiff's burden of proof with the prospective jurors and differentiate it from the burden in a criminal case. You could do so as follows:

**Plaintiff's counsel:**

*Q:* This is a civil rather than a criminal case. In this civil case, Darcy has to prove the case by only a preponderance of evidence. Proof beyond a reasonable doubt applies only in a criminal case. Is there anyone here who could not follow the court's instructions that the plaintiff needs to prove its case by only a preponderance of the evidence? Raise your hand if you could not do that.

However, in a criminal case, you might want to discuss trial duty concepts. Imagine you are the defense attorney and want to voir dire about two concepts: "reasonable doubt" and the criminal defendant's constitutional right to choose not to testify and to have no negative inferences drawn by the jury as a result of that choice.

Questions can focus on obtaining the jurors' traditional reasonable doubt commitment using a customary set of questions such as these.

*Q:* You understand that my client has no obligation to prove anything?

*Q:* Do you agree with the proposition under our Constitution that the prosecution must prove every element of a charged crime beyond a reasonable doubt before you can find my client guilty?

*Q:* Would you be willing to promise my client that you will hold the prosecution to proving every element of each crime charged beyond a reasonable doubt?

*Q:* If you have a reasonable doubt at the end of all the evidence as to *any* element of the charged crime, would you have any trouble acquitting my client of that crime?

However, you may be able to achieve something beyond just the juror acquiescence to the reasonable doubt concept, to which admittedly you can refer in closing argument ("Remember when I talked to you at the beginning of trial about reasonable doubt? You all promised me and my client . . ."). Imagine instead that you ask the following single question.

*Q:* If you believed at the end of all the evidence that my client was probably guilty, but nevertheless had a reasonable doubt as to his guilt, would you be able to find him not guilty?

This single question, besides committing the jurors to acquitting if they have a reasonable doubt—which effectively holds the prosecution to proof beyond a reasonable doubt—accomplishes two other strategically important things. First, it mentally prepares the jurors for the possibility that because of the law regarding the burden of proof, they may have to acquit someone they confidently believe is probably factually guilty. Second, it gives particular context to the somewhat amorphous concept of reasonable doubt.

The defendant's right not to testify offers another example of an area where you can accomplish something beyond rote commitment by a juror.

*Q:* Do you agree with the fact that my client has a constitutional right not to take the stand?

*Q:* If my client does not take the stand, how will you feel?

*Q:* Will you be more prone to think he's guilty?

*Q:* If the judge instructs you that in your deliberations you are not to take into consideration if my client chooses to exercise his right not to testify, would you have any difficulty following that instruction?

Once in a while, these standard questions can reveal information worthy of rigorous follow-up questions, but usually all the juror might be willing to say is "yes," "sure," "I agree," or such. The jurors will not talk, so you will not get any information about their attitudes toward this particular issue, or about their personalities or thought processes in general. Remember: In some sense, you don't really care what jurors talk about just so long as they talk. So think of this alternative (or complementary) approach to the topic of your client not testifying ("Some people would say that if someone is innocent, they'll testify and say so. How do you feel about that?").

## H. Case-Specific Questions

To intelligently exercise challenges, you need to obtain information from prospective jurors as to how they feel about your case, your case theory, your client, your witnesses, and you. These questions are designed to assist you in deciding how to exercise challenges. At the same time, your questions can instruct the jury about the case theory. Usually, there are specific case-related areas that you wish to probe.

### Core Factors

To formulate case-specific questions, begin by isolating key factors in your case theory and juror profiles; these are factors on which your case may rise or fall. List the topics specific to your case and then select those you believe are of particular importance, keeping in mind how much time the judge allows for voir dire.

---

**Jury Selection**

**Using Core Formulas for Formulating Case-Specific Questions**

- People and witnesses (police officers, salespersons, students);
- Organizations (corporation, law enforcement);
- Places (where the incident—that is, the focus of the lawsuit—took place);
- Legal principles (presumption of innocence, self-defense, comparative fault, proximate cause, damages);
- Pieces of evidence (knife, poison, contract, autopsy photographs, airplane parts);
- Events similar to the one involved in the lawsuit (landlord-tenant dispute, consumer fraud);
- Issues (drugs, gun ownership, careless driving, alcoholic beverages, eyewitness identification, death by violent means, pain and suffering); or
- Client identification traits (wealth, poverty, nationality, corporate status, race, region of the country).

---

### People, Organizations, Places, and Events

Questions about people, organizations, and places provide illustrations of how jury selection questions can be designed to both explore reasons for exercising challenges and persuade the jury to be receptive to the case theory at the same time.

#### Juror Knowledge and Bias

Jury selection questions will inquire about whether the prospective jurors know any of the parties, participants involved in the subject matter of the lawsuit, and the witnesses. For jury selection, trial counsel needs to prepare a list of witnesses they may call to testify. Either the judge or the lawyers, depending on court practice, will read the lists and ask whether the jurors are acquainted with the witnesses. If you are criminal defense counsel, you can ask the judge to merge your list with the prosecution's, thereby not identifying particular witnesses as defense witnesses. Since you may decide not to even put on a case, you do not want the jurors from the start to expect you to call witnesses. Similarly, if an organization such as a corporation is involved, inquiry can be made into whether the jurors are or have been employed by or otherwise affiliated with the organization. If a prospective juror responds in the affirmative, follow-up questions are asked to determine the nature of the relationship with the person or organization. Also, counsel should inquire into whether the prospective jurors are familiar with locations that play a part in the lawsuit. For instance, in a wrongful death case, they may know the intersection where the cars collided.

Prospective jurors may harbor biases about the witnesses based upon their occupation. For instance, they may tend to believe or disbelieve a law enforcement officer. As an example, assume that in the *Blue Moon News Robbery* case (page 81), the prosecution intends to call police officer witnesses who will testify to investigating the scene, collecting a latent fingerprint, arresting the defendant, and taking witness statements. While the prosecutor would not want jurors who are unduly skeptical of police officers, the defense attorney would not want jurors who would give excessive deference to them.

---

## Juror Questions

### Bias Toward Police
### The *Blue Moon News Robbery* Case

**Prosecutor:**

General Questions to the Panel

Q: Have you, a member of your family, or a close friend ever had contact with a law enforcement officer?

(Juror nine raises her hand.)

Specific Questions Addressed to Juror Nine

Q: Can you tell me about the circumstances in which you or your family or good friend had a contact with law enforcement?
A: Yes. My younger brother, 14 years of age, ran away. My mother contacted the police to report him missing. The police found him two months later and brought him home.
Q: What is your impression of the police?
A: Positive. The police were very helpful. They kept us informed and they did a thorough investigation.

Defense counsel, in an effort to test the depth of prospective juror nine's views and to neutralize any bias, might ask:

**Defense counsel:**

*Q:* Do you think police officers are more truthful than other people?

*Q:* Do you think police officers can be mistaken?

*Q:* Just because one of the prosecutor's witnesses is a police officer doesn't mean you will give more attention to his testimony than to that of other witnesses, does it?

**Prosecutor:**

Objection. This may be a factor relevant to the jurors' deliberation.

**Judge:**

Overruled. You may answer.

*A:* No.

**Defense counsel:**

*Q:* In other words, you can put aside any personal feelings you may have because the police were helpful to your family and judge a police officer's testimony in this case just as you would that of any other witness?

*A:* Yes. I can do that.

### The Surrogate

A technique for educating and persuading prospective jurors about the case theory and the people involved is to enlist one or more of them to tell a story or discuss what happened in an event resembling the one that is the subject of the lawsuit. This can be done while probing for bias. For example, in the *Wrongful Death Collision* case, plaintiff's counsel could ask about whether the prospective jurors are familiar with the intersection where the plaintiff claims the defendant ran a stop sign, colliding with the plaintiff's car. Follow-up questioning could elicit information from individual prospective jurors indicating that the intersection is clearly marked with stop signs and otherwise safe. Let's illustrate the surrogate concept in the *Blue Moon News Robbery* case.

## Jury Questions

### The Surrogate
### The *Blue Moon News Robbery* Case

The prosecutor might ask a prospective juror about the experience of being a robbery victim.

*continued* ▶

---

**Prosecutor:**

General Questions to the Panel

*Q:* Have you or a member of your family or a close friend ever been the victim of a robbery?

(Juror 11, an elderly man, among others, raises his hand.)

Specific Questions Addressed to Juror 11

*Q:* Mr. Narvaez, can you tell us who was robbed?
*A:* I was.
*Q:* When was that?
*A:* About five years ago.
*Q:* What happened?
*A:* I own a coffee shop, Happy Go Latte, and I was robbed just as I was opening up for the day.
*Q:* Were you alone at the time?
*Q:* Go ahead and describe what happened.
*Q:* How did you feel when the man pointed the gun at you?
*Q:* Would the fact that it is alleged that Mr. Newman was robbed at gunpoint prevent you from being fair and impartial in this case, if you were selected as a juror? (Note: The prosecution is asking this question to insulate this witness from a defense challenge for cause.)

---

## V. STRATEGIES

### A. Exercising Challenges

Three factors are fundamental in determining how to, and whether to, exercise a challenge for cause or a peremptory challenge: appearance of fairness, the relationship between peremptory and for-cause challenges, and comparing prospective jurors.

#### *Appearance of Fairness*

If the legitimacy of the opposing counsel's challenge for cause is obvious to you, consider your obligation to ensure the process seats jurors who are fair and impartial. Beyond that, you will gain credibility with both the judge and the jury if you join in the challenge for cause or the judge's decision to excuse the prospective juror. At least do not resist opposing counsel's challenge for cause. Also, you do not want to risk a mistrial or reversal on appeal if the person clearly should not sit on the case. However, a criminal defense attorney may be compelled to oppose a challenge by the prosecutor or the judge's decision to excuse a juror. Defense counsel's primary duty is to prevent or reverse a conviction in every conceivable and ethical way, and because defense counsel operates in a system where jeopardy prevents appeal after acquittal.

### *Relationship Between Peremptory and For-Cause Challenges*

When considering whether to assert a challenge for cause, think of the relationship between challenges for cause and peremptory challenges. Challenges for cause are unlimited, but peremptory challenges are limited in number. Thus, you first must consider whether the objectionable juror could be excused through the exercise of a challenge for cause instead of expending a valuable peremptory challenge. On the other hand, you must consider the consequences if you do not succeed in your challenge for cause. If the challenge is asserted with the prospective juror present, which is the general procedure, this is likely to have an adverse effect on the prospective juror. Generally, you will be accusing the juror of being too biased to sit on the case, and this assertion may engender hostility toward you or your client. Therefore, you probably will have created a situation where you must exercise one of your peremptory challenges against the prospective juror if your challenge for cause fails.

### *Comparing Prospective Jurors*

You should compare the people seated in the jury box and those in the panel. When a lawyer exercises a challenge for cause against a prospective juror seated in the jury box, a new prospective juror is seated in the chair. Then the juror is subject to the exercise of a challenge. If the persons in the panel could be the same or worse than those already in the jury box, the lawyer might want to exercise care if peremptory challenges are limited. Instead, the lawyer may want to consider not challenging (passing) a seated prospective juror.

### Strategies in a Criminal Case

A defense attorney's strategy in a criminal case is of critical importance. If the law in the jurisdiction requires a unanimous verdict, the defense needs only one juror to hang a jury (obtain a mistrial). Practically speaking, it usually, though not invariably, takes two to three jurors to hold out. Therefore, defense counsel may be willing to leave a few persons on the jury whom counsel does not especially like if there are some jurors she does like. In that way, defense counsel does not use peremptory challenges and leaves it to the prosecution to challenge. This then places the prosecution in the position either of passing and ending jury selection. This strategy would leave defense counsel with the jurors defense counsel likes, or of using up challenges. In the latter situation, should the prosecution exercise a peremptory challenge after you pass—that is, accept the panel—the prosecution will have fewer peremptory challenges left to excuse prospective jurors who are later seated. In a jurisdiction where you can challenge after you pass if the other side then exercises a challenge, defense counsel will have a greater number of peremptory challenges left compared with those left to the prosecution. These extra challenges will mean that near the end of the selection process, defense counsel will be able to remove several seemingly pro-prosecution jurors at once. This strategy will not work in a jurisdiction where the law does not allow you to accumulate peremptory challenges. (Also keep in mind that in some jurisdictions, if you do not use all your peremptory challenges, you may not be able to appeal the court's refusal of a challenge for cause.)

A prosecutor's approach to jury selection is influenced by the fact that it only takes one juror to hang the jury. The prosecutor will be scrutinizing jurors to see whether they are likely to work well in a group situation and will be concerned about those who may not. Also, the prosecutor will be on the lookout for the antiauthority, or disaffected person who might hold out.

### Strategies for Exercising Challenges

To explain the strategic processes underlying the exercise of challenges, let's examine the *Hill Moveit Personal Injury* case.

---

#### Jury Selection Strategies for Exercising Challenges
#### The *Hill Moveit Personal Injury* Case

Imagine that you are defense counsel in the *Hill Moveit* case. Your client is contesting liability. Prospective juror Jamal Fleming revealed during the judge's general questioning and plaintiff counsel's specific questioning that he was a plaintiff in an automobile accident personal injury case just two months before trial began. You have concluded, even before you begin your questioning of Mr. Fleming, that he more than likely will not be disposed to the defense case. He is the type of juror you do not want. Under the law of your jurisdiction, a prospective juror may be excused for cause if the juror has "an actual or implied bias that renders the person incapable of reaching a fair and impartial verdict." In civil cases in your jurisdiction, each side is allotted four peremptory challenges. The procedure for exercising challenges is in an alternating manner with the plaintiff declaring the first peremptory challenge.

---

Now let's explore the defense potential strategies for when and how to exercise challenges in *Hill Moveit* jury selection. To get Mr. Fleming excused, you seemingly have five options.

- First, convince Mr. Fleming that he should request to be excused from the case.
- Second, have the judge excuse Mr. Fleming.
- Third, challenge Mr. Fleming for cause, asserting he is biased and cannot be fair and impartial.
- Fourth, exercise a peremptory challenge.
- Fifth, entice the plaintiff to exercise a peremptory challenge to excuse Mr. Fleming.

What should you do? You could begin by exploring the possibility of establishing a foundation (1) for Mr. Fleming to request to be excused, (2) for the judge on his own to excuse Mr. Fleming, or (3) for you to challenge Mr. Fleming for cause.

### Prospective Juror Requests to Be Excused

The first and best option is that Mr. Fleming recognizes his own bias and asks to be excused. But as good a plan as this is, it is more than probable that Mr. Fleming will state, "Of course I can be fair and impartial to the defense." In other words, it may be a very difficult task to accomplish and require so many questions that you appear argumentative.

### The Judge Excuses the Prospective Juror

The second option is for the judge to determine that Mr. Fleming should be excused. This requires the judge to be astute, so that you as the lawyer will not need to exercise a challenge for cause. But as good a plan as this strategy is, again, it may be a difficult task to accomplish, requiring so many questions of the prospective juror that you appear argumentative.

### Making a Challenge for Cause

Strategy three, whether you should challenge for cause, requires you to consider the strategic ramifications of such a challenge. For instance, even though you have the right to challenge the jurors for cause, if you do so, you will be perceived as the lawyer who is "kicking people off the jury." As previously discussed, the jurors who are left may feel antagonism toward you. You must also consider what your position will be if you challenge Mr. Fleming for cause and the challenge is not sustained. Ordinarily, you would be placed in the position of being bound to exercise a peremptory challenge against him because of both his potential antagonism toward you, and the grounds on which you made the challenge for cause in the first place. Consequently, you probably will *not* challenge Mr. Fleming for cause *unless* and *until*, after a series of your questions, he commits himself to a stance from which—realistically—it does not appear that he can be rehabilitated and your reason for trying to remove him from the jury will be clear.

On the other hand, you could question Mr. Fleming so that he will acknowledge that his recent personal injury case so prejudiced him that he could not be fair and impartial in this personal injury case. If you encourage him to express a firm commitment to a position beyond the point where the plaintiff's counsel could rehabilitate him, then you could challenge for cause. With this approach, you may be able to accomplish two objectives: First, Mr. Fleming may recognize he harbors a bias and then perceive that others doubt his impartiality. Second, as a result of this new self-awareness, he may decide that he should bend over backwards to show an impartial state of mind. But, again, it is *unlikely* that you will alter a person's beliefs in a few minutes of jury selection.

### Exercising a Peremptory Challenge

In regard to whether you should exercise a peremptory challenge, a tactical consideration is whether you will expend all of your challenges and be unable to challenge another prospective juror who may be even worse than Fleming. Remember that you have only four peremptory challenges, and each juror you challenge will be replaced by another from the panel. So think about whether Mr. Fleming is really at the bottom or top of your ranking scale in terms of jurors you do not want. Again, if you exercise a peremptory challenge against Mr. Fleming, down the line you may run out of peremptory challenges and end up with a juror who is even worse.

Also consider that if your effort to develop a foundation for a challenge for cause failed, you could try to turn the juror's ostensible bias to your advantage in an effort to preserve one of your peremptory challenges. You could have Mr. Fleming acknowledge that he was recently injured in an automobile accident and implicitly establish that his sitting in judgment on a personal injury case requires that he give assurances that he will be fair. Then, through your questions, you could seek to have him state that despite his injuries and lawsuit, he will make every effort to be fair and impartial to your client.

*Enticing Opposing Counsel to Exercise a Peremptory Challenge*

This is the most difficult strategy because it entails rehabilitating Mr. Fleming so that he appears to be leaning toward the defense position. Second, and most important, you may raise a question in the mind of the plaintiff's attorney about whether Mr. Fleming will end up with a reverse bias, by exercising an abundance of caution to appear fair. If you conclude that you may have planted a seed of doubt in your opponent's mind, you could hold off challenging Mr. Fleming and exercise your peremptory challenges to excuse other prospective jurors first. This would conserve your peremptory challenges in the hope that plaintiff will exercise a peremptory challenge to excuse Mr. Fleming.

---

### Jury Selection Strategies: Overcoming Bias

#### The *Hill Moveit Personal Injury* Case

The questions you might ask as defense counsel to get the prospective juror to commit to being fair and impartial could include the following.

*Q:* If you were a juror in this case, could you decide the case on the evidence in the courtroom and only on that evidence?

*A:* Yes.

*Q:* Would it make it more difficult to be impartial and fair to Hill Moveit, the defendant, because you were a plaintiff in a highway accident case?

*A:* No.

*Q:* Even though you were a plaintiff in a highway accident lawsuit, could you set aside your feelings and decide this case just on what happens in the courtroom?

*A:* Yes.

*Q:* In your case, your position was obviously well founded?

*A:* I won.

*Q:* But you don't believe that everyone who sues is in the right, do you?

> *A:* No. Surely not.
> *Q:* Now, in this case, Mr. Fleming, do you believe you can listen to the evidence and be fair and impartial in assessing the evidence?
> *A:* I think so.
> *Q:* Can you promise me that you will be fair and impartial?
> *A:* Yes. I can.
> *Q:* Are you sure?
> *A:* Yes.

## B. Analyzing Prospective Jurors

Before exercising any challenges, you need to analyze the information you obtained from your background investigation and from observing and listening to juror responses. You then should evaluate this information against juror profiles and grounds for a challenge for cause. This process is fast moving and allows little time for reflection. Therefore, jury seating and challenges charts, with your codes for rating the jurors and your "good" and "bad" juror profiles noted on them, are particularly helpful. The jury seating chart will enable you to organize information during the voir dire. The jury profiles will guide your judgment as to whether to challenge a juror because you believe the juror will not be favorably disposed to your client's case.

Jury consultants also can be hired to conduct juror surveys, develop juror profiles, and attend trial to evaluate and provide advice about prospective jurors. These experts can be expensive but beneficial in jury selection. Ultimately, the decision concerning whether to exercise a challenge rests with the trial lawyer, in consultation with the client.

### Deselecting Prospective Jurors

Jury selection is a process in which you deselect a jury. Opposing counsel will be striving to eliminate any prospective juror whom you would select and who matches your good juror profile. You are constrained in the process by having only a limited number of peremptory challenges. Therefore, your work involves identifying and challenging those prospective jurors whom you have concluded are risks to decide against your client.

Besides screening prospective jurors with your juror profiles, you must be mindful of the group dynamic and how the jurors fit into it, because the group dynamic will affect jury deliberations. Prospective jurors fall into categories: foreperson, leaders, followers, outsiders, and oddballs. Life experience will enable you to tell who fits into which category. For instance, the leaders, who usually have been leaders in their business or community lives, will speak up during voir dire. They will have amicable interactions with fellow prospective jurors. Leaders will play a dominant role in deliberations (and you can often spot the foreperson among the leaders). A leader who is against you will play a dominant role during deliberations and can turn the jurors against your side. Outsiders, whom you spotted during jury selection because they might have dressed inappropriately for court, never spoke up, and never interacted with others, may follow or may be contentious in the jury room. The oddball is the one you don't want to miss. This type of juror can seem fine until after the jury is sworn. Then the person brings in his own coffee because he can't tolerate what is in the jury room, or for the first time begins looking at you like you're his worst enemy, and so on. On the other hand, the oddball or the outsider can be your best ally if you are defense counsel in a criminal case requiring a unanimous verdict, and you most likely will be satisfied with a mistrial resulting from a hung jury.

### Listening and Watching

The primary way that you identify those prospective jurors whom you think are against your case is by carefully watching and listening to them, and listening to co-counsel or other team members who are aiding you in jury selection. As we stressed earlier in this chapter, when you are questioning jurors, you want to get them talking so that you can listen and watch. However, there is an even better time to watch and listen, and that is when opposing counsel is questioning the jurors. At that time, you are free from having to question, take notes, and so on. You can concentrate on the prospective jurors and notice the verbal and nonverbal signals.

### Verbal and Nonverbal Signals

Most of your evaluation of prospective jurors will be based on a juror's verbal and nonverbal responses, both individually and in comparison to the responses you are getting from the panel.

To evaluate the verbal response of a juror, consider both the content of the juror's answer and the way it is phrased. The response might be reluctant, qualified, equivocal, argumentative, or inconsistent. For example, defense counsel in a criminal case might ask, "If the court were to instruct you that the law presumes a person innocent until proven guilty beyond a reasonable doubt, would you have any quarrel with that idea?" If the juror answered, "I will try to follow the court's instructions," the juror's use of the word *try* suggests the juror might not believe in this principle of law or have difficulty applying it. Compare the juror's responses to your questions and those by opposing counsel; differences may provide you with clues as to the inclination and thinking of the juror. Is the juror friendlier to opposing counsel than to you?

Because a prospective juror might in a verbal answer mask her true beliefs, another indication of the juror's inclinations may be gleaned from the person's body language. There exists an accumulation of literature on the subject of nonverbal communication, some of which is based on scientific research and experimentation. Many of these studies of nonverbal communication can assist you if you wish to interpret the nonverbal reactions of prospective jurors. The "bible" for jury selection is V. Hale Starr and Mark McCormick's *Jury Selection* (4th ed., Aspen Publishers 2009). This book contains an extensive discussion, along with illustrative photographs of body movement communication.

Understanding nonverbal communication is a talent many lawyers have. For instance, if the prospective juror avoids eye contact with you and crosses his or her arms, but smiles and talks directly to opposing counsel, you have some hints that there is a communication barrier between you and the prospective juror.

You may obtain information by observing other nonverbal traits. How the prospective juror dresses might give you some idea about how important he considers jury duty. What the prospective juror carries or wears (reading material, rings, or lapel pins) might provide insight into the person's personality and beliefs. How the person interacts with other prospective jurors, such as chatting or standing apart, can provide insight as to how they will behave during deliberations.

### Your Instincts

We acquire a feel for a person. It is something you have done your entire life, so do not be afraid to trust your instincts, your accumulated life wisdom. Your reaction and your client's reaction to a prospective juror should be given great weight. If you have a sense of uneasiness about the prospective juror or how the person seems to be responding to you or your client, beware. This sense is an indispensable source of information on which you should rely. It indicates the juror likely will be unreceptive to you and therefore to your case theory. It is better to be safe than sorry, so you should be inclined to exercise a challenge to a juror that gives you this impression.

## VI. ETHICAL CONSIDERATIONS

Trial lawyers have ethical obligations to the jurors before, during, and after the jury selection. Because our legal system is founded on the principle that cases are to be decided by juries free from entangling influences, it is imperative that you be professionally responsible in safeguarding that principle.

## A.  Trial Publicity

Front-Page News

---

RUSTON GLOBE

---

# Freck Point Murder Charges

**By MARGO GORDON**
September 8, 20XX

First degree murder charges have been filed against well-known mystery author Samuel L. Griffith for the death of his wife Sondra Griffith. In announcing the filing of criminal charges, Jamner County Assistant Prosecutor Michael Gonnif accused Griffith of the "cold-blooded slaying of his wife in order to collect on her life insurance."

Dispelling the earlier reports that Mrs. Griffith had been killed by a burglar, Assistant Prosecutor Gonnif said, "The forensic blood spatter evidence combined with Samuel Griffith's false statements on the night of the murder are conclusive proof. Besides, why would he hire a lawyer the next day if he were not charged and had done nothing wrong?" Ruston Chief of Police Donald Torrie was also present at the press conference, and he confirmed the prosecutor's opinion, stating that the evidence "shows that Griffith, not some intruder, stabbed Mrs. Griffith to death. Griffith staged the break-in."

*SEE MURDER CHARGES, A5*

---

An attorney's extrajudicial statements about the case to media representatives can present ethical and legal issues. Pretrial publicity in a criminal case may rise to such a level that there is a probability that jurors selected from the community will be prejudiced. To avoid a violation of due process, this situation forces the court to grant a motion for change of venue or grant a continuance, or at least extensive voir dire regarding pretrial publicity. The ABA Model Rules set out the guidelines for an attorney's ethical code of conduct regarding pretrial publicity.

## Ethical Rules For Trial Publicity

### ABA Model Rules of Professional Conduct

ABA Model Rule of Professional Conduct 3.6 on Trial Publicity

(a)   A lawyer who is participating or has participated in the investigation or litigation of a matter shall not make an extrajudicial statement that the lawyer knows or reasonably should know will be disseminated by means of public communication and will have a substantial likelihood of materially prejudicing an adjudicative proceeding in the matter.

(b)   Notwithstanding paragraph (a), a lawyer may state

(1)   the claim, offense or defense involved and, except when prohibited by law, the identity of the persons involved;

(2)   information contained in a public record;

(3)   that an investigation of a matter is in progress;

(4)   the scheduling or result of any step in litigation;

(5)   a request for assistance in obtaining evidence and information necessary thereto;

(6)   a warning of danger concerning the behavior of a person involved, when there is reason to believe that there exists the likelihood of substantial harm to an individual or to the public interest; and

(7)   in a criminal case, in addition to subparagraphs (1) through (6):

(i)   the identity, residence, occupation and family status of the accused;

(ii)   if the accused has not been apprehended, information necessary to aid in apprehension of that person;

(iii)   the fact, time and place of arrest; and

(iv)   the identity of investigating and arresting officers or agencies and the length of the investigation.

(c)   Notwithstanding paragraph (a), a lawyer may make a statement that a reasonable lawyer would believe is required to protect a client from the substantial undue prejudicial effect of recent publicity not initiated by the lawyer or the lawyer's client. A statement made pursuant to this paragraph shall be limited to such information as is necessary to mitigate the recent adverse publicity.

(d)   No lawyer associated in a firm or government agency with a lawyer subject to paragraph (a) shall make a statement prohibited by paragraph (a).

## Ethical Rules for Trial Publicity

### ABA Model Rule of Professional Conduct 3.6, Comment 5

Official Comment 5 to Model Rule of Professional Conduct 3.6 provides practical examples of the types of statements likely to create prejudice. Prohibited are statements concerning

*continued* ▶

(1) the character, credibility, reputation or criminal record of a party, suspect in a criminal investigation or witness, or the identity of a witness, or the expected testimony of a party or witness;

(2) in a criminal case or proceeding that could result in incarceration, the possibility of a plea of guilty to the offense or the existence or contents of any confession, admission, or statement given by a defendant or suspect or that person's refusal or failure to make a statement;

(3) the performance or results of any examination or test or the refusal or failure of a person to submit to an examination or test, or the identity or nature of physical evidence expected to be presented;

(4) any opinion as to the guilt or innocence of a defendant or suspect in a criminal case or proceeding that could result in incarceration;

(5) information that the lawyer knows or reasonably should know is likely to be inadmissible as evidence in a trial and that would, if disclosed, create a substantial risk of prejudicing an impartial trial; or

(6) the fact that a defendant has been charged with a crime, unless there is included therein a statement explaining that the charge is merely an accusation and that the defendant is presumed innocent until and unless proven guilty.

Assume that the *Ruston Globe* newspaper accurately reported the comments of Jamner Assistant County Prosecutor Gonnif. He violated his ethical responsibilities in several ways, including stating opinions about the defendant's credibility and guilt, information about forensic tests, and improper comments on defendant's exercise of his right to an attorney.

### Prosecutor's Special Responsibilities

Model Rule 3.6 allows a prosecutor to disclose some information in the interest of the public's right to know, such as the charge and matters of public record. However, the rule generally prohibits pretrial disclosure of other more prejudicial information (for example, defendant's confession) that would unduly create a climate of adverse publicity such that the defendant probably would be denied a fair trial in the community.

This provision is designed to keep law enforcement and others assisting or associated with the prosecutor from doing what the prosecutor is prohibited from doing, even though the prosecutor has no authority over them. To accomplish the purpose of the rule, the prosecutor can communicate the rule to law enforcement and others assisting in the criminal case. Jamner prosecutors clearly had not gotten this message across to police chief Torrie, who commented on the case in a way that the prosecutor would have been prohibited from doing in the *Freck Point Murder* case.

## B. Jury Impartiality

Before and throughout the trial, trial counsel must remain at arm's length from any prospective juror, such as those listed in your jury panel. Counsel must avoid even the appearance of influencing the prospective juror privately, either directly by conversing with the juror or indirectly by encouraging a friend of the juror to discuss the case with the juror. Counsel must report any information about a juror's misconduct or improper interest in the case.

Trial counsel may not communicate with the jurors during the proceedings unless authorized by court order or law. And while most jurisdictions permit you to interview jurors after the verdict, you have ethical duties to neither talk to them if they decline to be interviewed, nor to harass, coerce, or make misrepresentations to them.

## Ethical Rules for Impartiality of the Tribunal

### Model Rules of Professional Conduct

Under Model Rule of Professional Conduct 3.5, a lawyer must not

(a)   seek to influence a judge, juror, prospective juror or other official by means prohibited by law;

(b)   communicate ex parte with such a person during the proceeding unless authorized to do so by law or court order;

(c)   communicate with a juror or prospective juror after discharge of the jury if

(1)   the communication is prohibited by law or court order;

(2)   the juror has made known to the lawyer a desire not to communicate;

or

(3)   the communication involves misrepresentation, coercion, duress or harassment. . . .

Under Model Rule of Professional Conduct 3.5(a), if the jurors remain in the jury pool and thus are prospective jurors for future cases, the lawyers should not influence their actions in future cases. For example, after the verdict, neither prosecutor nor defense counsel should discuss with a juror who has not been permanently excused from jury service—one who remains on the panel and may sit on another case—evidence that was excluded from the trial, such as the defendant's prior specific instances of misconduct, which the court had ruled inadmissible. Such a discussion could be seen as influencing the prospective juror.

## CHECKLIST: JURY SELECTION

### Judicial Expectations: Jury Selection

Counsel understood and followed the court's approach to jury selection:

☐ Whether the judge uses a judge-run, attorney-run, or hybrid approach;

☐ Whether the court permits a preliminary statement by counsel; and

☐ Types of questions the court considers improper and proper.

### Understanding the Procedure

Counsel understood the jury selection process:

☐ The order of questioning;

☐ How to make a record;

☐ The grounds for a for-cause challenge and how to exercise it;

☐ How to rehabilitate a prospective juror challenged for cause; and

☐ How to exercise peremptory challenges, including:

   • *Batson* challenge and requirements,

   • mechanics of exercising peremptories, and

   • the number of peremptory challenges allotted.

### Organization

Counsel was organized and used a

☐ jury selection binder,

☐ juror seating chart,

☐ challenges chart,

☐ case summary sheet, and

☐ list of witnesses.

### Building a Positive Relationship with the Jurors

Counsel developed a positive relationship by

☐ projecting honesty and sincerity, and

☐ achieving a conversation with the prospective jurors by

   • asking open-ended and closed-ended questions where appropriate,

   • speaking so the questions were easily understood,

   • using a conversational and friendly tone,

   • listening attentively,

   • managing the discussion, and

   • remaining nonjudgmental.

### Questioning

☐ Lawyer used introductory remarks to relax the jurors and give them a snapshot of the case.

☐ Lawyer used concluding questions and, if permitted, closing remarks.

☐ Questions elicited information that would aid in exercising challenges and cause the jurors to be receptive to the case theory.

- [ ] Questions covered:
  - Challenge for cause areas,
  - Case weaknesses,
  - Advancement of the case theory and theme,
  - Trial questions (burden of proof), and
  - Case issues (damages).

## Exercising Challenges

- [ ] Challenges were exercised against prospective jurors who probably would not reach the desired verdict.

## Ethical Considerations

- [ ] Counsel did not make an extrajudicial media statement likely to prejudice the trial or other proceeding.
- [ ] In a criminal case, the prosecutor took reasonable steps to prevent law enforcement and others associated with the prosecution from making statements that the prosecutor would be prohibited from making.
- [ ] Counsel did not try to influence a prospective juror or juror by means prohibited by law, and, after discharge of the jury, did not communicate with the juror when the juror indicated a wish not to communicate, when prohibited by law or the court, or when the communication involved misrepresentation, coercion, duress, or harassment.

# OPENING STATEMENT
## Storytelling

*"Well, when I was an attorney, uh, a long time ago, young man, I uh, realized after much trial and error in the courtroom, whoever tells the best story wins. In unlawyer-like fashion, I give you that scrap of wisdom free of charge."*

—**John Quincy Adams**, portrayed by
Anthony Hopkins in *Amistad* (1997)

*"Human memory, in contrast, is more like the village storyteller; it doesn't passively store facts but weaves them into a good (coherent, plausible) story, which is re-created with each telling—like oral epics, the chansons de geste, of the Middle Ages."*

—**Judith Hooper & Dick Teresi**, *The Three-Pound Universe* 194-195 (Macmillan 1986)

## I. DEVELOPING OPENING STATEMENT

Opening statement is your first and best opportunity to fully communicate your case theory, particularly the factual theory—the story—to the jury. Opening statement should bring the case alive in the courtroom and provide jurors with a narrative story that will help them assemble and understand the evidence as it is fragmentally presented throughout the trial. Opening statement, like any first impression, can have a powerful influence over the jurors' thinking about your case and client. A compelling opening statement is crucial to persuading the jury.

In this chapter, we show you the practical aspects of developing an opening statement: how to select the content of your opening statement, how to structure that content, and how to prepare the opening so that it will be convincing. Then we explore how to effectively deliver the opening statement and how to persuade using trial visuals. Our discussion examines the ethical boundaries of an opening statement—what *not* to say during opening.

Throughout this chapter, we rely heavily on the application of case theory as a structure for your opening statement. See Chapter 3, Case Theory and Theme Development.

## II. SELECTING THE CONTENT

### A. Setting the Objectives

We best recall what we hear first and last, the middle tends to be lost; this concept has been articulated as the principles of primacy and recency. What jurors hear from you at the outset of the case falls under the principle of primacy. The opening statement has two major purposes:

- To communicate your case theory to the jury convincingly through storytelling and a brief explanation of legal principles; and
- To provide an overview of the trial, including witnesses and evidence.

Your opening statement should lead the jury both intellectually and emotionally to the conclusions you wish them to reach. Your aim at the end of your opening statement is that the jury will be ready to render the sought-after verdict if the evidence comes out as you contend. Thus, your primary concern in composing a persuasive opening statement is deciding which information to include. That decision is guided by your case theory, which, as discussed in Chapter 3, is made up of two components: the legal theory and the factual theory. In the next sections, we discuss how you can use your and your opponent's case theories as guides for formulating the content of your opening statement.

## B. Legal Theory

Most courts permit a brief and accurate statement of basic legal principles in the opening statement. Therefore, you should seek to identify core legal points that are essential to your case theory—such as the elements of negligence, or the definition of an affirmative defense. Then you can analyze those points and determine how to discuss them briefly and impartially. However, you want neither to invade the judge's prerogative to instruct the jury on the law nor to engage in argument. Therefore, confine your discussion of the law to pattern jury instructions, be concise, and preface your remarks with a statement that the judge will instruct the jury on the law.

To illustrate how to briefly state the legal theory and other aspects in opening statement, we use the *Blue Moon News Robbery* case (see Chapter 4, page 81).

Both prosecutor and defense counsel will need to select a legal theory for their cases.

---

### Legal Theory Statements

#### The *Blue Moon News Robbery* Case

To show how counsel in the *Blue Moon News Robbery* case might express their legal theories, observe the two opening statements.

##### Prosecutor

If you were the prosecutor, you may wish to discuss the elements of the crime of robbery in the first degree. You might recite the contents of the charging document (information or indictment), charging the defendant with robbery in the first degree. The charging document concisely states the legal elements of the crime. Or you could summarize the prosecution's legal theory:

*continued* ▶

> "Ladies and gentlemen, the defendant is charged with robbery in the first degree. In essence, the charge is that on January 15 of this year in Jamner County, the defendant, Mike Ryan, took money from the Blue Moon News clerk, Gardner Newman, against his will and by force. During this robbery, the defendant displayed what appeared to be a firearm."

### Defense Counsel

At this point, defense counsel in a criminal case may choose to waive opening statement or reserve it until the beginning of the defense case. These strategic choices are discussed in detail on page 145. However, as defense counsel, if you decide to make an opening, you might simply state:

> "To prove the charge of robbery in the first degree, the state must prove each element of the crime beyond a reasonable doubt. One element of the crime that the prosecutor [pointing to the prosecutor] must prove is the identification of the defendant as the perpetrator of the robbery. The state cannot prove that identification element beyond a reasonable doubt."

This brief statement of the law by defense counsel in the robbery case communicates the misidentification legal theory. It also focuses the jury from the start on the central issue in dispute in the case—misidentification.

## C.  Factual Theory: The Story

### The Essential Elements

A persuasive opening is storytelling at its best. It communicates the factual theory component of the case theory in such a way that the jury will be compelled to reach the verdict the attorney desires. It provides the story framework that the jury can use to understand and organize the evidence as it is introduced during the trial.

The factual theory is conceptualized as having two subparts: (1) *sufficiency* to support the legal theory, and (2) *persuasiveness*.

**Factual Theory**

Sufficient  +  Persuasive

### Factual Sufficiency

Opening statement is an opportunity to present your factual theory by describing the evidence that you believe will be presented in the trial. Planning the factual content of your opening statement requires that you determine the essential factual points that compose your story.

In crafting the story, plaintiff's counsel must be concerned with factual sufficiency. If you are plaintiff's counsel, generally you must present sufficient information in your opening statement to show that you can prove the elements of your claim or offense. Dismissals on the grounds of insufficiency are rare. However, be aware that at the conclusion of opening, the defense may move for dismissal because plaintiff's counsel failed to assert sufficient facts to support the plaintiff's legal theory, and the court may grant the motion.

### Persuasive

When you choose the content of your opening statement, your task is to analyze the case and identify the story you want to tell. Concentrate on including these five persuasive story elements to opening statements.

---

### CHECKLIST

#### Persuasive Story Elements

- ☐ Human values and human needs,
- ☐ Human story,
- ☐ Believable and understandable story,
- ☐ Quantity of evidence, and
- ☐ Quality of evidence.

---

#### Human Values and Human Needs

Focus on human values, the ones that most in our culture share and hold dear. In our culture, we care about honesty, fairness, family, community. We root for the underdog. David and Goliath and Rocky Balboa stories also appeal to us because we value striving and overcoming what seem to be overwhelming odds.

Lawsuits are usually about the deprivation of human needs. These are needs that we as human beings have in common—to have enough food and water; to have a safe place to sleep; to be safe from harm; to be free; to belong; to be valued and thus to enjoy high self-esteem. A story about the loss of these essential needs resonates with the jurors. A story that is grounded in human values and needs is one that the jury can relate to and be swayed by.

#### Human Story

Tell a story about one or more real human beings with whom the jury can empathize. The challenge in preparing the opening is selecting who is the central person or persons in the story. Usually, that person is your client. You want the jury to like and care about your client, and you want to relate favorable facts about him or her. For example, in the *Enron* criminal trial for conspiracy, fraud, and insider trading, defense counsel strove to tell the human stories of defendants Kenneth Lay and Jeffrey Skilling, while the prosecutors concentrated on the lives of stockholders who were harmed.

### Believable and Understandable Story

Like any story, it should be believable. To be credible, the story must make common sense to the jurors. Preferably, it is a familiar story, one that the jurors know from common experience. However, even if the story is unfamiliar to jurors, the evidence, often through expert testimony, could establish that the story is realistic. For instance, an expert on child abuse could explain that the child's failure to promptly report the abuse is not an uncommon phenomenon.

### Quantity of Evidence

The story for opening statement involves enhancing believability by focusing on the amount of evidence supporting the story. For instance, in the *Blue Moon News Robbery* case, the story that identifies the defendant as the robber because the defendant's fingerprint was found on the magazine that was left on the counter is more persuasive than if the only evidence were the victim's eyewitness identification. Or, the defense opening statement story becomes all the more plausible and persuasive if the defense can attack the vulnerabilities in victim Newman's identification, and also point to the defendant's expected testimony that he did not commit the robbery and to alibi witnesses who will testify that Ryan was with them at the time the crime was committed. Of course, this story has now committed defense counsel to having her client to testify before the prosecution has presented even a single witness; plainly a serious, strategic decision, requiring careful analysis of all reasonable options likely to present themselves as the case unfolds.

### Quality of Evidence

Focus on the pedigree of your evidence. For example, in the robbery case, the story you tell about Mr. Newman should be designed to persuade the jury that he is a person who is credible and without any reason to mislead the jury with his testimony. On the other hand, different strategic approaches are required if lower-pedigree evidence is needed to present the case (e.g., the prosecution's use of a former codefendant who is testifying in return for a "deal").

### Applying the Five Persuasive Story Essentials

Let's consider the *Deyoung Wrongful Death Collision* case.

## Human Values, Needs, and Human Story

### The *Deyoung Wrongful Death Collision* Case

On May 19, Kerry Deyoung was driving her seven-year-old daughter, Katie, to school. According to the complaint, Chris Edwards ran a stop sign and hit the passenger's side of Deyoung's car. Although Kerry Deyoung was not hurt, Katie was critically injured and died the next day in the hospital.

Defendant Edwards was on his way to a meeting at 9:00 A.M. It was 9:05, and the defendant was traveling in his SUV at 45 miles per hour in a 25 miles per hour residential area. He drove through a stop sign at Natalie and Main Streets and into the passenger's side of the Deyoung's car.

Plaintiff's counsel wants to put a human face on the deceased seven-year-old Katie Deyoung in the opening statement.

---

### Communicating Essentials of the Story

#### The *Deyoung Wrongful Death Collision* Case

Plaintiff's counsel's opening statement begins:

"You walk down Crawford Street today and you see that it is a tree-lined, wide residential street, like many other streets in our town. As you approach the end of the street, there is a large oak tree in front of a modest two-story home. The home is painted a grayish-green color with white trim."

"Going through the front door, you see a comfortable living room to your left, and straight ahead is a stairway to the second floor. As you ascend the stairs, the wall on your right is covered with family photographs, many black-and-white photographs of earlier generations."

"At the top of the stairs, the first room on your right is Katie Deyoung's bedroom. Katie was seven years old when she died. This is a picture of Katie in her soccer uniform. Entering her room, you see her things, which include a soccer ball, dolls, and clothes in her closet. Her bed is made."

"Katie's room hasn't been touched since May 20 three years ago—the day Katie died. It has become a shrine to her."

"The day before, May 19 three years ago, Katie's mother was driving her to school."

---

This excerpt is an example of building a compelling opening that begins with the human story of the child Katie, who loved soccer, played with dolls, and lived in a modest home. The human values of family and the loss of a child are given paramount placement with the story of her room being turned into a shrine. This word-picture of the child's world is believable and makes sense. Now that the listeners care about the child and about the case, the lawyer can describe the collision. The description of the collision should have a story that makes sense—how the defendant failed to stop and T-boned the Deyoung's car, killing Katie.

*Believable Story with Sufficient Quantity and Quality of Evidence:* You want to choose a few critical facts to form the core of your factual theory and create a narrative that includes enough details to make the story real and compelling to the jury. One technique for determining how much factual information to cover in opening statement is to select critical facts and then organize them in a chronological narrative. The opening should contain enough facts for a full, realistic narrative; then you can insert additional facts that you expect to come out in evidence to round out the opening statement.

To demonstrate constructing the story, think again about the *Blue Moon News Robbery* case, where the central issue is misidentification, page 81. As the defense attorney, you want to present sufficient information to the jurors so they can understand how misidentification occurred. The defense might select some essential facts to support the defense claim that there is at least a reasonable doubt that Mr. Newman misidentified the defendant. Defense counsel could then weave key facts about misidentification into a compelling narrative story for opening statement.

---

### Believable Story

#### The *Blue Moon News Robbery* Case

**Defense attorney:**

"It was dimly lit in Blue Moon News that night. *Very dim* in the store. The store has only a couple of lights, and the one by the cash register is set back away from the counter. The robber's face was not fully visible to Mr. Newman; the robber had pulled his hat down to cover his face. He obviously was concealing his face so he couldn't be identified. Also, you will hear Mr. Newman testify that the man who robbed the convenience store was six feet tall. Look at Mike Ryan (pointing to the client). He is 5 feet 7 inches tall."

The defense factual theory of misidentification is evident from this narrative.

---

*Complex Cases:* Some cases are technically complex. That complexity may dictate that you use part of your opening statement to simplify technical terms so your factual theory remains understandable as the evidence progresses. For instance, in a toxic tort case, you may need to explain important toxicological terms such as *exposure, dose*, and *response* in lay terms.

> Some of Mr. Hoffman's injuries were caused by two things: exposure and dose. Exposure occurs when you walk through a field that has been sprayed with an insecticide. As you walk, you notice a slight mist in the air, like a fog or cloud. You are getting exposed to that insecticide. Now let's relate that to Mr. Hoffman's exposure at the factory.

After technical terms are explained, you can then discuss the plaintiff's claim.

### Opening Statement Is Not Argument

Opening is a factual statement, told persuasively, not an argument. Being argumentative will result in interruptions by opposing counsel's objections, possible judicial admonitions, or worse. Well-presented factual descriptions that incorporate the essential ingredients are far more persuasive than a string of conclusions and judgments. We next illustrate how using particular language results in an argumentative opening statement. Consider plaintiff attorney's opening statement in the *Deyoung Wrongful Death Collision* case. The argumentative language is italicized.

---

### Opening Statement

#### Objectionable Argumentative Factual Theory Statements
#### The *Deyoung Wrongful Death Collision* Case

Excerpt from opening by plaintiff's counsel:

"Defendant Edwards didn't want to be late for a meeting at 9:00 A.M. It was already 9:05, and the defendant was racing at 45 miles per hour in a 25 miles per hour residential area to get to his office. And he *deliberately and callously* blew through a stop sign at Natalie and Main Streets, smashing into the passenger's side of the Deyoung's car. The impact crushed Katie's body, broke her neck, and, the following day, took her life. *The defendant put his meeting before the life of Katie Deyoung. That May morning he sacrificed the little girl's life for his business interests. His weapon—an SUV.*"

---

For example, plaintiff's attorney could have avoided being argumentative by cleansing the statement of value-laden words such as "deliberately and callously" and by eliminating the comparison to a sacrifice.

Recognizing the line between when an opening is a factual statement and when it becomes an argument is necessary to avoid the objection "argumentative." Individual judgment is a factor here, but some principles may help identify arguments with value-laden or judgmental words such as *stingy, greedy, wanton, mean,* or *angry,* which generally convert your factual statement to an argument. Phrases that characterize a claim or defense—*meaningless, worthless, ridiculous*—or descriptions cast in extravagant or judgmental terms may do likewise.

But you might then ask: Isn't this just an example of an attorney employing vividly descriptive language? Yes, it is, but these dramatic words are really the attorney's emotional comments and conclusions about the story rather than the story itself. Some might say that each of these words and phrases is objectionable. Others would contend that, in this instance, it is not that any one of the individual words or phrases should not be used because it is argumentative, but rather it is the total effect of such language that, in these circumstances, would be viewed as argument appealing to the jury's passion and prejudice.

An approach that you can employ to avoid sounding argumentative is to use customary phrases to introduce your point.

*The evidence will show* that the defendant was driving 45 miles per hour in a residential neighborhood.

*We will present evidence* that the result of defendant's driving was the death of Katie.

Generally, the occasional use of the introductory phrase will make an opening sound less like argument and more like a statement of the evidence that will be presented at trial. Finally, if possible, before making your opening statement, consult case law, other attorneys, the judge's clerk, and others about the permissible parameters for opening statement for the particular judge.

### Not Too Detailed

Hone your story to the essential facts, because the jury can get lost in minutia. First, the story must include facts that prove the legal theory—for example, the existence of a contract in a breach of contract suit. Second, the story should contain the requisites of a persuasive story: human values and needs, a human story, believable, understandable, and so on. Omit the rest. For example, in the opening statement, the jury does not need to know the names of all the participants. It would be like introducing them to people at a cocktail party; it is unrealistic to believe they will remember all the names. A technique that works well is to identify lesser participants in the story by their titles or job descriptions, such as *babysitter, teacher, operating room nurse*, and so on. Titles can be impressive when referring to some of your witnesses who play a significant role in the story, such as your expert, by title—*chief surgeon*—instead of just by name.

## D.  Admissible Evidence

In opening statement, you are entitled to mention admissible facts and substantive information in evidence that you expect to prove. Usually, you will be able to predict with confidence what evidence will or will not be admitted. You can do this by researching evidentiary law or, in appropriate circumstances, presenting a motion in limine. However, sometimes you may be in doubt as to whether a fact you wish to mention in opening statement will be admissible. If so, you must consider whether you will discuss that information.

More broadly, you should never make claims in opening about matters you may not be able to prove. Consider the position of the prosecutor in the *Blue Moon News Robbery* case if she tells the jurors in opening, "You will hear evidence that the defendant's fingerprint on the magazine could *only* have been left at the time of the robbery." Imagine if the prosecutor then cannot present such evidence. It is certain that defense counsel will focus on that portion of the prosecution's opening in closing argument.

> Remember when this trial began? The prosecutor stood in front of you and said, "You will hear evidence that the defendant's fingerprint on the magazine could only have been left at the time of the robbery." That evidence was crucial to the state's case, given the weak identification we've been discussing. If that print could have been left earlier that day or even the day before, it doesn't mean much. The prosecutor promised you she was going to give you evidence that those prints were left at the time of the robbery. But she didn't keep her promise. We all know

this because there is not a shred of evidence tying that print to any particular time. That crucial piece of evidence talked about by the prosecutor does not exist.

## E.  Weaknesses and the Other Side's Case

### Candor About Weaknesses

In planning your opening statement, identify case weaknesses and calculate how to disclose them to the jury in the best way possible to minimize their impact. Weaknesses might include your client, who you intend to call to the stand, having a prior criminal record, a key witness having made a plea bargain, or having only a single witness to testify about a critical factual event. You can introduce such weaknesses during jury selection: "Mr. Newman was convicted of shoplifting a few years ago. Will that so prejudice you that you could not be fair to the prosecution and Mr. Newman?" You could then discuss the weaknesses again in your opening statement.

By disclosing weaknesses as early in the case as possible, you make your case theory less vulnerable to attack. You also have an early chance to present a plausible explanation for the weaknesses. At least you diminish the psychological impact of having the harmful information exposed by opposing counsel along with the resulting inference that you tried to conceal it. By providing the jurors with your explanations for possible weaknesses in your case before your adversary has the opportunity to exploit them, you in effect provide the jurors with the material to align with your position. This technique is referred to by the medical term *inoculation*, meaning that by exposing the jurors to weaknesses and providing your responses, the jury will be able to resist opposing counsel's arguments when made. Jurors may think that since you are willing to keep talking about the weaknesses, they can't be that serious. By presenting the weaknesses yourself and mentioning them strategically throughout trial, you may desensitize the jury to their impact. Your willingness to be open about the case's weaknesses reinforces the fair and candid character you wish to project to the jurors. The jurors should see you as a seeker of justice and truth who discloses both the good and the bad about your case.

To illustrate, suppose you are the prosecutor in the *Blue Moon News Robbery* case. Your case rests on whether Mr. Newman correctly identified Mike Ryan, the defendant, as the robber. You have recognized two potential weaknesses in Mr. Newman's identification that you want to acknowledge during your opening statement:

- The convenience store was not well lit, and
- The robber had his hat pulled down to hide his face.

By confronting these weaknesses, you believe you may be able to defuse their importance and enhance your case theory and its credibility.

| Discussing Weaknesses in Opening Statement |
| --- |

### The *Blue Moon News Robbery* Case

Excerpt from prosecutor's opening statement:

> "When the defendant approached Mr. Newman from the less-lit back part of the store, the defendant walked forward to stand under an overhead light. His face was within a yard of Mr. Newman's and was illuminated enough by the bright overhead light. While it took the defendant just a few moments to confront Mr. Newman at the counter and get the money from him, the defendant had been in the store for a few minutes and Mr. Newman had a good opportunity to view him.
>
>   "The defendant left his fingerprint on the magazine on the counter. . . ."

### Other Side's Case

If plaintiff's attorney delivers opening statement first, counsel faces the question of whether to anticipate and address defenses in the opening statement. This is both a legal and a strategic issue. Law or evidence rules may prohibit counsel from discussing the defenses.

In a criminal case where the prosecution has the burden of proof, the defendant is presumed innocent and has a Fifth Amendment privilege. The prosecutor, as a general rule, may not anticipate what the defense testimony will be and should not comment on it. Should the prosecutor do so, the comment may be met with a defense objection and mistrial motion on the grounds that the prosecutor is attempting to improperly shift the burden of proof to the defense.

In a civil case, plaintiff's counsel may decide not to mention the defense claims in opening statement for two reasons. First, that effort would expose weaknesses defense counsel might not have identified and that defense counsel can then fix during trial. Second, the very act of discussing the defense would lend credibility to the particular defense. Also, plaintiff's counsel risks mischaracterizing the adversary's case. To the extent that the weaknesses actually appear different at trial from how they did in plaintiff's characterization, defense counsel can argue that plaintiff's entire position from opening to closing was premised on a misconception of the defense.

### F.  Case Theme

The most critical component of the opening—the theme—is also the most challenging to develop, requiring creativity and a mastery of the whole case. The theme is the crystallization of your case theory. The theme is a memorable word or phrase. It is a hook that the jurors will remember. A theme provides a thread that you can weave through the trial to unify your case. You can introduce the theme in jury selection, include it in opening, develop it during the presentation of evidence, and come back to it in closing. See Chapter 3, Case Theory and Theme Development. The following excerpt from the prosecutor's opening statement in the *Enron* case provides a good illustration of using a theme in opening.

---

### Case Theme

#### The *Enron* Case

In the *Enron* case, the heart of the government's case against corporate executives revolved around broken trust and falsification.

Excerpt from prosecutor's opening statement:

> "The victims in this case, the investing public, their employees, those who did not have that information, those who were not able to sell their stock before Enron entered bankruptcy were not as fortunate as these two men. These two men are Defendants Ken Lay and Jeffrey Skilling. This is a simple case. It is not about accounting. *It is about lies and choices.* The case will show you that these Defendants worked to lie and mislead. They violated the duty of trust placed in them. They violated it by telling lie after lie about the true financial condition of Enron."

Transcript of Proceedings Before the Honorable Sim Lake and a Jury at 347, *United States v. Skilling*, H-04-CR-025SS (S.D. Tex. 2006) (Prosecutor John Hueston's opening statement).

---

Now we illustrate defense counsel's theme in the *Blue Moon News Robbery* case.

---

### Case Theme

#### The *Blue Moon News Robbery* Case

The defense theory of misidentification in the *Blue Moon News Robbery* case could be capsulated into a double-tragedy theme. *Double tragedy* could be the descriptive phrase that expresses the core set of ideas that will be returned to at different times during the trial.

Excerpt from defense counsel's opening statement:

> "This case involves a double tragedy. Late one evening, Gardner Newman was threatened and robbed while he was working at a convenience store. That was a tragedy. The robber had his hat pulled down over his face. Mr. Newman mistakenly identified my client as the robber—a second tragedy."

---

In closing argument in the *Blue Moon News Robbery* case, defense counsel could expand the theme by harkening back to the opening statement theme and adding another potential tragedy:

> You'll recall that in opening statement I referred to this as a case involving double tragedies. The first tragedy was when Mr. Newman was robbed. The second was when Mike was misidentified as the robber. There is a potential third tragedy—a verdict that Mike is guilty of a crime he did not commit. It is in your hands to prevent that ultimate tragedy. Don't let it happen.

### Useful Points for Creating a Theme

- **Short:** Use a phrase, a line of poetry, a sentence.
- **Memorable:** Capture the essence of your case theory in a way that sways the jurors and will be easily remembered.
- **Convey Values:** Express a value that resonates with the jurors. For example, in the *Enron* case, the value was being truthful, and in the *Blue Moon News Robbery* case, it was double tragedy—not convicting an innocent person.
- **Match the Case and Fact Finder:** Tailor the theme to the type of case and fact finder. If your opening statement is to a judge in a bench trial, you would want to gauge the appropriateness of using the poem or the reference to "double tragedy." Know your judge; some judges may be offended.

Watch plaintiffs' counsel's opening statement in the *Freck Point* trial demonstration movie for the introduction and development of a case theme on the website *http://www.aspenlawschool.com/books/berger_trialad4e.*

## G.  Damages

It is not easy to talk about money with a jury. Should plaintiff's counsel deal with damages in his opening statement? The position on this issue is varied. Naturally, the decision as to whether to discuss damages depends on the nature of the case. One view is that this is too early in the case to delve into this subject. The jury does not yet have enough information to be convinced as to the award. Instead, plaintiff's counsel should omit a discussion of damages and use the sales approach of first persuading the jury that plaintiff deserves damages and of the gravity of the harm done. Later, when counsel determines the jury is ready, counsel will reveal the price tag.

However, other attorneys believe that if liability is clear and damages are large, damages may be discussed. Yet another view holds that damages should be discussed in opening so the jurors will not suffer sticker shock.

## H. Waiver and Reserving Opening

Except in a simple bench trial, it is rare for plaintiff's counsel (in a civil case) or the prosecutor (in a criminal case) to waive opening statement. To the contrary, plaintiff's attorney or the prosecutor, cognizant of the plaintiff's burden of proof, the rule of primacy, and the influential nature of the opening statement, will use the opportunity to full advantage.

Defense counsel must make the strategic decision either to make an opening statement right after that of the plaintiff's attorney or reserve it until the commencement of the defense case. This decision is of more importance in a criminal case than it is in a civil case. Defense counsel in civil cases make their opening statements at the beginning of trial. There are good reasons for this. In civil litigation, generally both sides' positions will be in the pleadings, and most information underlying those positions will have been revealed in discovery. Also, civil litigation is not constitutionally circumscribed in the same way that criminal litigation is. It is accepted that the defendant in a criminal case may sit back, not put on a case, and force the prosecution to meet its burden of proof.

While criminal defense counsel may recognize the benefits of making an opening statement right after the prosecutor's, counsel must balance the risks against the benefits. One risk attendant on delivering an early opening statement is that the defense discloses and commits to a defense case theory. This early disclosure, particularly when the defense attack is based on the anticipated failure of the prosecution to prove the case, notifies the prosecutor of the issues the defense intends to raise and allows the prosecutor to try to meet the declared defense during the prosecution's case-in-chief. Furthermore, the defense's decision whether to put on a case may be a function of how the prosecution case proceeds. In other words, defense counsel may plan to have the defendant testify, but, after cross-examination of the prosecution's witnesses, defense counsel may decide that enough doubts have been raised and that the defense should rest. If defense counsel has already told the jury that the defendant will testify, however, the decision to now rest, while perhaps still the best strategy, may be an uncomfortable one. An early statement of the defense case may result in an overstatement of the deficiencies in the prosecution's case. Some advantages of reserving opening statement include communicating the defense case theory in close proximity to the presentation of the defense case, making the presentation easier for the jury to follow, and affording the chance to interweave the defense case theory with a discussion of the weaknesses in the prosecution's evidence. Defense counsel can always waive opening if, after hearing the prosecution case, the defense decides not to put on a case and to rest.

## I.  Bench Trial

Now, let's turn to the bench trial and the judge's likes and dislikes.

---

### Judicial Expectations: Opening Statement

#### Bench Trial

The judge, wishing to conserve time and knowing that opening statements are not evidence, wants a succinct, to-the-point opening. The judge may even tell you that an opening is not needed. If an opening statement is permitted, focus on what the court wants, which is a description of your case theory (your legal theory and the facts supporting it) and identifying issues in the case. Tell a persuasive story with a plot, a protagonist, and values. Judges, like jurors, will organize, understand, and decide the case through a narrative. The story is most persuasive if it fits a pattern of cases with which the judge has experience. A story told chronologically and explaining relationships of the parties and other players is best.

Keep your opening brief, unless it is a complex case. Do not overdramatize. An effective opening in a bench trial is a concise and engaging story that informs the court of what the case is about, rather than the more elaborate and emotional story told to a jury.

---

## III.  CRAFTING THE OPENING

In this section, we cover five practical steps for crafting an opening statement: gathering information and refining the opening statement, writing it, structuring it so it is easily understood and convincing, applying storytelling techniques, and making it the right length.

### A.  Gathering Information and Refining the Opening Statement

Preparing your opening statement is an ongoing process of gathering information and ideas for its content. Begin when you first learn about the case. We recommend that you take notes on information and ideas for your opening statement—even notes on napkins and scraps of paper. You can put your notes in a file folder, in a computer file, in a section of a notebook, or whatever else suits you as a place to collect ideas for opening statement. Your initial reaction to a witness or piece of evidence is likely to be one that the jurors will experience. You should record it because it is that emotion that you may wish to communicate to the jury. As you progress in case preparation and discovery, you will be able to gather more information to add to your notes for opening. Make your gathering and recording of information and thoughts an ongoing process.

As the trial date approaches, you want to refine your statement. Write it in final draft form long before trial so that you can begin rehearsing the opening.

## B. Writing the Opening Statement

It is good practice to write your opening statement. When you write it, you force yourself to organize the information and to concentrate on the wording. The opening statement should be written as "speaking words" for the jury, not a formal communiqué. It is helpful to use the components of a persuasive story, such as human story, values, and so on, as headings, and list supportive facts that apply to each heading. In this way, you will marshal the critical facts for the story. For instance, under the heading "Human Story," you could list facts favorable to your client. Once you have the persuasive facts, then you can weave them into a story line. Pay particular attention to crafting the beginning and conclusion. Later, you can reduce your written opening statement to outline notes that you can glance at during opening. If you use your fully written opening statement as a reference during opening, you will invariably begin reading it and lose eye contact with the jurors.

Use the storytelling devices described in the next section when crafting the opening. Write the statement, and then continue to rewrite it until you are satisfied that when you conclude your opening the jury will want to render the verdict you are requesting.

## C. Structuring the Opening Statement

The opening statement's structure should present the case theory in a convincing, clear, and simple manner. Think of an opening statement as having three parts: beginning remarks, a body, and a conclusion. Each one of these parts should flow and relate smoothly to each other.

### A Strong Beginning

Holding the jury's attention is an art. Carefully craft those first few words that begin your opening. As soon as possible, you should get to the heart of the matter—a clear statement of the theory of your case, expressed as emphatically as possible. The following are some attention-getting techniques.

#### *Dramatic Scene*

It's your story, so you can start it anywhere you wish. If you want to start with attention-getting facts, the beginning of a faithfully chronological narrative may not be that dramatic. Therefore, you may adopt the structure in which opening statement begins with a description of a dramatic scene and then moves forward or backward in time and places these facts within a larger chronological narrative. This approach has the advantage of beginning with a vivid image intended to catch the jury's attention. The *Deyoung Wrongful Death Collision* case illustration gives such a dramatic-scene beginning: Plaintiff's counsel describes a visit to the deceased child's bedroom, which has been left exactly as it was on the day she died. See page 137.

Another example of this approach is found in the *O.J. Simpson* case, only this time we visit the civil wrongful death case and see how counsel for the family and estate of the deceased Nicole Brown began opening—not at the beginning when O.J. Simpson was married to Nicole Brown, but instead with a description of what happened shortly before the murder.

---

**Beginning Remarks: What To Do in Opening Statement**

*The O.J. Simpson Civil Wrongful Death Case*

Plaintiff's attorney, Mr. Petrocelli:

> "On a June evening, the 12th of June, 1994, Nicole Brown just finished putting her ten-year-old daughter, Sidney, and her six-year-old son, Justin, to bed. She filled her bathtub with water. She lit some candles, began to get ready to take a bath and relax for the evening. The phone rang. It was 9:40 P.M. Nicole answered. And it was her mother, saying that she had left her glasses at the restaurant nearby in Brentwood, where the family had all celebrated Sydney's dance recital over dinner, just an hour before. Nicole's mother asked if Nicole could please pick up her glasses from the restaurant the next day. Nicole said, of course, good-bye, and hung up. Nicole then called the restaurant and asked to speak to a friendly young waiter there. Nicole asked this young waiter if he would be kind enough to drop her mother's glasses off. The young man obliged and said he would drop the glasses off shortly after work on his way to meet his friend in Marina Del Rey. The young man's name was Ron Goldman. He was 25 years old . . . ."

Transcript of Attorney for Plaintiff Frederic Goldman, *Brown, Goldman, Rufo v. Simpson*, 1996 WL 694142 (Cal. Super. Ct.), available at *http://walraven.org/simpson/oct23-96.html* (Daniel M. Petrocelli's opening statement).

---

We want to hear the rest of that story. Every juror in the civil *O.J. Simpson* case probably knew the basic facts of the case, and yet these introductory remarks capture attention and make the listener want to hear more. It works because it paints a word-picture of events with enough detail to make the scene come alive in the courtroom. You can see Nicole lighting the candles, taking the phone call, calling Ron Goldman. You can feel the momentum of fate turning the innocent event of forgetting your glasses in a restaurant into the horror that awaits. We want to hear more. This is the goal of the initial remarks—to grab the jurors' attention, draw them into the case, and make them want to hear more.

*Abbreviated Story*
Begin opening with a theme.

## Using the Case Theme

### The *Freck Point Wrongful Death* Case

Plaintiff's counsel in the *Freck Point Wrongful Death* case, could begin:

"This is not a case about love. It is not about hate. It is about greed."

No matter what plaintiff's counsel says next, the jurors surely will want to hear more. They are wondering, "What greed? Tell us about that." According to the plaintiff's case theory, greed was Samuel Griffith's motive for killing his wife, for his ultimate betrayal. He killed her to collect the proceeds from her life insurance policy. The word *greed* encapsulates that case theory.

Another approach is to grab the jurors' attention by summarizing the facts that make the story persuasive. This is best achieved in a short paragraph that briefly and dramatically presents the factual theory. In the *Deyoung Wrongful Death Collision* case, plaintiff's counsel describes in the opening how the defendant's car sped through the stop sign, collided with the plaintiff's car, and fatally injured Katie. This is an example of the abbreviated-story beginning.

This approach of beginning with the defendant's fault, rather than the plaintiff's injuries, is consistent with two concepts the plaintiff's counsel wants. First, to focus on the defendant's misconduct and convince the jury that the plaintiff was wronged and that they want the plaintiff to prevail. Second, the jury understands this is a legitimate lawsuit about a tragic wrong, rather than just a pursuit for money. Only after establishing that there is a wrong to be remedied and convincing the jury of the defendant's fault will plaintiff's counsel discuss damages.

Applying this technique to the *Hill Moveit Personal Injury* case, plaintiff's counsel would first paint a picture of the corporation's failure to both design and construct a safe trailer and to provide appropriate warnings. Counsel would then discuss how those failures caused the furniture to fall off the trailer. Later, counsel would discuss the plaintiff's injuries and damages. The defendant's opening could begin with the plaintiff's request for inflated damages: "Ladies and gentlemen of the jury, we can't turn back the clock and have things as they were for Darcy Rutherford before the accident. We all wish we could. We are here because of money. The plaintiff is seeking . . . ." If defense counsel is successful in showing that the plaintiff is seeking an unjustified amount of money, the jury may well be motivated to correct that wrong.

### The Body

Like the first act of a play, the body of the opening statement introduces the players, the story, and the scenes. Most of all, it tells the story. Failure at this juncture can be devastating, for just as dissatisfied theatergoers would, your audience, the jurors, can close their minds to your case. But, no matter how you order the body of the statement, you want to accomplish the goals of maintaining the jury's interest and making the story clear, understandable, and convincing. At least three structures or combinations of them may be adopted for organizing the body of the opening statement and presenting the factual story: chronological narrative, flashback of the story, or the witness-by-witness format. Whichever approach you use, your factual theory should be the unifying element.

---

**Opening Statement**

#### Overall Structure of the Body

The body of the opening should convincingly cover the content, be organized, and be easy to follow. The body may include the following topics:

1. A brief explanation of the legal theory (see pages 133-134, 167-168),
2. Identification of the parties and key witnesses (see page 151),
3. Factual theory—the story (see pages 134-138),
4. Inoculation of the jurors against case weaknesses (see pages 141-142),
5. Refutation of the opponent's case theory (see page 142), and
6. Damages (see pages 144 and 145).

The order in which you place these subjects could be as listed here. Alternatively, you could begin the storytelling right after your beginning remarks or put them in another order. Usually, the most effective way of including topics four and five, inoculation and refutation, is to build them into the story along with explanations, as was illustrated on pages 141-142, where the prosecutor addressed the issue of dim lighting in the Blue Moon News convenience store.

---

#### *Story Structure*

*Chronological Narrative:* Telling the order in which events happened is the most common way a story is told. For instance, in the *Blue Moon News Robbery* case, the prosecutor can use a chronological narrative that begins with Mr. Newman beginning his shift at the store. Later, Mr. Newman notices the defendant in the back of the store. Then the defendant approaches Mr. Newman's counter, and so on.

*Flashback:* A flashback seizes the jurors' attention and is a dramatic scene technique. You pick a dramatic point in the story, describe it, and then move back or forward in time to tell a chronological story. Illustrations of the flashback approach include the *Deyoung Wrongful Death Collision* case at page 136 and the *O.J. Simpson* civil wrongful death case at pages 148, 155. Essentially, the flashback model duplicates the chronological approach, but it has a dramatic introduction. To keep the chronology straight for the jury, you can use a poster showing the timeline or a computer slideshow with a timeline.

*Witness-by-Witness Approach:* Although some lawyers use this approach, it is the least effective storytelling structure:

> We will be calling Mr. Poe and he will testify . . . . Next, a forensic chemist Ray Lynn Graftin will testify . . . . And then, Margaret Dupin will tell you that . . . .

This repetitive method of reciting the facts by witnesses breaks up the flow of the opening and fragments the narrative rather than forming a cohesive story.

*Illustrating Opening Statement—The Body:* Notice how in the *Freck Point Murder* case opening statement, the story is one in which chronology is mixed with a flashback technique and presented in the form of an imaginary tour of the crime scene.

What follows is a compressed example of the body of an opening statement in the *Freck Point Murder* case that illustrates incorporating a theme and case theory, storytelling, a brief introduction to the principle parties, refutation of the other side's case theory, and careful word choice for this core section of the opening.

## Opening Statement Theme

### The *Freck Point Murder* Case

The prosecutor weaves the theme of *betrayal* into these opening remarks:

> "In your mind's eye, travel to the Freck Point area of Ruston. It's Sunday morning, October 16, approximately 1:10 A.M., and we're standing in front of 4187 Alter Street, a well-kept frame house that belongs to Samuel and Sondra Griffith. Go inside through the hallway. Now you're walking up the steps to the master bedroom, and inside the room the couple shared for 12 years of their marriage, you see the queen-size bed where they shared the events of their lives, their hopes, their fears. But as we slowly open the bedroom door, we stop [pause]. Sondra will never share her life with anyone again. She is lying on her back, covered with bloody sheets, and she is still . . . terribly still. Seven separate stab wounds have torn through her flesh, and each of the wounds is a separate opening from which her lifeblood has rushed . . . then slowly drained and soaked the sheets and carpet while splashing the ceiling and walls red.
>
> "Leave—don't worry, you won't go back into that room for now [tone indicates reacting to the horror]; instead, we'll take the stairs down into the

*continued* ▶

kitchen. Look at the knife block on the counter; one of the knives is missing. Where could it have gone? Oh, look! There it is, three blocks away in a hedge of bushes. It's the missing knife from the kitchen set [holds up the knife], and it's covered with Sondra's blood. Nearby, there's a can of Sprite with blood on it [pause], Sondra's blood—and something else [pause]. It's the defendant's saliva loaded with his DNA on the same soda can as his dead wife's blood.

"Look for the defendant in the house. There he is talking to the police. His bathrobe, lying on the bathroom floor, is spattered with Sondra's blood, dry now. From the nature of the spatter, he was there when Sondra's body was stabbed again and again. But if he was there, why couldn't he protect her as she would have trusted him to do? [Pause.] Because he was the one who killed her. There he is in the living room telling the police that he never saw her stabbed. He's telling them that he was not in their bedroom when his wife of 12 years was repeatedly stabbed with her own kitchen knife. Once, twice, three times, four times [attorney demonstrates slowly, deliberately]. Now the defendant recounts a tale of walking upstairs only to have a stranger wielding a bloody knife push him aside and flee from the house.

"What actually happened this night in this house was an ultimate betrayal of trust—a betrayal of trust for money."

Now the prosecutor tells the story about the couple's financial situation. The prosecutor will talk about the death of defendant's previous wife, Marian (assuming the judge has ruled in limine that the event is admissible), to carry on the theme of betrayal out of greed—how Samuel also betrayed his first wife for money. We later discuss how this portion of the opening statement may be enhanced with visuals.

### Conclusion

Concluding remarks should state the desired verdict. In a criminal case, both the prosecution and defense will generally have a straightforward request—a verdict of guilty or not guilty. An effective technique for finishing is to go back to the theme and state why the jury should reach a favorable verdict for your client.

*Criminal Case*

## Opening Statement

### Conclusion in a Criminal Case
### The *Blue Moon News Robbery* Case

The prosecutor and the defense in the *Blue Moon News Robbery* case might conclude:

**Prosecutor:**

"Based on the evidence that I just outlined, at the conclusion of this case, I will ask you to return a verdict that truth and justice dictate, and find the defendant guilty of robbery in the first degree."

**Defense counsel:**

> "What happened to Mr. Newman when he was robbed was tragic. At the end of this case, I will ask you to prevent another tragedy—that tragedy would be to find Mike guilty of a robbery he didn't commit. I will ask you to prevent a double tragedy and find Mike not guilty."

### Civil Case

In a civil case, counsel will also want to state the desired verdict. Here, for example, counsel could refer back to the abbreviated story.

---

**Opening Statement**

#### Conclusion in a Civil Case
#### The *Deyoung Wrongful Death Collision* Case

Plaintiff's counsel in the *Deyoung Wrongful Death Collision* case could introduce the opening statement and couple that with the verdict:

> "The defendant was late for a business meeting, so he sped through a stop sign at Natalie and Main Streets, smashing into the passenger's side of the Deyoung's car. The impact crushed Katie's body, broke her neck, and, the following day, took her life. At the end of the case, you will be satisfied by a preponderance of the evidence that the defendant should be held accountable and award plaintiff $10 million."

---

## D. Storytelling

### Pick Persuasive Language

Words and phrases should be carefully selected for each segment of the opening, but particularly those describing critical facts that underpin your case theory. They should be the words of a storyteller that will connect with everyone on the jury, no matter what their ages or educational backgrounds.

### Legal Terms and Legalese

Explain legal principles in plain English. Avoid legalese or police-ese: *exited the unit* (for "got out of the patrol car"), *hereinwith, aforementioned party, prior, subsequent.*

### Words with Connotations

Search for words with favorable connotations and those that vigorously express ideas to the jury. For example, if you were the prosecutor in the *Blue Moon News Robbery* case, you might refer to Gardner Newman as the *victim* rather than *Mr. Newman.* Plaintiff's attorney in a civil case might refer to the injured plaintiff as *scarred*. Use strong imagery, such as describing a plaintiff's injuries in a personal injury case as having "her arm torn off and her neck broken in the collision."

You also want to guard against using words that have connotations that undercut your case theory. For example, in this chapter, the word *story* is used in its best sense. On the other hand, *story* can have a negative connotation (a fictional story). Therefore, you never want to refer to your recitation of facts or what your client will testify to as a *story* because it could be received by the jurors as referring to a fictional one.

### Nonargumentative

Avoid judgmental argumentative words that can be taken as opinions or argumentative conclusions. ("It is clear the defendant willfully avoided his responsibilities.")

### Point of View

In delivering your opening, it is important that it be given from a point of view. When the story is told from your client's point of view, you will be inclined to tell it with passion. Having a perspective is valuable to you as the storyteller. You will readily remember what happened by visualizing the events from that person's vantage point as they transpire in your mind. In the *Deyoung Wrongful Death Collision* and the *Blue Moon News Robbery* cases, the stories could be told from the points of view of Katie's mother and the robbery victim Mr. Newman. In the *O.J. Simpson* opening statement, the story is told from the deceased Nicole Brown Simpson's point of view. The jurors in the *O.J. Simpson* case heard about what she perceived: putting her two children to bed, filling the tub, lighting candles, receiving a call, and so on. When the jurors receive the story from that point of view, they are more empathetic to the person from whose perspective they view the facts.

Besides telling the story from your client's viewpoint, you could tell it from the perspective of an eyewitness to the events. This method puts the jury at the scene witnessing what took place. This technique was common in Greek tragedies, where the Greek chorus of actors would describe the events and background. This approach is the equivalent of telling the story so the jurors become eyewitnesses to what took place. This, too, can have a dramatic emotional impact.

### Tense Shifting

Another effective storytelling technique is to shift the story from the past tense to the present tense. This enhances the juror-as-witness viewpoint approach mentioned before. The story is told as though it is happening as it is being told. The effect on the jurors is to take them to the event and bring the story to life. Notice what happens if we revise the *O.J. Simpson* opening statement just by changing the tense.

## Opening Statement: Tense Shifting

### The *O.J. Simpson Civil Wrongful Death* Case

On a June evening, the 12th of June, 1994, Nicole Brown just finished putting her ten-year-old daughter, Sidney, and her six-year-old son, Justin, down to bed. She *fills* her bathtub with water. She *lights* some candles, *begins* to get ready to take a bath and relax for the evening. The phone *rings*. *It's* 9:40 P.M. Nicole *answers*. And it *is* her mother . . . .

Transcript of Attorney for Plaintiff Frederic Goldman, *supra*.

## E.  Choosing Length

In preparing your opening statement, anticipate how long it can and should be. Determine the time limitation, if any, that the judge will put on your opening. You can inquire about this with the judge or court personnel when you are assigned to the judge for trial. If the court has a time limit, practice and time your presentation so you are not cut off or chastised if you exceed the time limit. Even if the court does not impose a time limit, you should create one for yourself. An overly long opening statement can be a disadvantage as jurors lose interest. Because the length of the opening will depend on the complexity of the case and the communication skills of the attorney, we do not suggest a strict time limit but do suggest a half-hour limit as a general guideline in an uncomplicated case.

## F.  Avoiding Noise

Wouldn't it be wonderful if you could present your case theory to the jury without interference? You would give your opening statement, move directly to putting on your case-in-chief, and then deliver your closing argument. In this way, your message—your case theory—would be communicated to the jury in a clear and convincing manner without interruption. However, in communication theory, there is the concept called *noise*. Noise is anything that interferes with the communication of the message (your case theory) to the receiver (the jury). Every attorney expects that opposing counsel will do her best to create noise. That noise may be the presentation of the other side's case theory or efforts to obstruct or blur your communication with arguments, objections, or cross-examinations. But some noise is of the attorney's own doing.

As you read through the following excerpt from the *O.J. Simpson* transcript, assume you have a seat on the jury and ask, "Is there any noise interfering with the lawyer's message, and, if so, where is the noise coming from?"

## Opening Statement Noise

### Beginning Remarks in Opening Statement: What to Avoid
#### The *O.J. Simpson Criminal* Case

*Judge Ito:*     "Let me remind you from my instructions to you yesterday that any statements made to you by the attorneys during the course of their opening statements are not evidence and should not be considered as such by you. These opening statements are normally given by the attorneys to sort of give you an overall view of the evidence that they intend to present. It's to give you a road map so to speak as to how to evaluate the evidence. This case as you know will be relatively long and by necessity some of this evidence will be presented to you out of chronological or logical order so they'll need to explain to you the case that they intend to present.

"All right. Are both sides prepared to go forward? Mr. Cochran?"

*Mr. Cochran:*   "We are, Your Honor"

*Ms. Clark:*     "Yes, we are, Your Honor."

*Judge Ito:*     "You may proceed. Mr. Darden."

*Mr. Darden:*    "Your Honor, Judge Ito, Mr. Cochran, Mr. Shapiro and Dean Ulman. And to my colleagues seated here in front of you and to the real parties in interest in this case—the Brown family, the Goldman family and the Simpson family. And to you ladies and gentlemen of the jury, good morning."

*Jury:*          "Good morning."

*Mr. Darden:*    "I think it's fair to say that I have the toughest job in town today. Except for the job you have. Your job may be just a little tougher. But your job, like my job, both have a central focus—a single objective. And that objective is justice obviously."

"It's going to be a long trial, and I want you to know how much we appreciate your being on the panel. We appreciate the personal sacrifices you're making by being sequestered. . . ."

"We are here today obviously to resolve an issue, to settle a question. A question that has been on the minds of people throughout the country these past seven months. . . ."

"And I'm sure you'll be wondering why as the trial proceeds on and I'm sure you're wondering why right now. As the Judge instructed you already, opening statements are not evidence. Opening statements are given by lawyers, and in an opening statement we inform the jury of what we think the evidence will show in this case. Or, what we believe the evidence will show. But, we are lawyers; we're not witnesses. We're not under oath. Nothing we say is evidence. The things we say to you today are not the things you should carry into the jury room and into deliberation. . . ."

"But, that raises another question. And that question is: Do you know O.J. Simpson? We've seen him play football for USC. We've watched him thrash UCLA and play in the Rose Bowl. We watched

> him win the Heisman trophy. He may be the best running back in the
> history of the NFL. We watched him leap turnstiles and chairs and
> run to airplanes in Hertz commercials. And we watched him with a 50
> inch Afro in *Naked Gun 33 and a Half.* . . ."

1995 WL 25440 at 17 (opening statement by Christopher Darden).

The unedited version of those beginning remarks in the *O.J. Simpson* opening statement took about five minutes. Five precious minutes. What did you, as
an imaginary juror in the case, want to know when the prosecutor stood before
you? Like any juror, you want to know what the case is all about. Did you get
that message? No, instead you got a preamble—noise—telling you among other
things what the judge had already told you a couple times—"any statements
made to you by the attorneys during the course of their opening statements are
not evidence." The prosecutor was so persuasive on this point that you may have
been convinced not to listen to another thing he had to say. In essence, counsel
created his own noise that blocked the communication of his case theory to the
jury for an important five minutes.

At the outset of your opening statement and elsewhere during your trial
work, you want to eliminate the noise and certainly avoid creating it.

The judge normally will have told the jury what the purpose of opening statement is, so you do not need to tell them that it is like a roadmap, a picture on the
jigsaw puzzle box, or some other analogy. You can go right to your task—grab-
bing the jurors' attention and telling them what you expect to prove.

## IV. DELIVERING THE OPENING

### A. Staging in the Courtroom

#### Center Position

Judge: "Counsel, do you wish to make an opening statement?"

The moment arrives, and you begin: "Your Honor [nodding toward the
court], counsel [turning to opposing counsel], ladies and gentlemen of the jury
[looking the jurors in the eye] . . . ." If you are inclined toward such courtesies,
which we are, or custom requires, you can speak to them after rising at counsel
table or as you walk to your central position, or you can address them when you
reach your position in front of the jury. Then, again, you may expand the opening remarks to include such things as "I'm proud to represent . . . [if courtroom
custom permits]" and/or "It is now my opportunity to address you on behalf
of . . . in opening statement. Opening statement is like a sketch for a painting. It
gives you the broad outline . . ." (if the unusual situation arises where you think
that the court has not covered this sufficiently). Whatever amplifying you do, do

not create noise. Ideally, you would step to your position and start your storytelling with the attention getter.

### Purposeful Movement

Can you move around the courtroom? That depends on the jurisdiction and courtroom custom. Again, you may be leashed to the podium by court protocol (federal court decorum). Even if you are required to use a podium, the court's "wingspan rule" may allow you stand to the side of the podium as long as you can reach out and touch it. In other courts, you are allowed to roam freely around the courtroom. If you can move freely, should you? What if you are a nervous pacer? If you are a pacer, we have some advice for you: Don't do it. If you pace, you are making noise, distracting the jurors from the story.

Generally, you should remain center stage and tell the story. However, when you want to shift the jurors' attention, you can move to another place in the courtroom. Another time to move is usually when you want the jurors to look at a trial visual. For instance, you may want the jurors to look at a chart that you will place on a flipchart easel that is behind the witness chair, as shown below. You would walk up, place the chart on the easel, and discuss what is on the chart from that location. When finished, you return to your original position before the jury.

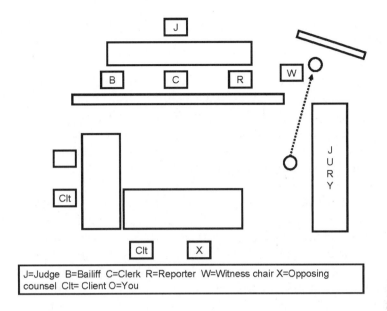

J=Judge  B=Bailiff  C=Clerk  R=Reporter  W=Witness chair  X=Opposing
counsel  Clt= Client  O=You

There are innumerable variables in how you can move around the courtroom and alter the focal point of the jurors' attention. You could walk over and
put your hand on your client's shoulder to shift attention to the client. You could
step aside so the jurors will concentrate on a television monitor that you have
placed in front of the jury box so they can watch an animated video of the event.
The critical points are these:

- Prepare the courtroom (for example, have the television monitor ready to
  be pulled over to in front of the jurors) before the jurors come out of the
  jury room to listen to your opening statement, and
- Plan and choreograph your movement like a dancer before a performance.

## B.  Your Performance

Your appearance, demeanor, and behavior are all important to the delivery
of your opening statement. In Chapter 2, we discussed the importance of these
matters and offered techniques for effective delivery. These include rehearsal,
coping with nervousness (pages 24-25), and sincerity (pages 7-12). We discuss
two other considerations—pacing the story and using notes.

### Pacing the Story

Professional storytellers say that no one ever complains about their pacing
of the story. This is despite the fact that the speaker may slow to a snail's pace.
The reason that no one complains is because the good storyteller knows to slow
down when the facts are dramatic. The slow pace allows the mind to keep up
with and visualize what is happening. By rereading the *O.J. Simpson* civil case

opening statement (page 156) both quickly and slowly, you will realize how effective the slow-pace technique can be.

### Notes

In a perfect world, you would present your opening statement without notes. This should be your goal. Notes, if you refer to them, can handicap you. The more notes you have on the page, the more likely that the notes will act like a magnet pulling your eyes down and toward them. This causes you to lose eye contact with your jurors and hampers your communication. Additionally, under the stress of performance, you will have difficulty locating information if the page or note card is filled with words.

You can free yourself from your notes. The remedy, again, is laborious preparation and several rehearsal sessions. By the time the trial begins, you should know your case so well that you can deliver your opening statement without or almost completely without notes. If you need notes for moral support, reduce your written opening to outline form (in large font) so that you can just glance at your points and keep eye contact with the jurors. An exception to this "don't-read" rule is when you are quoting from a document, such as a written statement or jury instruction. Then it is wholly appropriate to read because it assures the jury that you are concerned with accurately reporting the quotation.

A valuable technique is to use your visuals as your notes. For example, you can create a timeline with brief descriptions of the events at different points in time. You can blow up that timeline and adhere it to foam-core board. Then you can use the timeline as notes as you take the jury through the chronology of facts using the timeline. People will be amazed that you delivered your opening statement without relying on notes, when, in fact, your notes are on the visuals that you have in plain sight in front of the jury. Another tip is to put a cup of water near your notes. When you need to glance at your notes, take a sip of water and peek at the notes.

---

View the opening statements in the *Freck Point* trial demonstration movie to see how to structure and deliver an opening statement (see the website *http://www .aspenlawschool.com/books/berger_trialad4e*).

---

## V.  VISUALS IN OPENING

Bring your opening statement story to life in the courtroom with visuals. Chapter 2 outlines all the reasons for enlisting visuals to persuade the jury. Here we stress that one of the best times to use visuals is when you are storytelling. What better way to imprint the story on the jurors' minds? Visuals displayed in opening should enrich, simplify, and advance your story. What you use is limited only by the admissibility of the evidence at trial and your imagination.

## A. Permissibility

If you can say it in your opening statement, you should be able to show it. You usually can. You are entitled to tell the jury what you expect to prove in opening, so you should be able to tell them and show them admissible evidence, such as a timeline. The corollary here is the same one we have already discussed—you can neither tell the jury nor show them anything that would be inadmissible.

You must be acquainted with the legal authority in your jurisdiction concerning the use of visuals in opening—does the trial court allow the use of visuals before you commence your opening? Otherwise, you may well encounter an objection during your opening statement and have the court excuse the jury to the jury room while you argue over whether you can use the visual. The worst repercussion could be a mistrial as a result of the judge's ruling that you should not have exposed the jurors to inadmissible evidence in your opening.

### Strategy

Be aware of court practice in your jurisdiction regarding what the court will allow and what, if anything, you need to do before you can avail yourself of using visuals in your opening statement. Even within a particular jurisdiction, practices can vary from judge to judge.

Seek an agreement, such as a stipulation from opposing counsel that you may use the visual or other evidence in opening. If counsel agrees, you can inform the trial judge of the stipulation before you commence opening and gain the court's approval to use the visual. Generally, you should inform the court and opposing counsel of your intent to display exhibits in opening, because you want to be able to give your opening statement without the interruption of an objection and argument about the use of the exhibit. Should the court rule that the exhibit cannot be shown, you may face additional difficulties, such as now having a PowerPoint presentation containing a slide that cannot be shown and needing to take measures to prevent the jury from seeing that slide. If opposing counsel will not agree to your use of the exhibit in opening, you can move to preadmit the visual or other evidence. This issue usually can be resolved in a pretrial hearing out of the jury's presence. At the hearing, the proponent calls the witnesses who will lay the foundation for the visual or other exhibit. On the other hand, the court may still prohibit the use of the visual if the party wishing to employ the visual cannot establish its admissibility before trial. Your jurisdiction's court rules may facilitate the resolution of objections to exhibits prior to trial. For example, a common approach that is used by courts is shown by Local Civil Rule 16 for the United States District Court, Western District of Washington. Rule 16 requires counsel prior to trial to identify pretrial exhibits (except for impeachment), state the party's position regarding the other party's exhibits ("stipulate to admissibility, (2) stipulate to authenticity but not admissibility, or (3) dispute authenticity and admissibility"). Further, the Western District's Local Civil Rules provide for premarking of exhibits and a pretrial order on the admissibility of exhibits. Wash. Ct. R. 16.1.

### Legal Authority

Provided that you can establish admissibility at a hearing outside the jury's presence, the court should allow you to show the evidence or some other visual indicating what the evidence will show. Some judges are reluctant to allow the use of visuals in opening statement, citing nothing but custom ("We don't allow that."). To convince the court, you can rely on cases that permit visuals in other jurisdictions. A sampling of some legal authority supporting the use of trial visuals in opening statement is as follows: *State v. Sucharew*, 66 P.3d 59 (Ariz. App. 2003) (PowerPoint presentation); *State v. Smith*, 130 P.3d 554 (Haw. 2006) (PowerPoint in opening and closing); *State v. Caenen*, 19 P.3d 142 (Kan. 2001); Paul Zwier & Thomas C. Galligan, *Technology and Opening Statements: A Guide to the Virtual Trial of the Twenty-First Century*, 67 Tenn. L. Rev. 523 (2000).

## B.  Planning and Preparation

Advance planning and preparation are critical to effectively using visuals during opening statement or any other part of trial. Although there are tremendous benefits to using visuals in your opening statement, they must be shown effortlessly or they will be distractions.

Suppose that you want to use a computer slideshow in your opening and the court is not equipped for this. You will need to have the necessary equipment (which includes the computer; remote; and either a television monitor, a screen, or a projector). You will also have to decide where to place the equipment in the courtroom. If you have not contracted with a visuals consulting firm that provides courtroom assistance, make sure that you know how to operate the equipment and that you have resolved technical problems prior to your opening (availability of extension cords, location of outlets for plugging in the equipment, placement of projection screen, and so on). If the equipment malfunctions, you will need a backup plan, such as printed slides and a document camera that you can use to project the slides onto the screen or providing hard copies for the jurors, judge, and attorneys.

## C.  Storytelling with Visuals

The opening statement is an opportunity to bring reality into the courtroom so the people discussed come alive and the events make sense. There is no better way to do that than with pictures. See Chapter 2, pages 18-20.

As an example, assume that you are the prosecutor in the *Freck Point Murder* case. You are prosecuting Samuel Griffith for murder in the first degree for stabbing his wife Sondra to death on October 16 of last year in the early morning hours. Assume further that you won the motion, and the court has ruled that the circumstances of Samuel Griffith's first wife's death are admissible to prove motive and modus operandi. Consider how you could deliver that portion of your opening statement that focuses on the death of Samuel's first wife, Marian Griffith.

### Photographs

Begin your opening statement by introducing the jurors to Marian Griffith by projecting a computer slide photograph of her on a big screen. As the jurors look at this photograph, tell them about Marian. "Marian and Samuel Griffith were married over 25 years ago, they had two children, and Marian had grown up vacationing at Priest Lake. Here she is at the lake the summer she died."

Then explain, "on August 20th, 16 years ago, while their children were at camp, the defendant and Marian went to Gun Lodge at Priest Lake, Oregon." Here, you move to the next slide showing the scene and Gun Lodge.

Gun Lodge

You show the jury the dock: "This is where Samuel and Marian Griffith launched their Sevylor raft." Use an arrow pointing to the place on the dock in this photograph. In the same photograph, using another animated arrow, you explain, "Samuel Griffith rowed around this point of beach at the right side of the photo and entered Portage Bay."

Then, with the aid of the next photograph of Alexandra Torres's cabin, you tell the jurors: "When the raft entered Portage Bay, Ms. Torres was sitting on her front porch reading."

Here you relate the defendant's story: "After they arrived in Portage Bay, they were swimming near the raft. Marian developed a leg cramp and was clinging to the raft. Then the wake from a speedboat 25 yards away caused the raft to over-turn. The defendant said he heard Marian cough and then she went underwater. Sam said that he righted the raft and pulled his wife into it. Marian was not con-scious, and he attempted CPR but got no response from her."

Moving to the next photo, you recount what happened from Ms. Torres's viewpoint. "Ms. Torres saw the couple swimming near the raft, but the raft never capsized. Ms. Torres saw the man pull a woman into the raft. She thought the man was helping her into the raft. The man then began rowing in the direction of Gun Lodge."

Showing this slide of the Gun Lodge dock, you describe how "the defendant slowly rowed back to the resort. At no time did he call out for assistance to anyone on the then crowded dock." The arrow shows where the defendant docked the raft.

To orient the jurors, you emphasize what happened through repetition. "There is an aerial photograph of the scene showing where Portage Bay is located, and this animated dotted line indicates the course the raft took from the Gun Lodge dock to the bay and back."

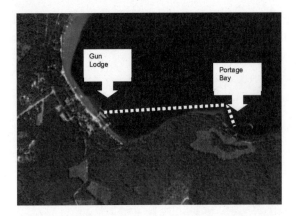

Next, you describe the investigation. "Two lifeguards the same size as the defendant and Marian got in the water in Portage Bay and attempted to reenact what the defendant had described. The raft didn't capsize. Several boats were run by the raft to create the largest waves they could, but the raft never capsized. You can see this still picture of the attempted reenactment. You will see a video-tape of the reenactment during the trial."

So far this opening statement, fortified by photographs, has brought what happened to Marian Griffith to life in the courtroom. The jurors saw what Marian looked like; she is no longer just a name. Jurors could see as well as hear what happened: what Gun Lodge looked like, where Portage Bay is in relationship to the lodge, how far the defendant rowed rather than rowing to shore in the bay, and so on. Also, you have piqued the jurors' interest so that they will be anticipating viewing the videotape of the reenactment. As you now turn to the explanation of how Marian Griffith died from asphyxia due to drowning, you again can display the picture of her.

So far we have concentrated on integrating photographs into the opening statement. Now, let's continue with the prosecutor's opening statement in the *Freck Point Murder* case to illustrate how additional visuals might be incorporated into an opening statement.

### Charts

#### Indebtedness Charts

As the prosecutor, your case theory is that Samuel Griffith murdered his wives to collect the insurance money. You will tell the jury that while he and Sondra appeared prosperous, they were deeply in debt when he killed her for the $2 million life insurance proceeds. One way to support this assertion is to show the jury indebtedness charts on computer slides that are animated so that each line appears one at a time. Alternatively, instead of a computer slideshow with the charts on the slides, the information could be displayed on a poster put on an easel. The top of the chart could show the Griffiths' annual income coupled with a listing of major annual expenditures, which indicates that the couple was spending $120,000 more than their combined income. The next chart could list their debts—the house mortgage of $850,000, more than $140,000 in credit card debt, and college loan debts. After revealing the debts piling up, line by line on the poster or computer slide chart, you explain that the Griffiths were in the eye of a financial tornado. That the major asset Sondra possessed was her $2 million life insurance policy. You point out that within three weeks after her death, Samuel Griffith made a claim to the insurance company as her beneficiary.

#### Legal Theory: The Elements Chart

During the opening statement, you want to explain the legal theory of murder in the first degree. You could display this in a chart or a computer slide where you have listed the elements of murder in the first degree:

---

#### Elements Chart Murder First Degree

1. On or about October 16, the defendant, Samuel Griffith,
2. In the State of Major,
3. Killed Sondra Griffith.
4. The defendant acted with intent to kill Sondra Griffith.
5. The intent was the result of premeditation.
6. Sondra Griffith died as a result of defendant's acts.

---

#### Case Summary Chart

A case summary chart lets the jurors see your conception of the case on one page. Developing this chart can be a challenge in a complex case. However, with this chart on a computer slide, the trial lawyer can build the trial visual piece by piece with the software's animation feature so that when all the pieces are shown on the screen, the case will make sense as a totality.

### Timeline

A timeline serves dual purposes. The purposes are to enable the jurors to understand the chronology of events in the case and to highlight important occurrences. When the case involves several events for the jury to grasp, a timeline is a particularly beneficial device. Second, a timeline facilitates the trial lawyer's communication of the facts. In opening statement, the lawyer can begin the story with events that will have an attention-getting effect on the jurors no matter where the events were in the case chronology. The lawyer can then employ the timeline to explain when the just-described facts took place and provide the jurors with the big picture. For instance, the prosecutor in the *Freck Point Murder* case could begin with the stabbing death of Sondra Griffith, and then, with the timeline, first show when Sondra was stabbed, and then go back more than 17 years ago to when Samuel Griffith was facing bankruptcy. An animated digital slideshow allows the lawyer to reveal events on the timeline when desired, so that as the story unfolds, new events are added to the timeline.

**TIMELINE**

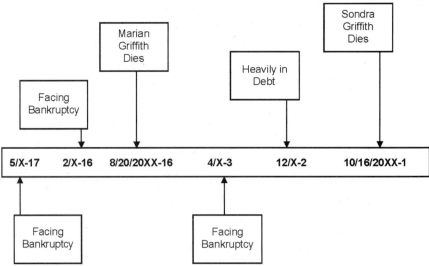

Timelines can be simple, easily created one-line form, or they can be much more elaborate. CaseSoft (*http://www.casesoft.com/timemap*) produces Time-Map software that creates timelines.

The following is another sample of a timeline. Created using Naegeli Trial Technologies software (*http://www.naegelitrialtech.com*), it shows the healing process occurring in a medical malpractice case.

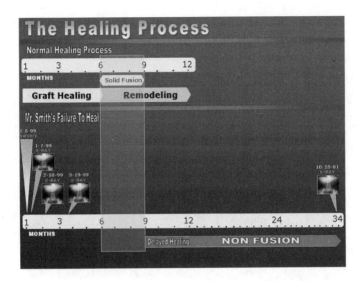

## Scene Diagram

Scene diagrams enable the lawyer to show the jurors what happened during the event that is the focal point of the lawsuit. The diagram can be of either the interior of a house, office, or other structure, or the exterior of a building, street, or vehicle. In the *Freck Point Murder* case, the prosecutor could use the diagram of the bedroom showing how Sondra Griffith was killed, where she lay on the bed, where the blood spatters were, and so on. It would be as if the jury were present with the detectives at the murder scene.

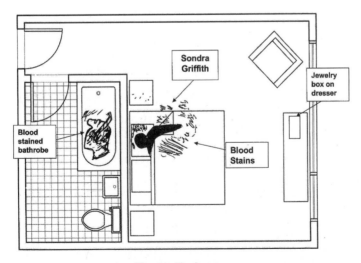

**Master Bedroom**
**4187 Alter Street**

Following is a traffic collision scene, created by using software from Borrowed Ladder Media Services, Inc. (*http://www.borrowedladder.com*).

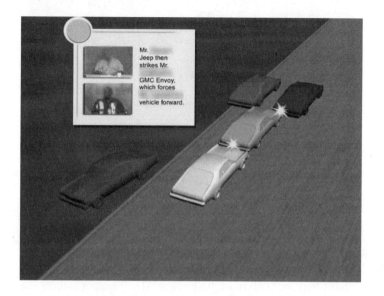

### Documents

In opening statement, you may wish to show the jurors portions of documents, such as a clause in a contract. To emphasize the significant clauses, computer software can highlight them just as you would mark a book with a highlighter. Among other techniques, you can either insert an arrow to point at the passage or magnify it on the digital slide. The next example uses software from Borrowed Ladder Media Services, Inc.

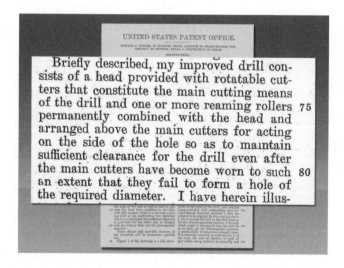

We have only begun to scratch the surface in this discussion of trial visuals. What you use is limited only by rules governing the admissibility of evidence and your imagination. The possibilities are endless.

## VI. ETHICAL CONSIDERATIONS

### A. Personal Opinion

**What to Avoid in Opening Statement: Opinion**

#### Criminal Case

**Prosecutor:**

"The state will call Mr. Ethridge, who has tendered a plea of guilty to attempted strong-arm robbery. And I'll say this from the bottom of my heart, that there is one soul, who was at one time unclean and is now clean. . . . That's good for the soul, and he is looking forward to this. As much as someone tragically is, he's at a point where he wants to be clean. That's really what it's all about. And there will be evidence in this case that Mr. Ethridge is wanting to let it all out. This is his day to let all these things fly. He's beyond that now. Hallelujah."

*Gilchrist v. State*, 565 S.E.2d 281, 285 (S.C. 2002), the court held that the prosecutor was improperly vouching for the witness, "implying his personal opinion concerning the witness's truthfulness."

**Ethical Rules: Fairness to Opposing Party**

#### Model Rule of Professional Conduct 3.4

ABA Model Rule of Professional Conduct 3.4 on Fairness to Opposing Party and Counsel lays out important parameters for opening statement as follows:

A lawyer shall not: . . .

(e)  in trial, allude to any matter that the lawyer does not reasonably believe is relevant or that will not be supported by admissible evidence, assert personal knowledge of facts in issue except when testifying as a witness, or state a personal opinion as to the justness of a cause, the credibility of a witness, the culpability of a civil litigant or the guilt or innocence of an accused. . . .

In the criminal case opening statement illustration, the prosecutor stepped over the line by expressing an opinion about Mr. Ethridge's credibility ("And I'll say this from the bottom of my heart, that there is one soul, who was at one time unclean and is now clean"). While all lawyers are prohibited from expressing a personal opinion of the type described by the rule and risk receiving a court rep-rimand and possible bar sanctions, ramifications for the prosecution in a crimi-nal case may also include mistrial, dismissal, or reversal on appeal.

The lawyer's axiom derived from this ethical prohibition is "Never say *I.*" Whenever a trial lawyer uses the first person, the lawyer may find that the words that follow are a statement of opinion. But the statement need not contain the word *I* to run afoul of the prohibition. Dogmatic statements ("their witness lied") can also be statements of personal opinion. Appellate decisions have so consis-tently condemned prosecutors' referral to witnesses as liars that the adage could be amended to be "Never say *I* or *lie.*" A few cases and commentary discussing the personal-opinion rule are *State v. Pabst*, 996 P.2d 321, 326 (Kan. 2000); *State v. Horton*, 68 P.3d 1145 (Wis. App. 2003); James W. Gunson, *Prosecutorial Sum-mation: Where Is the Line Between Personal Opinion and Proper Argument?* 46 Me. L. Rev. 241 (1994).

The Commentary to ABA Standard on the Prosecution Function 3-5.8(b) states:

> Expressions of personal opinion by the prosecutor are a form of unsworn, unchecked testimony and tend to exploit the influence of the prosecutor's office and undermine the objective detachment that should separate a lawyer from the cause being argued. Such argument is expressly forbidden by the ABA model eth-ics codes, and many courts have recognized the impropriety of such statements. This kind of argument is easily avoided by insisting that lawyers restrict them-selves to statements such as "The evidence shows" . . . or something similar.

However, does this mean that counsel is prohibited from discussing the credibility of the witnesses? Clearly not. But counsel must discuss *evidence* from which the jurors should discount the witness's credibility. Attorneys are prohib-ited from expressing their personal opinions.

## B. Overpromising

Promising to prove something during opening statement and later failing to do so damages not only the lawyer's credibility, but also the lawyer's case. The best strategy is to underpromise; this will boost your standing with the jury and help maintain juror interest during your presentation of the case, as they learn new information favorable to your case.

Overpromising can constitute an ethical breach. ABA Model Rule 3.4 prohib-its counsel from alluding "to any matter . . . that will not be supported by admis-sible evidence." When counsel comments on matters that will not be supported by admissible evidence, counsel risks venturing outside the record.

Referring to the prosecutor's opening statement in the *O.J. Simpson* case on pages 156-157, you will note that he repeatedly went beyond what he could rea-sonably expect to prove ("[A question] certainly has been on the minds of my people in Richmond, California, and friends in Fayetteville, Georgia . . . ," and,

"We've seen him play football for USC. We've watched him thrash UCLA and play in the Rose Bowl. We've watched him win the Heisman trophy. He may be the best running back in the history of the NFL. We watched him leap turnstiles and chairs and run to airplanes in Hertz commercials. And we watched him with a 50-inch Afro in *Naked Gun 33 and a Half.*"). For obvious reasons including that the prosecutor's remarks praised Simpson, the prosecutor did not draw objections. And while, if they had been objected to, the prosecutor might have lamely claimed these were matters of common knowledge, the comments were beyond what the prosecutor could reasonably expect to prove.

## C. Introducing Irrelevant Matter

A third prohibition stated in ABA Model Rule 3.4 is that counsel shall not refer "to any matter that the lawyer does not reasonably believe is relevant." The *Gilchrist* case illustration, where the prosecutor vouched for his witness's credibility ("And I'll say this from the bottom of my heart . . ."), runs afoul of both the rule against expression of personal opinion and also this rule. The prosecutor's view about the credibility of a witness is indisputably inadmissible and irrelevant. See page 171.

Although unethical conduct is less common during opening statement than closing argument, misconduct that arises in opening usually violates the same ethical principles as misconduct in closing argument. In Chapter 13, closing argument, you will find additional examples of jury statements that overstep ethical boundaries. See pages 493-496. These examples could just as well have been expressed during opening.

---

### Ethical Rules Pertaining to Opening: Summary

#### ABA Model Rules of Professional Conduct

Under ABA Model Rule of Professional Conduct 3.4, a lawyer in trial is prohibited from doing the following.

**Personal Opinion:** Prohibited from stating "personal knowledge of facts in issue except when testifying as a witness, or personal opinion as to the justness of a cause, the credibility of a witness, the culpability of a civil litigant or the guilt or innocence of an accused."

**Overstating:** Counsel shall not mention "any matter . . . that will not be supported by admissible evidence."

**Injecting Irrelevant Matter:** Counsel shall not allude to matter that counsel "does not reasonably believe is relevant."

*Gilchrist v. State*, 565 S.E.2d 281, 285 (S.C. 2002), held that the prosecutor was improperly vouching for the witness, "implying his personal opinion concerning the witness's truthfulness."

## CHECKLIST: OPENING STATEMENT: STORYTELLING

### Content

The **Jury Trial** opening statement:

☐ Concisely states the legal theory without arguing or invading the judge's prerogative to instruct on the law;

☐ Includes sufficient facts to support the legal theory;

☐ Incorporates the essentials of a persuasive story:

- Human values,
- Human needs,
- Human story—usually about the client,
- Believable and understandable story,
- Quantity of evidence described is compelling, and
- Quality of evidence is convincing.

☐ Is a statement of fact, not argument;

☐ Is not too detailed;

☐ Covers only admissible evidence that counsel expects to prove;

☐ Candidly addresses case weaknesses;

☐ Anticipates and refutes the other side's case theory when permissible (prosecutor may not attempt to shift the burden to the defense); and

☐ Has a well-crafted case theme.

The **Bench Trial** opening statement:

☐ Succinctly states your case theory and identifies the issues;

☐ Gets to the heart of the matter;

☐ Assists the court in making findings of fact and conclusions of law;

☐ Incorporates the essentials of a persuasive story, without being emotional or overly dramatic; and

☐ Tells the story so that it fits the pattern of cases with which the judge is familiar or explains why it differs from the norm.

### Structure

☐ The opening statement begins with an attention getter (theme, dramatic setting of the scene).

☐ The body of the opening flows smoothly and tells the story with a clear and understandable structure (flashback, chronological).

☐ The opening statement concludes by referring to the theme and reasons for the requested verdict.

### Storytelling, Staging, and Delivery

☐ Counsel projects sincerity.

☐ Counsel avoids distracting behavior (pacing back and forth).

☐ Counsel uses eye contact with jurors.

☐ Counsel does not read the opening.

☐ Counsel uses effective storytelling techniques, such as

- choosing persuasive language;
- eliminating legal terms and legalese;

- employing words with connotations;
- adopting a point of view, such as the client's;
- shifting tenses for effect (present);
- delivery at an appropriate rate (slowed when covering dramatic facts); and
- avoiding noise (anything that obstructs or interferes with clear and convincing communication).
☐ Opening is an appropriate length of time.
☐ The opening is staged successfully.
  - Counsel positions herself to hold the jury's attention.
  - Counsel makes purposeful movements that do not distract (pacing).
☐ The opening uses trial visuals effectively.
  - Counsel ensures use is permissible.
  - Visual is persuasive.
  - Counsel positions equipment and visuals appropriately.
  - Counsel has a backup plan if equipment malfunctions.

### Ethical Boundaries

☐ Counsel does not state a personal opinion.
☐ Counsel does not overpromise something that cannot be proved.
☐ Counsel does not introduce irrelevant matter.

# MAKING AND MEETING OBJECTIONS

---

*Vinny Gambini:* I object to this witness being called at this time. We've been given no prior notice he'd testify. No discovery of any tests he's conducted or reports he's prepared. And as the court is aware, the defense is entitled to advance notice of any witness who will testify,

particularly those who will give scientific evidence, so that we may
properly prepare for cross-examination, as well as give the defense
an opportunity to have the witness's reports reviewed by a defense
expert, who might then be in a position to contradict the veracity of his
conclusions.

*Judge Chamberlain Haller:*  Mr. Gambini?

*Vinny Gambini:*  Yes, sir?

*Judge Chamberlain Haller:*  Mr. Gambini, that is a lucid, intelligent, well
thought-out objection.

*Vinny Gambini:*  Thank you.

*Judge Chamberlain Haller:*  Overruled.

—*My Cousin Vinny* (1992)

## I. OVERVIEW

During pretrial preparation, you identified potential evidentiary issues and pretrial motions or trial objections. Now you are on the brink of trial, and it is time
to concentrate on planning, making, and meeting objections during trial. This
chapter covers the essentials of making and meeting trial objections.

### A. Objectives

An objection is a mini-motion. An objection asks the court to exercise its
power on your client's behalf (sustain your objection). The objectives of trial
objections are in many respects identical to those of motions. Objections

- control information that the fact finders can consider, normally excluding
  testimony or exhibits offered by opposing counsel;
- control opposing counsel's conduct; and
- preserve error for appeal.

### B. Objection Theory

Objection theory is a conceptual framework for determining the basis for
objections and how to make and argue them. An objection may be thought of
as having a legal component and a factual component (like a case theory or
a motion theory). The legal theory is the legal authority or legal basis for your
objection. Your factual theory is made up of the facts that support the legal basis.
You are concerned with the legal and factual sufficiency and persuasiveness of
the objection, just as you are with your case theory.

**Objection Theory**

Legal Basis   **AND**   Factual Basis

### Legal Basis

The legal basis for an objection is your legal authority. Generally, the legal basis is derived from evidentiary law, local courtroom practice, statutes, codes of professional responsibility, and federal and state constitutions. Many objections that are based on evidentiary rules are identified by the name or purpose of the rule—irrelevant, unfairly prejudicial, hearsay, and so forth.

### Controlling Information

As an objecting party, your concern is with controlling information flowing to the jury and the admissibility of evidence. To determine the legal authority underlying your objection, you will reply on evidence rules, statutes, constitutions, and case law. Examples of objections to control information include hearsay, privileged communication, and irrelevant information.

### Controlling Opposing Counsel Conduct

Controlling your adversary's conduct is primarily based on professional responsibility rules because they provide legal authority for your objections. While your jurisdiction's rules of professional conduct describe unethical behavior that is subject to bar sanctions, they also constitute persuasive authority for trial objections. If the conduct is seen as an ethical breach, the judge is not likely to permit it. Two important sources for such objections are ABA Model Rules of Professional Conduct 3.4 and 3.5.

---

## Ethical Rules Relating to Impermissible Conduct

### ABA Model Rules of Professional Conduct

**Impermissible Conduct:** Model Rule of Professional Conduct 3.4 provides: "A lawyer shall not . . . in trial, allude to any matter that the lawyer does not reasonably believe is relevant or that will not be supported by admissible evidence, assert personal knowledge of facts in issue except when testifying as a witness, or state a personal opinion as to the justness of a cause, the credibility of a witness, the culpability of a civil litigant or the guilt or innocence of an accused. . . ."

---

Rule 3.4(e) can be converted into "fairness" objections:

*Objection. Counsel is*

- *stating a personal opinion,*
- *outside the record,*
- *asserting personal knowledge of a fact,*
- *assuming a fact not in evidence, or*
- *referring to something that won't be supported by the evidence.*

ABA Model Rule of Professional Conduct 3.5 deals with attorney behavior:

## Ethical Rules Relating to Impermissible Conduct

### ABA Model Rules of Professional Conduct

**Impermissible Conduct:** Model Rule of Professional Conduct 3.5 provides that a lawyer shall not:

(a) seek to influence a judge, juror, prospective juror or other official by means prohibited by law;

(b) communicate ex parte with such a person during the proceeding unless authorized to do so by law or court order;

(c) communicate with a juror or prospective juror after discharge of the jury if:

(1) the communication is prohibited by law or court order;

(2) the juror has made known to the lawyer a desire not to communicate; or

(3) the communication involves misrepresentation, coercion, duress or harassment; or

(d) engage in conduct intended to disrupt a tribunal.

Rule 3.5 is the authority for objections such as these:

*Objection. Your Honor, counsel is*

- *engaging in ex parte contact, or*
- *disrupting the proceedings.*

### Factual Basis

Generally, you will state your legal grounds: "Objection. Hearsay." This is enough (without making an argument laying out the factual basis in support of your objection), and the court will either sustain or overrule your objection.

However, sometimes you need to assert the factual basis supporting your objection. Such argument usually takes the form of a simple factual story. It may also include an offer of proof. An offer of proof is an attorney's statement as to the content of evidence that is being offered or will be offered, making clear its relevance and purpose. Your factual story should be sufficient and persuasive to support the legal basis of the objection: You must state enough facts to establish the legal basis of the objection, and those facts must be convincing. For instance, consider the following illustration from the *Freck Point Murder* case discussed in Chapter 3.

## Factual Basis Objection Theory

### The *Freck Point Murder* Case: The Sprite Can

The prosecutor is offering into evidence a Sprite can, which is an item of physical evidence that is not readily identifiable.

**Defense counsel objects:** "Objection. Prosecution exhibit number 39 hasn't been properly identified. Rule 901."

**The prosecutor responds:** "Your Honor, the foundation is complete; we have established a chain of custody."

**Judge:** "The jury will be excused to the jury room. . . ."

**Defense counsel** supports the objection with a factual basis showing that the chain of custody has been broken: "The evidence slip attached to the bag containing the exhibit shows that detective Mitchell checked it out of the evidence room and returned it the following day. He did this before the exhibit went to the crime lab. No showing has been made that the detective kept the exhibit in a place where it could not be contaminated or switched with another can. No showing has been made that the exhibit is in the same condition when detective Mitchell returned it to the evidence room as it was when he removed it. A link in the chain is missing."

**The prosecutor,** in response, could supply a factual basis for admissibility by making an offer of proof that the detective will testify later in trial that the exhibit was kept in a secure place and that it was not altered in any way. Then, the prosecutor could seek to have the judge admit the Sprite can subject to the condition that the detective would later testify as stated in the offer of proof.

## II. JUDGMENT

You are strolling along the downtown sidewalk, and you come to a four-way intersection controlled by a stoplight. You look across the street at the sign to see if you can cross. The do not cross symbol shifts to the walking stick figure. You notice that the intersection light on your crosswalk side is red. You have a legal right to step off the curb and cross the street. Do you exercise your legal right just because you can? Not if you value your personal safety. Instinctively, because of prior experience, you look to see whether traffic will allow you to cross—to make sure a driver doesn't run the light or the driver coming from your left doesn't fail to stop at the crosswalk line and hit you while taking that free right turn.

Similarly, just because you have a legal basis to object does not mean you should. Good sense may dictate that you withhold the objection. You are not the objections police in charge of objecting every time you have a legal basis to do so. In this section, we offer three factors that you should take into consideration in deciding whether to object. Ask yourself whether the objection is sound, consistent with your case theory, and suitable to the audience.

### A. Sound Basis

The legal basis may exist for the objection, but is it solid? The benefits of making objections only when the grounds are solid are at least threefold. First, it is likely that the trial judge will sustain your objection if your grounds for it are sound.

Second, if the case is appealed, the judge's ruling on the objection should be upheld. On the other hand, the ramification of making an objection on questionable grounds may include having your objection overruled and, if done too often, leaving the judge with a lack of confidence in your legal assertions. In a regime where evidence rulings are subject only to an abuse of discretion standard, you don't want to lose a judge's confidence in either your legal knowledge, preparation, or integrity. Equally bad, if the court sustains your ill-founded objection and the evidence is excluded, error is built into the record and the case is vulnerable to reversal on appeal. (Defense counsel in criminal cases need not be so concerned about soundness of the grounds because of counterbalancing obligations to the defendant, and, more important, because the prosecution cannot appeal an acquittal.)

Third, in contrast to the negative consequences of making unsupportable objections, counsel who objects only when the grounds are firm gains significant collateral benefits. Counsel can build a reputation of being a lawyer who is trustworthy, someone who objects only when there is a solid basis for doing so, and someone who does not waste the court's time. When an attorney has such a reputation, the judge is more likely to listen carefully to counsel's objections and rely on well-made arguments.

## B. Case Theories

If it hurts your case theory or helps your adversary, object. Otherwise, don't. As we have discussed, through trial objections you seek to prevent the jury from considering either an exhibit, testimony, or an opposing counsel's words or conduct that is harmful to your case theory or that bolsters your opponent's case theory. By preventing your opponent from using certain evidence central to the issues, you can affect the sufficiency and persuasiveness of the other side's factual and legal theories. You can also prevent presentation of evidence that can undermine your case theory.

Let's return to our previous example from the *Freck Point Murder* case where the prosecutor wants to offer the Sprite can into evidence. Defense counsel in a murder case should not object if the exhibit neither harms the defense case nor advances the prosecution's case, even though a chain of custody foundation has not been established. In fact, withholding an objection makes good sense if the exhibit helps the defense case theory (an unknown third person's DNA was on the can). On the other hand, if the laboratory's DNA analysis has determined that the defendant's saliva and the victim's blood are both on the Sprite can and the can was located near the murder weapon, that would hurt the defense case theory and calls for an objection raising the lack of authentication. Fed. R. Evid. 901.

## C. The Audience: Jury and Judge

### Jury

Making objections sparingly is also advantageous depending on your audience. Jurors normally see themselves as seekers of justice and truth, and they are hungry for information. Despite the court's and counsels' efforts to educate them on the significance of objections, jurors still tend to see objections as an effort to withhold evidence. Delays caused by objections and sidebar arguments can make jury service tedious and boring.

Think back once more to the chain of custody in the Sprite can illustration. If defense counsel's objection is sustained, what effect will it have on the jury and on the case? For the moment, the fact finders will not learn of the evidence, and the objection, therefore, satisfies the objective for making objections—controlling the information that the jury receives. However, will this be only a short-lived victory? First, when the objection is sustained, it will peak the jury's interest about what was excluded; they will be wondering what was in the bag that the witness was testifying about.

Second, the sustained objection may just delay matters until after the prosecution calls Detective Mitchell to provide the missing link in the chain. When the Sprite can eventually does come into evidence, defense counsel will have highlighted its significance for the jury. Thus, if defense counsel assesses that ultimately the Sprite can will probably come into evidence, defense counsel may be wise to withhold an objection to it.

### Judge

It is important to reflect upon what the judge expects of counsel concerning the proper appearance and demeanor of counsel when making and meeting objections. Generally, the court requires the following:

---

### Judicial Expectations: Objections

**Stand:** Judges expect you to stand when stating an objection unless you are disabled or practice in a court that prefers counsel to remain seated.

**Speak to the Judge:** Judges want counsel to direct the objection to the bench and to refrain from arguing with opposing counsel.

**One Attorney:** When there are multiple lawyers for the same party, only the lawyer who is conducting the witness's examination may object.

**Preferred Form:** Generally, the preferred way to object is to say, "Objection," followed by a concise statement of the basis for the objection, such as, "Objection. Hearsay." Avoid speaking objections that are disfavored, which are speeches by counsel often in an argumentative or suggestive manner rather than objections stated in the preferred form.

*continued* ▶

> **Bench Conferences:** Recognizing that jurors do not like sidebar conferences, generally judges want counsel to request a bench conference only if absolutely necessary.
>
> **Bench Trial:** In a bench trial, some judges are intolerant of objections, even when an objection is solid and is specific to the case theories. In bench trials, many lawyers have had an objection rebuked by a trial judge with the aside, "Counsel, let's just move along. I can sort out what's admissible and what's not." A good practice is to learn in advance from colleagues, court personnel, or some other reliable source what the judge wants. In the absence of this information, you can test the waters with objections. However, if the judge appears irked and wants to hasten the bench trial along, then only object when absolutely necessary, such as when counsel wants to preserve error for appeal.

## III. MAKING OBJECTIONS

To effectively make an objection, it must be made in a timely manner and be phrased correctly.

### A. Timing

#### Timeliness Rule

Federal Rule of Evidence 103(a) provides that objections should be made in a timely manner, as follows:

> (a) **Preserving a Claim of Error.** A party may claim error in a ruling to admit or exclude evidence only if the error affects a substantial right of the party and: (1) if the ruling admits evidence, a party, on the record: (A) timely objects or moves to strike; and (B) states the specific ground, unless it was apparent from the context; or (2) if the ruling excludes evidence, a party informs the court of its substance by an offer of proof, unless the substance was apparent from the context.

Therefore, the evidentiary rules dictate that you should strive to make timely objections. But an even more important reason exists for this tenet—you cannot unring the bell.

#### The Bell Has Rung

Opposing counsel is cross-examining your witness. Counsel asks a patently improper question, introducing inadmissible evidence that cuts your case theory to the core. You object and ask the judge to admonish counsel and instruct the jury. The judge sustains your objection, admonishes counsel, and tells the jury to disregard counsel's question. Opposing counsel announces proudly, "No further questions."

What opposing counsel has done—referring to inadmissible evidence in the jury's presence—was both unethical and a violation of the evidence rules. ABA Model Rule of Professional Conduct 3.4 on Fairness to Opposing Party and

Counsel states that an attorney in trial shall not "allude to any matter that the lawyer does not reasonably believe is relevant or that will not be supported by admissible evidence." Federal Rule of Evidence 103(d) states:

> (d) **Preventing the Jury from Hearing Inadmissible Evidence.** To the extent practicable, the court must conduct a jury trial so that inadmissible evidence is not suggested to the jury by any means.

The trial judge's ruling and instruction to the jury were correct. But can the jury follow the court's instructions and disregard what they've heard? It's doubtful. Offending counsel cannot refer to the evidence in closing, and a juror who raises the testimony in deliberation may be admonished by fellow jurors that they were told by the judge that they must not consider it; but the jurors still heard it. You cannot unring the bell once it has sounded. Harm has been done to your case. For that reason, making an objection in a timely fashion is required by Rule 103(d) and is also necessary to shield the jury from receiving information harmful to your case theory.

Making objections in a timely manner requires active listening and immediate responses. Four strategies will enable you to take action before the bell is rung: (1) Consider filing motions in limine, (2) prepare ahead with a pocket brief, (3) learn to recognize repetitive patterns of speech that can trigger an objection, and (4) make a practical list of objections and have it with you in trial.

### Motions in Limine

Many of the objectionable matters identified before trial can be the subjects of motions in limine. For example, in the *Freck Point Murder* case, the defense could file a motion prior to trial to exclude any evidence relating to the death of Sam Griffith's first wife, Marian Griffith, on the grounds that it is inadmissible propensity evidence. An illustration of a memorandum of law in support of that motion in limine is in the Appendix at the end of this chapter, pages 206-212.

When an evidentiary or other matter can be ruled on pretrial, it is generally preferable to do so pretrial than making a motion during trial. If the court rules that the evidence is excluded, the jury is protected from the harmful information. If the court denies the motion and the evidence is admitted, the moving party still gains to a degree, because now counsel knows the court's ruling and can adjust trial strategy accordingly, such as discussing the harmful information in jury selection and opening statement in an effort to inoculate the jury against it.

### Pocket Brief

Advance preparation can also assist in making timely objections. This requires researching legal authority, planning your factual arguments, and preparing a short evidentiary pocket brief and any offers of proof that may be required. It is good practice to prepare a pocket brief (so called because you figuratively keep it in your pocket until needed) and any offers of proof that may be required. A well-researched pocket brief can be effective in persuading the judge to render a favorable ruling. Also, the judge is likely to be impressed with the lawyer's thorough preparation and useful research.

### Recognizing Patterns

If you lived anywhere near a railroad track when you were growing up, you very likely learned that when you heard the train's whistle in the distance, it was time to get off the tracks. The whistle was a clear warning of what was to come, an unmistakable, recognizable pattern. Generally, before objectionable and harmful information is presented in trial, it also is preceded by an audible warning of what is approaching.

You can learn to recognize these repetitive patterns—ones that could trigger an objection. By listening carefully you will attune your ear and be prepared to object if you want to. Consider creating a list of patterns that signal the coming of objectionable matter. The following is a nonexclusive list of patterns that warn, like a train whistle, what is probably coming so an objection may be made before it is too late.

---

## Objections: Recognizable Patterns

### Warning of Oncoming Objectionable Information

*Pattern*

| | |
|---|---|
| Counsel: | "In summary, Ms. Munch, you've testified that . . ." |
| Likely objections: | Argumentative. |
| | Misquoting the witness. |
| | Asked and answered. |

*Pattern*

| | |
|---|---|
| Counsel: | "Mr. Brauchler, what if I told you that Ms. Fent testified . . ." |
| Likely objections: | Calls for speculation. |
| | Argumentative. |
| | Violates the sequestration rule. |

*Pattern*

| | |
|---|---|
| Counsel: | "Doctor, when you consider the statements that the defendant made to the police or the statements he made to you three days later, what conclusions do you come to regarding . . ." |
| Likely objection: | Compound question. (Words *or* and *and* signal compound question.) |

*Pattern*

| | |
|---|---|
| Counsel: | So, besides you, both Mr. and Mrs. Fontes were in your living room, correct? |
| Witness: | Yes. |

| | |
|---|---|
| Counsel: | For how long were you there? |
| Witness: | Ten minutes. |
| Counsel: | During that time, what . . . |
| Likely objection: | Hearsay. (The time frame indicates that they probably talked and that counsel may well ask about the conversation.) |

Pattern

| | |
|---|---|
| Counsel's conduct (has the clerk mark an exhibit) or questioning indicates that an exhibit is about to be offered. | |
| Likely objections: | The exhibit has not been authenticated. |
| | The exhibit has not been identified. |
| | The exhibit is irrelevant. |
| | The exhibit is unfairly prejudicial. |
| | (The objection should be made before the jury sees the exhibit.) |

Notice that the probable objections could be determined before the question was completed. This is significant because often the question, not the answer, is objectionable or because the answer is objectionable and the objection must be made before the harmful answer is given. If an objection is made before the question is completed or the witness's answer is given, counsel may state that the question has not been completed or that the answer should be able to be heard before the court rules on the objection. When this happens, counsel who has made the objection can direct the court to Federal Rule of Evidence 103(d), which provides that in a jury trial, "[t]o the extent practicable, the court must conduct a jury trial so that inadmissible evidence is not suggested to the jury by any means." As you gain trial experience, you will learn to anticipate—the patterns of questioning and conduct—so that you can object before the bell is rung.

### A Practical List of Objections

Objections can be categorized to fit trial stages—opening statement, direct examination, and so forth. You will find this type of list at pages 188-191. We prefer this list because it is practical. During your pretrial preparation, you can anticipate the information your opponent will present. The list of objections, coupled with this information, can provide you with ideas for objections that could arise. You can also use the list to remind yourself of pitfalls to avoid in your own trial performance. Then, just before and during trial as you approach a particular stage of trial, you can review the list of objections so they are fresh in your mind as you enter that trial phase. For example, the list of jury selection objections would be reviewed just before jury selection begins. This practice is like charging your cell phone so it is ready to go when needed.

## Objections by Stage of Trial

### Jury Selection Objections

Objection. The question

- anticipates instructions on the law that have not been given.
- asks the juror to speculate on the verdict if certain facts are proven and attempts to get the juror's commitment to a verdict.
- is unfair and embarrassing to the juror.
- is unnecessarily probing.
- is an argument of the case.
- poses an improper hypothetical question.
- asks for a verdict from a previous trial.

### Opening Statement Objections

Objection. Counsel

- is arguing the case.
- is unethically stating a personal opinion.
- is misstating what will be contained in the evidence.
- is making a statement that is inflammatory and improper.
- is stating facts outside the record.
- is making a statement that comments on privilege.

### Closing Argument Objections

Objection. Counsel

- is improperly stating a personal opinion.
- is making a statement that is inflammatory and improper.
- is misstating the evidence.
- is discussing punishment.
- is stating facts outside the record.

### Direct Examination Objections

FORM OF THE QUESTION
Objection. The question

- is ambiguous/vague. I ask that it be clarified to avoid misunderstanding.
- is argumentative.
- is not a question but a comment on the evidence.
- is a jury speech.
- assumes a fact not in evidence. It suggests that [assumed fact] is true. This witness has not said that, and neither has any other.
- is compound/contains two parts. I ask that it be separated for better understanding.
- is confusing.
- is cumulative.
- is irrelevant/has nothing to do with anything the jury has to decide. Federal Rule of Evidence 401.
- is leading. Counsel is suggesting how the witness should answer. Federal Rule of Evidence 611(c).
- misquotes the witness. The witness said [testimony]; defense counsel said [misquote].

- misstates the evidence.
- calls for lay opinion that is (not reasonably based on the witness's perception; not helpful; misleading; in an area not recognized for lay opinion testimony).
- is repetitive.
- has been asked and answered.
- has been asked again and again. Counsel is going over and over the same ground with the witness.
- calls for a narrative response. The witness is being asked to tell a story rather than respond to questions; that prevents me from objecting to inadmissible evidence.
- calls for speculation and asks the witness to guess rather than testify as to what the witness knows. Federal Rule of Evidence 602.

HEARSAY
Objection. The question

- calls for hearsay. The jury can't evaluate the credibility of the person who talked to this witness. Federal Rules of Evidence 801-807.
- calls for self-serving testimony.
- calls for hearsay within hearsay.
- calls for hearsay by conduct.

PREJUDICIAL
Objection. The question

- is improper because any probative value of the testimony is substantially outweighed by prejudicial nature.
- is improper because it will inflame.
- is improper because it will mislead the jury.
- is improper because it will confuse the jury.
- is a waste of time, will cause undue delay, or is cumulative.

CHARACTER EVIDENCE
Objection. The question

- calls for improper character evidence. Federal Rules of Evidence 404, 405.
- calls for character evidence, and the witness has not been shown (to be familiar with So-and-So's community reputation/to be acquainted with the witness he/she seeks to support).
- calls for evidence on a character trait that is not in issue here.

PRIVILEGE
Objection. The question

- calls for disclosure of privileged communication.

EXPERT WITNESS
Objection.

- The witness has not been sufficiently qualified in the field of . . .
- The area of expertise is beyond the scope of the witness's expertise.
- The area of expertise is not generally recognized in the scientific community. *Frye v. United States*, 293 F. 1013 (1923). OR

*continued* ▶

- This purported expert testimony is not sufficiently reliable. Federal Rule of Evidence 702 and *Daubert v. Merrell Dow Pharmaceuticals Inc.*, 509 U.S. 579 (1993).
- Question calls for improper expert opinion because
  - it asks the witness to guess and would not be sufficiently certain.
  - it calls for opinion on a question of law.
  - it would be of no assistance to the jury. The facts are not sufficiently clear.

EXHIBITS

FOUNDATION

Objection.

- Chain of custody hasn't been shown. Federal Rule of Evidence 901.
- Exhibit hasn't been authenticated.

WRITINGS

Objection.

- Best evidence rule has not been complied with. The exhibit offered is not the best evidence because . . . Federal Rules of Evidence 1002, 1003.
- Business records are inadmissible because they are not shown to have been routinely made/recording was not made near the time the information was received/record not relied on in day-to-day business/custodian was not called to authenticate/sources of the information lack trustworthiness.
- Public record is inadmissible because it was not prepared by public officer under statutory duty/is not properly certified/contains prejudicial opinion. Federal Rule of Evidence 902.
- Document speaks for itself; oral testimony is unnecessary.
- Summary chart is inadmissible because it does not accurately incorporate underlying data/the original is not so voluminous as to require a summary.
- Witness's familiarity with the handwriting has not been demonstrated. Federal Rule of Evidence 901(b)(2).

PHOTOGRAPHS

Objection.

- The photograph distorts . . .
- The exhibit is inflammatory.
- The exhibit has not been shown to be an accurate representation of . . .

TREATISES

Objection.

- The use of the treatise is improper because it is not a standard in the field/is not established as reliable/cannot be used to impeach because it does not contradict the witness.
- The treatise should not be received as an exhibit. Federal Rule of Evidence 803(18).

Cross-Examination Objections

COUNSEL'S MISCONDUCT

Objection. Counsel is

- harassing and arguing with the witness.
- badgering the witness.

- misquoting the witness.
- asking a bad-faith question.
- has no factual basis for the insinuation.

PRIOR INCONSISTENT STATEMENT
Objection.

- Does not contradict the witness on a matter that is material to this case; it therefore is collateral and the party should not be permitted to put on extrinsic (evidence other than from the witness testifying) impeaching evidence.
- Is not inconsistent with the testimony of the witness. Federal Rule of Evidence 801(d).

SCOPE
Objection.

- Question goes beyond the scope of matters covered on direct.

FORM OF THE QUESTION: See Direct Examination.

## B. Phrasing the Objection

Objections should be phrased so that they convince the judge and do not offend the jury. How the objection is phrased can be either helpful or harmful to you and your case in the eyes of the jurors. Objections can be phrased in three ways or a combination of them: preferred, hypertechnical, or understandable.

### Preferred Phrasing

The preferred phrasing is simply to state, *"Objection, Your Honor,"* and follow that with the legal grounds for the objection: *"Objection. Hearsay." "Objection. Irrelevant."* And so on. This phrasing informs the judge of the grounds without elaboration. If the judge wants more, she can ask for it. This phrasing is preferred by lawyers and judges for its brevity and for being devoid of any unnecessary argument. Barring exceptional circumstances, we recommend this phrasing to you.

### Hypertechnical Phrasing

Hypertechnical phrasing of an objection to a leading question would be, *"Objection. Evidence Rule 611(c)."* Phrasing objections in a hypertechnical way should be avoided because they are not helpful to the court and can appear to the jury and judge to be an effort to impress. Citing legal authority to the court can be appropriate if the court wishes authority or when coupled with the preferred form stating the legal grounds for the objection: *"Objection. Leading, Your Honor, Evidence Rule 611(c)."*

### Understandable Phrasing

An objection is partially pitched to the jury when it is phrased in a way so that the grounds are announced in nonlegal terms to make it clear to the jury why the objection is being made. Generally, counsel should not use this type of objection because it can border on or be considered to be a *speaking objection*, one that effectively converts a legal objection into an argument to the jury ("Irrelevant. This case is about whether the jury has a reasonable doubt about my client's self-defense claims; this evidence, however . . ."). Instead, counsel should use the brief preferred phrasing.

However, some extraordinary circumstances call for making objections so that the jury can clearly understand why they are being made. An exceptional situation calling for this phrasing is when opposing counsel has made it look like objecting counsel is attempting to hide information from the jury or is deliberately delaying the proceedings. For example, opposing counsel repeatedly asks leading questions or continues to elicit hearsay despite sustained objections. When it is clear that opposing counsel is in this way trying to leave an unfavorable impression of objecting counsel with the jury, objecting counsel may consider phrasing objections in a way that jurors can clearly understand why they are being made. Again, this is only a retaliatory measure to preserve counsel's integrity in the eyes of the jury and to correct the situation. In the following examples, a *preferred phrasing* of an objection is converted into an *understandable phrasing*.

## Understandable Phrasing of Objections

- "Objection. Argumentative," becomes: "Objection. Counsel's not asking a question. She's making a speech."
- "Objection. Leading," becomes: "Objection. Counsel is testifying. He's leading the witness, again."
- "Objection. Irrelevant," becomes: "Objection. This has nothing to do with thing the jury has to decide. It's irrelevant."
- "Objection. Hearsay," becomes: "Objection. It's hearsay. The jury won't hear and assess the testimony of the person who spoke to this witness."

## C.  Requesting a Remedy

Ordinarily, you will state your objection and the grounds as, "Objection. Leading." However, you may decide that the situation calls for further action by the court. When that occurs, couple the objection and legal grounds with a request for relief from the court.

For example, if objectionable information is seen or heard by the jury before you can make an objection, you can still request that the judge take remedial steps after the information has been revealed. This might occur when a witness gives a nonresponsive answer or volunteers a statement, or when a statement or exhibit is admitted subject to its being connected later, but it never is. You can proceed with your objection by stating the objection and the grounds, interposing a motion to strike the testimony, and requesting that the judge instruct the jury to disregard the information. Suppose a witness has just responded to a question. If you wish to object, you could proceed as follows:

> *Your Honor, we move to strike the previous testimony by Peggy Clifton that plaintiff slipped on the grease. Ms. Clifton lacked personal knowledge of the facts. She didn't see what happened.*

Other examples of circumstances where additional remedial measures could be sought include these requests

- for a bench conference to argue over the objection;
- that the jury be excused because you want to argue about the objection or make a motion, such as a motion for a mistrial;
- that the judge admonish opposing counsel for improper behavior, such as stating a personal opinion; and
- for a limiting instruction (that the out-of-court statement of the witness not be considered for the truth of the matter).

## IV. MEETING OBJECTIONS

### A. Pretrial Preparation

Rather than having to respond to an objection, it is preferable to not draw an objection. To a great degree, you can accomplish this by planning your trial work so that it is not objectionable. Even if you are not successful in staving off the objection, your pretrial preparation can ready you to meet and overcome the objection. For example, if counsel wishes to introduce a computer animation, pretrial preparation would include research to determine what evidentiary foundation must be established. Counsel could prepare a motion in limine or pocket brief outlining the evidentiary requirements and how the testimony supports admissibility. Then, when counsel's direct examination asks questions necessary to lay the foundation for the admissibility of the computer animation, opposing counsel may not object. However, if opposing counsel objects, then counsel can respond, stating the law and handing the brief to the judge.

### B. Silence and Principles for Phrasing

#### Silence

When opposing counsel objects, that doesn't mean you should answer the objection. Often judges will rule on the objection without asking for a response. So, when you hear an objection, look to the court for an indication of whether you should speak. If the judge looks at you and says something like, "Counsel, any response?" or just looks at you like you need to respond, then you should. Some lawyers like to interrupt the flow of a presentation, such as a closing argument, with objections. These objections can be so meritless and their obstructionist purpose so obvious that the best response is to just look to the judge in a knowing way and say nothing. When the judge has overruled a series of these objections, opposing counsel may realize the futility of the tactic and the potential backlash from the jury and desist.

### Principles for Phrasing

The principles applicable to phrasing an objection are applicable to responding to an objection as well. Generally, the preferred response is to briefly state the legal reason that the judge should overrule the objection. For example, opposing counsel says, *"Objection. Hearsay."* Counsel who is conducting the direct examination could respond, *"Your Honor. It's not hearsay; the evidence is not offered for the truth of the matter asserted."* It is good practice to avoid a lengthy response. Judges prize brevity. In fact, you risk mentioning inadmissible evidence or confusing the court during a prolonged response. Just as with phrasing objections, it may be necessary to state your response to an objection in either the technical or understandable way, but that would only be under exceptional circumstances, such as those outlined on page 192.

## C.  Erroneous Objections

Understanding evidentiary rules and law is a prerequisite of being a trial lawyer. Armed with that knowledge, it is possible to unscramble objections that are based on misstatements of evidence law and convince the court to overrule an objection.

---

### Meeting Erroneous Objections

#### "Speaks for Itself"

**Counsel on direct examination:**
"I'm handing you Exhibit Number 30, a letter that you testified you recovered at the scene. Now that it has been admitted into evidence, please read paragraph 3 of Exhibit 30 to the jury."

**Opposing counsel:**
"Objection, Your Honor. Exhibit 30 speaks for itself."

**Counsel:**
"Your Honor, first, 'speaks for itself' is not a legal ground. Second, the exhibit does not speak. If the witness is not allowed to read from the exhibit, we will have to either pass the exhibit juror to juror or put it on the document camera so the jurors can read it."

---

"Speaks for itself" is not a legal ground that can be found in any evidence book. It is learned through courtroom practice. The judge sustains an objection when counsel asks a witness to read from a document that already has been admitted into evidence. The flawed concept is that the document is in evidence, and, therefore, it is repetitious for the witness to read from it. The mistake is that until the contents of the document are communicated to the jury, the document has not spoken. It is not repetitious. The soonest that the jurors will learn what the document says is during argument or when they are in the jury room.

---

### Erroneous Objections

#### "Prejudicial"

**Plaintiff's counsel on direct examination:**
"What did the defendant say then?"

**Witness:**
"He said that Mrs. Sanchez got what she deserved. And then he laughed."

**Defense counsel:**
"Objection. Prejudicial, Your Honor."

**Counsel:**
"What we offer will be prejudicial to defendant's case. Evidence Rule 403 provides that prejudicial evidence is admissible unless its probative value is substantially outweighed by unfair prejudice. There is nothing unfair about the witness's answer."

---

This objection is based on a partial reading of Federal Rule of Evidence 403, and an accurate and complete recitation of the rule meets the erroneous objection. When meeting these and other objections based on flawed evidentiary grounds, counsel needs to point the court either to the absence of legal authority or to the misused evidence rule.

---

### Erroneous Objections

#### "Not the Best Evidence"

**Defense counsel on direct examination:**
"Could you describe the area including the intersection where the accident took place and the adjacent streets?"

**Plaintiff's counsel:**
"Objection. Not the best evidence. If counsel wants to prove what the area looks like, she can offer a map of that section of town."

**Defense counsel:**
"Your Honor, of course the best evidence rule doesn't apply here. That rule applies to documents and when a copy can be used instead of the original. The witness should be allowed to answer."

---

Just like the "speaks for itself" objection, the "not the best evidence" objection sounds correct, but once again is based on a mistaken understanding of the Evidence Rules, 1002-1004, dealing with what traditionally was referred to as the "best evidence rule." To meet this and other erroneous objections, you first need to identify for the judge that it neither is supported by a legitimate legal ground nor properly interprets the evidence law.

While incorrectly stating the legal grounds is most common when making an objection, it can also occur when counsel tries to make an objection. An example of this is counsel's response to a hearsay objection by stating that it is not hearsay because it is not offered for the truth of the matter stated when it surely is. In answering the "not offered for the truth of the matter" claim, objecting counsel can answer by stating that if it is not offered for the truth of the matter stated, then it is irrelevant.

## D.  Perseverance

You offer the exhibit. Opposing counsel objects: *"Objection. No foundation."* The judge rules: *"Sustained."* You are puzzled and ask yourself, "What did I miss?" There are two ways to stave off this "no foundation" objection. First, you can grow old and grizzled as a trial lawyer, and then opposing counsel may not toy with you. Second, you can do what we suggested earlier in this chapter: Carefully research the foundation for the exhibit and present it perfectly.

This is not the time to give up. You may respond to the objection by arguing that it lacks specificity and that the legal grounds are not apparent from the context, as required by Federal Rule of Evidence 103(a)(1)(B). This might force opposing counsel to identify the missing foundational requirements. If that works, you can rectify the missing foundation link. Otherwise, this is the time to press on and seek to cover the missing link in the evidentiary foundation. You can go back and lay the foundation again. Yes, you may be met with "ask and answered" objections, but don't be deterred. You will get there. Keep a clear head. Perhaps if you rephrase the question, that will solve the problem. Think also about whether you will need to call another witness to satisfy the judge's concerns.

While we have been discussing the "no foundation" objection, which can be one of the most troublesome, the need to be persistent and not give up applies to responses to other objections. This need for tenaciousness is equally applicable to making objections as well. Just as the ruling sustaining the no-foundation objection can be troublesome, so can one like this: *"Objection is overruled on the grounds stated,"* which can leave you wondering, "What is a proper grounds then?" It is time to think again and identify the correct legal grounds. Don't give up.

The one caveat to this tenacious approach is that you must be courteous and respectful of the judge. When you have exhausted your options and the court has finally ruled, you should stop. An exception exists even to this caveat, and that is when you are convinced you are right and you are willing to live with the consequences of the judge holding you in contempt. Then, bring your toothbrush and wallet and be prepared for a stay in the county jail! Better to be courteous and ethical.

## V. OBJECTION STRATEGIES

Four trial strategies are essential to both successfully making and meeting objections: (1) protecting the record; (2) having the proper appearance and decorum; (3) arguing out of the jury's presence; and (4) responding to dirty, rotten tricks.

### A. Protecting the Record

While a paramount goal in objecting is to have the trial court sustain your objection, you also must think about protecting the record for appeal if the judge does not sustain your objection. Equally important in meeting objections, you will need to protect the record if the judge sustains the other party's objection. For example, if the judge excludes evidence and it is not clear from the record what the substance of the excluded evidence was, an offer of proof is required.

State law determines both how to preserve an objection for appeal and the appellate court's standard for determining whether to reverse the trial court (abuse of discretion, automatic reversal).

#### Ensuring that a Trial Record Exists

Whether making or meeting an objection, counsel should always be thinking about making sure that the trial record (for example, the court reporter's transcript and/or a video of the event) reflects the proceedings. It is helpful to think of the presence of an appellate court judge hovering over one's shoulder. With that specter in mind, counsel will make sure that the record both exists and is in proper form. Sidebar and in-chambers conferences should be made part of the record if they are of any significance. A conscientious judge will make the record. If the jury must be shielded from the discussions, the judge should make the record at the earliest opportunity when they are absent. If the judge does not do so, it is good practice for counsel who wants a record to ask the court to make a record. If the judge does not do so, counsel should do so. For instance, counsel could state, *"Your Honor, with your permission, I would like the record to show that Your Honor and all counsel have just met in chambers and discussed . . . ."* If, for some reason, the judge refuses your request to put your position on the record, put it into a written statement and file it with the clerk of the court. Consistent with this approach, do not waive the reporting of parts of the trial, such as jury selection or closing, unless there is an exceptional reason for doing so.

For visual activities in the courtroom, such as a witness's testimony about markings on a diagram that illustrate where the witness was standing when the witness observed the collision, make sure the record reflects what happened. Counsel: *"Could you take this blue marking pen and mark the diagram where you were standing and then put your initials next to the X?"*

### Making an Objection: Timely Made, Specific Grounds, Motion to Strike

Federal Rule of Evidence 103(a)(1), which was referred to earlier in the discussion of the importance of making a timely objection, spells out how to make a record of an objection. The rule states:

> (a) **Preserving a Claim of Error.** A party may claim error in a ruling to admit or exclude evidence only if the error affects a substantial right of the party and: (1) if the ruling admits evidence, a party, on the record: (A) timely objects or moves to strike; and (B) states the specific ground, unless it was apparent from the context . . .

*Timely:* An objection should be made in a timely fashion, before the answer is given, unless there is no opportunity to object or it is not apparent from the question that the answer will be inadmissible. A late objection normally should be coupled with a motion to strike. Here, we stress that to create a record for appeal, the objection must be timely or a motion to strike must be made.

*Specific Grounds:* The specific grounds for an objection should be stated: *"Objection, Your Honor. The exhibit is not the best evidence of the contents of . . . ,"* to allow the trial judge to make an informed ruling and to preserve any error for appeal.

### Meeting an Objection to Exclude Evidence: Offer of Proof

Federal Rule of Evidence 103 states:

> (a) **Preserving a Claim of Error.** A party may claim error in a ruling to admit or exclude evidence only if the error affects a substantial right of the party and: . . . (2) if the ruling excludes evidence, a party informs the court of its substance by an offer of proof, unless the substance was apparent from the context.

If an objection is made in an effort to exclude evidence that you offered and the objection is sustained, your argument against the objection generally should be accompanied by an offer of proof, except where the nature of the evidence is apparent from the questions asked. An offer of proof makes it clear on the record the relevance and purpose of the evidence that you intended to present. It also gives the trial judge another opportunity to consider the admissibility of the evidence and reverse the ruling.

Although you should be aware of and utilize an offer of proof where appropriate, there are some situations where you might not make an offer of proof. For instance, you might forgo making one if the offer is futile, the judge ruled that all evidence on the issue is inadmissible, and you do not believe you have grounds to establish reversible error on appeal, or if the record shows that the judge's ruling is clearly erroneous.

Almost universally, offers of proof are made outside the presence of the jury. Generally, they are made after the judge rules on the objection and excludes the evidence. Sometimes, however, the court may request an offer of proof prior to ruling, or you may request to present your offer of proof prior to a ruling on the objection. There are three ways to make an offer of proof: (1) written affidavit or brief, (2) testimony, or (3) oral statement by attorney.

### Written Affidavit or Brief

An offer of proof can be made in writing. That might be accomplished by sworn affidavits from witnesses or by short briefs that the attorneys would exchange and submit to the judge. Or, if the attorney anticipates that the testimony may be objectionable, the testimony could be prepared in writing, together with a brief, and the attorney would be ready to hand them to the judge prior to the objection being ruled on.

### Testimony

An offer of proof can also be made in question and answer form, Federal Rule of Evidence 103(c), or the offer can be made through live testimony. Counsel can request permission to call the witness to testify as the witness would have testified if the testimony were not excluded. If the judge grants this request, then counsel examines the witness to make a record of the offer of proof.

### Oral Statement

The easiest way to make an offer of proof is for counsel to make an oral statement to the court as to the testimony that would have been elicited from the witness if the witness had been allowed to testify on the subject. Counsel could state to the court, *"Your Honor, if I were permitted to question the witness about what plaintiff said on the date in question, the witness would testify . . . ."* When trial counsel, as an officer of the court, makes an offer of proof, the court is to presume that the offer of proof would be supported by the evidence. *People v. Lyle*, 613 P.2d 896, 898 (Colo. 1980). Usually, this is done out of the jury's presence and in open court (not at sidebar or in chambers), because the oral statement should be on the record.

### Limiting Instructions

A limiting instruction is an oral cautionary instruction that a judge may be requested to give at trial. The instruction directs the jury that the evidence may be considered by them, but only for a limited purpose. For instance, a prior conviction is admissible only for the purpose of judging the credibility of the defendant witness.

When you are meeting an objection and the court has overruled your objection, the controlling law in your jurisdiction may require you to request a limiting instruction, also referred to as a cautionary instruction. If you fail to request a cautionary instruction, some jurisdictions will find that the error is not preserved for appeal by the objection. Also, if you are meeting an objection, the evidence may not be admissible for one purpose but admissible for another. Under such circumstances, you can offer the evidence subject to a limiting instruction that it be used for the other purpose. Pattern jury instructions are often used to limit the jury's consideration of evidence to a particular purpose.

---

## Objections

### Limiting Instructions

**Civil case** typical pattern jury instruction:

Limited-Purpose Evidence—Generally

Evidence on the subject of former accidents is about to be introduced. You may consider this evidence only for the limited purpose of whether it tends to show that the common cause of the claimed damage was a dangerous condition and the defendant had knowledge of that condition. You must not consider the evidence for any other purpose.

**Criminal case** pattern instruction if a prior conviction is admitted only for impeachment:

Limited-Purpose Evidence—Prior Convictions

Before the witness is permitted to answer this question, the court advises you that the answer may be considered by you only for the purpose of deciding what weight or credibility should be given to the testimony of the witness and for no other purpose.

---

## B.  Courtroom Appearance and Decorum

The effective presentation of an objection or response to an objection requires a proper courtroom manner. You should confidently and clearly state the objection. For instance, counsel states, *"Objection, Your Honor. The question calls for a hearsay response."* This succinct statement is easily understood by the judge. Standing when you object will gain the court's attention and usually stop whatever behavior you are objecting to—generally testimony. Become familiar with courtroom customs regarding whether you need to stand when objecting or meeting an objection.

Tone of voice and counsel's demeanor can have other effects on both the judge and jury that should be considered. For instance, a vigorously declared objection can highlight the significance of the issue and information objected to for the judge. Also remember that if you appear to be involved in an all-out fight with opposing counsel over some issue, the natural inference for the jury to draw is that the matter is important and the consequences harmful to your case if you lose.

Always address the judge with your objection and arguments on the objection. No matter what opposing counsel says or does, you should not argue directly with other counsel. That means only face and address the judge. Judges detest squabbling between counsel.

Counsel should control any reaction to the judge's ruling. The best practice is to not register any visible reaction. Hide your disappointment or anger and proceed in a businesslike manner. If the court's ruling is against you, you only highlight for the jury the harm and the importance of the evidence by grimacing or showing any sort of dissatisfaction. Neither will you endear yourself to the judge with such behavior.

While courtesy toward the judge is important, this in no way implies timidity. When an objection is made, generally the judge will rule on the objection. Rather than ruling, the judge may not rule on the objection and simply say, "Just move along counsel. Ask another question." If that makes sense, then counsel should do so. On the other hand, if it does not, counsel may state, *"Could I please have the court's ruling?"*

---

### Making or Meeting Objections

#### Courtroom Decorum

In making or meeting an objection, counsel should

- confidently and clearly state the objection or response;
- know whether courtroom custom requires counsel to stand when addressing the court concerning an objection;
- stand when addressing the court to emphasize the objection or response;
- use a businesslike tone of voice and demeanor;
- address the court, never opposing counsel;
- not register a visible reaction to an adverse ruling by the judge; and
- politely insist on a ruling on the objection if the judge does not state one.

---

See the direct and cross-examination of the defendant in the *Freck Point* trial demonstration movie for how to make and meet objections on the website *http://www.aspenlawschool.com/books/berger_trialad4e.*

---

## C. Arguing out of the Jury's Presence

Counsel should not inject inadmissible evidence or comment into the trial. Federal Rule of Evidence 103(d) supports this proposition, stating that the proceedings should be conducted "[t]o the extent practicable, the court must conduct a jury trial so that inadmissible evidence is not suggested to the jury by any means." To avoid this jury contamination, counsel can either request a sidebar (also referred to as a bench conference), where counsel go to the other side of the judge's bench away from the jury and discuss the matter outside the jury's hearing, or have the jury excused to the jury room.

There are several downsides of requesting these measures. Jurors do not like secrecy. They particularly do not like sidebars. Further, if you are the counsel making the demand, it can appear that you are trying to conceal something, which in fact you are. There is always an attorney involved in the sidebar who has a stage whisper that can be heard a block away. For at least these reasons, it is good practice to avoid requesting a sidebar or to have the jury excused unless absolutely necessary.

You may have alternatives to these measures. The circumstances may permit you to reserve argument until the court takes a scheduled recess and then make the argument or motion while the jury is in the jury room. For instance, the court might sustain your objection to counsel's speaking objection, and then during the recess, you could move the court for additional remedial action, such as moving to have opposing counsel sanctioned. You can also anticipate what counsel is likely to do next and present your concern and argument to the judge in chambers or on the bench before the trial resumes, or after lunch before the jury is seated.

## D. Defeating Dirty, Rotten Tricks

Counsel should be prepared to handle unscrupulous behavior by opposing counsel in making and meeting objections. Some conduct that you must guard against is either on or over the line separating ethical and unethical behavior. In a perfect world, both the judiciary and the disciplinary arm of the bar association would protect against this behavior. However, in the real world of trial work, it is usually up to counsel to defend the client and to seek justice by not allowing unprincipled behavior to have the desired effect. The responses suggested here should be resorted to only in retaliation and then only to maintain your position and ensure a fair trial for your client.

We began our discussion of trial strategies by pointing to the necessity of making a timely objection before opposing counsel injects inadmissible evidence or improper comment into the trial (ringing the bell). A timely objection is the remedy that protects against the impropriety. Here, we offer additional illustrations of archetypal underhanded tactics and suggest remedies. We begin with objections.

### Objections: Defeating Dirty Tricks

#### Coaching the Witness

**Defense attorney interrupting cross-examination:** "Objection. The witness couldn't possibly know that."

**Witness:** "I don't know."

While an objection phrased, "Objection. Lack of personal knowledge," normally would be legitimate, counsel should not use objections to coach the witness. Repeated hints to the witness can be met by highlighting the behavior for the court. Federal Rule of Civil Procedure 30(c)(2) governing depositions requires that an objection be concise, nonargumentative, and nonsuggestive. Although no Federal Rule of Evidence counterpart exists, it is persuasive support for the response to the coaching. Plaintiff's counsel in the described situation could state: *"Your Honor, counsel is coaching the witness. We request the court to instruct counsel not to continue helping the witness."*

## Objections: Defeating Dirty Tricks

### Calming the Witness

**Defense counsel** is cross-examining the witness, who has become angry.

**Plaintiff's attorney:** "Objection. Judge, may we have a sidebar?"

Realizing that the witness has lost control and concerned that the witness is losing credibility with the jury, counsel seeks a sidebar conference not to make a genuine objection, but to give the witness an opportunity to become composed. To counter this, defense counsel can withdraw the question and move to another area of cross-examination.

## Objections: Defeating Dirty Tricks

### Voir Dire on Expert's Qualifications

**Plaintiff's attorney:** "Your Honor, may I voir dire the witness on qualifications?"

**Judge:** "You may."

**Plaintiff's attorney** begins questioning the expert witness on qualifications, such as number of times the witness has testified on this area of expertise. But then, counsel shifts to asking about the testing done in the case.

Counsel may request an opportunity to voir dire a witness to determine whether the witness is qualified to testify. In the illustration, the questioning was permitted so that counsel could determine whether the expert was qualified to testify as an expert. Counsel may request to voir dire the witness on other preliminary questions, such as whether the witness has sufficient knowledge of a person's reputation in the community to give testimony about the witness's character, or voir dire to find out whether the witness had the requisite personal knowledge to testify. If counsel under the guise of voir diring the witness begins to cross-examine the witness, the attorney who called the witness should object and seek to resume direct examination. Defense counsel here could state: *"Objection. Counsel is no longer questioning on qualifications. Counsel is cross-examining the witness. May I proceed with our direct examination?"*

---

### Objections: Defeating Dirty Tricks

#### Speaking Objection

**Defense attorney:** "Objection, Your Honor. Calls for a narrative response. This witness is being asked to tell a story rather than respond to questions, and that prevents me from objecting to inadmissible evidence—and counsel knows it. Ever since this trial began, counsel has . . . ."

---

Speaking objections are improper because they are likely to introduce inadmissible evidence and comments into the trial. Unless the judge cuts off counsel who begins making a speech, the only remedy opposing counsel has is to speak up and try to stop the speaking objection or, failing this, talk over counsel. Speaking objections or speaking responses can do irreparable harm to the other side's case. Plaintiff's counsel in this situation could attempt to speak over and drown out defense counsel: *"Objection to counsel's comments—he's making a speaking objection rather than just stating his grounds. Your Honor, speaking objections have contained unsupportable . . . ."*

## VI.  ETHICAL CONSIDERATIONS

In both making and responding to objections, you must guard against ethical abuses by opposing counsel. As you progressed though this chapter, you have learned the wiles of some counsel—for example, speaking objections, introducing inadmissible evidence, and so on—and how they can breach both ethical and legal rules. As you have also seen, the ABA Model Rules of Professional Conduct prohibit much of those tactics.

We adhere to the view that using objections merely to harass your opponent or to break the flow, such as interrupting argument or witness testimony, is unprofessional conduct. Although the ABA Model Rules do not expressly discuss this behavior, Rule 3.2 states that a "lawyer shall make reasonable efforts to expedite litigation consistent with the interests of the client," and the result of such interruptions is to delay litigation for no legitimate reason. You should recognize, however, that some attorneys believe, or at least act as if they do, that interrupting the flow of the opposing counsel's examination is a proper trial strategy and engage in this type of conduct. In that case, you can object to your opponent's conduct, especially if the bulk of the objections are not well founded.

## Ethical Rules Pertaining to Objections

### ABA Model Rules of Professional Conduct

**Rule 3.2:** Rule 3.2 provides that counsel "shall make reasonable efforts to expedite litigation consistent with the interests of the client."

**Rule 3.4:** Rule 3.4 prohibits various acts of lawyer misconduct:

PERSONAL OPINION: Counsel shall not state "personal knowledge of facts in issue except when testifying as a witness, or . . . personal opinion as to the justness of a cause, the credibility of a witness, the culpability of a civil litigant or the guilt or innocence of an accused."

OVERSTATING: Counsel shall not mention "any matter . . . that will not be supported by admissible evidence."

INJECTING IRRELEVANT MATTER: Counsel shall not allude to matter counsel "does not reasonably believe is relevant."

**Rule 3.5:** Rule 3.5 prohibits counsel from disrupting the proceedings.

APPENDIX
SAMPLE MEMORANDUM OF LAW
IN SUPPORT OF DEFENDANT'S MOTION IN LIMINE

Hon. Sarah Lympus
Trial Date: Monday October 11, 20XX+2

SUPERIOR COURT OF MAJOR
JAMNER COUNTY

| | | |
|---|---|---|
| KATHLEEN BRENNEMAN, | ) | |
| | ) | Case No.: XX-4-44922-RUS |
| Plaintiff, | ) | |
| | ) | |
| vs. | ) | DEFENDANT SAMUEL L. GRIFFITH |
| | ) | MOTION IN LIMINE MEMORANDUM |
| | ) | OF LAW |
| SAMUEL L. GRIFFITH, | ) | |
| | ) | |
| Defendant | ) | |
| _____ | ) | |

## I. RELIEF REQUESTED

Defendant Samuel L. Griffith requests this court in limine to exclude any reference to the death of Mr. Griffith's first wife, Marian Griffith, during the trial of the above-entitled cause.

## II. STATEMENT OF FACTS

**A.  The murder of Mr. Griffith's current wife, Sondra Griffith**

Mr. Griffith's wife Sondra was killed by an intruder who entered their home and stabbed her to death in her own bed. (Ex. B, Decl. Samuel L. Griffith ¶2-3.) On Saturday night, October 16, two years ago, the defendant, Samuel Griffith, then 55, and his wife Sondra, 51, spent the evening together in their home on Freck Point, a neighborhood in Ruston, Major. They had been married 12 years. The defendant, a Marine Corp veteran, is a writer of mysteries who has had some success. His wife, Sondra, was a high-paid executive with Shepard Pharmaceuticals Corp. After dinner, they watched a DVD of an old movie, *A Place in the Sun*. (Ex. B ¶4.)

Following the movie, the two changed into bathrobes and went out to their hot tub in the gazebo. The gazebo was situated some 30 yards behind the house and separated from the house by a tall hedge. There they sat and drank wine

MOTION IN LIMINE MEMORANDUM OF LAW-1 of 7

LAW OFFICES OF RICHARDSON, FARMER & DAY
962 Hood Ave.
Ruston, Major 98102
(206) 328-1748

until midnight, when Mrs. Griffith said that she was going to bed. Mr. Griffith stayed by the pool reading a book. (Ex. B ¶5.)

Around 1:00 A.M., Mr. Griffith went inside the house, entering through the back door. As he was heading to the stairs leading up to their bedroom, he noticed the front door open and heard a sound upstairs. He ran up the stairs, and at the top of the stairs he saw a man approximately 6 feet 2 inches tall coming from their bedroom. The man, who had a knife in his right hand, pushed Mr. Griffith aside, ran down the stairs, and escaped out the front door. (Ex. B ¶6.)

Mr. Griffith entered his bedroom and found his wife lying on the bed. She had multiple stab wounds. Mr. Griffith tried to revive his wife, but she was dead. He called 911 at 1:10 p.m. Mr. Griffith saw that his wife's wedding ring was missing from her left-hand index finger and that the drawers in the dresser and the bedside table were open. A jewelry box on the dresser was open, and, at a glance, Mr. Griffith could see that jewelry was missing. When the Ruston Police arrived eight minutes later, Mr. Griffith told them what happened. (Ex. B ¶7-8.)

Following Sondra Griffith's death, Kathleen Brenneman filed a wrongful death complaint alleging that Mr. Samuel Griffith killed his wife, Sondra Griffith.

Kathleen Brenneman, the plaintiff, is the adopted daughter of Sam and Sondra Griffith. During Sam Griffith's nine-year marriage to his first wife, Marian, they lived with Marian Griffith's daughter, Kathleen, from her first marriage. Together, Sam and Marian had a son, Matthew, who was 8 years old, and a daughter, Molly, who was 13 years old on the day their mother died. After Marian died, the three children lived with Marian's first husband. When he died in a car crash, Sam and Sondra adopted Kathleen as well as Marian and Sam's children, Matthew and Molly. (Ex. A, Pl.'s Resps. Def.'s Interrogs., Interrog. 5.)

Plaintiff seeks, under the State of Major's "slayer statute," to be declared the beneficiary of Mrs. Sondra Griffith's life insurance policy and to gain the proceeds from that policy. (Ex. A, Pl.'s Resps. Def.'s Interrogs., Interrog. 5.)

Mr. Griffith anticipates that plaintiff will attempt to offer evidence of and refer to circumstances of the death of Mr. Griffith's first wife, Marian. It is this evidence that Mr. Griffith moves in limine to exclude as unfairly prejudicial and improper propensity evidence. (Ex. B ¶8.)

**B. The death of Mr. Griffith's first wife, Marian Griffith**

Marian Griffith died in a boating and swimming accident on August 20, 16 years before Mr. Griffith's second wife was murdered. (Ex. C., Or. Med. Examiner Autopsy Report.) On that day, Mr. Griffith and his wife Marian were boating at Priest Lake, Oregon, where they were on vacation. Their children were visiting relatives. The couple, in an inflatable raft at first, then got in the water to swim. Marian developed a leg cramp and clung to the raft. A wake from a speedboat caused their raft to overturn. Marian Griffith coughed and went underwater. Mr. Griffith rescued her, righted the raft, pulled her into it, and then

LAW OFFICES OF RICHARDSON, FARMER & DAY
962 Hood Ave.
Ruston, Major 98102
(206) 328-1748

attempted CPR. Mr. Griffith rowed to shore; however, by the time they reached shore, Marian was dead. (Ex. D, Richland County Sheriff's Report, ¶10.)

Richland County Sheriff detectives thoroughly investigated the circumstances of Marian Griffith's death. (Ex. D.) The Oregon Medical Examiner determined that Marian Griffith died from asphyxia due to drowning and classified the death as "possible accident." (Ex. C.) The Richland County, Oregon, District Attorney's Office reviewed the case. Proof of homicide was insufficient as evidenced by the Richland County District Attorney, which never filed charges against Mr. Griffith. (Ex. E, Decl. Carey Hubbard, Dist. Atty.) Mr. Griffith collected proceeds from his first wife's life insurance policy. (Ex. B ¶11.)

## III. ISSUES PRESENTED

Issue 1: Is evidence relating to the death of Mr. Griffith's first wife inadmissible because the plaintiff has not proved by even a preponderance of the evidence the alleged prior misconduct, that Mr. Griffith killed his first wife, when Mr. Griffith has never been charged with causing the death and the evidence is consistent with an accidental drowning?

Issue 2: Is evidence relating to the death of Mr. Griffith's first wife inadmissible when the plaintiff cannot establish a legitimate purpose for admitting the evidence other than to show propensity?

Issue 3: Is evidence relating to the death of Mr. Griffith's first wife inadmissible when the admission of that evidence is unfairly prejudicial?

## IV. EVIDENCE RELIED ON

Last year, the Major Supreme Court held that an evidentiary hearing is not required for the trial court to decide the question of admissibility under Rule 404(b) and that a narrative offer of proof was sufficient. *State v. Inouie*, 154 Maj. 2d 211, 219 (20XX-1). Discovery has been completed, and Mr. Griffith relies on a documentary record. This motion is based on the Declaration of Laura Richardson with attached Exhibits A-F:

Exhibit A: Plaintiff's Responses to Defendant's Interrogatories
Exhibit B: Declaration of Samuel L. Griffith
Exhibit C: Oregon Medical Examiner Autopsy Report
Exhibit D: Richland County Sheriff's Report
Exhibit E: Declaration of Carey Hubbard, District Attorney
Exhibit F: The records and files of the Jamner County Clerk, Case Number XX-4-44922-RUS

MOTION IN LIMINE MEMORANDUM OF LAW-3 of 7

LAW OFFICES OF RICHARDSON, FARMER & DAY
962 Hood Ave.
Ruston, Major 98102
(206) 328-1748

## V. ARGUMENT

Major Evidence Rule 404(b)(1) provides, "Evidence of a crime, wrong, or other act is not admissible to prove a person's character in order to show that on a particular occasion the person acted in accordance with the character." MER 404(b) is applicable to civil cases. *Ainsworth v. McDermott*, 255 Maj. 3d 122 (20XX-4). Rule 404(b)(1) codifies the well-established evidentiary principle that prior acts of misconduct are inadmissible to establish that a defendant is immoral or a criminal and because of this, is the "kind of person" who is likely to have committed the alleged act. The concept is that the defendant is to be tried based on the acts he is alleged to have committed. He is not to be tried for unproven past misconduct, which is likely to be more prejudicial than probative. A serious risk exists that the jury will misuse it as character evidence.

The State of Major's seminal case interpreting the meaning of Rule 404(b)(1) is *State v. Ward*, 290 Maj. 2d 333 (20XX-25). *Ward* promulgated a three-tiered analytical approach with stringent foundational requirements that must be met before misconduct evidence may be introduced under Rule 404(b)(1):

> The trial court must make three preliminary findings. *First*, the trial court must find by a preponderance of evidence that the bad acts, other than the crime charged, occurred. On this issue we agree with the appellant and impose a higher burden of proof than *Huddleston v. United States*, 485 U.S. 681 (1988), which calls only for evidence sufficient for the jury to conclude the act occurred and that the defendant committed the act. *Second*, the trial court must find the evidence materially relevant to an identifiable, legitimate purpose. *Third*, under MER 403, the trial court must balance the unfair prejudicial effect of the evidence against its probative value. (Emphasis added.)

### 1. Evidence relating to the death of Mr. Griffith's first wife should be excluded because the plaintiff cannot prove by a preponderance of the evidence that Mr. Griffith killed his first wife.

*State v. Ward* makes it clear that the trial court must find that any prior bad acts, in this case the alleged murder of Mr. Griffith's first wife, occurred by a preponderance of the evidence.

Applying the first *Ward* test, evidence of Marian Griffith's death is irrelevant and in violation of Rules 401 and 402's relevancy requirements that must be satisfied before misconduct evidence is admissible. *State v. Ward*, 290 Maj. 2d at 338, and *State v. Cox*, 154 Maj. App. 24, 30 (Div. 2 20XX-1). "In the MER 404(b) context, misconduct evidence is relevant only if a preponderance of evidence proves the misconduct." *State v. Ward*, 290 Maj. 2d at 338. Plaintiff

LAW OFFICES OF RICHARDSON, FARMER & DAY
962 Hood Ave.
Ruston, Major 98102
(206) 328-1748

Brenneman cannot prove by a preponderance of evidence that Marian Griffith's death was the result of a homicide.

No significant evidence, let alone a preponderance of evidence, proves that Marian Griffith' death was the result of a homicide. Mr. Griffith was never charged with murdering Marian Griffith. The evidence, consistent with the medical examiner's findings (Ex. C), points to a tragic accidental death. While Marian Griffith was swimming with her husband, she developed a leg cramp. She went underwater and drowned when the wake from a nearby boat capsized the inflatable raft that she was clinging to for safety. (Ex. B ¶10.) Marian Griffith died from asphyxia due to drowning. The Oregon State Medical Examiner classified the death as "possible accident," not homicide. (Ex. C.)

### 2. Evidence relating to the death of Mr. Griffith's first wife is inadmissible because it has no legitimate purpose other than to show propensity.

It would be mere speculation to conclude that evidence of Mr. Griffith's first wife's accidental death was probative to show a legitimate purpose, such as intent or common scheme or plan. Therefore, the death of Marian Griffith is neither probative for a proper purpose in the current trial nor relevant to any issue raised by allegations against the defendant in the wrongful death complaint.

Evidence of the death of Samuel Griffith's first wife Marian fails to satisfy the second *Ward* prerequisite that the evidence serves an identifiable, legitimate purpose. Misconduct evidence may be admissible provided it is relevant to another purpose besides showing that the defendant is a generally dangerous person. Rule 404(b)(2) expresses this limited exception as follows: "[t]his evidence may be admissible for another purpose, such as proving motive, opportunity, intent, preparation, plan, knowledge, identity, absence of mistake, or lack of accident . . ." While the plaintiff may attempt to claim that Marian Griffith's death reveals a modus operandi, some overall "scheme or plan," a careful look at these claims reveals that neither is logically nor materially probative to any legitimate purpose.

Misconduct may be admissible to prove modus operandi. Under this doctrine, the similarities of the alleged acts and the other unalleged acts can be used to prove that the same person committed alleged acts, such as identity. However, this doctrine demands that the unalleged acts must be so distinctive as to be a "signature." *State v. Canova*, 10 Maj. App. 215, 121 (Div. 1 20XX-7). The circumstances of the defendant's first and second wives' deaths were strikingly dissimilar.

- His first wife died by drowning; the second wife by stabbing.
- The first death allegedly resulted from an accident; in the second death, an intentional act.

LAW OFFICES OF RICHARDSON, FARMER & DAY
962 Hood Ave.
Ruston, Major 98102
(206) 328-1748

- In the first death, only the defendant and his wife were involved; in the second death, a third person was central.
- In the first death, the defendant was with his wife at the time of the alleged accident; in the second death, he arrived after the fatal stabbing.
- In the first death, the alleged accident happened in full public view; in the second death, within the privacy of the home.

Therefore, the modus operandi doctrine is inapplicable.

Plaintiff might contend that the misconduct evidence proves a common scheme or plan that the defendant was motivated to kill Sondra Griffith for the insurance money. Divisions 3 and 4 of the Major Court of Appeals differ on the interpretation of this exception to Rule 404(b)(2). Division 4 in *State v. Matovich*, 90 Maj. App. 60 (20XX-4) held that for this exception to apply, the crime charged must have as an element the proof of common scheme or plan. Because wrongful death does not have common scheme or plan as an element, this exception can be summarily dismissed.

However, in *State v. Tilly*, 125 Maj. App. 296 (20XX-5), Division 5 held that the scheme or plan need not be an element but can be an overarching one and that the charged crime must be a part that comes under the umbrella plan. Applying the *Tilly* analysis to this case, the circumstances of Marian Griffith's death are also inadmissible. No evidence suggests that Mr. Griffith had an overarching plan to defraud life insurance companies. It is inconceivable that he murdered his first wife to collect insurance and then waited 16 years to complete his scheme by murdering his second wife for the insurance money. The evidence does not support an allegation that Mr. Griffith killed either wife.

Plaintiff cannot rely on *State v. Linde*, 95 Maj. App. 332 (Div. 1 20XX-4), where misconduct evidence was admissible to "rebut a claim of accident" raised at trial. Defendant has never contended that his wife Sondra's death was the result of an accident; she was murdered by an intruder.

### 3. Under MER 403, the trial court must balance the unfair prejudicial effect of the evidence against its probative value.

Before prior misconduct evidence is admissible, Major Evidence Rule 403 requirements must be met. *State v. Ward*, 290 Maj. 2d at 340. MER 403 provides in part:

> The court may exclude relevant evidence if its probative value is substantially outweighed by a danger of . . . unfair prejudice . . .

In conducting this balancing, the plaintiff has nothing to place on its side of the scales. The plaintiff cannot prove by a preponderance of evidence that Mr. Griffith killed his first wife. Consequently, circumstances surrounding

LAW OFFICES OF RICHARDSON, FARMER & DAY
962 Hood Ave.
Ruston, Major 98102
(206) 328-1748

the death of his first wife are not probative for any legitimate purpose under Rule 404(b)(2). Further, assuming, but not conceding, that sufficient evidence exists to prove that the defendant killed his first wife, as discussed in regard to the second *Ward* test, the misconduct evidence would not be probative on any legitimate purpose under Rule 404(b)(2).

Even if the court were to find the death of Marian Griffith marginally relevant in the current case, the unfair prejudice would be overwhelming, "substantially" more unfairly prejudicial than any possible probative inferences. The jury would not even focus on the issues in the current case. To the jury, defendant would be a "killer" and more, "a wife killer" who got away with it the first time. It would be all but impossible for them to fairly weigh the evidence concerning Sondra's death once they hear about Marian.

Finally, plaintiff may argue that as a safeguard against the unfairly prejudicial nature of the bad character evidence, the jury could be given an instruction that they should use the evidence only for a specified purpose. However, any limiting instruction that the jurors not misuse this evidence in question would be ineffectual. Once the jurors have been poisoned, they will not be able to ignore it.

## VI. CONCLUSION

Rule 404(b)(1) prohibits the introduction into evidence of propensity evidence. Admitting any reference to Marian Griffith's death into the trial of this cause would interject propensity evidence and create a grave danger that the jury would misuse it. Rule 404(b)(1) states the well-established evidentiary principle that prior acts of misconduct are inadmissible to establish that a defendant is the "kind of person" to commit such a crime and therefore is likely to have committed the alleged act. The defendant must be tried based on the acts he is alleged to have committed. He is not to be tried for unproven past misconduct, which is unfairly prejudicial.

Mr. Griffith respectfully requests that the Court preclude the plaintiff from referring to or offering any evidence regarding the circumstances of his first wife's death during the trial of the above-entitled cause.

DATED: August 2, 20XX + 2

RICHARDSON, FARMER & DAY, PLLC
By *Laura Richardson*
Laura Richardson, MSBA No. 23544

MOTION IN LIMINE MEMORANDUM OF LAW-7 of 7

LAW OFFICES OF RICHARDSON, FARMER & DAY
962 Hood Ave.
Ruston, Major 98102
(206) 328-1748

## CHECKLIST: MAKING AND MEETING OBJECTIONS

**Making Objections**

*Purpose*

The objection is intended to accomplish:

☐ Controlling the information to the jury (exclude evidence),
☐ Controlling opposing counsel from alluding to inadmissible evidence, or
☐ Preserving error for appeal.

*Judgment*

Counsel exercises judgment in objecting, ensuring that

☐ the objection is made on legal and factual grounds,
☐ the objection is consistent with counsel's case theory, and
☐ the objection considers the audience—jury and judge.

*Meet Judicial Expectations*

Counsel meets the judge's expectations:

☐ Stands when objecting unless physically challenged;
☐ Addresses the court, does not argue with opposing counsel;
☐ Only the attorney handling the witness objects;
☐ Uses the preferred form of objecting unless circumstances require a different form; and
☐ In a bench trial:
   • Determines what the judge wants during pretrial; or
   • If counsel does not know the judge's practice, counsel objects only when necessary.

*Trial Strategies*

☐ The objection is timely made, shielding the jury from inadmissible evidence.
☐ The objection is stated appropriately either in preferred, technical, or understandable phrasing, depending on the situation.
☐ The objection is coupled with a request for a special remedy if one is needed (for example, strike the testimony, a cautionary instruction).
☐ When the objection is designed to protect the record, counsel
   • makes sure that the record exists,
   • states specific grounds for the objection, and
   • requests a limiting instruction if necessary.
☐ Counsel's demeanor, tone of voice, and behavior are proper (for example, counsel does not engage in banter with opposing counsel).
☐ Counsel requests a sidebar or to have the jury excused when argument or evidence should not be heard by the jury.
☐ Counsel objects to improper behavior of opposing counsel.

*continued* ▶

## Meeting Objections

### Preparation

☐ Counsel is prepared to meet the objection with factual and legal arguments.

☐ Counsel has prepared a pocket brief for major issues.

### Silence or Phrasing

☐ Counsel remains silent, awaiting the court's ruling, when no response is necessary.

☐ Counsel's response to the objection succinctly states the legal response, unless the court requests argument or an explanation.

### Trial Strategies

☐ Counsel protects the record by making sure there is one.

☐ Counsel makes an offer of proof when evidence is excluded, unless the evidence is evident from the context.

☐ Counsel requests a limiting instruction if necessary.

☐ Counsel's demeanor, tone of voice, and behavior are proper (for example, counsel does not engage in banter with opposing counsel).

☐ Counsel requests a sidebar or to have the jury excused when argument or evidence should not be heard by the jury.

## Ethical Boundaries: Making and Meeting Objections

In objecting or responding, counsel does not

☐ state an improper personal opinion,

☐ mention any matter that is not supported by admissible evidence,

☐ inject irrelevant information, or

☐ engage in conduct that causes an unwarranted delay in the proceedings.

# INTRODUCING EXHIBITS

*"If it doesn't fit. If it doesn't fit, you must acquit."*

—**Johnnie Cochran**, referring to gloves
found at the crime scene in the 1995
*O.J. Simpson* murder trial

## I.  GETTING EXHIBITS ADMITTED

Exhibits can prove elements of your case theory, and they can refute the other side's case theory. They can explain, highlight, and enliven both testimony and the presentation of the case. They can be used at any stage of trial as we indicate in other chapters of this book—from jury selection through closing argument.

In this chapter, we explore the decision-making process for determining when you should use an exhibit at trial and, equally important, when you shouldn't. We discuss evidentiary foundations for introducing an exhibit into evidence, and the courtroom mechanics for introducing an exhibit into evidence and displaying it to the jury. As such, this and the next chapter, which covers the visual trial and technology, are extensions of Chapter 2, Persuasion Principles, where we discuss at length why visual exhibits are so critical to trial persuasion. Accompanying this book are these supplementary materials about exhibits:

- Trial Movie: On our website (URL below), you can watch experienced lawyers introducing exhibits and displaying them for the jury.
- Website: The website for this book, *http://www.aspenlawschool.com/books/berger_trialad4e,* contains additional trial visuals.

## II.  PLANNING TO USE EXHIBITS

### A.  Objectives for Introducing Exhibits

A primary objective in introducing exhibits at trial is to communicate substantive information supporting your case theory or weakening the other side's case theory. Visuals are essential in persuading a jury, engaging the jury, and assisting the jury in retaining information. Exhibits bring a realistic quality to case presentation and highlight important factual or legal matters. The use of exhibits and visuals are also essential persuasion in alternative dispute resolution. Our reference to trial applies equally to alternative presentations.

### B.  Preparation

Preparation is at the core of proficient use of exhibits. Planning begins in the pretrial process. Early in your preparation, you should begin to identify and obtain potential exhibits. As you approach closer to the trial, you will need to determine which items you will actually offer at trial. In this section, we present a two-part preparatory process: (1) identifying and creating potential exhibits, and (2) selecting exhibits that you intend to offer into evidence at trial.

## 1. Identifying and Creating Potential Exhibits

During your preparation, you want to identify and examine all potential exhibits currently in existence. For instance, to examine all of the evidence in existence, you must visit the scene of the incident—for example, the place where the crane collapsed or the cars collided. In the *Freck Point* case, you want to visit both Sam and Sondra Griffith's residence and Priest Lake, where Marian's drowning occurred. You, your investigator, and a professional photographer will then photograph pertinent objects or conditions. You will also dispatch your investigator to collect evidence—a public record, for example. Discovery in a civil case further enables you to gain possession of potential exhibits. For example, your requests for production can provide access to documents, electronically stored information, and entry onto premises for inspection and testing.

---

### Creating Exhibits

The search for exhibits does not stop once you have gathered existing evidence. Instead, think about and create demonstrative evidence. Review your case with these questions in mind.

- **What significant aspects of the case need to be persuasively presented?** For example, how could a diagram of the Griffith house and surrounding area assist in showing the jury where the knife and Sprite can were found in relationship to the house?
- **What is complex and needs simplification?** For instance, how can a computer slideshow, such as PowerPoint, aid a DNA expert to explain DNA evidence to the jury?
- **What is missing?** For example, if the weapon used to kill Sondra were missing, would it help to find one like it that could be offered as demonstrative evidence to show what the weapon looked like?

---

Perhaps in consultation with experts, you decide to use an exhibit. You will need the exhibit created. This may involve employing others to develop the exhibit or doing it within your law office.

## 2. Selecting Exhibits

You will need to evaluate the exhibit's likely effect on the case before actually creating the exhibit. The initial impact that the potential exhibit made on you is a good indicator of how it will affect the jury. Consider the following before using an exhibit.

## When Exhibits Should Be Used
### *Accentuate the Positive and Eliminate the Negative*

The value of an exhibit lies in its persuasive power to bolster your case theory and undercut the other side's case theory. The analysis centers on those ingredients that make up your legal and factual theories. Consider whether the exhibit supports or enriches these aspects of the persuasive factual theory:

- Human values,
- Human needs,
- Human story,
- Believable and understandable story,
- Quantity of evidence, and
- Quality of evidence.

Examples of how visuals can achieve these ends of accentuating the positive and eliminating the negative are found throughout this book.

### *Complex Information*

Typically, information offered at trial can be complex in two ways. First, the subject, such as expert testimony, can be conceptually difficult in a scientific field such as DNA. Or second, the quantity of information presented to the jury can be too much to grasp. For example, the case may involve numerous transactions involving several parties. Under either circumstance, demonstrative evidence is effective in simplifying the complicated. Edward R. Tufte, author, professor, and expert in information design, puts it this way: "What is to be sought in designs for the display of information is the clear portrayal of complexity. Not the complication of the simple; rather the task of the designer is to give visual access to the subtle and the difficult—that is—the revelation of the complex." Edward R. Tufte, *Visual Display of Quantitative Information* (2d ed., Graphics Press 2001). For example, a summary chart can be used to condense and summarize a mound of hospital records. Similarly, a computer slideshow with illustrations can simplify an explanation of scientific evidence. Examples of how visuals can achieve this end of simplifying the complex with a summary chart are found at pages 250-251, 257-258, and 327-328.

### *Integrity*

To be convincing and of value, the exhibit must be believable. Should it prove to be other than trustworthy, it can damage your case: A model that collapses or a computer-generated animation that is admitted into evidence over an objection. Or an exhibit that is inaccurate or visually misleading can backfire against the attorney who offers it. The exhibit's lack of integrity can undermine the fact finder's belief in the trustworthiness of the case. Generally, the impact that the potential exhibit makes on you is a good indicator of the effect that it will have on the jury. It is also beneficial to show the potential exhibit to others for their comments.

### When Exhibits Shouldn't Be Used

Knowing when not to offer an exhibit that will damage your case is at least as important as knowing when to use an exhibit that will be advantageous. Here are some guidelines.

#### *Exhibit Lacks Integrity*

If the exhibit appears inaccurate or in any way misleading, it should not be offered into evidence.

#### *Exhibit Accentuates the Negative and Eliminates the Positive*

Because the goal of introducing exhibits in trial is to support your case theory or undercut your opponent's, it is axiomatic that if the reverse could result from an exhibit, it should not be offered. For instance, the defense in the *Blue Moon News Robbery* case offers a photo of the scene that actually gives the impression that the lighting was better than what the defense has been asserting.

#### *Attorney or Witness Is Unprepared*

If the attorney or the witness is unprepared to work with the exhibit, the exhibit is likely to be ineffective. If, for example, the attorney using a complex timeline to explain the chronology of events points to the exhibit and reveals a lack of knowledge about what happened on the date marked on the timeline, neither the lawyer nor the timeline are of much use in imparting information. Preparing the witness to both lay the foundation for admission of and then display of the exhibit is likewise essential. Never risk an unrehearsed courtroom demonstration. See "Prepare Your Witness" at page 221.

#### *Too Many*

Exhibits, particularly of the demonstrative kind, can be overused. The potential effect of overusing exhibits is that they will confuse the case and overwhelm, confound, or even bore the jury.

## C. Legal Research and Briefing

You must determine whether each exhibit is admissible. Many exhibits, such as photographs, require minimal research because their evidentiary predicates (also referred to as foundation questions) are easily understood and met. Generally you should prepare a trial brief on any problematic and key evidentiary issues, such as a computer animation. Research will reveal the necessary legal requirements for a proper evidentiary foundation. Briefing the issues gives you legitimate opportunities to present the court with a favorable recitation of the facts in addition to serving the primary function of providing persuasive legal authority for admitting the exhibit.

### Motion in Limine

When you intend to offer a significant exhibit, opposing counsel may file a motion in limine to exclude it prior to trial. When that happens, you can file a responsive brief. Or you may take the initiative and employ a motion in limine to move the admission of the exhibit and file a legal memorandum supporting its admissibility. This proactive strategy can generate a clear pretrial ruling and a chance to remedy an exhibit that the court finds in part inadmissible. By redoing the exhibit, you can eliminate aspects the court finds objectionable.

### Pocket Brief

What can you do if opposing counsel has not filed a motion in limine, and you are unsure about whether opposing counsel will object when you offer the exhibit? If you flag the issue of admissibility by submitting a brief, you increase the likelihood that opposing counsel will object or move in limine to exclude the exhibit. The strategic solution to this dilemma is to prepare a pocket brief on the admissibility of the exhibit (you figuratively keep it "in your pocket" until needed). You can present the brief to the court if opposing counsel objects to admissibility of your exhibit. Naturally we assume here that the court rules or practices do not require pretrial resolution of issues of admissibility regarding exhibits. See pages 185-186 about objections and pocket brief.

### Evidentiary Foundation Questions

You want your presentation of an exhibit to flow and have impact. You want to avoid having your presentation interrupted by objections and arguments over whether a proper foundation for admissibility has been laid. The way to accomplish this is to know how to lay a proper evidentiary foundation for a variety of pieces of evidence.

Legal research can construct an effective set of foundation questions (also referred to as predicate questions). Look at model evidentiary foundations. You can then reshape and mold questions to your case and style. In this chapter, at pages 244-251, we provide you with a sample foundation.

Several resource books exist for drafting predicate questions. Many states have courtroom handbooks with foundational predicate questions designed for compliance with the particular state's evidence law. They are often accompanied by a commentary annotated with the state's case law. One of the best books is Edward J. Imwinkelried, *Evidentiary Foundations* (8th ed., LexisNexis 2012). Another valuable resource is Steven Guy Goode and Olin Guy Wellborn III, *Courtroom Evidence Handbook* (Thomson/West 2007). Another source for model foundations is 86 Am. Jur., *Proof of Facts*. For more elaborate and unique foundations, you might look to your colleagues who have successfully laid a similar foundation and review their relevant trial transcripts.

In the case files on the website, *http://www.aspenlawschool.com/books/ berger_trialad4e*, you will find excerpts of *Morgan's Evidentiary Foundations Courtroom Handbook for State of Major Trial Lawyers. Morgan's Evidentiary Foundations* is a fictional yet useful handbook with evidentiary foundations and case law; it can be used in doing this chapter's assignments, which involve laying foundations and introducing exhibits.

## D. Prepare Your Witness

Imagine this scene: Counsel shows the witness an enlarged aerial photograph of the witness's business district for the first time when the witness is testifying at trial. In response to the question of whether the witness can identify what is in the photograph, the witness says: "I'm not sure." The witness then tilts her head trying to get another angle view of the scene, but to no avail. The judge looks at counsel quizzically. Opposing counsel suppresses a grin. The jury waits. You *never* want to experience this. The rule is to *never* surprise your witness with an exhibit. Prior to trial, you should show the witness any exhibit that the witness will testify about or use in trial.

Your pretrial discussion should include everything you will call on the witness to do with the exhibit in trial. This discussion should include how the exhibit will be displayed. For example, if the witness is right-handed and is going to be marking on a diagram on an easel, the lawyer should instruct the witness to stand to the left side of the diagram and write with the right hand to avoid obstructing the jury's view of the diagram with the witness's body. Further, the lawyer can instruct the witness how the witness will be asked to mark on the diagram: "Please mark the diagram with an X where the witness stood, and place the witness's initials next to the X, and use a dotted line to show a path of motion on the diagram." Of course, you will not go word for word through this with the witness, but you can give the witness examples of how it will be done in the courtroom so the witness will be accustomed to the process.

If you plan to have the witness engage in a courtroom reenactment, you will need to practice the demonstration repeatedly. This rehearsal should include other participants who may be called on to play a part with the witness.

## E. The Exhibit List

To organize your exhibits and keep track of them and rulings on their admissibility during trial, you will need an exhibit list. The form of the list should be one with which you are comfortable. This is an example of an exhibit list you might consider:

| EXHIBIT LIST | | | | | |
|---|---|---|---|---|---|
| *Exhibit Description* | *Exhibit Number* | *Foundation Witnesses* | *Offered Date/Time* | *Admitted/ Refused* | *Comments* |
| | | | | | |
| | | | | | |

An exhibit list can track all actions taken with your exhibits as well as the other side's exhibits. You can note when an exhibit is offered and whether it is admitted or refused, noting the time and date. When anyone questions what happened with an exhibit, you can respond with details, such as the hour it was received into evidence and who the sponsoring witness was.

While the list seems foolproof, errors by you or the clerk are possible. Therefore, before you rest your case, you must check with the court clerk to make sure that your list comports with the clerk's record. You do not want to neglect to get an exhibit into evidence through inadvertence.

## F. Judicial Expectations

It is common for judges to have particular ways that they want exhibits prepared and presented. The following are some of them:

### Judicial Expectations: Exhibits

**Do Not Display Until Admitted:** Counsel is expected to shield the jurors from seeing an exhibit until the judge admits it into evidence.

**Premarking:** Judges like to save court time by having counsel mark exhibits prior to trial. The judge may have a preferred method of premarking and submitting the exhibits. For example, King County Superior Court Judge Timothy Bradshaw developed the following instructions for counsel appearing before him:

> Counsel/parties will present two sets of Exhibits. The first (original set) will be marked by the Clerk and used at trial. The second (copy) set is a working copy for the Judge. Plaintiff/Petitioner's Trial Exhibits shall begin with the Number "1" and shall be numbered consecutively up to the last proposed Exhibit. Defendant/Respondent's Trial Exhibits will begin with the number which follows Plaintiff/Petitioner's last proposed Trial Exhibit. Exhibits presented during trial will be marked and designated by the Court Clerk. Once the Clerk has marked an Exhibit, it is officially in his/her custody.

**Depositions:** The judge may have preferences as to how counsel should prepare and offer depositions. For example, United States District Court Judge Stephen P. Friot published these procedures for depositions:

> Depositions: If rulings will be necessary with respect to any testimony to be read from depositions, transcripts of the depositions shall be delivered to chambers not later than noon on Thursday of the week before the week the trial is scheduled to start. (If rulings are necessary as to any prerecorded deposition testimony that counsel intend to present with audio-visual equipment, the transcripts, marked as set forth below, should be submitted to the court at least seven days before the edited testimony is intended to be presented, unless other arrangements are discussed with and approved

by the court, so as to assure sufficient time for any necessary editing of the video record.) The passages that the proponent of the deposition testimony intends to read shall be highlighted in green. The passages counter-designated by any other parties shall be highlighted in yellow. (Passages more than one page long may be marked with a vertical highlight of the appropriate color in the left margin.) To the cover of each such deposition transcript there shall be attached a list of objections, by page and line number, stating the basis for the objection. The objections shall also be noted with handwritten notations at the appropriate places within the deposition transcript. Use good judgment (and be realistic) when lodging objections to deposition testimony. Bear in mind that deposition testimony does not become objectionable just because you wish the witness had not said what he said.

*http://www.okwd.uscourts.gov/files/jfriotrules.pdf.*

**Bench Trial:** Use exhibits and visuals during a bench trial just as you would in a jury trial. Judges are human and are thus influenced by visual information.

## III. INTRODUCING AN EXHIBIT

### A. The Song and Dance Routine

Smoothly introducing an exhibit requires something like a song and dance routine. The trial attorney must know the lyrics—the words to the song that the judge expects and likes to hear before admitting an exhibit. The *words to the song* that are music to a judge's ears are *italicized*. Also, the lawyer must know the dance steps—the gliding movement around the courtroom necessary to getting the exhibit introduced. The **descriptions of the dance steps are in bold type.** The routine should be rehearsed and memorized. Nothing detracts more from the impact of an exhibit than a faltering performance by the lawyer. Once you have mastered the song and dance routine, you will comfortably and effectively get exhibits into evidence. See pages 224-226 for the dance steps.

The conventional song and dance for introducing an exhibit into evidence involves five activities:

## CHECKLIST

### Introducing an Exhibit into Evidence

☐ 1. Getting the exhibit marked for identification,
☐ 2. Showing the exhibit to opposing counsel,
☐ 3. Laying the foundation,
☐ 4. Offering the exhibit, and
☐ 5. Meeting objections.

The song and dance routine may be shortened and even eliminated alto-gether. When exhibits are premarked (see Judge Bradshaw's instructions to counsel about premarking at pages 222-223), step one above is eliminated. If prior to trial the trial judge rules that an exhibit is admitted, no need exists to go through steps one and three through five. Instead, counsel shows the exhibit or identifies the exhibit for opposing counsel, the court, and the witness, such as when counsel, the judge, and the witness have all of the exhibits in notebooks before them. Or, as will be discussed later in this chapter, the exhibit may be stored electronically and called up and projected on monitors or a screen.

In the next chapter, The Visual Trial and Today's Technology, we discuss how to effectively display exhibits for the jury once they have been admitted into evi-dence. At this point, we focus on first gaining admission of the exhibit.

## 1. Getting the Exhibit Marked for Identification

The first step is to **approach the court clerk** to mark the exhibit for identification:

*"Would you mark this for identification, please."*

The lawyer hands the exhibit to the clerk, who adheres a label or tag to it marked according to who offered it (Plaintiff's Exhibit 5). The clerk then records the num-ber and description of the exhibit on an exhibit list and announces, "Plaintiff's Exhibit 5 has been marked for identification." You would note on your exhibit list the nature of the exhibit and the number of the exhibit (such as, "Photo: Front of Griffith's house," Plaintiff's Exhibit 5). This step can be skipped if the exhibits have been premarked as discussed above. While the clerk generally supplies the number for the exhibit, you could ask for specific numbering. For example, if a number of items belong together, you could request subnumbers (for photo-graphs of the Griffith house—Plaintiff's Exhibit 5A, 5B, and so on). If you have a number of exhibits that you are going to introduce through the witness, such as several photographs, you could hand them all to the clerk for numbering at the same time.

At this point, the exhibit is not in evidence and should not be shown to the jury. On the other hand, if the court has already ruled that the exhibit is admis-sible, for instance at a pretrial hearing on a motion in limine, then it may be seen by the jury.

## 2. Showing the Exhibit to Opposing Counsel

Now that the exhibit has been marked for identification, the next step is to **show the exhibit to opposing counsel** so counsel knows what the exhibit looks like and can make a determination of whether to object to it. In the alternative, have the witness lay the foundation for the exhibit and then show it to oppos-ing counsel before offering it. However, this breaks the flow of testimony from the witness who has just laid the foundation. Also, counsel may forget to show the exhibit at this point, and when counsel offers the exhibit, either the court or opposing counsel will point out counsel's misstep.

### 3.  Laying the Foundation

Counsel next approaches the witness with the exhibit, still concealing it from the jury's view. Alternatively, in some local courts and federal courts, counsel is confined to a podium, and exhibits are digitally stored and displayed on courtroom monitors or a screen. The lawyer identifies the exhibit for the witness, the judge, and opposing counsel to view on their monitors. If the court admits the exhibit into evidence, then the judge will have the image projected on monitors or a screen for the jurors to see. In such a jurisdiction, examining counsel obviously does not physically approach the witness. Where counsel must physically show or hand the exhibit to the witness, court courtesies vary from court to court. Courtroom practice may require that counsel request permission before approaching the witness:

> *"May I approach the witness, your Honor?"*

Ask the judge, court personnel, or attorneys familiar with the court practices whether such a request is required and whether it is necessary to repeat the request every time the lawyer wishes to approach. For example, in some local state courts and in federal courts, counsel might be confined by court rules or conventions to the podium unless the judge gives permission otherwise.

**The next dance move is to go to the witness and hand or otherwise show the exhibit to the witness.** It is good practice to show the exhibit to the judge and provide the judge with a copy of it if practicable, such as a copy of a document.

If the court requires counsel to stand at a podium, and exhibits are digitally stored and displayed on courtroom monitors or a screen, the exhibit is called up by the lawyer for the judge and opposing counsel to view. If the court admits the exhibit into evidence, then the judge will have the image projected on monitors or a screen for the jurors to see.

Once the witness is looking at the exhibit, counsel lays an evidentiary foundation for the admission of that exhibit into evidence. Later, we provide you with the lyrics to the foundation-laying songs for the different types of exhibits. However, routinely the foundation-laying song begins with the refrain:

> *"Showing you what has been marked for identification as Plaintiff's Exhibit 5. Do you recognize it?"*

These words perk up the judge because they signal that a foundation is about to be laid for admissibility of the exhibit, and the judge will be required to rule on it. Also, the witness's answer "yes" establishes part of the identification or authentication element of the foundation for admissibility of the exhibit.

After the foundation, the lawyer moves to the next step.

## 4. Offering the Exhibit

After the evidentiary foundation has been laid, counsel offers the exhibit into evidence by simply stating:

*"Offer Plaintiff's Exhibit 5, Your Honor."*

Phrasing may differ depending on court custom: *"Move the admission of Plaintiff's Exhibit 5."* Again, it is a matter of knowing the court's practices. The most common mistake is for counsel to state: *"I'd like to admit Plaintiff's Exhibit 5,"* or something to that effect because the judge, not counsel, either admits or rejects the proposed exhibit.

## 5. Meeting Objections

The judge will now await opposing counsel's response, sometimes inquiring: "Any objection?" Opposing counsel is given an opportunity to state an objection. If counsel objects, it is good practice to look only at the judge and observe whether the judge summarily overrules the objection. If the court wants a response to the objection, the judge may, either by looking at or verbally, invite counsel who offered the exhibit to argue in favor of its admission into evidence. This exchange in front of the jury should be perfunctory. If the argument is going to be extended, the court may hear argument at sidebar or excuse the jury and ask counsel to proceed with argument and then rule on admissibility of the exhibit.

When the exhibit is offered, opposing counsel may also request to voir dire the witness regarding the foundation. The questioning, if permitted, should not become a cross-examination. If the voir dire ventures away from the evidentiary foundation, trial counsel should object.

When the court rules to admit or refuse the exhibit, counsel notes the date and time of the ruling on the exhibit list. Also, the name of the sponsoring witness should be noted.

---

Watch direct examinations of plaintiffs' witnesses in the *Freck Point* trial demonstration movie to see how to introduce and display a variety of exhibits located on our website, *http://www.aspenlawschool.com/books/berger_trialad4e.*

---

## B. Making a Record

As you and the witness work with an exhibit, it is important that a record be made for an appeal, closing argument, and jury deliberations. If it does not exist in the trial transcript, it does not exist for an appellate court to review. A trial attorney is always mindful of the record when working with an exhibit. Making a record by marking it during the trial creates a visual record that counsel can point to in closing or that jurors can refer to when they discuss the exhibit during jury deliberations.

For example, counsel says: *"Mr. Griffith, could you take this blue marking pen and put your initials, S.G., on Defendant's Exhibit 3, to show where you were when you were shoved? Now could you write the word 'shoved' on the place on the diagram you just initialed?"* In summation, counsel can remind the jury that they can look to the markings on the diagram to see where Mr. Griffith said he was shoved. In the jury room during deliberations, the jurors can refer to the marked diagram to remember where Griffith said the shoving took place. If the appellate court examines Exhibit 3, the place where Griffith testified he was shoved will be apparent on the exhibit.

## C. Timing of an Exhibit

How you structure the order of witnesses and time the introduction of an exhibit can make the introduction into evidence and display of an exhibit flow smoothly, and increase the exhibit's persuasive impact on the jury. Federal Rule of Evidence 104(b) states:

> **Relevance That Depends on a Fact.** When the relevance of evidence depends on whether a fact exists, proof must be introduced sufficient to support a finding that the fact does exist. The court may admit the proposed evidence on the condition that the proof be introduced later.

One implication for this federal rule and its state rule counterparts is that the trial judge is vested with the discretion to admit an exhibit conditionally on trial counsel's assurance that counsel will establish relevancy or the foundation later. When there is an objection to offering an exhibit because you need additional testimony to complete a foundation or establish relevancy, just say, *"Your Honor, I'll connect it up later."* Of course, you must have a good-faith belief that you can connect it up. If you fail to do so, the judge, on opposing counsel's later motion, may exclude the exhibit, strike all testimony regarding it, and instruct the jury to disregard the exhibit and testimony about it.

On the other hand, when you offer the exhibit and inform the court that you will connect it up later, the judge may require that you lay the complete foundation and establish relevancy before admitting the exhibit. For example, presenting a chain of custody may require that you present witnesses in a specific sequence so that you can introduce the exhibit only after the evidentiary foundation is laid.

Suppose you are the prosecutor in the *Freck Point* case. You wish to call a housekeeper who worked in the Griffiths' kitchen and was familiar with her set of knives to introduce the knife used to kill Sondra Griffith. But the housekeeper cannot identify the knife that Officer Marchese recovered from a bush as the knife from the set, but only as one that "looked like the knife from the set." You have various options. You can offer the knife and assure the judge that you will call Marchese later to lay the evidentiary foundation. Or you could start with the housekeeper and ask the court to interrupt her testimony long enough to present the foundation by calling Marchese to testify and reserve the right to recall Marchese later. Or you could call Marchese first. Timing is a strategic consideration here. To heighten juror interest concerning the knife that is in an evidence bag marked as Plaintiff's Exhibit 8, you could delay introduction of the exhibit until later in the trial, though some jurors might feel you led them to the well and left them waiting for a drink of water.

Yet another strategy is to skip the foundation and just offer the exhibit. When it is clear that counsel can and will, if necessary, lay the foundation, opposing counsel may decide not to object. If opposing counsel objects, this may result in not only appearing that counsel is prolonging the time necessary to admit the exhibit, but also enhancing the importance of the exhibit by increasing the jury's anticipation to view the exhibit. The downside to this strategy is that if opposing counsel objects, the objection will be sustained and you may appear to be inept.

## IV.  LAYING A FOUNDATION

### A.  Stipulation

Before discussing evidentiary foundations, it is important to note that counsel can *stipulate* to the admissibility of an exhibit. A stipulation is an agreement between you and opposing counsel. As to tangible evidence, a stipulation can be a mutual agreement that an exhibit be admitted into evidence. This process bypasses the requirements of witness testimony or proof of self-authentication to establish the foundation for admissibility. You might decide to stipulate if the exhibit is not an important issue in the case, you want to save time and money, or you and opposing counsel know that, if put to the test, the exhibit will be admitted. On the other hand, your stipulation can be partial. You might stipulate to the exhibit's identification or authenticity, but not to its relevance or to any other evidentiary concerns. For example, you might stipulate to a document being a contract between the parties, but not to its relevance in the case. Stipulations can be oral or written. If written, a stipulation can be in the form of a signed and dated letter, a formal request for admissions, or as part of a written pretrial order.

## Written Stipulation

### The *Freck Point* Case

Dean Lukens
Lukens & Lum
220 Thicket Drive
Ruston, Major 10000

> Re:   *Brenneman v. Griffith*

Dear Mr. Lukens:

This letter is to confirm our stipulations concerning the admissibility of the following exhibits listed with the clerk's premarked identification numbers. We have agreed these exhibits can be admitted for all purposes.

*Plaintiff's Exhibits*

1) ID #27 Sondra Griffith's Mariche Life Insurance policy, 5/18/20XX-5.

*Defense Exhibits*

3) ID #3 Oregon Medical Examiner's autopsy report on Marian Griffith, 8/26/20XX-16

The undersigned agree to the above statement.

_____*Gary Lark*_____   Dated: November 18, 20XX
Gary Lark
Attorney for plaintiff Kathleen Brenneman

_____*Dean Lukens*_____   Dated: November 27, 20XX
Dean Lukens
Attorney for defendant Samuel L. Griffith

## B.  Court Ruling on Admissibility

The court, either in accordance with evidentiary rules or custom, will follow certain procedures in deciding whether an exhibit will be admitted into evidence. Under Federal Rule of Evidence 104, the judge decides preliminary legal questions concerning admissibility of evidence, such as authenticity or privilege (constitutional, attorney-client, and so on) or on the foundation for an exception to the hearsay rule. In making this decision, under Rule 104(a), the judge is not bound by the rules of evidence, except those relating to privilege. Evidentiary rules, such as Federal Rule of Evidence 104(b), grant the judge discretion to admit evidence subject to further proof.

## C.  Essential Evidence Rules

The Federal Rules of Evidence are discussed because most states (except California and New York, which have their own codes) have adopted them, sometimes with variations. Despite differences among the rules, an exhibit is usually admissible if you can answer yes to the following four questions.

1. Is it relevant?
2. Does it pass the Federal Rule of Evidence 403 test (probative vs. unfairly prejudicial)?
3. Is it authentic or identified?
4. Is it otherwise admissible?

### Relevant

To be admissible, an exhibit must be relevant to the case. To establish relevancy, the proponent of the exhibit must show that it makes the existence of a material fact in the case more or less probable.

Federal Rule of Evidence 401 provides:

> Evidence is relevant if: (a) it has any tendency to make a fact more or less probable than it would be without the evidence; and (b) the fact is of consequence in determining the action.

Federal Rule of Evidence 402 provides:

> Relevant evidence is admissible unless any of the following provides otherwise: the United States Constitution; a federal statute; these rules; or other rules prescribed by the Supreme Court. Irrelevant evidence is not admissible.

However, before any exhibit is admitted into evidence, it must pass the Rule 403 test—more probative than prejudicial, not misleading, delay or cumulative. That rule states:

> The court may exclude relevant evidence if its probative value is substantially outweighed by a danger of one or more of the following: unfair prejudice, con-

fusing the issues, misleading the jury, undue delay, wasting time, or needlessly presenting cumulative evidence.

### Authenticated or Identified

The rule regarding authentication or identification of an exhibit is simple requiring this element of the foundation set out in Federal Rule of Evidence 901(a), which states:

> (a) **In General.** To satisfy the requirement of authenticating or identifying an item of evidence, the proponent must produce evidence sufficient to support a finding that the item is what the proponent claims it is.

All that is needed for this aspect of the foundation is to prove that the exhibit is what the party claims it to be. The standard of proof is low; the party need only provide sufficient evidence that a reasonable juror could find that the exhibit is what it is claimed to be. For instance, counsel asks the witness, *"Showing you what has been marked for identification as Plaintiff's Exhibit 5. Do you recognize it?"* The witness responds, *"Yes, that is a photograph of the front of the Griffiths' house."* Now it is claimed to be a photograph of the front of the house. Counsel asks, *"How do you know it's a picture of the front of the Griffiths' house?"* Witness answers, *"Because I live next door to Mr. and Mrs. Griffith and see the front of their house every day."* That is sufficient evidence to support a finding that the exhibit is a photograph of the front of Griffith's house. Rule 901(b) merely provides more illustrations of the application of the rule, such as its application to the identification of handwriting.

With some exhibits, it is not necessary to call a witness to prove that it is what it is claimed to be because the exhibit is self-authenticating. Federal Rule of Evidence 902 provides a list of self-authenticated exhibits. These are evidentiary items that are so trustworthy that no witness needs to be called. Included are things like certified copies of public records. See page 242 for the complete list. With a self-authenticating exhibit, you need only offer it into evidence.

### Otherwise Admissible

The foundation for any exhibit must satisfy the preceding three requirements: relevance, authentication or identification, and Rule 403. But often another evidentiary requirement must be met for the exhibit to be held admissible. For instance, with a document, both hearsay and best evidence rules must be considered. Now we turn to laying foundations for particular types of exhibits.

## V. REAL EVIDENCE

### A. Definition and Overview

Real evidence is the actual evidence in a case. Some practitioners and commentators designate real evidence as original or physical evidence. When discussing real evidence, we are referring to an actual object that played a direct role in the incident that is the subject of the trial. In the *Freck Point* case, examples of real evidence would include, among other things, the knife and the Sprite can that are covered with blood and saliva. These real evidence exhibits in combination with the testimony of the DNA expert and the detective's testimony that the Sprite can was located near where the knife was found constitute circumstantial evidence of the defendant's responsibility for his wife's death.

Witness testimony is the common manner of authenticating real evidence and requires that the witness testify that the exhibit is what it is claimed to be. There are two categories of real evidence with which you will be dealing:

- Readily identifiable real evidence (the thing is unique, singular), and
- Fungible real evidence (lacks unique characteristics, not readily identifiable).

## B.  Readily Identifiable Real Evidence

### Foundation Points

To introduce an exhibit of real evidence, counsel needs a foundation to establish: (1) that the exhibit is relevant (Rules 401-402); (2) it is what the witness claims (Rule 901(a)); (3) any changes to the exhibit are explained, which represents a mix of Rules 401 and 403; and (4) it passes the Rule 403 test. See pages 230-231.

*The Gun*

---

### Real Evidence

#### Laying the Foundation for Readily Identifiable Real Evidence
*Shooting Assault* Case

Imagine that you are the prosecutor in a shooting assault case and you intend to get the handgun into evidence. Now you begin the exhibit song and dance routine. Pick up the bag containing the handgun, which your lead detective obtained from the evidence room and brought to court this morning. **Go to the court clerk** and ask, *"Would you please mark this?"* The clerk affixes an exhibit tag to the bag that reads "State's Exhibit 11." Once it is marked, **show it to defense counsel.** Then, **go to the witness** (requesting the court's permission if need be) and **hand the bag to the officer.** The questions and answers proceed as follows:

**Prosecutor:**

Q:  Officer Glock, *handing you what has been marked for identification as Plaintiff's Exhibit 11. Can you identify it?*

A:  Yes, this a bag that I placed into evidence; it bears my initials and the case number that I wrote on it.

Q:  Officer, could you cut open the bag? Remove what is in the bag and look at it, but do not show the contents of the bag to the jury. Can you *tell us whether you recognize what is in the bag?*

---

*A:* Yes, I recognize it.

*Q:* What is it?

*A:* It is the handgun that I just said that I took from the defendant's bag after I arrested him.

*Q: How do you know it is the same gun that you took from the defendant?*

*A:* This is a Smith and Wesson revolver—the same kind that was in defendant's bag. It bears the serial number 67432, which is the number that I saw on the weapon and noted in the case file. Also, I placed the weapon in an evidence bag, sealed the bag, wrote my initials on the seal, and logged it into the evidence room when I got back to the station.

*Q:* Looking at the handgun, Exhibit 11 now, *is it in the same condition that it was when you took it from the defendant, bagged, and logged it into the evidence room, or is it different?*

*A:* It does have a white powder on the handle and barrel that was not on the gun when I took it from the defendant's bag. Also, it has a trigger guard that I put on it this morning when I checked it to see whether it was safe.

*Q:* Is it loaded? Is it safe?

*A:* It is unloaded and safe.

*Q:* Was it unloaded when you recovered it from the defendant's bag?

*A:* No. It had five live rounds in it. I unloaded the weapon and bagged the ammunition separately.

*Q:* Officer, other than the fact that it's now unloaded, has powder on it, and now has a trigger guard on it, can you please tell us whether Exhibit 11 is in the same condition now as it was when you took it from the defendant's bag?

*A:* It is in the same condition.

*Q:* Officer Glock, do you know how what is now marked as Plaintiff's Exhibit 11 got to this courtroom?

*A:* Yes, this morning I picked it up from the evidence room.

**Prosecutor:**

Your Honor, I offer Plaintiff's Exhibit 11.

**Judge:**

Any objection?

**Defense Counsel:**

No, Your Honor.

**Judge:**

Plaintiff's Exhibit 11 will be admitted.

**Prosecutor:**

Officer Glock, will you come down here in front of the jury and show the jurors Exhibit 11?

## C.  Fungible Real Evidence: Chain of Custody

The foundation for fungible evidence requires proof of relevancy and that it passes the Rule 403 test. In addition, because no witness can readily identify the exhibit, you must develop through witness testimony a chain of custody. By proving the chain of custody, you establish for the court the same ultimate fact you established with readily identifiable real evidence. You show the real evidence is what it is claimed to be.

Because fungible real evidence cannot always be made unique, must be maintained in a particular condition (for instance, refrigerating blood samples), or could be mixed up with other fungible real evidence (a powdery white substance alleged to be powdered cocaine, for instance), you must trace the custody of the real evidence over time to establish that it has not been switched for a similar object, contaminated, or altered.

A chain of custody establishing the whereabouts of an exhibit during all relevant times of the case is an essential part of an evidentiary foundation when the exhibit has passed through several hands, and it is important that it is kept in the same condition, has not been mixed up with another exhibit, or the like. Drug prosecutions, where, for example, the government must establish that the white powder found in defendant's briefcase is the same white powder a forensic chemist has determined to be cocaine, are cases where establishing a chain of custody is necessary. Witness testimony should establish that the exhibit has been kept safe, unaltered, and uncontaminated during the time it has been in custody.

Be mindful that you also want to enhance the persuasiveness of the exhibit. By using the testimony to show that there are no significant breaks in the links of the custody chain, the testimony should convince the jury that this is the real evidence that was involved in the case. There has been no tampering, no mix-up, or no unexplained change. As you plan to emphasize the reliability of the chain of custody, we suggest you adopt the approach we also applied to documentary evidence.

---

### Evidentiary Foundation

#### Chain Of Custody
#### *Controlled Substance* Case

Suppose that the exhibit is a powdery substance that a police officer seized from the defendant in a possession of controlled substances case. In a model foundation, the prosecutor would call the officer to testify about seizing the drugs and packaging them in State's Exhibit 20, which is a sealed envelope. The officer would testify that he placed his initials on the envelope, sealed it, and delivered it to the evidence room. The officer would testify about how evidence is stored and that the envelope has been opened and that someone else's initials are on the envelope.

So far, only a partial chain of custody has been laid. The prosecutor would call a forensic scientist from the crime laboratory to testify to taking the Exhibit 20 from the evidence room to the lab, and then opening the envelope, testing the powdery substance, determining it to be cocaine, resealing the envelope, initialing it, and returning it to the evidence room. The expert would also testify about lab procedures used to ensure the contents of the envelope are not contaminated or exchanged. This is one model of how a chain of custody for fungible evidence can be laid, and then the exhibit can be offered into evidence.

## VI. DOCUMENTARY EVIDENCE

### A. Definition and Overview

Documentary evidence refers to things in writing or things recorded that are offered to prove their content. These include e-mails, written statements, letters, memorandum, contracts, leases, and recordings such as videos.

In the *Freck Point* case, examples of documentary evidence relevant to the defendant's motive to kill his wife include insurance policies showing that Sondra was heavily insured and that her husband was the beneficiary. Bank and credit card statements reveal the extent of the couple's indebtedness.

Three essential evidentiary questions applicable to documentary evidence are the same as those for real evidence.

1. Is it relevant?
2. Does it pass the Fed. R. Evid. 403 test (probative vs. unfairly prejudicial)?
3. Is it authentic or identified?

Added to these are the following three.

4. Is it admissible under the original writing rules—Fed. R. Evid. 1001-1003?
5. Will it survive a hearsay objection?
6. Is it otherwise admissible?

Meeting objections that the document is irrelevant or unfairly prejudicial depends upon the facts of the individual case. We focus on laying foundations to establish that the document is authentic, satisfies the best evidence rule, and is not inadmissible hearsay.

## B. Authentication

The evidentiary foundation for a document must establish that it is authentic. Formulating a foundation for authenticity, like any other foundation, begins with applicable court rules and case law, which not only outline the evidentiary predicates but also often contain the lyrics to the familiar song that the judge likes to hear before admitting the exhibit.

Federal Rule of Evidence 901(a) states the rule regarding the quantity of evidence needed to lay the foundation:

> (a) **In General.** To satisfy the requirement of authenticating or identifying an item of evidence, the proponent must produce evidence sufficient to support a finding that the item is what the proponent claims it is.

Federal Rule of Evidence 901(b) lists examples of sufficient evidence that complies with the rule:

> (1) **Testimony of a Witness with Knowledge.** Testimony that an item is what it is claimed to be.
>
> (2) **Nonexpert Opinion About Handwriting.** A nonexpert's opinion that handwriting is genuine, based on a familiarity with it that was not acquired for the current litigation.
>
> (3) **Comparison by an Expert Witness or the Trier of Fact.** A comparison with an authenticated specimen by an expert witness or the trier of fact.
>
> (4) **Distinctive Characteristics and the Like.** The appearance, contents, substance, internal patterns, or other distinctive characteristics of the item, taken together with all the circumstances.
>
> . . .
>
> (7) **Evidence About Public Records.** Evidence that:
>
> (A) a document was recorded or filed in a public office as authorized by law; or
>
> (B) a purported public record or statement is from the office where items of this kind are kept.
>
> (8) **Evidence About Ancient Documents or Data Compilations.** For a document or data compilation, evidence that it:
>
> (A) is in a condition that creates no suspicion about its authenticity;
>
> (B) was in a place where, if authentic, it would likely be; and
>
> (C) is at least 20 years old when offered.
>
> (9) **Evidence About a Process or System.** Evidence describing a process or system and showing that it produces an accurate result.
>
> . . .

With Rule 901 in mind, we examine and provide model foundations for authenticating e-mails, text messages, website printouts, and traditional documents, such as letters, contracts, or memoranda.

### 1. E-Mails

E-mail is today's primary mode of communication, and consequently e-mails are commonplace trial exhibits. The foundation for authenticating an e-mail may be laid either by testimony that the e-mail is what the party claims (Fed. R. Evid. 901(b)(1)); by comparison (Fed. R. Evid. 901(b)(3)); or by its distinctive characteristics (Fed. R. Evid. 901(b)(4)).

### Testimony by the Sender

The foundation for an e-mail may be laid by calling a witness who sent the e-mail to testify, in accordance with Federal Rule of Evidence 901(b), "that the matter [e-mail] is what it is claimed to be." For example:

---

#### Laying the Foundation for E-Mail: Sender's Testimony

*Q:* Handing you what has been marked as Plaintiff's Exhibit 45 for identification. *Do you recognize it?*

*A:* Yes.

*Q:* *What is it?*

*A:* It is a printout of an e-mail that I sent Barbara Schwab.

*Q:* *How do you recognize it?*

*A:* It is what I wrote, and it is addressed to Barbara Schwab's e-mail address. We frequently exchanged e-mails.

---

### Circumstantial Evidence

A foundation for introduction of an e-mail can be laid with circumstantial evidence. For example, when defendant David Safavian was prosecuted for making false statements and concealing facts during an investigation into his golfing trip with lobbyist Jack Abramoff while Safavian was chief of staff of the U.S. General Services Administration, the government sought to introduce 260 e-mails between Safavian, Abramoff, and others. *United States v. Safavian*, 435 F. Supp. 2d 36 (2006). The defense challenged the authenticity of the e-mails, and the court decided there was sufficient circumstantial evidence for the jury to determine that they were authentic. The district judge noted that the "threshold for the Court's determination of authenticity is not high," and that it is not incumbent upon the court to "find that the evidence is necessarily what the proponent claims, but only that there is sufficient evidence that the jury ultimately might do so." *Safavian* at 38.

Based upon circumstantial evidence, the district judge found that the e-mails in the *Safavian* case met the authentication requirements of Rule 901. *Safavian* at 39-41. For many of the e-mails, the court relied upon Rule 901(b)(4), stating:

> One method of authentication identified under Rule 901 is to examine the evidence's "distinctive characteristics and the like," including "[t]he appearance, contents, substance, internal patterns, or other distinctive characteristics of the item, taken together with all the circumstances." Fed. R. Evid. 901(b)(4). Most of the proffered exhibits can be authenticated in this manner. The emails in question have many distinctive characteristics, including the actual email addresses containing the "@" symbol, widely known to be part of an email address, and

certainly a distinctive mark that identifies the document in question as an email. See *United States v. Siddiqui*, 235 F.3d 1318, 1322 (11th Cir. 2000). In addition, most of the email addresses themselves contain the name of the person connected to the address, such as "abramoffj@gtlaw.com," "David.Safavian@mail. house.gov," or "david.safavian@gsa.gov." *See, e.g.,* Exhibits 101, 105, 106. Frequently these emails contain the name of the sender or recipient in the bodies of the email, in the signature blocks at the end of the email, in the "To:" and "From:" headings, and by signature of the sender. The contents of the emails also authenticate them as being from the purported sender and to the purported recipient, containing as they do discussions of various identifiable matters, such as Mr. Safavian's work at the General Services Administration ("GSA"), Mr. Abramoff's work as a lobbyist, Mr. Abramoff's restaurant, Signatures, and various other personal and professional matters.

The court then decided that the other e-mails that were "not clearly identifiable on their own" were also admissible, relying on Rule 901(b)(3):

> Those emails that are not clearly identifiable on their own can be authenticated under Rule 901(b)(3), which states that such evidence may be authenticated by comparison by the trier of fact (the jury) with "specimens which have been [otherwise] authenticated"—in this case, those emails that already have been independently authenticated under Rule 901(b)(4). For instance, certain emails contain the address "MerrittDC@aol.com" with no further indication of what person uses that email address either through the contents or in the email heading itself. *See, e.g.,* Exhibit 134. This email address on its own does not clearly demonstrate who was the sender or receiver using that address. When these emails are examined alongside Exhibit 100 (which the Court finds is authenticated under Rule 901(b)(4) by its distinctive characteristics), however, it becomes clear that MerrittDC@aol.com was an address used by the defendant. Exhibit 100 is also an email sent from that address, but the signature within the email gives the defendant's name and the name of his business, Janus-Merritt Strategies, L.L.C., located in Washington, D.C. (as well as other information, such as the business' address, telephone and fax numbers), thereby connecting the defendant to that email address and clarifying the meaning of both "Merritt" and "DC" in it. The comparison of those emails containing MerrittDC@aol.com with Exhibit 100 thereby can provide the jury with a sufficient basis to find that these two exhibits are what they purport to be—that is, emails to or from Mr. Safavian.

This is an example of how to lay the foundation for the admissibility of an e-mail with circumstantial evidence:

---

### Laying the Foundation for E-Mail: Circumstantial Evidence

*Q:* I am handing you what has been marked for identification as Plaintiff's Exhibit 46. *Do you recognize it?*

*A:* Yes.

*Q:* *What is it?*

---

*A:*  It is a printout of an e-mail that I received from Barbara Schwab.

*Q:*  Is there anything about Exhibit 46's *appearance, contents, substance, or anything else* that causes you to recognize it as an e-mail from Barbara Schwab to you?

*A:*  Yes. It is addressed to me, and it has her e-mail address, Bschwab@comayak.net, in the "from" line.

*Q:*  How do you know that's Barbara Schwab's e-mail address?

*A:*  We have carried on a regular exchange of e-mails for the past three years with her using that address.

*Q:*  Is there anything else about *contents* of the e-mail that indicates that it is from Barbara Schwab?

*A:*  Yes. We had been discussing her homeowner's insurance around the date on which this e-mail was sent, and she discusses that insurance in this e-mail. Besides, it has her name, name of her business, address, and phone number at the bottom of the e-mail.

## 2.  Text Messages and Other Electronic Messages

When the Supreme Court of North Dakota was faced for the first time with the issue of the foundational requirements for admissibility of text messages, it turned to case law in multiple jurisdictions. These jurisdictions held that other electronic messages, including e-mails, chat room printouts, instant messages, and text messages were authenticated by "circumstantial evidence establishing the evidence was what the proponent claimed it to be." *State v. Thompson*, 777 N.W.2d 617, 624-625 (2010). Upholding the trial court's ruling that a text message had been properly admitted into evidence, the North Dakota Supreme Court observed the low threshold of proof required to authenticate an electronic message—"the proponent must provide proof sufficient for a reasonable juror to find the evidence to be what it purports to be"—and that an argument that electronic messages are inherently unreliable because of their "relative anonymity" should be rejected. The court held the witness's testimony about his "knowledge of Thompson's cell phone number and signature on the text messages" was sufficient to authenticate the text message under North Dakota's Rules of Evidence 901(b)(1) and (4), which are the same as the Federal Evidence Rules. *Id.* at 624-626.

An excellent source for case law on the authentication of e-mails, text messages, websites, Web pages, and other electronically stored evidence and an analysis of those cases can be found in Jay M. Zitter, *Authentication of Electronically Stored Evidence, Including Text Messages and Email*, 34 A.L.R. 6th 253 (originally published 2008).

The template of predicate questions for other electronic messages, such as faxes, text messages, and chat room printouts mirrors those for e-mails. For example, this is an illustration of how to lay a foundation for a text message:

---

### Laying the Foundation for a Text Message

Q: I am handing you what has been marked as Exhibit 48 for identification. *Do you recognize it?*

A: Yes.

Q: *What is it?*

A: It is a printout of a cell phone text message that I received from Barbara Schwab.

Q: Is there anything about Plaintiff's Exhibit 48's *appearance, contents, substance, or anything else* that causes you to recognize it as a text message from Barbara Schwab to you?

A: Yes. It says "Fr: Barb" at the beginning, and I have her cell phone number stored in my cell phone under "Barb." And at the end of the message, it has her cell phone number and her signature, "Bschwab."

Q: How do you know that Bschwab is Barbara Schwab's signature?

A: I've seen it over and over again when she texted me in the past.

---

### 3. Websites and Web Pages

Websites and printouts from websites can be circumstantially authenticated in the same way as has been shown for e-mails and other electronic communications. For instance, in *Griffin v. State*, 995 A.2d 791 (2008), the Maryland Court of Special Appeals found that a MySpace profile printout was circumstantially authenticated based upon the context and content of the communication. The court relied upon Md. Rule 5-901(b)(4), the state's counterpart to Federal Rule of Evidence 901(b)(4), which is the rule most commonly relied upon to authenticate e-mails and other electronic communications. *Id.* at 803. In *Griffin*, among the circumstances laid out in the foundation for authentication of the MySpace profile as belonging to Ms. Barber were the following: a photograph of a Ms. Barber on the profile; testimony by Ms. Barber that her boyfriend's nickname was "Boozy"; references in the profile to "Boozy"; and Ms. Barber's birth date matching the birth date on the profile.

### 4. Traditional Documents and Signatures

Authentication of handwriting on traditional documents, such as letters, contracts, wills, and the like may be proven by calling as a witness either a person who saw the person sign the document (Fed. R. Evid. 901(b)(1)), a nonexpert who is familiar with the handwriting of the person whose signature is on the document (Fed. R. Evid. 901(b)(2)), or by having the trier of fact or a handwriting expert compare the exhibit with authenticated specimens (Fed. R. Evid. 901(b)(3)).

This is how to lay a foundation with a nonexpert witness who is familiar with the signature on the document:

---

### Laying the Foundation for Handwriting
### Lay Testimony

Q:  Handing you Defense Exhibit 12, *do you recognize it*?

A:  It's a letter.

Q:  Tell us whether you recognize the signature on the letter?

A:  It is my brother's signature.

Q:  *How do you know that he signed it?*

A:  Pretty easy. It's signed Terry Dunham, my brother's name. I've seen him sign his name over the years, and he sends me signed holiday and birthday cards—when he remembers to send one.

---

The foundation for an expert's authentication of handwriting commences with qualifying the witness as a handwriting expert. See generally, Chapter 11, Experts: Yours and Theirs. The foundation may be laid as follows:

---

### Laying the Foundation for Handwriting
### Expert Testimony

[The expert has been qualified, and has explained the methodology applied in her field.]

Q:  Handing you Defense Exhibit 15. *Do you recognize it?*

A:  Yes. It is a sample of Terry Dunham's handwriting.

Q:  *How do you recognize them as samples of his handwriting?*

A:  He came to my office and I had him provide these samples of his handwriting in my presence.

Q:  Now, I'm handing you Defense Exhibit 4. Do you recognize it?

A:  It is a letter—a questioned document—that defense counsel provided to me for examination.

Q:  *Did you compare the handwriting on Defense Exhibit 15 with the handwriting on Exhibit 4?*

A:  Yes.

Q:  Could you describe *how you compared* the known handwriting on Exhibit 15 with the handwriting on the questioned document Exhibit 4?

A:  I used a microscope to examine and compare the distinctive characteristics of the handwriting on each, including how the letters were formed, misspellings, and so on.

Q:  Were you able to reach an opinion as to whether or not the Gary Clark whose handwriting is on Exhibit 15 is the author of Defense Exhibit 4 for identification?

A:  Yes, I was. The author of both Defense Exhibits 4 and 15 are the same person—Terry Dunham.

---

Having laid the foundation for the admissibility of the two defense exhibits, defense counsel offers them into evidence. Then, counsel has the expert testify that they were enlarged and placed side by side, and counsel offers this demonstrative exhibit. Once admitted, the expert uses this visual aid to show the jury how points of comparison on Exhibits 4 and 15 match and to establish that the handwriting on Exhibit 4 is Terry Dunham's.

### 5. Self-Authentication

Introducing a self-authenticated document into evidence at trial is as simple as saying, *"Offer into evidence what has been premarked for identification as Plaintiff's Exhibit 3."* It is that easy because by law the document is self-authenticating, and any objection can be met by pointing to that applicable rule of evidence. The pretrial work to come up with the self-authenticating document is not always simple; it requires that counsel obtain the document in a timely manner and in a form that complies with the jurisdiction's rules for self-authentication. For instance, the document may need a particular seal or custodian's signature.

While it is unnecessary to call a witness to authenticate a self-authenticating document, it is often the case that a document needs to be explained so that the jurors understand its significance. Counsel can explain its significance in closing argument, or counsel can wait to display the exhibit to the jury until a witness is on the stand who can talk about the exhibit.

Federal Rule of Evidence 902 lists the self-authenticated documents that do not require extrinsic evidence of authentication:

(1)  Domestic public documents that are signed and sealed
(2)  Domestic public documents that are not sealed but are signed and certified
(3)  Foreign public documents
(4)  Certified copies of public records
(5)  Official publications
(6)  Newspapers and periodicals
(7)  Trade inscriptions and the like
(8)  Acknowledged documents
(9)  Commercial paper and related documents
(10) Presumptions under a federal statute
(11) Certified domestic records of regularly conducted activity
(12) Certified foreign records of regularly conducted activity

## C. Original Writing Rule

The common law best evidence rule is history. The antiquated best evidence rule required that the proponent had to offer the original document into evidence. Now, Federal Rules of Evidence 1001-1004 and their state counterparts allow a duplicate of the original to be admitted into evidence unless either a genuine question is raised as to the document's authenticity, such as when opposing counsel claims it is a forgery, or it would be unfair to admit the duplicate, such as when part of the original had been erased. Federal Rules 1001-1004 provide:

### Rule 1001. Definitions That Apply to This Article

In this article:

(a) A "writing" consists of letters, words, numbers, or their equivalent set down in any form.

(b) A "recording" consists of letters, words, numbers, or their equivalent recorded in any manner.

(c) A "photograph" means a photographic image or its equivalent stored in any form.

(d) An "original" of a writing or recording means the writing or recording itself or any counterpart intended to have the same effect by the person who executed or issued it. For electronically stored information, "original" means any printout—or other output readable by sight—if it accurately reflects the information. An "original" of a photograph includes the negative or a print from it.

(e) A "duplicate" means a counterpart produced by a mechanical, photographic, chemical, electronic, or other equivalent process or technique that accurately reproduces the original.

### Rule 1002. Requirement of the Original

An original writing, recording, or photograph is required in order to prove its content unless these rules or a federal statute provides otherwise.

### Rule 1003. Admissibility of Duplicates

A duplicate is admissible to the same extent as the original unless a genuine question is raised about the original's authenticity or the circumstances make it unfair to admit the duplicate.

### Rule 1004. Admissibility of Other Evidence of Content

An original is not required and other evidence of the content of a writing, recording, or photograph is admissible if:

(a) all the originals are lost or destroyed, and not by the proponent acting in bad faith;

(b) an original cannot be obtained by any available judicial process;

(c) the party against whom the original would be offered had control of the original; was at that time put on notice, by pleadings or otherwise, that the original would be a subject of proof at the trial or hearing; and fails to produce it at the trial or hearing; or

(d) the writing, recording, or photograph is not closely related to a controlling issue.

This is an illustration of how to lay a foundation for a duplicate:

> **Laying the Foundation for a Duplicate Document**
>
> *Q:* Handing you what has been marked for identification as Plaintiff's Exhibit 3. *Do you recognize it?*
>
> *A:* Yes. It is a copy of a lease for a condominium—number 21—located at 2344 Eastlake, and it is signed by the defendant, Ms. Watson, and by me.
>
> *Q:* *How do you recognize the lease and the defendant's signature?*
>
> *A:* First, I drafted the lease. Second, Ms. Watson was in my office, and I watched her sign the lease, Exhibit 3. And third, that is my signature on it.
>
> *Q:* You said that Exhibit 3 is a copy of the lease. *How was this copy made?*
>
> *A:* I walked over to the office copy machine and ran three copies of it. I gave Ms. Watson a copy, and we retained the original and two copies. Exhibit 3 is one of the two copies we kept.
>
> *Q:* Please tell us whether Plaintiff's Exhibit 3 *is an accurate reproduction of the original* lease.
>
> *A:* It's exactly the same.

Federal Rule of Evidence 1004 provides the conditions under which a witness can discuss the contents of a writing without compliance with the originals rule. Generally this is used if both the original and duplicate are unavailable to the proponent who wishes to offer the writing, recording, or photograph. While this rule, when read in isolation and without consideration of Rule 1003, seems to require that a foundation be laid that the original is unavailable for one or more of the listed reasons before a duplicate is admissible, this is not the case.

For a witness to be able to discuss the contents of a writing, such as a lease, counsel would have to lay a foundation under Rule 1004 that the original lease and duplicates are lost, destroyed, not obtainable by judicial means, or in the possession of opposing party, who did not produce them when required to prove the contents with testimony. If, for example, counsel offers evidence that the original lease was destroyed in a house fire, a witness who had read the lease would be permitted to relate her recollection of its contents to the jury without contravening the originals rule.

## D.  Hearsay

When you intend to introduce a document into evidence, you should think about potential hearsay objections that may be raised against it. We concentrate on foundations for these prevalent exceptions relating to documents: recorded recollections, business records, public records, and Rule 1006 summary charts. Other common hearsay exceptions applicable to documents include prior inconsistent statements and party admissions, which are covered in Chapter 10 on cross-examination at pages 345-346, 365-367, and learned treatises, which are explored in Chapter 11 on experts at pages 422-424.

The complete list of hearsay exceptions applicable to documents under Federal Rule of Evidence 803 includes:

The following are not excluded by the rule against hearsay, regardless of whether the declarant is available as a witness:

. . .

(5)  Recorded recollection.
(6)  Records of a regularly conducted activity.
(7)  Absence of a record of a regularly conducted activity.
(8)  Public records.
(9)  Public records of vital statistics.
(10)  Absence of public record.
(11)  Records of religious organizations concerning personal or family history.
(12)  Certificates of marriage, baptism, and similar ceremonies.
(13)  Family records.
(14)  Records of documents that affect an interest in property.
(15)  Statements in documents that affect an interest in property.
(16)  Statements in ancient documents.
(17)  Market reports and similar commercial publications.
(18)  Statements in learned treatises, periodicals, or pamphlets.
. . .
(22)  Judgment of a previous conviction.
(23)  Judgment involving personal, family, or general history, or a boundary.

*Police Report*

### 1. Refreshed Recollection and Recorded Recollections

As an exception to the hearsay rule, a witness's recorded recollections may be introduced into evidence if the prerequisites of Federal Rule of Evidence 803(5) have been met. Rule 803 states:

The following are not excluded by the rule against hearsay, regardless of whether the declarant is available as a witness:

(5)  A record that:
(A)  is on a matter the witness once knew about but now cannot recall well enough to testify fully and accurately;
(B)  was made or adopted by the witness when the matter was fresh in the witness's memory; and
(C)  accurately reflects the witness's knowledge.

If admitted, the record may be read into evidence but may be received as an exhibit only if offered by an adverse party.

Specifically, the elements of the foundation include: (1) The document contains information; (2) that information is about something the witness once knew; (3) the witness made or adopted the document when the information was fresh in the witness's memory; (4) the document accurately reflects the witness's knowledge; (5) the witness at trial cannot testify fully and accurately about the contents of the matter.

The following line of questioning shows how to lay a foundation for admissibility of a recorded recollection, and along the way, how to lay a foundation for refreshing a witness's memory.

---

### Laying the Foundation for Refreshed Memory and Recorded Recollection

*Q:* What did you discuss at the meeting?

*A:* It was brief, and we all exchanged e-mail addresses, business addresses, and cell phone numbers.

*Q:* What contact information did you get from the others at the meeting?

*A:* That was three years ago. I don't recall. But I did note it in my report about the meeting.

*Q: When did you enter the information in your report about the meeting?*

*A:* As they gave me the information, I jotted it down right then, and right after the meeting I wrote the report.

*Q:* Would it *refresh your recollection* if you looked at your report?

*A:* I think so.

*Q:* Handing you what has been marked for identification as Plaintiff's Exhibit 87. *Do you recognize it?*

*A:* Yes, it is the report we've been discussing.

*Q:* Please read the exhibit to yourself, and when you are through, let us know.

*A:* I'm done.

*Q:* May I have the exhibit please? [Witness hands it to counsel.] Now, without reference to the Exhibit 87, can you tell this jury *fully and accurately* what the contact information was that they gave you? [If the witness answers in the affirmative, then in accordance with Federal Rule of Evidence 612 regarding refreshed recollection, counsel would have the witness testify to the information.]

*A:* I'm sorry, I can't accurately remember all that information so that I could give it to you without looking at the journal.

*Q:* Can you tell us *whether the information you wrote in Exhibit 87 was, at the time you wrote it, fresh in your memory, and was what you wrote in the journal, Exhibit 87, an accurate account of what you knew of the contact information?*

*A:* It was accurate.

*Q:* Your Honor, offer Plaintiff's Exhibit 87 into evidence.

**Judge:**
Plaintiff's Exhibit 87 is admitted.

*Q:* Please *read* Exhibit 87 for the jury. [Under Federal Rule of Evidence 803(5) the exhibit is read into evidence, but is not received as an exhibit unless offered by an adverse party.]

---

## 2. Business Records

*Hospital Records*

Business records kept in the manner required by Federal Rule of Evidence 803(6) are inherently trustworthy and therefore admissible as an exception to the hearsay rule. Rule 803(6) provides:

> The following are not excluded by the rule against hearsay, regardless of whether the declarant is available as a witness:
>
> **(6) Records of a Regularly Conducted Activity.** A record of an act, event, condition, opinion, or diagnosis if:
>
> (A) the record was made at or near the time by—or from information transmitted by—someone with knowledge;
>
> (B) the record was kept in the course of a regularly conducted activity of a business, organization, occupation, or calling, whether or not for profit;
>
> (C) making the record was a regular practice of that activity;
>
> (D) all these conditions are shown by the testimony of the custodian or another qualified witness, or by a certification that complies with Rule 902(11) or (12) or with a statute permitting certification; and
>
> (E) neither the source of information nor the method or circumstances of preparation indicate a lack of trustworthiness.

The elements of the foundation for business records are: (1) The witness who is testifying to the foundation is the custodian of the records or is otherwise qualified and personally has knowledge of the filing system; (2) the record must be made at or near the time of the acts, events, conditions, opinions, or diagnoses; (3) by a person with knowledge or by a transmission from the knowledgeable person; (4) the record is kept in the regular course of business; and (5) it was a regular part of the business activity to make the record.

Under this rule, a foundation for a business record—such as a medical record—can be laid as follows:

---

### Laying the Foundation for Business Records

**Plaintiff's counsel:**

[Plaintiff's counsel has already obtained the witness's qualifications, including training, experience, and scope of responsibilities as chief medical records clerk.]

*Q:* Ms. Richardson, as chief medical records clerk of Ruston Medical Center, are you familiar with the process for creating, storing, and retrieving patient medical records?

*A:* I am; that's my job.

*Q:* Tell us whether you are the *custodian of those records.*

*A:* I am the custodian.

*Q:* Please explain what is contained in a patient's medical records.

---

*continued* ▶

*A:* [Witness explains the contents of records and procedure for creating records, emphasizing the vital importance of accuracy, how records are used, how they are stored, how they are retrieved, and so forth.]

\* \* \*

*Q:* Ms. Richardson, if I wanted to obtain a particular patient's medical records, could you locate those records?

*A:* Sure, if I had the right information.

*Q:* What would that be?

*A:* Name and date of birth or social security number. We need the date of birth or social security number because we often have more than one patient with the same name.

*Q:* Did I ask you to locate and copy a particular patient's records for me?

*A:* Yes, you did.

*Q:* What information did I give you?

**Defense counsel:**

Objection, hearsay.

**Plaintiff's counsel:**

Not for the truth, Your Honor, for authentication. I would add that the date of birth I provided is already in evidence.

**Judge:**

Overruled.

**Plaintiff's counsel:**

You may answer.

*A:* The name Darcy L. Rutherford and a date of birth of 10/16/XX.

*Q:* Did you locate the file?

*A:* Yes, I did.

*Q:* And did you make a copy of that file?

*A:* Yes, and I brought it to court.

[Counsel has the exhibit marked, shows it to opposing counsel, and with the court's permission approaches the witness.]

*Q:* Ms. Richardson, I'm showing you what's been marked as Plaintiff's Exhibit 6 for identification. *Do you recognize what this is?*

*A:* Yes. This is a copy of Ms. Rutherford's medical records that I just told you about, the ones I copied for you. [This satisfies the best evidence rules, Federal Rules of Evidence 1002, 1003.]

*Q:* How do you know these are Darcy Rutherford's records?

*A:* Well, I recognize our hospital's records—I've seen thousands—and I got this from our storage files.

*Q:* Anything else?

*A:* Yes. It has the name and date of birth you requested—Darcy L. Rutherford, 10/16/XX. It's all here on the first sheet of her records. [This satisfies the requirement of authentication, Federal Rule of Evidence 901.]

Q: Can you tell us whether this record was *created in the same way as the process we've already discussed for creating patient medical records at Ruston Medical Center?*

A: Yes.

Q: Is this record *kept in the regular course of the hospital's business?*

A: Yes.

Q: Is it from *information by or from someone with knowledge?*

A: Of course—doctors, nurses, and techs.

Q: *When is it entered?*

A: Right when the information is learned or right after.

Q: *Tell us whether it was the regular practice of the hospital to make such records.* [If the records are computer generated, you might instead want to frame your foundational questions in terms of "data" being kept in the regular course of business, entered at or near the time, and so on, rather than "records." In a computer-based system, the paper records may not even exist until printed out months later.]

A: We regularly keep these records.

**Plaintiff's counsel:**

Your Honor, I offer what has been marked as Plaintiff's Exhibit 6 into evidence as a business record.

## 3. Public Records and Reports

Public records and reports that satisfy Federal Rule of Evidence 803(8) are admissible under the exception to the hearsay rule because they are considered trustworthy based upon the care taken in keeping them. Rule 803(8) states:

The following are not excluded by the rule against hearsay, regardless of whether the declarant is available as a witness:

(8) **Public Records.** A record or statement of a public office if:
(A) it sets out:
(i) the office's activities;
(ii) a matter observed while under a legal duty to report, but not including, in a criminal case, a matter observed by law-enforcement personnel; or
(iii) in a civil case or against the government in a criminal case, factual findings from a legally authorized investigation; and
(B) neither the source of information nor other circumstances indicate a lack of trustworthiness.

Usually, the public record is self-authenticating and counsel need only offer the exhibit into evidence without calling a witness.

Another exception to the hearsay rule is codified in Federal Rule of Evidence 803(10). Rule 803(10) permits a party to establish that a public record or entry that is regularly made and preserved by a public office or agency is missing either by calling a witness to testify or introducing evidence in the form of a certification in accordance with Federal Rule of Evidence 902. Rule 803(10) states:

> The following are not excluded by the rule against hearsay, regardless of whether the declarant is available as a witness:
>
> **(10)  Absence of a Public Record.** Testimony—or a certification under Rule 902—that a diligent search failed to disclose a public record or statement if:
>
> (A)  the testimony or certification is admitted to prove that
>
> (i)   the record or statement does not exist; or
>
> (ii)  a matter did not occur or exist, if a public office regularly kept a record or statement for a matter of that kind; and
>
> (B)  in a criminal case, a prosecutor who intends to offer a certification provides written notice of that intent at least 14 days before trial, and the defendant does not object in writing within 7 days of receiving the notice—unless the court sets a different time for the notice or the objection.

For example, the absence of the recording of a real estate deed is offered to prove that the person claiming title to the property did not have it. Laying a foundation for the absence of the deed requires proof by testimony or through proper certificate that the person doing the title search conducted a diligent search for the deed.

## 4.  Rule 1006 Summary Chart

Federal Rule of Evidence 1006 is commonsensical; it allows the fact finder to receive volumes of information in a convenient and comprehensible format. A summary chart that satisfies the rule is substantive evidence that the jury may consider; it is not just a demonstrative evidence exhibit. The original material upon which the chart is based must be both authentic and not inadmissible hearsay. Rule 1006—Summaries states:

> The proponent may use a summary, chart, or calculation to prove the content of voluminous writings, recordings, or photographs that cannot be conveniently examined in court. The proponent must make the originals or duplicates available for examination or copying, or both, by other parties at a reasonable time and place. And the court may order the proponent to produce them in court.

Elements of a foundation for a Rule 1006 summary chart are: (1) the original writings, recordings, or photographs are so voluminous that they cannot be conveniently examined in court; (2) the originals would be admissible; (3) the chart accurately summarizes the originals; and (4) the originals or duplicates must be made available to the other parties for examination. A foundation for a summary chart of bank records follows:

## Laying the Foundation for a Summary Chart

**Defense counsel:**

[Defense counsel has qualified the witness as a certified public accountant and had the witness discuss his examination of the defendant's bank records, credit card statements, and tax records for a five-year period.]

Q: Mr. Carroll, you've told us that you examined all these records and statements. What would you *estimate the number of these documents to be*?

A: I didn't count them, but they fill ten packing boxes and run into the hundreds at least.

Q: Could they be *conveniently examined here in court*?

A: Hardly—it would take days to go over them.

Q: Have you *made duplicates of those documents available to the defendant*?

A: Yes, they were provided.

Q: Handing you what has been marked for identification as Exhibit 34. *Do you recognize it?*

A: Yes. It is a chart that I prepared, and it summarizes the defendant's income and expenditures over the five years we have been discussing.

Q: Upon what did you base your summary?

A: I based it on the records and statements we just discussed.

Q: Tell the jury whether or not Defense Exhibit 34 *accurately reflects* the contents of those records and statements that you examined.

A: It does.

## VII. DEMONSTRATIVE EVIDENCE

### A. Definition and Overview

Demonstrative evidence refers to evidence that demonstrates, or illustrates, a fact or condition to be proved in a case. Demonstrative evidence is created evidence used in a trial to assist a witness in testifying, to make the testimony more persuasive, and to aid the jury fact finder in understanding the case. Examples of demonstrative evidence are a computer-generated slideshow (PowerPoint), photographs, charts, graphs, models, diagrams, timelines, anatomical drawings, computer animations, videos, and in-courtroom demonstrations. In civil cases and for the criminal defense, an attorney or attorney-agent creates demonstrative evidence. Generally, the government's demonstrative evidence in criminal cases is created by a law enforcement agency or the prosecutor's office. Demonstrative evidence is often admitted into evidence; however, some judges do not permit demonstrative evidence in a jury room because it isn't real evidence in the case. Demonstrative evidence may also be used in mediation and arbitration proceedings.

Let's return to the *Freck Point* case. In that case, the demonstrative evidence could include: photographs of the Griffiths' home, a mock-up model of the bedroom where Sondra Griffith was killed, a picture of Sondra when she was alive, a diagram of the scene, a computer slideshow to aid the expert to explain DNA, and so on.

Just as with real and documentary evidence, the essential evidentiary questions applicable to demonstrative evidence include.

1. Is it relevant?
2. Does it pass the Fed. R. Evid. 403 test (probative vs. unfairly prejudicial)?
3. Is it authentic or identified?
4. Is it otherwise admissible?

In this section, we cover how to lay a foundation for many types of demonstrative exhibits. Because relevancy is case specific, we focus on authentication of the exhibit under Federal Rule of Evidence 901(a) (is the evidence sufficient to support a finding that the exhibit is what the proponent claims it is) and whether it passes the Rule 403 test.

## B. Photographs, Videos, Diagrams, and Models

### 1. Photographs

*Pictures + Diagrams*

To introduce a photograph, video, diagram, and the like, counsel needs to lay a foundation sufficient to establish that the photograph is relevant (Rules 401-402) and that shows what the witness claims (Rule 901(a)) and is not misleading (Rule 403). Elements of the foundation are: (1) the subject matter in the exhibit is relevant; (2) the witness has *seen* the subject matter in the exhibit; (3) the exhibit fairly and accurately shows what is in it at a relevant time; and (4) changes to what is shown are explained.

---

**Laying the Foundation for a Photograph**
**The *Blue Moon News Robbery* Case**

**Prosecutor:**

Q: Mr. Newman, I'm showing you what's been marked as State's Exhibit 11 for identification. *Do you recognize what that is?*

A: Sure.

Q: *What is that?*

A: It's a photograph of the convenience store.

Q: What view does it show?

A: It's the view from the cash register looking at the front door.

Q: Does this photograph *fairly and accurately represent that view* as it looked on the night of the robbery?

A: Yes.

---

*Q:* Is it *different in any way?*

*A:* The magazines are probably different.

*Q:* Other than that?

*A:* No. Everything's the same.

*Q:* *Would this photograph help the jury better understand your testimony about the night of the robbery?*

*A:* Yes.

**Prosecutor:**

Your Honor, move the admission of State's Exhibit 11 into evidence.

## 2. Videos

Laying a foundation for a video uses the same key questions as laying the foundation for a photograph.

---

### Laying the Foundation for a Video
#### The *Blue Moon News Robbery* Case

**Prosecutor:**

*Q:* Mr. Newman, I'm handing you what has been marked as State's Exhibit 9 for identification. *Do you recognize what that is?*

*A:* Yes. It's a video showing the general layout of the new store.

*Q:* *How do you know that?*

*A:* Well, I watched it yesterday . . . .

*Q:* And these initials and date on the DVD?

*A:* They're mine. I put my initials and wrote the date on the disk right after I watched it.

*Q:* Please tell us whether the video on the DVD *fairly and accurately shows* the general layout of the store as it was on the night of the robbery.

*A:* Absolutely.

*Q:* *Is it different in any way?*

*A:* Maybe there's a newspaper or two in a different place on the racks, but it all looks the same to me.

*Q:* Other than the possible location of a few newspapers, is it different in any way?

*A:* No.

*Q:* *Do you think this video would help the jury understand what happened that night?*

*A:* Yes.

**Prosecutor:**

Your Honor, offer State's Exhibit 9 and request that I be able to play it for the jury at this time.

---

### 3. Non-Scale Diagram of the Store

---

**Laying the Foundation for a Non-Scale Diagram**
**The *Blue Moon News Robbery* Case**

**Prosecutor:**

*Q:* Mr. Newman, could you please step off the stand and come down here by the easel?

[At this point, the diagram is turned so the jury cannot see it. If the diagram is on a CD, the jurors' monitors will be off.]

*Q:* Looking at what's been marked as State's Exhibit 14 for identification, *do you recognize it?*

*A:* Sure.

*Q:* *What is it?*

*A:* That's a diagram of my store.

*Q:* Generally, what does the diagram show?

*A:* The front door, register area, and general location of the magazine stands and racks.

*Q:* Does this diagram *fairly and accurately show* the layout of the news store on the night of the robbery?

*A:* Absolutely.

*Q:* Is this diagram drawn to scale?

*A:* No.

*Q:* Other than the fact that it is not drawn to scale, *is the layout of the store different in any way from how it looked on the night of the robbery?*

*A:* No. Not that I can see.

*Q:* *Do you think that this diagram would help the jury understand your testimony today?*

*A:* Yes. I think it would help.

*Q:* Your Honor, I offer State's Exhibit 14 into evidence.

**Judge:**

Any objection?

**Defense counsel:**

No.

**Judge:**

Very well. It will be admitted as State's Exhibit 14 into evidence.

**Prosecutor:**

[Prosecutor turns the easel toward jurors. If instead of an easel, the diagram is on a CD, at this point the diagram will appear on the monitors in front of the jury, and the witness will mark the diagram from his own monitor on the witness stand.]

---

## 4. Model of the Store

---

### Laying the Foundation for a Model
### The *Blue Moon News Robbery* Case

**Prosecutor:**

*Q:* Mr. Newman, I'm showing you what has been marked as State's Exhibit 4 for identification. [Counsel shows exhibit in such a way that jury cannot see the model.] *Do you recognize what this is?*

*A:* Yes.

*Q:* *What is it?*

*A:* It's a model of my store viewed from the top—as if there was no roof.

*Q:* What basically does it show?

*A:* Almost everything—the entrance, cash register area, the magazine racks and stands. There are even little miniature newspapers and magazines . . . of course, not all the ones we sell.

*Q:* Does this model *fairly and accurately show* what the store looked like on the night of the robbery?

*A:* Yes.

*Q:* *Would it help the jury understand what you're telling them about what happened that night?*

*A:* It sure would.

**Prosecutor:**

Your Honor, I offer State's Exhibit 4 into evidence.

---

## C. Computer Animations

Computers can generate animations that illustrate what happened during the event that is the subject of the lawsuit. Generally, the animations presented in law cases are drawings created from software for the computer and then assembled so when the animation is run it looks like a movie. With an animation, the jury can see a recreation of events such as an automobile collision, a plane crash, or a product failure. On pages 170, 406-407, and 492-493, we list several company's websites that you can visit to view animations, or you can watch animations by visiting this book's website at *http://www.aspenlawschool .com/books/berger_trialad4e.*

A valuable resource that analyzes cases involving computer animations is Kurtis A. Kemper, *Admissibility of Computer-Generated Animation,* 111 A.L.R. 5th 529 (originally published 2003).

The Colorado Court of Appeals lists essential evidence rules that must be complied with to lay a foundation for a computer animation, which is another form of demonstrative evidence, as follows:

> A computer animation is admissible as demonstrative evidence if the proponent of the video proves that it: 1) is authentic under CRE 901; 2) is relevant under CRE

401 and 402; 3) is a fair and accurate representation of the evidence to which it relates; and 4) has a probative value that is not substantially outweighed by the danger of unfair prejudice under CRE 403. . . . An item of demonstrative evidence is authenticated if there is evidence to support a finding that the item is what its proponent claims it to be. CRE 901. Once authenticity is established, defects in physical evidence go to the weight of that evidence, not its admissibility. . . .

In addition, appellate courts have encouraged trial courts to give cautionary or limiting instructions to the jury when admitting computer generated evidence. . . .

*People v. Cauley*, 32 P.2d 602, 607 (2001).

Because an animation is demonstrative evidence, like a chart or diagram, and unlike a scientific device, the party offering it need not lay a foundation showing the validity of its underlying principles and data. *People v. McHugh*, 476 N.Y.S.2d 721, 760 (Supp. 1984); *People v. Hood*, 53 Cal. App. 4th 965, 969 (4th Dist. 1997).

## 1. A Witnessed Event

If the event was witnessed, the proponent of showing the animation need only call the eyewitness to lay the evidentiary foundation for admissibility. The foundation for authenticating the animation is similar to the foundation required for a video, discussed at page 253. The witness testifies that the animation is a fair and accurate portrayal of what the witness saw. For example, a motorist who witnessed a collision could testify to seeing what happened; that the animation fairly and accurately shows what happened; and the animation would be admissible as a demonstrative exhibit.

## 2. Animation to Assist an Expert

Computer animations are admissible as demonstrative evidence to assist an expert in explaining those witness's findings and opinions to the jury. For example, in *State v. Farner*, 66 S.W.3d 188 (Tenn. 2002), a negligent homicide case, the Supreme Court of Tennessee admitted a computer animation to illustrate and explain the accident reconstructionist's expert testimony. The foundation for admissibility of an animation to assist an expert would resemble that used for a video, discussed at page 253.

When an animation is admitted into evidence, the court should give a limiting jury instruction along the lines of this one given in *Hinkle v. Clarksburg*, 81 F.3d 416, 425 (1998), in accordance with Federal Rule of Evidence 105 or its state rule counterpart:

> This animation is not meant to be a recreation of the events, but rather it consists of a computer picture to help you understand Mr. Jason's opinion which he will, I understand, be giving later in the trial. And to reenforce the point, the video is not meant to be an exact recreation of what happened during the shooting, but rather it represents Mr. Jason's evaluation of the evidence presented.

## D. Computer Simulation

*State v. Farner*, 66 S.W.3d 188, 208 (Tenn. 2002) explains the difference between a computer animation and a computer simulation—the former being illustrative of testimony only, while the latter is substantive evidence that reconstructs an event in virtual space—and the additional foundational requirements for a simulation are as follows:

> Computer generated evidence is an increasingly common form of demonstrative evidence. . . . If the purpose of the computer evidence is to illustrate and explain a witness's testimony, courts usually refer to the evidence as an animation. . . . In contrast, a simulation is based on scientific or physical principles and data entered into a computer, which is programmed to analyze the data and draw a conclusion from it and courts generally require proof to show the validity of the science.

Keeping this distinction in mind, it is useful to examine the foundation for a computer simulation approved by the court in *Commercial Union Ins. Co. v. Boston Edison Co.*, 591 N.E.2d 165, 168 (1992). That case concerned a dispute over whether the plaintiff was overcharged for steam supplied by the defendant. Plaintiff offered a computer simulation, generated by a computer program called TRACE, to prove that the calculation of actual steam provided was less than what they were charged. The defendant objected to the simulation. The Massachusetts Supreme Court found that the simulation was properly considered by the trial court and outlined the foundational requirements for the admission of a simulation as follows:

> The function of computer programs like TRACE "is to perform rapidly and accurately an extensive series of computations not readily accomplished without use of a computer." *Schaeffer v. General Motors Corp.*, 372 Mass. 171, 177, 360 N.E.2d 1062 (1977). We permit experts to base their testimony on calculations performed by hand, cf., e.g., *Anthony's Pier Four, Inc. v. HBC Assocs.*, 411 Mass. 451, 478, 583 N.E.2d 806 (1991); *Kroeger v. Stop & Shop Cos., Inc.*, 13 Mass.App.Ct. 310, 323, 432 N.E.2d 566 (1982). There is no reason to prevent them from performing the same calculations, with far greater rapidity and accuracy, on a computer. Therefore, as we indicated in *Schaeffer, supra*, 372 Mass. at 177-178, 360 N.E.2d 1062, we treat computer-generated models or simulations like other scientific tests, and condition admissibility on a sufficient showing that: (1) the computer is functioning properly; (2) the input and underlying equations are sufficiently complete and accurate (and disclosed to the opposing party, so that they may challenge them); and (3) the program is generally accepted by the appropriate community of scientists. See *Commonwealth v. Fatalo*, 346 Mass. 266, 269, 191 N.E.2d 479 (1963).

## E. Summary Charts

There are two types of summary charts: the Federal Rule of Evidence 1006 chart and the Rule 611(a) chart. The Rule 1006 chart is substantive evidence, not demonstrative, and it is admitted into evidence and may be present in the jury room during deliberation. A discussion of the Rule 1006 chart and an illustration of the evidentiary foundation for its admissibility are at pages 250-251 and 327-328.

By contrast, a Rule 611(a) chart is merely a teaching or illustrative device; it is inadmissible and does not go to the jury room. If the summary chart does not qualify under Rule 1006 because, for instance, the volume of the documents is insufficient, it may still be admissible under Rule 611(a). A Rule 611(a) chart summarizes the testimonial or documentary evidence that has been presented in the trial. For example, in *United States v. Baker*, 10 F.3d 1374 (9th Cir. 1993), an FBI agent testified to the values of drug transactions with the aid of summary charts that were based on her notes of the trial testimony. The summary charts were admitted for illustrative purposes to aid the agent's testimony.

Summary charts are nowhere mentioned in Rule 611(a); rather they are permitted under the theory of Rule 611(a) that authorizes the judge to "exercise reasonable control over the mode . . . of . . . presenting evidence so as to (1) make those procedures effective for determining the truth; (and) (2) avoid wasting time."

When the court allows the use of a summary chart, it may instruct the jury along these lines:

> Certain charts and summaries have been shown to you solely to help explain the facts disclosed by the books, records and documents which are evidence in this case. These charts and summaries are not evidence or proof of any facts. You should therefore determine the facts from the evidence.

*United States v. Ogba*, 526 F.3d 214, 225 (5th Cir. 2008).

*State v. Yates*, 168 P.3d 359 (2007) outlines the foundation necessary to introduce a Rule 611(a) summary chart into evidence. In *Yates*, the prosecution offered a 7-by-13-inch chart with a list of the 13 murder victims listed horizontally across the top, and 15 categories of evidence listed vertically down the left side. Information was added to the chart once the evidence was admitted. The *Yates* court found the chart to be admissible under the foundational requirements for admission of a Rule 611(a) chart. To be admissible, the court must be satisfied that: (1) the chart is based on competent evidence already before the jury; (2) the chart fairly represents that evidence; and (3) the opposing party has a full opportunity to object before the jury sees it. Also, *Yates* requires that the jury be instructed that the "chart is not itself evidence, but is only an aid in evaluating the evidence." *Id.* at 391.

## VIII.  ETHICAL CONSIDERATIONS

Ethical issues that arise concerning real, documentary, or demonstrative evidence frequently focus on the disclosure of such evidence.

Prosecutor

*Brady v. Maryland*, 373 U.S. 83 (1963) involved a prosecution for murder where the defendant requested records of extrajudicial statements of the defendant's accomplice in which the accomplice admitted committing the murder. The Supreme Court held:

> We now hold that the suppression by the prosecution of evidence favorable to an accused upon request violates due process where the evidence is material either to guilt or to punishment, irrespective of the good faith or bad faith of the prosecution.

This ethical obligation extends to the prosecution team. "This in turn means that the individual prosecutor has a duty to learn of any favorable evidence known to others acting on the government's behalf in the case, including the police." *Kyles v. Whitley*, 514 U.S. 419 (1995).

Besides the constitutional obligation to disclose exculpatory information, the prosecutor has an ethical obligation.

---

### Ethical Rules Pertaining to Prosecutor: Exculpatory Evidence

#### ABA Model Rule of Professional Conduct 3.8(d)—Accused Person

The prosecutor in a criminal case shall . . . make timely disclosure to the defense, of all evidence or information known to the prosecutor that tends to negate the guilt of the accused or mitigates the offense, and, in connection with sentencing, disclose to the defense and to the tribunal all unprivileged mitigating information known to the prosecutor, except when the prosecutor is relieved of this responsibility by a protective order of the tribunal.

#### ABA Model Rule of Professional Conduct 3.8(g) and (h)—Convicted Person

    (g)  When a prosecutor knows of new, credible and material evidence creating a reasonable likelihood that a convicted defendant did not commit an offense of which the defendant was convicted, the prosecutor shall:

        (1)  promptly disclose that evidence to an appropriate court or authority, and

        (2)  if the conviction was obtained in the prosecutor's jurisdiction,

            (i)  promptly disclose that evidence to the defendant unless a court authorizes delay, and

            (ii)  undertake further investigation, or make reasonable efforts to cause an investigation, to determine whether the defendant was convicted of an offense that the defendant did not commit.

    (h)  When a prosecutor knows of clear and convincing evidence establishing that a defendant in the prosecutor's jurisdiction was convicted of an offense that the defendant did not commit, the prosecutor shall seek to remedy the conviction.

### Other Lawyers

While other lawyers are not subject to the stringent disclose requirements imposed on prosecutors, they also have disclosure obligations imposed by the ABA Model Rules of Professional Conduct. Rule 3.4(a) provides:

---

## Attorney Obligation for Disclosure

### ABA Rule 3.4(a)

Disclosure by Attorneys:

> A lawyer shall not unlawfully obstruct another party's access to evidence or unlawfully alter, destroy or conceal a document or other material having potential evidentiary value. A lawyer shall not counsel or assist another person to do any such act.

The official Comment to the Rule explains counsel's obligations:

> Documents and other items of evidence are often essential to establish a claim or defense. Subject to evidentiary privileges, the right of an opposing party, including the government, to obtain evidence through discovery or subpoena is an important procedural right. The exercise of that right can be frustrated if relevant material is altered, concealed or destroyed. Applicable law in many jurisdictions makes it an offense to destroy material for purposes of impairing its availability in a pending proceeding or one whose commencement can be foreseen. Falsifying evidence is also generally a criminal offense. Paragraph (a) applies to evidentiary material generally, including computerized information. Applicable law may permit a lawyer to take temporary possession of physical evidence of client crimes for the purpose of conducting a limited examination that will not alter or destroy material characteristics of the evidence. In such a case, applicable laws may require the lawyer to turn the evidence over to the police or other prosecuting authority, depending on the circumstances.

---

## CHECKLIST: INTRODUCING EXHIBITS

### Planning to Use Exhibits

☐ Identify exhibits in existence and collect and preserve them.
- Determine if other exhibits and trial visuals are called for and create them.
- Incorporate the essentials of a persuasive story:
  - Human values,
  - Human needs,
  - Human story—usually about the client,
  - Believable and understandable story,

- Quantity of evidence described is compelling, and
- Quality of evidence is convincing.
- Conduct legal research and move in limine to admit the exhibit or prepare a trial brief if needed.
- Plan to establish the foundation for admissibility of the exhibit.
- Prepare your witnesses to work with exhibits in trial (show them the exhibits and rehearse).
- Have an exhibit list.

### Meet Judicial Expectations: Exhibits

☐ Do not display the exhibits until admitted, and
☐ Premark the exhibits.

### Introducing an Exhibit

☐ Have the clerk mark the exhibit if it is not premarked.
☐ Show the exhibit to opposing counsel.
☐ Establish the evidentiary foundation for the exhibit.
☐ Offer the exhibit and meet any objections to it.
☐ Make a record.

### Laying a Foundation

☐ Will the other side stipulate to the exhibit's admissibility so that you do not have to lay a foundation?
☐ Essential evidence rules.
- Is the exhibit relevant under Fed. R. Evid. 401 and 402?
- Does it pass the Fed. R. Evid. 403 test (probative vs. unfair prejudice)?
- Is it authentic or identified under Fed. R. Evid. 901 or 902?
- Is it otherwise admissible?
☐ Real evidence.
- Regarding identification of real evidence, is it readily identifiable or is it fungible, requiring a chain of custody?
☐ Documentary evidence.
- Is it relevant?
- Does it pass Rule 403?
- Is it authentic under Rule 901 or self-authenticated under Rule 902?
- Is it admissible under the original writing rule, Fed. R. Evid. 1001-1004?
- Will it survive a hearsay objection?
- Is it otherwise admissible?
☐ Demonstrative evidence.
- Is it relevant?
- Does it pass Rule 403?
- Is it authentic or identified?
- Is it otherwise admissible?

### Ethical Considerations

☐ A prosecutor must disclose exculpatory information including exhibits.
☐ Counsel cannot obstruct opposing party's access to exhibits.

# THE VISUAL TRIAL AND TODAY'S TECHNOLOGY

*If you have tears, prepare to shed them now.*
*You all do know this mantle: I remember*
*The first time ever Caesar put it on;*
*'Twas on a summer's evening, in his tent,*
*That day he overcame the Nervii:*
*Look, in this place ran Cassius' dagger through:*
*See what a rent the envious Casca made:*
*Through this the well-beloved Brutus stabb'd;*

*And as he pluck'd his cursed steel away,*
*Mark how the blood of Caesar follow'd it,*
*As rushing out of doors, to be resolved*
*If Brutus so unkindly knock'd, or no;*
*For Brutus, as you know, was Caesar's angel:*
*Judge, O you gods, how dearly Caesar loved him!*
*This was the most unkindest cut of all. . . .*

—**Mark Antony**, in William Shakespeare's
(1564-1616) *Julius Caesar* (1600-1601),
Funeral Oration, 3.2

## I.  VISUALS AND THE HIGH-TECH TRIAL

In this chapter, we discuss the high-tech trial; when you should and should not use visuals; available hardware, software, and other computer equipment; companies that create and display visuals; how to retrieve and display visuals in trial; and the criteria for good and bad visuals.

This chapter is augmented by the companion website, *http://www.aspen lawschool.com/books/berger_trialad4e,* which provides additional information on the visual trial and today's courtroom technology. The website is continually updated with useful information about visuals. For instance, it has links to resources that create ADR and trial visuals, provides courtroom technological assistance, and offers a link to a virtual tour of courtroom technology. Also on the website you can watch a visual trial—the *Freck Point* trial—that includes computer slideshows, a witness being impeached by counsel using clips from a video deposition, diagrams, photographs, and real evidence. On this video you can observe experienced trial lawyers introducing these exhibits and then effectively displaying them for the jury.

> To see a demonstration of how to interrelate a scene diagram with photographs, watch the plaintiff's direct examination of the detective in the *Freck Point* trial demonstration movie on the website *http://www.aspenlawschool.com/books/ berger_trialad4e.*

## II.  REASONS TO USE OR NOT USE VISUALS

A lawyer must evaluate the effectiveness of visuals at trial or in an alternative dispute resolution process (mediation, arbitration, or negotiation)—whether you created them or you had them created by a consulting visuals company. There are some essential criteria for determining whether a visual will be effective. In our discussion, we are concentrating on computer slideshows such as Power-

Point, but the same standards apply to most other visuals as well. Although each visual must be evaluated on its own merit and the situation in which it will be offered, certain fundamental dos and don'ts exist.

---

## The Dos and Don'ts of Using Visuals

### Use Visuals

- **Perception and Retention:** Jurors retain more of what they see than what they hear. Jurors are accustomed to computers and to receiving information visually.
- **Time Saver:** Technology saves time for the lawyer with the creation and use of visuals.
- **Storytelling:** Visuals can help convey your story to the jury.
- **Complexities:** Visuals simplify information and assist an expert in explaining technical information.
- **Story Is Implausible:** Visuals can reveal the implausibility of the other side's story.
- **Explain Legal Theory:** A visual can help explain the legal theory, such as when the jury instruction is incomprehensible.

### Do Not Use Visuals

- **Too Many:** Do not overload with visuals, because that distracts from communication. Visuals should complement you or your witness's words. Use a reasonable number of visuals to suit the trial.
- **Too Dark, Too Light, Wrong Color:** Words or images should be easy to see. Avoid dark lettering or images on a dark background. Light colors may wash out in a bright room unless they are on a dark background. Avoid red, because some people are color-blind and cannot see red. Instead, use light or white lettering on a dark background, which work well in a well-lit room.
- **Too Small:** The lettering and image should be large enough to be easily seen at a distance.
- **Too Cluttered:** The visual should not be too wordy or complicated. Irrelevant information should be culled from the visual. (KISS—Keep it simple, stupid.)
- **Too Noisy:** Sound effects are distracting—avoid them unless the sound is part of the event being portrayed, such as a video deposition, a police chase, or a 911 call.
- **Too Ugly:** A visual should be nice looking and professional. Poor design is distracting.
- **Unprepared:** When the attorney and/or witness is unprepared to work with the technology or visual, should it be a surprise if disaster ensues?

---

## III. DISPLAYING THE EXHIBIT

Getting the exhibit admitted into evidence is only part of the trial lawyer's job when working with exhibits. Generally, up until that point the exhibit should not have been shown to the jury, because it is not yet in evidence. However, after the court has ruled that it is admitted, the lawyer's task is to show the exhibit to the jury and have the witness discuss it in the most persuasive way. There are multitudes of ways to display an exhibit. The method you select depends on three factors:

1. Technology available in the courtroom,
2. Courtroom practices, and
3. The type of exhibit (audio recording would be played while a photograph would be shown).

## A. Courtroom Technology

How the exhibit is displayed depends on the technology available in the courtroom. Many courtrooms are equipped with the latest technology: a document camera; television monitors for the jurors, counsel, and the judge (enabling the judge to regulate what the jurors will see and when); a large screen onto which a computer slideshow, a video, and other visual media may be shown; and even a remnant of the traditional courtroom—the flipchart on an easel.

However, you may be assigned to a courtroom that was designed at the turn of the century—the twentieth century. A flipchart on an easel may be the only method available for displaying visuals. In this case, assuming that you wish to and can afford to use a document camera or computer visuals, you must make prior arrangements—with permission from the judge and opposing counsel—to bring and use your own technology. Determine, among other things, where to place a screen or television monitor, projector, or document camera. Locate the power source—and whether extension cords are needed. Technology can fail. We've witnessed presentations where the video, the PowerPoint presentation, or audio wouldn't play, or even where a computer crashed. Always be prepared with a backup plan to accomplish your objectives.

## B. Courtroom Practices

Courtroom practices also govern how you will be able to display exhibits. Ultimately, the judge will determine how you may display the visual. For example, if the court is equipped with state-of-the-art technology, the judge may require that an image be projected on juror monitors rather than having the image enlarged and displayed on an easel.

What follows is a discussion of some of the ways to display an exhibit, along with some trial techniques for implementing the methods.

## C. Using a Document Camera

A document camera, also referred to as a "digital visual presenter," enables a lawyer to project an image of an exhibit onto a large screen or a television monitor. This is ideal for anything from a photograph to an object the size of a penny.

Some document cameras allow transparencies such as x-rays to be placed on the bed of the document camera and the light source switched from above to below, projecting the transparency. Using a document camera replaces the need to publish an exhibit to the jury (see the next section) or to admit blowups of exhibits large enough for the jurors to see.

Photo by J. Barratt Godfrey

## D. Publishing or Parading the Exhibit

Another method for displaying the exhibit to the jury is to ask the judge to pass the exhibit among the jurors: *"May I publish Plaintiff's Exhibit 5 to the jury?"* With the court's permission, you hand the exhibit to a juror, and the jurors pass it from hand to hand. This method works well for an important exhibit that you want to emphasize. The drawback is that it takes time for the exhibit to be passed hand to hand. It does not work as well as a document camera for writings because it can take time for individual jurors to read the document. When the exhibit is being passed around, make sure that the jurors can concentrate on the exhibit. In particular, because you are conducting a direct when the exhibit is being passed, suspend asking questions of the witness until the exhibit has been passed to all the jurors and you have been able to retrieve it from them.

You can also highlight an exhibit by parading it in front of the jurors so that they can get a close look at it. Ask the judge, *"Your Honor, may I show this exhibit to the jury by walking in front of the jury?"* If the exhibit is dramatic and you are the plaintiff's attorney or the prosecutor, parading an exhibit, such as a photograph from the *Freck Point* trial of Sondra Griffith laying stabbed to death in her bed, can have a particularly powerful effect and create a human connection between the victim, the jury, and the attorney. To show the exhibit, walk slowly in front of the jury box, stopping every few feet so the jurors in both the front and back rows can see. Try to catch the jurors' eyes when you stop to show the exhibit, and see and feel the impact the exhibit has on them. When the jurors look in your eyes, they will understand the importance of the exhibit.

> For an example of how to parade an exhibit, watch Detective Montgomery parade the knife during his direct examination in the *Freck Point* demonstration movie on the website *http://www.aspenlawschool.com/books/berger_trialad4e.*

### E.  Showing or Reading the Exhibit

The most frequent way an exhibit is communicated to a jury is by either showing it or reading it to the jury. Once the exhibit, such as the photograph of Sondra Griffith, has been admitted, ask the witness: *"Could you hold up Plaintiff's Exhibit 8, please, so the jury can see it?"* Then you have the witness use the exhibit to amplify on his testimony: *"Could you tell the jury what can be seen in the photograph, Plaintiff's Exhibit 8?"* Or you can ask that the exhibit of the defendant Samuel Griffith's statement be read by him: *"If you would, could you read paragraph five of Plaintiff's Exhibit 12?"*

### F.  Display for the Jury

One way to display a chart, diagram, enlarged photograph, or another admitted exhibit is to place it on an easel. The easel can be placed in front of the jury or at the end of the jury box near the witness stand so the jury can get a good look at the exhibit. In the staging diagram below, you move to the clerk to mark the exhibit (Step 1), walk to opposing counsel to show the exhibit (Step 2), walk to the witness for identification (Step 3), offer the exhibit and meet objections (Step 4), display the exhibit on an easel (Step 5), and make a record (Step 6).

While the witness is still seated in the witness chair, counsel takes the exhibit that has just been admitted and places it on the easel. For example, assume the exhibit is a diagram of the stairs leading upstairs to the Griffiths' bedroom and that the witness is defendant Samuel Griffith. Defendant's counsel could say, *"If you would, Mr. Griffith, please step over here to the easel where I've placed Defense Exhibit 3."* Griffith's lawyer has the witness stand on the left side of the exhibit, because in this position the right-handed witness will not obstruct the jury's view when she writes on the exhibit.

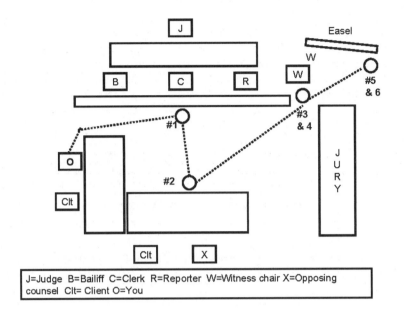

J=Judge  B=Bailiff  C=Clerk  R=Reporter  W=Witness chair  X=Opposing counsel  Clt= Client  O=You

When working with an exhibit, first ask the witness to generally tell the jury about the exhibit, because up until now, even if the witness is repeating what was said during the laying of the evidentiary foundation, the jurors will not have seen the visual. Counsel may begin: *"Mr. Griffith, could you describe for the jurors what they can see in Defense Exhibit 3?"* After the witness has oriented the jurors to the exhibit, counsel can ask more specific questions, such as: *"Mr. Griffith, you testified before that you ran up the stairs and saw a man come from your bedroom. He then shoved you as he pushed past. Could you take this blue pen and draw a line showing you coming up the stairs, and then place an X where you were when the man shoved you? Also, please put your initials by the X and write shoved."* When the testimony relating to the exhibit is concluded, remember to say, *"You may resume your seat,"* or your witness will remain standing at the easel while you move on to other topics.

## G. Using a Computer

Slideshows of exhibits, documents, photographs, depositions, and other media can be digitized to display in an electronic format. Once the media is created or converted to an electronic format, it can be presented to the court using a digital projector or other display, depending upon the sophistication of the particular courtroom's technology. Later in this chapter, we discuss computer visuals in depth.

In the *Freck Point* demonstration movie, you can watch both counsels use computer slideshows during opening statements and closing arguments. You can also see how a slideshow is used during the direct examination of Detective Montgomery by viewing the movie on the website *http://www.aspenlawschool.com/books/ berger_trialad4e.*

If you are bringing equipment into the courtroom, use a rolling cart with the monitor and other equipment on it. Where to station the equipment depends on the courtroom layout, but a good placement for the projection screen or display is near either end of the jury box. In this way, you can stand in the center for opening and closing, and then direct the jurors' attention to the display when you wish to show an exhibit or other visual. A handheld remote will allow you to advance the slides no matter where you move in the courtroom. If you use a remote, be sure to practice working with it and to check the battery.

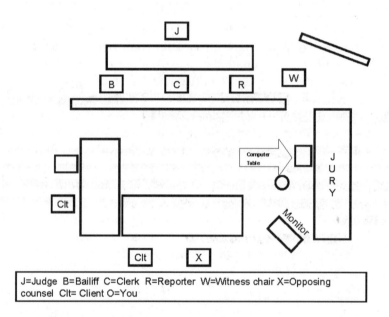

J=Judge  B=Bailiff  C=Clerk  R=Reporter  W=Witness chair  X=Opposing counsel  Clt= Client  O=You

## H. Demeanor

Related to the method of displaying an exhibit is the attitude counsel projects to the jury in dealing with the exhibit. To illustrate, consider how the prosecutor or plaintiff's lawyer could behave with the knife in the *Freck Point* case. If counsel handles the knife with respect and care, this projects an impression to the jury that the weapon is dangerous. On the other hand, if counsel casually handles it, and even inappropriately hands it to the defendant on cross-examination, counsel may subliminally suggest to the jury that the knife and the person who holds it are not threatening. Some exhibits should be handled gently and respectfully, such as the bloody nightgown and bedsheets of Sondra Griffith, in order to reflect the solemnity of the victim's injury.

## IV. TODAY'S TECHNOLOGY

### A. Software and Courtroom Presentations

There are several software programs for creating visuals. This book's accompanying website shows you ways to use that software. Our goal is to inform you about the software and courtroom technology that is available and what it can do for you.

Manuals and other resources on how to design slides for PowerPoint and other types of computer presentation software are readily available. Three particularly good books on designing visuals with computer software are Ronald E. Bowers, *Visuals for Today's Prosecutors* (NCDA 2003) (for prosecutors); Ann E. Brenden & John Goodhue, *The Lawyer's Guide to Creating Persuasive Computer Presentations* (2d ed., ABA 2005) (accompanying CD contains 12 self-guided tutorials on basic PowerPoint techniques); and Mike Rogers, *Litigation Technology: Becoming a High-Tech Trial Lawyer* (Aspen Publishers 2006). The companies that design these software products commonly offer manuals and free trial periods, during which you can first download the software from the Internet and then try it for free for a limited time.

Other popular trial software programs are Trial Director by inData and Sanction by LexisNexis. These programs enable the lawyer or trial support assistant to retrieve an image, such as an individual document, by a Bates number, a bar code, or a given name or number at any time. Then the document can be enlarged and pertinent portions of it highlighted as it is projected on a screen.

Tom Mighell, *iPad in One Hour for Litigators* (ABA Law Practice Management Section 2013) is a useful handbook, covering such things as apps for the courtroom, presenting digital evidence, and storing and reviewing documents.

### B. The Creator

The creation of the visuals may be done by you, your law firm staff, or a company that you employ to design the visuals. However, for complex visuals, such as a computer-animated video showing the collapse of an apartment staircase, you may need to hire a computer programmer, a visuals company, and scientists to do the physics on which the visual is based.

> ## Trial Visuals Creators
>
> On the Internet, you can locate companies that create demonstrative evidence. The following are some websites you can visit.
>
> - Borrowed Ladder Media Services, Inc.: *http://www.borrowedladder.com*
> - Naegeli Trial Technologies: *http://www.naegeliusa.com*
> - High Impact: *http://www.highimpactlit.com*
> - Legal Art Works: *http://www.legalartworks.com*
> - MediVisuals: *http://www.medivisuals.com*
> - Prolumina: *http://www.prolumina.net*

Even if someone else prepares the visual, you must maintain oversight and control of the final product, because it will be used in your case.

## C. The Equipment

What equipment, if any, will you need to bring to the courtroom? If the court does not have what you need and you plan to bring equipment to the courtroom, the first step is to ask the judge for permission to bring in equipment. Then ask the judge where to position the equipment. Some equipment that you may consider bringing to the courtroom:

> ## Equipment
>
> The following is a list of equipment that could be brought into court.
>
> - Document Camera
> - Computers:  Two computers in case one fails.
> - Remote:  To advance or reverse the slideshow or to black out the screen (with extra batteries).
> - Monitor or Screen:  Images can be projected onto a screen with a digital projector or shown on a monitor to which the computer is connected.
> - Touch Screen:  A large monitor that allows digital annotations (e.g., a witness can draw on a scene diagram displayed on the touch screen); technology may be available to save the markings on the exhibit so they will be preserved for appeal. A variation of this technology includes interactive rear projection whiteboards, such as a SMART Board or StarBoard.
> - Digital Projector:  With an extra bulb.
> - Bar Code Scanner:  Software allows for the scanning of a bar code on an exhibit to retrieve and project an image of the exhibit on the screen.
> - Cables, Extension Cords, and Tape:  To tape the cords to the floor, wall, and so on.

### Tablets for Trial

Trial lawyers are increasingly utilizing tablets, such as iPads or similar types of tablets, during trials. There are good reasons for this trend. First, displaying documents and other exhibits with a tablet is simpler than learning how to operate a computer program such as TrialDirector. Second, utilizing a tablet is less expensive than employing staff to run complex software.

Operating with a tablet in the courtroom requires a projector, a screen, an adapter, and a long VGA cord so that counsel can move around the courtroom. For example, TrialPad is an application that is much less expensive than traditional software, and it enables counsel to convert exhibits into PDFs. An exhibit can be shown to a witness on the tablet, and then to the judge before it is shown to the jury. These exhibits can be displayed to the jury from the tablet. With the TrialPad app, a witness can annotate an exhibit, and counsel can expand a paragraph from a document with a callout device so that it is easily read.

Tablets can be used for other purposes in trial. For example, iPads come with Keynote, which is a software app similar to PowerPoint, that can show a computer slideshow during opening statement, closing argument, or expert testimony. Tablets allow you to conveniently carry and retrieve case documents and exhibits. Also, you can do on-the-spot legal research online with a tablet.

### The Fully Equipped Courtroom

If you are in a fully equipped courtroom, the court will expect that you come prepared to use the equipment. Federal courtrooms have equipment such as monitors, document cameras, projection screen, a projector, and so on. Take a look at this federal courtroom.

Courtroom: U.S. District Court, Western District of Washington.

The above picture is a view from the jury box. Note that the jurors will view the exhibits on monitors in front of them. The lawyer stands behind the podium that is between the two counsel tables. (Standing at a podium is a requirement in all federal district courts.) If an attorney wishes to show the jurors a portion of a deposition, the attorney can use a laptop to display the deposition portion, and because the computer is linked into the court's system, the deposition shows on the jurors' monitors. The same method works for exhibits. To show an exhibit on the monitor, the lawyer or support person would type the premarked exhibit number into the computer. As previously mentioned, alternative ways to retrieve and display exhibits include using a bar code on the exhibit or putting it on the document camera, which from this view is on the right side of the podium. On the far wall behind counsel table is a screen that may descend from the ceiling in order for counsel to project a larger image.

Here is another view of the same federal courtroom, this time from behind the podium. The jury box is to the left. On the left shelf of the podium is the document camera. While counsel might use the document camera to show a document on the jurors' monitors, this can be troublesome because the image may have to be focused and papers may have to be removed from a notebook. Instead, counsel can use the computer hooked into the court's system. An object—for instance, a handgun—could be placed on it, and then the camera could be zoomed in to show the serial numbers clearly on the monitors. Or an x-ray can be placed on the document camera and be illuminated with the light underneath. While this courtroom is equipped with state-of-the-art technology, there is also a flipchart easel on which counsel can write and place visuals.

Federal courts provide counsel with in-person training sessions, online tutorials, and an online virtual tour of the courtroom that allows you to inspect and receive a description of the equipment. For more information about technology in a federal courtroom, visit the U.S. District Court Western District of Washington on the Internet at: *http://www.wawd.uscourts.gov/attorneys/trial-support/courtroom-technology*.

## D. The Display

### The Displayer

You can hire a trial support company to operate the equipment for you when you are in trial (if you can afford it). Otherwise, a colleague or legal assistant may be able to operate the equipment and display the trial visuals for you. Some attorneys prefer to handle the exhibits themselves, if possible, because they don't want their personal connection with the jurors to be in any way diluted or fragmented by having another person displaying the exhibits.

### Backup Plans

Some lawyers avoid using computer presentations because they fear, with some justification, equipment or software failure. Generally, judges will not recess to fix the problem. Therefore, the trial lawyer should always have a backup plan, such as showing slide printouts on the document camera or parading a slide copy to the jury.

### Retrieval and Display in High-Tech Fashion
*Exhibits and Trial Visuals*

Counsel must promptly retrieve and show the desired visual or exhibit. The low- or no-tech means of accomplishing this is to have a well-organized system. It all begins by loading the exhibits and trial visuals into a computer database with the necessary software. Sanction by LexisNexis is an example of a storage and retrieval software program. Another method is to bar code the exhibit so that a scanner hooked to the computer will read the bar code and project the image on the screen. If the exhibits have not been premarked, then when the exhibit is offered, an image is shown only on the judge's monitor so the judge can rule on its admissibility. Once the judge has admitted the exhibit, the image is displayed so the jury can see it.

*Transcripts*

In the absence of computer assistance, the lawyer who wants to have a transcript, usually a deposition, admitted into evidence will be working with the paper transcript. The lawyer, with the aid of a deposition summary, can search for the pertinent section of the transcript. Then the lawyer, with either a notebook or bound deposition, elicits the prior testimony from the witness. If it is a preservation witness, the lawyer can read the questions from the transcript, and a designated person who is the surrogate for the absent witness reads the responses. However, this can be tiresome.

A better approach is to transcribe depositions in real time. A real-time deposition is where the court reporter's notes are instantaneously turned into text and transmitted to computer, where software, such as LiveNote, captures it. The lawyer can mark places in the transcript where particular words are used or where the passage relates to a particular issue. This enables the trial lawyer to search and find the wanted passage in the transcript and display it on a screen. The transcript also can be hyperlinked to exhibits.

The following is what an annotated LiveNote transcript looks like:

LiveNote, *http://www.livenote.com.*

The transcript can be synchronized with video and sound. If the deposition was videoed, the transcript can be synchronized to the video so that on the screen, the jury will see the transcript scroll, and also the video of the deposition. A further benefit is that the exhibit being discussed by the witness can be timed to be shown when it is discussed in the transcript. Then the jury sees the transcript scroll on the screen, hears and sees the witness testify, and sees in a third part of the screen the exhibit that is being discussed. This method is superior to having the preservation deposition testimony read into the record by the lawyer and a stand-in for the absent witness.

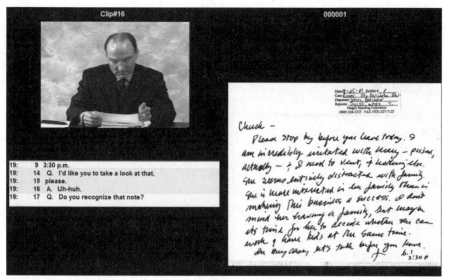

Naegeli Trial Technologies, *http://www.naegelitrialtech.com.*

## E. Computer-Created Visuals

The computer is an economical and timesaving tool for creating visuals that the lawyer can use in alternative ways. A lawyer with PowerPoint can create slides of drawings, photographs, scanned-in documents, or other images. Slides can be printed in color or black and white, and can be enlarged with an office poster maker or at an office supply store. The poster-sized paper can then be adhered to foam core to create a board-backed enlargement. Another approach is to place the letter-sized visual on a document camera, which will project the image so the jurors can see it in an enlarged form.

## F. Disclosure and Court Approval

Although the rules in your jurisdiction may not require that you disclose your computer presentation to opposing counsel, it is generally good practice to do so. For example, if you are planning to show a PowerPoint slideshow in opening statement, you can provide opposing counsel with either a paper printout of the slides or a CD containing the presentation. Once opposing counsel has had a chance to review the slides, you can seek a stipulation that all or part of it may be shown. If opposing counsel objects, you can make a motion in limine to the court to be able use the slideshow in opening statement. Whether in limine or with a stipulation, you should provide the judge with printouts or a CD of the slides, because you do not want to surprise the judge.

At the hearing on the motion, you may be required to call witnesses to lay a foundation for the exhibit shown in the slideshow. With this full-disclosure approach, objections can be resolved out of the presence of the jury, and your presentation will move in a smoother manner than if it were interrupted by objections.

## G.  Software Sampler

The following is a checklist of those visuals, along with page numbers where they appear in the book, so that you can draw from this list when brainstorming for visual ideas.

---

**CHECKLIST**

### List of Trial Visuals

The following is a list of visuals that you might consider, along with page numbers where they appear in this book.

- ☐ Photographs (pages 163-166)
- ☐ Charts
  - Legal elements (pages 167, 490)
  - Case summary (page 76)
  - Summary—Fed. R. Evid. 1006 (page 327)
- ☐ Timeline (pages 168-169)
- ☐ Scene diagram (page 169)
- ☐ Document callouts (page 170)
- ☐ Deposition (pages 276-277)
- ☐ Medical illustration (page 406)
- ☐ Animation (pages 170, 406-407, 492-493)
- ☐ Argument visuals (pages 490-493)
- ☐ Models (page 407)

---

## V.  ETHICAL CONSIDERATIONS

A lawyer must be concerned about displaying tangible evidence to the jury before the evidence is admitted into evidence; to do so is unprofessional. Tangible evidence should not even be brought into view of the fact finder unless you have a good-faith belief that it will be admissible. If you harbor a doubt about admissibility, you should make an offer of proof to the judge in the absence of the jury or during a bench conference. ABA Model Rule of Professional Conduct 3.4(e) provides that a lawyer, in trial, shall not "allude to any matter that the lawyer does not reasonably believe is relevant or that will not be supported by admissible evidence. . . ."

## Ethical Rules Pertaining to Exhibits: Summary

### ABA Model Rules of Professional Conduct

**Disclosure to the Other Side**

**Prosecutor:** Under Model Rule of Professional Conduct 3.8(d), the prosecutor must disclose to the defense any evidence tending to negate the guilt of the defendant, mitigate the degree of crime, or reduce punishment.

**Other Counsel:** Model Rule of Professional Conduct 3.4(a) prohibits a lawyer from obstructing another party's access to evidence or unlawfully altering, destroying, or concealing a document or other material having potential evidentiary value. A lawyer shall not counsel or assist another person to do any such act. Counsel may, according to the Rule's Comment, take temporary custody of the material for examination, and local law may require turning it over to the other party.

**Display**

Model Rule of Professional Conduct 3.4(e) provides that a lawyer, in trial, shall not "allude to any matter that the lawyer does not reasonably believe is relevant or that will not be supported by admissible evidence. . . ." Therefore, counsel should not expose tangible evidence (e.g., exhibits) to the jury unless the lawyer has a good faith belief that the thing will be admissible.

## CHECKLIST: VISUAL TRIAL AND TECHNOLOGY

**Pros and Cons of Trial Visuals**

- ☐ Pros:
  - Aids juror perception and retention,
  - Saves time,
  - Tells the story better than words,
  - Explains complexities,
  - Reveals the implausible, and
  - Explains the law.
- ☐ Cons:
  - Overload of visuals can distract from communication,
  - Can be unreadable,
  - Can be too cluttered,
  - Too noisy,
  - Too ugly, or
  - Counsel can be unprepared to work with the visual.

**Effectively Display the Exhibit**

- ☐ Scout the courtroom to determine what equipment is available.
- ☐ Gain permission from the judge to bring in and use equipment for displaying exhibits, such as a document camera.

*continued* ▶

☐ Make arrangements to bring equipment to court.

☐ Determine how to display the exhibit with these alternatives, among others:
  • Document camera;
  • Publishing or parading the exhibit;
  • Placing the exhibit, such as a diagram, on an easel; or
  • Projecting the computer image on a screen or monitor.

☐ Display the proper demeanor and behavior when working with the exhibits.

☐ Time the introduction of the exhibit so it has impact on the jury.

### Software and Trial Presentations

☐ Computer software, such as PowerPoint, can be used to create and display visuals.

☐ Have a backup plan, such as printing the computer slides on letter-sized paper so they can be displayed with a document camera in case of a computer failure.

☐ A trial visuals consulting business can create the trial visuals, and also appear in court as trial support to display the visuals.

☐ Obtain court permission to display court visuals.

### Ethical Considerations

☐ Do not display an exhibit to the jury before the court has ruled on its admissibility or when it is otherwise permissible to do so, such as during opening statement.

# DIRECT EXAMINATION
## Building the Case

---

*"A trial is intended to be a search for truth. Knowing what is true is a necessary first step, but it is not enough. A lawyer must prove those truths, and prove them with admissible evidence."*

> —**David Boies**, *Courting Justice: From NY Yankees v. Major League Baseball to Bush v. Gore, 1997-2000* (Hyperion 2004)

*"Any fact is better established by two or three testimonies, than by a thousand arguments."*

> —**Nathaniel Emmons**, *A Dictionary of Thoughts, Being a Cyclopedia of Laconic Quotations* (Tyrone Edwards ed., F.B. Dickerson Co. 1908)

---

## I.  UNDERLYING PRINCIPLES

This chapter explains how to build direct examination and how direct examinations serve as the building blocks and mortar for constructing a persuasive case for the jury. When you call a witness for direct examination, it is your opportunity both to present factual information that is sufficient to support your case theory and to persuade the jury to accept your case theory. Direct examination also provides you with an opportunity to weaken your opponent's case theory by presenting evidence that contradicts it.

Of course, the defendant's entire case theory may be a challenge to the plaintiff's ability to meet its burden of proof. In this situation, the defense may call few or even no witnesses for direct examination and raise defense points solely through cross-examination of the plaintiff's witnesses. The defense strategy of relying on cross-examination of plaintiff's witnesses and presenting no defense case (calling no witnesses for direct examination) is used in criminal cases, but is seldom a defense strategy in civil cases.

Direct examination should fulfill two major objectives:

- Support your case theory by conveying sufficient and persuasive information through credible witness testimony and exhibits, and
- Meet the other side's case theory.

We explore how to achieve these objectives by determining the content of a direct examination, structuring the direct so that it is compelling, focusing on witness preparation, and effectively conducting both direct and redirect examinations.

To see demonstrations of how to conduct direct examination, watch the direct examination of lay witnesses in the *Freck Point* trial demonstration movie on the website *http://www.aspenlawschool.com/books/berger_trialad4e.*

## II. SELECTING CONTENT

### A. Case Theory as a Guide

It is imperative that you use your case theory to decide what testimony to elicit on direct. This ensures that you present all the information you can from the witness to support your case theory. It also confines direct examination to information supporting those points that are relevant to the case theory. If direct examination produces information that goes beyond your case theory, it risks cluttering the trial with extraneous details that may obscure and confuse your case theory for the jury. Or, worse, it may fling open the door for a cross-examination that otherwise would be outside the scope of direct examination.

How do you prepare your case theory so that it helps you determine the evidence you want to present? Then, having carried out this analysis using the case theory, what are the essential pieces of evidence you want to impart in a specific, direct examination? Finally, having decided what evidence you want to present through a particular witness, what is the best way to present this evidence during direct examination? This section addresses how to develop these essential points.

A direct examination should be consistent with your case theory. As you plan the direct of each witness, consider whether it is consistent with the context of your case theory. This ensures that the testimony from various witnesses and your exhibits are consistent. By preparing with your entire case in mind, any individual direct examination can present an opportunity to actually explain or eliminate any apparent inconsistencies between your witnesses.

### Closing Argument and Trial Plan as a Guide to Direct Examination

Pretrial preparation is the key to building an effective direct examination, and that preparation of a direct examination is the product of your formulation of your case theory. See Chapter 3, Case Theory and Theme Development. To prepare your direct examination, begin by using (1) your tentative closing argument, and (2) a trial plan.

- **Tentative Closing Argument as a Guide:** How you intend to present the case theory in closing argument should guide you to list all the points from your witnesses and exhibits that you anticipate presenting at trial to support your legal theory, factual theory, and theme. Your tentative argument pulls together the legal and factual theories, because the essence of a good closing is the trial lawyer making suggestions to the jury about how they should apply the law to the facts during jury deliberations.
- **Trial Plan as a Guide:** In your trial plan, list the witnesses, the tangible evidence (documentary, real, and demonstrative), the anticipated evidentiary objections of opposing counsel, your responses, the alternatives to the particular witness or tangible evidence that you could use to support your legal theory, if needed, and proposed jury instructions. See examples of a trial plan on pages 285 and 389.

## B. Legal Theory

Your initial concern in planning direct examination is to present sufficient evidence to support the elements of your legal theory. Of course, information elicited in direct examination of one witness may support only one element of your legal theory, more than one element, or every element. In other words, you may have to call multiple witnesses in your case-in-chief before the testimony and exhibits produced through the combined direct examinations establish the elements of your legal theory by sufficient evidence. Those elements will be familiar to you because you will have concentrated on them in preparing your trial plan; and in developing proposed jury instructions, a tentative closing argument, your opening statement, and voir dire questions.

You can craft your direct examination using a trial plan, as illustrated on page 285, to assist you in determining what testimony and exhibits to present in direct examination in order to prove the elements of your legal theory. Your plan for trial, which is based on your case theory, can serve as your guide for organizing your direct examination. It can also function as your checklist of the evidence to elicit from the witnesses.

To illustrate how a trial plan can help you decide on the content of direct examination, assume you are the prosecutor preparing for direct examination in the *Blue Moon News Robbery* case. (See pages 81 and 286 for information on this case.) Imagine that you are preparing the direct examination testimony of Mr. Gardner Newman, the clerk at the Blue Moon News convenience store, where

## Preparing Direct Examination

### Using the Trial Plan
#### The *Blue Moon News Robbery* Case

**PROSECUTION'S TRIAL PLAN**

| Claim (Defense) | Legal Elements (Legal Theory) | Facts (Factual Theory) | Witness | Evidence | Weakness | Evidence Objection | Response to Objection | Jury Selection | To Do |
|---|---|---|---|---|---|---|---|---|---|
| First degree robbery | Identification of defendant | Clerk can identify defendant as robber | Clerk Newman | Newman saw robber | Short time to observe | Suggestive show-up | Show-ups are permissible, show-up not suggestive | General major witness credibility instruction | Speak to Newman |

One of the elements of the crime is that the defendant is the person who committed the robbery. Your trial plan lists Mr. Newman, the robbery victim, as the person who can testify on the element of identity—that the defendant is the person who robbed the store. That testimony is critical to establishing that the defendant is guilty of the offense.

the robbery occurred. Your trial plan indicates what you must prove to fulfill the legal elements of robbery in the first degree, including identification of the defendant.

Now, consider the questions you will need to ask to ensure obtaining factually sufficient information to establish the element of identification.

---

**Direct Examination**

### Legal Theory
### The *Blue Moon News Robbery* Case

As the prosecutor, you might include the following questions in your direct examination of the convenience store clerk, Mr. Gardner Newman, who can identify the defendant, Mike Ryan, as the person who robbed him:

*Q:* Mr. Newman, were you able to see the person who robbed you?
*Q:* Can you describe what the robber was wearing?
*Q:* If you saw that person again, could you identify him?
*Q:* Is that person in court today?
*Q:* Could you point him out?

This testimony is essential for presenting a prima facie case for first degree robbery and establishes the defendant's identity as the robber, a legal element of the crime charged.

---

## C. Factual Theory

Direct examination witness testimony must also be persuasive. Will the direct examination or amalgamation of direct examinations in your case-in-chief compel the jury to reach the desired verdict? The persuasive factual story entails at least these five key essential components:

* Human values and needs,
* Human story,
* Believable and understandable story,
* Quantity of evidence, and
* Quality of evidence.

See Chapter 3, Case Theory and Theme Development, at pages 38-42, where we discuss these five key essentials of a persuasive story.

### Human Values and Needs, and Human Story

As you review what your witness could testify to on direct, you are looking for facts, opinions, and tangible evidence that will highlight the human values and needs, and human stories that exist in the case. This aspect of direct examination will assist your audience—the jury—to understand and relate to the case.

Continue to assume that you are the prosecutor in the *Blue Moon News Robbery* case and are planning the direct examination of the clerk.

## Direct Examination

### Human Values and Needs, and a Human Story
### The *Blue Moon News Robbery* Case

Direct examination of the convenience store clerk, Mr. Gardner Newman, could focus on the two factors of human values and needs, and a human story.

**Human Values and Needs:** The community—in particular, the jurors—are concerned about personal safety. Everyone has a need to be safe from harm. The direct examination of Mr. Newman could be designed to bring out these aspects:

*Q:* Mr. Newman, when the man produced the handgun, where was it pointed?

*A:* At my chest.

*Q:* What were you thinking when the gun was pointed at your chest?

*A:* I was thinking that I would give him anything he wanted so he wouldn't shoot me.

*Q:* How did you feel at the time?

*A:* I was afraid that he'd shoot me.

*Q:* Did you say anything?

*A:* I begged him to not shoot me and to just take the money from the register and leave.

**Human Story:** The story told through Mr. Newman's direct examination could be about a grandfather who was working two jobs to support both him and his wife, or about being alone at night in the store and being vulnerable to robberies.

How you refer to a person—by label, by title, by last name, by first name—can affect how a jury perceives the person. Referring to the person in a familiar way can be a technique for humanizing the person and a component of telling a human story. At the outset of trial, the prosecutor should refer to the clerk as Mr. Newman. However, once the jury is acquainted with the witness, counsel can begin to call him by his first name.

> *Q:* Gardner, did you ever notice anything unusual about the robber's clothing?

If the client is a corporation, you can still make an effort to tell a human story and humanize the client. You can focus attention on the people working for the corporation, particularly the people who represent the corporation in the courtroom and who are sitting at counsel table.

Should you attempt to depersonalize the party on the other side by referring to the person with a label, "the defendant"? We believe that the need for courtesy in the courtroom overrides any benefit that might be derived from this ploy. Simply refer to the person formally using Mr., Ms., or other appropriate title, followed by their last name. If the opposing party is a young child, referring to them by their first name is typically acceptable.

### Believable and Understandable Story

We suggest you use a story format in presenting your case, because jurors benefit from being able to fit the pieces of evidence into a coherent, logical structure. As you present evidence in direct examination, the evidence is often presented in fragments, like a jigsaw puzzle. Jurors, like most people, will struggle to arrange these fragments into a coherent story so they can understand them. The more that you arrange these pieces of evidence so they fit into a logical and comprehensive story, the more likely it is that the jury will comprehend and accept *your story*. There are two important factors in telling your story through direct examination of witnesses: (1) The individual witness tells a complete and logical story, and (2) the case as a whole fits together and tells a complete and consistent story.

#### *Individual Witness's Story*

Even though a witness may have perceived only a portion of the entire factual story, you should attempt to construct each witness's direct examination so it works as a self-contained story for that particular witness while remaining consistent with the stories of other witnesses and the tangible evidence. After all, for the witness, his story is a complete story.

To illustrate the idea of having each witness tell a self-contained story, imagine again that you are the prosecutor in the *Blue Moon News Robbery* case.

---

### Direct Examination

#### Individual Witness Story
#### The *Blue Moon News Robbery* Case

Felix Gutterez, a witness for the prosecution, told you that he observed a man running from the store to a car parked nearby. Felix then told you that he entered the store and learned that the clerk had just been robbed. Felix neither saw the robbery nor can he identify the defendant as the man who committed it. Yet Felix can tell a complete story of what he perceived from his vantage point.

Begin direct examination by having Felix identify himself, give some personal background information, and explain how he happened to be in the vicinity of the store that night. You could focus on the crux of his testimony—approaching the store, being outside the store, seeing a man wearing a blue jean jacket running away from the store to a car, entering the store, learning about the robbery, and later talking to the police and giving them a rough description of the robber and car—all conceived, structured, and presented to support your case theory.

### Case as a Whole

The second important factor is that your entire case, including all the direct examinations of your witnesses and the tangible evidence, should fit together and tell a complete and consistent story. The story itself must also be believable. It must appear coherent and comport with the fact finder's common sense and everyday experience with human nature. In short, it must make sense.

To illustrate the second factor in storytelling, the entire story of the robbery must be logical, sufficiently detailed, and fit together.

## Direct Examination

### Case as a Whole: Witnesses' Testimony
### The *Blue Moon News Robbery* Case

To tell the complete story in the *Blue Moon News Robbery* case, as the prosecutor, you will need testimony from Mr. Gardner Newman, Felix Gutterez, the police, and the fingerprint expert. The clerk saw the defendant commit the robbery, Felix saw the defendant fleeing the store, the police arrested the defendant, and the fingerprint expert compared and found a match between the defendant's fingerprints and a partial print on a magazine left on the counter in the Blue Moon News store. The complete story consists of their combined direct testimony.

The clerk, Mr. Gardner Newman, describes the defendant, the person browsing in the store prior to the robbery; he relates the particulars of how the robbery was carried out, identifies the defendant as the man who committed the robbery, and connects the robber with the magazine found on the counter, which was later examined by the fingerprint expert.

Eyewitness Felix Gutterez continues the robbery story by relating how he saw a man fleeing from the store to a car, which then headed south. He gives a general description of the man, his clothing, and the car.

The officers supply information by describing how they stopped the defendant's car in the early morning hours of the following day because he matched the description, arrested the defendant, and took him to the store where Newman identified Ryan as the robber.

The fingerprint expert finishes the story by testifying that the defendant's fingerprints match those found on a magazine left on the counter at the convenience store.

By telling the complete story and interrelating the specific pieces—the man running south, the defendant arrested south of the store during the early morning hours, and the defendant identified by Newman as the robber—the pieces of the story appear logical, consistent, and therefore persuasive.

### Quantity of the Evidence

To persuade the jury, you will need to meet the burden of proof—a preponderance of the evidence in a civil case and beyond a reasonable doubt in a criminal case. Therefore, you are concerned about the quantity of evidence that supports your case theory. In the *Blue Moon News Robbery* case, the prosecutor has a single eyewitness, Mr. Gardner Newman, who will identify the defendant, Mike Ryan, as the robber. Additional evidence supporting the identification element is testimony of the fingerprint expert that the latent partial print on the magazine left on the counter matches the defendant's left index fingerprint. While this is more than sufficient evidence to take to trial and seek a conviction, it is hardly a slam-dunk conviction. Eyewitnesses can be inaccurate, fingerprint analysis can be incorrect, or, even if correct, the defendant may have left the prints when he was in the store earlier, and Newman is really identifying him from a prior visit. Contrast this fact pattern with a convenience store robbery where the robber is caught on video by surveillance camera and two people are available to testify that they can identify the defendant. Obviously, all else being equal (both cases present the same quality of evidence), the latter case with a greater quantity of evidence is more persuasive.

### Quality of the Evidence

To successfully support your case theory or to refute your opponent's, the direct examination must convince the jury that the evidence presented is true and accurate. Merely presenting the evidence to satisfy your legal theory does not ensure that the jury will believe it. Both the witness and the testimony must be perceived as believable. Ultimately, you wish to elicit testimony that will allow you to argue in closing argument that both your witnesses and evidence are credible. Let's now examine how to make a witness appear credible during direct examination, as well as how to present information from which this credibility can later be argued in closing.

#### *Witness Credibility*

What makes a witness believable? If the witness is presented in human terms, as a person with attributes the jury finds appealing, the jury is more likely to believe the witness. The process of presenting the person as a believable witness is referred to as accrediting the witness. Accrediting your witness means eliciting some background information about the person, such as family history, education, and work experience. Accrediting a witness also requires preparing your witness's courtroom presentation, including physical appearance, demeanor, and responses to questions. Knowing what specific accrediting information to present in direct examination requires common sense and an ability to relate the credibility information to your case theory. To illustrate this and other aspects, assume you are the attorney representing the plaintiff in the *Medical Malpractice* case.

> ### The Medical Malpractice Case
>
> Plaintiff Shawny Kixskiller, a ten-year-old girl, was hit by a car and suffered multiple injuries. Medic One rushed her to the Soundview Hospital emergency room. Plaintiff alleges that Dr. Clancy acted negligently by waiting too long to operate, and as a consequence, Shawny suffered a permanent disability—the loss of use of her left leg.

Accrediting the witness involves conveying information about the witness that jurors can directly relate to, respect, or be sympathetic to. For instance, suppose that the defense attorney in the *Medical Malpractice* case wants to accredit nurse Jean Grahn.

### Direct Examination

#### Accrediting the Witness
#### The *Medical Malpractice* Case

One way to build the credibility of Nurse Grahn, an employee in the Soundview Hospital emergency room, is through a series of questions that personalize, humanize, and substantiate her competency.

*Q:* Ms. Grahn, how long have you lived in Spencer?
*A:* My entire life, 45 years.
*Q:* Are you married?
*A:* Yes, 25 years next month.
*Q:* Do you have any children?
*A:* Yes. Two. A daughter who graduated from law school last year and is practicing with the attorney general's office in the consumer fraud division. My son, Andrew, is an accountant with Bear and Co.
*Q:* How long have you been a registered nurse?
*A:* Twenty years.
*Q:* Where are you regularly employed?
*A:* In the emergency room at Soundview Hospital.
*Q:* Could you describe for the jury the education and training that you went through to become a registered nurse?
*A:* [Witness describes her education and training.]

As with all presentations, you must keep within the limitations of evidentiary rules. Most courts allow, and opposing attorneys usually do not object to, some accrediting background information if you keep it within reasonable bounds. If, for instance, counsel had begun to explore Grahn's unrelated activities in the community, such as her work with a homeless center, the court is likely to sustain a relevancy objection. On the other hand, if counsel was qualifying Grahn as an expert, counsel could elicit a wide range of information, such as training and experience as a nurse relating to her area of expertise.

If the background information includes specific instances of the witness's prior acts of good conduct, and such evidence is inadmissible under the evidentiary rules, you should not offer it. Furthermore, if you introduce evidence of good conduct, you risk opening the door and allowing your adversary to present evidence of the witness's prior acts of misconduct. For instance, in accrediting Grahn by having her discuss her charitable work and other good conduct, you may open the door to discrediting evidence, such as complaints filed against her, on the grounds that you have put her character in issue.

### Credibility of the Witness's Testimony

Now think about how to present your witness so that the substantive information, the witness's testimony, is believable. The information that the witness provides should be a logical, detailed, and complete story. Additionally, the direct examination testimony of all the witnesses and exhibits, collectively, should tell a logical, commonsense story. Two trial techniques that bolster the credibility of witness testimony are (1) the use of broad and narrow questions, and (2) the ordering of witnesses so that they corroborate each other.

*Broad and Narrow Questions:*  Develop the story of each witness in detail by asking a series of questions that, taken together, relate a complete story to the jury. We recommend combining broad with narrow questions. The broad, open-ended questions allow the witness to tell the story in narrative form to the jury. The narrow, specific questions slow down the narrative story and enrich the testimony with details.

To illustrate, imagine again that you are defense counsel for Dr. James Clancy, the surgeon in the *Medical Malpractice* case. You are examining nurse Jean Grahn regarding Dr. Clancy's decision to wait four hours before operating on the plaintiff. You want to show that the plaintiff arrived at the hospital in critical and unstable condition. You will then combine this evidence with the testimony of other witnesses to argue in closing that it would have been medically unreasonable to operate on the plaintiff while she was in such a condition.

---

### Direct Examination

#### Credible Testimony: Broad and Narrow Questions
#### The *Medical Malpractice* Case

As defense counsel, instead of asking one question—"Nurse Grahn, please describe plaintiff's condition when she arrived at the hospital"—a series of questions creates a credible and vivid picture of the critical nature of plaintiff's condition:

> *Q:* Nurse Grahn, where were you when you first saw Shawny Kixskiller at the hospital?
> *A:* I met the Medic One van at the door to the emergency room.
> *Q:* Please describe Shawny's condition when she arrived at the hospital.
> *A:* She was in critical condition.
> *Q:* Can you describe how Shawny looked then?
> *A:* She was not breathing on her own. She had an oxygen mask over her face.
> *Q:* Did you notice if anyone was monitoring the oxygen delivery?
> *A:* Yes. Paramedic Robert McElhanney appeared to be in charge of the oxygen.
> *Q:* Could you describe Shawny's injuries?
> *A:* Yes. There was a laceration over her right eye and . . . .

*Order of Witnesses:* The sequence in which the witnesses and exhibits are arranged also enhances the credibility of each witness's testimony. Counsel should plan the witness order so that the witnesses can corroborate one another. Providing corroborative details through several witnesses enhances the believability of witness testimony. You may create an order of witnesses to tell a chronological story. Or you may choose to call strong witnesses at the beginning and end of the sequence, and then sandwich more problematic witnesses in the middle to deemphasize weak points. See page 331 for a further discussion of the order of witnesses.

## Direct Examination

### Credible Testimony: Order of Witnesses
### The *Medical Malpractice* Case

Defense counsel might consider first calling Nurse Grahn followed by paramedic McElhanney. In this way, Nurse Grahn's testimony that the plaintiff was in critical condition when she arrived at the emergency room will be corroborated by the paramedic's testimony. Nurse Grahn, after being appropriately qualified as an experienced surgical nurse, could testify that Dr. Clancy responded appropriately when diagnosing and treating plaintiff in the emergency room. Nurse Grahn would first testify that it was essential to safeguard plaintiff's life: for Dr. Clancy to give plaintiff oxygen and wait four hours before operating. If an operation was performed immediately on plaintiff's arrival at the hospital, the doctor would have risked plaintiff's life. The paramedic can corroborate the testimony of Nurse Grahn. Paramedic McElhanney could testify as follows:

> *Q:* What did Dr. Clancy do when Shawny Kixskiller was admitted at the emergency room?
> *A:* Shawny Kixskiller could not breathe on her own. Dr. Clancy gave the order to immediately transfer Shawny from the portable oxygen to a respirator in intensive care. He then ordered the surgical team to stand by, because as soon as Shawny stabilized, Dr. Clancy wanted to be ready to operate.

## D. Case Weaknesses

Direct examination provides a unique opportunity to reckon with your opponent's case theory or blunt a cross-examination attack on your case theory, witnesses, and evidence. There are a few advantages to eliciting the damaging information during direct examination. You can defuse cross-examination because you are the one who has first presented the harmful information to the jury and thus deprived your opponent of the revelation. You also may have the opportunity to explain the harmful information. The jury may be impressed by the candor both you and the witness show concerning the weaknesses.

But there are reasons for you to consider why you might want to exclude case weaknesses in your direct. First, overemphasis on meeting your opponent's case theory or explaining weaknesses in your case theory can lead the jury to discount your theory or conclude that your opponent's theory has more merit than yours.

Second, opposing counsel may forget or completely overlook the opportunity to bring out the weakness on cross, or may not wish to risk going into the area for fear that it could open the door to evidence harmful to counsel's case.

Third, you could forgo covering the weakness in direct and deal with it on cross by preparing the witness for the attack or by responding to the weakness during redirect examination.

### Deciding Whether to Include the Information
#### Anticipating Attacks

The first step in deciding whether you will seize the opportunity in your direct examination to deal with your case frailties is to anticipate your adversary's attacks. Step into the shoes of opposing counsel. If you were opposing counsel, would you discredit this witness or the witness's version of events? Would you seek concessions supporting your case theory? If so, what are they? Now shift back into your own role. How significant are these attacks in terms of hurting your case theory? Suppose you decided that if you were opposing counsel you would attack your witness, and that the attack you would choose could be harmful. Your second step is to resolve the substantive information, if any, that can be included in direct examination to protect your witness or your witness's testimony from damage on cross-examination. Your best means of protecting your witness may be to have the witness candidly expose the weakness during direct examination.

#### Admissibility of the Evidence

Whether you will include harmful information in your direct examination also depends on the admissibility of that evidence. If you believe that the evidence that you anticipate your opponent would like to introduce on cross-examination of your witness is inadmissible, then you may not need to include that evidence in your direct examination. Rather, you could move in limine to exclude the evidence. If the court grants your motion, then you can proceed with your direct examination without that damaging information. For example, you could move to exclude prior bad acts of your witness that opposing counsel would like to elicit on cross of your witness.

Some rehabilitating evidence is admissible only after the witness or testimony has been attacked on cross-examination. For instance, suppose you anticipate that on cross-examination opposing counsel will attempt to discredit your witness with a prior inconsistent statement. However, under some jurisdiction's evidentiary law, you cannot on direct examination present your witness's prior consistent statements, such as, *"Dr. Clancy, did you say the same thing to anyone else on September 12th?"* If evidentiary law in your jurisdiction does not permit you to offer the prior inconsistent statement during direct examination and have the witness explain why it was made, you will have to wait until your witness's credibility has been attacked on cross-examination before you can present the witness's explanation of the prior statement to rehabilitate your witness in redirect examination or rebuttal.

### Dealing with Weaknesses

You should integrate into the direct examination's factual story the points that deal with case problems by including sufficiently detailed explanations. Thus, the testimony about the weaknesses becomes a natural part of testimony. You will also have to be sure that the explanations do not detract from the persuasiveness of your overall case theory.

### *Painting a Detailed Picture*

Suppose as prosecutor that you decide to address your opponent's case theory in direct examination. Imagine you are the prosecutor in the *Blue Moon News Robbery* case, and the defense theory is misidentification. You anticipate that the defense may try to impeach the clerk's positive identification of defendant Mike Ryan as the robber by attacking the clerk's perceptual ability. Among other things, you anticipate defense counsel will dwell on the lateness of the hour, implying the clerk was tired and thus mistaken, and the clerk's limited opportunity to observe the robber.

---

### Direct Examination

#### Dealing with Weaknesses
#### The *Blue Moon News Robbery* Case

As the prosecutor, you can focus on counteracting any potential attack that Mr. Newman was physically exhausted and therefore mistaken in his identification of the defendant by incorporating questions similar to the following into the clerk's direct examination:

*Q:* Mr. Newman, can you describe what you did the day and evening of the robbery?

*A:* I worked the 10:00 P.M. to 7:00 A.M. shift. The morning of the robbery, I got off from work at 7:00 A.M. That's 7:00 A.M. on the day of the robbery. I got home at

*continued* ▶

---

> 7:30 A.M., had breakfast with my family, did some gardening. Then I ate a light lunch. I went upstairs to bed around 12:30 P.M. and slept until about 8:30 P.M. I took a shower, had a light dinner, and watched a little television. I left to go to work at 9:30 P.M.
>
> *Q:* Is that a routine day for you before going to work for the night shift?
> *A:* Yes, it is. I always sleep seven to eight hours during the day.
> *Q:* How did you feel when you went to work?
> *A:* Just fine.
> *Q:* What time did you arrive at the store?
> *A:* About 9:50 P.M.
>
> The technique used here paints a picture of a well-rested, alert man. Likewise, details can be used to establish the clerk's opportunity to observe the robber (lighting, distance, particular motive for focusing on the man prior to the robbery, time spent looking at his face, and so on) and, in turn, the accuracy of his identification of the defendant as the robber:
>
> *Q:* Were there any others in the store at the time?
> *Q:* Where was the man?
> *Q:* Did you notice what he was doing?
> *Q:* Any particular reason you noticed the man?
> *Q:* Did you notice what he was wearing?
> *Q:* How long was he at the magazine rack?
> *Q:* How long did you watch him when he was at the magazine rack?

### *Explaining the Weaknesses*

Another way of dealing with weaknesses, including potential attacks on your witnesses or their testimony, is to have a witness explain or justify her actions. You also may be able to have your witness explain or justify testimony during redirect and rebuttal.

## Direct Examination

### Explaining or Justifying Case Weaknesses
### The *Medical Malpractice* Case

Suppose you represent the defendant, Dr. Clancy, in the malpractice case. Dr. Clancy received a prior warning by officials at another hospital for failure to follow professional procedures. You believe that opposing counsel probably will ask about the warning during cross-examination of Dr. Clancy and that the court will permit the inquiry. On direct examination, you might ask the following question, which allows the doctor to explain the warnings:

*Q:* Dr. Clancy, you have told us that while you worked at Mt. Mason Hospital, the administrator, Dr. McKeta, issued a warning to you about hospital procedures. Could you tell the jury about that complaint?

## E. Admissibility

In deciding on the content of direct examination, consider evidentiary law; it determines whether the evidence you want to introduce is admissible. No matter how probative and credible your witness's information is, it will not assist your case theory if it is inadmissible. You need to understand the relevance of each piece of information your witnesses present for your own and your adversary's case theories, as well as any other evidentiary requirements for that information. (Section IV on essential evidence rules discusses the admissibility of evidence in detail.) Looking at this from opposing counsel's prospective, you must be equipped with arguments detailing the factual basis and legal authority for refuting anticipated objections. You need to know how to lay the proper foundation for exhibits. You also need to think of alternative ways for introducing information if evidence is ruled inadmissible.

Of course, you will not be able to plan for all contingencies. You must be flexible to respond to unanticipated objections or to withdraw a line of questioning or an exhibit once you recognize its inadmissibility.

# III. STRUCTURING DIRECT EXAMINATION

Customarily, direct examination is structured in the same manner as the opening statement and the closing argument: It has an introduction, a body, and a conclusion. Each of these parts should carry out specific purposes.

## A. Introduction

Your introductory questions should accomplish three specific purposes. First, they should get the jurors' attention. Second, they should entail either qualifying the witness (if an expert) or accrediting the witness (eliciting the information that builds credibility). Third, they should put the witness at ease and introduce the witness to the jury within the context of your case. Confidence-building background questions, such as those focusing on occupation, marital status, and so forth, serve these last two purposes. See the questions that introduced Nurse Grahn in the *Medical Malpractice* case, at page 291.

An effective way to commence direct examination, particularly of a central witness, is to begin with the question on the minds of the jurors. Starting in this fashion captures the jury's attention, demonstrates a willingness to face the issue, and avoids the risk that the jury will only halfheartedly listen to the testimony until the witness answers that central question. For example, plaintiff's counsel might begin the direct examination of Dr. Clancy by asking: *"Doctor, let's get to the heart of the matter. Did you wait too long to operate on Shawny Kixskiller?"* Then, of course, you can turn to the introductory questions that humanize your witness and paint a human story, as discussed above.

## B.  Body

The body of the direct examination is normally the focal point of your case. The body should contain substantive information that supports your case theory or refutes your adversary's case theory. The organizational structure of the body should make your case theory readily apparent to the jury. There are a variety of ways in which to organize the body:

- Chronology of events,
- Subject areas,
- Legal elements, and
- Straight narrative.

### Chronology of Events

Organizing by chronology of events makes it easy for listeners to follow. This is particularly helpful when the sequence of events is critical to understanding issues in the case. You can use chronology as a guide so the testimony is logically structured and, at the same time, use the chronology as an integral part of the testimony, such as in the malpractice case, where the exact timing and the sequence of events are central to the respective case theories. In the following direct examination by defense attorney in the *Medical Malpractice* case, you can see how the chronology is integrated into the testimony.

---

### Direct Examination

#### Chronological Structure
#### The *Medical Malpractice* Case

*Q:*  Dr. Clancy, what time did the Medic One van arrive at the hospital?

*Q:*  Please tell us what happened in the emergency room.

*Q:*  How long did Shawny Kixskiller spend in the emergency room?

*Q:*  What time did she arrive in intensive care?

*Q:*  How many doctors were directly involved with her surgery?

---

Sometimes, there are a number of relevant time periods, making it important that you give the jury a time frame for the particular period the witness is referring to: *"Let's focus on before Ms. Kixskiller was put in the ambulance." "Now, let's talk about what happened immediately after she was taken out of the ambulance . . . ."*

### Subject Areas

Another approach is to organize the information into subject areas or modules (general hospital procedures, emergency room treatment, surgery, recovery room, intensive care). You could sequence the subject areas chronologically and, as the prior example illustrates, arrange the direct examination so as to present information chronologically within each subject area. Transitional language helps the jury follow the direct as it changes from one module to another, such as: *"Now, let's focus on the recovery room procedures. Could you tell the jury . . . ?"*

### Legal Elements

Alternatively, you could structure direct examination by legal elements as stated in your proposed jury instructions. This format is similar to organization by subject matter since it arranges information by topic. The advantage of this arrangement is that the information can be easily translated into a closing argument, matching information in the direct to the legal elements. In the malpractice example, the sequence could be based on the elements of negligence—duty, breach, proximate cause, and damage. That approach may lead to a sequence that could begin with the general hospital procedures, then follow with treatment or the lack of treatment, and so forth.

### Straight Narrative

Another organizing device, sequencing testimony to tell a story, takes advantage of all the devices that have been discussed. We suggest that you refer to your final draft of your closing argument when organizing direct examination to tell a story. You will also be including information that is more comprehensive than information that simply proves your claims or defenses or refutes those of your adversary:

> *Q:* Mr. Kixskiller, did you ride in the Medic One van with your daughter?
> *Q:* Where were you sitting in the van?
> *Q:* Could you see your daughter?

Our preference is that direct examination testimony should be structured to tell a complete, logical, and consistent story for each witness, and that all the testimony and exhibits together should mirror your closing argument.

## C. Conclusion

The conclusion of direct or redirect examination ideally should be the logical culmination of your examination or a high point in the testimony. A powerful introduction and finish are compatible with the rules of primacy and recency—that people usually remember and are influenced most by what they hear first and last. Consequently, when organizing the body of each witness's direct examination testimony, consider within your organizational framework the possibility of presenting a particularly interesting, important, or memorable piece of information (yes, there is one) at the end of the witness's testimony:

> Dr. Clancy, one final question. Today, reflecting back on your decision to wait until Shawny's condition stabilized before operating, do you still consider that to have been the correct medical decision?

Apply this idea of an effective conclusion to your total case—specifically, the order of witnesses you will call, because your entire case builds toward a strong conclusion. As noted, begin with a strong witness, conclude with a strong one, and relegate the weaker witnesses to the middle of your case-in-chief.

---

### CHECKLIST

**Structuring Direct Examination**

*Introduction*

☐ Accredit your witness with human values and human needs, and a consistent, believable, human story.
☐ Put the witness at ease.
☐ Elicit information to build the witness's credibility.
☐ Use a dynamic beginning—the central question, theme, or story line.

*The Body Structure: Choices*

☐ Chronology of events.
☐ Subject areas.
☐ Facts supporting legal elements.
☐ Straight narrative.

*Conclusion*

☐ Culmination of the testimony.
☐ Finish on a high note.

---

## IV. ESSENTIAL EVIDENCE RULES

This section covers the essential evidence rules that you must know for planning and conducting a direct examination.

### A. Witness Competency

While Federal Rule of Evidence 601 provides that all witnesses are competent except as provided by the rule, appellate courts usually have held that the trial court has the discretion to decide that the witness does not have the sufficient capacity to testify. *United States v. Gates*, 10 F.3d 765, 766 (11th Cir. 1993). Generally, the test is whether the person understands the duty to testify truthfully and was capable of perceiving, recalling, and communicating about the event. *United States v. Davis*, 306 F.3d 398 (6th Cir. 2002); *State v. Karpenski*, 971 P.2d 553 (Wash. App. 1999). The court, under Federal Rule of Evidence 104(a), makes this preliminary decision. Examples of people who may be found not to meet the test are children (presumptive age of competency), those of unsound mind, or those who are intoxicated at the time of the testifying. Later in the chapter we discuss in more detail how to prepare problematic witnesses to testify.

## B. Impeaching Your Own Witness

On direct examination, counsel may impeach his own witness. Federal Rule of Evidence 607 provides: "Any party, including the party that called the witness, may attack the witness's credibility." This rule abandons the traditional requirement that the party seeking to impeach his own witness must be surprised by the witness's testimony. Under this rule, trial counsel may also blunt anticipated impeachment evidence by eliciting it on direct examination. See Chapter 10, Cross-Examination, on impeaching with a prior inconsistent statement, pages 345-346, 357-359.

## C. Leading Questions

Federal Rule of Evidence 611(c) prohibits the use of leading questions on direct except as may be necessary to develop the witness's testimony. Also, this rule provides that "when a party calls a hostile witness, an adverse party, or a witness identified with an adverse party," the court should ordinarily allow leading questions. A leading question has been defined as a question that "suggests to the witness the answer desired by the examiner." McCormick, *Evidence* 14 (6th ed. 2006). Leading questions are usually allowed when directed to children and those with memory difficulties, and when the questions regard preliminary or undisputed matters.

## D. Present Recollection Refreshed

Your witness is testifying on direct examination. You are asking questions when, all of a sudden, your witness responds, "I don't remember." Federal Rule of Evidence 612 governs the use of a writing to refresh the memory of a witness. The process is referred to as "present recollection refreshed." Any writing can be used, but only to refresh the witness's memory so that the witness can then testify. The writing itself is not evidence.

### Direct Examination

#### Refreshing the Memory of a Witness

- Ask whether anything would refresh the witness's memory.
- Show the witness the writing and allow the witness to read it silently.
- After the witness has read the statement silently, ask whether the witness now remembers what happened.
- Take the statement back from the witness so the witness is not testifying with the aid of the writing.
- Proceed with the questioning (assuming that the court does not conclude that the witness is now testifying from the writing).

Now we are ready to apply the steps for refreshing a witness's memory in the *Blue Moon News Robbery* case.

---

### Direct Examination

#### Present Recollection Refreshed
#### The *Blue Moon News Robbery* Case

As the prosecutor, you are conducting direct examination of Mr. Gardner Newman, the clerk, to establish the accuracy of his identification of the defendant as the robber.

*Q:*  How long did you watch the man when he was at the magazine rack?
*A:*  I can't remember.
*Q:*  Is there anything that would refresh your recollection as to the amount of time you observed him?
*A:*  Yes, the statement I gave to the police that night.

Prosecutor shows the defense counsel the statement Mr. Newman made to the police, and then shows the witness the statement by handing it to the witness and letting the witness read it silently to himself.

After the witness has read the statement silently, the prosecutor asks the witness:

*Q:*  Do you now remember how long you observed the man at the magazine rack?
*A:*  Yes, I do.

The prosecutor approaches the witness and takes the statement back from him so that the witness is no longer testifying with the aid of the written statement.

*Q:*  So, tell us how long you observed the man at the magazine rack.
*A:*  Five minutes.

---

Federal Rule of Evidence 612 sets out the rights of the adverse party when a witness has had her memory refreshed either at trial or before "to have the writing produced at the hearing, to inspect it, to cross-examine the witness about it, and to introduce in evidence any portion that relates to the witness's testimony."

## E.  Past Recollection Recorded

Now imagine that your witness still can't remember even after you tried to refresh the witness's recollection. You reach for another life preserver: past recollection recorded. Keep this piece of rescue equipment handy because you never know when you might need it. The evidentiary foundation is as follows:

## Direct Examination

### Past Recollection Recorded

The evidentiary foundation to get a past recollection recorded into evidence is an exception to the hearsay rule under Federal Rule of Evidence 803(5), which allows into evidence:

- A record that (A) is on a matter the witness once knew about but now cannot recall well enough to testify fully and accurately; (B) was made or adopted by the witness when the matter was fresh in the witness's memory; and (C) accurately reflects the witness's knowledge.
- If admitted, the record may be read into evidence but may be received as an exhibit only if offered by an adverse party.

Now for an illustration of past recollection recorded and how you lay a proper foundation. Imagine you are defense counsel in the *Medical Malpractice* case.

## Direct Examination

### Past Recollection Recorded
### The *Medical Malpractice* Case

Defense counsel is questioning Dr. Clancy about Shawny's condition when she was admitted to the hospital.

*Q:*  Dr. Clancy, describe in detail what condition Shawny was in when you entered the emergency room.

*A:*  She had multiple injuries, and her condition was very serious. She didn't appear to be stable.

*Q:*  Can you be specific, Dr. Clancy?

*A:*  I don't exactly remember what her multiple injuries were.

*Q:*  You don't remember?

*A:*  Only generally that she was in very critical condition.

*Q:*  I will show you Exhibit 29, marked for identification. Did you write that?

*A:*  Yes, indeed, just after the patient was in the emergency room.

*Q:*  When you wrote it, was it correct?

*A:*  Yes.

*Q:*  Please read to the jury the part about the patient's condition in the emergency room.

*A:*  "The patient was not breathing on her own," and I intubated her . . . .

## F. Lay Witness Opinion

Federal Rule of Evidence 701 provides that a lay witness may testify in the form of opinions if these opinions are

- rationally based on the witness's perception;
- helpful to clearly understanding the witness's testimony or to determining a fact in issue; and
- not based on scientific, technical, or other specialized knowledge within the scope of Rule 702.

Lay opinions that have been held to meet these standards include ones such as sanity or insanity, intoxication, and vehicle speed.

## V. CONDUCTING DIRECT EXAMINATION

In this section, we continue the process of how to successfully conduct a direct examination. An effective direct examination calls for attention to the following:

- Judicial expectations,
- Witness preparation,
- Staging,
- Your preparation,
- Jury instructions,
- Form of the questions,
- Highlighting the important information,
- Listening to the answer,
- Providing markers for the jury,
- Audience interest,
- Real and demonstrative evidence, and
- Problematic witnesses.

## A. Judicial Expectations

Judges want the presentation of evidence to go smoothly, and they want to conserve court time. They believe that counsel should do what is necessary to meet these goals. Consequently, the bench has the following expectations for counsel when it comes to calling witnesses to testify.

### Judicial Expectations: Direct Examination and Witness Testimony

**Witness List:** The judge will expect you to provide the court and opposing counsel with your witness list. The judge will read the list to the jury during voir dire to see if any juror recognizes a witness's name. It is good practice to provide a list to the court reporter so that it will not be necessary to ask the witness to spell their name.

Ready to Go: Witnesses should be available when needed to testify. Judges are disinclined to grant continuances when witnesses fail to appear. You need to give your witnesses an entire day, if necessary, and have them ready to testify when called.

Informed of the Rules and Rulings: Judges expect that counsel will inform witnesses of the court's orders that apply to the witnesses. For instance, if the judge has granted a motion in limine excluding a particular subject matter that the witness might possibly mention when testifying, counsel must inform the witness not to mention it. Counsel also should inform the witnesses of sequestration orders, and that they are neither to enter the courtroom until called nor to discuss their testimony with a witness who has yet to testify.

Stand: When questioning a witness, counsel should stand except when either incapacity prevents counsel from standing or the court observes another custom, such as requiring counsel to sit at counsel table when examining a witness, as is the norm in North Carolina.

Give Notice: Do you need to inform the court or opposing counsel of the order in which you will call witnesses or of the estimated time for direct and cross? While some courts will require that you notify opposing counsel by a deadline, such as the end of the day, of whom you intend to call during the next court day, other courts do not. Some courts require more. For example, King County Superior Court Judge Cheryl Carey requires that counsel confer not later than ten days prior to trial and submit either the following form or one with the same information by five court days prior to trial. Failure to complete the form can result in the exclusion of witnesses or imposition of sanctions.

**Submission of the following information is required by Judge Carey not later than five court days prior to trial. DO NOT FILE THIS DOCUMENT WITH THE CLERK'S OFFICE.**

Use tenths of hours for estimates: 1, .2, .5, 1.0, etc.

_____ v. _____

Estimate of Time for Witness Examinations

### PLAINTIFF(S)

| Witness Name | Direct Exam | Cross-Exam | Redirect Exam | Total |
|---|---|---|---|---|
|  |  |  |  |  |
|  |  |  |  |  |
|  |  |  |  |  |
|  |  |  |  |  |

_continued_ ▶

| Witness<br>Name | Direct<br>Exam | Cross-<br>Exam | Redirect<br>Exam | Total |
|---|---|---|---|---|
| | | | | |
| | | | | |
| | | | | |
| | | | | |

DEFENDANT(S)

*http://www.kingcounty.gov/courts/SuperiorCourt/judges/carey.aspx*

**Bench Trial:** In a bench trial, the judge expects that you will get to the crux of the matter and not waste court time on peripheral witnesses. Therefore, shorten direct examinations by seeking stipulations, eliminating what you can without harming the case, such as offering a curriculum vitae rather than having the expert testify to qualifications, or eliminating some peripheral witnesses. However, retain witnesses who are needed to tell a persuasive factual story through direct examinations.

## B.  Witness Preparation

A successful direct examination is the product of a well-prepared witness. Your central goal is to prepare the person to effectively communicate her story, project confidence, testify clearly, and demonstrate credibility.

### Preparing the Witness for the Trial Setting

The courtroom can be an intimidating setting for a witness, even an experienced expert witness. The more you help the witness know what to expect in the courthouse and courtroom, the less likely the person is to appear nervous and the more likely they will appear comfortable, confident, and credible.

In dealing with a novice witness, you should begin with fundamental matters of how a trial functions—jury selection, the opening statement, direct and cross-examination, and the closing argument. Then explain the function and role of the judge, jury, counsel, witnesses, court clerk, court reporter, and bailiff. Discuss where the witnesses, the parties, and you and your opponent will sit or stand in the courtroom. Discuss the role of objections. For instance, to prevent the introduction of inadmissible evidence, you should explain the function of objections and the meaning of the terms *overruled* and *sustained*; you should also explain how the witness should respond when an objection is made. Practicalities concerning travel, such as the location of the courthouse and courtroom, parking or public transportation areas at or near the courthouse, places to wait before being called to testify, and other such matters should also be discussed. You want to dispel apprehension about the trial and alleviate as many concerns as possible for your witness. Anything that you can say or do to help your witness visualize the courtroom and be comfortable with the trial process should be done—within reason and, of course, your economic constraints.

### Preparing the Witness on the Substance

#### *The Witness's Role*

Explain to the witness where his testimony fits in the case. This will give your witness an understanding of his role and where you and opposing counsel may be headed with the questions. Discuss the necessity of the witness telling the truth. Explain that you need to know about any damaging information, because you can only protect the witness if you know the information. For instance, you could file a motion in limine to exclude from the trial the witness's prior act of misconduct that has no bearing on the case. Make sure you ask if your witness has any concerns and address those concerns.

#### *Substantive Details*

Discuss all of the substantive information in support of your case theory that you expect the witness will testify to on direct examination. Delve into the details to learn how the witness will respond to your direct examination questions. As you go through the witness's testimony, probing the information critical to the case theories and the witness's credibility, check for inaccuracies, inconsistencies, and previously unrevealed information. Pay attention to the witness's estimates of time, distance, and other measurements. Some witnesses are particularly bad at estimating. For instance, a witness may tell you that an event could not have taken more than a minute, when it actually took a half hour. To get an accurate estimate of the time it took, have the witness look at her watch to see what time it is, think back to the event, then have her look away from the watch and say "start" and then say "stop" when the witness says the same period of time passed by. Then, have the witness look at the watch to see how long it took.

#### *Reviewing Prior Witness Statements and Depositions*

Your witness should review each of her prior statements and any deposition line by line, explaining that at trial a witness may be examined on prior statements (and any other discovery that is relevant). Then review the content of the testimony with the witness. If there are any inconsistencies between the expected direct testimony and the prior statement, discuss them to determine why. Tell the witness that if any part of the prior statement or deposition is inaccurate, the witness should explain to you why it is inaccurate or why this statement differs from another statement. Explain that the prior statement is not binding; the witness is bound only by a responsibility to tell the entire truth.

Take special care in choosing what to use to refresh a witness's recollection while preparing them for testifying at trial. Under Federal Rule of Evidence 612, if a writing is used to refresh a witness's memory for testimony, and the court in its discretion determines it is necessary in the interests of justice, the opposing party "is entitled to have the writing produced at the hearing, to inspect it, to cross-examine the witness about it, and to introduce in evidence any portion that relates to the witness's testimony . . . ." If the writing would otherwise be protected as privileged, such as attorney-client or work product, the protection is lost if it is used to refresh the witness's recollection and the court orders its production under Rule 612.

### Preparing the Witness on How to Testify

While you are prohibited by ethical rules such as ABA Model Rule of Professional Conduct 3.4(b) ("A lawyer shall not . . . counsel or assist a witness to testify falsely") from coaching a witness as to what to say, you may advise your witness on *how* to testify. In essence, you prepare your witness to be a good communicator—confident, clear, and credible. You should cover at least the following three points.

#### Appearance

Appearance does matter. The witness should dress appropriately for the courtroom. You could explain that the lawyers will be dressed in business attire. If appropriate, a witness may dress in uniform. If you believe your witness needs assistance in selecting proper clothes for the courtroom, consider taking an active role with the witness (shopping, clothes on loan, and so on). However, an appropriate courtroom appearance depends on more than just clothing. You should discuss sitting up straight, avoiding distracting habits such as chewing gum or jingling coins in a pocket, attending to personal hygiene, and looking directly at the jury when testifying on direct.

#### Communication on Direct Examination

You can discuss how to behave on direct examination, explaining that this is the witness's opportunity to communicate with the jury. The witness is talking to the jurors, the people who will decide what happens, and no one else in the room matters as much as they do in a jury trial. This is a good opportunity to explain to the witness that jurors are just members of the community whose job it is to decide what happens in the case. They are looking to the witness to provide her story. They have no axe to grind with the witness, and they can be trusted to listen fairly to the witness's testimony. This may put the witness at ease.

#### Communication on Cross-Examination

Explain how to behave on cross-examination. Cover the difference between direct and cross. On cross-examination, the witness is not telling the jury what happened as much as responding to opposing counsel's questions. Consequently, the witness usually should look at opposing counsel, not the jury, listen carefully to each question, and answer it directly and briefly. The witness should not volunteer information.

The witness should behave in a courteous manner and never become provoked. You can explain that quarreling with an attorney gains little. Tell the witness that if she does become angry, after the witness finishes testifying and leaves the courtroom, the attorney remains and can argue at the end of the case that the witness's angry demeanor showed that the witness had an interest in the case. You can also alleviate some of the witness's trepidation about cross-examination by explaining that as long as the witness tells the truth, the witness has nothing to fear because the jury will believe that she is being trustworthy.

You may review some of what the witness might encounter from opposing counsel on cross-examination—the tricks. For instance, on cross, counsel may ask whether the witness discussed the case with anyone. The way the question is asked may suggest some impropriety in discussing testimony prior to trial. You can then explain that it is perfectly proper to discuss testimony with you pretrial. Then make the point that the witness should not try to figure out where counsel is going with the question, but should just listen to the question and answer it directly.

### Methods for Witness Preparation

The best way to prepare your witness is an in-person meeting. In the alternative, or in conjunction with the face-to-face meeting, you can provide written materials (letter or brochure) or a DVD to prepare your witness.

#### Meeting with the Witness

You should never have a critical witness testify if you have not had a face-to-face meeting to prepare your witness for trial. The amount of time for the meeting depends on the witness's prior court experience, other scheduling conflicts, the witness's level of comfort, and the importance of the testimony. Your meeting can be structured in the same manner as your initial client and witness interviews. Perhaps begin with more general points and then progressively focus on more specific ones.

#### Provide Written Material

You might begin your witness preparation by sending the witness a letter or brochure that discusses the practical and substantive aspects of being a witness. Your letter could include substantive information that the witness should be familiar with: prior written statements, a deposition, diagrams, and so on. It also can ask the witness to review these materials before you meet. But keep in mind the potential risks. You do not want to overload or confuse your witness with too much information. And you must consider whether your opponent will be able to obtain a copy of the letter. Although the letter may be considered a privileged communication, in some jurisdictions it may be discoverable and admissible if the letter is referred to for preparing or refreshing the witness's memory. Therefore, before sending a letter, you should be aware whether, or under what circumstances, the letter and supporting documents could be discoverable by the other side and possibly admissible into evidence.

#### View a DVD

In addition to or instead of a letter or brochure, you could have the witness view a DVD, either at home or in your office. The video can include directions to the courthouse, a tour of the courtroom, a mock direct examination, and so forth. A letter and DVD are two tools that can help prepare the witness before your face-to-face meeting. However, they are not substitutes for the meeting.

### Practicing Direct Examination

If you are preparing a novice, critical, or possibly problematic (hard-of-hearing, argumentative) witness for direct, rehearse the direct examination. You can do this by role-play. Explain to your witness why this is an important aspect of witness preparation and how it can help your witness correct communication problems. Practice direct examination with the witness so they know what you will ask and so that you know the answers. Some attorneys video the role-play and then play it back to the witness, pointing out both helpful and harmful aspects of the performance.

If the witness will be using real, documentary, or demonstrative evidence, such as performing a courtroom demonstration, drawing on a chart in court, or using a diagram, practice the activity during your preparation.

A particular problem that can occur with any witness is loss of memory. Preparing for this problem requires familiarity with evidentiary rules already discussed concerning refreshing the witness's recollection or gaining admission of a prior statement by the witness (past recollection recorded). Fed. R. Evid. 612, 803(5). You should prepare all of your witnesses for how they will handle this contingency. Keywords will be important in presenting a proper evidentiary foundation for either refreshing recollection or past recollection recorded, and you might familiarize your witness with these words: *"Do you remember...," "If I showed you your statement, would that refresh your recollection?"* and so on. For illustrations, see pages 301-303.

### Practicing Cross-Examination

Preparation for cross-examination is essential. Explain why it is necessary to practice cross-examination, because this aspect is worrisome for many witnesses. To prepare the witness for cross-examination, you need to step into opposing counsel's shoes and think of the questions that your opponent may ask on cross-examination. Then, practice the cross-examination with the witness. During your practice cross, you can use the techniques that opposing counsel may use on the witness, such as trying to get the witness rattled or angry or to say inconsistent things.

## C.  Staging

In a properly conducted direct examination, the witness speaks directly to the jurors, just as in a normal conversation. The less interference with this dynamic, the better. The following three courtroom positions are preferred because they facilitate direct communication from your witness to the jurors and reduce interference.

Unless you are in a courtroom where you are required to stay behind a podium, you will not remain stationary in one of the three preferred positions during direct. You will move around the courtroom with purposes in mind, such as moving to the clerk to have an exhibit marked, approaching the witness to show the witness an exhibit, and so on. As mentioned before, courtroom practice may require you ask permission of the judge to approach the witness, and you should determine what the custom is before commencing trial.

### Position 1

If your jurisdiction allows you to move around the courtroom, the best way to facilitate this communication between your witness and the jurors is to move to the far end of the jury box—Position 1 as shown in the courtroom diagram. When you take this position, the witness naturally looks at the jurors. You can prepare the witness for this before trial, telling her that when you go to the end of the jury box, it is a reminder for the witness to look at the jurors, establish eye contact, and tell them what happened. Your positioning also causes the witness to speak up so that the jurors farthest from the witness can clearly hear what the witness has to say. To get the witness to speak up and at the same time inform the jurors of why you are standing where you are, you can, at the beginning of one of your early direct examinations, say something to this effect, *"Nurse Grahn, I'm going to stand back here so that you will speak up so the jurors on the far end over here can hear what you say."* Once said, you don't need to repeat this with other witnesses; the jury will understand why you stand there.

Again, the court may have a customary practice that prohibits you from doing this, such as requiring counsel to use a podium or to remain seated at counsel table.

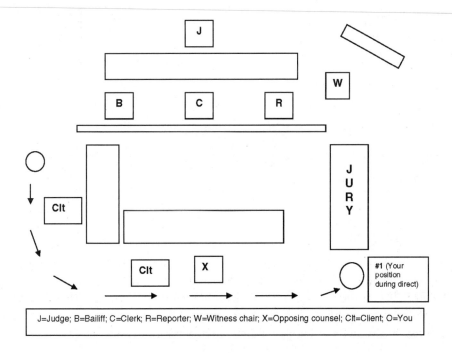

J=Judge; B=Bailiff; C=Clerk; R=Reporter; W=Witness chair; X=Opposing counsel; Clt=Client; O=You

### Positions 2 and 3

Two other preferred courtroom placements also work well to put the spot-light on the witness during direct. Have the witness step out of the witness chair and join you in front of the jury, as shown in Position 2 on the diagram below. The reasons for having the witness do this are numerous, including having the witness demonstrate, showing the jurors an injury, working with an exhibit, and so on. This is an ideal position for an expert witness, because from this position the expert can shift into an instructor's role to teach the jury about the area of expertise. As the expert takes over, the examining attorney can step away to the end of the jury box so the expert has center stage. Another spotlight position is at an easel at the end of the jury box—Position 3 on the diagram below. Merely ask the witness to step to the easel and discuss the exhibit. The attorney can remain at the end of the jury box or move forward to stand by the witness, who talks directly to the jurors.

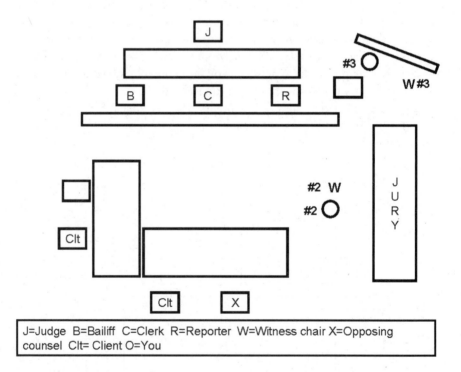

J=Judge  B=Bailiff  C=Clerk  R=Reporter  W=Witness chair  X=Opposing counsel  Clt= Client  O=You

## D.  Your Preparation

To prepare for direct, you should meet with all accessible witnesses; review their statements, depositions, and interrogatories; examine your tangible exhib-its; and visit the scene. When you are ready to prepare a particular witness exam-ination, we suggest that you write down your direct examination questions. One approach is to draw a line down the center of a page. Place the questions on the left side. During direct, you can use the right side to jot notes of significant answers. Put notations in the margins to indicate the legal authority supporting admission of the evidence if there is any question about it. Also, in appropriate places in your notes, indicate the exhibits you wish to introduce or use to illustrate the points you need to present.

---

## CHECKLIST

### Preparation

☐ **Legal Research:** Conduct all necessary legal research.

☐ **Scene Visit:** Visit the scene of the incident.

☐ **Witness Contacts:** Meet with and prepare all accessible witnesses.

☐ **Prior Statements:** Review all witness statements and discovery materials (interrogatories, depositions, admissions, and so forth).

☐ **Exhibits and Pleadings:** Know and understand the potential exhibits and be familiar with the pleadings.

☐ **Notes for Direct:** Write questions, notes, outline for direct examination.

☐ **Organization of Direct Examination Notes:** Organize the notes for each direct into a separate file, section of a notebook, or other readily accessible place for each witness.

☐ **Organization of Exhibits and Documents:** For each witness, organize the witness's deposition, prior written statements, and subpoena for trial and return into a file, notebook section, or other place where it is readily accessible and retrievable.

---

## E. Mirroring Jury Instructions

When language from jury instructions is incorporated into a direct examination, the direct becomes persuasive by familiarizing the jurors with how the direct examination satisfies the law the court will read to them at the end of the trial. Jury instructions are often difficult to follow and to understand. The more the jurors hear the words used from the instructions, the more likely it is that they will follow and understand them. This use of repetition to familiarize and persuade is a strategy that is critical to advocacy. If permitted by the judge, your jury selection questions may employ phrasing from the jury instructions (reasonable doubt, preponderance of evidence). See Chapter 4, pages 102-104 and 111-112, for examples of jury selection questions.

Likewise, direct examination provides another opportunity to mirror your case presentation with the jury instructions. Therefore, your direct examination questions should reflect the words the court is likely to include in the jury instructions. This repetition is likely to help persuade the jury that the evidence you elicited on direct examination fulfills the requirements of law as expressed in those instructions. Of course, you should avoid using any confusing or stilted legalese from the instructions in direct examination.

Keep in mind that if your witnesses do not present evidence on a particular point, or if you fail to gain the admission of a particular exhibit, it may affect whether a jury instruction on a particular issue will be given by the court. For instance, if you fail to present evidence on a principal-agent relationship, the court cannot give your proposed respondent superior liability instruction, and you cannot argue that issue in your closing argument.

To illustrate the use of jury instructions to develop the content of direct examination, let's return to the *Blue Moon News Robbery* case. You are again the prosecutor. You wish to familiarize the jury with one of the legal elements of first degree robbery: force or fear of force.

---

## Direct Examination

### Mirroring Jury Instructions
### The *Blue Moon News Robbery* Case

You are the prosecutor planning how to make the clerk's testimony echo the court's probable jury instruction: "The state must prove that the victim's property was obtained by the defendant through force or fear of force." Consequently, you might ask the manager:

*Q:* Describe what the defendant first said to you.
*A:* He yelled, "Give me the money or you're a dead man!"
*Q:* When the defendant said, "Give me the money or you're a dead man," did you have any fear that he *might use force* if you did not do what he said?
*A:* I was scared to death. I feared for my life. That's why I gave him the money.

---

You also can use the same jury instruction and use the direct examination testimony to argue in closing.

---

## Using Direct Examination Mirroring Jury Instruction to Argue in Closing

### The *Blue Moon News Robbery* Case

The judge has instructed you on the elements of first degree robbery, and one of the elements is that the defendant had to use force, or the clerk of the convenience store had to be in fear of the use of force. That means that no one has to actually be killed or injured for the crime of robbery to have been committed. Remember that during jury selection I asked you if you would follow that rule of law, and each one of you said you could follow that law. . . .

---

> Remember what Mr. Newman, the clerk of the convenience store, told you about his fear of force. Mr. Newman said that after the defendant yelled, "Give me the money or you're a dead man," he was "scared to death." Mr. Newman went on to say, "I feared for my life. That's why I gave him the money." Beyond a reasonable doubt, Mr. Newman was in fear of force.

## F. Form of the Questions

You should strive for a direct examination that sounds like a conversation in which you are seeking information from the witness. Several guidelines ensure that your direct examination flows like conversation. Questions should be

- brief and simple,
- understandable,
- open-ended,
- without negatives,
- designed to comply with the evidentiary rules, and
- without follow-up affirmations.

### Brief and Simple

Ask brief and simple questions, such as, *"Where do you live?"* Avoid compound questions, such as, *"Where do you reside* and *who pays the rent?"* Whenever the question includes the conjunctive *and* or the disjunctive *or,* it is usually a compound question. Compound questions are objectionable, and such questions are confusing to the jury.

### Understandable

Be sure that your questions are understandable. Generally, your question and the witness's response should not contain technical terms. An exception may occur where your case involves technical matters. In such a case, your witness should explain the meaning of the terms before you begin to use them freely in your questions. While the terms are being defined by the witness, you or your witness can write a glossary, perhaps using on a flipchart as demonstrative evidence.

### Open-Ended Questions

One of the best-known evidentiary rules for direct examination is to avoid using leading questions, Federal Rule of Evidence 611(c): *"Isn't it true that you were awarded the Doctor of the Year award?"* When you use leading questions, you permit your direct examination to be interrupted by opposing counsel's objections. But more importantly, you should avoid leading questions during direct examination because with leading questions *you* will be testifying, not your witness. A technique that you can use to avoid leading questions is to employ the phrase *"whether or not,"* as in, *"Doctor, can you tell this jury whether or not you have received any awards for your service as a physician?"*

Although leading questions are generally prohibited on direct examination, they are permitted by evidentiary rules in exceptional circumstances. You can use leading questions when presenting preliminary matters such as background information about the witness (name, address, age, occupation) and other accrediting information. After you present a proper foundation, the court also will allow you to ask leading questions when developing testimony of special problem witnesses, such as children or hostile witnesses.

There are two types of open-ended questions: (1) general questions, and (2) directive open-ended questions.

### General Questions

General questions are likely to elicit a narrative response—for example, *"Can you tell me what happened next?"* Consciously thinking about the language you use to ask questions will result in obtaining the responses you want from your witness. For instance, introductory words are important in a general open-ended question:

Q: Can you explain . . .
Q: Please tell the jury . . .
Q: How did that happen?
Q: What happened next?
Q: When did that occur?

Select phrases that invite your witness to communicate with the jury and make the delivery flow in the witness's own words, if a reasonably articulate, well-prepared witness is being examined. Ideally, the witness will look at the jury and tell them in a conversational tone what happened. If the witness is not articulate, a more controlled question-and-short-answer format can be better. Be aware that in some jurisdictions you will draw an objection when you use a general open-ended question that allows your witness to respond in a narrative, such as, *"Could you tell the jury what happened that day?"* The objection to narrative responses is founded on the notion that such a response precludes opposing counsel from having a fair opportunity to object in a timely fashion.

### Directive Open-Ended Questions

Less articulate witnesses may need guidance and direction. Therefore, you may want to use the directive open-ended question. This type of question points the witness to the specific subject matter you want discussed: "Do you recall where you were late in the evening on June 5, 20XX?" Although the question directs the witness, it is not leading because it does not suggest the answer. The directive open-ended question gives the witness a frame of reference and a structure for responding. This device can be extremely useful to direct the witness to begin his story of a particular incident. Let's use an example from the *Blue Moon News Robbery* case.

Q:  *Mr. Newman, do you recall where you were late in the evening on June 5, 20XX?*

A:  Yes, I was at work at the convenience store.

Q:  *Did anything unusual happen?*

A:  Yes. A man came in and robbed the store.

Q:  *Let's talk about that. When was the first time you noticed the man?*

### No Negatives

Avoid negative questions, such as, "You can't tell the jury whether or not it was left or right, can you?" They are confusing and produce confusing responses. Double negatives are even worse: "Did you or did you not ask him not to go?"

### Designed to Comply with the Evidentiary Rules

Meticulously prepare evidentiary foundation questions, such as authentication of an exhibit. If you do this, you will be able to smoothly introduce your exhibits into evidence. You also deter opposing counsel from interrupting your direct examination with objections, or opposing counsel's voir dire on the exhibit by asking questions about the foundation.

### Without Follow-Up Affirmations

Lawyers can fall into the habit of affirming their witness's answers to direct examination questions. The most common affirmations are probably "okay" and "uh-huh," sometimes uttered after almost every answer. This verbal hiccup is not only unnecessary, but also can become irritating and distracting.

## G.  Listening to the Answer

During direct examination, you must listen closely to each answer and decide what, if any, follow-up questions need to be asked, or if other adjustments need to be made. Direct examination is not just going through a set of questions as if you were playing a lawyer in some movie where everything is scripted.

It doesn't do much good to ask the right question if you don't listen carefully to the answer. For example, if in response to your question, your medical expert witness responds in medical terminology that the jury cannot understand and you move on to your next question, you might as well have not asked the question. You must concentrate on every answer from your witness, assessing in literally a few seconds whether

- the witness understood the question,
- the answer was clear,
- the answer was complete,
- the witness has jumped ahead in the story, and so on.

You must then make appropriate corrections, including stopping and redirecting your witness: *"Mr. Newman, let me stop you. I think you've gotten a bit ahead. So, could you go back and tell the jury what happened after the defendant came to the counter, but before you saw the gun?"*

## H.  Providing Markers for the Jury

In literature and film, a story can flash back and flash forward as long as the readers or audience are provided with cues and markers as to where they are in the story. With declarative sentences, you let the jurors know your organization and where the particular testimony fits into the witness's overall story. For example:

- *"Mr. Newman, before we discuss the actual robbery, I'd first like you to focus on the store lighting. What kind of lighting is in the store?"*
- *"Doctor, you've just told us that there are four steps in the procedure. Could you please list these steps, and then we'll discuss them one at a time."*
- *"Mr. Newman, I'd like to move ahead to the identification at the police station, and then we'll go back to the robbery itself."*

In each of these examples, the attorney makes a short statement before asking a question. But the statement is not being made to gain any unfair advantage; it is to help the jury follow the testimony. If you use this technique of markers fairly, the judge and jurors will know where the testimony they are hearing fits into the witness's overall story, and will be able to fully concentrate on the testimony. Used this way, the technique is unobjectionable.

## I.  Highlighting the Important Information

Not all of the information you elicit on direct is of equal importance. You can use various trial techniques to stress the witness's testimony on important points. Without attempting to introduce needlessly cumulative evidence, repetition is one effective way to emphasize testimony.

### Looping

You could use what is called *looping*—incorporating part of a witness's reply into your next question to give emphasis to the reply.

---

**Direct Examination**

### Highlighting: The Looping Technique
### The *Blue Moon News Robbery* Case

When the prosecutor in the convenience store robbery case wants to emphasize the robber's display of a pistol, the prosecutor incorporates Mr. Newman's response into the next question:

---

> Q: Please tell the jury what occurred next.
> A: Then the defendant pointed the pistol at me.
> Q: When the defendant pointed the pistol at you, which hand did he use?

### Utilizing Exhibits and Courtroom Demonstrations

Exhibits and demonstrations can be used to highlight information. First, the trial attorney has the witness testify about what happened. Second, using an exhibit or demonstration, the direct examination goes over the same subject matter. For example, counsel could use a diagram, chart, or photograph to explain an event in greater detail.

## Direct Examination

### Highlighting with a Crime Scene Diagram
### The *Blue Moon News Robbery* Case

The prosecutor first has Mr. Newman describe how the robbery took place. Next, after Mr. Newman authenticates the crime scene diagram, the prosecutor introduces the diagram into evidence. Then, the prosecutor has Mr. Newman show the jury what happened with the aid of the diagram.

> Q: Mr. Newman, could you use this blue pen and put an *X* on State's Exhibit 6 to indicate where you first saw the person you've identified as the defendant?
> Q: Could you draw a dotted line showing where the defendant walked to the counter where you were?
> Q: Mr. Newman, would you show the jury on State's Exhibit 6 where you were standing when the defendant pointed the pistol at you? Just mark on Exhibit 6 with your initials, *G.N.*, where you were.

Courtroom demonstrations to emphasize testimony should be rehearsed. For instance, the prosecutor in the *Blue Moon News Robbery* case could have Mr. Newman show the jury how the defendant pointed the pistol at him. The prosecutor could have Mr. Newman demonstrate the distance that the robber was from him at the time the robber pointed the pistol by having Mr. Newman direct the prosecutor to stand as far away from him as the robber stood from him at the time of the robbery.

### Stop-Action Direct

Another highlighting technique is the stop-action direct. You can slow down the action by asking short questions intended to have the witness narrate the action gradually and in great detail. This technique is helpful to call the jury's attention to important points that you want them to focus on or to give the sense that an event took a long time. However, if you use the technique indiscriminately, direct examination that is too detailed can become monotonous, boring, and confusing.

---

### Direct Examination

#### Highlighting: Stop-Action Direct
#### The *Medical Malpractice* Case

The stop-action direct technique can be used to highlight the conduct of the medics in the *Medical Malpractice* case.

Q: Let's go step by step. Explain how the medics carried your daughter Shawny to the Medic One van.

Q: When the medics arrived at the van, what did they do with your daughter?

Q: After your daughter was placed in the van, what, if anything, did the medics do for your daughter?

Q: Could you describe for the jury the oxygen mask that the medics used on your daughter?

Q: Can you describe for the jury how your daughter looked when the oxygen mask was placed on her face?

Q: Were her eyes open or closed?

---

## J.  Audience Interest

Strive to make direct examination interesting so that it maintains the jury's attention. Repeatedly asking the general question, *"And what happened next?"* has been called the "windshield washer" approach. It usually produces the information, but it is as boring as trying to concentrate on your windshield wipers.

---

### Direct Examination

#### Creating Juror Interest

Strive to keep the jurors engaged and interested in the direct examination. Trial techniques to accomplish this include the following:

- Energy: Ask questions as though you want to know the answer even though you know it (unless the witness surprises you). Counsel should be energetic and interested. Actively listen to the answers and ask follow-up questions when called for.
- Variation: Vary how you do things during your examination:
  - Vary the form of the question, particularly the introductory part of the question.
  - Change your voice tone and volume.
  - Inject silence, particularly after a good answer (or when Juror 4 falls asleep— amazing how that works to wake them up).

---

- If permitted, move purposefully around the courtroom to display an exhibit, examine a witness, or for another reason.
- Have the witness move around the courtroom, step down from the witness stand and demonstrate, mark a diagram, show an exhibit, and so on.
- **Exhibits and Demonstrations:** Enrich direct examination with exhibits and demonstrations. Conduct a demonstration to create reality in the courtroom. Space out the introduction of exhibits so that introducing them changes the pace and injects interest into the direct.
- **Tense Shift:** Bring the case alive in the courtroom by shifting from the past to present tense, and have the witness paint a word picture of what is happening: "Mr. Newman, the man came from the back of the store. What do you see happen now?"

## K. Exhibits

### Dual Purposes

An exhibit serves essentially two purposes:

- Evidence that proves your legal theory, and
- Evidence that persuades the jury to accept your case theory or to discount the other side's case theory.

### Proving Your Case

First, you introduce an exhibit into evidence to prove your legal theory. You may be required to introduce it to prove a sufficient prima facie case. For instance, in a breach of contract case, plaintiff's counsel will have the written contract admitted into evidence to prove the existence of a contract between the parties. Or, in a drug prosecution, the prosecutor will introduce the controlled substances to prove possession of a controlled substance.

### Persuasive

Second, an exhibit can enhance the persuasiveness of your case theory, or highlight weaknesses in your opponent's case theory. In this section, we highlight this dual role of tangible evidence in direct examination and explain how to make the tangible evidence an integral part of your direct examination. See Chapter 8 for a fuller discussion of the use and admissibility of exhibits, and Chapter 2, pages 18-20, for a discussion of the role of visuals in persuasion.

### Pretrial Investigation and Preparation

During your pretrial investigation and preparation, think about the tangible exhibits you potentially have available, and the relevance of the information expressed in and by those things to your legal theory.

Your trial plan can help you think about how to integrate exhibits into your direct examination so the tangible evidence can tell your story, while emphasizing, highlighting, or making understandable key points in a witness's testimony.

### Illustrating the Dual Purposes

To illustrate how exhibits serve two purposes—to prove an element of your legal theory and to persuade—let's return to the *Blue Moon News Robbery* case. When Officer James Phalen investigated the scene, he found a gun just outside the store. It turned out to be a toy gun.

As the prosecutor, you will contend that this toy gun was used in the robbery. Your trial plan indicates that you want to use the toy gun that the defendant used in the robbery because, together with the clerk's testimony, it satisfies two elements of robbery in the first degree: (1) that the victim's fear of force was used by the defendant to obtain the property, and (2) that during the commission of the robbery, the defendant displayed what appeared to be a firearm. The second element is important because it elevates what would otherwise be second degree robbery to first degree robbery, and first degree robbery carries a greater penalty than second degree robbery.

---

**Direct Examination**

The Dual Purposes: Proving Legal Theory and Being Persuasive
The *Blue Moon News Robbery* Case

The prosecutor will ask Mr. Newman, the clerk, to testify that the robber threatened him with what appeared to be a gun and said, "Give me the money or you're a dead man!" The toy gun, because it looks real, *visibly demonstrates why the clerk was in fear of force* and also demonstrates that the robber displayed what appeared to be a firearm. As such, *the toy gun also adds to the persuasiveness* of the clerk's testimony.

To maximize the impact of this particular portion of the clerk's direct examination, you plan to introduce the toy gun through the store clerk at the point in his testimony where he is discussing his fear.

Q: Did the defendant do anything else to try to get you to produce the money?
A: Yes. He pulled out a gun from his jacket and threatened me with it.

---

You will, however, have to present a foundation for the gun, including a reasonable basis for the clerk's identification of the toy gun as either the actual gun or one that looks like the gun; the actual gun's chain of custody must establish it as the one held by the robber. The chain of custody foundation would require another witness or witnesses to show that the toy gun in court is the same one recovered outside the store. Because the police took possession of the gun, labeled it, stored it, and brought it to court, you would need to present the chain of custody through police testimony. Then you need to decide the sequence of the testimony. Do you have the police testify before the clerk? When will you have the gun admitted as evidence, and through which witness? Of course, even if the police had not recovered the actual toy gun used in the robbery, you could locate a toy fitting the clerk's description and then have him testify that the gun "fairly and accurately" looks like the gun the robber used. The toy gun could then be used at trial as demonstrative evidence.

Looking at these questions from a slightly different angle than evidentiary and organizational concerns, the questions should alert you that you must also think about the persuasive nature of the gun. Think creatively about how to use the toy gun to make the clerk's fear for his safety and his belief that the object was a real gun more persuasive, even though the robber had only a toy gun to threaten him. You have a variety of choices. You could show that the police officer on the scene initially handled the gun as if it were real. You could handle the toy as though it were a real gun. Or you could rely on the common sense and experience of the jurors by displaying the toy gun and passing it among them.

## Direct Examination

### Persuading with an Exhibit
### The *Blue Moon News Robbery* Case

As the prosecutor, you could use Officer Phelan to *persuade the jury that the toy gun looked so real that it was reasonable for the clerk to be fearful*. Assume that the gun has been admitted into evidence.

Q: Officer Phelan, when you first picked up this gun, State's Exhibit 9, from the ground, what did you do?

A: I took a plastic bag from my pocket to pick up the gun. I then turned the gun downward to check the barrel to see if it was loaded.

Q: Then what did you do?

A: I tried to open the gun barrel. That was when I discovered that it was a toy.

Q: What was your reaction to your discovery that the gun was a toy?

A: At first I laughed. Then I got very angry that a toy marketed for children was so real that it fooled me. I consider myself to be a person who is quite familiar with guns. I carry a gun eight to ten hours a day. This toy really fooled me.

The police officer's direct examination establishes the foundation for the admissibility of the gun and shows that the toy gun was found near the store. It also provides persuasive testimony that the gun appeared to be real and could actually cause a person to fear harm. You would plan the content of the clerk's testimony to show that he believed the gun was real, was threatened with it, and feared for his life. Clearly, having two people, and in particular an experienced police officer, testify during their direct examinations that they believed the gun was real enhances the persuasiveness of the first degree robbery case theory.

## L.  Problematic Witnesses

Certain witnesses present special problems because of their demeanor, appearance, manner of testifying, background, memory, or other such personal factors that can reflect negatively on their testimony. Among problematic witnesses are those who are very young, very old, biased, adverse, hostile, scared, boring, long-winded, overly confident, or have a severe infirmity. These human problems can, to a degree, either be resolved or compensated for with a witness by preparing the witness carefully, conditioning the jury to listen to the testimony (by discussing in voir dire problems inherent with a child witness), and tailoring your approach in direct examination to fit the problem the witness poses.

### Problem Solving

Usually if you spend extra time in preparing problem witnesses, you can improve their performance. For instance, people who speak in a monotone, are soft-spoken, or have dull information to impart may have their testimony enhanced thorough preparation, practice, and the incorporation of visuals into the direct examination. A soft-spoken or mumbling witness may be aided by calling attention to the problem during your meeting with the witness. You may be able to prevent this problem during the actual examination by standing at a distance from the witness (provided that the court protocol allows you to do this) so the witness will naturally speak up, or by having the witness speak into the courtroom microphone.

To fully illustrate the approach, suppose you are plaintiff's attorney in the *Medical Malpractice* suit. You plan a direct examination of plaintiff's father, Mr. Kixskiller, and must prepare him. Mr. Kixskiller presents special witness problems. Although he is an important witness who can testify about plaintiff's condition, Mr. Kixskiller has a hearing impairment.

Because Mr. Kixskiller has a hearing impairment, he may have difficulty with questions posed both by you and opposing counsel. His responses to questions may not be precise or on point if he cannot fully hear the questions. A juror may not listen fairly to Mr. Kixskiller's testimony because he speaks in an excessively loud voice due to his impairment.

During witness preparation, you could work with Mr. Kixskiller to overcome the problems caused by his hearing impediment. To enable him to hear you, you could speak as slowly and as loudly as is necessary. You could advise him that if he has trouble hearing either you, opposing counsel, or the judge during the trial, he should ask the speaker to speak louder. You also could make an effort to get him to lower the volume of his voice. By spending several sessions practicing direct examination, you may be able to ensure that he hears your questions and can respond appropriately.

Then, beginning with jury selection, you can lay the groundwork for Mr. Kixskiller's problematic testimony by asking whether each prospective juror can carefully and fairly listen to a witness despite an excessively loud voice and hearing impairment.

Mr. Ichiro, a witness for plaintiff, Mr. Kixskiller, has difficulty hearing and may at times appear to be nonresponsive to my questions or defense counsel's questions. Will you be able to consider his testimony fairly and impartially and in accordance with the court's instructions?

When you conduct direct examination, you can show concern for Mr. Kixskiller's ability to hear; your consideration toward the witness may guide them to be particularly tolerant in listening to and deliberating over Mr. Kixskiller's testimony. If Mr. Kixskiller has difficulty hearing either the judge or opposing counsel, you could urge the judge or counsel to speak up so as to be heard. If you are concerned that the judge or jury may perceive Kixskiller's loud voice as irritating or disrespectful, you might say:

> Your Honor, Mr. Kixskiller may have difficulty hearing me. Therefore, I will be using a loud voice. Likewise, Mr. Kixskiller might respond loudly. No disrespect is meant to Your Honor or the jury.

## VI. OTHER SOURCES OF TESTIMONY

### A. Deposition

The Federal Rules of Civil Procedure and the Federal Rules of Evidence or state counterpart rules govern whether deposition testimony will be admissible in trial. Two instances when a deposition may be used in lieu of direct examination include these:

- **Preservation Deposition:** Federal Rule of Civil Procedure 32(a)(4) provides that the preservation deposition testimony of an unavailable witness (the witness is dead, lives more than 100 miles away, or cannot testify due to age, illness, or imprisonment) is admissible in lieu of the witness's live testimony.
- **Admission of a Party-Opponent:** Under Federal Rule of Evidence 801(d)(2), an admission of a party-opponent is admissible if it is the party's own statement, is adopted by the party as true, is made by a person authorized by the party to make it, or is one made by an agent or a co-conspirator of a party.

At trial, the judge will commonly preface the introduction of the deposition into evidence with an oral instruction to the jury containing both an explanation of what a deposition is and how the jury should receive it.

To present the testimony at trial, a stand-in for the deponent can be called to read the deponent's portions of the transcript. Or, if counsel sought a videoed deposition, the video can be shown to the jury. Reading from a deposition transcript is to watching a video deposition what reading a critic's review is to seeing the play, or reading a wine menu is to drinking a glass of pinot noir. With a video, the jury can evaluate the witness's demeanor, take cues from her facial expressions, and see the place where the deposition was taken and how it was conducted. For an excellent model of a deposition, see the DVD accompanying the companion book, Berger, Mitchell, and Clark, *Pretrial Advocacy: Planning, Analysis, and Strategy* (4th ed., Aspen 2012).

## B.  Other Pretrial Case Documents

In a civil case, facts that would otherwise be the subject of your direct examination are often admitted in pleadings, interrogatories, and requests for admissions, or at a pretrial conference where they are incorporated into a pretrial order. You or the judge must read such admissions into the record for the benefit of both the jury and the trial record. However, you must be prepared for how your particular trial judge will want you to proceed in presenting admissions from those various sources. One common method is for the judge or attorney to explain the process and read the admissions given in response to requests for admissions to the jury. The judge or attorney then reads the admitted facts. The same approach generally applies to the explanation and submission of interrogatories to the jury. Also, when dealing with discovery admissions, if a document such as an interrogatory contains the admission but also contains many inadmissible facts, you will need a clean excised copy for trial.

## C.  Stipulation

A stipulation is an agreement between the parties that is read to the jury. It could be a stipulation to a fact, to a witness's testimony, or to some element. For instance, in the *Medical Malpractice* case, Shawny Kixskiller's father could have become ill and the parties could stipulate to Mr. Kixskiller's testimony. The testimony could be reduced to a written statement. At the appropriate time in the plaintiff's case, plaintiff's counsel informs the court of a desire to inform the jury of the stipulation. The judge would then instruct the jury. Following the court's instruction, plaintiff's counsel would read the stipulation to the jury. Naturally, court procedures may differ (the judge may wish to read stipulations to the jury), so be certain to check with the court. See pages 228-229 for an example of a written stipulation in the *Freck Point* case.

## D.  Judicial Notice

Federal Rule of Evidence 201 governs judicial notice. The court may take judicial notice when the fact is "not subject to reasonable dispute" and is either

*   generally known within the trial court's territorial jurisdiction, or
*   can be accurately and readily determined from sources whose accuracy cannot reasonably be questioned.

In a civil case, the court must instruct the jury that the judicially noticed fact is to be conclusively accepted. In a criminal case, the judge shall instruct the jury that it may, but is not required to, accept as conclusive the noticed fact.

## VII. VISUALS FOR DIRECT EXAMINATION

Direct examination involves working with the full assortment of exhibits and trial visuals. In this section, we concentrate on how to take advantage of exhibits and trial visuals in direct examination to persuade the jury.

### A. Direct Examination in Complex Cases

Two principal ways that direct examination can be complex and hard for the jury to follow are when

- technical information is involved; and/or
- the case involves a large quantity of information (numerous actors, events, or both actors and events).

When faced with presenting complex information, the lawyer should think of employing visuals to simplify and clarify the information. Here we concentrate on direct examination that potentially could confuse the jurors because it imparts a mass of information. See also Chapter 11 on expert witnesses.

#### Federal Rule of Evidence 1006: Summary Chart

Summary charts are especially effective in assisting the jury to clarify and understand a mountain of information. The first type of summary chart is the kind authorized by Federal Rule of Evidence 1006. Under that rule, the contents of voluminous writings, recordings, or photographs that cannot be conveniently examined by the jurors may be presented by a chart, summary, or calculation. Rule 1006 charts are admissible as substantive evidence. One example of voluminous records is a corporation's accounting records, which the chart that follows shows.

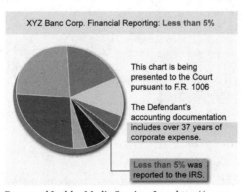

Borrowed Ladder Media Services Inc., *http://www .borrowedladder.com.*

### Federal Rule of Evidence 611(a): Summary Chart

Federal Rule of Evidence 611 is also the rule relied on for using summary charts:

> (a) Control by court. The court shall exercise reasonable control over the mode and order of examining witnesses and presenting evidence so as to (1) make those procedures effective for determining the truth; (2) avoid wasting time; and (3) protect witnesses from harassment or undue embarrassment.

However, the rule makes no mention of summary charts. Rather, a body of case law developed under Rule 611(a) provides that summary charts are pedagogical devices offered to help in the presentation and comprehension of the evidence and may be shown to the jury. *United States v. Janati*, 374 F.3d 263 (4th Cir. 2004). A summary chart can contain, among other things, witness conclusions. Generally, the chart is not admitted into evidence. See page 250 for discussion of a summary chart, and page 251 for laying a foundation for a summary chart.

## B. Courtroom Demonstrations

Courtroom demonstrations can be effective in bringing a story to life. For example, as shown in the courtroom demonstration below, the prosecutor could have the witness step down from the witness chair and show the jury how the defendant approached him in an assault case.

Courtroom demonstrations must be rehearsed during trial preparation. The participants should practice the demonstration, and the attorney should carefully plan how and where it will be conducted in the courtroom. If you are thinking about conducting a demonstration with a witness called by the opposing party, the demonstration will not have been rehearsed. It is a gamble. It very well may backfire, or at least be met with resistance.

## VIII. APPELLATE RECORD

It is critical to think of conducting direct examination as speaking through the record to the appellate court, your other audience. You are building a record of substantive information for review by an appellate court if the case is appealed.

---

### Direct Examination

#### Making a Record for Appeal
#### The *Blue Moon News Robbery* Case

The prosecutor has asked the clerk whether the man who robbed him is in the courtroom. Mr. Newman responds yes. Then, in response to the prosecutor's request that the witness point to the person, Mr. Newman points to the defendant. That's not enough. The prosecutor needs to establish an appellate record on the identity element, because the transcript will not reflect it until the prosecutor says:

> "Your Honor, may the record reflect that the witness, Mr. Newman, has pointed to a man seated at the defense counsel table, Mike Ryan, who is the defendant in this case."

---

Similarly, you want the transcript to reflect proof of all the elements of your claims or defenses, even those that are obvious: the date of the crime, the use of force or threat of force, the defendant's taking of property, and the venue. You will want to review your trial plan and your proposed jury instructions to ensure that you have introduced sufficient evidence through witnesses on direct examination to establish a prima facie showing on each legal element of your claim or defense.

## IX. REDIRECT AND REBUTTAL

### A. Redirect

Redirect examination permits the trial attorney who conducted the direct to respond to opposing counsel's cross-examination attack. Redirect, however, is limited to the scope of cross-examination and is subject to re-cross.

### The Successful Redirect

The ideal redirect examination is one that succinctly deflates the hot-air balloon that was inflated during cross-examination. Some of this will be planned in advance: *"Mr. Newman, is there any doubt in your mind that the defendant is the person who robbed you?"* And some will be the result of your assessment of the impact of various points brought out in cross-examination. The quicker the air is let out, the better the redirect is because it exposes the emptiness of the cross.

To accomplish this effect, counsel must listen carefully to the cross, analyze the main thrusts of the examination, find the flaws in them, and then expose the flaws on redirect. For example, suppose your expert witness was cross-examined showing the expert was paid an exorbitant fee. Your opponent wants to use this testimony to show bias. However, this testimony alone might not sway a jury to believe that the expert was biased. Your redirect examination question, *"What are you doing with your fee?"* and the answer, *"Donating it to charity,"* would burst the cross-examination balloon.

### Case Weaknesses

Counsel may either include a case weakness in direct examination or leave the matter for redirect or rebuttal. See pages 294-296. Developing a strategy depends on many factors. As always, you need to consider the advantages and risks that exist in any decision you make. For example, if you have a witness explain a case weakness, you open the door for opposing counsel to delve deeper into the area in cross-examination. Moreover, had you not brought out the matter on direct, opposing counsel may not have broached the subject.

Suppose you save your powerful response to a case weakness for redirect. Certainly, if the evidence is significant, producing it on redirect could provide a strong conclusion to the witness's examination. However, this possible advantage must be weighed against several disadvantages. The court may rule that the information is inadmissible because it is improper redirect or otherwise in violation of evidentiary law. Such a ruling may then deprive you of the significant information unless you can think of an alternative way to present it, such as another witness, cross-examination of an opposing witness, and so on. Also, if permitted on redirect, the strategy could lead to a damaging recross-examination and result in a weak finish to your witness's examination.

## B.  Rebuttal

Rebuttal allows the plaintiff (or prosecutor) to present testimony to refute the other side's case by calling new witnesses or recalling witnesses. This includes rebutting attacks on plaintiff's witnesses. So, rebuttal offers another avenue to rehabilitate your witness after cross-examination. But again, rebuttal is limited to matters introduced by the defense and, if allowed, may be subject to the defense responding in surrebuttal.

While you may consider presenting the rehabilitating information in rebuttal, that decision has a number of strategic dimensions. If you wait for rebuttal and attempt to recall your witnesses to respond to the evidence produced by the opposing party, a number of problems may ensue, including the court ruling that the information is not proper rebuttal, or is collateral. Additionally, you may have difficulty relocating your witnesses, or be faced with a fatigued jury who by this point may not be able to give full attention to the evidence. Further, if the judge permits rebuttal testimony, surrebuttal by the other side may also be permitted. The advantage to waiting for rebuttal is that you can take a wait-and-see attitude, and, if the information that your adversary has presented is not very damaging, you may not want to highlight it at all by calling rebuttal witnesses. Rather, you could argue your response in closing argument.

## X. ORDER OF WITNESSES

Direct examinations are the building blocks for a persuasive case. It follows that those building blocks must be arranged properly or the whole structure may be faulty. We would like it if all of our witnesses were solid witnesses—articulate, invulnerable to impeachment, with significant information to impart—just as we would hope that all the building blocks for a structure were of the same shape and sturdy composition. However, life is not like that; some of our witnesses will not be as strong as others, and some will have little substantive information to offer. So we must arrange the order of our witnesses to ensure that the whole case-in-chief is convincing.

The traditional approach for witnesses is to start strong, end strong, and bury weak witnesses in the middle of the case-in-chief. You want to begin strong with a solid witness so that your case has a firm foundation. If the first witness crumbles, this can weaken the remainder of your case. Under the rule of primacy, what the jurors hear first tends to make a greater impression on them than what is heard in the middle of the case-in-chief. However, jurors are also impressed with what they hear last. Therefore, you should end on a high note with a solid witness, one who is not likely to be impeached and who has valuable information to impart to the jury.

Another important principle in deciding on the order of witnesses is to tell the story of your case in a logical way. A chronological story is easy to follow. Another way to arrange witnesses so the information is presented in a logical order is to arrange it by subject matter.

## XI. ETHICAL CONSIDERATIONS

Most of the ethical dilemmas concerning direct examination involve a lawyer's communication with witnesses.

## A. Coaching

What are the ethical boundaries of what a lawyer can say to a client or witness? For example, can the lawyer explain the law describing what constitutes the defenses to murder, suggest which ones are not likely to apply to the client's case, and leave it to the client to tell the lawyer what defense might apply? Can counsel suggest a defense? Can counsel tell the witness which words to use for the witness's testimony to be most effective? ABA Model Rules of Professional Conduct have two provisions that regulate what trial counsel can say to a witness, Rule 3.3(a)(3) and Rule 3.4(b).

---

### Ethical Rules for Communicating with a Witness

#### ABA Model Rules of Professional Conduct

Under the Model Rules of Professional Conduct, two provisions provide that while it is permissible for the lawyer to counsel the witness on the applicable law and significance of the witness's testimony, the attorney may not counsel or assist the witness in testifying to anything but the truth.

**Candor Toward the Tribunal:** Model Rule of Professional Conduct 3.3(a)(3): Counsel shall not "offer evidence the lawyer knows to be false."

**Fairness to Opposing Party and Counsel:** Model Rule of Professional Conduct 3.4(b): An attorney shall "not falsify evidence, counsel, or assist a witness to testify falsely, or offer an inducement to a witness that is prohibited by law."

---

## B. False Evidence

### The Rule

ABA Model Rule of Professional Conduct 3.3 on Candor Toward the Tribunal covers the prohibitions against offering false evidence and remedial measures as follows:

(a) A lawyer shall not knowingly: . . .

(3) offer evidence that the lawyer knows to be false. If a lawyer, the lawyer's client, or a witness called by the lawyer, has offered material evidence and the lawyer comes to know of its falsity, the lawyer shall take reasonable remedial measures, including, if necessary, disclosure to the tribunal. A lawyer may refuse to offer evidence, other than the testimony of a defendant in a criminal matter, that the lawyer reasonably believes is false.

(b) A lawyer who represents a client in an adjudicative proceeding and who knows that a person intends to engage, is engaging or has engaged in criminal or fraudulent conduct related to the proceeding shall take reasonable remedial measures, including, if necessary, disclosure to the tribunal.

(c) The duties stated in paragraphs (a) and (b) continue to the conclusion of the proceeding, and apply even if compliance requires disclosure of information otherwise protected by Rule 1.6.

The Comments to the Model Rules offer directions regarding how to deal with situations where false evidence may be or has been offered: The lawyer must "refuse to offer evidence that the lawyer knows to be false, regardless of the client's wishes." If the attorney knows that the client intends to testify falsely or wants the lawyer to offer false evidence, the lawyer may try to persuade the client against this, and, failing that, the lawyer must refuse. If only a part of the testimony is false, the lawyer can present the rest, but not the false part.

### Defense Counsel in Criminal Cases

Comment 7 to Model Rule of Professional Conduct 3.3 states that the rules just discussed apply equally to criminal defense counsel, as well as further explaining:

> The duties stated in paragraphs (a) and (b) apply to all lawyers, including defense counsel in criminal cases. In some jurisdictions, however, courts have required counsel to present the accused as a witness or to give a narrative statement if the accused so desires, even if counsel knows that the testimony or statement will be false. The obligation of the advocate under the Rules of Professional Conduct is subordinate to such requirements. . . .

If counsel other than criminal defense counsel does not know that the evidence is false and only reasonably believes it is false, counsel can still refuse to offer it. However, Comment 9 to the rule recognizes the difference between defense counsel in a criminal case and other lawyers as follows:

> Because of the special protections historically provided criminal defendants, however, this Rule does not permit a lawyer to refuse to offer the testimony of such a client where the lawyer reasonably believes but does not know that the testimony will be false. Unless the lawyer knows the testimony will be false, the lawyer must honor the client's decision to testify.

### Remedial Measures

If after the fact the lawyer learns that he has offered false evidence, the lawyer is to take remedial measures. The comment states that the proper course of action is "remonstrate with the client confidentially, advise the client of the lawyer's duty of candor to the tribunal and seek the client's cooperation with respect to the withdrawal or correction of the false statements or evidence. If that fails, the advocate must take further remedial action." Depending on the circumstances, the action may be withdrawal or disclosure of the information to the judge.

## Ethical Rules Pertaining to Direct Examination: Summary

### ABA Model Rules of Professional Conduct

Coaching: Model Rule of Professional Conduct 3.3(a)(3) provides: A lawyer shall not "offer evidence the lawyer knows to be false." Rule 3.4(b) states an attorney shall "not falsify evidence, counsel or assist a witness to testify falsely. . . ."

False Evidence: Model Rule of Professional Conduct 3.3(a)(3) provides: "A lawyer shall not knowingly . . . offer evidence that the lawyer knows to be false. If a lawyer, the lawyer's client, or a witness called by the lawyer, has offered material evidence and the lawyer comes to know of its falsity, the lawyer shall take reasonable remedial measures. . . ." Rules for criminal defense counsel may differ, however, including a requirement that counsel allow the defendant to testify as long as counsel does not know the evidence is false. Other than the testimony of the defendant, counsel may refuse to offer false evidence if counsel reasonably believes it to be false.

## CHECKLIST: DIRECT EXAMINATION

### Content

The attorney conducting the direct:

☐ Advances the case theory;
☐ Elicits evidence that supports elements of the legal theory (claim, defense, or counterclaim);
☐ Delivers a compelling story by concentrating on the five essentials of a persuasive factual story:
  • Human values that the jury cares about (fairness) and human needs (personal safety),
  • Human story (facts that will sway the jury to care about the client),
  • Believable and understandable story (makes common sense),
  • Quantity of evidence (the facts testified to by the witness contributes to the evidence required to meet the burden of proof), and
  • Quality of evidence (the facts elicited show that the witness is credible);
☐ Where appropriate, reveals case weaknesses to inoculate the jury; and
☐ Seeks to elicit admissible evidence under applicable evidence law.

### Structure

☐ Introductory questions accomplish these objectives.
  • Get the jurors' attention (start with the first question that is likely on the jurors' minds).
  • Accredit the witness.
  • Put the witness at ease and introduce the witness to the jurors.
☐ The body of the direct is readily understandable by the jury because it uses one or more organizational structures:

- Chronological,
- By subject area,
- By legal elements, or
- Straight narrative.
☐ The conclusions of direct and any redirect are on a high note.

### Essential Evidence Rules

☐ The witness is competent.
☐ The witness has personal knowledge.
☐ Counsel impeaches his own witness if need be.
☐ Counsel does not ask leading questions unless on preliminary matters, uncontested matters, or where they are addressed to a hostile witness or adverse party.
☐ Direct delves only into relevant material.

### Conducting a Successful Direct

☐ The witness is well prepared to testify.
☐ Counsel is positioned in the courtroom so the witness is the center of attention and enabled to communicate directly to the jury.
☐ Language from crucial jury instructions is incorporated into the questioning.
☐ The form of each question is designed to facilitate communication and make the testimony flow smoothly. Each question
  - is brief and simple,
  - is understandable (open-ended for well-prepared and articulate witnesses),
  - omits negatives,
  - complies with evidence rules, and
  - does not include follow-up affirmations by counsel ("Uh-huh," "Okay").
☐ Counsel listens to the witness's answer and responds accordingly (asks follow-up questions to clarify an answer).
☐ Direct highlights important information using techniques such as
  - looping,
  - using exhibits and courtroom demonstrations, and
  - stop-action.
☐ Direct maintains the jury's interest with trial techniques such as
  - maintaining energy in asking questions, listening, and responding;
  - varying voice volume and tone, form of the question, positioning in the courtroom, and so on; and
  - conducting a rehearsed courtroom demonstration and working with exhibits so as to highlight the testimony and maintain jurors' interest.

### Exhibits

☐ Direct examination introduces exhibits necessary to prove the case theory.
☐ Exhibits are used persuasively.

### Problematic Witnesses

☐ Direct takes the witness's special problems into account (elicits testimony from a very young child to show the witness is competent and treats the witness gently).

*continued* ▶

**Visual Trial**

☐ Direct employs visuals to make the direct persuasive and understandable.

**Appellate Record**

☐ Counsel makes a record for appeal.

**Redirect**

☐ Successfully undercuts damage done by cross-examination.
☐ Ends on a high note.

**Order of Proof**

☐ The order in which the witnesses are called in the case-in-chief is the most effective way of convincingly communicating the case theory.

**Meet Judicial Expectations: Direct Examination**

☐ Counsel prepares a witness list for the court and opposing counsel.
☐ Counsel is ready to call witnesses when needed.
☐ Counsel informs witnesses of pertinent court orders and rules regarding sequestration.
☐ Unless local custom is different, the lawyer stands when questioning the witness.
☐ If required, counsel gives notice of witness order, length of cross and direct, and so on.
☐ In a **bench trial,** counsel
  • drops peripheral witnesses,
  • seek stipulations,
  • gets to the heart of the matter,
  • uses exhibits and visuals, and
  • has witnesses testify to only what is needed to tell the essence of a persuasive story.

**Ethical Boundaries**

☐ The examination does not offer evidence that counsel knows to be false.
☐ Counsel remedies the situation if the witness introduces false evidence.

# CROSS-EXAMINATION
## Concession Seeking

*"It requires the greatest ingenuity; a habit of logical thought; clearness of perception in general; infinite patience and self control; power to read men's minds intuitively, to judge of their motives; ability to act with force and precision; a masterful knowledge of the subject matter itself; an extreme caution, and above all, the instinct to discover the weak point in the witness under examination."*

> —**Francis L. Wellman**, *The Art of Cross-Examination* 28 (new ed., Book Jungle 2007) (originally published 1903)

*Kaffee:* Did you order the Code Red?
*Col. Jessep:* I did the job I . . .
*Kaffee:* [shouting] Did you order the Code Red?
*Col. Jessep:* [shouts] You're goddamn right I did!

> —**Daniel Kaffee**, portrayed by Tom Cruise, and **Col. Nathan Jessep**, portrayed by **Jack Nicholson**, in *A Few Good Men* (1992)

## I. THE FOUR C'S OF CROSS-EXAMINATION

You may be thinking that cross-examination is a daunting task, particularly when Wellman says it requires, among other things, the "greatest ingenuity" and the "power to read men's mind intuitively." However, while those innate talents are helpful, you can formulate and conduct a successful cross-examination with the methodology we cover in this chapter. Specifically, you will learn these four C's of cross-examination:

- Content: Determining the content of the cross-examination,
- Construction: Constructing the examination so that it will persuade the jury,
- Character: Comporting oneself, and
- Control: Controlling runaway and evasive witnesses.

> To see demonstrations of the four C's of cross-examination, watch the cross-examinations in the *Freck Point* trial demonstration movie on the website *http://www.aspenlawschool.com/books/berger_trialad4e.*

## II. CONTENT

### A. Purpose of Cross-Examination

The content of cross-examination flows from the purpose of the cross. The seminal book written on cross-examination, Francis Wellman's *The Art of Cross-*

*Examination* (new ed., Book Jungle 2007), was originally published in 1903, and it is freely available in its entirety on Google Books. Wellman observes that "more cross-examinations are suicidal than homicidal." Wellman explains that cross-examinations often yield disastrous results because cross-examiners do not understand the primary purpose of cross. That primary purpose of cross-examination is to uncover the truth—to gather concessions that either help your case theory or undermine your adversary's case theory. Usually, cross-examination responses are beneficial. Impeachment of the witness and the witness's testimony remains an objective, but only a secondary one.

## B.  Case Theory as Guide

### Your Theory

Planning the content of cross-examination begins with your and the other side's case theories. Start with a firm understanding of your factual theory—the persuasive story. What are the strengths of your evidence and the values that your factual theory communicates to the jury? The examination should be designed to obtain concessions compatible with your case theory. Think of cross as aimed at persuading the jury of your case theory and gathering concessions that you can argue in closing argument to support your case theory.

### Your Adversary's Case Theory

Carefully analyze the other side's case theory to determine what favorable concessions you may be able to gain. Those concessions are concessions supporting your case theory, and also admissions pointing out the deficiencies in the other side's case theory. To illustrate how this process works, consider these common defenses illustrated in diverse criminal cases.

---

### Cross-Examination

#### Analysis of Your Adversary's Case Theory

- **Alibi—Defense Argument:** "My client was across town at the time of the robbery, attending a party."
- **Consent in a Sexual Assault Case—Defense Argument:** "Yes, he had sex with her, but she consented."
- **Self-Defense—Defense Argument:** "Sure, he stabbed him. If he hadn't, my client would have been killed."
- **Insanity—Defense Argument:** "Yes, she killed her sister, but she was insane at the time and she didn't know the difference between right and wrong."

---

These potential case theories employ a confession and avoidance strategy. They concede some facts crucial to proving the elements of the charged crime, but provide a viable defense. From a defense vantage point, confession and avoidance is an effective strategy because it removes much of the taint from the defendant: "Yes, the death happened, but the defendant was not responsible." From the prosecutor's view, concession and avoidance is advantageous because the defense concedes important facts. The truths that defense witnesses will concede prove elements of the prosecution's legal theories. For example, an alibi witness would concede that she does not contest that the robbery took place. The defendant in the self-defense case will concede to having stabbed the other person.

## C. Tentative Closing Argument

The process of preparation, planning, and performance of cross-examination is done by focusing on your and the other side's case theory, theme, and the other phases of the trial, primarily closing argument.

A crucial planning tool for designing cross-examination, just as in direct examination, is to examine your tentative closing argument that embodies your theory and a refutation of the other side's case theory. The cross-examination process begins by looking forward, examining your tentative closing argument, and then planning shifts backward to the potential cross-examination. Looking ahead, you explore the points to present in closing argument to support the case theory and to discredit the other side's witness or witness's story. Then ask yourself, "What information might I obtain through cross-examination to argue these points in closing argument?" Working from the tentative closing argument, it is possible to figure out the points to cover in cross-examination. Going back and forth using the tentative closing argument as a guide, cross-examination objectives for each witness will take shape.

In the *Blue Moon News Robbery* case, consider the prosecutor, who is expecting to deal with an alibi defense to the charge of robbery. The usual defense approach would be two-pronged: (1) undercut the prosecution's proof that the defendant committed the crime (show vulnerable eyewitness identification), and (2) present testimony that the defendant was elsewhere when the crime was committed.

The prosecutor's tentative closing argument to refute the alibi defense stresses the prosecution's evidence that the defendant committed the robbery and secondarily deals with the alibi defense. The evidence can be developed on cross-examination to support these arguments:

- Alibi witness is mistaken,
- Alibi witness is fabricating, and/or
- So what? The witness does not establish an alibi.

Consider the first alternative—arguing that the alibi witness is mistaken. Where does this lead the prosecutor in planning cross-examination? An alibi witness may be honestly mistaken in believing that the defendant was in his presence when the defendant was committing the crime in another place.

Cross-examination of such a witness can stop when the primary objective is met—obtaining concessions. If the witness is shown to be mistaken, the examiner need not show the witness lacks credibility. The following are some areas where the prosecutor may be able to gain favorable concessions in these areas of vulnerability.

- **Relationship and Collaboration:** The witness's relationship with the defendant may have motivated the witness to selectively recall the defendant's presence, and the defendant may have planted the idea. Cross-examination could cover any relationship between defendant and the witness, contacts between the witness and defendant since the crime, whether the alibi was discussed, and who first mentioned they were together at the time of the crime.
- **Admission of Uncertainty:** The honestly mistaken witness may be uncertain that it was the exact date and time of the crime that the witness was with the defendant. Cross-examination would concentrate on obtaining concessions from the witness that it could have been a different date or time that the witness was with the defendant. The cross-examination leading into an attempt to obtain this acknowledgment could include questions about the details of the circumstances under which they were together, a test of the witness's memory of other days before, and after the date and time of the crime.
- **When First Contacted:** If the witness was contacted by the defense a significant period of time after the crime, the witness would necessarily have to attempt to reconstruct from distant memory the circumstances of the contact with the defendant. The closer in time between the crime and the defense contact with the witness, the more likely the witness would more accurately recall. Assuming that the defendant committed the crime, this analysis will assist the prosecutor in determining whether she will approach the witness as being untruthful, or sincere, but mistaken.

## D. The Concession-Seeking Question

To identify what you want to obtain during cross-examination, ask yourself this key question: "What must the witness *concede* or face having her answer labeled a lie, mistaken, or preposterous?" Two operational words in this sentence need further elaboration.

- **Must:** The witness must make the concession because the cross-examiner can prove it or because to not make the admission defies common sense. For example, in our *Blue Moon News Robbery* case, the alibi witness must admit that there were 40 to 50 people at the party because other credible witnesses will testify to this.
- **Concede:** The concession in this question is one that supports your case theory or undercuts the other side's. The concessions you want are the

ones you have identified by constructing your tentative closing argument, such as the witness is uncertain about being with the defendant at the time of the crime. Or that the defendant contacted the witness a couple months after the crime and asked the witness to vouch for the alibi.

The significance of this key question (what the witness *must* concede) is that it both illuminates how concession-seeking cross-examination works and provides a device for identifying the type of concessions you want. Because the concession being sought is the truth (the cross-examiner can prove the proposition), either the witness will grant the concession or deny the truth and be impeached.

Shana Alexander's book, *The Pizza Connection: Lawyers, Money, Drugs, Mafia* 318-320 (Weidenfeld & Nicholson 1988), about a $1.65 billion heroin and money laundering conspiracy case trial that lasted 18 months, provides an illustration of how this key question technique can work to formulate a line of cross-examination of an alibi witness.

---

### Cross-Examination

#### The Concession-Seeking Question
#### The *Pizza Connection* Case

Place: Courtroom in New York                                  When: January 1987

(Defense counsel) Larry Bronson's defense of (defendant) Sal Greco is focused on his client's need to prove that he was not in a Bagheria farmhouse in early March 1980 watching a heroin quality-control test. Bronson will show he [Greco] was quietly, busily at home in New Jersey. He calls Greco's good friend and tax accountant, Justin Pisano, a man who keeps detailed date books.

Under patient examination by Bronson, the witness goes through a precise account of driving to the Jersey Shore three Sundays in March to go over Greco's accounts and to visit nearby pizzerias with his client in order to compare their business with that of the Greco pizzeria in Neptune City.

Stewart's cross-examination of Pisano becomes this prosecutor's finest hour. He concentrates on the March date-book entries.

"On March 2, yes, I drove down to see Greco," Pisano says, "and we had a leisurely dinner."

"You told us yesterday you were in no rush, right?"

"Yes."

"And that's the truth, the whole truth, and nothing but the truth?"

"Yes."

"Then what is this appointment for 7:00 P.M., with Troviatta?"

"Just a tax appointment. Early March is income tax time, and I made many Sunday and night appointments to service all my tax clients."

"What is Troviatta's first name? Where does he live?"

"I don't remember. I don't even think I do their taxes anymore."

---

Stewart remembers. He says Pisano was thirty-five miles away from Greco's pizzeria that night, in the heart of Manhattan, at Lincoln Center, at the opera.

Pisano emphatically denies this. He has only been to Lincoln Center once in his life, to hear Pavarotti.

"Are you an opera fan?"

"Nope. Only been to one opera in my life, when I was in high school."

Stewart shows the witness, and the jury, the Sunday-evening newspaper opera listing for March 2, 1980, at the New York State Theater at Lincoln Center: *La Traviata*.

Bronson objects. "Misleading the witness, your Honor. His witness's tax client is named Troviatta—with two t's."

"And the advertisement for the opera is spelled *T-R-A-V-I-A-T-A*, right?" Stewart asks.

"No. It's *La* Traviata," says Pisano gamely.

"La Traviata?"

"Right. I don't see the comparison to Troviatta."

"Except for the time. *That's* a coincidence. Isn't it?"

Pisano agrees, and Stewart directs him to look at the entry for two Sundays ahead, March 16, at one in the afternoon.

"Are you referring to Carmen? Carmen Sangari, who I no longer do?"

"Carmen Sangari?" Stewart produces the *New York Times*, and asks him to read aloud the opera listing for that Sunday afternoon. Pisano looks, and agrees that this is truly an amazing coincidence.

Spectators have begun to giggle. But Stewart is not finished. He directs the witness's attention to his diary entry for the following Sunday at 7:00 P.M. "Is that a tax client of yours?"

The giggling turns to guffaws. The notebook says, "Barber of Seville."

The cross-examiner started with the truth—the alibi witness Pisano was at the opera at the time that defendant Sal Greco was witnessing the heroin quality-control test. Stewart could prove it with Pisano's diary and the *New York Times* opera listings. The answer to the question, "What must this witness concede to stamp the answer a lie, mistaken, or preposterous?" is that he was at the opera and not with Greco. When Pisano did not give the concession, he stamped his answer laughable. If he had made the admission, he would have conceded that he could not be an alibi witness for Greco.

## E. Brainstorming for Content

Once you have a firm grasp of the case theories and have prepared a tentative closing argument, you have a vision of what you want to achieve in cross-examination. You can brainstorm to identify the content of your examination. To accomplish this, make two lists:

- A list of concessions the witness must make that bolster your case theory or undercut the other side's or label the answer false, mistaken, or ridiculous; and
- A list of ways in which the witness is impeachable.

### Brainstorming Concessions

The brainstorming process involves finding a place away from friends, family, colleagues, and others—a place where you can think without interruption. Then, write answers to our concession-seeking question: "What must the witness concede or face having her answer labeled a lie, mistaken, or preposterous?" Concentrate on the information possessed by the witness whom you will cross-examine.

Next, think about the points you want to make in your tentative closing argument. In reality, this will be an interactive process where your list of concession points trigger how those points can be used in closing. Your ideas for closing will lead you to concession points. Now think about cross-examination. What witness information would you be able to elicit on cross that could support the argument point? You want to identify specific facts that you can use in argument. For example, in a case in which your client is suing for breach of contract, a concession you might obtain from the other side's witness is the fact that there was a signed contract.

### Brainstorming Impeachment

Brainstorm to determine how you could impeach the adverse witness. List areas of impeachment and note on the list the ones that apply to the witness. The following is a list of areas of impeachment that you can review during your brainstorming process.

---

## CHECKLIST
### Topics for Impeachment for Cross-Examination

**All Witnesses**
- ☐ 1. Improbability
- ☐ 2. Prior inconsistent statement
- ☐ 3. Prior convictions
- ☐ 4. Lack of personal knowledge
- ☐ 5. Mental and sensory deficiencies
- ☐ 6. Bias and interest
- ☐ 7. Prior bad acts probative on untruthfulness
- ☐ 8. Contradiction
- ☐ 9. Character witness—"Have you heard . . . ?"

**Expert Witness**
- ☐ 1. Qualifications
- ☐ 2. Reliability of the field

---

□ 3. Basis for opinion
□ 4. Opinion
□ 5. Learned treatises

You are brainstorming to find and write single facts that will support your argument, rather than conclusions. For example, rather than writing "the witness is biased," which is the argument you want to make at the end of the case, you would note facts that would lead the jury to that conclusion, such as, "the witness has known the opposing party for ten years," "the witness eats lunch with opposing party twice a week," "the witness was the party's bridesmaid at her wedding," and so on.

### Brainstorming the Content

Now, let's apply this methodology to the *Blue Moon News Robbery* case. Review the case on page 81.

Assume you are the prosecutor. You are planning the cross-examination of a defense alibi witness. Your theory is that Mike Ryan committed the robbery. The defense theory is reasonable doubt based upon misidentification and alibi. With the case theories in mind, you brainstorm for concessions that Delaney, the alibi witness, must make, because you can prove these assertions with witness testimony or by inferences from the evidence. If Delaney does not make the concession, then Delaney can be impeached by your proof. A thorough development of Delaney's cross is provided on pages 348-359.

#### Impeachment Areas

Now, turn to brainstorming whether there are any areas in which Delaney is vulnerable to be impeached by looking at the list of nine areas of impeachment. Bias or interest of the witness seems to apply. The task here is to brainstorm and make a list of concessions that the witness must make regarding bias. (Delaney worked with the defendant; Delaney saw defendant socially.)

#### Prior Inconsistent Statement

Another potential area of impeachment is a prior inconsistent statement. Delaney, when speaking to the detective, indicated that he was unsure whether Ryan was at the party from 10:00 P.M. to 3:00 A.M. Should Delaney testify that he is sure that the defendant was at the party that entire time, the prosecution could impeach him with his prior inconsistent statement. As a general rule, prior inconsistent statements are used to impeach a witness by showing that the witness gave conflicting statements. The prior statement when offered for impeachment purposes is not hearsay because it is not offered for the truth of the matter stated. It merely bears on the witness's credibility. However, a prior inconsistent statement can be offered to impeach the witness, and in some instances to tell the truth about the matter stated. When the evidence rules define the prior statement as nonhearsay or an exception to the hearsay rule, the prior inconsistent statement can be used to tell the truth about the matter stated. For example, a prior inconsistent statement under oath or a prior statement of a party are non-hearsay under Federal Rule of Evidence 801(d)(1). Therefore, in the *Blue Moon News* case the cross-examination can be designed to show that the earlier statement was more accurate by getting the *nonparty witness* to provide details about how the prior statement was given. It would be improper for the prosecutor to argue that the prior statement was truthful. However, if the witness were the defendant (that is, a *party*) then the prior statement would not be hearsay and could be offered into evidence as substantive evidence—a truthful statement. In the following illustration, Delaney must concede certain facts if he testifies that he was "certain" that defendant was with him all evening.

## III.  CONSTRUCTION

Now it is time to dispel an often-mistaken notion about cross-examination: Cross-examination is not the time for the witness to testify. You have brainstormed and identified the witness's fact, opinion, and impeachment concessions that you want to communicate to the jury. During cross-examination, your questions will be predominantly (some would contend always) leading in form, and you will know what the answer will be (or, very rarely, won't care what the answer will be). During this type of examination, you are not exploring for information. Rather, the witness will make statements that you are confident the witness will make. Simply put: This in effect is your opportunity to testify; you are making the affirmative substantive statements, and the witness is just confirming. Your next preparation task is to construct cross-examination so your testimony is clear and persuasive for the jury. Of course, you are not under oath and are not really testifying, but this is a mind-set that will assist you in designing an effective cross.

Construction of effective cross-examination involves a four-step process.

- Step 1: Imagine the portion of your tentative closing argument that will involve this witness's testimony.
- Step 2: Make a rough list of the points you will want to obtain from this witness (concessions, impeachment) to make your closing argument.
  (*Note:* These first two steps are interactive—ideas from your tentative closing leads you to seek certain facts from the witness; facts you realize you can obtain from the witness will lead to further concepts for your closing.)
- Step 3: Take the rough list of points you created in Step 2 (adding more points as your understanding of the case evolves) and organize your list into the format we suggest below.
- Step 4: Use the information, organized into our suggested trial format, to conduct the cross-examination of the witness.

## A. Formulating Cross-Examination Questions

### The Suggested Format

Write your cross-examination. Yes, you will hear from experienced trial lawyers that they never write their cross-examinations. We have watched experienced lawyers who did not write their cross-examinations. They should have.

Writing the cross-examination forces the lawyer to think clearly and to organize the material so that the jury will understand it. When the cross is written, the lawyer is not likely to resort to open-ended questions, or to ask questions that fail to accomplish the lawyer's goals of gaining concessions (and secondarily, if necessary, discrediting the witness or witness's testimony). Additionally, when the cross is written, possible objections that could interrupt the flow of the cross are more readily identified and can be researched so the objection can be met at trial.

A technique we've found to be effective is to write the examination using the following trial format for actual performance of the cross-examination.

### Trial Format for Cross-Examination

| ARGUMENT<br>(Witness Is Biased) | |
| --- | --- |
| FACTS | REFERENCES & NOTES |
| | |

At the top of the page, put the argument that you will make at the end of the case, such as, "Witness is biased." This heading is important because it will keep you focused on your subject during the cross-examination, curbing any tendency you might have to wander. Number each page relating to that subject. When you start a new topic, start with a new page one. On the left side, write short statements of fact. These statements of fact are the fact concessions that you have settled on after brainstorming and then organizing the resulting information.

The right column is available to write references to the file (a statement in the witness's deposition or e-mail) in case the witness does not provide the desired answer and you need to promptly access your proof. Also, the right column can be used to take notes of any of the witness's answers that you find remarkable or noteworthy for closing argument.

You will have four advantages by following this method.

First, writing short statements reinforces that you are not engaging in an exploratory examination designed to discover something. Rather, you are stating facts that the witness must concede or else be impeached.

Second, it forces you to use leading questions. You need only add words such as "isn't that correct?" to the end of the statement *or* raise your voice to make the statement into a question.

Third, the one-fact-per-question approach creates a persuasive examination on the facts because it avoids conclusion and leads the jury to come to the conclusion on their own. Having reached the conclusion on their own, it is more likely they will have a proprietary interest in it and cling to it.

Fourth, it compels ends-means thinking. The statements (questions) are designed to carry forth your case theory during closing argument and to discredit the other side's case theory.

### Applying the Four-Step Process

Let's apply our four-step process to the *Blue Moon News Robbery* case and the cross-examination of defendant's alibi witness. We'll use the four steps—imagining tentative closing, listing needed points, placing the list of needed points in our trial format, and formulating questions—to illustrate, we provide three different examples: (1) concession-seeking cross, (2) cross aimed at bias, and (3) cross-examination bringing out a prior inconsistent statement.

#### a. Concession-Seeking Cross-Examination

### Step 1: Developing Tentative Closing Argument

#### Delaney—Mistake or Lack of Perception that Defendant Was at the Party
#### The *Blue Moon News Robbery* Case

We all understand why Delaney so desperately wants to believe that his friend never left the party, because we'd feel the same way if we were in his situation. But we also understand that given the circumstances of the party, it is all but impossible for Delaney to vouch for where defendant was at every moment from 10 P.M. to 3 A.M.

Look at the diagram Delaney drew of his apartment; look at the photos on the monitor of Delaney's patio and backyard, the living room, dining area, family room area, the kitchen, and the outside deck and backyard with a walkway leading around the complex to the street. This was not a sit-down dinner for eight. Between 40 and 50 people were mingling throughout the space, talking and drinking. And Delaney wasn't just another guest; he was the host.

Delaney was busy making certain that people got drinks, that food was replenished, that he mingled around talking to everyone. He did not have defendant on a leash. And you heard him say that from one area of his apartment you can't see another area. From the kitchen, you can't see the living room or family room. From the patio, you can't see the living room or kitchen. Most important, you can walk out on the patio and walk right around the building to the street. There is simply no way that Delaney, as much as he would wish to believe otherwise, could have noticed if the defendant slipped out for a while—particularly if the defendant did not wish to be noticed.

Step 1, the envisioned closing, is the product of having the central argument idea for closing that Delaney was mistaken and could not have perceived that the defendant was at the party the entire time. With that argument in mind, the prosecutor proceeds to the second step—brainstorming the known information in the case to obtain facts supporting the argument. In this way, the envisioned tentative argument is fleshed out so it is like the one above.

## Step 2: Rough List of Points to Support Closing

### The *Blue Moon News Robbery* Case

- The party was at Delaney's apartment complex.
- At the party, people were in several rooms.
- People were milling around.
- Between 40 and 50 people attended the party.
- Delaney was the host.
- Delaney moved around and mingled.
- People were drinking.
- Delaney was drinking.
- Delaney did not keep track of when people arrived or left the party.

## Step 3: Placing Rough List and Further Obtained Information into Trial Format

### The *Blue Moon News Robbery* Case

**ARGUMENT**
**(Mistake-Perception Problem)**

| FACTS | REFERENCES & NOTES |
|---|---|
| People weren't only in one place—living room. | Diagram it |
| People milling around. | |
| 40-50 people there. | Delaney's written statement |
| You were host. | |
| You moved around and mingled. | |
| Party was at your apartment complex. | |
| People were drinking. | |
| You were drinking. | |
| You were drinking throughout the evening. | Photos |
| You did not know when each person arrived or left the party. | Photos |

*continued ▶*

> Did not check watch or write the
>    times. No reason to do that.
> When in one room can't see into
>    other rooms.
> Can walk out back and around
>    front to street.

Look at the prosecutor's organization of information using our trial format. It is designed to elicit the facts that the witness must concede (or be impeached), supporting the prosecution's position that the witness could not have perceived that the defendant was at the party for the entire time. With this format, the cross-examination questions will be formulated as in the next illustration. We have decided to place the questions in a full transcript so that you will get a feel for the rhythm and be able to see how this four-step process results in construction of actual cross-examination questions. Because the prosecutor is working from the concept that it is the prosecutor's time, in effect, to testify (not to explore to find out what happened or to repeat direct examination), observe that in the cross-examination transcript the witness almost always answers the leading question as the cross-examiner wishes.

## Step 4: Formulating Cross-Examination Questions

### Prosecutor's Cross-Examination of Alibi Witness (Delaney) Regarding Lack of Perception of Defendant's Whereabouts The *Blue Moon News Robbery* Case

*Q:* Now, this party went on from 10 P.M. to 3 A.M.?

*A:* Uh-huh.

*Q:* And once it got going, there were 40 to 50 people there?

*A:* I guess.

*Q:* This was at your apartment on 116 Bay Street?

*A:* Yes.

*Q:* Your Honor, may Mr. Delaney step down to the easel?

**Judge:**

You may step down, Mr. Delaney.

*Q:* The blank page has been marked State's Exhibit 6 for identification. I'm handing you a magic marker. Mr. Delaney, could you please give us a rough diagram of your apartment?

*A:* I can't really draw very well.

*Q:* No problem. Nothing artistic or to scale. Just give us a rough sketch.

*A:* Okay. [Proceeds to draw.]

*Q:* Could you label each room?

*A:* Sure.

*Q:* Okay, take us through your apartment.

*A:* Well, here's a small entry hall. To the left is the living room . . . . [Witness goes on to explain all the rooms in his apartment.]

*Q:* Thank you. Please return to your seat on the witness stand. Now, your apartment is on the first floor?

*A:* Yes.

*Q:* So, in addition to the rooms you've shown us on the diagram, you've got a patio off the family room?

*A:* Yes.

*Q:* And from there you can step right into the backyard of the apartment complex?

*A:* Yes.

*Q:* May I approach the witness, Your Honor?

**Judge:**

You may approach.

*Q:* Mr. Delaney, I'm showing you what has been marked as State's Exhibit 7 for identification. That's a photo of your patio and the backyard?

*A:* Yes.

*Q:* That fairly and accurately represents what the patio and backyard look like?

*A:* Sure.

*Q:* There's this walkway here across the backyard? [Showing photo.]

*A:* Uh-huh.

*Q:* That goes all the way around the complex to the street?

*A:* Yes.

*Q:* So, if you wanted to, you could walk out the family room onto the patio and then go on that walkway around the building to the street in front of the apartment complex?

*A:* I guess.

*Q:* At this point, I offer State's Exhibits 6 and 7 into evidence for demonstrative purposes.

**Judge:**

Any objection?

**Opposing counsel:**

No.

**Judge:**

So admitted.

*Q:* Thank you, Your Honor. Now, Mr. Delaney, this was not a sit-down dinner, was it?

*A:* No.

*Q:* Those 40 to 50 people were going all through your apartment?

*A:* Not my bedroom.

*Q:* But the living room?

*A:* Yes.

*continued* ▶

*Q:* They went in the kitchen?

*A:* Some.

*Q:* The family room?

*A:* Yeah.

*Q:* Dining room?

*A:* Yes.

*Q:* Out on the patio?

*A:* Uh-huh.

*Q:* You're a good host?

*A:* I try.

*Q:* So, as they say, you mingled among your guests?

*A:* Yes.

*Q:* Made people feel welcome?

*A:* I guess.

*Q:* Introduced people?

*A:* Most of these people knew each other.

*Q:* You were talking to people?

*A:* Yes.

*Q:* Making sure they had drinks?

*A:* Yes.

*Q:* And food?

*A:* Sure.

*Q:* You had a few drinks yourself?

*A:* Sure.

*Q:* You were in different rooms over the course of the evening?

*A:* Yes.

*Q:* And when you're in the kitchen, you can't see the family room?

*A:* No.

*Q:* Or the living room?

*A:* No.

*Q:* And from the living room, you can't see the family room?

*A:* No.

*Q:* Or the dining room?

*A:* No.

*Q:* Now let's talk about other people who attended your party. Name a couple other people who were in attendance.

*A:* *X* and *Y*.

*Q:* When did *X* arrive?

*A:* Early in the party. Maybe around 10:30 P.M.

*Q:* What did you talk to *X* about?

*A:* The Super Bowl, I think.

*Q:* When did *Y* arrive?

*A:* I'm not sure.

*Q:* What did *Y* have to drink?

*A:* He likes Scotch.

*Q:* You testified that the defendant was at your party from 10 P.M. on January 15 until 3 A.M. the following morning, correct?

*A:* Yes.

*Q:* You didn't check your watch when he arrived, did you?

*A:* No.

*Q:* You didn't write down the time he arrived, correct?

*A:* No.

*Q:* The defendant wasn't the first to arrive, was he?

*A:* No.

*Q:* You had no reason to note the time of his arrival?

*A:* No.

*Q:* You didn't keep track of when the 40 to 50 people arrived, did you?

*A:* No.

*Q:* You had no reason to?

*A:* No.

*Q:* The first time you were asked to remember when you saw the defendant at your party was when the defendant called you, correct?

*A:* I guess.

*Q:* He called you two months after your party?

*A:* Yes.

*Q:* Couldn't the defendant have come to your party, left, and come back again without you noticing?

*A:* Maybe. But he didn't.

*Q:* With all the people there and the drinking, you're not sure when you saw the defendant at your party, are you?

*A:* Not every second. But I know he was there the entire time.

If Delaney had conceded that he was unsure of when he saw the defendant at the party, this is where you would stop your cross-examination, state, "No further questions," and then take your seat at counsel table. The defendant has just lost an alibi witness. As it is, you have still obtained information that, in the context of the jury's experience and common sense, makes Delaney's insistence that he is certain that defendant never left the party seem implausible.

### b. Cross-Examination Revealing Bias

**Step 1: Developing Tentative Closing Argument**

**Witness Bias**
**The *Blue Moon News Robbery* Case**

Some people work in the same place and barely even pass each other. So it wouldn't mean all that much to say they worked together. But that wasn't the case with the defendant and his alibi witness, Delaney.

For over two years, they worked together with only four other people in the showroom of Tire Universe. They ate lunch together and talked about their lives almost every day. And they saw each other socially outside of work. So when Delaney threw

*continued* ▶

> a party on January 15, it's no surprise he invited the defendant; the defendant was his friend. And it is no surprise that when defendant arrived at the party, Delaney was happy to see him and to talk with him for a while. So it's no surprise that last week, when he testified sitting in that seat on the witness stand [counsel points to the witness chair], Delaney would want to help a friend.
>
> Here was a friend who was in so much trouble, and who Delaney, naturally, did not want to believe was capable of doing anything as terrible as sticking a gun in another human's face. This is not a criticism of Delaney. Surely, if defendant were our close friend, we'd want to believe that he was at that party every moment from start to finish.

The tentative closing illustrated above is composed of the facts that were identified by brainstorming the evidence in the case (gained through discovery and investigation). Delaney had to admit these facts that support the argument or be impeached.

## Step 2: Rough List of Points to Support Closing

### Impeachment for Bias
### The *Blue Moon News Robbery* Case

- They both worked at Tire Universe.
- Until December 15 of last year, defendant Mike Ryan also worked there.
- Delaney and the defendant worked there for two years together.
- Tire Universe is a small business.
- There are few employees.
- Delaney worked in the same room as the defendant.
- For two years they saw each other almost every day at work.
- They ate lunch together.
- They talked daily.
- The two socialized when they worked at Tire Universe.
- On January 15, the witness threw a party.
- The defendant attended the party.
- The witness and defendant spoke at the party.
- The witness was happy the defendant attended the party.
- The witness invited the defendant to the party.
- The witness considered the defendant a friend.
- The witness wants to help the defendant.

## Step 3: Placing Rough List and Subsequently Obtained Information into Trial Format

The *Blue Moon News Robbery* Case

**ARGUMENT**
(Bias)

| FACTS | REFERENCES & NOTES |
|---|---|
| You work at Tire Universe. | |
| Until 12/15 of last year the defendant, Mike Ryan, also worked there. | |
| You and the defendant worked there for two years together. | |
| Small business. | |
| Few employees. | Delaney's written statement, p. 3, l.4 |
| You worked in same room as the defendant. | |
| For two years you saw each other almost every day at work. | |
| Ate lunch together. | Delaney's written statement, p. 3, l.7 |
| Talked daily. | |
| You socialized with the defendant when both worked at Tire Universe. | |
| January 15, you threw a party. | |
| Defendant was there. | |
| You and he spoke. | |
| Happy he was at the party. | |
| You invited him. | |
| Considered him a friend. | |
| Want to help him here. | |

The next illustration shows Step 4, the formulation of cross-examination questions. The difference between the attorney's notes and the transcript are that the notes are statements (a reminder to the lawyer that cross is not the time to explore for information but rather the time to gather information that the witness must provide). However, in the transcript, the statements are now questions. This is accomplished by simply adding words such as *"isn't that true"* or *"isn't that correct,"* or just raising your voice at the end of the sentence, which converts a statement into a question.

> ## Step 4: Formulating Cross-Examination Questions
>
> ### Cross-Examination of Alibi Witness (Delaney)
> ### Regarding Bias and Motive
> ### The *Blue Moon News Robbery* Case
>
> *Q:* Mr. Delaney, you work at Tire Universe?
> *A:* Yes.
> *Q:* You work in the showroom?
> *A:* Yes.
> *Q:* The defendant also worked in the showroom?
> *A:* For a while.
> *Q:* In fact, you and Ryan worked together in that showroom for two years, until he left on December 15?
> *A:* I'm not sure about the date he left.
> *Q:* But you did work together for two years?
> *A:* Yes.
> *Q:* Besides you and the defendant, there were only four other employees who also worked on the floor?
> *A:* Yes.
> *Q:* So, for two years, you and the defendant saw each other almost every weekday?
> *A:* Pretty much.
> *Q:* You ate your lunch together most days?
> *A:* I guess.
> *Q:* You talked together?
> *A:* Well, sure . . . we were working together; you have to talk.
> *Q:* But you also talked about personal things?
> *A:* Yeah.
> *Q:* You talked about what was going on in your lives?
> *A:* Sometimes.
> *Q:* You went out with defendant after work sometimes?
> *A:* Yes.
> *Q:* You socialized together on some weekends?
> *A:* Sometimes.
> *Q:* You became friends?
> *A:* Yes.
> *Q:* So when you threw a party on January 15, you invited your friend, the defendant?
> *A:* Sure.
> *Q:* And he came?
> *A:* Yes.
> *Q:* You were happy he was there?
> *A:* I guess.
> *Q:* You took time to talk to him?
> *A:* Yeah.

While Delaney is vulnerable to being impeached by showing that he is the defendant's friend and therefore biased in favor of the defendant, all is not so simple. This is an interesting area because it illustrates the need to remain focused on your case theory. Your cross should always be consistent with that theory. Just because bias is on the list of impeachment areas does not mean that it should routinely be explored on cross, even if the facts support an argument that the witness is biased. Perhaps the witness is not biased, and, even more important, a contention that bias exists may be inconsistent with the case theory. Here, the prosecutor's theory is that the defendant and the witness were not together throughout the time of the party. But if the witness were a close friend of the defendant, it is more likely that they would have spent significant time together at the party than if they were just work acquaintances, and therefore more likely Delaney would be aware of his whereabouts.

### c. Impeachment with Prior Inconsistent Statement

## Step 1: Developing Tentative Closing Argument

### Inconsistent Statement
### The *Blue Moon News Robbery* Case

Delaney is *positive* today that the defendant never, ever left his party. But when he talked to Detective Malcomb on April 15, in the familiar surroundings of his own apartment, he was anything but positive. Delaney told you on the stand that he wanted to be as accurate as possible with what he told the detective and certainly would never have lied to the detective. So, that night, when Delaney wanted to be as honest and accurate as could be, he did not tell the detective he was "positive" the defendant had been with him all evening; he did not say he was "certain." When indicating that the defendant had been at the party all evening, Delaney qualified his statement—"At least I *think* so." In that single phrase, he really said: "I think he was there, but I could be wrong."

## Step 2: Rough List of Points for Closing

### Impeachment with a Prior Inconsistent Statement
### The *Blue Moon News Robbery* Case

Delaney, a friend of the defendant, is one of the defense's alibi witnesses. Assume he is the witness testifying. He must concede certain facts concerning his statement to the detective.

- The detective came to Delaney's house.
- Delaney spoke to the detective on April 15.
- Delaney was aware that the detective was seeking the truth from witnesses during the investigation.
- Delaney knew it was important to tell the truth to the detective.
- The detective asked Delaney about the January 15 party.
- Delaney said to the detective, "Mike was at my party from 10 P.M. until the end at 3 A.M., at least I think so."

## Step 3: Placing Rough List and Subsequently Obtained Information into Trial Format

The *Blue Moon News Robbery* Case

**ARGUMENT**
**(Inconsistent Statement—Unsure)**

| FACTS | REFERENCES & NOTES |
|---|---|
| Delaney—Prior Inconsistent Statement—Unsure about defendant's presence. | Delaney witness statement |
| Ever make a statement to anyone indicating that you were not sure about the time? | |
| Sure about that, too. | |
| You spoke to detective on April 15. | |
| Defendant was at your home. | |
| It was 7 in the evening. | |
| He asked you about the January 15 party. | |
| You said to the detective, "Mike was at my party from 10 p.m. until the end at 3 a.m., at least I think so." | |

The prosecutor's notes now form the basis for the cross-examination questions of Delaney in the following transcript of the cross on the prior inconsistent statement.

## Step 4: Formulating Cross-Examination Questions

Prosecutor's Cross-Examination of Alibi Witness (Delaney)
with Prior Inconsistent Oral Statement
The *Blue Moon News Robbery* Case

*Q:* So, you're telling the jury that you have no doubt the defendant was at your party for every moment from 10 P.M. to 3 A.M.?

*A:* None. He was there!

*Q:* [*Prosecutor focuses witness on prior conversation with detective.*] On April 15, you had a conversation with Detective Malcomb?

*A:* April 15? I'm not sure about that date.

*Q:* But you did talk to the detective around mid-April?

*A:* Yeah.

*Q:* He came over to your apartment?

*A:* Yes.

*Q:* Around 7 P.M., after dinner?

*A:* I guess.

*Q:* The detective wanted to talk about the defendant and defendant's alibi that he was at your party?

*A:* Yes.

*Q:* [*Now prosecutor does buildup, bringing out commonsense reasons why Delaney's statements to the detective would be accurate.*] When you talked to the detective, you knew this was a serious matter?

*A:* Yes.

*Q:* A serious crime was charged, armed robbery?

*A:* Yes.

*Q:* So, you were not going to lie to a member of law enforcement, were you?

*A:* Of course not.

*Q:* You were going to try to be as accurate as possible?

*A:* Of course.

*Q:* The detective asked you the time during which the defendant had been at your party?

*A:* Uh-huh.

*Q:* You told him, "Mike was at my party from 10 P.M. until the end at 3 A.M."?

*A:* Yeah, that's what I've been telling you.

*Q:* [*Now the prosecutor begins the impeachment.*] But you didn't follow that with saying something like, "I'm certain," did you?

*A:* No need. That was clear.

*Q:* Really? Didn't you then say to the detective on April 15 [*prosecutor slowly says the following*], "At least I think so"?

*A:* [If Delaney answers yes, undoubtedly accompanied by some explanation, the impeachment is complete. If he denies making the statement, the prosecutor will have to recall the detective on the rebuttal to get out Delaney's statement and thereby complete the impeachment.]

Note that with the concessions obtained from cross-examination during closing argument, the prosecutor can refer to the fact that Delaney was unsure about how long the defendant had been at the party: "At least I think so." Delaney is not certain.

## B. Types of Questions, Sequencing, and Transitioning

The form of the question, order of questions, and transitions between lines of questions are always designed to accomplish the same goals—to make the cross-examination understandable and persuasive. The following are some techniques.

## Four Types of Questions

### 1. Leading

Leading questions are authorized for cross-examination by Federal Rule of Evidence 611(c). Most of your cross-examination questions should be leading. For an example of using leading questions, see pages 350-353.

### 2. Anticipatory

The anticipatory question when asked on cross-examination is often designed to elicit an answer opposite to the seemingly sought-after answer. The desired effect of the anticipatory question is to highlight the answer. A classic example that could be asked in the *Blue Moon News Robbery* case would be the prosecutor's question directed at the alibi witness: *"So, Mr. Delaney, when you learned that your friend Mike Ryan had been arrested for robbery and you knew he was at your party when the robbery was committed, you immediately went to the police and told them he was with you at the time?"* This behavior would be human nature—a tendency to save a friend. But when the alibi witness answers no to this question, as the prosecutor knows he will, the anticipatory form of the question highlights the answer and discredits the witness's current claim that he is certain the defendant was at the party at the time of the robbery.

### 3. Accusatory

This form is a subtype of the leading question, and it accuses the witness of something. For instance, the prosecutor could ask witness Delaney, *"The fact of the matter is you have no idea where the defendant was during most of the time of the party, isn't that right?"*

### 4. Interrogatory

By *interrogatory* we refer to nonleading, open-ended questions. The interrogatory type of question required for direct examination generally should be avoided during cross-examination. Because of its open-ended nature, an interrogatory question such as, *"Why would you do such a thing?"* allows the witness to expound and, more likely than not, damage your case.

## Sequencing

### Concessions First

As a general principle, cross-examination should begin with questions designed to obtain concessions. You can begin in a pleasant, nonconfrontational manner that is likely to elicit the "yes" answers. This approach is sometimes referred to as the "pet the dog" technique. In the *Blue Moon News Robbery* case, the defense attorney might begin to attack the identification of the defendant with questions such as, *"That must have been really scary when you saw the gun? You must have been thinking that this person might panic or be crazy and shoot you?"* Pet the dog first and a tail wags, but abuse the dog and you risk getting bitten. If you appear amiable when you begin to cross-examine the witness, it is more likely that you will get the responses you want. If you are able to get the concessions you want—to turn the witness to your advantage—you can forgo impeaching the witness.

### Topical or Chronological

Cross-examination can be organized in at least three ways: chronological, topical, or both. In the *Blue Moon News Robbery* case, an example of a combined chronological and topical cross would be to focus questions on the relationship (bias argument) between the alibi witness and the defendant and then trace their relationship forward from when they first met.

### Finish on a High Note

Last impressions are lasting impressions. Cross-examination should finish strong. Select a strong point that is not objectionable to finish your cross. If you happen to hit on a better line of cross-examination that proves productive, you can decide to end earlier than you otherwise planned.

### Organizational Tools

The format that we recommend to you—in which each subject area is numbered sequentially—allows you to move the sections around as you plan your cross-examination (pages 359-360). You can tab the sections and move them around in a notebook until you are satisfied with the order.

### Transitions

As you move from topic to topic or event to event, use transitional language. These statements of transition are like signposts that show where you are going next so the jury can follow. For example, in cross-examining Delaney, the prosecutor could say, *"Now, Mr. Delaney, let's discuss your relationship with the defendant."* This same technique is discussed in Chapter 9 on direct examination, page 298.

---

Watch the cross-examination of the defendant in the *Freck Point* trial demonstration movie to observe formulating questions, sequence, and transition on the website *http://www.aspenlawschool.com/books/berger_trialad4e.*

---

## IV.  BEHAVIOR OF COUNSEL

The behavior of the cross-examiner is important, though the literature and seminars on cross-examination hardly dwell on it. Jurors are inclined to protect witnesses, and they do not want to see lawyers attack or in any way abuse them. Therefore, the general rule is that you should be courteous and professional toward the witness and avoid clashing with the witness. In Chapter 2, in discussing the significance of an advocate's professional manner, we explain the importance of sincerity (see pages 7-12). This principle also holds true during cross-examination. The cross-examiner's demeanor should be that of the sincere seeker of truth who is fair to all, even the other side's witnesses.

In the *Art of Cross-Examination*, Francis Wellman describes the manner of the cross-examiner, and that description holds true today (although we would now use gender-neutral language, which few writers in 1903 thought to do):

> It is the love of combat which every man possesses that fastens the attention of the jury upon the progress of the trial. The counsel who has a pleasant personality; who speaks with apparent frankness; who appears to be an earnest searcher after truth; who is courteous to those who testify against him; who avoids delaying constantly the progress of the trial by innumerable objections and exceptions to perhaps incompetent but harmless evidence; who seems to know what he is about and sits down when he has accomplished it, exhibiting a spirit of fair play on all occasions—he it is who creates an atmosphere in favor of the side which he represents, a powerful though unconscious influence with the jury in arriving at their verdict. Even if, owing to the weight of testimony, the verdict is against him, yet the amount will be far less than the client has schooled himself to expect.
>
> On the other hand, the lawyer who wearies the court and the jury with endless and pointless cross-examination; who is constantly losing his temper and showing his teeth to the witnesses; who wears a sour, anxious expression; who possesses a monotonous, rasping, penetrating voice; who presents a slovenly, unkempt personal appearance; who is prone to take unfair advantage of witness or counsel, and seems determined to win at all hazards—soon prejudices a jury against himself and the client he represents, entirely irrespective of the sworn testimony in the case.

Francis L. Wellman, *The Art of Cross-Examination* 28 (new ed., Book Jungle 2007) (originally published 1903).

However, there is an exception to that part of the general rule that holds that the cross-examiner should avoid sparring with the witness. A clash is appropriate when the witness deserves it, but you should only go after the witness when you are confident that the jurors believe that the witness deserves a comeuppance. Never get ahead of the jurors and take on the witness before they are ready for you to do so. And when you do, maintain your professional and sincere demeanor. Examples of situations where you might challenge the witness include those where the witness is clearly lying, refusing to answer the question, or injecting information into the answer that the examiner did not ask for. In the next section, we offer techniques for addressing some of these problems that arise with witnesses being intentionally difficult.

## V.  CONTROLLING A WITNESS

Professor Irving Younger, now deceased, was and still is nationally recognized for his Ten Commandments of Cross-Examination. He taught a generation of lawyers to adhere to them when conducting cross-examinations. Irving Younger,

*Ten Commandments of Cross-Examination,* summarized from *The Art of Cross-Examination* (ABA 1976) (from a speech given by Irving Younger at the ABA Annual Meeting in Montreal, August 1975). These lectures have been issued on DVD by the ABA.

These Ten Commandments are still taught to lawyers.

---

### Irving Younger's Ten Commandments of Cross-Examination

1. Be brief.
2. Short questions, plain words.
3. Always ask leading questions.
4. Don't ask a question, the answer to which you do not know in advance.
5. Listen to the witness'[s] answers.
6. Don't quarrel with the witness.
7. Don't allow the witness to repeat direct testimony.
8. Don't permit the witness to explain answers.
9. Don't ask the "one question too many."
10. Save the ultimate point of your cross for summation.

---

An attorney who strictly follows these Ten Commandments during a cross-examination will maintain control of even a witness who is intent on evading or deflecting the questions. This is not to say that we agree that you should follow these literally as commandments, because exceptions exist. When the witness is lying and the examiner can prove the lie, the interrogatory (nonleading) question gives the prevaricator plenty of latitude to spin the deception, which the examiner can later reveal as a falsehood. Or the examiner may be willing to ask a question whose answer she does not know because she does not care what answer the witness gives, particularly when common sense dictates the answer (*"Doctor, when doing open-heart surgery, the operating room should be sterile?" "Officer, you try to be accurate in writing your reports?"*). We do recommend that you use Professor Younger's commandments as useful guidelines to follow unless you have a good reason not to.

Some witnesses will not respond as you expect. Inevitably, you will encounter the rambling, evasive witness who will backhand your question with a quick answer and then launch into a monologue that serves the opposing party's case theory. How do you control the evasive witness? Besides adhering to Younger's commandments, we offer some techniques that we have found effective. Some of these are confrontational, and, thus, they may offend jurors if not done properly. The following techniques are listed in increasing confrontational tone to meet escalating levels of evasiveness by the witness. You, as plaintiff's attorney, are cross-examining Mr. Dale Dirks, the defense expert on damages, whom you know from reading trial transcripts can be an evasive witness.

> ## Cross-Examination
>
> ### Control Techniques for the Evasive, Rambling Witness
> ### The *Hill Moveit Personal Injury* Case
>
> **Technique #1**
>
> **Securing an Agreement:** Mr. Dirks, I'm going to try to make my questions simple. Most all of them will be able to be answered yes or no. When I'm through, Ms. Rutherford's lawyer will be able to ask you questions so that you can elaborate or explain your answers to my questions. Can we agree that you will answer my questions with a yes or no if that is what the question calls for?
>
> **Technique #2**
>
> **Repeat the Question:**
>
> *Q:* Mr. Dirks, did you speak with Dr. Donhow before you reached your opinion in this case?
> *A:* Ramble, ramble, ramble . . . .
> *Q:* Did you speak with Dr. Donhow before you reached your opinion in this case? [Note: If the witness continues to ramble and evade your question now, it should be clear to the jury.]
> *Q:* Can you repeat the question that I asked you, Mr. Dirks? [Note: This and the following questions are increasingly confrontational.]
> *Q:* Are you ready to answer the question now?
> *Q:* Mr. Dirks, is there something preventing you from answering the question?

If the witness not only evades and rambles, but also sneaks in harmful information, you can "move to strike as nonresponsive." Ask the court to instruct the jury to disregard what the witness has said. At some point, after you've used all your techniques and the witness continues evading, you probably will have created a sufficient atmosphere to request the court to intercede and order the witness to respond directly to your questions. A final technique that you can use to control the runaway witness is to resort to the physical. Raise your hand, palm facing the witness, in the universally recognized signal to stop. It usually works.

## VI.  EVIDENCE RULES

In this section, we discuss both the evidence rules applicable to cross-examination generally and to the nine principal areas of impeachment and accompanying trial techniques for discrediting a witness or the witness's testimony. See pages 344-345 for an impeachment checklist that lists nine areas of impeachment for all witnesses. (In the next chapter, on experts, we will discuss evidence law and techniques for cross-examination for impeachment of experts.)

## A. Scope of Cross and Leading Questions

Federal Rule of Evidence 611(b) governs the scope of cross-examination, saying that it "should not go beyond the subject matter of the direct examination and matters affecting the witness's credibility." Under the rule, the judge has the discretion to allow questioning into other matters as if on direct. Leading questions are permitted on cross-examination under Federal Rule of Evidence 611(c).

## B. Improbability, Bias, Motive, Perception, or Ability to Relate

This cross-examination can be designed to reveal the improbability of the witness's testimony. An example of this type of cross-examination was used in the *Pizza Connection* case where the examiner revealed the improbability of the alibi witness's story that he was servicing tax clients when his diary entries revealed the titles of operas scheduled at the same times he claimed to be with tax clients (see pages 342-343). Cross-examination also is commonly designed to reveal bias, motive, difficulties with perceptions, and/or problems with ability to relate (witness calls a fleece jacket "denim," because he thinks that's what the fabric is called). The evidentiary rules that come into play include Federal Rules of Evidence 401 and 611(b). Rule 401 defines relevant evidence as that which has the tendency to make the existence of any fact that is of consequence in determining the action more or less probable. Rule 611(b) states that the scope of cross-examination includes matters within the scope of direct, matters affecting credibility, and, within the court's discretion, additional matters.

### Extrinsic Evidence

The Federal Rules of Evidence have no required foundation before the cross-examiner may offer extrinsic evidence of bias. However, some appellate courts have required that the witness be given an opportunity to admit or deny the facts or statements showing bias before extrinsic evidence (evidence not from the witness's mouth; generally from another witness) will be admitted. See *United States v. Weiss,* 930 F.2d 185, 197-198 (2d Cir. 1991). If the witness admits the bias, then the court, under Federal Rule of Evidence 403, may preclude the introduction of extrinsic evidence as being cumulative.

## C. Prior Inconsistent Statements

### Importance of the Method

Cross-examination with a prior inconsistent statement can severely damage a witness's credibility. An example of impeachment with a prior inconsistent statement is the impeachment of the alibi witness in the *Blue Moon News Robbery* case at pages 357-359. But only use this form of impeachment if the inconsistency is significant. Impeaching with prior inconsistent statements can take some time, even if the witness admits the impeachment. The jury naturally expects that if you are spending time on the buildup, something important will come at the end. If an eyewitness testifies that "it was dark," impeaching with a prior statement in which the witness said "it was very dark" will leave the jurors shaking their heads at you.

### Rules of Admissibility

Under Federal Rule of Evidence 613, a witness may be examined about prior inconsistent statements, either oral or written, to impeach the credibility of that witness if the following conditions are met.

#### Inconsistency

The prior statement must be inconsistent with the witness's trial testimony. For this reason, before attempting impeachment with a prior inconsistent statement, it is vital to lock down the witness's current testimony. Literal inconsistency between the current testimony and the prior statement is not required. For instance, *McCormick on Evidence* cites this test: "[C]ould the jury reasonably find that a witness who believed the truth of the facts testified to would have been unlikely to make a prior statement of this tenor?" Charles T. McCormick, *McCormick on Evidence* 63 (Kenneth S. Brown & George E. Dix eds., West 2006).

#### Confrontation with Prior Statement

At common law, the cross-examiner was required to confront the witness with the prior statement by asking about the circumstances of the making of the prior statement, such as the time, place, and person to whom the statement was made. If the prior statement was written, the cross-examiner was required to show the writing to the witness. *Queen Caroline's Case,* 2 Br. & B. 284, 313, 129 Eng. Rep. 976 (1820).

Under Federal Rule of Evidence 613(a), the cross-examiner need not lay a foundation by confronting the witness with the prior statement. Even though confrontation is not required, it is a good technique because it shows the fairness of the cross-examiner. On request, the statement shall be revealed or shown to opposing counsel.

#### Extrinsic Evidence

*Witness Admits:* If the witness admits to having made the prior statement, it can be argued that impeachment has been completed and extrinsic evidence should be inadmissible. Federal Rule of Evidence 403 provides the court with discretion to exclude cumulative evidence or evidence that would cause undue delay or waste of time, and most jurisdictions hold that extrinsic evidence of an inconsistent statement already admitted by the witness is inadmissible.

*Witness Denies:* If the witness denies making the prior statement, extrinsic evidence is admissible to prove the prior inconsistent statement unless that statement concerns a collateral matter (something too unimportant to merit the time required to put on the impeaching evidence), *United States v. Roulette,* 75 F.3d 418, 423 (8th Cir.), *cert. denied,* 519 U.S. 853 (1996). If it involves a collateral matter, then the cross-examiner is stuck with the witness's denial. But what constitutes a denial? If the witness claims not to be able to recall the prior statement or equivocates about it, the court also may admit the extrinsic evidence. *United States v. Dennis,* 625 F.2d 782 (8th Cir. 1980).

The extrinsic evidence proving the prior statement can be either the prior written statement itself if it is authenticated, a witness who can authenticate the statement, or, in the case of an oral statement, a witness who heard the statement.

### Rule 613(b) Fairness Requirements

Federal Rule of Evidence 613(b) requires only that for extrinsic evidence to be admissible, the following two events must occur.

- At some time, the witness must be given an opportunity to deny or explain the statement. Rule 613(b) is satisfied if the witness can be recalled. The witness need not be confronted with the statement at the time of the examination.
- Opposing counsel must have an opportunity to question the witness.

The idea behind this aspect of Rule 613(b) is that several witnesses who are colluding could be cross-examined before they are confronted with the prior statement. Rule 613(b) does not apply to party opponent admissions qualifying under Federal Rule of Evidence 801(d)(2).

## D. Prior Convictions

### Rules of Admissibility

Prior convictions are admissible under Federal Rule of Evidence 609 to attack the credibility of a witness if the following conditions are met:

- Type of crime and balancing,
- Time limit,
- Not a juvenile conviction, and
- Issues around the appeal.

### Type of Crime and Balancing

*Felony and Witness Other Than the Accused:* Evidence of a felony (a crime punishable by death or imprisonment over one year) may be admitted subject to Federal Rule of Evidence 403 (probative value of the conviction is substantially outweighed by unfair prejudice). Fed. R. Evid. 609(a)(1).

*Felony and the Accused Is the Witness:* Evidence of a felony (a crime punishable by death or imprisonment over one year) may be admitted conditional on the court determining that the "probative value of admitting this evidence outweighs its prejudicial effect to the accused." Fed. R. Evid. 609(a)(1).

It is important to note that while the court engages in a balancing test for both the witness and the criminal defendant, the burden is different. For a witness, including parties in a civil case, the usual Rule 403 burden of showing unfair prejudice substantially outweighing probative value applies. When the witness is not the defendant, the danger of unfair prejudice is slight since the usual Rule 609 concern that the jury may find the defendant guilty of the current offense because of prior crimes does not exist.

However, for impeachment of the defendant, the cross-examiner has the burden of showing that probative value exceeds prejudicial effect. The jurisdiction's case law should be researched to determine what factors the court is to consider in performing this balancing test to determine admissibility. Some pertinent factors that courts have considered include impeachment value of the prior crime, remoteness of the prior conviction, similarity between the prior crime and the current charge, the age and circumstances of defendant, and the centrality of the credibility issue.

*Crimes of Dishonesty or False Statement and Any Witness:* Any witness, including the accused, may be attacked by evidence of a prior conviction of a felony or misdemeanor crime of dishonesty or false statement. Fed. R. Evid. 609(a)(2). Here the court does not engage in a balancing of factors, nor does the court have any discretion. If the crime is found to be one of "a dishonest act or false statement," the conviction "must" be admitted if the witness testifies. While crimes of violence generally do not qualify, crimes such as embezzlement, perjury, and so on do meet the definition. Again, the jurisdiction's law should be researched to determine whether the prior crime qualifies under this rule.

### Time Limit: Less Than Ten Years

For the conviction to be admissible, less than ten years must have elapsed since the conviction or release from confinement, whichever is later. Note that this rule trumps both Rule 609(a)(1) and Rule 609(a)(2). However, a conviction over ten years old is admissible if (1) the judge finds, in the interests of justice, that the probative value supported by specific facts substantially outweigh the prejudicial effect; and (2) the adverse party gives advance notice of intent to use the conviction. Fed. R. Evid. 609(b).

### Not a Juvenile Conviction

The prior conviction is inadmissible if it is a juvenile adjudication. However, in the interest of justice the court may admit juvenile convictions to impeach a witness, other than the defendant, if the conviction would be admissible if the witness were an adult and if the court decides that the prior conviction is "necessary to fairly determine guilt or innocence." Fed. R. Evid. 609(d)(4).

### Appeal

The fact that the case is on appeal does not render the prior conviction inadmissible, but the evidence of the pendency of the appeal is also admissible. Fed. R. Evid. 609(e).

### Proving the Prior Conviction

Cross-examination of a witness regarding a prior conviction normally must be confined to questioning about the facts contained in the record of the prior conviction: the fact of conviction, the type of crime, and the punishment imposed. Examination beyond these matters, such as asking about the facts of the crime of conviction, is prejudicial and inadmissible. *State v. Coe,* 684 P.2d 668 (Wash. 1984). If the witness admits the prior conviction, the cross-examiner may be precluded from offering a prior conviction document because it is cumulative evidence. Fed. R. Evid. 403.

Alternatively, the cross-examiner may offer the prior conviction document as a self-authenticated document (certified copy) of the prior conviction document under Federal Rule of Evidence 902(4).

## E. Prior Bad Acts Probative of Untruthfulness

### Rules of Admissibility

Under Federal Rule of Evidence 608(b), cross-examination may cover specific acts of conduct if they are probative to show untruthfulness. The specific acts of misconduct that the court may permit under Rule 608(b) are those of fraud or deceit or otherwise indicating a lack of honesty. Counsel may not ask whether the witness was arrested or convicted of the act. The cross-examiner must have a good-faith basis for the question (*United States v. Zaccaria,* 240 F.3d 75, 81-82 (1st Cir. 2001) and *Chavies v. Commonwealth,* 374 S.W.3d 313, 322 (Ky. 2012)), and may only ask the question if the court permits it in its discretion.

### Examples of Prior Bad Acts

Some examples of prior bad acts include:

- Cross-examination into defendant's lying responses on income tax return and financial disclosure statements was held proper. *United States v. Sullivan,* 803 F.2d 87 (3d Cir. 1986).
- Previous use of a false name. *United States v. Ojeda,* 23 F.3d 1473, 1476-1477 (8th Cir. 1994).

### No Extrinsic Evidence

If the witness denies the prior bad act, the cross-examiner is stuck with the answer and may not introduce extrinsic evidence.

## VII. CONDUCTING CROSS-EXAMINATION

In this section, we touch on a few additional trial techniques for conducting a winning cross-examination.

## A.  No Questions

Throughout direct examination, the cross-examiner is assessing the impact of the witness and witness's testimony on the case. Usually, counsel will decide to conduct a cross. However, sometimes when a witness has neither hurt the cross-examiner's case nor contributed much to the other side's, counsel can rise and, with a not-too-obvious "this witness offered nothing" expression, say, *"No questions, Your Honor,"* and sit down. Jurors like this, and judges like it even more. Generally, though, even these witnesses have some useful concession that can be obtained in a question or two.

## B.  Staging

*Opposing counsel: "Your witness."*
Now what do you do? Do you stand? Sit? Stand behind a podium? Move around? In federal and some state courts, convention dictates that you question the witness from behind a podium. In some state courts, you sit at counsel table. Custom may require that you seek the court's permission before approaching the witness, for example, by saying, *"May I approach the witness, Your Honor?"*

If the cross-examiner has the freedom to move around the courtroom, that movement can enhance the cross-examination. On direct examination, trial counsel can focus the spotlight on the witness, who is the person delivering the message (case theory) by moving behind the jury box so that the jurors naturally look at the witness, not counsel. However, on cross, the cross-examiner wants much of the attention focused on the cross-examiner. Recall that cross-examination is trial counsel's opportunity to testify.

So that the cross-examiner can garner the jurors' attention, the best position is right in front of the jurors and up toward the witness. From that position, the jurors can look to the cross-examiner when the question is asked and then to the witness for the answer. This position of close proximity to the witness also gives trial counsel a good view of the witness's demeanor and behavior during the questioning. The witness's demeanor and behavior (glancing down or fidgeting) can not only telegraph to the jury whether the witness is being truthful, but also provide evidence of deception that counsel can comment on during closing argument. These "folk beliefs" about what a truthful or untruthful person looks like and how they behave are powerful, and even if incorrect or misleading, must be recognized and contended with by counsel for all parties.

The farther the cross-examiner is from the witness, the less stress the witness will feel. Trial counsel can use this dynamic to her advantage. When counsel is seeking concessions with a relaxed, friendly approach, the best position to facilitate this approach is one that has the lawyer at some distance from the witness. For instance, counsel may question from the counsel table or back by the end of the jury box away from the witness. However, if counsel wishes to challenge and pressure the witness because, for example, the witness is evading or fabricating,

the cross-examiner can move closer to the witness. Or counsel may begin at a distance and then close in on the witness, not only with challenging questions, but also by physically moving closer to the witness.

## C.  Demeanor

You don't need to be cross to cross-examine. In fact, an aggressive, angry cross can be counterproductive. Your demeanor and behavior will have an impact on the witness, judge, and jury. Make it a favorable one. At various times during cross-examination, you likely will feel frustrated, angry, or elated. Unless you are careful, your voice, facial expressions, or other body language will reveal your feelings or state of mind. You should think about whether any display of your emotions will be harmful or helpful. Keep in mind that everything you do while representing your client should be done for a reason, a reason that ultimately connects to your achieving your client's objectives. Do you wish to display emotion in reaction to a witness's response to your questions? Should you raise your voice? Show a pained expression? If you show distress when the witness gives an answer that hurts your case, your reaction may increase the answer's significance. If the answer is harmful, you will have all the more reason to hide your emotions. Consciously try to control your reaction. The best practice is to control your emotions and not show facial expressions.

Your demeanor and conduct toward a witness may well influence how the jurors feel about you and the witness. If you are overbearing, or you badger or attack a witness by raising your voice, standing too close to the witness, or firing your questions rapidly, you may cause jurors to sympathize with the witness and regard her testimony approvingly. Conversely, when you examine a hostile and argumentative witness courteously, the jury may be more likely to regard the witness as biased, evasive, or untruthful. Therefore, we suggest you adhere to the suggested demeanor and behavior that is described earlier, at pages 361-362. Again, the best practice is to control your emotions and not show facial expressions.

## D.  Notes and Note Taking

Earlier in this chapter we stressed the importance of writing your cross as a way of organizing it and ensuring that you take full advantage of the techniques for concession-seeking and impeachment cross. However, when it comes to performing the cross, you do not want to read your questions or, even worse, write the answers to the questions. There are at least two reasons for not having your eyes glued to your notes.

- Watch the Witness:  As you watch the witness, you will be able to tell when the witness is evading, unsure, or deceiving. This behavior (twitching, looking away) can cause you to react to the perceived behavior, such as delving further into a subject when it is apparent that the witness may be hiding something.

   Even more important, if you are looking at your notes rather than the witness, it is likely you are going to be focused on the next question and not listening.
- Watch the Jury: Ordinarily, jurors are poker-faced and hard to read. However, you can sometimes see their reactions, such as when boredom sets in or they are upset with a witness or with you.

By the time of trial, you should be familiar with your cross-examination notes and should not have to do more than glance down. The technique is to refer to your notes to see the topic that is at the top of the page and the line of short statements with keywords highlighted. Then, look up at the witness, ask the question, and listen to the answer. Don't look down when the witness starts to answer.

Some occasions call for you to read your notes during cross-examination, and that is usually when you want to correctly state a quotation or a reference source, or use precise language in laying an evidentiary foundation—laying the foundation for a prior inconsistent statement. Another time you might do this is when you want to tether the witness to his deposition so he will not vary from it. You can look at the witness's deposition as you frame a question to the witness so he knows that a variance from it will allow you to use the deposition transcript to impeach him.

Recall that on the right side of your cross-examination notes, you have space where you can take notes. This does not mean that you should write every answer or even most answers. What you want to record are the golden nuggets—the concessions that you can refer to in closing argument.

## E. Listening to the Answer

Listening to the witness's answer on cross is even more important than listening to your own witness's answer when you conduct direct. You generally know what your witness will say on direct, but you never know for sure what will come out of the witness's mouth when you conduct cross. Concession-seeking cross is founded on the concept that you know the answer that the witness should give, but who knows what may happen? As previously mentioned, cross-examiners often do not listen to the answer because they are intent on the next question. So it is crucial that you pay close attention to the answer. It may prove to be a valuable admission. Or it may open up a line of questions that you explore with follow-up questions. After all, the difference between a witness saying "I generally go . . ." rather than "I always go . . ." may be the difference in the outcome of a case; if you're not listening carefully, however, you may hear only "I go . . . ."

## F. Highlighting Important Information

Most of the trial techniques that we describe for highlighting important direct testimony apply equally to cross-examination. See pages 318-320 for a fuller discussion of them.

### Highlighting Important Testimony on Cross-Examination

You can use a variety of methods to highlight important testimony.

- **Looping:** Incorporate part of a witness's reply into your next question to give emphasis to the reply.
- **Silence:** Stop after the answer, count to ten, and look at the jury to see if the answer sunk in.
- **Write the Answer:** Write the witness's answer on a board or flipchart with a marker, making sure to quote the witness accurately.
- **Exhibits and Demonstrations:** Enrich cross-examination with exhibits and demonstrations. Conduct a demonstration to create reality in the courtroom so the jury can see what happened—show how far the robber was from the victim when he pointed the gun at him. Or the cross-examiner can have the witness work with an exhibit, like handling the murder weapon. Space out the introduction of exhibits in order to change the pace and inject interest into the cross.

## G. Bench Trial

When cross-examination is conducted in a bench trial, it should be tailored to the judge's wishes.

> ### Judicial Expectations: Cross-Examination
>
> #### Bench Trial
>
> While good advocacy dictates the single-fact-per-question approach when the jury is the audience, judges do not need to be gradually led to a conclusion. Rather, judges, conscious of the need to save time, and with experience in assessing witness credibility, would like to have counsel cut to the chase and avoid any efforts to impeach with minor matters.

## VIII.  USING VISUALS IN CROSS-EXAMINATION

Exhibits and trial visuals can be employed productively in cross-examination to gain concessions and to impeach a witness. However, some risks are inherent in using them on cross. If, for example, the prosecutor were trying to gain a concession that a piece of clothing associated with the crime scene fit the defendant, the lawyer could take a chance and ask the defendant to put it on during cross-examination. In doing so, counsel may become a footnote in history.

A lawyer may effectively impeach by confronting the witness with an exhibit or visual. For example, if the plaintiff has testified that a disability caused by the defendant kept him from work, defense counsel could impeach the witness with a photograph of him playing tennis. Prior inconsistent statements are powerful impeachment evidence. The impeachment can be done by reading the document or, far better, by retrieving the prior statement electronically and projecting it on a screen or monitor. The approach for using a video deposition to impeach with a prior inconsistent statement is much the same as with a deposition transcript, except for the last step.

1. Lock the witness into the current testimony.
2. Inquire about whether the witness ever gave a prior inconsistent statement.
3. Give the witness a chance to change the response.
4. Ask the witness about being deposed (taking the oath, having a chance to review the transcript, and so on).
5. Confront the witness—"Is this the question I asked and the answer you gave?"
6. With the deposition in hand, direct the witness to the page and line, and then read the relevant portion of the deposition. With a video deposition, the lawyer plays the video.

Showing that the witness gives an answer on a video deposition that is inconsistent with what the witness has just testified to is usually quite effective.

## IX. ETHICAL CONSIDERATIONS

We would venture to say that on any given day in any given courthouse in this nation, ABA Model Rule of Professional Conduct 3.4(e) is violated more often than any other ethics rule pertaining to trial, and particularly during cross-examination. Rule 3.4(e) states that "a lawyer shall not in trial, allude to any matter that the lawyer does not reasonably believe is relevant or that will not be supported by admissible evidence, assert personal knowledge of facts in issue except when testifying as a witness. . . ." Frequently, under the guise of asking a question, cross-examiners advance facts and theories that cannot be proven. One flagrant example is the cross-examiner who asks a final question of this type, and when opposing counsel objects, counsel, knowing that the damage to the other side's case has been done, smugly withdraws the question and states, "No more questions." This behavior is unacceptable, and it is reserved only for lawyers on television or in movies. Remember: The judge will see what you are doing—the same judge who will rule on virtually all the legal issues in your case within an abuse of discretion standard. You do not want this judge to doubt that you know what you are doing or whether you can be trusted.

---

### Ethical Rules Pertaining to Cross-Examination: Summary

#### Model Rules of Professional Conduct 3.3(a)(3) and 3.4(e)

**Irrelevant or Inadmissible:** Under Model Rule of Professional Conduct 3.4(e), "a lawyer shall not in trial, allude to any matter that the lawyer does not reasonably believe is relevant or that will not be supported by admissible evidence, assert personal knowledge of facts in issue except when testifying as a witness. . . ." Under Rule 3.4(e) counsel should not inject irrelevant or inadmissible evidence during cross.

**False Evidence:** Under Model Rule of Professional Conduct 3.3(a)(3), "a lawyer shall not knowingly offer evidence that the lawyer knows to be false. If a lawyer, the lawyer's client, or a witness called by the lawyer, has offered material evidence and the lawyer comes to know of its falsity, the lawyer shall take reasonable remedial measures. . . ." Under Rule 3.4(e), counsel should not seek false evidence during cross.

---

### CHECKLIST: CROSS-EXAMINATION

**Content**

Cross-examination should:

- ☐ Serve the primary purpose of advancing counsel's case theory or undercutting the other side's case theory.
- ☐ Seek concessions supporting counsel's case theory or undercutting the other side's.

*continued* ▶

☐ Serve the secondary purpose of impeachment.
☐ Impeachment cross explores one of the nine principal areas of impeachment:
1. Improbability,
2. Prior inconsistent statement,
3. Prior convictions,
4. Lack of personal knowledge,
5. Mental and sensory deficiencies,
6. Bias and interest,
7. Prior bad acts probative on untruthfulness,
8. Contradiction, and
9. Character witness ("Have you heard . . . ?").

### Construction

Cross examination should:

☐ Flow smoothly and be understandable.
☐ Question appropriately: almost always leading with *"Isn't it true that . . ."* and *"Didn't you . . . ,"* sometimes anticipatory or accusatory under special circumstances, and seldom, if ever, use an interrogatory question (*"How?"* and *"Why?"*).
☐ Be short and comprehensible.
☐ Be sequenced effectively, using this order:
1. Concessions first,
2. Topical and/or chronological, and
3. Finish on a high note.
☐ Label transitions clearly ("Now let's talk about . . .").

### Character

☐ Cross-examiner should appear as a sincere seeker of truth who shows courtesy and professionalism toward the witness.

### Control

☐ Counsel should control the witness using Irving Younger's Ten Commandments, and vary the approach only when counsel has good reason to do so.
1. Be brief.
2. Use plain words and short questions.
3. Leading questions only.
4. Be prepared—know the answer.
5. Listen to the answer.
6. Don't quarrel with the witness.
7. Don't ask the witness for an explanation.
8. Don't repeat the direct examination.
9. Limit examination—avoid too many questions.
10. Persuade during closing, not during cross-examination.
☐ Use control techniques.
• Secure an agreement.
• Repeat the question.
• Ask the witness to repeat the question.

- Become more confrontational.
- Palm toward witness "stop" gesture.

### Essential Evidence Rules

Counsel should:

☐ Ask leading questions.
☐ Abide by evidentiary law applicable to these areas of impeachment:
  - Improbability, bias, motive, perception, and ability to relate;
  - Prior inconsistent statements;
  - Prior convictions; and
  - Prior bad acts probative of untruthfulness.

### Strategies

☐ Do not cross-examine when it serves no purpose.
☐ Counsel's position in the courtroom should direct the jury's attention to counsel, allow counsel to observe, and have an effect on the witness.
☐ Counsel's demeanor toward the witness should be as a sincere seeker of truth who is courteous to the witness but does not tolerate witness deception or evasion.
☐ Counsel seldom should read from notes and infrequently take notes.
☐ Counsel should highlight important aspects of the testimony by using the following techniques:
  - Looping,
  - Exhibits and demonstrations,
  - Silence, and
  - Writing the answer so the jury can see it.

### Bench Trial

☐ Counsel should go directly to the crux of the matter; the one fact-per-question approach is not required.
☐ Do not impeach on minor matters.

### Visuals

☐ Use visuals during cross.

### Ethical Boundaries

☐ Counsel never should allude to any matter that trial counsel cannot reasonably believe is relevant or that won't be supported by admissible evidence.

# EXPERTS
## Yours and Theirs

*"A witness who has special knowledge in a particular matter may give an opinion on that matter. In determining the weight to be given such opinion, you should consider the qualifications and credibility of the witness and the reasons given for the opinion. You are not bound by such opinion. Give it the weight, if any, to which you deem it entitled."*
> **—Idaho Criminal Jury Instruction 104**
> *available at http://www.isc.idaho.gov/*

*"There are as many opinions as there are experts."*
—**Franklin D. Roosevelt**, Address, "The
Scrap Rubber Campaign" (June 12, 1942)

*"Okay, bear with me. I mean, you're one of only ten guys in the country*
*who understands this stuff."*
*"I think there's at least fifteen, but go on . . . What don't you get?"*
*"Insects arrive at a corpse in a specific order. Right?"*
*"Like summer follows the spring."*
*"And you can pinpoint time of death, based on the type and age of insects*
*present on the body."*
*"I watch the insects mature. From eggs to larvae to adults. Then count*
*backwards."*
*"Linear regression."*

—**Sara Sidle**, portrayed by **Jorja Fox Born**, &
**Gil Grissom**, portrayed by **William**
**Petersen**, in *Crime Scene Investigation*
(CSI), "Sex, Lies, and Larvae" (CBS,
Dec. 22, 2000)

## I. OVERVIEW

In this chapter, we discuss both direct and cross-examination of expert witnesses. We concentrate on how to take advantage of the opportunities that can
arise when expert witnesses testify at trial. You will learn the evidentiary requirements for expert testimony and how to prepare and present the essential components of an expert's direct examination, such as qualification of the expert,
reliability of the field of expertise, and the factual basis and opinion. We also
examine how to prepare for and conduct an effective cross-examination of an
expert witness. This discussion centers on how to gain favorable concessions
from the other side's experts and how to impeach expert testimony in ways that
are not available for lay witnesses.

## II. ESSENTIAL EVIDENCE RULES: EXPERTS

An understanding of the law of evidence concerning expert witnesses is required
for preparing and presenting expert testimony that supports your case. It is also
important that you understand this body of law to be able to attack your opponent's expert testimony on cross or through motions or objections. Here we
examine those rules that apply only to expert witnesses and expert testimony.
Also, even if expert testimony meets these evidentiary requirements, the trial
court will still apply the other evidence rules. The court will make a relevancy
inquiry (Fed. R. Evid. 401) and will make a determination of whether the expert
testimony's probative value is substantially outweighed by danger of unfair prejudice (Fed. R. Evid. 403).

To conduct a direct examination, you must know how to qualify your witness as an expert (lay a foundation) and how to elicit expert witness testimony in a way that your jury will find useful and persuasive. To attack the other side's expert testimony, you will need to know when and on what grounds you can disqualify a witness from testifying as an expert, how to make your opponent's expert less believable, and how to question your opponent's expert to draw out concessions that support your case.

We review evidentiary law using the Federal Rules of Evidence because those rules apply in federal courts and, with some variations, in most state courts. Later, we offer suggestions concerning how you can persuasively present expert testimony while meeting these evidentiary requirements.

## A. Qualifications and Ultimate Opinion

Under Federal Rules of Evidence 702 and 704, a witness who is qualified as an expert by knowledge, skill, experience, training, or education may testify in the form of an opinion or otherwise, including an opinion on an ultimate issue to be decided by the jury, if

(a) the expert's scientific, technical, or other specialized knowledge will help the trier of fact to understand the evidence or to determine a fact in issue (e.g., expert testimony in a criminal case would assist the jury by explaining about how a pipe recovered from the defendant was used to smoke crystal methamphetamine);

(b) the testimony is based on sufficient facts or data;

(c) the testimony is the product of reliable principles and methods; and

(d) the expert has reliably applied the principles and methods to the facts of the case.

Opinion testimony may embrace the ultimate issue to be decided by the fact finder. However, experts are not permitted to tell the fact finder what result to reach, or to render an opinion on the law (except in those rare cases involving a standard of care in the interpretation of the law, such as in a case involving a claim of legal malpractice). Under Federal Rule of Evidence 702, moreover, an expert does not need to provide an opinion, but in the proper case may be a "pedagogical expert" providing the jury with expert information that counsel will use in arguing the case.

## B. Reliability of the Expert's Field

Before an expert can render an opinion, the lawyer who called the expert to testify must prove to the court that the field of expertise for the expert's opinion is reliable. Usually, the evidentiary component of reliability is not a major issue. Many scientific fields are so widely accepted in the scientific community that a trial lawyer can rely on the willingness of the court to take judicial notice of the scientific reliability of the discipline (such as ballistics, psychiatry, and so on).

However, other fields are not so widely accepted and require proof of reliability. Issues concerning the reliability of the area of the expert witness's testimony generally arise in a motion in limine to exclude the expert testimony. This motion, which is made outside the presence of the jury, may require argument or written briefs, and frequently is supported by discovery, depositions, affidavits, and expert witness testimony.

### *Frye* Test

For more than half a century, *Frye v. United States,* 293 F. 1013 (D.C. Cir. 1923), enunciated the classic test for a novel science. Under *Frye,* the proponent of the expert testimony was required to prove that the scientific technique in question conformed to the standard generally accepted in the scientific community. Thus, on direct examination, the lawyer would question the expert whether the scientific theory, protocol, and/or technology meets the standards in *Frye* as follows:

**Sample Questions**
- *Has the technology of brain imaging been generally accepted in the scientific field of forensic psychology by the scientific community?*
- *The technology of brain imaging has not been generally accepted in the forensic psychology field by the scientific community, correct?*

### *Daubert* Test

The U.S. Supreme Court, in *Daubert v. Merrell Dow Pharmaceuticals Inc.,* 509 U.S. 579 (1993), set aside *Frye* in federal courts, holding that Federal Rule of Evidence 702 replaced it. Under *Daubert,* the trial court acts as a gatekeeper and makes a Federal Rule of Evidence 104(a) preliminary inquiry whether the proffered expertise is methodologically reliable. In subsequent cases, the Supreme Court held that *Daubert* applies not just to science, but to all forms of expertise under Federal Rule of Evidence 702. Judicially relevant factors under *Daubert* include

- whether the theory or technique can be and has been tested,
- whether the theory or technique has been subjected to peer review and publication,
- the known or potential rate of error and the existence and maintenance of standards controlling the technique's operation, and
- the level of acceptance in the scientific community.

*Daubert* controls in the federal system. On the state level, some states adhere to the *Frye* test, others adopt *Daubert,* while other states craft their own test. Even if expert testimony passes *Daubert* muster, the trial court will still make a Federal Rule of Evidence 401/702 inquiry to decide whether the expert has scientific knowledge that will help the fact finder decide or understand a fact in issue. Finally, Federal Rule of Evidence 403 comes into play to exclude scientific evidence when its probative value is substantially outweighed by danger of unfair prejudice. See pages 391-395 for an illustration of how to structure the Rule 702 qualifications.

## C. Basis for Opinion

Federal Rule of Evidence 703 governs the types of data or facts on which an expert may base an opinion. The categories of data or facts include the following:

- Those perceived by the expert or made known to the expert at or before the hearing:
  - Perceived by the expert: Such as a doctor performs a physical examination of a patient;
  - Made known at trial: For example, at trial, a hypothetical question is posed containing a description of a person's physical condition or the expert is made aware of other testimony presented to the finder of fact.
- Otherwise inadmissible evidence, if such evidence is reasonably relied on by experts in a particular field in forming opinions or inferences, such as when a doctor renders an opinion in part based on a discussion with a radiologist (which is inadmissible hearsay). So long as other experts in the doctor's field would reasonably rely on such a conversation, it may form the basis for the doctor's expert opinion. Federal Rule of Evidence 703, however, bars the expert from revealing the otherwise inadmissible evidence unless its "probative value in helping the jury evaluate the opinion substantially outweighs their prejudicial effect." Of course, cross-examination could open the door for the doctor to reveal her conversation with the radiologist.

## D. Hypothetical Questions

Traditionally, based on the common law of evidence, an expert who lacked personal knowledge had to learn the facts by either listening to the testimony or hearing a hypothetical question that fairly summarized the trial evidence. Federal Rule of Evidence 705 permits the expert to testify in terms of inferences and opinions without first testifying to underlying facts and data. Consequently, Rule 705 provides the party presenting the expert with the strategic option to present the expert's opinion before presenting the underlying reasons and analysis. The advantage of proceeding in this manner is that the jury is given context within which to appreciate the series of questions about the basis for the opinion.

Q: *Doctor, have you formed an opinion to a reasonable degree of medical certainty as to the cause of Mr. Smith's illness?*

A: Yes.

Q: *What is that opinion?*

A: Exposure to substance Z.

Q: *Now, let's talk about how you arrived at that conclusion . . . .*

However, Federal Rule of Evidence 705 also grants the judge the discretion to require that the expert testify to the underlying facts and data before rendering an opinion. Under Rule 705, hypothetical questions are not required. However, in a particular case, you may need to pose a hypothetical to which the expert can respond with an opinion. A hypothetical question is useful if you wish to summarize the facts that have or will be presented. A hypothetical question asks your expert to assume certain facts that are admissible in evidence or that you know will be introduced into evidence, and then to base an opinion on those facts. Hypothetical questions are often met with an objection from opposing counsel. Failure to include a material piece of evidence, misstating evidence, or including inadmissible evidence may draw an objection from opposing counsel that, if sustained, will bar your expert from rendering an opinion unless you can rephrase it as a nonobjectionable hypothetical.

## Hypothetical Question

A hypothetical question might be phrased as follows:

"Dr. Hollingsworth, I want you to assume the following facts. A 12-year-old boy consumed five eight-ounce glasses of Judi Cream Cola during each day of the week for a period of two months. The Judi Cream Cola is made with the sweetener gooloss. He had an eight-ounce glass for breakfast at 7:00 A.M., eight ounces for lunch at noon, eight ounces mid-afternoon at 3:00 P.M., eight ounces for dinner at 6:00 P.M., and another eight ounces before bedtime at 9:00 P.M. He did this for two months. Do you have an opinion as to whether that would cause the boy to have a case of hysterical hyperactive syndrome caused by the ingredient gooloss?"

This hypothetical question appears to be well constructed, but it may well be met with an objection. If evidence were introduced that the boy ate or drank anything else during that period of time, then the opposing counsel may object on the grounds that you failed to include that material evidence for the expert's consideration. Or, if evidence had not been introduced that the glass the boy drank from was eight ounces in size, the question would be flawed. The question also may be objected to because it failed to include evidence of the boy's health, weight, or height. Or the question could be attacked because the facts in evidence are insufficient on which to base an expert opinion. These represent just a sampling of the type of objections that might be voiced. We suggest that you not use a lengthy hypothetical question because of the potential risks involved. However, if you need to construct and use a hypothetical question, you should review the evidence rules in your jurisdiction and study local practice by speaking with experienced trial attorneys, and then you should carefully prepare the question in writing and practice it with your expert witness.

## III. STRUCTURING DIRECT EXAMINATION

### A. Preparing Yourself

#### Legal Research

Your preparation for direct examination of an expert begins with gaining a firm understanding of evidentiary law relating to expert testimony and researching the case law that has a bearing on the area of expertise that you will be covering during the direct examination.

#### Understanding the Field

You will need a fundamental understanding of the expert's field of expertise. Your best source for learning about the particular field is your expert. You can learn from your expert's report, your interview of your expert, and by talking with others familiar with the specialty, such as other attorneys and other experts.

The Internet is a source that is ripe with information, but should be approached cautiously. While the Internet is a valuable starting place to obtain general information about many areas, be wary of the reliability of information gleaned from a casual search. Do not assume that the information you find is considered accurate by experts in the field.

You can also learn by reading about the field of expertise. To gain a general understanding of the field, your reading can consist of specialized periodicals that include articles on the subject; treatises in the field; and your own expert's works, such as articles, reports, books, and so on. Some particularly helpful reference books are available that are devoted to specific subject areas and contain models of direct and cross-examination questions in those specialized areas. For example, Robert L. Habush, *Cross Examination of Non-Medical Experts* (Matthew Bender 1995), contains extensive transcripts of testimony given by technical and engineering experts. David Faust, *Coping with Psychiatric and Psychological Testimony* (6th ed., Oxford University Press 2011) contains discussion and transcripts. A multivolume series, *American Jurisprudence Proof of Facts* (Lawyers Cooperative Publishing 2006) provides hundreds of model transcripts of direct and cross-examination questions of such experts as doctors, engineers, collision reconstructionists, police officers, and dentists. These transcripts of expert witnesses can be valuable preparation resources.

#### Interviewing the Expert

To understand how to guide the jury to value the testimony of your expert, it is important to understand how the expert's field contributes to your case. Understand how your expert's training and experience (qualifications) contribute to his authority in this field. To fully understand these issues, you should interview your expert. The following is a checklist for interviewing your expert witness.

CHECKLIST

**Topics for Interviewing Your Expert**

☐ **Meet Where the Expert Works:** Meeting at a busy expert's office or laboratory, for example, is a courtesy that may provide you with insight into his work that will prove valuable at trial.

☐ **Qualifying Information:** It is common for an expert to already have a set of questions designed for you to ask to qualify the expert. Find out what experiences and training your expert has that is specific to the issues he will address in this case.

☐ **The Field of Expertise:** A discussion and explanation of theories, methodology, laboratory protocols, technology, and so on that the expert covered.

☐ **What the Expert Did:** Questions about what was done in the case (testing, laboratory work, and so on).

☐ **Problematic Areas in the Field:** An explanation of the problems and limitations of the expert's field.

☐ **Problematic Areas in the Case:** Issues the other side might raise.

☐ **What the Expert Can Offer:** To prove elements of the case theory or to undercut the other side's case theory.

☐ **Visuals:** PowerPoint slides, anatomical drawings, charts, and other visuals that will assist the expert.

## B.  Preparing Your Expert

The preparation of your expert witness is critical to a persuasive direct examination. Although many experts are experienced and adept at testifying, your expert may be unacquainted with the role of being an expert witness. For instance, a doctor might be thrust into the role of an expert witness because the witness was the treating physician in a case involving medical issues. If that is so, you will need to have a discussion like the one you would with a novice lay witness that covers trial procedures, exhibits, direct and cross, and so on.

You may want to discuss your case theory with the expert so that the expert knows where she fits into the case. The expert may also be able to help you identify additional supporting evidence for your case theory, as well as problems that you will need to address. While this discussion is important, be wary. Remember, anything you say to a testifying expert, other than the necessary conveying of attorney-client information, may be discoverable by your opponent.

You and your expert should review key publications, including treatises and the expert's own works. Your witness may need to respond to cross-examination questions about his work or learned treatises. You also need to prepare your expert to use exhibits to the best advantage during direct examination.

While the preparation of an experienced expert may not involve providing all of the background information about trial that you would offer a fledgling expert, even very seasoned experts must be prepared. Ultimately, each case is different and must be judged accordingly. Although experts know their fields better than you do, you know your case and trial strategies. You must prepare your expert for both your case and what you expect to accomplish with the expert. While some experts may resist your efforts to prepare them, remember that preparation is a two-way street. As you prepare your witness, he is educating and preparing you to conduct a persuasive examination. Even the most jaded expert will be receptive to your request that he help you prepare.

---

**Expert Witness**

### Preparing Your Expert Witness to Testify

When preparing your expert witness to testify for both direct and cross-examination, you will want to cover these areas:

- **The Significance of the Expert Testimony:**  Acquaint the expert with both your and the other side's case theories so the expert understands where her testimony fits in the full picture.
- **The Court Process:**  Discuss how it works.
- **Manner of Testifying:**  For a new expert witness and even an experienced expert, discuss how to be a good witness.
- **Prepare the Expert for Cross-Examination:**  Include questions about the expert's written works and treatises, if any, that express different views. Discuss how to react if you object during cross-examination.
- **Schedule:**  Review your expert's placement on the list of witnesses.
- **Demonstrative Exhibits:**  Prepare exhibits with enough time to have the expert verify their accuracy and to discuss how they will be used in testifying.
- **Potential Exhibits:**  Show and go over each exhibit with the expert.
- **Rehearse Direct Examination and the Other Side's Anticipated Cross-Examination:**  Even experts who are accustomed to testifying will benefit from rehearsal.

---

## C.  Selecting Content

You are concerned with eliciting expert testimony that will prove the legal sufficiency of your case theory and persuade the jury to render a verdict in your client's favor. Developing the content of your expert's testimony requires referring to

- your trial plan, and
- the tentative draft of your closing argument.

These two tools can guide you in focusing on the opinions and facts that you wish to elicit from your expert witness during direct examination to support your case theory. By examining the end product you wish to achieve—that is, your closing argument—you can work backward to identify the points you need to obtain from your witness's direct examination. Throughout this chapter, the examples illustrate how your tentative closing argument, which is an embodiment of your case theory, and potential direct and cross-examination, are planned simultaneously prior to trial.

To illustrate how to plan the content and presentation of direct examination of an expert, we use the *Hill Moveit Personal Injury* case. Review the facts on pages 45-47.

### Trial Plan

The trial plan you draft as the defense attorney in the *Hill Moveit Personal Injury* case might look like the table shown on page 389. Your trial plan indicates that one element of your legal theory that you need to establish is comparative fault (contributory negligence) by the plaintiff. According to your trial plan, you have a few pieces of evidence, including photographs of Ms. Rutherford's SUV, a facsimile of the entertainment center, and the investigative report. No other witnesses saw what happened, and Ms. Rutherford cannot remember. Only an expert witness, a collision reconstructionist, can examine the evidence and provide testimony that Ms. Rutherford's car was following too closely behind the trailer.

### Tentative Draft of Closing Argument

Now turn to your factual theory. This factual theory will be expressed in your tentative closing argument when you argue that the facts and expert's opinions establish that Darcy Rutherford's contributory negligence caused her injuries because she was following too closely behind the Hill Moveit trailer. If she had been a safe distance back, she would not have been injured because her SUV would not have struck the furniture. To illustrate how the tentative closing argument embodies your case theory and guides the development of your direct examination of an expert, here is an abbreviated excerpt of a closing argument in the *Hill Moveit* case. This illustrative excerpt contains a more fully developed closing argument than the draft closing you would likely have for use in planning the direct or cross-examination of an expert prior to trial.

---

**The *Hill Moveit Personal Injury* Case**

#### Closing Argument Re Defense Expert

Why should you believe this accident reconstruction as scientific evidence? As Dr. Riley testified, collision reconstruction is routinely done and relied on by law enforcement agencies across this county. It is based on the immutable laws of physics. Expert testimony concerning how an accident has occurred is common in civil lawsuits such as this one as well.

Dr. Riley has explained the science of collision reconstruction, testifying at length about the methods and procedures he used to reach his conclusions in this case. He explained to you that the damage pattern on plaintiff's SUV, when compared

**TRIAL PLAN CHART**

**Plaintiff's Trial Plan for the *Hill Moveit* Case**

| Legal Theory (Claim or Defense) | Factual Theory (Legal Elements) | Facts | Witness | Exhibits | Weakness in the Evidence | Evidence Objections | Response to the Objections | Jury Instructions | Things to Do |
|---|---|---|---|---|---|---|---|---|---|
| Comparative fault | Duty owed | Driving on highway—duty not to tailgate | Collision reconstruction expert—opinion that plaintiff was following too closely, and but for that the furniture would not have struck the windshield | Moveit trailer<br><br>Facsimile of furniture<br><br>Photographs of damage to plaintiff's SUV<br><br>State patrol investigation field diagram | No one witnessed the collision<br><br>Furniture destroyed in collision<br><br>SUV destroyed after the collision | Daubert—insufficient evidence of collision to reconstruct | Sufficient information for reconstruction | Comparative negligence is negligence on the part of a person claiming injury that is the proximate cause of the injury claimed (pages 458 and 460-461) | |
| | Breach of duty | Followed too closely | | | | | | | |
| | Proximate cause of injury | Following too closely caused plaintiff to be struck | | | | | | | |
| | Injury | Plaintiff injured | | | | | | | |

with the entertainment center's construction, shows that the furniture piece was upside down when the SUV hit it. The base of the entertainment center was above the hood when Ms. Rutherford drove into it. It is that base that went through the windshield. As Dr. Riley testified, the entertainment center was intact when it fell out of the trailer, and the plaintiff's vehicle hit it before the furniture could tumble and break apart. As he put it, "If she had been two seconds back—which is the State of Major Department of Transportation's rule—the accident would not have occurred because she would not have hit the furniture."

But we are not asking you to merely rely on Dr. Riley's say-so. You will have these photographs to examine yourself in the jury room so you can confirm independently that the plaintiff was following too closely. You can see how the facsimile entertainment center lines up with the damage on the SUV. You can see the board in the driver's side of the vehicle. It makes common sense that that baseboard was sent through the windshield when the plaintiff's SUV hit it right after it fell upside down on the pavement and before it had a chance to tumble and disintegrate.

The plaintiff's collision reconstruction expert, Janett Strait, claims that "it's impossible for a reasonably prudent collision reconstruction expert to determine what happened because no evidence exists that can be scientifically analyzed." The plaintiff's expert is mistaken. As Dr. Riley has shown, evidence of what took place does exist. It is shown here in Exhibits 76, 81, and 85. Granted, it was necessary to find a facsimile to the entertainment center that was destroyed, but as this photograph, Exhibit 81, shows, it can be done. As you will recall from the testimony of Stanley Luby, this entertainment center in the photograph is just like the one he had in the trailer. Also, as you will recall, the reason that the SUV and the entertainment center were not available for Dr. Riley to examine is because the plaintiff disposed of them.

Based on the physical evidence and Dr. Riley's expert analysis and opinion, the plaintiff was following too closely and that contributed to her injury.

With the *Hill Moveit* defendant's case as an illustration, the following discussion explains how your trial plan and closing argument can assist you in planning a direct examination that both fits within the legal context of presenting a legally sufficient case and is persuasive.

## D.  Components of Expert's Direct

The structure of an expert witness's testimony has five components:

1. Qualifying the witness as an expert,
2. Establishing the reliability of the field of expertise,
3. Presenting the factual basis for the expert's opinion,
4. Meeting the opposing party's attack, and
5. Having the expert render the opinion.

These components of expert testimony correspond to the evidentiary requirements for admissibility of expert testimony. However, here we focus on structuring and delivering the expert witness's testimony so that it is convincing to the jury.

## 1. The Expert's Qualifications

You have two objectives when presenting your expert's qualifications: (1) to satisfy the evidentiary requirements so that the expert may testify as to his opinion, and (2) to present credibility-building information that makes the expert's opinion trustworthy and thus persuasive.

We now emphasize how to accomplish the second objective: credibility-building information that makes the expert's opinion trustworthy and persuasive.

### Stipulating to the Expert's Qualifications

You are about to begin your questioning to qualify your witness as an expert, and opposing counsel addresses you and the judge: *"We'll stipulate to Dr. Riley's qualifications as a collision reconstructionist."* If you respond that you accept the stipulation, you can save time, which usually will ingratiate you to the judge and allow you to move to other parts of the witness's testimony. Stipulating can be strategically wise if your expert's qualifications appear weak to you when contrasted with those of your opponent's expert.

Usually you will want to forgo stipulating and instead use the opportunity to build your witness's credibility with the jury. For the jury to understand the context and quality of your expert's opinion, they need to hear what it is about your expert's training, experience, and credentials that are specific to the opinion that she is offering.

If you do not want to stipulate, thank opposing counsel for the offer, respectfully decline the offer, and continue to qualify your witness.

### Establishing the Expertise

Federal Rule of Evidence 702 specifies that an expert may be qualified by knowledge, skill, experience, training, or education. Using these topics, you can then develop specific questions that qualify your expert witness to give an opinion. In doing this, you should develop questions that reflect the specific area of the expert's knowledge that relates to your case.

In the *Hill Moveit* case, the defense would want to stress Dr. Riley's knowledge and experience in collision reconstruction. When focusing on his scholarly activities, such as writing papers, conducting seminars, and delivering lectures, you would want to concentrate primarily on Riley's activities that deal with the specialty of reconstructing vehicle collisions.

When you are qualifying a nonscientific expert witness, such as an automobile mechanic, you would concentrate on the appropriate aspects of the expert's employment and experience in the particular area of automobile mechanics about which you wish the expert to testify. Generally, the more specific the witness's qualifications to the issue on which he opines, the more persuasive the qualifications will be.

*Introducing and Humanizing the Witness*

It is helpful to think about this portion of direct examination as your opportunity to introduce your expert as a person to the jury. Through your questions, you have the witness talk about himself. When presenting your expert's qualifications, you also have an opportunity to humanize your witness. The more human and appealing a witness appears to the jury, the more compelling his testimony is likely to be. This process is called *accrediting* your witness. In this regard, an expert is similar to a lay witness.

In the following example of how to qualify Dr. Riley, he is questioned about his donation of time to oversee car seat impact studies by Tot Seat Corp. However, be careful when eliciting this personal information; you do not want to seek to introduce evidence that is too far afield the expert's qualifications, because your adversary might interrupt with an objection.

Experts, like most witnesses, can be nervous when they testify. This segment of the expert's testimony can serve to relax the witness and enable the witness to develop a rapport with the jury. The expert can swivel in the witness chair, look at the jury, and talk about her background and experience—subject matter with which she is comfortable.

*Illustration of Questions for Qualifying an Expert*

Often, an expert will provide the lawyer with a series of qualifying questions that the expert prefers to be asked. If your expert does not offer this, take the initiative and ask the expert for suggestions. The following is a pattern of questions that can be modified to qualify your expert.

---

## Expert Witness

### Pattern Questions for Qualifying an Expert

**Introduction**

*Q:* Please state your name.

*Q:* What is your business address?

*Q:* What is your title?

*Q:* Who is your employer?

**Tickler**

*Q:* Have you come here today prepared to state an opinion as to [the specific area of expertise, such as "the speed of the plaintiff immediately prior to the collision"]? [Note: This question must be a yes or no question, and the expert must be prepared to answer only yes or no. Because the witness has not yet been qualified to give an opinion, such a question, however, might give the jurors a context for appreciating the reasons for your qualification directions.]

*Q:* Your opinion on this question is the subject of your expertise. Before we explore that momentarily, first let's discuss your qualifications in this area.

---

Expertise

Q: What is your particular field?

Q: Please explain what this field of . . . involves.

Q: As a(n) [criminalist, accident reconstructionist], what are your primary responsibilities?

Education

Q: Where did you obtain your education in the field of . . . ?

Q: Please describe your educational background in this area.

Q: What degree did you receive after completing . . . ?

Q: After receiving your degree in . . . , were you in a further educational program [for a doctor: intern and residency]?

Certification

Q: What is board certification [in the field of medicine]?

Q: What are the requirements to become board certified?

Q: Are you board certified in . . . ?

Licensing

Q: Are you licensed in this state to practice [medicine, law]?

Training

Q: Could you describe for the jury the other training you received in . . . ?

Experience

Q: Have you received any on-the-job training as a . . . ?

Q: How long have you worked as an . . . expert?

Q: Over the years that you have worked as an expert in this field, roughly how often have you [done accident reconstructions, performed autopsies]?

Professional Organizations

Q: Do you belong to professional organizations in the field of . . . ?

Q: How are members of that organization selected? [If being a member is only a matter of paying $25 annual dues, you probably don't want to give much focus, if any, to the membership.]

Q: Have you held any office in the organization?

Teaching

Q: What, if any, teaching experience do you have in your area of expertise?

Q: What is your academic title, if any?

Q: What subjects have you taught?

Q: Please explain the process of how you achieved the position of . . .

Publications

Q: What, if anything, have you written on the subject of . . . ?

Q: What written works of yours have been published?

*continued* ▶

> **Honors**
>
> *Q:* What, if any, honors have you received in the field of . . . ? [Your expert may appear far more likeable if, rather than asking the witness to list all awards, you probe into awards and honors because this will avoid having the expert sound like he or she is bragging. An example follows.]
>
> *Q:* Please tell us whether you were one of two people in this country to receive that grant.
>
> **Prior Experience Testifying**
>
> *Q:* Have you testified before as an expert in the area of . . . in [Superior Court, District Court]?
>
> *Q:* How often have you testified in those courts?
>
> *Q:* What other states, if any, have you testified as a(n) . . . expert?
>
> *Q:* Which side have you been called to testify for?
>
> *Q:* How often would you estimate that you have been called by each party?

The questions should always be modified to fit the particular expert. The following illustrates a portion of the defense attorney's direct examination of Dr. Riley that, by establishing that Riley is qualified to testify in the specific field of collision reconstruction, is calculated to persuade the jury to adopt his opinion.

## Expert Witness

### Qualifying the Collision Reconstructionist
### The *Hill Moveit Personal Injury* Case

*Q:* Please state your name and occupation.

*Q:* Dr. Riley, where do you reside?

*Q:* Dr. Riley, have you come here today prepared to state an opinion as to how closely Darcy Rutherford was following behind the Hill Moveit trailer at the time of the accident?

*Q:* Doctor, we will get to your complete opinion in a moment, but first, let's discuss your qualifications in the area of reconstructing accidents of this nature.

*Q:* What is your particular field of expertise?

*Q:* What is your educational background as it relates to the science of collision reconstruction?

*Q:* What are the academic requirements that you had to fulfill to obtain your Ph.D. in engineering science?

*Q:* Please tell the jury about your employment background as it relates to the science of collision reconstruction.

*Q:* Are you familiar with Tot Seat Corp.?

*Q:* How, if at all, are you associated with the child car seat company? [Dr. Riley explains that he donates his time to oversee the testing of child car seats for safety.]

*Q:* What is collision reconstruction?

> Q: Dr. Riley, please describe the type of training you have had in the area of collision reconstruction.
> Q: What certifications can be obtained as a collision reconstructionist?
> Q: Are you certified in collision reconstruction?
> Q: What steps did you go through to become certified as a collision reconstructionist?
> Q: Dr. Riley, have you written any articles concerning collision reconstruction?
> Q: Could you list approximately how many lectures you have presented related to collision reconstruction and generally what they were about?
> Q: What honors, if any, have you received in the field of accident reconstruction?
> Q: Who employs you to do collision reconstruction work?
> Q: Do you consult and testify as an expert more often for plaintiffs or defendants?
> Q: How long have you worked in the field of collision reconstruction?
> Q: How many accidents or collisions have you investigated?
> Q: What are the different types of accidents that you have investigated?
> Q: Have you been qualified as an expert witness in collision reconstruction?
> Q: How many times have you testified as a collision reconstruction expert?

### Tendering the Witness as an Expert

In some jurisdictions, when counsel has concluded the testimony to qualify the witness as an expert, counsel would "tender" or offer the witness to the court as an expert. The theory is much the same as offering an exhibit after you have laid a proper foundation. You have laid the foundation for the expert, and so you offer or "tender" the expert for the court to accept or reject their "expertness."

To make a tender in the *Hill Moveit* case, defense counsel would address the judge and state, "Your Honor, I submit Dr. Terrence Riley as an expert in the area of collision reconstruction."

This process of tendering the witness signals the right of your opponent to do one of three things: object, not object, or voir dire.

In most jurisdictions, the formal tendering of the witness as an expert is not necessary. In many of these jurisdictions, the affirmative tender of the witness to the judge is actively disapproved by the courts. The theory here is that counsel is inviting the judge to comment on the evidence by describing the witness as expert. In these jurisdictions, defense counsel would simply continue with the direct examination of Dr. Riley. Obviously, you will need to learn the court's practice in this regard before you put your witness on the stand.

### Voir Dire on Qualifications

Opposing counsel may seek to voir dire the witness after you have completed asking questions to qualify the witness. Opposing counsel will make a request to the court, *"May I voir dire the witness, Your Honor?"* If this occurs, you should make sure the questions are confined to the witness's qualifications. If opposing counsel ventures outside this area of inquiry, you can object on the ground that the question does not go to the witness's qualifications and that counsel will have an opportunity to cross-examine later.

## 2. Reliability of the Expert's Field

Developing testimony underpinning the reliability of the expert's field, whether or not it is required for the admissibility of the expert testimony in your particular case, also serves the purpose of making the expert's opinion persuasive. Look back at the closing argument at pages 388-390. Notice that an important element in the presentation was to convince the jury that collision reconstruction is considered a reliable discipline.

To illustrate questions used to establish the scientific reliability of the field of collision reconstruction, examine those questions that defense counsel might ask Dr. Riley. These questions may be in response to a motion in limine to exclude Dr. Riley's testimony under *Daubert,* based on an assertion that both his and his field's methodology is unreliable, or on direct examination, to persuade the jury that your expert's opinion is scientifically reliable.

---

### Reliability of the Expert's Field: Satisfying *Daubert*

#### The *Hill Moveit Personal Injury* Case

Q: Please describe to the jury the science of collision reconstruction.

Q: Dr. Riley, please describe briefly the history of collision reconstruction to the jury.

Q: Dr. Riley, how many years has the science of collision reconstruction been used?

Q: Are there books and articles on collision reconstruction?

Q: Are there any educational programs devoted to training collision reconstruction experts?

Q: Are there any certification programs that test and accredit persons trained in the science of collision reconstruction?

Q: Can you explain when experts reconstruct collisions?

Q: Explain the scientific tests and procedures collision reconstructionists employ when reconstructing a collision.

Q: How reliable is collision reconstruction?

---

## 3. Procedures and Factual Basis for the Expert's Opinion

For the jurors to rely on the expert's opinions, they must understand that a sound basis exists for the opinion testimony. So, during the expert's direct examination, you should have the witness explain

- what the expert did,
- why it was done in a particular way, and
- the basis for the expert's opinion.

Even though Federal Rule of Evidence 705, which obviated the necessity of hypothetical questions, does not require the disclosure of the underlying facts and data and procedures that your expert used before testifying to an opinion, you may still want to do so for two related reasons. First, such testimony will make it easier for the jury to understand your expert's opinion. Second, by discussing your expert's procedures, facts, and data that she considered, the opinion is generally more convincing. In fact, it is hard to imagine an expert examination that goes like this.

Q: *What is your opinion?*
A: She was 60 feet behind the trailer.
Q: *Thank you. No further questions.*

When you conduct the direct examination concerning how the expert arrived at the opinion, discuss the procedures, techniques, and tests generally used in the field. Then, your expert should explain the procedures, techniques, and tests used in this particular instance.

### Types of Factual Data

There are three types of factual data that an expert might rely on in forming his opinion: data created through expert investigation, data provided by the attorney, or data created by others.

*Data Created Through Expert Investigation:* Data can be created by the expert either through experiments or investigation. For instance, a doctor could perform a medical examination and, if permitted, order medical tests of the plaintiff. Or, the collision reconstructionist could examine the scene, measure skid marks, and do further investigation as needed.

*Data Provided by the Attorney:* An attorney can give factual data to the expert before trial, such as records, reports, other documents, depositions, transcripts or statements from witnesses, and so forth.

*Data Prepared by Others:* Data may be prepared by others and used by most experts in the particular field. This data is not specifically prepared by the expert. An expert can rely on any source of information, including otherwise inadmissible evidence such as hearsay, as long as the information is of the type that is reasonably relied on by experts in the particular field. Fed. R. Evid. 703. Such information could include census statistics, labor statistics, x-rays, hospital records, mortality tables, or other such materials recognized in the field as being proper for drawing expert conclusions or findings.

### Organizing the Factual Data

Whichever combination of these three sources of data your expert used to arrive at an opinion, at some point you must present that opinion and data to the jury. It is critical that you organize information about the expert's opinion and its basis for the jury so the information is easy to follow, especially if your expert is testifying in a technical area. To organize this portion of the expert's testimony, we suggest grouping the expert's testimony into six categories:

1. The subject of the opinion;
2. The theoretical aspects of the expert area that underlie the opinion;
3. Data given to the expert by the attorney or investigator;
4. Data developed or relied on other than that supplied to the expert;
5. General procedures, techniques, and tests used in the field; and
6. Specific procedures or tests used in this case.

After dividing the testimony into these six categories, determine what sequence of topics to use by your sense of what provides clarity in your case.

The following example illustrates questions that could elicit information falling into the six categories. In this example, expert witness Dr. Riley is being asked by the defendant's counsel about collision reconstruction procedures, his investigation and the test procedures and techniques he used, and the meaning of the tests he used. In the process, he will use exhibits to illustrate his testimony. You might choose a different topic sequence to fit your case.

---

**Expert Witness**

### Organization of the Factual Data
### The *Hill Moveit Personal Injury* Case

1. Subject Area and Theoretical Underpinnings

Q:  Please explain to the jury what a collision reconstructionist does.

Q:  What types of cases involve collision reconstruction?

Q:  Have you ever analyzed and reconstructed an accident like the one here where an object fell off the back of a trailer and struck a following driver's vehicle?

Q:  How are motor vehicle accidents reconstructed?

A:  Every case is different. But basically, an accident reconstructionist analyzes the scene and vehicle or vehicles to determine what happened by applying engineering principles—and the immutable laws of physics.

Q:  When you say "immutable laws of physics," what do you mean?

A:  The three laws of Newtonian physics, inertia, force, and action/reaction, as well as the science of gravitational attraction.

Q:  When you say "the science of gravitational attraction," what do you mean?

A:  Gravity is the same anywhere on the surface of the earth. Objects fall at a precise speed. Using this, we can calculate with great precision what happened in many auto accidents. [We would have the expert either explain each of the three laws of Newtonian physics or let the jury know that these terms will be defined later: "Dr. Riley, we'll ask you about those three laws in a few minutes."]

Q:  Dr. Riley, what are you trying to determine?

A:  Commonly, we determine, among other things, point of impact, where the vehicle went after impact, stopping distance, and speed at impact.

2. General Procedures and Techniques Used in the Field

Q:  What techniques, tests, and measurements are required to reconstruct an accident?

*Q:* Please explain the techniques, tests, and measurements to the jury.

*Q:* Are these techniques, measurements, and tests that were used in this case the ones generally used by other accident reconstruction experts?

### 3. Expert's Data and Sources

*Q:* Please describe the beginning of your involvement in this case.

*A:* You called me in to consult on the case.

*Q:* What materials did you use to reconstruct the collision, and, if you did, could you describe what you received?

*A:* I examined the Major State Patrol investigative file and witness statements, pictures of the trailer pulled behind the vehicle driven by Stanley Luby, photographs of Darcy Rutherford's SUV, as well as witness depositions.

### 4. Tests, Calculations, and Procedures Actually Employed by the Expert

*Q:* Dr. Riley, you stated you began reconstructing the accident by examining photographs taken by the police of Darcy Rutherford's SUV and a facsimile of the entertainment center, correct?

*Q:* Dr. Riley, here are exhibits that have already been admitted into evidence. First is Exhibit 76, a photograph of the damaged front of the SUV, and next is Exhibit 81, which is a picture of the SUV with the exemplar entertainment center in front of the front bumper, and finally Exhibit 85, showing the board in the driver's side of the SUV. Can you identify them?

*Q:* Tell us whether or not these were photographs that you used in reconstructing this collision.

*Q:* Dr. Riley, could you step over here to the document camera and, with the use of the photographs, could you explain to the jury what you found? [In some courtrooms, the photos will appear on computer screens in front of the jurors, in others as blowups on an easel.]

[Dr. Riley explains with the aid of the photographs placed on the document camera how, when the furniture item is upside down, its edges line up with the damage to the front of the SUV and how the baseboard of the entertainment center shown in Exhibit 81 is at a height that matches the height of the inverted entertainment center. Dr. Riley explains how this leads to the conclusion that the SUV hit the entertainment center within half a second after it tumbled over the tailgate of the trailer. He then goes on to explain how much distance the SUV would cover in half a second and why that distance represents the distance that Ms. Rutherford was following the Moveit trailer.]

## 4. Counteracting the Opposing Party's Attack

Strategically, you want to use your expert's direct examination to undercut the other side's case theory and to blunt opposing counsel's cross-examination of your expert. In this section, we concentrate on meeting those specific aspects of your opponent's theory that call your expert's opinion into question. Thus, you should think about those areas where your expert witness and the expert's testimony may be subject to attack. The following are common areas of vulnerability:

- The reliability, accuracy, and completeness of the underlying data used by the opposing expert;
- The opposing expert witness's qualifications;
- The appropriateness of the expert's opinion;
- The scientific reliability of the field and opinion;
- The procedures and techniques used for obtaining, analyzing the data, and determining the opinion; and
- The credibility factors of the particular expert witness, such as bias in testifying for one side, interest in the case, or payment.

To conduct direct examination to counteract those aspects of the opposing party's case theory that are designed to undercut information provided by your expert, imagine you are the defense attorney and you are planning direct examination of Dr. Terrence Riley. You anticipate the plaintiff will call Janet Strait, who will testify that no reasonably prudent expert would attempt to reconstruct the collision given the limited evidence. The case now will involve a battle of the experts.

Note how this anticipated attack changes the areas of opinion that you will have Dr. Riley testify. Before we consider this anticipated attack, we anticipate qualifying Dr. Riley and having him express an opinion solely on the issue of how the collision occurred.

Now, he will present an opinion on these elements:

- The process of collision investigation and reconstruction,
- The amount of evidence needed to form an opinion, and
- How the collision occurred.

Each of these areas requires subtly different qualifications and careful construction.

As defense counsel, you wish to refute any attack on Dr. Riley's opinion that might be made during opposing counsel's direct examination of Janet Strait, or in cross-examination of Dr. Riley. With the assistance of Dr. Riley, you have analyzed the Strait report and deposition and concluded that the potential area of vulnerability in Dr. Riley's testimony is the destruction of both the SUV and the entertainment center. The following illustrates the type of questions you might include in direct examination of Dr. Riley to blunt your opponent's anticipated attacks.

---

### Expert Witness

#### Counteracting the Opposing Party's Attack
#### The *Hill Moveit Personal Injury* Case

*Q:* Dr. Riley, after the accident, were the parts of the entertainment center preserved?

*Q:* Who last had possession of the entertainment center? [Dr. Riley explains that the Major State Patrol released the remains of the entertainment center to the

---

plaintiff and that, according to the discovery he reviewed, the pieces were not preserved.]

Q: Was it critical that you examine the actual entertainment center? [The witness explains that an exemplar, an entertainment center of the same size and make, was obtained and is in evidence as Exhibit 24. The witness states that with the aid of the exemplar, he was able to reconstruct where the SUV struck this furniture piece.]

Q: Doctor, were you able to examine Darcy Rutherford's SUV?

Q: Would it have helped your efforts to reconstruct what happened in the accident if you could have examined the SUV? [The witness explains that while it might have been useful, it was not necessary because he was able to examine the damage using the photographs.]

Q: Do you know what happened to that vehicle? [Dr. Riley explains that he understands that the vehicle was repaired and sold by the plaintiff.]

Now reexamine the closing argument on pages 388-390. Examine how the closing argument incorporated this direct examination testimony, which was intended to blunt the attack on Dr. Riley's opinion.

### 5. The Expert's Opinion

**Expert Witness Testimony**

#### Opinion Testimony
#### The *Hill Moveit Personal Injury* Case

Q: Dr. Riley, based on the evidence available, do you have an opinion to a reasonable scientific certainty as to whether Ms. Rutherford was following too closely when the entertainment center fell over the tailgate on the Hill's Moveit trailer?

A: I do.

Q: And what is that opinion?

A: It is my opinion that she was following too closely—within 60 feet. If she had been farther back, in compliance with the Major State Transportation's two-second rule, she never would have hit the entertainment center.

Q: Could you explain how you reach that opinion for the jury.

There are at least three ways you can organize the body of testimony, assuming each is permitted by controlling evidentiary law.

*Opinion First*

First, similar to the illustration above, you can elicit the expert's opinion before having the expert explain the basis for the opinion. The benefit of using this approach is that by presenting the opinion first, it provides the jury with a framework within which to assimilate the expert's testimony. Your expert can then adopt the role of a teacher and explain the opinion.

### Opinion Last

Second, the expert can build to her opinion as a climax to direct examination. You can begin by discussing the data, procedures, and analysis behind the expert's determination, concluding with the opinion itself.

### First and Last

Third, you could begin with your expert's opinion. Then you present data, procedures, analysis, and the basis for the opinion, and conclude by having the expert reiterate the opinion. A risk inherent in this approach is that when you attempt to again elicit the opinion at the end of the expert's testimony, opposing counsel may object on the grounds it is repetitious.

## E.  Conducting Direct

Because experts have a depth of knowledge on their areas of expertise and often have experience testifying, they provide the trial lawyer with both opportunities and challenges beyond those offered by lay witnesses. You should also review the principles discussed in Chapter 9 at pages 297-300, 304-325 on how to conduct an effective direct examination; these principles apply equally to expert witnesses. Next, we discuss how to take full advantage of an expert on direct examination.

> To see how to conduct a direct examination of an expert witness, watch the direct of the plaintiffs' expert in the *Freck Point* trial demonstration movie on the website *http://www.aspenlawschool.com/books/berger_trialad4e.*

### Staging

A first-rate expert is a first-rate teacher. With that principle in mind, your goal in staging the body of the expert's direct is to provide the expert with the visual aids needed to teach, and give the expert the floor. Let your expert engage the jury and educate them about the particular specialty. Your job is to ask your expert open-ended questions that let your expert teach the jury. You want to ask these questions as if you do not know the answers and you are interested in learning. Think of yourself as an inquisitive juror who has been given a chance to ask questions of the expert.

For example, in the *Hill Moveit Personal Injury* case, the visuals that Dr. Riley can use to teach the jury are Exhibit 76 (a photograph of the damaged front of the SUV), Exhibit 81 (a picture of the SUV with the exemplar entertainment center in front of the front bumper), and Exhibit 85 (a photograph showing the board in the driver's side of the SUV). As the transcript of the direct examination quoted on page 399 shows, after these exhibits have been admitted into evidence, the defense attorney provided the expert with a way to display these exhibits to the jury. Dr. Riley placed the photographs on a document camera so that they would be projected on a screen in an enlarged image. In this way the expert becomes the center of attention in front of the jury. The defense attorney then can stand to the side or move to the end of the jury box so that the expert is in the spotlight talking to the jurors. If courtroom practice restricts movement, requiring, for instance, that counsel stand behind a podium or that the expert stay on the stand as the exhibit is placed on the document camera, the principle remains the same: Find a way to put your expert in the spotlight, even if it is only by asking open-ended questions.

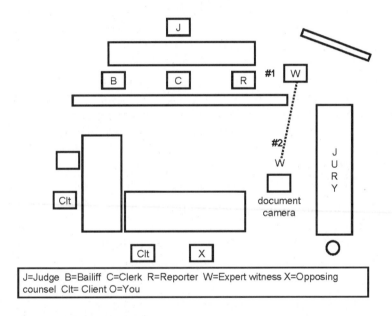

### Translating

One of the challenges in working with expert witnesses is that they use language unfamiliar to most jurors. When you prepare your expert to testify, emphasize that the expert needs to use terminology that will be understood by jurors who are unfamiliar with the field. The expert can resort to analogies to explain concepts.

Even when counsel has prepared the witness well, the expert may lapse into technical terminology. When this happens, counsel's job is to make sure that the expert translates the words into language that the jury will understand. For example, direct examination in the *Hill Moveit* case could include these exchanges:

*Q: Dr. Riley, you used the words "instrumented anthropometric dummies."
What are instrumented anthropometric dummies?*
*Q: Can you explain what you mean by a "damage pattern" to the car?*

We emphasize that you must have your expert define technical terms for the jury. The jurors must be able to clearly follow and understand the testimony or they will become frustrated that you are presenting them with what is to them gibberish and, thus, showing no respect for them in their role of ultimate decision makers. For example, while puzzling over what a term means ("Did he say 'damage pattern'? Is that the marks on the car, or all of the evidence taken as a pattern?"), a juror may miss your next three to four questions, and when he returns from his reverie, he will be lost and perhaps unable to catch up.

### Storytelling

The principles for conducting a direct examination for lay witnesses discussed in Chapter 9 should be used for direct examination of experts. The most important principle is to apply storytelling techniques so that the direct is understandable, interesting, and persuasive. Recall how Dr. Riley was qualified as an expert. The defense lawyer proceeded in a structured manner that presented Riley's scientific education, training, and employment chronologically. The testimony essentially tells the story of Riley's professional life and development. Recall that the attorney employed the funnel method of questioning, proceeding from the general to the specific in discussing the factual data, and then eliciting Dr. Riley's opinion. Applying a storytelling technique will ensure that your audience, the jury, will not get lost in following the expert's testimony.

### Keeping the Jury from Getting Lost

The challenge in direct examination of an expert is to make the testimony clear and easy to follow. There are a variety of techniques, some of which we have already discussed, that in combination can achieve this goal.

---

### Keeping the Jury from Getting Lost

- **Provide context** for the jury by asking the expert why he is testifying and stating his opinion as soon as he is qualified, but before bringing out the basis for the opinion.
- **Use natural organization** if possible. Some areas of expertise follow a set of steps in arriving at conclusions. For example, testing for the presence of cocaine involves an initial screening test to exclude non-narcotics, followed by a series of increasingly specific confirming tests. These steps provide a natural organization for your direct.
- **Create organization** if there is no natural organization. Work with the expert to create an organization to describe what she does. For instance, when discussing how an expert reaches a conclusion, have her list the five different things she does.

Organize by telling the jury about the five factors (tests, steps, and so on), applying each to the facts of the case (or explaining how they must be considered together to reach a conclusion), and arriving at her opinion.

- Provide the jury with markers, as discussed in Chapter 9, page 298. ("Dr. Jones, you've listed three things you look for in deciding whether a bullet was fired from a particular gun. I'd like to start with what you've called 'class characteristics,' and then we'll examine the other two.")
- Define terms by using analogies and examples. Have the terms and definitions on flipcharts or computer slides.
- Listen with the jury's ear. Imagine a juror listening to this expert's testimony. What is the next question following the previous answer? If you were a juror, what would you want to hear next? If an expert testifies that "the first thing I do is drop the sample in dry ice," the next two questions that follow, in either order, are, "Could you describe how you do that?" and, "Why do you do that?" If an expert says, "The residue was red," a juror would next want to ask, "What does it mean that the residue was red?"

## F. Visuals

When the subject matter is complex, the best way to make the information understandable is by using visuals. Visuals are especially valuable with an expert witness because the testimony can be technical and difficult for jurors to understand. For instance, the expert testimony may be about injuries and medical treatment, the operation of equipment, economic losses, blood spatter evidence, and so on. Visuals can assist the expert in explaining the subject matter to the jury so that it is understood. See pages 218 and 256 in Chapter 7.

In the *Hill Moveit* case, demonstrative evidence can be used by Dr. Riley, in the role of teacher, to explain and illustrate the scientific field, tests, data, and his ultimate opinion. Dr. Riley can use photographs to explain how he reconstructed the collision, as well as to show the jury how he used that data in arriving at his opinion.

### Technical Information

Technical information is daunting for many jurors. Using a visual may impart the information in a much more comprehensible way. For example, this book's accompanying website, *http://www.aspenlawschool.com/books/ berger_trialad4e*, contains trial demonstrations of expert testimony that is aided by the use of visuals. Also, in this section, we offer some illustrative visuals so that you can see what can be created to help your expert communicate to the jurors in a meaningful way.

Our website also offers visuals that are designed to clarify technical information for the jury.

### Medical Illustrations

When your case involves medical testimony, you will want to introduce a demonstrative exhibit that assists the physician in explaining his testimony to the jurors. For example, in the *Freck Point Murder* case, the pathologist could use a medical illustration of Sondra Griffith's head to show the jury where she was stabbed. MediVisuals (*http://www.medivisuals.com*) is one company that provides trial medical illustrations of all the different parts of the human body. MediVisuals has developed virtual reality visuals, such as an illustration of a brain that can be rotated 360 degrees with the aid of arrows on the visual.

With the aid of this first illustration, the medical expert can show the jury how the plaintiff suffered injuries to both the front and back of the skull.

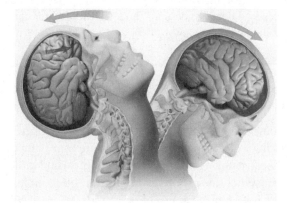

High Impact Litigation, Inc., *http://www.highimpactlit.com.*

### Animation

Computer-generated animations can be used to recreate the event and show the movement of people and things.

Legal Artworks, *http://www.legalartworks.com.*

## Models

Another very effective visual is a model. Models allow the jury to see the object in three dimensions, which gives the object real-life aspects that a photograph cannot. Models can be particularly valuable in showing how something works or happened. For instance, this large model of a handgun can be used by the expert to explain how a hammer lock would prevent accidental firing if the hammer was pulled back and then jarred, such as by dropping the gun.

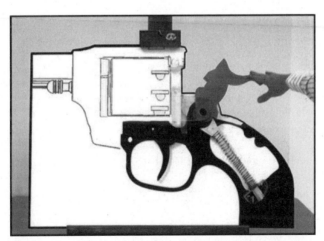

Demonstrative Evidence, Inc., *http://www.demonstrativeevidenceinc*
*.com.*

## IV.  CROSS-EXAMINATION OF EXPERTS

### A.  Preparing

#### Legal Research and a Motion to Exclude

Preparing for an effective cross-examination begins with an understanding of evidentiary law relating to expert testimony, and researching the case law on the expert's field.

While most of this chapter assumes the admissibility of expert testimony, the first line of defense against expert testimony is a motion in limine to exclude it because of noncompliance with the evidence rules and case law. For a discussion of in limine motions, see Chapter 6, pages 185 and 206-212. The exclusion of the expert's testimony usually is a favorable alternative to having to cross-examine the expert. However, there are occasions when you may conclude that you will forgo the motion to exclude the opposing party's expert, because the expert may do more good for your case than harm. This can occur when the expert is vulnerable to being thoroughly impeached on cross or gives overall support to your position, thus offering the benefit of using the opposition's expert for support.

The following is a checklist of grounds for moving to exclude the expert's testimony.

---

### CHECKLIST

#### Grounds for Excluding Expert Testimony

Counsel can consider making a motion in limine to exclude expert testimony on the following grounds (references are to the Federal Rules of Evidence).

- ☐ The witness lacks sufficient qualifications to be an expert—Rule 702.
- ☐ The subject is not beyond the common understanding of the fact finder and therefore will not assist the fact finder—Rule 702.
- ☐ The field is not sufficiently reliable—Rule 702, *Frye, Daubert.*
- ☐ The opinion would render an opinion on the law or on a witness's credibility, or dictate to the jury what decision to reach—Rule 704.
- ☐ The testimony's probative value is substantially outweighed by unfair prejudice—Rule 403.
- ☐ The testimony would be a waste of time or presentation of cumulative evidence—Rule 403.
- ☐ The testimony is irrelevant to any issue at trial—Rule 401.
- ☐ The expert lacks a basis in fact or data on which to render any opinion—Rule 703.
- ☐ The opinion is too speculative ("could have," failing to be expressed in certain terms)—Rules 401, 403.

---

You must be alert to the opposing party's expert straying too far from her particular field. This is common. An expert qualified to testify in one area will slip in an opinion on a related but distinctly different area of expertise. For instance, a collision reconstruction expert qualified to reconstruct the speed of a vehicle at impact might then slip in the opinion that the plaintiff could not have been hurt at such a low speed. Such medical testimony is clearly beyond the scope of the collision reconstructionist's expertise.

An example of a more subtle but equally inappropriate attempt to stray outside an expert's qualifications is a collision reconstruction expert who is qualified to estimate the speed of a vehicle involved in a collision based on skid marks, but instead attempts to make a speed estimate based on impact damage on the vehicle and mathematical calculations. Should this occur, you can object on the grounds that the witness is not qualified to provide such an opinion.

### Your Expert and Other Sources

Your expert is the best source for gaining an understanding of his field of expertise. Likewise, when it comes to planning a cross-examination of the other side's expert, your expert is your best resource.

After you have identified the other side's potential expert and have received discovery (opposing party's expert report), you should consult with your expert about potential areas for cross-examination. Your expert can point out areas of vulnerability in the other side's expert, such as deficiencies in qualifications, faulty testing and procedures, learned treatises expressing views contrary to those of the other side's expert, and so on. Your expert may be able to suggest ideas and insights for cross-examination. Also consider consulting other lawyers who have encountered the expert.

### Discovery and Collecting and Reading

#### Discovery

The more discovery you have of your opponent's expert, the better. Under Federal Rule of Civil Procedure 26(a)(2)(A)-(D), a party planning on calling an expert must provide the opposing party with the identity of any expert witness it may use in the trial to present evidence under Federal Rules of Evidence 702, 703, and 705. A written report that includes the expert's opinion, data, or information used to form an opinion, exhibits, qualifications, including a list of publications authored in the last ten years, a list of cases during the last four years, and a statement about compensation must also be provided to the opposing party. See our DVD on depositions in the back of our *Pretrial Advocacy* book.

#### Collecting and Reading

You will want to research and read everything the opposing expert has written or testified to that is pertinent to the subject that the expert will testify to at trial. As a result of both formal and informal discovery and investigation, you may be able to obtain a great deal of information pertinent to the expert that either supports your case theory or undercuts or impeaches the other side's expert. This can include, among other things:

- Books;
- Articles;
- Reports in other cases;
- Transcripts from prior trials;
- Depositions in other cases (indexed transcripts of trial and deposition testimony of thousands of experts are now available through online services for a fee);
- Papers presented at conferences; and
- Blogs and Internet postings of papers, articles, and videos.

## B.  Selecting Content of Cross

The objectives for expert witness cross-examination are the same as for any other witness. You want to

- obtain concessions that bolster your case theory or your expert's testimony;
- obtain concessions that undercut the other side's case theory; or
- discredit the adverse expert witness, the witness's opinions, or her versions of the facts.

### Concession-Seeking Cross-Examination

As with other witnesses, the primary goal of cross-examination should be to gain concessions—to gather facts, opinions, and inferences that the witness must concede. Expert witnesses are especially susceptible to the concession-seeking cross-examination approach covered in Chapter 10, pages 341-343. Because experts usually want to continue being retained by the legal community, many forensic experts want to maintain their credibility and will not exceed the bounds of reasonableness in their field of expertise. They want to avoid becoming readily impeachable. So, assuming that your case theory is reasonable and your experts are correct in their conclusions, and further assuming that the other party's expert is honest and qualified as an expert, you should be able to obtain some favorable concessions. Under the right circumstances, you may even be able to turn the expert to your advantage.

Where the opposing expert has an emotional attachment to your opponent's case or to a specific issue, do not expect the same degree of logical concessions. However, the expert's failure to make logical concessions may form the basis of an effective impeachment.

### Impeachment

There are nine areas of impeachment that are available for impeaching any witness, lay or expert, that were covered in Chapter 10, on pages 344-345. Here we emphasize five areas for impeachment that are applicable only to experts. Remember that the nine areas of impeachment in the checklist have equal force when used to cross-examine experts. In addition, because experts must be qualified and are allowed to render opinions and discuss inferences, cross-examination can be used to attack witnesses' credentials as well as to impeach them, for instance, by using learned treatises that reveal deficiencies both in the experts' opinions and their bases for them.

---

### CHECKLIST

#### Impeachment Topics for Cross-Examination

**All Witnesses**

- ☐ 1. Improbability
- ☐ 2. Prior inconsistent statement
- ☐ 3. Prior convictions
- ☐ 4. Lack of personal knowledge
- ☐ 5. Mental and sensory deficiencies
- ☐ 6. Bias and interest
- ☐ 7. Prior bad acts probative on untruthfulness
- ☐ 8. Contradiction
- ☐ 9. Character witness—"Have you heard . . . ?"

**Expert Witness Areas**

- ☐ 1. Qualifications
- ☐ 2. Reliability of the field
- ☐ 3. Basis for opinion
- ☐ 4. Opinion
- ☐ 5. Learned treatises

---

In the following sections, we provide examples of how to plan and conduct cross-examination to gain concessions and to impeach. However, here is one last principle before we turn to illustrations of how to plan and conduct cross-examination:

#### Danger Zone

Beware of the temptation to challenge the expert in the expert's area of expertise. The expert is trained and experienced in the field and, ordinarily, the trial lawyer has only a surface knowledge of the subject. Consequently, cross-examinations that match wits with the other side's expert are rarely fruitful, and can and commonly do lead to disastrous results. Generally, the less you let them talk, the better. Ask short, crisp leading questions, make your points, and stop. Before venturing to cross-examine within the expert's field, it is advisable to have had a prior consultation with your expert. Such a cross-examination should be entered into only with the greatest caution.

You can keep your distance from the adverse expert by concentrating on the areas where it will be easier to expose vulnerabilities, points that are outside the expert's technical expertise. This can be some of your most effective cross-examination. For examples of this type of attack, see pages 419 and 422. Alternatively, you can concentrate on gaining admissions to accepted common principles in the area of expertise.

## C.  Concession-Seeking Cross

To develop a concession-seeking cross of an expert witness, you would follow the steps outlined in Chapter 10 on cross-examination: Develop a tentative closing argument that expresses your case theory and contains the elements of how you will refute the other side's case theory, use that tentative closing argument as a guide, brainstorm to identify concessions the witness should make that will bolster your case theory, and then construct your cross so it will persuade the jury.

To illustrate how to obtain substantive information during cross-examination that supports your case theory, let's assume that you represent plaintiff Darcy Rutherford in the *Hill Moveit* case. The defendants have alleged the affirmative defense of plaintiff's intoxication being the proximate cause of her injuries. This is a complete defense barring recovery. The three elements of the intoxication defense that the defendants must prove are as follows.

1. The plaintiff was under the influence of alcohol at the time of the injury.
2. Plaintiff's intoxication caused her own injury.
3. Plaintiff was more than 50 percent comparatively at fault in causing her injuries.

Hill Moveit International Corporation employed an expert in forensic toxicology, Byron Bird, to testify in support of this intoxication defense. On direct examination, Mr. Bird testified that he is a private forensic toxicologist consultant and has served in that capacity for the past 10 years. For 15 years before establishing his own consulting business, he was a forensic toxicologist for the Major State Toxicology Laboratory. Mr. Bird testified that throughout his career he has performed more than 35,000 blood analyses for drugs and alcohol. He stated that he has been qualified as an expert in the effects of alcohol impairment on human cognition and motor skills, and that he has testified as a forensic toxicologist more than 1,000 times in the State of Major and federal courts regarding alcohol findings in blood.

Mr. Bird testified that he reviewed the police reports, the medic reports, Darcy Rutherford's medical records and laboratory test results, and related data. He also stated that he is familiar with Ruston Medical Center, as well as Major State Toxicology Laboratory toxicological methods and protocols for analyzing blood samples. He testified that while the state toxicology laboratory uses a high-precision gas chromatography method that enables the forensic toxicologists in the lab to certify blood alcohol test results to a high degree of certainty, the medical center uses a different method—enzymatic testing of the patient's blood serum to detect alcohol. Mr. Bird testified that he compared the two methods and concluded that the enzymatic analysis is accurate and reliable. Also, he testified that the enzymatic testing methods are based on sound scientific principles and have gained general acceptance in the medical and scientific communities.

Mr. Bird testified that he reviewed the test control data for the particular analyzer machine used by the medical center to test Ms. Rutherford's blood serum, and found the analyzer machine to be properly calibrated and in working order. The test results showed that Ms. Rutherford's serum alcohol concentration level was 70 to 124 mg/dl; applying the generally accepted scientific conversion to whole blood measurements, the range would be between .06 and .10. Based on this range, Mr. Bird rendered this opinion:

> My opinion, to a reasonable degree of scientific probability, is that Ms. Rutherford's ability to drive a motor vehicle was likely impaired as a result of alcohol intoxication. At this level, a driver has reduced coordination, diminished ability to track moving objects, more difficulty steering, and compromised ability to respond to emergencies.

You represent Darcy Rutherford. Plaintiff's case theory is that Darcy Rutherford was not intoxicated, she did not cause her own injury, and the Ruston Medical Center test results are unreliable. The best way to prepare to cross-examine an expert is to consult with your experts. Your main expert is Dr. Varda Nevins, who is a professor of medicine at University of Major Medical School and the director of the Emergency Department at Ruston Medical Center. Dr. Nevins has told you that the enzymatic testing done at the medical center is not appropriate for later forensic use in criminal or civil proceedings. Moreover, because of the trauma to Ms. Rutherford's body, the patient's metabolic and physiological processes at the time she entered the hospital rendered the reading unreliable. The high buildup of lactic acid in her blood due to the deprivation of oxygen would lead to false-positive elevated alcohol readings. Trauma also produces elevations in the serum concentration of the enzyme LDH, which can also cause the overestimation of alcohol in the blood serum. Dr. Nevins has also told you that the state toxicology lab does not use the enzymatic tests because they are not reliable in some circumstances, particularly those involving trauma. Rather, the state lab tests with gas chromatography.

### Brainstorming for Concessions

You have mapped out your closing argument to meet the defense contention that your client was intoxicated and she should be barred from recovery. You will argue that the defense has the burden of proving she was intoxicated, and that no reliable evidence proves that she was intoxicated. You will point to the testimony of Dr. Nevins and her conclusion that no reliable scientific evidence supports the proposition the patient Rutherford was intoxicated. You will also argue that the opinions of the defense expert, Mr. Bird, are not worthy of belief.

The next step is to brainstorm for concessions that will support your case theory. You ask yourself: "What factual concession(s) must this witness concede or face having his answer labeled a lie, mistaken, or preposterous?" The answer to your question will be those factual points where the witness must provide the concession, because you can either prove the fact, or draw the inference from the proven facts or common sense. Just a few of the concessions that Mr. Bird must make are included in the following illustration.

---

**Expert Witness**

### Concession-Seeking Cross-Examination
### The *Hill Moveit Personal Injury* Case

*Q:* Mr. Bird, the State of Major Toxicology Laboratory uses gas chromatography testing, correct?

*Q.* What is gas chromatography?

*Q:* Is gas chromatography highly precise?

*Q:* If Ms. Rutherford's blood had been tested with gas chromatography, the results would be reliable, right?

*Q:* The State of Major Toxicology Laboratory does not use enzymatic testing, does it?

*Q:* The state laboratory does not use enzymatic testing because it's not as accurate as gas chromatography, correct?

*Q:* Blood-sample testing at Ruston Medical Center is for the purpose of medical assessment and treatment?

*Q:* What is forensic testing of a blood sample?

*Q:* Blood sample testing at the medical center is not designed to comply with requirements for forensic testing, is it?

*Q:* Blood sample testing at the medical center is not designed to comply with requirements for civil or criminal proceedings, is it?

*Q:* Lactic acid will build up in the blood when someone is oxygen deprived?

*Q:* High concentrations of lactic acid in the bloodstream could lead the analyzer machine to falsely find more alcohol than was actually present in the blood?

*Q:* Trauma to the body also produces elevations in the serum concentration of the enzyme LDH?

*Q:* LDH can cause overestimation of alcohol in the blood?

*Q:* Mr. Bird, Ruston Medical Center does not attempt to comply with requirements of the Major administrative code for quantitative analysis of blood samples, is that right? [Questioning continues to describe what the administrative code requires.]

*Q:* Mr. Bird, you understand the term *chain of custody,* correct?

*Q:* You have received training on the importance of a chain of custody as it relates to a blood sample and testing?

*Q:* Tell us about that training.

*Q:* You would agree that it is important to the integrity of blood alcohol testing that a proper chain of custody be maintained?

> *Q:* The reason that chain of custody is important is that it ensures that the right sample is tested, true?
>
> *Q:* Chain of custody is also important because it ensures that the actual results of those tests are reported, correct?
>
> *Q:* Mr. Byrd, you are aware that the chain of custody for Darcy Rutherford's blood sample is unknown, right?

Note that this area of inquiry is both supportive of your case theory and a method of discrediting the witness.

## D. Discrediting

Discrediting or exposing weaknesses in an adverse expert witness or in the witness's testimony is a challenging task. Realistically, you will seldom destroy the adverse expert witness. Rather, you may be able to weaken the expert's credibility or persuasiveness with the jury. Here, we discuss and provide examples of categories that can guide you in cross-examining the expert witness. First, you can use any of the standard nine areas available to cross-examine any witness, expert or not. Then, we will explore the five other categories applicable to experts:

1. Lack of qualifications to testify as an expert witness,
2. Unreliability of the scientific area,
3. Deficiencies in the procedure and factual data used,
4. Limits and problems with the opinion, and
5. Learned treatises.

When you plan the content of cross-examination, think about these as five potential areas you might explore, but be mindful that a successful cross-examination can be based on any one of these and the nine standard categories. Also, throughout this section there is a continuum between admissibility and weight. For example, the same attack on qualifications by which you seek to exclude the expert's testimony will, if your objection to admissibility is overruled, serve as the basis for an attack in cross-examination geared to diminishing the weight the jury should give the expert's opinion.

> For a cross-examination designed to discredit an expert, watch the cross-examination of the plaintiffs' expert in the *Freck Point* trial demonstration movie on the website *http://www.aspenlawschool.com/books/berger_trialad4e.*

### Nine Standard Impeachment Areas

As you plan cross of an expert, consider the nine standard impeachment areas that are available for all witnesses. For instance, in a product liability suit against the manufacturer of a ladder, a cross-examination of an expert could be framed around the expert's lack of personal knowledge if the expert relied on a written description of the ladder and testing rather than personally examining the ladder and conducting tests.

As an illustration, suppose you are considering discrediting the expert by exposing the witness's bias. How much compensation is the expert receiving in the case? If the expert witness's fee is unreasonable based on the work done, the witness may be biased. Or, instead of monetary compensation, there may be an exchange of services. But keep in mind that jurors do not expect experts to work for free. If an expert did work for free, she would be labeled as biased, as someone promoting some cause. More significant is whether the expert may be a professional expert who testifies either just for plaintiffs or for defendants. The expert may be a professional expert for a particular client—a law firm, government, or industry. If so, the expert may have testified in many cases, providing an identical or a similar opinion. The more her business, or at least a significant percentage of her income, involves expert testimony, the greater the particular expert's motive to win for this client with an eye to getting the next client.

For example, in the *Hill Moveit* case, the defense retains the expert Dr. Darvus Juno, who consistently has been retained by manufacturing companies in product liability cases and always finds that the plaintiff's negligence, not a manufacturer defect, caused the collision. In the following example, we illustrate how you can construct a series of questions tailored to establish bias. To plan the cross, you prepare a tentative closing argument that you, as defense counsel, would like to deliver. From this tentative closing, you can foresee the points you wish to obtain in cross-examination.

---

### Tentative Closing Argument

#### Expert Witness Standard Impeachment Area: Bias
#### The *Hill Moveit Personal Injury* Case

"Dr. Juno is what you might call a professional defense witness. He has testified in 150 cases—all for defendant manufacturing companies. He has never once found fault with a defendant's actions. How believable is this type of witness? Recall that I asked him about the 150 cases in which he appeared as an expert witness for defendants. Ten different products were involved that were manufactured by 30 different manufacturing companies located throughout the United States. But Dr. Juno never found even one defendant at fault. How much is his opinion worth?"

Now, using this tentative closing argument as your guide to the points you wish to include in cross-examination concerning bias, you might ask the following cross-examination questions.

---

**Expert Witness**

### Standard Impeachment Area: Bias
### The *Hill Moveit Personal Injury* Case

*Q:* You have testified in other cases where defendants were represented by the law firm of McDermott & Stewart, haven't you?

*Q:* You have done so more than once, correct?

*Q:* You have appeared in product liability cases as an expert witness for defendants represented by McDermott & Stewart on six or seven cases?

*Q:* Besides those six or seven cases, you also testified in other trials?

*Q:* In fact, in the past ten years, you've testified in approximately 150 cases?

*Q:* In each of those 150 cases, you gave an opinion about whether a product was defectively manufactured?

*Q:* In each of those 150 cases, you were called as a witness for the defendant, right?

*Q:* You have never testified as a plaintiff's expert witness, have you?

*Q:* In each of those 150 cases, it was alleged by the plaintiffs that there was a design defect?

*Q:* But in each of those 150 cases, you testified for the defense that there was no design defect?

*Q:* In each of those 150 cases, you were retained by the defense, correct?

*Q:* In each of those 150 cases, the defense paid you for your time?

*Q:* They paid you for your analysis time?

*Q:* You are paid $300 per hour for your analysis time, is that right?

*Q:* They paid you for your deposition time?

*Q:* They paid you for your courtroom time?

*Q:* You are paid $400 per hour for testimony time, correct?

*Q:* As a result of those 150 cases, you have declared over $335,000 in income?

---

Notice how the example above ties bias with the type of self-interest we've discussed when being a forensic expert is the expert's business. A word of caution: Do your homework well. Find out how many total cases Dr. Juno has consulted on. If it's 150 or so, you are fine. If it's a thousand, be careful—on redirect, the expert might testify, *"I found design defects in more than 800 cases and told my clients that. Those did not go to trial."*

### Qualifications

Your purpose in cross-examination is designed to persuade the jury to give little weight to the expert's testimony. Your efforts at keeping the expert off the stand will already have taken place during an in limine motion or in voir dire during direct examination.

---

### Expert Witness: Qualifications of an Expert

#### An Area of Vulnerability for an Expert

The following are some areas where the expert may be vulnerable to a cross-examination designed to discredit the expert.

- The expert is *deficient* in education, experience, or other areas generally associated with qualifying the particular type of expert.
- There are *inaccuracies* in credentials (a law enforcement officer claims to have a master's degree in biology, but had only a bachelor's degree).
- The expert *lacks* credentials compared to your expert. For example, the witness lacks practical experience in laboratory work, whereas your expert works in a lab. This approach sets up closing argument that contrasts the two expert's qualifications.
- The credentials are *exaggerated or hollow* (the expert belongs to professional organizations that require only the payment of dues to belong).
- The expert is testifying *outside the witness's area of expertise* (the expert is knowledgeable about respiratory physiology, but has little experience in neurophysiology).

---

### Reliability of the Expert's Field

Even if you do not present your own expert in the same field, you can attack the reliability of your opponent's expert's field. Or, you may cross-examine the expert on the subject if you intend to offer an expert in the field who will testify that those in that field should not venture the type of opinion the other side's expert intends to render.

---

### Expert Witness: Unreliability

#### An Area of Vulnerability for an Expert

Some components of a discipline that may provide fruitful topics to explore on cross-examination are as follows:

- The training that persons in the field have ("There is no particular training required to do what you do?" "No degree required?" "And there's no certification or licensing?");
- The imprecise nature of the tests and procedures used ("So, you consider ten factors, none of which has more weight than any other?" "Then you decide if there's a match?" "But your field has no set standards for how to assess those

---

factors?" "And you do not need all ten factors to find a match?" "You just know it's a match?");

- The unreliability of instruments used;
- The field's failure to gain acceptance by other professional disciplines.

Cross-examination regarding the unreliable nature of the field can convince the jury to adopt a skeptical frame of mind about the expert's results and opinion, thus giving the opinion little or no weight.

### Procedures and Factual Data

Cross-examination assailing the data or procedures used by the expert challenges the reliability and trustworthiness of that expert's opinion. In this regard, urging the jury to discount your opposing party's expert opinion because of deficiencies in the underlying basis for the expert's opinion is often the strongest point you can make. It also allows you to attack the expert's opinion without actually taking on the expert. As you recall, an expert relies on three kinds of data: data created by the expert through experiments and investigation, information that is given to the expert about the case, and data prepared by others and relied on by experts in the field.

## Expert Witness: Procedures and Data

### Areas of Vulnerability for an Expert

The expert's opinion may be vulnerable in the following areas:

- The *time* the expert had or used in analyzing the data (the doctor examined the patient for ten minutes; psychiatrist did not examine criminal defendant until ten weeks after the crime);
- *Information was incomplete* (the engineer did not receive all the blueprints);
- Expert is making an *incorrect assumption about the data* (the expert assumes that the core soil sample he was given was from "quadrant 4"; you will present evidence that the sample was from "quadrant 3," which invalidates the expert's calculation);
- Expert received *faulty or biased data* (much of the data is from an interested party);
- Expert's procedures or experiments for analyzing the data are *faulty, unreliable, left undone, or wrong* (a metallurgist failed to heat the metal to the appropriate temperature).

The concession-seeking cross-examination of Mr. Bird at pages 414-415 serves as an illustration of a cross-examination designed to convince the jury that the expert's opinion is faulty. The basis for his opinion was an unreliable and unscientific enzymatic test, and, further, the samples from your client may have been switched or contaminated. Note that we assume here that the medical reports for Darcy Rutherford contain the alcohol reading, and that is admissible because the hospitals' doctors relied on the enzymatic reading. Fed. R. Evid. 703.

Another technique in this area involves asking the expert witness either to assume additional facts or to substitute different facts that you know will be presented at trial. You can then ask the adverse expert whether different or additional facts might change the expert's opinion. If the expert answers in the affirmative, the expert's opinion is weakened because the expert reached an opinion without all the facts or with inaccurate information. If, on the other hand, the witness is reluctant to change or modify her testimony no matter how you change the facts, it may become apparent to the jury that the witness is biased, inflexible, and really advocates an unrealistic position.

### The Expert's Opinion

The most difficult area to explore when cross-examining an adverse expert witness is the expert's opinion. Getting an expert to concede that his opinion is wrong is improbable. When the cross-examiner ventures into the expert's field, as will happen when the examiner challenges the expert's opinion, the cross-examiner enters into perilous territory.

Nevertheless, it is possible for a well-planned cross-examination to be effective if it follows one of the following four lines of inquiry.

---

### Expert Witness: Expert Opinion

#### An Area of Vulnerability for an Expert

The expert's opinion may be vulnerable in the following areas:

- Uncovering *inconsistencies;*
- Getting the expert to take an *extreme position;*
- Establishing that the opinion is a matter of the *expert's judgment,* not unalterable principles; and
- Establishing that the *opinion is limited.*

---

#### Inconsistencies

You may be able to expose inconsistencies in the expert's opinion by showing the expert's opinion is at odds with the expert's prior opinion (as expressed in interrogatories, deposition testimony, published articles, and so on). Or you can show that the factual data in the case or in similar cases, the literature in the field, or the expert's own notes and records in the case are inconsistent.

#### Extreme Position

The second cross-examination technique is to make the expert go to an extreme in defending her opinion. In the following illustration, we outline the type of questions you might plan as defense counsel in the *Hill Moveit* case. Keep in mind that the illustration represents your first questions, on which you would then need to build follow-up questions.

---

**Expert Witness**

Extreme Position: Attacking the Expert's Opinion
The *Hill Moveit Personal Injury* Case

*Q:* You stated during your direct examination, and I quote you, "Enzymatic serum testing is generally accepted in the medical community and is an accurate and reliable method of testing," correct?

*A:* Yes.

*Q:* It is as reliable and accurate as gas chromatography?

*A:* Yes.

*Q:* If you had the option of either enzymatic serum testing or gas chromatography, you would select enzymatic testing?

*A:* Yes.

---

Another line of questions would lead Mr. Bird to defend his opinion that the enzymatic test reading was accurate despite Ms. Rutherford's elevated levels of LDH and lactic acid. Recall that your expert told you that these will lead to high false-positive readings. You could ask Mr. Bird to assume higher and higher levels of LDH and lactic acid, and pose this question with each higher level: *"Would you change your opinion that the test's reading would be accurate?"*

### Expert's Judgment

A third line of inquiry is to show that the expert's opinion is a matter of judgment based on many factors and not a matter of immutable doctrine. This will be particularly useful if you call an expert who has come to a different conclusion. For example, when representing the plaintiff, you can seek a concession from Dr. Riley that whether the collision could be reconstructed in the *Hill Moveit* case is a matter of judgment for an expert. You could venture further to obtain the concession from Dr. Riley that the plaintiff's expert could reasonably come to the conclusion that there was insufficient evidence to permit the reconstruction of the collision.

### Opinion Is Limited

The fourth line of inquiry is to establish that after extensive qualifications and detailed tests, the expert is not really saying very much concerning the case. To illustrate, let's examine the *Shooting Homicide* case.

> ### The *Shooting Homicide* Case
>
> Imagine a murder prosecution where the defendant is accused of shooting the victim with a handgun. The murder weapon has not been found. The defendant does own several guns. The defense is misidentification. When the defendant is arrested, a pair of his gloves are seized by the police and sent for laboratory analysis. At trial, an expert witness for the prosecution testifies on direct examination that a Neutron Activation Analysis test revealed traces of gunpowder residue on the gloves.

Imagine now that as defense counsel in the *Shooting Homicide* case, you cross-examine the expert to limit her opinion.

### Expert Witness

#### Attacking the Expert's Opinion as Limited
#### The *Shooting Homicide* Case

*Q:* This test doesn't show what specific weapon was used?
*A:* No.
*Q:* It doesn't show what caliber weapon?
*A:* No.
*Q:* It doesn't show the type of ammunition?
*A:* No.
*Q:* It doesn't show how many shots were fired?
*A:* No.
*Q:* It doesn't show when the shots were fired?
*A:* No.
*Q:* It doesn't show what the shots were fired at?
*A:* No.
*Q:* It doesn't show who fired the shots?
*A:* No.

### Learned Treatise

Unique to the examination of expert witnesses is the use of learned treatises. Federal Rule of Evidence 803(18) provides that learned treatises are not excluded under the hearsay rule. Under this rule, an expert may be cross-examined concerning the content of learned treatises if

- it is called to the attention of the witness on cross, or it was relied on by the witness on direct; and
- it is reliable authority established by (a) admission on cross, (b) judicial notice, or (c) testimony by another expert.

After the treatise is admitted into evidence, it may be read to the jury, but it is not admitted as an exhibit. The information read is substantive evidence. This allows a lawyer to use learned treatises in dynamic ways. In cross-examination, the lawyer can employ an opinion in an authoritative publication to contradict the opinion of the witness under examination.

Let's return to the *Hill Moveit* case, where you represent the plaintiff, Darcy Rutherford. The defense has called Mr. Bird to testify that the enzymatic test reading for Ms. Rutherford's blood serum was reliable, and that from that reading the expert could render an opinion that Ms. Rutherford was impaired by alcohol at the time of the collision. You want to rely on the views expressed by Barry Purcell in his article in the *Journal of Pediatric Gastroenterology.* Mr. Purcell's view corresponds with the view of your expert, Dr. Varda Nevins. You plan your cross-examination of Mr. Bird by drafting the following tentative closing argument.

---

### Tentative Closing Argument

#### Expert Witness Standard Impeachment Area: Bias
#### The *Hill Moveit Personal Injury* Case

"The eminent Dr. Varda Nevins, director of Ruston Medical Center's Emergency Department and a professor at the University of Major's Medical School, told you that the blood serum test conducted by the hospital was unscientific and unreliable. She explained to you that the trauma to Darcy's body would lead to an unreliable reading. Another expert, Barry Purcell, also supports this opinion that trauma can lead to false-positive results. Even the plaintiff's witness, Dr. Riley, described Barry Purcell as an authority on blood sample testing. Recall what Barry Purcell wrote in his article on enzymatic procedures, and I quote: 'Certain metabolic disturbances such as lactic acidosis create problems when automated enzymatic assays are used, which may lead to false-positive test results.'"

---

Even though Dr. Riley will disagree with Barry Purcell's opinion, at least you can predict that Dr. Riley will concede that Barry Purcell's article is authoritative and that Mr. Purcell's opinion is in agreement with your expert's.

---

### Expert Witness

#### Learned Treatise
#### The *Hill Moveit Personal Injury* Case

Cross-examine Dr. Riley on a learned treatise as follows:

Q: Dr. Riley, are you familiar with the current literature concerning the enzymatic and gas chromatographic procedures?

*continued* ▶

> *Q:* I noticed from your latest article in the *Journal of Clinical Toxicology* that you cite the article "Endogenous Ethanol Production in a Child with Short Gut Syndrome," published in the *Journal of Pediatric Gastroenterology,* written by Barry Purcell and A.W. Jones, correct?
>
> *Q:* Dr. Riley, would it be fair to say that Barry Purcell's article is an authoritative source on enzymatic and gas chromatographic procedures?
>
> *Q:* Barry Purcell's article is relied on by forensic toxicologists such as yourself, correct?
>
> *Q:* Doctor, I'm going to place a page from that article on the document camera so you can read along with me from Barry Purcell's article that we've been discussing. The article states: *"There are important differences between gas chromatography and enzymatic procedures, which have an impact on this case. Gas chromatography (GC) is the preferred method because of its higher selectivity for ethanol, which allows positive identification by comparison of retention time with known standards. Mass spectral analysis would definitely prove the presence of ethanol. Enzymatic assays are less specific than GC for the analysis of ethanol. For example, both n-propanol and isopropanol are good substrates for ADH. Certain metabolic disturbances such as lactic acidosis create problems when automated enzymatic assays are used, which may lead to false-positive test results."*
>
> *Q:* Do you subscribe to the position by Barry Purcell that certain metabolic disturbances, such as lactic acidosis, create problems when automated enzymatic assays are used, which may lead to false-positive test results?

## E. Structuring Cross

The best approach is a concession-seeking cross-examination. This is especially true for expert witnesses, because of the hazardous nature of efforts to discredit an expert and to contest an expert's opinions. During cross-examination of an adverse expert witness, you can get portions of learned treatises that are supportive of your case theory read into evidence. Therefore, because a concession-seeking cross is most likely to be fruitful, it is best to begin your cross-examination with this approach. If it succeeds, perhaps by even turning the witness to your advantage, you can forgo discrediting the witness.

Another reason to begin cross-examination by gaining admissions is that, generally, at the outset of cross the witness will be more obliging. To foster the expert's cooperativeness, trial counsel should be courteous and nonconfrontational. Once challenged, the expert may well become combative and less likely to grant concessions. See Chapter 10, pages 361-362.

## F. Conducting Cross

The techniques for conducting cross-examination of lay witnesses also apply to expert witnesses. Controlling the witness, however, can be even more problematic when dealing with an adverse expert witness. See Chapter 10, pages 362-364.

The expert has a point of view and opinions to express. The skilled expert will advocate for those views and opinions if given any chance. The problem is compounded by the fact that many experts have extensive experience in the witness chair. Some of them have more courtroom time than the attorneys trying the case.

The witness may evade your questions, or jump from giving quick answers to your questions to lecturing you. Remain courteous and calm. Keep your ego out of your cross-examination. Do not try to show everyone that you know as much as, if not more than, the expert. Just focus on obtaining information and you will be fine.

Choose a few points to establish in your cross-examination of the adverse expert witness, and then know when to stop, particularly if the cross-examination has produced a favorable concession.

## V. ETHICAL CONCERNS

The ethical concerns for expert witnesses in direct and cross-examination are generally the same ones that pertain to lay witnesses. See Chapter 9, pages 331-334, and Chapter 10, page 375.

Be aware that the circumstances that lead to the expert serving as an expert in the case may create an environment where the expert is formulating testimony to meet a specific need. Whether the expert is being paid for his time or is a treating physician with a relationship with his patient, be cognizant of the potential for the expert to change his testimony based on his perception of what the attorney wants to hear.

Here, we summarize the applicable ethical principles and ABA Model Rules of Professional Conduct.

---

### Ethical Rules Pertaining to Direct and Cross-Examination of Expert Witnesses: Summary

#### ABA Model Rules of Professional Conduct

**Direct Examination**

Coaching: Model Rule of Professional Conduct 3.3(a)(3) provides that a lawyer is prohibited from offering false evidence. Under Rule 3.4(b), an attorney shall "not falsify evidence, counsel or assist a witness to testify falsely. . . ."

False Evidence: Model Rule of Professional Conduct 3.3(a)(3) provides that "a lawyer shall not knowingly offer evidence that the lawyer knows to be false. If a lawyer, the lawyer's client, or a witness called by the lawyer, has offered material evidence and the lawyer comes to know of its falsity, the lawyer shall take reasonable remedial measures. . . ." Rules for defense counsel in a criminal case may differ, including a

*continued* ▶

requirement that counsel continue to represent the defendant as long as counsel does not know the defendant's testimony is false.

### Cross-Examination

**Irrelevant or Inadmissible:** Model Rule of Professional Conduct 3.4(e) provides that "a lawyer shall not in trial, allude to any matter that the lawyer does not reasonably believe is relevant or that will not be supported by admissible evidence, assert personal knowledge of facts in issue except when testifying as a witness. . . ." Under Rule 3.4(e), counsel should not inject irrelevant or inadmissible evidence during cross.

**False Evidence:** Model Rule of Professional Conduct 3.3(a)(3) provides that "a lawyer shall not knowingly offer evidence that the lawyer knows to be false. If a lawyer, the lawyer's client, or a witness called by the lawyer, has offered material evidence and the lawyer comes to know of its falsity, the lawyer shall take reasonable remedial measures. . . ." Under Rule 3.4(e), counsel should not seek false evidence during cross.

## CHECKLIST: EXPERTS

### Expert Direct Examination

*Content*

- ☐ The direct examination of the expert advances the case theory.
- ☐ The direct examination elicits evidence that supports elements of the legal theory (claim or defense or counterclaim).

*Components of an Expert's Direct Examination*

The direct effectively covers these five components:

- ☐ The expert's qualifications,
- ☐ Reliability of the field of expertise,
- ☐ Factual basis supporting the expert's opinion,
- ☐ Counters the other side's attack, and
- ☐ The expert's opinions.

*Conducting the Direct*

Counsel should do the following:

- ☐ Put the expert center stage and enable the expert to teach the jury (assuming a good expert);
- ☐ Have the expert testify in understandable terms and, when necessary, seek translations of technical terminology;
- ☐ Provide the expert with exhibits and technology that allow the expert to visually explain findings and opinions to the jury; and
- ☐ Utilize storytelling techniques to make the expert's testimony understandable, interesting, and persuasive.

*Ethical Boundaries*

Counsel should ensure that:

- ☐ The direct examination does not offer evidence that counsel knows to be false.
- ☐ Counsel remedies the situation if the witness introduces false evidence.

**Expert Cross-Examination**

*Excluding the Testimony*

As an alternative to cross-examination, counsel should make a motion to exclude the expert's testimony.

*Preparation*

Counsel prepares well for the cross-examination by

- ☐ consulting with her own expert;
- ☐ obtaining full discovery; and
- ☐ researching and reading the expert's published work, reports, transcripts, and other pertinent literature in the field.

*Content*

Counsel should ensure that

- ☐ the cross-examination serves the primary purpose of advancing counsel's case theory or undercutting the other side's case theory,
- ☐ the cross seeks concessions supporting counsel's case theory or undercutting the other side's case theory,
- ☐ the cross-examination serves the secondary purpose of impeachment, and
- ☐ counsel's impeachment cross explores one of the 14 areas of impeachment.

*Construction*

Counsel should prepare the following:

- ☐ Cross-examination that flows smoothly and is understandable;
- ☐ Questions that are framed appropriately—almost always leading, sometimes anticipatory or accusatory under special circumstances, and seldom, if ever, interrogatory;
- ☐ Short and comprehensible questions;
- ☐ Effectively sequenced questions, using this order:
  - Concessions first,
  - Topical and/or chronological, and
  - Finishing on a high note.
- ☐ Clearly labeled transitions ("Now let's talk about . . .").

*Character*

- ☐ Cross-examiner should appear as a sincere seeker of truth who shows courtesy and professionalism toward the witness.

*Control*

- ☐ Counsel should control the witness using Irving Younger's Ten Commandments and vary the approach only when counsel has good reason to do so.

*continued* ▶

1. Be brief.
2. Use plain words and short questions.
3. Leading questions only.
4. Be prepared—know the answer.
5. Listen to the answer.
6. Don't quarrel with the witness.
7. Don't ask the witness for an explanation.
8. Don't repeat the direct examination.
9. Limit examination—avoid too many questions.
10. Persuade during closing, not cross-examination.

☐ Counsel uses control techniques.
- Secure an agreement.
- Repeat the question.
- Ask the witness to repeat the question.
- Become more confrontational.
- Palm-toward-witness "stop" gesture.

*Impeachment*

☐ Counsel should successfully impeach the witness and/or witness's testimony.
- Expert witness areas:
  1. Qualifications,
  2. Reliability of the field,
  3. Basis for opinion,
  4. Opinion, and
  5. Learned treatises.

*Ethical Concerns*

☐ Counsel should not allude to matter that trial counsel cannot reasonably believe is relevant or that won't be supported by admissible evidence.

# JURY INSTRUCTIONS
## The Jury's Law

*"Ladies and Gentlemen: I will take a few moments now to give you some initial instructions about this case and about your duties as jurors. At the end of the trial I will give you further instructions. I may also give you instructions during the trial. Unless I specifically tell you otherwise, all such instructions—both those I give you now and those I give you later—are equally binding on you and must be followed."*

        **—Model Civil Jury Instructions**,
        Eighth Circuit District Courts (2008)

*"'We would like clarification of the term "reasonable doubt" . . . ' the jury wrote to U.S. District Judge Reggie Walton on the eighth day of deliberations. 'Is it necessary for the government to present evidence that it is not humanly possible for someone not to recall an event in order to find guilt beyond a reasonable doubt?'"*

        **—Jury in the I. Lewis "Scooter" Libby Trial**
        (verdict delivered Mar. 6, 2007), Jury

Notes, Doc. 311 (Mar. 2, 2007), United
States v. Libby, 1:05-cr-00394-RBW
(D.D.C. 2007)

## I. OVERVIEW

From the jury's perspective, the jury instructions are the law. Because your proposed instructions are the embodiment of the legal theory component of your
case theory, it is imperative that the court adopt them so the court's instructions
contain that legal theory.

The judge will read the instructions to the jury at the end of the case, either
just before or after closing argument, depending on the rules or customs in the
jurisdiction. As discussed in Chapter 3 (page 29), early in your trial preparation and formulation of a case theory, you will have researched the law, particularly the pattern jury instructions for your jurisdiction. The development of
a case theory begins by determining what law governs the case, and the jury
instructions, which is the only law the jury will know; this is the logical place to
start. You will design the presentation of your case around your legal theory as
expressed in your drafted proposed instructions. Recall our earlier discussion of
the integration of language and concepts from jury instructions in direct examination (pages 313-315). In Chapter 13, Closing Argument, you will learn about
the paramount importance of jury instructions in summation.

There are three points in time when you concentrate on drafting and arguing
jury instructions.

- **Pretrial:** First, you should draft proposed jury instructions before the trial
  begins to guide the development of your case theory.
- **Other Side's Proposed Instructions:** Second, you focus on instructions
  during the trial when you examine opposing counsel's proposed
  instructions. You either revise your instructions or plan exceptions
  to instructions (objections to the court's tentative instructions) and
  arguments on instructions.
- **Court's Instructions:** The third point occurs at or near the conclusion
  of the evidence, when the court finalizes the instructions it will give the
  jury. By this time the judge may have drafted a tentative set of instructions
  independently, and then will have compared the proposed instructions
  that each counsel submits. Before finalizing the instructions, most judges
  conduct a hearing during which they allow counsels' arguments and
  exceptions. Then, the judge finalizes the court's instructions that will be
  read to the jury.

In this chapter, we provide a comprehensive coverage of jury instructions.
You will learn how to research and draft proposed instructions, and how to

respond to the other side's proposed instructions. We explore the presentation and argument regarding jury instructions and ethical responsibilities pertaining to jury instructions. Although we are mindful of distinctions in procedures and formats throughout jurisdictions, we have included representative examples of some jury instructions.

## II.  DRAFTING PROPOSED JURY INSTRUCTIONS

Drafting proposed jury instructions that the trial judge is likely to adopt requires you to do the following:

- Thoroughly prepare,
- Write and organize instructions properly,
- Be guided by the legal theory,
- Correctly state the law, and
- Be guided by the factual theory.

### A.  Preparation

#### Procedures and Practices

In your preparation, you should research the following:

- Court procedures and practices,
- Deadlines for serving and filing instructions, and
- Procedures for objecting to and arguing instructions.

#### Pattern Jury Instructions

Counsel must research and analyze the controlling law, such as the legal principles reflected in statutes or case law that will form the basis for your proposed instruction. Read the cases in which a specific instruction has been approved. In most jurisdictions, counsel must cite authority when submitting proposed jury instructions that are original or modified pattern instructions.

Pattern jury instructions are standard, court-approved instructions that have been published. Pattern instructions exist for many substantive civil claims, crimes, and defenses. Most of the trial topics for which you will need instructions, such as credibility of witnesses, burden of proof, and verdict forms, are found in pattern instructions. You should consult your jurisdiction and others for applicable pattern instructions.

Pattern instructions, promulgated in the 1930s, ensure uniform, accurate, and understandable statements of law. Experienced attorneys and judges as well as academics who serve on jury instruction committees, draft and periodically update the pattern instructions. Generally, these instructions are regarded as models, and are rarely found objectionable in their content. Therefore, most judges prefer pattern instructions to ones specifically created for a particular case, because pattern instructions are rarely reversed on appeal. Pattern instructions also expedite the preparation of instructions because they save on research and drafting time.

Pattern instructions are not infallible, as we illustrate later in this chapter. Counsel should scrutinize them for misstatements of law as they pertain to your specific case.

### Briefing

If you wish to persuade the court to adopt a particularly important instruction that varies from the language in a pattern instruction or that is completely new, consider submitting a brief in support of your proposed instruction.

Because a jury instruction can be the heart of the case, it is worth the effort to submit a trial brief. For example, suppose that you represent the defendant in a prosecution for possession of narcotics. The defendant contends that he did not know that the substance was a narcotic. Your legal theory is that "knowledge of the narcotic content is a requirement for the crime of possession." You propose such an instruction. If the court gives the instruction you propose, your client, if believed, will be acquitted. The court, however, may not agree with your legal theory and refuse to inform the jury of the very existence of this defense. Because of the court's refusal to give your proposed knowledge instruction, your client could be convicted. The seriousness of the trial judge's refusal to give this jury instruction issue is evident. If the instruction is refused and the court is found mistaken on appeal, reversal of the conviction is certain.

## B.  Writing and Organizing Proposed Instructions

Jury instructions are often so poorly worded and organized that as far as jurors are concerned they are incomprehensible and might as well be written in a foreign language. You want the jurors to understand the law when the judge delivers the instructions to them. To accomplish this ultimate goal, you should strive to draft your proposed instructions in understandable terms that a jury can comprehend. In particular, your proposed jury instructions should be based on your legal and factual theories, and these theories should be clearly expressed.

Using pattern instructions is one way to achieve clarity and comprehensibility in drafting jury instructions. Look for applicable pattern instructions that also fulfill your desire for understandable instructions. To illustrate how to use a pattern instruction, assume you are the attorney representing the plaintiff in what has been called the *Speeding Train* case.

---

### The *Speeding Train* Case

A dense fog blanketed the area. You represent an injured passenger who claims that even though the train he was riding in observed the speed limit of 90 miles per hour at an intersection, the train conductor nevertheless should have slowed down because of the weather conditions at the time.

Plaintiff's attorney, after examining the facts and the law about speeding trains, would then proceed to locate any pattern instruction that may be applicable. Plaintiff might offer a proposed pattern instruction as illustrated.

---

**Pattern Jury Instruction**

### The Speeding Train Case

*Plaintiff's Proposed Jury Instruction No. 5 Speed at Which Trains Are Run*

A State of Major statute provides: The speed limit of trains approaching an intersection is 90 miles per hour.

The speed must be consistent with the exercise of the highest degree of care consistent with the practical operation of a railroad.

Citation: Major Pattern Instructions 73.00.

---

However, this instruction does not capture your legal theory that even though the train is proceeding within the 90 miles per hour speed limit, the conductor nevertheless breached the duty of care.

As plaintiff's attorney in the *Speeding Train* case, the pattern instruction you believe, does not reflect your case theory. Therefore, consider modifying the pattern instruction or drafting another proposed instruction. However, before you do any drafting, note that some jurisdictions require a pattern instruction to be given where one exists on a particular issue.

However, let's suppose you are in a jurisdiction where you can modify an existing instruction or draft an original one. There are four principles to adhere to in drafting a revision of a patterned instruction or original instruction and placing it in a set of proposed instructions. A proposed original instruction or modified pattern instruction should

1. state the legal theory,
2. be balanced,
3. be written in understandable language, and
4. be organized into a set of comprehensible proposed instructions.

### 1. Legal Theory

Your proposed original instruction or revised pattern instruction should effectuate your objective by stating your legal theory clearly and correctly. By consulting case law and statutes, you likely will have encountered words or phrases that express your legal theory in a manner that you want included in your jury instruction. But before you just transpose a court holding, dictum, or statute into a jury instruction, consider whether the language is a correct and understandable statement of the law. When discussing the train speed statute, you should either quote the statute or judicial opinion verbatim or, if paraphrasing for clarity, be sure to choose vocabulary that accurately reflects the statute's or case's intent.

In the modified pattern instruction in the following illustration, note how the first and third paragraphs incorporate the statute verbatim in the modified jury instruction. The second paragraph of the jury instruction illustrates how an instruction can be based on an interpretation of case law.

---

### Modifying a Pattern Jury Instruction

#### The *Speeding Train* Case

Plaintiff's Proposed Jury Instruction No. 5 *Speed at Which Trains Are Run*

A State of Major statute provides: The speed limit of trains approaching an intersection is 90 miles per hour.

[The duty of care that a railroad owes to a passenger is that of the highest degree because a railroad is a common carrier. Under certain circumstances, such as adverse weather conditions, a railroad, even though its train is traveling at the posted speed, can still be considered negligent.]

The speed must be consistent with the exercise of the highest degree of care consistent with the practical operation of a railroad.

---

Bracketed material indicates modification of pattern instruction MPI 73.00. *See Darvas v. Bailey*, 286 Maj. 3d 198, 199 (2005).

---

### 2. Balanced and Nonargumentative

Instructions are the court's statement of law to the jury; the language needs to be balanced. Although the instruction should reflect your case theory, it should not include argumentative words and phrases. In some jurisdictions, the judge is prohibited from commenting on the evidence. For example, the train-speed jury instruction would be argumentative and unlikely to be given by the judge if it described the speed of a train as follows:

> The speed limit of a train approaching an intersection is 90 miles per hour. Speeds exceeding that limit can be considered to be grossly inconsistent with the duty to exercise the reasonable degree of care required in the operation of a railroad.

Rather, plaintiff's proposed jury instruction number five, as modified in the illustration above, is worded in neutral and nonargumentative descriptive language.

### 3. Understandable Language

A combination of several principles of clear writing will make instructions intelligible. Some states have developed plain English pattern jury instructions that are written in simple, everyday language. The goal of plain English jury instructions is to improve their clarity and usefulness. In drafting your proposed instructions, strive to achieve the same goal.

Plain English, rather than legal jargon or seldom-used words, makes the instructions easier to understand. For example, consider observing a few plain English rules such as the following: instead of using the word *disregard,* substitute *ignore;* replace the phrase *entertain a reasonable doubt* with *have a reasonable doubt;* and instead of *infer,* use the word *conclude.* Furthermore, avoid negative constructions, because they tend to confuse jurors. To return to the train illustration, compare a negative statement that could have been used in the instruction with the affirmative one that is used:

Negative: The fact that the train was traveling at the posted speed is not the only consideration in determining negligence of the railroad.

Affirmative: [A] railroad, even though its train is traveling at the posted speed, can still be considered negligent.

Normally, the active voice ("The State of Major statute provides that the speed of trains . . .") is preferable to the passive voice ("The speed of trains . . . is provided by the State of Major statute."). Simple sentences with one independent clause are easier to comprehend than compound sentences that join two independent clauses with a coordinating conjunction, such as *and, or,* or *but.* Aim for a clear relationship between each part of a sentence, and avoid attaching too many dependent clauses and phrases.

### 4. Organizing Proposed Instructions

The relationship of each instruction to the others also affects the comprehensibility of your proposed instructions. Think about your proposed instructions as a set instead of a series of individual instructions. The topics and sequence of the instructions can aid the jurors in analyzing the case as a whole and in grasping their duties as jurors.

There are general instructions that you will propose in all cases, such as those telling the jury about the case, their responsibilities as jurors, summary of claims, burden of proof, definition of claims, defenses, injury, remedy, calculation of remedy, verdict, and so on. You should arrange the instructions in a meaningful sequence by grouping topics. Many pattern instruction books, such as the one described below, include a suggested list of instructions logically organized for different types of cases. Most jurisdictions have a set of pattern instructions for common types of cases.

The following is from the Washington Pattern Jury Instructions, which in this example provides the topics and a sequence of topics for a two-party automobile accident case.

## Organizing a Proposed Set of Instructions

### Instructions Involving Pedestrian and Motor Vehicle
### (No Affirmative Defense)

| Number | Instruction |
|--------|-------------|
| 1. | Introductory Instruction (Duties of Jurors) |
| 2. | Issues—Credibility of Witnesses and Weight of Testimony |
| 3. | Summary of Claims |
| 4. | Burden of Proof on the Issues—No Affirmative Defense |
| 5. | Meaning of Burden of Proof—Preponderance of the Evidence |
| 6. | Proximate Cause—Definition |
| 7. | Negligence—Adult—Definition |
| 8. | Ordinary Care—Adult—Definition |
| 9. | General Duty—Driver or Pedestrian |
| 10. | Right of Way—Pedestrian—Vehicle |
| 11. | Violation of Statute, Ordinance or Regulation—Evidence of Negligence |
| 12. | Measure of Damages—Personal and Property—No Contributory Negligence |
| 13. | Measure of Economic Damages—Elements of Past Damages |
| 14. | Measure of Damages—Elements of Damages—Nature and Extent of Injury |
| 15. | Measure of Damages—Elements of Noneconomic Damages |
| 16. | Concluding Instruction—for General Verdict Form |
| 17. | Use of General Verdict Form |
| 18. | General Verdict Form |

Adapted with permission from Washington Pattern Jury Instructions, Civil, pages 609-610, Copyright © 2006 by Thomson West Publishing Co.

Pattern jury instruction books are a source for ideas on the types of instructions you should include and their sequence.

## C.  Legal Theory as a Guide

Let's examine how to draft proposed instructions that will embody the legal theory. Assume that you are the prosecutor in a case involving an assault in the second degree. An essential element that you must prove is that the defendant "knowingly assaulted another with a weapon." Your theory is that the defendant intentionally drove into her ex-lover. The defendant claims that she did not even see her ex when she drove away. Therefore, hitting her ex with her car was an accident. You have witnesses who will testify that the victim was standing right in front of the idling vehicle in broad daylight when the defendant suddenly accelerated from a complete stop and hit the victim. You could adopt a pattern jury instruction on this element.

The State of Major has a pattern jury instruction, MPI 4.10, which states that the definition of *knowledge* and *knowingly* contains exactly the same wording as the relevant statute. You might propose the following pattern jury instruction.

---

### Adopting a Pattern Jury Instruction

#### The Second Degree Assault Case

Prosecutor's Proposed Jury Instruction No. 2

A person knows or acts knowingly or with knowledge when a person

(a) is aware of a fact, facts, or circumstances or result described by a statute defining an offense; or

(b) has information that would lead a reasonable person in the same situation to believe that facts exist that are described by law as being an element of a crime.

Citation: MPI 4.10.

---

Your legal theory might be better advanced if the jurors decide what *knowledge* meant rather than having them receive this somewhat technical definition. But some instructions, because they are so fundamental to your claim, must be given, even though you really do not want to request them. In this instance, you recognize that a conviction might be reversed if the court does not give a definition of the word *knowledge* that either repeats or closely follows the statutory definition.

As noted earlier, there are two points in time when you may draft your instructions prior to the court's finalization of jury instructions: The first is when you draft proposed instructions before trial; the second is when you receive the other side's proposed instructions. This second occasion is of particular importance, because you may want to revise your original proposed instructions once you've analyzed your opponent's. Imagine that defense counsel proposes a different "knowledge" instruction than the pattern instruction you proposed. Assume that in the *Second Degree Assault* case, defense counsel proposed the following "knowledge" instruction.

> ### Opposing Counsel's (Defense) Proposed Jury Instruction
>
> #### The *Second Degree Assault* Case
>
> Defendant's Proposed Jury Instruction No. 2
>
> A person knows or acts knowingly or with knowledge when he or she is aware of a fact, facts, or circumstances or result described by law as being a crime.
>
> If a person has information that would lead a reasonable person in the same situation to believe that facts exist that are described by law as being an element of a crime, the jury is permitted but not required to find that he or she acted with knowledge.
>
> Acting knowingly or with knowledge also is established if a person acts intentionally.
>
> ---
>
> Citation: *State v. Nevin*, 285 Maj. 3d 81, 84 (2004).

As the prosecutor, you should inspect the defense's proposed instruction, analyzing it for legal accuracy and comparing it with the jury instruction that you proposed. You then decide which "knowledge" instruction better supports your prosecution legal theory. Under your proposed instruction, the jurors might think they would be bound to find that the defendant acted "knowingly" if a "reasonable person in the same situation" would be led "to believe that facts exist that are described by law as being an element of a crime."

By contrast, the defense instruction allows the jury to make such a finding of knowledge, but does not require it. After a careful reading, you conclude that your proposed instruction would be more beneficial to your case theory than will the defense instruction. Thus, your position at trial could be to take exception (object) to the defense instruction if the court were to insert it in the court's tentative instructions. You will have both the statute and the pattern instruction as authority for your position. But all is not so simple.

## D. Correctly Stating the Law

A cardinal rule in drafting instructions: make sure they accurately state the law. The trial will be for naught if an appellate court finds (1) an instruction to be in error, and (2) the error to be harmful. Therefore, attorneys and trial judges tend to rely on pattern instructions. However, too much reliance on pattern jury instructions can be hazardous, because they may be unintelligible, not include all the essential factors of your legal theory, or misstate the law. Likewise, if you modify a pattern instruction or draft an original instruction, you also run the same risks. Therefore, carefully examine your instructions to ensure they are unassailable.

To illustrate the significance of careful legal analysis of an instruction, including pattern instructions, let's return to the *Second Degree Assault* case. Imagine that you are the prosecutor. You are drafting during the second phase when you are comparing your and defense counsel's proposed "knowledge" instructions. Your proposed instruction has some positive attributes of a pattern instruction: easy preparation, because the statute is quoted verbatim; probable adoption as a court instruction; and a helpful expression of a legal theory. But you need further analysis to determine whether your proposed instruction will withstand a legal attack.

The instruction that you proposed, which is identical to the pattern instruction, could be read by the jurors to create a conclusive presumption. In other words, if jurors believe the defendant received information that, had it been received by a reasonable person, would give that reasonable person knowledge, the jurors would be required to find the defendant likewise had knowledge. This interpretation of the instruction could be found by the appellate court to violate the constitutional due process requirement that the prosecuting authority must affirmatively prove each element of a crime. By creating a conclusive presumption, the pattern instruction directs the jury to find an element as proven when only circumstantial evidence has been shown.

By contrast, the defense's proposed instruction creates a rebuttable presumption; that is, jurors may find, but are not required to find, that the defendant had knowledge if a reasonable person with the same information would have believed relevant facts exist. Such a presumption can likely pass constitutional muster.

Based on this legal analysis, you conclude your proposed "knowledge" instruction is constitutionally flawed. You also decide that the defense's proposed instruction, which is less favorable to your legal theory, is more likely an accurate statement of law. Given that you, as the prosecutor, represent the people, the best course of action would be to withdraw your proposed instruction and not object to the defense's proposed instruction. Then you would be confident that the instructions could withstand an appeal of a guilty verdict.

## E. Factual Theory as a Guide

When you draft instructions, they should be based on your factual theory—the evidence supporting your legal theory. The instructions must accurately reflect that evidence. Also, instructions explain specific duties of the jury critical to determining the facts, such as assessing credibility. Let's examine these two: drafting instructions that reflect the evidence, and drafting instructions to guide the factual determination.

### Drafting to Reflect the Evidence

To illustrate the two principles of how the evidence influences the drafting of jury instructions, and guiding the factual determination, assume you are the plaintiff in a breach of contract case.

> ### The *Breach of Contract* Case
>
> Plaintiff is claiming loss of profits. You anticipate that your accountant will testify on direct examination about loss of profits as follows:
>
> *Q:* Do you have an opinion as to the losses suffered by plaintiff?
> *A:* Yes. In my opinion, plaintiff suffered greatly. Though she incurred expenses that in my opinion were reasonable, she also had a loss of profits that, according to my calculations, came to . . . .

As plaintiff's attorney, you will submit a proposed damage instruction that includes loss of profits.

## Plaintiff Drafting Proposed Jury Instructions to Reflect the Evidence

### The *Breach of Contract* Case

Plaintiff's Proposed Jury Instruction No. 15
The components of damages that you may find are as follows:

 a. Loss of profits
 b. Reasonable expenses

---

Citation: *Lum v. Hollingworth*, 279 Maj. 3d 82, 85 (1998).

Now suppose that you represent the defendant in the *Breach of Contract* case involving plaintiff McKay Copy-Kat Co. Defendant provided the sole source of sales for plaintiff during the year in question. You anticipate the following cross-examination of plaintiff's accountant intended to undermine the claim that there was a loss of profits.

## Defense Drafting Proposed Jury Instructions to Reflect the Evidence

### The *Breach of Contract* Case

Defense counsel's cross-examination of plaintiff's accountant:

*Q:* I am handing you Plaintiff's Exhibit 5. This is the accounting statement you prepared for the McKay Copy-Kat Co., correct?
*A:* Yes.
*Q:* It shows for the year in question that McKay had $600,000 in sales, correct?

*A:* Yes.

*Q:* It also indicates expenses of $120,000?

*A:* Yes.

*Q:* Liabilities for the same year were another $100,000?

*A:* Yes.

*Q:* According to this statement, Ms. McKay and one other employee were paid $100,000 each in salary?

*A:* Yes.

*Q:* So, after taxes, the McKay Co. had cash assets of $180,000, correct?

*A:* Yes.

*Q:* McKay then invested that money on December 4 by purchasing real property for $420,000?

*A:* Yes.

*Q:* Therefore, a real property purchase is shown as a liability of $420,000 on the balance sheet, correct?

*A:* Yes.

*Q:* As an accountant, you would agree that it is possible to consider the real property investment is in actuality an investment, correct?

*A:* Yes.

*Q:* People and companies generally make investments with assets or excess profit, correct?

*A:* Yes.

As defendant's attorney, you would exclude loss of profits in your proposed defendant damage instruction. The basis for exclusion is that the evidence shows that the plaintiff had a profit, not a loss. Note how the defense's proposed instruction matches the evidence for the defense.

### Defendant's Proposed Jury Instruction No. 15

The components of damages that you may find are as follows:

a. Reasonable expenses

---

Citation: *Ruffo v. Hollings*, 279 Maj. 3d 82, 85 (198X).

### Drafting to Influence Factual Determinations

Now let's look at how the drafting of an instruction on witness credibility might be used to influence the jury in making a factual determination favorable to the proponent's factual theory. Suppose that a key prosecution witness in the *Second Degree Assault* case is a police officer. As the prosecutor, you consider proposing the following credibility instruction, tailored for the particular case.

> ### Drafting Proposed Jury Instructions to Influence a Factual Determination
>
> ##### The *Assault in the Second Degree* Case
>
> ###### Prosecutor's Proposed Jury Instruction No. 5
>
> You are the sole judges of the credibility of the witnesses and of what weight is to be given to the testimony of each witness. In considering the testimony of any witness, you may take into account the opportunity and ability to observe the witness's memory and manner while testifying; any interest, bias, or prejudice the witness may have; the reasonableness of the testimony of the witness considered in light of all the evidence; and any other factors that bear on believability and weight.
>
> [The fact that a witness is a police officer can be considered as one of the factors in judging credibility.]
>
> ---
>
> Citation: Modified State of Major Pattern Instruction 3.0.
> (Bracketed material indicates modification.)

Now assume that you are defense counsel. Your legal theory focuses on attacking the persuasive sufficiency of the prosecutor's story. Specifically, you have tried to attack the credibility of a police officer and thereby the weight of that officer's testimony. You can argue that the court should eliminate the second paragraph of the prosecutor's instruction—"The fact that a witness is a police officer can be considered as one of the factors in judging credibility"—as misstating the law on witness credibility. Also, you can argue that the statement constitutes a judicial comment on the evidence in violation of the State of Major constitutional provision: "Judges shall not charge juries with respect to matters of fact, nor comment thereon, but shall declare the law."

Instead, you may even propose a replacement paragraph: "Just because a witness is a police officer does not entitle the witness to more or less belief than any other witness." The prosecutor would probably object, claiming this paragraph unfairly singles out police officers among all other witnesses. And so it will go, back and forth. The judge will likely use only the first paragraph of the prosecutor's proposed instruction.

Look at the proposed instruction once again from the prosecutor's viewpoint. Before proposing the modified portion of the instruction, the prosecutor would consider the defense objections and possible counterinstructions, and, as a matter of judgment, might well decide not to propose the modification to the instruction.

### F.  Guarding Against Juror Online Research

In their article "Online and Wired for Justice: Why Jurors Turn to the Internet (the 'Google mistrial')," *The Jury Expert* (Nov. 2009), Douglas L. Keene and Rita

R. Handrich recount how since 2001 jurors have been going online and upsetting trials. Instances include a lengthy 2009 federal drug trial ending in a mistrial because nine jurors had done Internet research. A California court excused a panel of 600 prospective jurors because several admitted to doing Internet research on the case. The authors conclude that jurors, who should know better, go online because

> . . .[w]e live in an era when access to information is ubiquitous. We are used to having a question cross our mind and checking for the answer. We do it without thinking. And jurors do, too.

*http://www.thejuryexpert.com/2009/11/online-and-wired-for-justice-why-jurors-turn-to-the-internet-the-google-mistrial/*

Several measures have been suggested to keep jurors from committing Internet juror misconduct, including: informing them in the jury summons not to do electronic research; asking voir dire questions about whether the jurors will follow the court's instructions about refraining from Internet research; having the jurors sign a declaration that they won't; and so on.

The primary prophylactic is a set of jury instructions explicitly prohibiting electronic research. In 2009, the Judicial Conference of the United States promulgated these model jury instructions for United States District Courts:

## Pattern Instruction for U.S. District Courts

### Prohibiting Electronic Research

**Before Trial**

You, as jurors, must decide this case based solely on the evidence presented here within the four walls of this courtroom. This means that during the trial you must not conduct any independent research about this case, the matters in the case, and the individuals or corporations involved in the case. In other words, you should not consult dictionaries or reference materials, search the internet, websites, blogs, or use any other electronic tools to obtain information about this case or to help you decide the case. Please do not try to find out information from any source outside the confines of this courtroom.

Until you retire to deliberate, you may not discuss this case with anyone, even your fellow jurors. After you retire to deliberate, you may begin discussing the case with your fellow jurors, but you cannot discuss the case with anyone else until you have returned a verdict and the case is at an end. I hope that for all of you this case is interesting and noteworthy. I know that many of you use cell phones, Blackberries, the internet and other tools of technology. You also must not talk to anyone about this case or use these tools to communicate electronically with anyone about the case. This includes your family and friends. You may not communicate with anyone about the case on your cell phone, through e-mail, Blackberry, iPhone, text messaging, or on Twitter, through any blog or website, through any internet chat room,

*continued ▶*

> or by way of any other social networking websites, including Facebook, My Space, LinkedIn, and YouTube.
>
> **At the Close of the Case**
>
> During your deliberations, you must not communicate with or provide any information to anyone by any means about this case. You may not use any electronic device or media, such as a telephone, cell phone, smart phone, iPhone, Blackberry or computer; the internet, any internet service, or any text or instant messaging service; or any internet chat room, blog, or website such as Facebook, My Space, LinkedIn, YouTube or Twitter, to communicate to anyone any information about this case or to conduct any research about this case until I accept your verdict.
>
> *http://www.wired.com/images_blogs/threatlevel/2010/02/juryinstructions.pdf*

Although in the past jurors have committed misconduct by doing their own independent research, today anyone with Internet access can do it easily and quickly. For these reasons, counsel is wise to propose jury instructions like these that are designed to make jurors refrain from doing electronic research.

Measures beyond jury instructions have been proposed, including:

- Threatening sanctions such as fines and contempt for disregarding the instructions,
- Having jurors turn in their electronic devices for the length of a short trial, and
- Having lawyers take the defensive move of doing their own online research to determine what could be learned about the client if jurors were to research.

Caren Myers Morrison, "Can the Jury Trial Survive Google?" 25 *Criminal Justice* 13 (Winter 2011).

## III. PRESENTING AND ADVOCATING FOR INSTRUCTIONS

The manner of presenting and advocating for instructions varies from jurisdiction to jurisdiction. The process also involves service of proposed instructions on the court and opposing counsel; informal discussions with the judge and opposing counsel; and formal, on-the-record objections to instructions and argument on instructions. Plan how you will perform these activities, keeping in mind that your ultimate objective is to convince the judge, in both a legally accurate and ethically proper manner, to adopt as the court's instructions those that best express your legal theory. We suggest focusing on the following:

- Court procedures and practices governing jury instructions,
- Organization, and
- Trial advocacy strategies.

## A. Court Procedures and Practices

Procedures and practices govern how jury instructions are to be presented to the court and how the court will decide which instructions will become the court's instructions. In turn, those procedures and practices dictate how you make a presentation on jury instructions.

### Format

The format for the proposed instructions and the process for submitting proposed instructions commonly are spelled out in local court rules, but can also be idiosyncratic to a particular judge.

If pattern instructions are used, some judges simply permit a list of relevant numbers. Other judges require that the full text, even of pattern instructions, be included. Most judges require that any modification to a pattern instruction be clearly shown. For example, the modifications can be delineated by brackets and contain citations to authorities. See the illustration on page 442.

### Conferencing

Even before receiving counsel's instructions, some judges prepare a tentative set of court jury instructions. Other trial judges may conduct an informal in-chambers meeting with both counsel to discuss jury instructions before drafting tentative court instructions. Despite the setting, plan to make points on desired instructions while still adapting to the more collegial, conversational manner. If possible, request an instruction conference either pretrial or early in the trial. Take the opportunity to inform the judge about your legal theory. As we suggested in the preparatory stages, be equipped with legal authority and reasons for the language you want to include in your proposed instructions. Explain to the judge why opposing counsel's proposed instructions do not accurately reflect the law, are not as well expressed as yours or the pattern instruction, or should not be adopted for some other reason.

### The Hearing

Near or after the close of evidence, you will be at the third point, where the jury instructions are the focus of your attention. At this time, the court is ready to finalize the court's instructions. Generally, the court will inform you as to the court's intended instructions by providing counsel with the court's tentative instructions. At a hearing on the record, both you and opposing counsel will be given an opportunity to take exceptions (object) to the court's jury instructions.

Local court rules may indicate how to take exception (object) to instructions. For example, the rules may provide an opportunity to object both to the giving of any instruction or verdict form and to the refusal to give an instruction that you proposed. Typically, both case law and court rules require stating the grounds and reasons for your objections. Failure to object with specificity may foreclose the issue on appeal. The following illustrates several ways you might present your objection.

> ## Arguing Instructions
>
> ### The *Breach of Contract* Case
>
> "Your Honor, I respectfully [take exception, object] to the court's instruction number 14 on the ground that it is an incomplete statement of the law. I respectfully request that instead of court instruction 14, plaintiff's proposed jury instruction 15 be adopted by this court.
>
> "In *Lum v. Hollingsworth*, cited at the bottom of plaintiff's proposed 15 and in our trial brief at page 4, a component for breach of contract damages is loss of profits according to proof at trial. In *Lum*, the court instructed the jury, I quote, 'You are the sole judges of the evidence and can read the balance sheet as reasonable persons and conclude that an investment could under certain circumstances be considered a liability against assets and thus a loss.'
>
> "Your Honor, we have an identical situation in this case. . . . Plaintiff's evidence on this issue was as follows. . . . For these reasons, the *Lum* case requires that the court adopt plaintiff's proposed jury instruction number 15."

After hearing counsel's objections, the court may change its tentative instructions or adopt its tentative instructions as the final court instructions.

### Alternative Proposed Instruction

When you believe that the judge may not accept your initial proposed instruction, you might propose alternative instructions. By doing this, you can fall back on your next best instruction. This falls under the same principle as developing backup case theories. Consider submitting an alternative instruction to the court either in your proposed jury instructions or held in reserve and presented at the hearing if the court is inclined not to adopt your initial proposed instruction.

### When Instructions Are Read

#### Final Instructions

In some jurisdictions the court reads the instructions after argument by counsel and just before the jury retires to deliberate. In other jurisdictions, the instructions are read before closing argument. In those jurisdictions where instructions are delivered after argument, generally you will want to obtain rulings on what instructions will be given before you begin closing argument. You can then formulate arguments around the law and not be discredited by a misstatement of law in your closing argument when the court delivers a different statement of law in the instructions.

As the judge reads the instructions to the jury, you will be tempted to focus elsewhere. Your mind may wander as the judge's soothing voice reads each instruction. Stop. Pay attention to what the judge is reading. Trial judges can make mistakes. The wrong instruction may have somehow found its way into the packet. Or an instruction somehow got lost. Or something else happened. If something does go wrong, rise and ask to approach the bench, where you can advise the judge of what went wrong. And, you hope, correct the problem.

Whether the judge gives the jurors a copy of the instructions to take to the jury room when they deliberate also varies among jurisdictions. You may wish, if it is not customarily done, to request that each juror be given a copy of the instructions as the judge reads them.

### Instructions During Trial

During various stages of the trial, the judge may decide that it is appropriate to instruct the jury. For instance, at the beginning of the trial, the judge can read preliminary instructions that caution the jury about discussing the case, explain the claims of counsel, explain the duties of jurors, provide criteria for analyzing credibility of witnesses, and so on. At times during the trial you also might want the judge to give instructions. For example, you may wish to have the judge read a limiting instruction that a piece of evidence may be considered only for a particular purpose (a prior act of misconduct may be considered only in determining the absence of accident or mistake and for no other purpose). Fed. R. Evid. 105. Or you may also want the judge to explain, at appropriate times, stipulations, depositions, interrogatories, and so on.

## B. Organization

Incomplete, inaccurate, or erroneous jury instructions can be the basis for appeal. You need a method to organize and account for your proposed jury instructions, those of the opposing party, the court's jury instructions, and authority for each set of instructions. A notebook that contains the relevant sets of jury instructions, supportive authority, and an organization chart will assist you in argument and in preparing or defending an appeal. We suggest that a chart can be immensely helpful. The chart on page 449, from the plaintiff's perspective, shows how to record the court's disposition as to the three proposed sets of jury instructions: the court's, the plaintiff's, and the defendant's. The numbers refer to those given by the court and to the parties as to their proposed instructions.

## C. Other Strategies

### Timing the Submission of Your Proposed Instructions

Consider when to submit instructions to the court and opposing counsel. If local rules or practice mandate that they be presented at a particular time (for example, at a pretrial conference or when a case is called for trial), and the rule is enforced, timing is not an issue. However, if there is latitude concerning when to serve the proposed instructions, weigh and balance different factors. The primary factor to consider is whether early service and filing of proposed instructions will give opposing counsel an advantage by disclosing your legal theory and trial strategy. The significance of such decision making is illustrated by the *Breach of Contract* case.

## Timing the Submission of Proposed Instructions

### The *Breach of Contract* Case

Assume that you are plaintiff's counsel. You have just received defendant's proposed instruction on damages. It excludes loss of profits as a component of damages. With this knowledge you can anticipate the other side's factual theory and potential attacks on your testimony and exhibits. This allows you to make adjustments in your presentation of evidence at trial for those anticipated attacks.

### Assessing Your Own (the Plaintiff's) Case

You plan to prove loss of profits by Exhibit 5, the accountant's balance sheet, and testimony by your client's accountant. Defense's proposed instructions telegraph that this may not be sufficient and that you have case weaknesses. You might discuss the issue with your witness. He might tell you he cannot anticipate any problems. But suppose he tells you that it is conceivable that one of the entries on the balance sheet, the purchase of real property, could be interpreted as a profit and not a liability. Your client tells you that the purchase of the real property was not an investment but was essential to build a warehouse instead of renting storage space. You can revise your trial strategy. You advise the accountant and your client that you will ask them a series of questions to reflect the purpose of the real property purchase. You plan to introduce documents that demonstrate that the real property purchase was an expense/liability and not an investment. You plan to select another expert, an economic appraiser of industrial markets, who could testify about expenses and liabilities in the copying business.

### Assessing the Defense Case

You now have a revised plan for the evidence you present for your case. Next, turn to the defense case. Ask yourself, "Is the potential cross-examination of the accountant and balance sheet the sole basis for defendant's proposed jury instruction?" Is there some other evidence that opposing counsel will use to refute your client's claim for loss of profits? Are there informal or formal means that you could use to learn about opposing counsel's trial strategy? You could telephone defense counsel and ask for an explanation of defense's proposed instruction. If you are scheduled to meet and negotiate a settlement, you might have an opportunity to ask opposing counsel. But these informal means might not yield any information. Though formal discovery is concluded, you could file a trial brief concerning proposed jury instructions. You could request that the judge order that the defense respond before trial. In that way, you might learn whether the defense strategy is based on the evidence the defense intends to present at trial. Otherwise, you might have to follow the strategy of bolstering your evidence on loss of profits, and prepare arguments for the jury instruction conference, where you will present your position as to the proposed damage instructions.

## JURY INSTRUCTIONS CHART

| Court Instruction by Number | | Jury Instruction Topic | Jury Instructions | | | | |
|---|---|---|---|---|---|---|---|
| | | | Plaintiff's Proposed Instruction | | Defendant's Proposed Instruction | | Notes |
| Proposed | Given (final court number) | | Submitted | Given | Submitted | Given | Action Taken |
| 1 (pattern) | 1 | Duties of Jury | 1 | Yes | 1 | Yes | Plaintiff, defendant, and court instructions number 1 were identical pattern instructions. |
| 3 (modified pattern) | 3 | Claims of the Parties | 2 | In part | 4 | In part | Court instruction number 3 was a composite of paragraph 1 from plaintiff's proposed 2 and paragraph 1 from defendant's proposed 4. |
| 5 | 5 | Definition of Duty for Negligence | 3<br><br>4 (alternative instruction for negligence) | No<br><br>No | 8 | Yes | The court rejected both plaintiff instructions 3 and 4. Reason given was use of the word carefully in both of plaintiff's instructions was not balanced. Court believes defendant's instruction 8 was balanced. |

Timing the submission of jury instructions might be critical in a criminal case. For instance, suppose the prosecutor were to propose a lesser-included-crime instruction early in the proceeding, such as second degree murder in a first degree murder prosecution. This would provide defense counsel with some information about how the prosecutor probably intends to present and argue the case. On the other hand, early service and filing of proposed instructions may work in your favor. Those proposed instructions provide the judge a legal framework within which to understand your case theory and presentation of the evidence. Moreover, you may rely on the proposed instructions in arguing evidentiary or other legal issues to the judge during the course of the trial.

### Argument

You must exercise judgment in arguing instructions. Decisions whether to argue vigorously in favor of an instruction, or to make a low-key presentation, or even to withdraw a proposed instruction are important. The *Second Degree Assault* case involving the "knowledge" instruction is an illustration of how judgment plays a role in your presentation. As you may recall from the discussion of the case, the prosecutor withdrew the prosecution's proposed instruction and did not object to the defense's proposed instruction. Deciding the course of action to follow requires analysis of your case theory, the law, ethical responsibilities, and then the exercise of judgment as to the best advocacy strategy to pursue.

## IV.  ETHICAL CONSIDERATIONS

Ethical considerations control the drafting, proposing, objecting to, and arguing of instructions. Generally, you have an ethical obligation to the court to be candid about the law of the case. Specifically, under ABA Model Rule of Professional Conduct 3.3(a)(1)(3), you may not knowingly make a false statement of law to the court or fail to disclose to the court legal authority in the controlling jurisdiction known to be directly adverse to your client's position and not disclosed by opposing counsel. These are continuing obligations, and if you become aware of the falsity of an assertion of law or contrary legal authority directly on point, you should promptly report it to the court.

To illustrate, reexamine the *Second Degree Assault* case from the prosecutor and defense counsel perspectives in light of the professional responsibilities of both lawyers. While the prosecutor might wish to have the court adopt the prosecutor's proposed instruction on "knowledge," the prosecutor is aware of a due process requirement that runs contrary to the prosecution's proposed instruction. Therefore, the prosecutor is obligated to disclose the legal authority. If the prosecutor knows the instruction is an incorrect statement of law, it would be unethical to rely on the instruction, hoping an appellate court will subsequently find the error harmless.

For the defense counsel, this issue is somewhat more complex. Generally, counsel must object to an instruction or waive the objection for appeal, although a "plain error" of constitutional magnitude such as exists here may be preserved even without objection. This issue then becomes one of how much effort must defense counsel devote to the objection. Specifically, can counsel object without citing convincing authority, hoping thereby to lose at the trial level while at the same time preserving the issue for appeal? Technically, that would not violate ABA Model Rule of Professional Conduct 3.3(a)(2), because the authority is not adverse to the defense position of wanting to build reversible error into the record. In fact, it supports it. Nevertheless, a number of attorneys might find this tactic in conflict with the spirit of Rule 3.3, which seeks to establish a duty of candor to the court.

## CHECKLIST: JURY INSTRUCTIONS

### Drafting and Organizing Proposed Instructions

☐ Adopt pattern jury instructions or modifications of them when possible,
☐ Write plain English,
☐ Embody counsel's legal theory,
☐ Use balanced expressions of the law,
☐ Be organized in a logical sequence,
☐ Correctly state the law,
☐ Reflect the evidence presented at trial, and
☐ Properly influence how the jury is to make factual determinations.

### Presenting and Advocating for Instructions

☐ The proposed instructions are in the proper form.
☐ Counsel advocates for proposed instructions during counsels' conference with the trial judge.
☐ Counsel properly offers alternative proposed instructions, or withdraws proposed instructions when necessary.
☐ Counsel effectively argues and takes exception to instructions during the hearing on instructions.
☐ Counsel should pay close attention during the reading of instructions and takes remedial steps if a problem arises.

### Ethical Considerations

Counsel advocates for a correct statement of the law in the instructions.

# CHAPTER 13

# CLOSING ARGUMENT
## Art of Argument

*"I've always considered final summation the most important part of the trial for the lawyer. It's the climax of the case, where the lawyer has his last and best opportunity to convince the jury of the rightness of his cause."*

—**Vincent Bugliosi**, *Outrage: The Five Reasons Why O.J. Simpson Got Away with Murder* (Norton 1997)

*"Are you kidding? Shelly Kates could convince a jury that Jeffrey Dahmer had an eating disorder."*

—**Jack McCoy**, portrayed by **Sam Waterston** in *Law and Order,* "Paranoia," Season 6, Episode 6 (Nov. 15, 1995)

*"All through the trial, it was the feeling that jurors number seven and number eleven were against Darrow. But when the accused attorney concluded his speech, the two men were openly weeping, as was everybody else in the courtroom including the judge.*

*"The jury was out thirty-four minutes. They had been ready to bring in a 'not guilty' verdict from the moment they went into deliberation. They took three ballots however—as one juror explained—so that no one would claim they had acted in 'undue haste.'"*

—**Clarence Darrow**, *Attorney for the Damned: Clarence Darrow in the Courtroom* (Arthur Weinberg ed., University of Chicago Press 1989)

## I. OVERVIEW

Closing argument is your final opportunity to convince the jury to decide in your client's behalf. This chapter explains the art of argument so you will know how to take full advantage of this opportunity. We discuss what jury instructions and evidence to talk about in your argument. Specifically, among other argument skills, you will learn how to argue persuasively by employing: proven model arguments, argument structures that keep the jury's attention, arguments that appeal to the jury (logical, ethical, and emotional appeal), argument visuals, and rhetorical devices.

Closing argument can be planned and delivered in a wider variety of ways than any other part of trial. This diversity stems from the latitude the law permits counsel in presenting closing argument and the unique nature of each attorney's personality, as well as analytical and rhetorical abilities. However, the strategies, principles, and practices presented in this chapter are adaptable by every attorney. They are the keys to delivering a compelling closing.

## II.  PLANNING CLOSING ARGUMENT

### A.  Preparation

Preparation of the content of your closing argument is a fundamental ongoing process, beginning when you first come in contact with the case and extending until the point you deliver your closing. Even so, there are three distinct points in time when you will concentrate on preparing the content of your closing argument: early in pretrial, as trial approaches, and during trial.

#### Three Stages
##### *Early in Pretrial: Closing as a Planning Tool*

The first time you will focus on preparing your closing argument is early in the pretrial stage. This begins when you first come in contact with the case. It may be either by reading about it in an article in the newspaper, seeing something on television, initially meeting with your client, or receiving the case file. During this stage, produce an outline of ideas for your closing argument. This requires a review of the available legal and factual information of the case. This initial, tentative closing argument can then be your roadmap for organizing further investigation, requests for discovery, cross-examination, and so on.

##### *As Trial Approaches*

Drafting and refining your closing argument is a continuous process. However, it becomes more focused as trial approaches. At this time, you will have a fairly solid understanding of the evidence that will be offered in trial. Therefore, your draft of closing argument will include what you think that evidence is, and your proposed jury instructions. The relationship between proposing jury instructions and drafting closing argument is symbiotic. Your jury instructions will provide guidance on the law and the facts you will include in your argument. Likewise, your closing argument provides guidance for determining which jury instructions best express your case theory and theme, because you will interpret those instructions for the jurors in your closing argument.

To illustrate how counsel drafts closing argument at this stage, consider the *Hill Moveit Personal Injury* case from the plaintiff Darcy Rutherford's perspective. Review pages 45-46.

As Ms. Rutherford's attorney, your legal theory against Hill Moveit continues to be what it was when you filed the complaint: product liability imposing strict liability for unsafe construction and design because of the trailer's open construction and lack of tie-downs, and failure to provide adequate warnings of unsafe conditions. You will draft your argument using this legal theory as expressed in your proposed jury instructions, your factual theory, the evidence that you intend to produce at trial through exhibits and testimony, and your theme. Your final draft of closing will also meet the other side's case theory, as well as attacks on your own case theory, which will require you to deal with case weaknesses.

### During Trial

During the third stage for preparing closing argument, the trial stage, listen to the testimony and view the exhibits. You will then make decisions, in light of the evidence, about whether to add to, delete, or refine your closing argument. Final touches to the closing, such as adding quotes from a witness's testimony or a sudden inspiration for a strong analogy or common life experience that will make one of your points, can be made during trial. For example, as plaintiff's counsel you observe that the defense's collision reconstruction expert witness opined that Darcy Rutherford's car was following too closely to the utility trailer. You conclude that the expert was evasive and argumentative during cross-examination; this might cause you to revise your closing to dwell on the court's credibility instruction and discuss the expert's demeanor while testifying, his reticence, and the implausibility of his testimony.

### Incorporating Ideas

As you amass information and ideas that you may eventually blend into your closing, record and organize that information so it will be accessible to you when you draft your argument. To accomplish this, maintain a closing argument file folder, a section of your trial notebook, a computer folder, or some other storage place where you can collect ideas and notes for closing argument. Whenever you have a thought or observation for closing argument, place a note concerning it in your storage place. Brilliant ideas for closing argument will come to you when you least expect—such as during the night. Write the thought on a tablet that you keep by your bedside. In the morning, transfer the notes to your repository, provided you can make sense out of your sleepless scribbling. Especially during trial, listen for words and phrases used by witnesses that ring true and support or generate a new argument. These are the gems that should be saved for inclusion in your closing.

Your notes will be extensive and may include, among other things, analogies, newspaper clippings, rhetorical questions, language from key instructions, lines of poetry, and important quotations from witness testimony. A likely source of ideas is Internet search, which will yield an abundance of information.

You might want to weave into your closing argument some inspiring ideas or quotes that are appropriate for your case and would be well known by jurors. Whether or not you decide to use such quotes or ideas, the time spent researching them and thoughtfully planning your closing is irreplaceable. Such research inspires your own creativeness. You can obtain ideas as to structure, choice of words, timing, and so on.

Consider this excerpt of Clarence Darrow's closing argument in *Illinois v. Nathan Leopold and Richard Loeb* (1924), where Darrow argues against the death penalty in one of the most sensational trials in the twentieth century. This trial was also the subject of a fictionalized book, *Compulsion*, by Meyer Levin (Simon & Schuster 1956), as well as a Broadway play and movie starring Orson Welles as Clarence Darrow. Leopold and Loeb kidnapped and murdered a 14-year-old boy; the prosecutor argued for the death penalty. This excerpt from the trial transcript and the famous trial are on the website of Professor Douglas O. Linder, Closing Argument: *Illinois v. Nathan Leopold and Richard Loeb* (Delivered by Clarence Darrow, Chicago, Illinois, Aug. 22, 1924), *http://www.law.umkc.edu/faculty/projects/ftrials/leoploeb/darrowclosing.html* (accessed Aug. 1, 2013).

### Closing Argument

#### Incorporating Ideas
#### The *Leopold and Loeb* Case

Excerpt of Clarence Darrow's Summation Against Imposition of the Death Penalty

"If these two boys die on the scaffold, which I can never bring myself to imagine, If [sic] they do die on the scaffold, the details of this will be spread over the world. Every newspaper in the United States will carry a full account. Every newspaper of Chicago will be filled with the gruesome details. It will enter every home and every family."

"Will it make men better or make men worse? I would like to put that to the intelligence of man, at least such intelligence as they have. I would like to appeal to the feelings of human beings so far as they have feelings—would it make the human heart softer or would it make hearts harder? "

"What influence would it have upon the millions of men who will read it? What influence would it have upon the millions of women who will read it, more sensitive, more impressionable, more imaginative than men? Would it help them if Your Honor should do what the state begs you to do?"

"What influence would it have upon the infinite number of children who will devour its details as Dicky Loeb has enjoyed reading detective stories? Would it make them better or would it make them worse? The question needs no answer."

"You can answer it from the human heart."

"What influence, let me ask you, will it have for the unborn babes still sleeping in their mother's womb? Do I need to argue to Your Honor that cruelty only breeds cruelty? That hatred only causes hatred; that if there is any way to soften this human heart which is hard enough at its best, if there is any way to kill evil and hatred and all that goes with it, it is not through evil and hatred and cruelty; it is through charity, and love and understanding."

## B. Case Theories as Guides

Planning the content of closing argument applies the same basic methodology that we suggested for opening statement. Rely on your case theory and the other side's case theory as guides for deciding what information to include. Closing argument, however, will differ from your opening. Now you can argue the inferences you want the jury to draw from evidence. You can characterize the evidence. You can discuss the law by referring to specific jury instructions. You can put the entire trial in perspective. In this section, we discuss how you can draw on your case theory to select the content of your closing argument.

### Legal Theory: Critical Jury Instructions

Closing argument is your opportunity to provide a roadmap of the law to the jury. That roadmap describes your legal theory, and if followed and properly applied to the evidence, it will lead the jury to a verdict favorable to your client. For example, defense counsel in a criminal case could select the reasonable doubt instruction and argue that when the reasonable doubt law, as expressed in the instruction, is applied to the lack of evidence, it leads to an acquittal.

Focus on those jury instructions that best express your legal theory and convey a picture of your case. Among the jury instructions, only a few will be vital to understanding your legal theory. Four jury instructions are usually pertinent to explaining a legal theory in closing:

- Elements of the legal claim,
- Burden of proof,
- Central issue in dispute, and
- The other side's case theory.

We discuss each of these and illustrate how to use them in selecting jury instructions for emphasis in closing.

#### *Elements of Your Claim or Defense*

If you are making a claim, such as when the plaintiff claims that defendant was negligent, or the defendant asserts comparative negligence, you need to make sure that the jury understands what you must prove. Because the plaintiff or prosecutor bears the burden of proving the elements of a claim for relief or crime, the plaintiff's attorney or prosecutor, in closing argument, usually will discuss instructions that set out and explain elements of the claim or crime. Likewise, the defense will select those jury instructions that define the elements of the crime or claim that defendant contends plaintiff has failed to prove. If the defense asserts an affirmative defense, the defendant will also wish to select the instructions explaining that defense.

To illustrate the selection and utilization of the elements of jury instruction in closing, imagine you represent the defendant Hill Moveit. Among defenses, Hill Moveit claims comparative negligence because plaintiff was following too closely and was intoxicated. You researched the law and drafted proposed jury instructions by modifying Major Pattern Jury Instructions. Consider your proposed instruction on intoxication.

## Closing Argument

Intoxication Instruction
The *Hill Moveit* Case

No. ___

It is a defense to an action for damages for personal injuries that the person injured was then under the influence of alcohol, that this condition was a proximate cause of the injury, and that the person injured was more than 50 percent at fault.

Begin your argument by explaining this complete defense of intoxication. So that the jury can understand the elements, you could create a chart to show the jury the requisite elements and place the chart on an easel in front of them.

## Intoxication

It is a defense to an action for damages for personal injuries:

1. Person injured under the influence of alcohol,
2. This condition was a proximate cause of the injury, and
3. The person injured was more than 50 percent at fault.

Provide the jury with an overview on the law and a brief discussion to the effect that the law in the State of Major provides that an intoxicated driver is not entitled to recovery if the driver is more than 50 percent at fault. Remind the jurors that they were sworn to follow that law. Then you could discuss each element of the intoxication defense and apply the law to the facts proven during the trial.

## Closing Argument

Using Jury Instructions in Closing Argument
The *Hill Moveit* Case

The first element of this defense is that the person was under the influence of alcohol. You have heard that Darcy Rutherford had a blood alcohol level between .06 and .10. The limit in the State of Major is .08. She was under the influence. The second element requires that her intoxication be a cause of the injury. Was Ms. Rutherford's condition a cause? You heard the testimony of the collision reconstruction expert that Ms. Rutherford was tailgating the utility trailer, and that if she had been at a legal

*continued* ▶

distance back she would have had time to evade the falling furniture. But she was too close, and her intoxication slowed her reaction time. If she had been sober and following at a legal distance, she would probably not be in the tragic condition she is in today. As hard a decision as it would be, you could conclude that she was 100 percent at fault. The evidence is conclusive that she was well in excess of 50 percent at fault, as required by the third element. It sounds callous and hard-hearted, but please recall when we discussed during jury selection that your deliberations should be free from sympathy for her. Now, the court has instructed you that you should not be swayed by sympathy. . . .

Now consider your other defense for Hill Moveit—comparative negligence. Your approach to drafting closing argument is the same as for the intoxication defense. Begin with your proposed jury instructions on negligence and comparative negligence modifying the Major Pattern Jury Instructions.

## Closing Argument

### Negligence Instruction
### The *Hill Moveit* Case

No. ___

Negligence is the failure to exercise ordinary care. It is the doing of some act that a reasonably careful person would not do under the same or similar circumstances or the failure to do some act that a reasonably careful person would have done under the same or similar circumstances. . . .

## Closing Argument

### Comparative Negligence Instruction
### The *Hill Moveit* Case

No. ___

Comparative negligence is negligence on the part of a person claiming injury that is a proximate cause of the injury complained of.

 If you find comparative negligence by the plaintiff, you must determine the degree, expressed as a percentage, to which plaintiff's comparative negligence contributed to the claimed injury. The court will furnish you a special verdict form for this purpose. Your answers to the questions in the special verdict form will furnish the basis by which the court will apportion damages, if any.

You could begin this segment of argument by explaining: *"Comparative negligence, as Her Honor has instructed you, is a defense to the product liability claims."* Then your argument turns to the elements of negligence using these instructions and/or an elements chart. You can argue: *"Ms. Rutherford failed to use ordinary care by following too closely and driving drunk."*

A verdict form can assist in the explanation of the claims, defenses (legal theories), damages, and how to approach deliberations. For example, either plaintiff's or defendant Hill Moveit's lawyer could use an enlargement of the verdict form to explain such issues as product liability, comparative negligence, and percentage of fault that the jury will be discussing during deliberations. The following is a sample verdict from the *Hill Moveit* case. (For simplicity, the verdict form contains only one of the product liability claims.) In closing argument, counsel can propose percentages of fault and dollar amounts for damages, and then fill in the chart with dollar amounts and percentages on an enlarged verdict form as counsel argues each point.

---

### SAMPLE SPECIAL VERDICT FORM

#### SUPERIOR COURT OF MAJOR IN JAMNER COUNTY

| | |
|---|---|
| Darcy Rutherford, | ) |
| | ) No.: XX – 01-549031 |
| Plaintiff, | ) |
| | ) |
| vs. | ) SPECIAL VERDICT FORM |
| | ) |
| Hill Moveit International | ) |
| Corporation, Stanley Luby, | ) |
| and Fergun GasPump | ) |
| | ) |
| Defendants | ) |
| _____ | ) |

We, the jury, answer the questions submitted by the court as follows:

QUESTION 1: Did the defendant Hill Moveit International Corporation supply a product that was not reasonably safe as designed?

ANSWER: _____ (Write "yes" or "no")

(INSTRUCTION: If you answered "no" to Question 1, sign this verdict form. If you answered "yes" to question 1, answer Question 2.)

*continued* ▶

QUESTION 2: Was the unsafe condition of the product a proximate cause of the injury to the plaintiff?

ANSWER: _____ (Write "yes" or "no")

(INSTRUCTION: If you answered "no" to Question 2, sign this verdict form. If you answered "yes" to Question 2, answer Question 3.)

QUESTION 3: What do you find to be the plaintiff's amount of damages? Do not consider the issue of contributory negligence, if any, in your findings.

ANSWER:
  (a)  Past Economic Damages        $ _____
  (b)  Noneconomic Damages          $ _____
  (c)  Future Economic Damages   $ _____

(INSTRUCTION: If you answered Question 3 with any amount of money, answer Question 4. If you find no damages, sign this verdict form.)

QUESTION 4: Was the plaintiff also negligent?

ANSWER: _____ (Write "yes" or "no")

(INSTRUCTION: If you answered "no" to Question 4, sign this verdict form. If you answered "yes" to Question 4, answer Question 5.)

QUESTION 5: Was the plaintiff's negligence a proximate cause of the injury to the plaintiff?

ANSWER: _____ (Write "yes" or "no")

(INSTRUCTION: If you answered "no" to Question 5, sign this verdict form. If you answered "yes" to Question 5, answer Question 6.)

QUESTION 6: Assume that 100% represents the total combined fault that proximately caused the plaintiff's injury. What percentage of this 100% is attributable to the plaintiff's negligence? What percentage of this 100% is attributable to the unsafe condition of defendant's product?

ANSWER:                                        Percentage
    To plaintiff Darcy Rutherford:        _____ %
    To defendant's product                _____ %
    TOTAL                                  100%

(INSTRUCTION: Sign and return this verdict.)

DATE:_____, 20_____  _____
                                    Presiding Juror

## Burden of Proof

In a criminal case, the burden of proof, beyond a reasonable doubt, generally is the subject of argument. In civil cases, attorneys often do not focus on the civil burden of proof, a preponderance of the evidence—defined in the jury instructions as enough evidence so that a proposition is "more probably true than not." The civil burden of proof places the two sides so procedurally close together that attorneys generally try to prove that their side is correct rather than risk relying on the burden. However, if counsel discusses the burden, plaintiff's counsel can argue that the difference is 51 versus 49 percent, or that it tips the scale of justice only so slightly toward the plaintiff's side. Defense counsel may argue, *"Plaintiff has only proven a 50-50 probability that the parties intended to enter into a contractual relationship. That's simply not preponderance."*

## Closing Argument

### Burden of Proof in a Criminal Case

#### Defense Argument

Criminal defense counsel might explain the reasonable doubt burden of proof by referring generally to how difficult and important a decision the jury has to make. Defense counsel might attempt to make the jurors believe that the "beyond a reasonable doubt" burden is like a religious canon and almost insurmountable. For instance, in closing argument defense counsel may suggest that jurors should find the defendant not guilty if they have "any doubt," and argue that the prosecution has the burden of proving guilt beyond "a shadow of a doubt." Or, in discussing the burden of proof, defense counsel may describe the jurors' role and how the jurors might approach the burden of proof. The defense attorney might explain why there is such a strong burden by highlighting the concern that an innocent person not be wrongfully convicted.

Even more important to the defense than the magnitude of the burden beyond a reasonable doubt may be the existence of the burden itself. It permits defense counsel to acknowledge negative inferences in the case (*"My client walked out of the store without paying for the razor blades, so maybe he did intend to steal them"*), and then balance these negative inferences with positive inferences (*"But he had $40 and credit cards, so maybe he didn't"*). Counsel can then rest on the burden in asking the fact finder for a defense verdict (*"So maybe he did, maybe he didn't, but you knew that before you heard any testimony, and the prosecution cannot carry any burden, let alone 'beyond a reasonable doubt,' with a 'maybe he did, maybe he didn't' case"*).

#### Prosecution Argument

The prosecutor will describe the burden as something that can be overcome. The duty of the prosecutor to do justice constrains prosecutors from interpreting the "reasonable doubt" concept to adversarial advantage: *"That's a reasonable doubt, not beyond a shadow of a doubt, not beyond all doubt, not just any doubt, but a reasonable one. As jury instruction five states: 'A reasonable doubt is one for which a reason exists.' Now, can one reasonably doubt Mr. Strait's guilt in this case in light of the uncontradicted evidence that . . . ?"*

*Issue in Dispute*

In most cases, one or two central issues are in dispute. You want to argue by referring to a jury instruction on these issues. Often, both plaintiff and defense counsel will include the same proposed instruction, because each attorney recognizes that that instruction expresses the law in the area of the case where there is a major dispute or conflicting evidence.

The approach that structures argument around instructions can be coupled smoothly with a jury instruction that centers on the issues in the case. This structure works well for plaintiff's counsel because the plaintiff has the burden to prove each element. This also simplifies the case for the jurors by making the claims more understandable. For example, plaintiff's counsel first discusses the elements of negligence with the exception of proximate cause. Then counsel asserts that the evidence establishes each of the other elements, and narrows the discussion to the one central issue—proximate cause. Counsel could state, *"The single issue in this case is: Was the defendant's failure to exercise ordinary care the proximate cause of plaintiff's injury?"*

*Other Side's Case Theory*

You will want to argue against your opponent's case theories. Select instructions you can employ to argue the weaknesses in the other side's case. Choose those instructions that best allow you to discuss those weaknesses. For instance, in the *Hill Moveit* case, as plaintiff's counsel you know that the defense is asserting comparative negligence and intoxication. Therefore, you need to argue based on the comparative negligence and intoxication instructions to refute the defense arguments.

---

Watch how to argue the burden of proof and attack the other side's legal theory for defense counsel's summation in the *Freck Point* trial demonstration movie on the website *http://www.aspenlawschool.com/books/berger_trialad4e.*

---

*Factual Theory: The Evidence*

A crucial function of planning closing argument is to marshal critical evidence that proves your legal theory as expressed in the jury instructions. Argument on the evidence consists of persuading the jury to follow and trust your analysis, witness testimony, and exhibits. Determining which witness testimony, exhibits, and credibility issues to argue requires focusing on essential points in your case theory. Just as with opening statement, you should avoid inconsequential evidence, because the jury will have a difficult time following your core facts if you also include the minutiae.

We suggest two methods for this sifting through the facts to find and arrange the important evidence for argument: (1) concentrate on the critical jury instructions, and (2) construct a story (narrative).

*Critical Jury Instructions*

By concentrating on the core jury instructions, you will naturally select the evidence to argue. This is because you will argue to the jury how to apply the law in those instructions to the facts, and thereby reach a verdict. Your organization of the significant facts will flow from the jury instructions.

For example, continue to assume you are plaintiff's counsel in the *Hill Moveit* case. You wish to determine which evidence you should discuss when arguing damages. Recall that you have two purposes in arguing damages: persuading the jurors that you have established damages within legally accepted categories of harm (that constitutes the damage element of your legal theory), and convincing the jurors of your view as to how damages should be calculated within such categories.

The following is an instruction on damages.

## Closing Argument

### Damages Instruction
### The *Hill Moveit* Case

No. ___

It is for the court to instruct you as to the measure of damages. By instructing you on damages, the court does not mean to suggest for which party your verdict should be rendered.

If your verdict is for the plaintiff, then you must determine the amount of money that will reasonably and fairly compensate the plaintiff for such damages as you find were proximately caused by the defendant, apart from a consideration of comparative negligence.

If you find for the plaintiff, your verdict must include the following **past economic damages** elements: (1) the reasonable medical care, treatment, and services received to the present time; (2) the reasonable value of earnings lost to present time; and (3) reasonable value of necessary nonmedical expenses that have been required to present time.

In addition, you should consider the following **future economic damages** elements: (1) the reasonable value of necessary medical care, treatment, and services with reasonable probability to be required in the future; (2) the reasonable value of salary and earning capacity with reasonable probability to be lost in the future; and (3) the reasonable value of necessary nonmedical expenses that will be required with reasonable probability in the future.

In addition, you should consider the following **noneconomic damages** elements: (1) the nature and extent of the injuries, and (2) the pain and suffering, both mental and physical, and the disability, disfigurement, loss of enjoyment of life experienced, mental anguish, loss of society and companionship, loss of consortium, and humiliation experienced and with reasonable probability to be experienced in the future.

*continued* ▶

> The burden of proving damages rests upon the plaintiff. It is for you to determine, based upon the evidence, whether any particular element has been proved by a preponderance of the evidence.
>
> Your award must be based upon evidence and not upon speculation, guess, or conjecture.
>
> The law has not furnished us with any fixed standards by which to measure noneconomic damages. With reference to these matters, you must be governed by your own judgment, by the evidence in the case, and by these instructions.

Using the jury instruction on damages, you could enlarge and project the instruction just as we illustrated with the verdict form that appears earlier in this chapter at page 461. However, this blowup of the damages jury instruction is visually complicated. You would be bogged down in complicated details trying to point to each of the three categories of damages. Instead, you want the jury to understand that there are three separate categories of damages and how to apply the evidence for each of the damages categories: past economic damages, future economic damages, and noneconomic damages.

Accordingly, in addition to, or in place of the blowup of the actual damages instruction, you could also use individual charts for each of the three damages categories. For instance, concerning the first category of damages in the instruction, past economic damages, your chart would list the elements for those damages.

---

### Closing Argument

#### Damages Instruction
#### The *Hill Moveit* Case

**Past Economic Damages**

1. The reasonable medical care, treatment, and services received to the present time;
2. The reasonable value of earnings lost to present time; and
3. The reasonable value of necessary nonmedical expenses that have been required to present time.

---

For each type of damage, you could then discuss evidence that you contend proves that category of damages. Among other things, as you explain the elements of each, you could itemize the medical expenses first at Ruston Medical Center and then of outpatient care, along with the loss of earnings, using Darcy's salary as a bartender as a starting place. You would talk about the evidence that proves those damages and justifies your calculations. This would include plaintiff's testimony, medical bills, W-2s, and so on.

*A Story*

Telling a story is an effective way of discussing the evidence during argument because juries approach a case from their human experiences. Jurors can best understand evidence that is structured in narrative form—this is what we mean by telling a story.

However, caution is in order. Closing argument is not an opportunity to tell prolonged stories or to reiterate your entire story of the case. In Chapter 5, on opening statement, we pointed out that it is a common fault of lawyers to give closing argument for an opening statement and opening statement for a closing argument. Opening statement is a time to tell a story and to relate the facts of the case, not to argue. Closing argument is the time to argue and use the story structure to weave together the factual story and legal theory of the case. By the time the jury has arrived at closing argument, they have heard the factual story in opening statement and during the presentation of the evidence, in addition to the smatterings of parts of the story told during jury selection. Belaboring by giving a litany of facts at this point in a narrative wastes the jurors' time and runs the risk of boring them.

However, a presentation of the facts in a short narrative form to bolster or make an argument can be successfully integrated into closing. For instance, relating an analogy can be effective. Alternatively, painting a word picture of the plaintiff's life before and after the injury while showing pictures of the plaintiff before and after, can drive home the human story aspect of your factual theory. Later in this chapter, we offer examples of storytelling designed to do just these things. See pages 476-477.

---

Watch the plaintiffs' counsel's summation in the *Freck Point* trial demonstration movie for how to use jury instructions and the case narrative on the website *http://www.aspenlawschool.com/books/berger_trialad4e.*

---

## C. Accentuating the Theme

You also can design your argument around your case theme. This theme should link the parts of the trial together. The theme is the memorable word, phrase, or sentence that captures your case theory. It is the thread that runs throughout the trial, and evolves from jury selection until now, when you come back to it in closing. Perhaps you recall the theme "rape is a secretive crime," which we mentioned in Chapter 3, page 55. Now, in closing argument, the prosecutor can refer again to this theme, which, like a thread, runs throughout the trial. Ten years after the trial, when a juror recounts the experience of serving on a jury, the theme is hopefully how the juror will describe what the case was about if asked about "a rape on a dark dirt road."

---

### Closing Argument

#### Using a Case Theme Throughout the Trial
#### The *Sexual Assault* Case

**Prosecutor in Jury Selection**

Ms. Enquist, you understand that rape is a secretive crime. It doesn't happen in a room like this with 40-some people watching. It can happen in an alley, a car on a dark road, in an empty house with only two people present. Would you, if you become a juror in this case, require the state to produce multiple eyewitnesses to what happened before you could find the defendant guilty of rape?

**Prosecutor in Opening Statement**

Rape is a secretive crime. On June 3 of last year, Zena Grant, the victim in this case, accepted a ride home with the defendant after they met at the Noble Restaurant and Lounge. The defendant turned off onto a dark dirt road . . . .

**Prosecutor in Closing Argument**

Members of the jury, it is not necessary to have multiple witnesses testify that they saw the defendant rape Zena. As you'll recall, we discussed in jury selection that rape is, by its very nature, a secretive crime, and that is why the law does not require proof by multiple witnesses. Here, you heard from Zena Grant, who testified that the defendant raped her. She was a thoroughly believable witness who had no reason to make up what happened. Beyond that, her testimony is corroborated by the witnesses who saw her leave the lounge with the defendant, witnesses who saw her in a beaten and bruised condition when she staggered onto the interstate . . . .

---

## D.  Responding to Your Adversary's Case Theory and Attacks on Your Case Theory

Another component of your closing argument consists of meeting your opponent's case theory and addressing assaults on your case theory. Planning this part of closing argument begins by envisioning the most devastating closing argument opposing counsel could deliver. Speculate about what opposing counsel will argue and then formulate your response to those arguments. When you make these arguments depends on whether you represent the plaintiff or the defendant, as discussed at pages 482-483.

### Anticipating Attacks

During pretrial, you will be able to anticipate attacks on your theory. After all, throughout case preparation you have thought about how the other side would respond to your case, especially those areas of potential vulnerability. Certain claims have predictable patterns of response or finite areas of attack that are dictated by experience and common sense. For example, the available avenues for attacking a claim for damages are credibility of the witnesses, inability to calculate accurately, excessive mistake in calculations, and exaggeration. Knowing these options and looking at the information in the case, you should have a good idea of where to expect the attack if you are claiming damages. There also are predictable techniques of attack—for example, attacking the credibility of a witness who is a relative of a party on the grounds of bias: *"She's the plaintiff's daughter; it is only natural that she would testify as she did about her mother's pain and suffering."* Accordingly, patterns or areas of attack and techniques for attack often meld together in practice.

### Meeting the Attack

Anticipating the attack is a part of the battle; meeting it in your argument is essential. You can meet the other side's case theory and accompanying attacks by

- stressing the strengths of your own case theory, and/or
- pointing out the weaknesses in your adversary's case theory.

Defense counsel may attack weaknesses in plaintiff's case theory by either arguing that the plaintiff failed to meet the burden of proof on an element, by asserting that the evidence establishes an affirmative defense, or both. Plaintiff's counsel may meet a defense theory that attacks the persuasive sufficiency of plaintiff's evidence by arguing that the evidence proves the elements, or by attacking weaknesses in the defense's evidence. If the defense raises an affirmative defense, plaintiff's attorney may either argue the vulnerable points in the defense's evidence or accentuate plaintiff's evidence refuting the affirmative defense.

### Emotion

Sympathy and emotion should not affect a jury's deliberations. The judge will instruct jurors to this effect. However, sympathy and emotion can be powerful, persuasive tools. To counteract an emotional appeal to jurors, you can stress the jury instruction. Bring the jury instruction to the surface in an attempt to diminish the sympathy and emotion. For example, counsel could argue:

> "Ladies and gentlemen, I expect that when it comes his turn, plaintiff's lawyer will bring you to tears by the time he is done. We all may be filled with sadness as we hear his argument on plaintiff's behalf. When that happens, remember the court's instruction that tells you in essence that you should neither be swayed by sympathy nor sidetracked by emotion."

## E. Juror Beliefs and Expectations

Unfortunately, some case weaknesses are often unspoken during the trial, and the lawyer learns about them only after the verdict. After a verdict is returned, the lawyer asks the jurors, *"Why did you decide to award the plaintiff $6 million?"* The lawyer finds out that the jury's verdict turned on something that neither trial attorney discussed in argument. Trial counsel is left with the question, "Why did the jury place so much weight on that evidence?" Here, we deal with answers to that question.

Jurors examine the evidence from their own experiences, understanding, and expectations of human behavior. They expect that people will have acted and events will have occurred according to certain norms with which the jurors are familiar. When the evidence is not in accord with their expectations, the jurors may conclude that the evidence is unsatisfactory and does not comport with common sense. A few of the illustrations we offered in earlier chapters were case-related expectations, such as the belief that a rape victim will attempt to escape given an opportunity, or that an abused child will report the abuse even if the abuser is an authority figure. Media-generated beliefs, such as the McDonald's coffee case, which contributed to the impression that there are too many frivolous lawsuits, and the "*CSI* effect" (from the television series *Crime Scene Investigation*), create the expectation that the prosecution will produce forensic science that will conclusively prove the defendant's guilt.

Another way of explaining jury decision making of this nature is that jurors are likely to understand and be persuaded by evidence in terms of the story it tells. If a piece of the story is missing or does not make sense, jurors may either finish the story according to their belief of how they think things occurred (or should have occurred), or reject the story because it does not sound correct.

Unspoken weaknesses that should have little or no connection to the claims or defenses also creep into jury deliberations—for example, negative aspects of the victim's or the defendant's personality, lifestyle choices of one of the parties that fall outside the mainstream community's norms or experiences, or race or religion may all affect the deliberations. Even if opposing counsel does not mention the elephant in the room, the jurors may not only see it, but also discuss and be swayed by it during jury deliberations. If and when such a "problem" appears in your case, acknowledge it. Argue that it should not be a consideration in the jury's deliberations.

To avoid these pitfalls, you should seek to identify what is missing or at odds with juror expectations. Then make your story complete, consistent, and correct. A simple way to uncover juror beliefs and expectations is to tell your case story to colleagues, friends, neighbors, or relatives. Alternatively, you could employ a focus group to hear your story; ask them for their opinions and listen to them. Neither argue with their positions nor readily disregard their assessments, criticisms, or suggestions. Chances are that a juror in your case will express the same difficulty with your case during jury deliberations, and you will not be there to argue the fallaciousness of that juror's belief. Once the problem area is identified, you can seek to complete the story with additional evidence and explanations, and distinguish the belief from what happened in your case.

Combating mistaken juror beliefs begins in jury selection, when you seek to get prospective jurors to acknowledge the existence of the belief, discuss it, and understand that the proposition they believe in is different from what the evidence may show in the case. Have them express a willingness to set aside the preconceived notion and decide the case by applying the law to the facts. For instance, in a child abuse case, questioning during voir dire can explore whether the prospective jurors believe that children who have suffered child abuse complain to others about the abuse. The effort to overcome juror beliefs and expectations continues throughout opening statement and the presentation of evidence. You can call witnesses to explain why something did or did not happen. Call an expert to testify that what happened is normal, although it is contrary to what one might expect. For example, an expert witness could explain that children do not, as a norm, report abuse by an authority figure (stepfather, priest, teacher). Or, to combat TV's "*CSI* effect," a prosecutor can call a forensic scientist to explain why certain scientific evidence does not exist in the case and that the television show does not reflect real life. Closing argument is your most powerful weapon against fallacious beliefs, because you can address them head on. *"Folks, CSI is a television show; it is not reality. You have heard from the criminalist who testified in this courtroom that what you see on CSI is pure entertainment, usually not based in reality. She also testified that under the circumstances of this case, you would not expect to detect DNA on the magazine. She testified . . . ."*

## F. Write It

We recommend that you write your closing argument. This process will force you to think about your arguments, carefully choose your words and phrases, and find a logical and clear organization for presentation. The writing process begins when you first enter the case; the product is polished during trial when, for instance, an answer from a witness has the ring of truth about it. The following are pointers about writing your closing.

---

### Writing Closing Argument

- **Write for the Audience:** Your closing should be written for the jurors (or the judge, if a bench trial), who will be listening and looking during your closing, not reading.
- **Don't Take It to Court:** The written closing has no place in court. If you take it to court, you will be tempted to read it. You will lose eye contact with your audience. Use an outline with keywords. Other techniques:
  - Use your visuals (elements chart, timeline) as substitutes for notes.
  - Put your notes near a cup of water so that you can take a sip of water. Glance at them. Or consider using a single page. List the main points you want to raise, using large, readable font.
  - Exception: Reading is fine when done for accuracy (quoting jury instructions, a document, or a witness).

---

## G.  Length

The judge may limit your time for closing. If so, rehearse it so that you will not run out of time and fail to cover important points. Otherwise, the length of closing will depend on the complexity of the case and the ability of the lawyer to maintain the jury's interest. To maintain that interest, the lawyer must have appealing arguments that jurors find valuable to their analysis of the law and evidence—like Aristotelian appeals, which are discussed in the next section.

## H.  Bench Trial

Delivering a closing argument to the judge is quite different from arguing to a jury. Judges and juries have different expectations of counsel. Understanding the judge's expectations can equip you to deliver an effective closing in a bench trial.

---

### Judicial Expectations—Closing Argument

#### Bench Trial

Judges have at least six expectations of counsel.

- First, although jurors can't ask counsel questions during summation, a judge can. The judge expects that you will give direct answers. Consider questions from the bench as an invitation to carry on a conversation with the judge with an eye toward alleviating any concerns the judge might have.
- Second, generally judges understand the law. Therefore, only when it is an uncommon or complicated area of the law is it necessary to explain it to the court. It is better to cover the law in a brief rather than argument.
- Third, the judge may be required to enter written findings of fact and conclusions of law at the end of the case. If so, the court will appreciate guidance in that regard. An argument that presents the facts and the conclusions of law can be effective.
- Fourth, the judge expects that counsel will make logical arguments, devoid of passion and emotion. Counsel is wise to let the facts tell the appealing story, leaving out adjectives and adverbs.
- Fifth, the court wants to conserve time and expects counsel's aid in that regard. The more concise and to the point the argument is, the better.
- Sixth, the court expects candor. Counsel should concede what must be conceded and be accurate in every statement of fact and law.

---

## III.  THE ART OF ARGUMENT

In this section, we offer a different method for the content to include in closing argument. This approach views closing argument from the perspective of choosing information that will sway the jury to reach a verdict for your client.

## A. Aristotelian Appeals

Aristotle formulated the three appeals that may be used to convince an audience: logos (logic), pathos (emotion), and ethos (ethics). In preparing your closing argument, you should concentrate on using all three appeals, because they sway an audience. Every human being is receptive to each of the three appeals. All three should be incorporated into closing argument. Some people are swayed more by one type of argument than another due to their training or life experience. For instance, because judges have been trained to think analytically, the logical appeal carries more weight than an emotional one. However, judges are human and can also be moved by a pathos argument. Jury argument tends to place more emphasis on pathos and ethos than would be used in argument to a judge, but logical arguments are essential to a good closing. Therefore, all three Aristotelian appeals should be incorporated into your closing argument.

---

### Closing Argument

#### Aristotelian Appeals
#### The *Blue Moon News Robbery* Case and
#### The *Hill Moveit Personal Injury* Case

- **Logos:** The first appeal is logic. Logical arguments stress patterns of thought, rational thinking, and a sense of logic. A jury will reach a verdict by applying the law to the facts. Therefore, arguments appealing to logic and the law are the centerpiece of the jury argument. In the *Blue Moon News Robbery* case, as the prosecutor, structure your argument in a logical pattern by using an elements chart for robbery in the first degree. Follow the list of elements one by one and argue that the evidence produced at trial has proven each of the elements. For example, you would argue that the fingerprint expert testifying that the latent prints on the magazine match the defendant's known print constitutes additional evidence that the defendant was the robber.
- **Ethos:** The second appeal is an ethical appeal. When making this argument, you appeal to the audience's highest moral sense. The argument speaks in terms of truth, duty, honor, justice, generosity, mercy, and the like. Nothing is more appealing to a jury than to correct an injustice or to do the right thing. In your arguments in the *Blue Moon News Robbery* case as defense counsel, you could repeatedly return to how the circumstances were conducive to a mistaken identification. The jurors' duty to uphold the law requires that the defendant's guilt be proved beyond a reasonable doubt. Or, as plaintiff's counsel in the *Hill Moveit Personal Injury* case, you will seek to portray the company as indifferent to the harm of unsecured loads and defectively designed trailers. Convince the jury that the company acted wrongfully. An incensed jury will be inclined to make things right by sending a message to Hill Moveit that what it did will not be tolerated.
- **Pathos:** Pathos, the emotional appeal, is the third type of argument. Of course, you cannot improperly appeal to the passion and prejudice of your audience,

*continued* ▶

whether judge or jury. In the *Blue Moon News Robbery* case, your emotional argument as defense counsel could center on the risk that your innocent client could be convicted of a crime he did not commit.

## B.  Sources for Argument

How do we determine how to argue in terms of both what to say and how to say it? In other words, how do we learn the art of argument? Judge Charles Moylan, former prosecutor, appellate judge, and teacher, once whimsically said that novice lawyers should spend some time traveling the country as evangelical ministers and then devote some time to selling previously owned vehicles. A stint selling on the Home Shopping Network might also serve lawyers well as a training ground for learning how to persuade.

Another way to learn what and how to argue is to study talented lawyers at work. Watch a trial lawyer argue. Pay close attention to what the lawyer argues and how. If an approach works, you may be able to adapt it to your case. However, if you do not feel comfortable with the style because it is not suitable to you, discard it.

You can also rely on books, DVDs, and websites that contain arguments by skilled trial lawyers. As an example, Vincent Bugliosi, who as a prosecutor tried the *Charles Manson* case, offers in his book, *Outrage,* his observations about the *O.J. Simpson* case. His editor for *Outrage* urged him to write the closing argument that he would have given if he had prosecuted the *Simpson* case. Although Bugliosi declined the offer because of the work it would have entailed given the time he would normally devote to preparing a closing, he did agree to write passages of what he would have argued, and commentaries along with these model arguments. Bugliosi's chapter on final summation, more than 100 pages, provides a collection of arguments that serve as models of how to argue. Vincent Bugliosi, *Outrage: The Five Reasons Why O.J. Simpson Got Away with Murder* (Norton 1997).

*Jury Argument in Criminal Cases* (2d ed., Azimuth 1993), by Professor Ray Moses, contains defense and prosecutor arguments; an associated website for the Center for Criminal Justice Advocacy (*http://www.criminaldefense.home stead.com*) offers a wealth of examples. *The Law as Literature* (Ephraim London ed., 1966) (originally published in 1901) contains about 50 contributors, with such notable authors as Supreme Court Justice Felix Frankfurter, Daniel Webster, Plato, Damon Runyon, and Albert Camus. Another outstanding resource is Joel Seidemann's *In the Interest of Justice: Great Opening and Closing Arguments of the Last 100 Years* (Harper Collins 2004).

Throughout the remainder of this chapter, we offer a sampling of well-crafted arguments by skilled lawyers that incorporate Aristotelian arguments.

### Logos

Vincent Bugliosi offers a lengthy logical argument that he believes could have been made in the *O.J. Simpson* case.

---

**Closing Argument**

#### Incorporating Aristotelian Logos in Argument
#### The Imaginary Closing in the *O.J. Simpson* Case

While Vincent Bugliosi's argument is more than five pages in the book *Outrage*, this two-paragraph excerpt from what can be described as the throw-it-out-the-window argument is sufficient to illustrate the logical argumentation.

"Ladies and gentlemen of the jury, the evidence of Mr. Simpson's guilt is so overwhelming in this case that you could throw 80 percent of it out the window and there still would be no question of his guilt. For instance, as we've previously discussed, we know that Simpson beat poor Nicole savagely, and she was in fear of her life at his hands. You recall she told officer Edwards, 'He's going to kill me, he's going to kill me.' I mean who else would have had any reason to murder these two young people, who apparently were both very well liked and popular, and particularly in such a brutal, savage way? But, let's throw this evidence out the window. Let's assume Mr. Simpson and Nicole got along well, just swimmingly, that he never laid a hand on her."

"When he was charged with these murders, if he were innocent, he would have been outraged, blazing mad, at being charged with murders he did not commit, and would desperately want to prove his innocence and find out who murdered the mother of his two children. Instead, he writes this suicide note that absolutely reeks with guilt. Show me an innocent person on the face of this globe charged with murder who would write a note like that. But let's assume there was no such suicide note; let's throw it out the window. After that slow-speed freeway chase, as you recall, the police found a gun, a passport, and a cheap disguise in Mr. Simpson's possession. And his closest friend, Al Cowlings, just happens to have $8,750 in currency stuffed in his pockets, which he told the police Mr. Simpson gave him in the Bronco. We all know what all of this means. We've already discussed it. Throw this evidence out the window. It doesn't exist."

---

### Pathos

A closing argument by plaintiff's attorney Gerry Spence in *Estate of Karen Silkwood v. Kerr McGee Corporation* incorporates the Aristotelian principle of pathos in argument. Karen Silkwood worked at Kerr McGee Nuclear Company as a chemical technician. As part of her union responsibilities she investigated health and safety at the plant, and she accused the company of safety violations and corporate cover-ups. Silkwood died in a car accident, and an autopsy of her body revealed contamination with plutonium. Her estate sued Kerr McGee.

## Closing Argument

### Incorporating Aristotelian Pathos in Argument
### The *Karen Silkwood* Case

Gerry Spence discusses corporate greed and neglect, Karen Silkwood, and, by analogy, the jury's responsibility.

"It was worse than the days of slavery. The owners of the slaves cared about their slaves, and many of them loved their slaves. It was a time of infamy and a time of corporate dishonesty. It was a time when men used men like disposable commodities. It was a time when corporations were more concerned with the public image than the truth. It was a time when the government held hands with these giants and played footsie with the greatest scientists. At the disposal of the corporation, to testify, to strike down the claims of people, and it was too late. The men are dying. The Gofmans and Morgans (plaintiff's expert witnesses) predicted it. They have long since passed on. But it was too late for many. They are fine men, open-faced, honest men, hardworking men who had hopes but whose lives were stolen from them for $3.50 an hour, taken under false pretenses. It was a sad time, the era between '70 and '79—they called it Cimarron syndrome."

"They are the nameless people now. One is a schoolteacher. One finally got a . . . welding certificate. One by one it is a tragedy so staggering I cannot imagine it, yet as Dr. Gofman said, 'If Karen Silkwood lived, she was doomed to cancer.' He could guarantee it."

"What is this case about? It is a case about Karen Silkwood, who was a brave, ordinary woman who did care. She risked her life—and she lost it. She had something to tell the world, and she tried to tell the world. What was it that Karen Silkwood had to tell the world? That has been left to us to say now. It is for you, the jury, to say it for her."

"I wish Karen Silkwood was standing here by me now and could say what she wanted to say. I think she would say, 'Brothers and sisters, they were just eighteen- and nineteen-year-olds. They didn't understand. There wasn't any training. They kept the danger a secret. They covered it with word games and number games.' And she would say, 'Friends, it has to stop here in Oklahoma City today.'"

"I'm going to tell you a simple story, about a wise old man and a smart-aleck young boy who wanted to show up the wise old man for a fool. The boy captured a little bird. He had the idea he would go to the wise old man with the bird in his hand and say, 'What have I got in my hand?' And the old man would say, 'Well, you have a bird, my son.' And he would say, 'Wise old man, is the bird alive or is it dead?'"

"The old man knew if he said, 'It is dead,' the little boy would open his hand and the bird would fly away. If he said, 'It is alive,' the boy would take the bird in his hand and crunch the life out of it and then open his hand and say, 'See, it is dead.'"

"So the boy went up to the wise old man and he said, 'Wise old man, what do I have in my hand?'"

> "The old man said, 'Why, it is a bird.'"
>
> "He said, 'Wise old man, is it alive or is it dead?'"
>
> "And the wise old man said, 'The bird is in your hands, my son.'"
>
> Joel J. Seidemann, *In the Interest of Justice* 252-253 (Harper 2004).

The jury returned a verdict of $505,000 in damages and $10 million in punitive damages. The verdict was later overturned, and then reinstated, and eventually the case settled.

### Ethos

The closing argument by Enron task force prosecutor Sean Berkowitz shows how an advocate can appeal to the jurors' highest moral sense.

---

### Closing Argument

#### Incorporating Aristotelian Ethos Argument
#### The *Enron* Case

During closing argument in the *Enron* fraud, insider trading, and conspiracy case in which Ken Lay and Jeff Skilling were the defendants, prosecutor Sean Berkowitz named the occupations of the jurors—dairy farmer, payroll manager, retired engineer, and so on. And then he pointed out:

> "The final word goes to people like the investors. You get to decide what's right. . . . You get the final word in this historic case. You get to decide whether they told truths or whether they told lies. Black and white."

With a large poster board with *truth* written in black on a white background and *lies* in white on a black background sitting on an easel behind him, Berkowitz argued:

> "These men lied. They withheld the truth. They put themselves in front of their investors, and I'm asking you to send them a message that it's not all right. You can't buy justice, you have to earn it."

---

## C. Selecting Persuasive Language

Closing argument frees you as a lawyer to draw on a broader way of expressing yourself than during any other phase of trial. In closing you are allowed to draw conclusions, to discuss the law, the evidence, and inferences from the evidence. By contrast, this is not opening statement, when you are restricted to stating the facts and are forbidden from arguing.

### Words with Connotations

Mark Twain put it this way: "The difference between the almost right word and the right word is really a large matter—'tis the difference between the lightning-bug and the lightning." Like most lawyers, you may not have the remarkable gift for delivery that Dr. Martin Luther King Jr. had. However, you can take the kind of care that he did in selecting the language to be used when addressing an audience. Listen to any of his speeches. You will recognize the care he took in phrasing his thoughts. Emotion and meaning are captured in the phrase *"I have a dream"* and in the sentence *"I have a dream that my four little children will one day live in a nation where they will not be judged by the color of their skin but by the content of their character."*

Your word choice will influence how your thoughts will be received by the jurors. For closing argument, you should employ a vocabulary that will best convince the jury. Your diction may be sternly logical, determinedly nonlegal, or bright and homespun. This is the opportunity to use value-laden words that you are prohibited from uttering in an opening statement. When choosing words, you must be mindful of their connotations and of the way they characterize the evidence.

Reread the excerpts from closings in this chapter and you can detect the care those lawyers took in selecting the words for their arguments. The words and phrasings are potent. In this excerpt, used earlier in the chapter, Clarence Darrow argues against the death penalty.

> Do I need to argue to your Honor that cruelty only breeds cruelty?—that hatred only causes hatred; that if there is any way to soften this human heart which is hard enough at its best, if there is any way to kill evil and hatred and all that goes with it, it is not through evil and hatred and cruelty; it is through charity, and love and understanding.

Words have connotations. The distinction between a neutral word and one with many connotations is the difference between "she said" and "she begged." It has been said, "What reaches the mind moves the heart." The word *begged,* with all of its connotations, registers in the mind and moves the heart.

As another example, consider the *Blue Moon News Robbery* case. The prosecutor could describe the defendant's testimony as his *story.* That word suggests defendant's testimony was concocted without quite explicitly declaring it to be fabricated. Or the prosecutor might frequently refer to the alibi witness as the defendant's *friend* to highlight Greg Delaney's interests in the case.

### Rhetorical Devices

A variety of rhetorical devices can enhance your argument. Illustrations of rhetorical techniques that you might choose for closing argument in the *Blue Moon News Robbery* case are as follows.

#### Postponement

Postponement is when the speaker touches on a subject briefly and holds it for later discussion. It is designed to retain the jurors' attention and give an important topic special treatment. The prosecutor in the *Blue Moon News Robbery* case may declare, *"The next element the state must prove is that the defen-*

*dant is the person who committed the robbery. This is the single issue in this case, so I will discuss this issue just a little later."*

### Concession

Concession is when the speaker concedes unfavorable information so as to acknowledge and thereby deemphasize a case weakness or harmful information. For example, the defense in the *Hill Moveit* case can argue, *"What happened to Darcy Rutherford is tragic. All of our hearts go out to her, but the defendant was not responsible."* Or the prosecutor in the *Blue Moon News* case can remark, *"Yes, it is possible that the defendant could have been in the store on another day and put his fingerprint on the magazine left on the counter, but does that make sense when you put it together with the other evidence in this case, such as Mr. Newman's identification of him?"*

### Antithesis

A speaker using antithesis places ideas in opposition to one another to emphasize differences or contrasts. The prosecutor in the *Blue Moon News Robbery* case could also use antithesis as follows.

---

**Closing Argument**

**Antithesis Argument**
**The *Blue Moon News Robbery* Case**

Alibi witness Mr. Delaney claims that he recalls that between 10:00 P.M. and 3:00 A.M. the following day, the defendant was at a party at his apartment. Mr. Delaney recalls when the defendant arrived, but he has no recollection of who arrived next at his party. He claims that the defendant wore a blue-and-white-striped shirt, but he cannot recall what any other guest wore. Mr. Delaney claims that defendant came to the party alone, but he cannot recall which of the other guests came alone to the party.

---

### Metaphors, Similes, and Analogies

Metaphors, similes, and analogies can effectively encapsulate the issues of the case or other concepts for the jury. Analogies are powerful arguments for at least three reasons. First, an analogy is persuasive because it relates the argument in a familiar way to the jurors. Second, it tells a story. We are all receptive to a good story that is well told. Third, an analogy enables the jurors to compare the analogy to the issue or situation before them and draw their own conclusions. The lawyer becomes an advisor who helps jurors reason by analogy, rather than telling them what to decide. For instance, if opposing counsel were to present arguments intended to divert the jury's attention from the central issue in the case, you might describe such tactics as "putting up a smoke screen," or the way Vincent Bugliosi does in his imaginary *O.J. Simpson* murder case argument in *Outrage* (page 475).

> ## Closing Argument
>
> ### Analogy Argument
> ### The Imaginary Closing in the *O.J. Simpson* Case
>
> I wonder if any of you folks have read Victor Hugo's account of the octopus. He tells us of how it doesn't have any beak to defend itself like a bird, no claws like a lion, nor teeth like an alligator. But it does have what could be called an ink bag, and to protect itself when it is attacked it lets out a dark fluid from this bag, thus making all of the surrounding water dark and murky, enabling the octopus to escape into the darkness.
>
> Now I ask you folks, is there any similarity between that description of the ink bag of the octopus and the defense in this case? Has the defense shown you any real, valid, legitimate defense reasonably based on the evidence, or has it sought to employ the ink bag of the octopus, and by making everything dark around Mr. Simpson, tried to let him escape into the darkness?
>
> I intend to clear up the water which defense counsel have sought to muddy, so that you folks can clearly see the evidence, the facts, the issues in this case, so that you can behold the form of the retreating octopus and bring this defendant back to face justice.

Analogies, like a malfunctioning firearm, can backfire. Opposing counsel will make every effort to find the flaw in the analogy, to convert the analogy to advantage, to mock it, or to distinguish it. For instance, if a prosecutor were to relate the octopus analogy in a self-defense case, defense counsel might respond: *"What does a story about an octopus have to do with this case? The prosecutor suggests that we have attempted to darken the water. Quite the contrary, we have done everything possible to make it clear that Rick acted to save his own life. It's the prosecution (faced with the lack of evidence here) who resorts to confusing matters by telling some story about an octopus. And incidentally, the prosecutor might want to get the facts straight here too—an octopus does have a beak."* Also, the analogy, simile, or metaphor should be suitable to the jury. Analogies involving war and sports can fall on deaf ears, and they are particularly susceptible to being manipulated by the other side. A reference to a basketball player may only obscure your argument for the juror who is unfamiliar with a player. Or a prosecutor's football analogy could be picked up by defense counsel, who converts it into an analogy that can be used against you (the evidence left the prosecution one yard short of the goal line, and that is a reasonable doubt).

To prevent a backfire, trial counsel should inspect the analogy for flaws and ways opposing counsel may alter it or distinguish it or otherwise turn it back on the teller. Carelessness in selecting an analogy, simile, or metaphor can end up harming your case, like a soldier causing a self-inflicted wound.

*Rhetorical Questions*

Rhetorical questions can be used to highlight an issue or to make transitions from one part of an argument to another. In the *Blue Moon News Robbery* case, the prosecutor might ask:

- "Did the defendant have a motive to rob the store?"
- "Was the defendant in the vicinity of the store when it was robbed?"
- "Did the defendant leave a fingerprint on a magazine on the counter?"
- "Was the defendant identified as a robber by Mr. Newman?"

*Tailored to the Case*

There is a caution implicit in using these rhetorical devices. They need to be appropriate for your case, within the frame of reference of the jurors, and invincible to being turned back on you.

One solution to such concerns is thorough preparation. Rehearse your argument with your rhetorical devices and without them. Try your argument on colleagues and non-lawyers to gauge their reaction. Find out which argument is more persuasive—the one with the rhetorical devices or the one without them? Think about how your opponent will react. Envision the worst possible use by your opponent of your rhetorical device.

### Stock Arguments

As a lawyer, you will collect stock arguments that you can reuse as you move from trial to trial. Included in this category might be your manner of explaining the burden of proof, the role of the jury, or damages. For instance, in arguing damages, many attorneys define pain in general. They discuss society's attitude toward pain, describe the pain suffered, discuss how it is difficult to compute, and suggest a formula for pain and suffering depending on the circumstances. As we suggested earlier, your best source for well-crafted arguments are experienced lawyers. Couple this research with your own imagination and you will have a stock of arguments that you can call on when needed.

## IV. STRUCTURING CLOSING

Closing argument must have a structure that the jury can follow and readily comprehend. The proven effective structure, paralleling the opening statement structure, has a beginning, a body, and a conclusion. Within this structure, you can choose among many approaches to argument. The content of the beginning-body-conclusion structure will vary widely, because attorneys' styles of wording and performance differ greatly. Keep in mind that these beginning remarks and the words that you speak to the jury at the conclusion of your closing are most important. Jurors pay the most attention to what you say first and last.

## A.  Beginning Remarks

We recommend that you begin closing argument by seizing the jury's attention. Because words are important, you should memorize and rehearse the words you will use to begin so they flow smoothly.

You might take a moment or two to thank the jurors for their service and their attention, particularly if it has been a long trial. However, to belabor this or to explain the purpose of closing argument is to create a pre-ramble, what we have termed *noise,* that interferes with your argument. See Chapter 5, Opening Statement, for an explanation and example of "noise," pages 155-157. You want to give them what they are waiting for: your argument for why they should vote a verdict in your client's favor. How you start will depend on whether you represent the plaintiff or the defendant.

Plaintiff

---

### Closing Argument

#### Plaintiff Counsel's Beginning Remarks
#### The *Freck Point Wrongful Death* Case

Theme

In the *Freck Point Wrongful Death* case, suppose you started with the greed theme. Now you could play it again and build on it based on the trial evidence.

> "In opening statement, I mentioned to you that this is not a case about love or about hate. It is about killing in the service of greed. Now that you have heard the evidence, you know that the defendant was driven by just plain greed."

A Quote

Or you might choose to begin with a quote, a figure of speech, or an analogy intended to catch the jurors' attention and interest:

> "It's often been said, 'The road to wisdom begins by asking the right questions.'"

Roadmap

Or you could give the jurors a roadmap of what you are going to argue. In other words, resort to the classic structure: Tell them what you are going to tell them, tell them, and then tell them what they've been told. In the *Hill Moveit Personal Injury* case, plaintiff's counsel could begin:

> "This discussion has two parts. First, it examines the legal elements of product liability. As we go over the elements of product liability, we will apply the law to evidence and show how it establishes the defendant's liability in this case. Second, we'll review the evidence proving damages."

---

### Defense

Because plaintiff's counsel has already set the stage, the defense's closing argument begins in a climate slightly different from the one plaintiff's counsel faced.

---

**Closing Argument**

#### Defense Counsel's Beginning Remarks
#### The *Hill Moveit Personal Injury* Case

**Fairness**

Some possible defense beginnings might use the following strategy of reminding the jury of its agreement to weigh the defense argument equally:

> "When I spoke to you in voir dire, you promised me you would keep an open mind until you heard all of the evidence and argument."

Or defense counsel could begin:

> "There are two sides to every coin."

**Pick Up**

Or defense counsel might consider picking up at the place where plaintiff counsel left off and then proceed into the defense argument:

> "Plaintiff's attorney just gave you a figure that would compensate plaintiff. We offer you this damage figure—zero [writes a big "0" on a blackboard]. Let me explain why . . . ."

---

As these illustrations suggest, beginning remarks vary. We are partial to attention-getting introductions because if done well, they pull the jury into your argument, rendering the argument more persuasive. But, you will need to assess what you are comfortable arguing.

## B. The Body

The body of your argument is where you apply the law in the jury instructions to the evidence in the case. Crafting these arguments is analogous to writing the concluding pages of a mystery story. Put yourself in the shoes of the author of a mystery story. You developed the motive and clues through many chapters. Now the reader needs guidance to gather the clues, see the motive, assemble the facts into a story, and draw the conclusions that point to the solution. Your job is like the author in the last pages of a mystery, you must tie all the strands together. Discuss how the law should be applied to the evidence and guide the jurors in the direction of the verdict you want them to reach.

This apply-the-law-to-the-facts organization can lead to an argument that fundamentally is an appeal to logic, or in Aristotelian terms, logos. Besides logic, the body of your argument should also, within ethical boundaries, contain ethical (ethos) and emotional (pathos) appeals.

### Organization and Subjects
#### Organization

Many approaches exist for organizing the body of closing argument. In practice, attorneys often blend these approaches in closing arguments.

- **Issues:** State the issue and frame it in your client's favor, if possible. Plaintiff's counsel, for example, could begin with an elements chart and, after applying the law in each element to the facts, reduce the issues to one element—proximate cause. Defense counsel could begin by agreeing that the issue is one of proximate cause.
- **The Evidence:**  Apply the law relating to the issue to the facts. For instance, apply the jury instruction on proximate cause to the evidence of the case. Each side contends that the evidence or lack of evidence supports its position.
- **Witness by Witness:** An organizational approach that reviews each pertinent witness's testimony in relation to your case theory is a choice we discourage. It is often tedious, disjointed, and hard to follow (particularly because it usually includes too much detail from the witnesses' testimony). However, it can be effective as a subpart of the body—particularly if it is to prove or cast doubt on an element in the case. In the *Blue Moon News Robbery* case, for example, defense counsel could argue reasonable doubt and misidentification by reviewing the testimony of each prosecution witness other than Newman. Defense counsel could then proceed by pointing out that the witness did not provide any evidence on the identity issue. In discussing the witness Newman, defense counsel could then argue that he misidentified the defendant because of poor lighting, the robber's face being partially concealed, and so on.

#### Topical Arguments

You can make arguments that center around subjects of argument. Topical arguments can center on the following:

- Critical jury instructions,
- Identifying issues in the case and then marshaling evidence on your side of the issue,
- Telling a narrative story,
- Meeting attacks on your case theory and/or attacking the other side's case theory,
- Arguing why damages are or are not warranted,
- Juror beliefs and expectations,
- Your case theme,

- The witness testimony, and
- A blend of these.

### Blending the Approaches

The approaches to organizing the body of closing argument are not mutually exclusive; they may and often are blended together. As an illustration, consider prosecutor's closing in the *Blue Moon News Robbery* case that blends the (1) by-the-issues, (2) by-narrative, and (3) by-the-numbers approaches.

We offer an illustration of one organizing tool, the blended approach, with the understanding that it is a broad structure and that you may find a better way to arrange closing argument for your individual case.

---

#### Closing Argument

**The Body: Blended Structure Argument**
**The *Blue Moon News Robbery* Case**

Body of the Prosecutor's Closing Argument

The single issue is: Did the defendant rob the store?

You have listened to Mr. Newman's eyewitness testimony. As you recall, on January 15 at approximately 11:30 at night, Mr. Newman was working as a clerk at the Blue Moon News convenience store. Mr. Newman saw the defendant browsing at the magazine rack. The defendant came to the counter area where Mr. Newman was. Although the defendant had his hat pulled down some, Mr. Newman got a good look at the defendant's facial features. The defendant's face was within three feet of Mr. Newman. The counter area was well lit. Mr. Newman identified the defendant in this court as the person who robbed him that night.

Based on Mr. Newman's testimony alone, the defendant is the person who committed the robbery. But this is not a case where all you have is the testimony of one eyewitness to consider during your deliberation. There is more. There are at least four more pieces of evidence pointing to that man as the person who robbed the store [pointing to the defendant].

First, you have fingerprint evidence. The defendant's latent fingerprint was left on the magazine that the robber placed on the counter. In the real world, that is more than mere coincidence.

Second . . . .

---

## C. Conclusion

A conclusion to your closing argument should be dynamic and memorable for your case. It might include telling the jury which verdict you request. Or take the form of a summary statement that emphasizes that the jury should review one witness's testimony, a particular jury instruction, and so on. For example, in the *Hill Moveit* case, your conclusion might be your discussion of damages, walking the jury through the Special Verdict Form (reprinted earlier in this chapter at pages 461-462) and explaining how they should fill it in. As defense counsel in the *Blue Moon News Robbery* case, you might conclude by going back to the reasonable doubt instruction.

Alternatively, your concluding remarks might be aimed at motivating the jury to embrace an emotional story by appealing to their highest moral character. For example, in the *Enron* case closing that appeared earlier in the chapter at page 477, the prosecutor refers to truth and justice. In the notorious *Charles Manson* case, the prosecutor concluded by motivating the jury.

---

**Closing Argument**

### Conclusion: Motivating the Jury
### The *Charles Manson* Case

In prosecuting the *Charles Manson* case, Vincent Bugliosi concluded his arguments in the following ways.

The initial closing was capped with these comments:

"Under the law of this state and nation these defendants are entitled to have their day in court. They got that."

"They are also entitled to have a fair trial by an impartial jury. They also got that."

"That is all they are entitled to!"

"Since they committed these seven senseless murders, the People of the State of California are entitled to a guilty verdict."

The prosecutor finished rebuttal argument with these words:

"Ladies and gentlemen of the jury, Sharon Tate . . . Abigail Folger . . . Voytek Frykowski . . . Jay Sebring . . . Steven Parent . . . Leno LaBianca . . . Rosemary LaBianca . . . are not here with us now in this courtroom, but from their graves they cry out for justice. Justice can only be served by coming back to this courtroom with a verdict of guilty."

---

To see how to deliver a motivational rebuttal, watch plaintiffs' counsel's rebuttal argument in the *Freck Point* trial demonstration movie on the website *http://www .aspenlawschool.com/books/berger_trialad4e*.

---

## D.  Rebuttal

The number of times you are permitted to argue to the jury also shapes the structure of your closing argument. Plaintiff's counsel in most jurisdictions is afforded both opening and rebuttal closing arguments, and has the choice of meeting the defense case theory and attacks in either or both arguments. Along with having the burden of proof, which justifies the allocation of another argument to plaintiff's counsel, comes the opportunity to refute defense arguments and have the last words. For these reasons, rebuttal has been referred to as "having the hammer." One plaintiff's strategy is to hold back a strong argument for rebuttal so that concluding remarks will be powerful. However, this strategic approach runs the risk of appearing to ambush the defense and diminishes the persuasiveness of the initial closing. The court might sustain an objection that in your particular case, the particular argument is beyond the scope of rebuttal; while this may not be likely to happen, it is a risk you must calculate.

Alternatively, plaintiff's counsel can reserve the motivational concluding remarks until rebuttal. This avoids finishing the initial closing on too high a note and making anticlimactic the concluding comments in rebuttal argument. Further, plaintiff has the advantage of having the last word before the jury retires to deliberate, during which counsel can exhort the jurors to reach a verdict for the plaintiff.

While rebuttal is restricted to responding to the other side's argument, that does not mean that counsel just waits to hear the closing and then extemporaneously answers it. Rebuttal is a powerful device—the last word. It cannot be left to inspiration. Rather, prior to trial you can fashion your rebuttal by anticipating what the other side will argue. Then polish your rebuttal during trial. By listening carefully to opposing counsel's argument, you will be able to identify the argument that provides you with an avenue to respond. You just bridge from opposing counsel's argument to your prepared remarks: *"Counsel just said that you should acquit his client if there is any doubt. Is that how Jury Instruction 5 defines a reasonable doubt? . . ."*

When the plaintiff has a rebuttal, defense counsel must anticipate plaintiff's rebuttal argument and try to undercut its potential impact. Therefore, defense counsel will need to analyze thoroughly what plaintiff's counsel will say in rebuttal about the defense case (*"If plaintiff's counsel says . . . , ask yourself how the plaintiff can explain why, under the circumstances, their witness did not come forward until almost a year later."*).

While the concept of "reasonable doubt" will play an important role in the criminal defense attorney's closing argument, the "presumption of innocence" plays an equally important part—but here the focus on this latter concept will be in blocking what we call "reversing the presumption of innocence." We'll illustrate with the *Freck Point Murder* case. Expert witnesses for the government will acknowledge that the killer was wearing gloves; police will concede that no gloves, bloody or otherwise, were found in the area. The defense will make strong points with this in support of its reasonable doubt defense—*unless* the prosecution or jurors are left free to "reverse the presumption." The portion of the defense closing argument calculated to block this possibility might go something like the following.

### Closing Argument

#### Blocking "Reversing Presumption"
#### The *Freck Point Murder* Case

When looking at the evidence in this case so that my client will get a fair trial, it is crucial that you don't let the prosecution in rebuttal or some juror in deliberations shift the presumption of innocence. Take the missing gloves I've talked about. If you reverse the presumption of innocence and presume my client guilty, then of course he must have done something to hide or destroy the gloves. But if you presume him innocent, then the absence of those gloves raises a doubt that cannot be made to disappear with speculation and excuses. It only disappears with *evidence*—like having an expert to testify that remnants in the fireplace are of the fiber composition of gloves, or a witness who saw my client take something off his hands and toss it in a ravine. So, if you hear the prosecutor or someone on the jury make excuses and offer speculations to fill in doubts in the prosecution's case, say on behalf of my client, "You're reversing the presumption of innocence."

While on the surface this "blocking reversing presumption" argument might seem appealing, the prosecutor in rebuttal may point out its fallaciousness with an argument along the following lines.

### Closing Argument

#### Rebutting the Reversing-the-Presumption Argument
#### The *Freck Point Murder* Case

Ladies and gentlemen, you will recall defense counsel's reversing-the-presumption-of innocence argument. Two things are very wrong with the argument.

The first thing wrong with the argument is that it misstates the law that you received from the judge in the instructions. The law regarding the presumption of innocence is contained in instruction number five, which states:

A defendant is presumed innocent. This presumption continues throughout the entire trial unless during your deliberations you find it has been overcome by the evidence beyond a reasonable doubt.

The law does not require, as defense counsel suggests, that evidence must be produced to explain the absence of, for example, the gloves. If that were the case, the law would reward murderers who successfully dispose of weapons and other evidence of their guilt.

Rather, the law requires that the defendant here, like any defendant in America, is to be presumed innocent. You might think of the presumption as a cloak that covers the defendant. That cloak of innocence, however, can be removed, as the instruction says, by evidence beyond a reasonable doubt. We gladly accept that burden.

The second thing wrong with the defense counsel's argument is that it is an invitation to abandon your common sense during deliberations. As the judge has told you, you may use your common sense during your deliberations. Let's apply the law on the presumption of innocence to the missing gloves example and see why the defense argument is an invitation to abandon common sense. During your deliberations you will have overwhelming evidence to overcome the presumption of innocence beyond a reasonable doubt—to remove the cloak of innocence from this defendant. Defense counsel hopes that a juror will say that the gloves are missing, that the absence of the gloves cannot be explained by the evidence, and, therefore, that the defendant did not murder Sondra. The common-sense explanation is that the defendant successfully disposed of the gloves. That's not speculation. Based on the ample evidence of the defendant's guilt, that's just plain common sense. Defense counsel hopes with the reversing-the-presumption argument that you will not use your common sense.

I urge you to follow the law on the presumption of innocence as given to you by the court, and to draw upon your well of common sense in reaching your verdict.

## V. DELIVERING CLOSING

Closing argument, like opening statement, is a speech, and the techniques described on pages 12-17 and 19-22 apply equally to closing argument. The following is a summary of pointers for delivering both opening and closing. You might also want to review the approaches, strategies, and techniques described in Chapter 2 on trial persuasion principles.

### Delivering Closing Argument

- **Take a Center Courtroom Position:** You want to take a position in the courtroom in front of the jury and at a distance comfortably back so that you don't invade the jury's space. Your movement around the courtroom should be purposeful. For instance, you may move to a chart, move to another position when you shift to another subject, and so on. (Be mindful of the rules and etiquette of the judge.)
- **Manage Nervousness:** Utilize these techniques: thoroughly prepare, practice, and concentrate on your message, not yourself.
- **Rehearse:** Rehearsing will make the closing flow smoothly and enable you to communicate with the jury.
- **Project Sincerity:** Believe in your case, be candid, and be courteous.
- **Tell a Story, Use a Theme:** Do this during those points in argument when you discuss the facts.
- **Use Visuals.**
- **Be Passionate, Be Fair, and Be Ethical.**

A final word of advice about your delivery: It is all right to be righteously indignant if either opposing counsel or another party steps out of bounds. It shows you care about fairness. But generally, be sincere in showing your indignation or it will appear to be a tactic.

## VI.  VISUALS FOR CLOSING

Visuals can serve several purposes in closing:

- Applying law to the facts,
- Explaining the law,
- Reviewing the facts,
- Defining terms,
- Showing relationships between the participants, and
- Arguing the case.

### A.  Illustrating the Use of Visuals

Let's return to the *Freck Point Murder* case to illustrate how visuals can create a persuasive closing argument. Assume for the following illustrations that you are the prosecutor.

#### Applying the Law to the Facts

You can show the jury the same elements chart that you introduced to them in your opening statement. With the aid of the chart, progress element by element, applying the law as stated in the jury instruction from which the elements chart is drawn to the facts proven during the trial. In this way you explain to the jury that the conduct of the person who stabbed Sondra Griffith to death fulfilled all the elements of murder in the first degree.

---

### Closing Argument Elements Chart

The *Freck Point Murder* Case
Murder—First Degree

1. On or about October 16, the defendant Samuel Griffith,
2. In the State of Major,
3. Killed Sondra Griffith.
4. The defendant acted with intent to kill.
5. The intent was the result of premeditation.
6. Sondra Griffith died as a result of defendant's acts.

---

#### Explaining the Law

To explain the law to the jury as the prosecutor, you could use a visual to explain the meaning of the word *premeditated*. The jury instructions define *premeditated* as "considered beforehand." Illustrate *premeditated* with a visual of a stop sign as you explain in everyday terms that people routinely premeditate action. *"When you come to a stop sign, you stop, then look to the left, then the right for oncoming cars. You consider beforehand whether to proceed. That's premeditation."* The visual of the stop sign will highlight your explanation.

### Reviewing the Facts

To review the facts for the jury, you could employ the timeline chart described on page 168. You could show photographs and the diagram of the bedroom where Sondra was stabbed to death, and so on.

### Arguing the Issue

As you apply the law to the facts with the aid of the elements chart, you reserve the discussion of one issue: "The single issue in this case is: Did the defendant do it?" Later, you can use a visual to present your arguments on that issue. The animation feature of a computer software program such as PowerPoint can facilitate your argument, because you can use your remote to make words and/or objects appear on the slide one at a time. You engage the jury's attention on your argument. When you conclude your arguments, the slide will show an accumulation of evidence proving your ultimate argument point. To illustrate, let's return to the *Freck Point Murder* case and examine a visual that could be used.

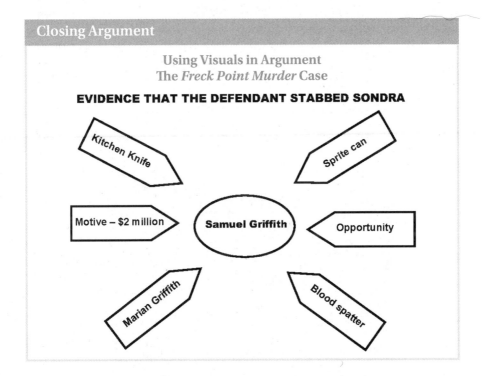

**Closing Argument**

Using Visuals in Argument
The *Freck Point Murder* Case

**EVIDENCE THAT THE DEFENDANT STABBED SONDRA**

Kitchen Knife — Sprite can — Motive – $2 million — Samuel Griffith — Opportunity — Marian Griffith — Blood spatter

It is not necessary to use a computer slideshow. Another approach is to use a board with the defendant's name in the middle and attach hook-and-loop-tape arrows to the board.

## B. Visuals in Diverse Cases

As you have seen with the *Freck Point Murder* case, you can be creative in designing visuals that support and enrich your argument. Now, examine some visuals to see what is possible. As you look at them, you will note two attributes. First, they are aimed at a particular issue that is at the heart of the case. Second, once the visual is complete, it is freestanding, requiring no explanation. Completion involves assembling all of the pieces with the use of a computer slideshow program using a custom animation feature or by pasting them onto a display board. By the time the visual has been assembled, it should be convincing on the issue.

*Visual 1: Prosecution for Fraud*

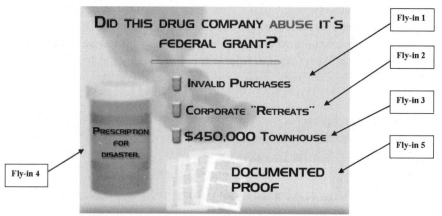

Borrowed Ladder Media Services Inc., *http://www.borrowedladder.com.*

*Visual 2: Defense of Antitrust*

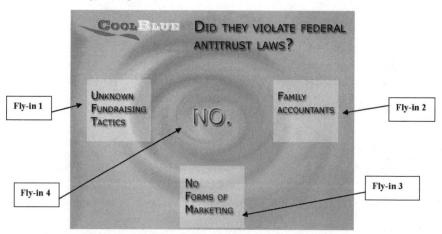

Borrowed Ladder Media Services Inc., http://www.borrowedladder.com.

The fly-ins in visuals one and two represent animations that will bring in the statements one by one until they are all assembled, showing how the jury should find on an issue. This technique is easily activated in PowerPoint or similar programs. (However, do not overly use this technique—it can distract jurors from listening to your argument.)

### Damages

Lawyers avail themselves of visuals to argue damages. This is a chart showing economic losses due to injury.

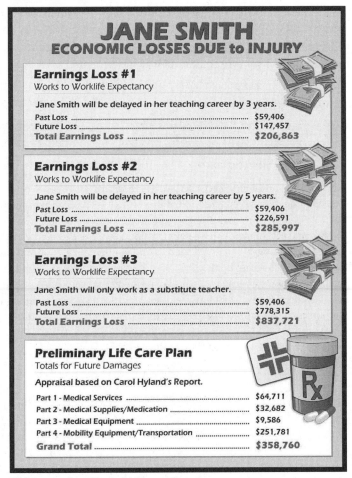

JANE SMITH
ECONOMIC LOSSES DUE to INJURY

**Earnings Loss #1**
Works to Worklife Expectancy

Jane Smith will be delayed in her teaching career by 3 years.

| | |
|---|---|
| Past Loss | $59,406 |
| Future Loss | $147,457 |
| **Total Earnings Loss** | **$206,863** |

**Earnings Loss #2**
Works to Worklife Expectancy

Jane Smith will be delayed in her teaching career by 5 years.

| | |
|---|---|
| Past Loss | $59,406 |
| Future Loss | $226,591 |
| **Total Earnings Loss** | **$285,997** |

**Earnings Loss #3**
Works to Worklife Expectancy

Jane Smith will only work as a substitute teacher.

| | |
|---|---|
| Past Loss | $59,406 |
| Future Loss | $778,315 |
| **Total Earnings Loss** | **$837,721** |

**Preliminary Life Care Plan**
Totals for Future Damages

Appraisal based on Carol Hyland's Report.

| | |
|---|---|
| Part 1 - Medical Services | $64,711 |
| Part 2 - Medical Supplies/Medication | $32,682 |
| Part 3 - Medical Equipment | $9,586 |
| Part 4 - Mobility Equipment/Transportation | $251,781 |
| **Grand Total** | **$358,760** |

High Impact, *http://www.highimpactlit.com.*

## VII.  ETHICAL CONSIDERATIONS

ABA Model Rule of Professional Conduct 3.4 on Fairness to Opposing Party and Counsel outlines the boundaries of professional conduct that are of particular significance for closing argument.

A lawyer shall not: . . .

(e) in trial, allude to any matter that the lawyer does not reasonably believe is relevant or that will not be supported by admissible evidence, assert personal knowledge of facts in issue except when testifying as a witness, or state a personal opinion as to the justness of a cause, the credibility of a witness, the culpability of a civil litigant or the guilt or innocence of an accused. . . .

The following four sections discuss Rule 3.4 and provide additional illustrations of closing arguments that exceeded the boundaries set by the Model Rules of Professional Conduct or ethical conduct. Rule 3.4 applies to all lawyers. Because prosecutors are charged with the duty to see that justice is done and must exercise particular care in how they phrase closing arguments, several of the illustrations come from prosecutors' closing arguments.

## A.  Personal Opinion

### Closing Argument

#### What Not to Do: Personal Opinion

**Prosecutor:** "Ladies and gentlemen, I believe it is very clear, and I hope you are convinced, too, that the person who committed this crime was none other than Christina Marsh." And later: "I'm sure she committed the crime." Referring to Marsh's testimony, the prosecutor states: "Use your common sense, ladies and gentlemen. That is not true. It's another lie. It's a lie, ladies and gentlemen, an out-and-out lie." Regarding the alibi witnesses' credibility, the prosecutor says: "You should entirely disregard their testimony because, if you will remember, every one of them lied on the stand. . . . I sincerely doubt if [the witness] had seen Christina Marsh there." Of another witness's testimony, the prosecutor states: "I find that awfully hard to believe."

*State v. Marsh*, 728 P.2d 1301, 1302 (Hawaii 1986), held:

> "The rationale for the rule is that '[e]xpressions of personal opinion by the prosecutor are a form of unsworn, unchecked testimony and tend to exploit the influence of the prosecutor's office and undermine the objective detachment that should separate a lawyer from the cause being argued.' ABA Standards for Criminal Justice, Commentary, at 3.89. The Supreme Court has observed that a prosecuting attorney's 'improper suggestions, insinuations, and especially, assertions of personal knowledge are apt to carry much weight against the accused when they should properly carry none.' *Berger v. United States*, 295 U.S. 78, 88 (1935)."

## B.  Venturing Outside the Record

Counsel should discuss only the admitted evidence. She should never state any facts or inferences other than those based on the evidence introduced at trial. To step beyond this boundary is to become an unsworn witness, which Model Rule of Professional Conduct 3.4 prohibits. The following excerpts illustrate closings that departed from the evidence.

## Closing Argument

### What Not to Do: Venturing Outside the Evidence

**Prosecutor:** "Those of you who have some medical knowledge know that cocaine is a downer, you get mellow on it. It's not like methedrine which strokes you up and causes you to do irrational acts. Cocaine is a downer. You don't go out and shoot people on cocaine. You make love: you mellow." *People v. Bell*, 778 P.2d 129, 149-150 (Cal. 1989).

**Prosecutor:** "Well, ladies and gentlemen, we can't tell you everything he did after his arrest and he knows it. Maybe when this is over, I will tell you what he did when he was arrested." *People v. Emerson*, 455 N.E.2d 41, 45 (Ill. 1983).

Personal stories can run afoul of the rule. In *People v. Barraza*, 708 N.E.2d 1256 (Ill. App. 1999), an aggravated sexual assault case, the prosecutor told a personal story in closing argument to refute the defense attorney's suggestion that the testimony of the two minor victims were not credible because they delayed reporting for two years. The prosecutor's story recounted a conversation with his ten-year-old daughter, in which she told him that she would not tell him if she were touched inappropriately despite his instructions to her that she should tell.

## C. Irrelevant Material

Arguments appealing to ethnic, racial, sexist, ageist, political, economic, or religious bias violate the fundamental principles of our justice system. Arguments calculated to inflame the passion, prejudice, or fear of the jurors should be avoided because they are morally and ethically wrong. Such arguments inject matters into the trial that may undermine a fair determination of the case. The following are some examples.

## Closing Argument

### What Not to Do: Introducing Irrelevant Matter

#### Religion

**Prosecutor:** "And this child embraced the Lord and embraced the word of God and tried to grow. And in the child's growth, he met Don McCary. It is the word of the Lord that this child was learning and that this man was corrupting, and that is what happened to this child."

*continued* ▶

> The Tennessee Court of Criminal Appeals in *State v. McCary*, 119 S.W.3d 226, 254 (2003), disapproved of the argument, stating, "In our view those arguments, replete with inappropriate religious references, were improper" and observed "[w]hether the defendant should be 'damned for eternity' is the exclusive jurisdiction of a far greater authority than the state courts."

## D.  The Golden Rule

A golden rule argument asks the jurors to put themselves into the place of the party. This type of argument is improper.

---

### Closing Argument

#### Do Not Place Yourself in the Case

**Civil Case**

A golden rule argument would argue to the jury that it should calculate damages by placing themselves in the plaintiff's shoes and award the amount they think it would be worth to undergo equivalent disability, pain, and suffering. *Brokopp v. Ford Motor Co.*, 71 Cal. App. 3d 841 (1977).

**Criminal Case**

An improper golden rule appeal to passion and prejudice occurred when the prosecutor asked the jurors to place themselves in the position of an innocent victim who was assaulted with a knife and sustained serious injuries. *People v. Simington*, 19 Cal. 4th 1374 (1993).

---

### CHECKLIST: CLOSING ARGUMENT

**Preparation**

☐ Preparation begins soon after entry into the case. Counsel should keep notes of ideas for closing.

☐ Prior to trial, write the closing argument, with final editing during trial. Reduce closing to outline notes.

☐ Rehearse closing argument. Just like opening statement, commit concluding remarks to memory so they will flow smoothly.

**Content**

☐ Case theories should serve as guides for planning closing.

☐ Regarding the legal theories, jury instructions, among others, serve as the core around which to craft closing argument:

- Elements of the claim or defense,
- Burden of proof,
- Issues in dispute, and
- The other side's case theory.

☐ In arguing the factual theory, counsel should use jury instructions that pertain to crucial facts, as well as a story embodying those facts.

☐ The case theme should be incorporated into the closing.

☐ Closing should meet the other side's case theory and attacks.

☐ Juror beliefs and expectations that could be detrimental to the case should be identified, met, or distinguished from your case.

### Length

☐ Length of closing should be suitable to the complexity of the case, and should not run overly long.

### Aristotelian Appeals

☐ Closing should make all three appeals: logical, emotional, and ethical.

☐ Persuasive language should include:
  - Words with connotations; and
  - Rhetorical devices, such as postponement, concession, antithesis, metaphors, similes, analogies, and rhetorical questions.

### Structure

☐ The closing should begin by seizing the jury's attention.

☐ The body of the closing should be well organized, emphasizing the strengths of the case before dealing with case weaknesses or the other side's attack.

☐ The closing should conclude by referring to the theme and reasons for the requested verdict, thus motivating the jury to make the right decision.

☐ Rebuttal should refute the other side's arguments and finish strong.

### Bench Trial

Counsel should

☐ be prepared to answer the judge's questions during closing;

☐ not spend an inordinate amount of time explaining the basic law in the case;

☐ assist the court in making findings of fact and conclusions of law;

☐ make logical and ethical arguments. Do not seek to appeal the judge's emotions, except as telling of the facts evokes emotion;

☐ be concise and to the point; and

☐ be candid, accurately stating the facts and law, and conceding what should be conceded.

### Delivery

Counsel should

☐ project sincerity;

☐ avoid distracting behavior, such as pacing back and forth;

☐ maintain eye contact with jurors or judge;

☐ deliver the closing with a minimal outline;

*continued* ▶

☐ position her body to hold the fact finder's attention; and
☐ make purposeful movements.

Counsel should use trial visuals effectively:

☐ Ensure use is permissible,
☐ Make visuals persuasive,
☐ Position equipment and visuals appropriately, and
☐ Have a backup plan if equipment malfunctions.

### Ethical Boundaries

☐ Counsel should not state a personal opinion.
☐ Counsel should not venture outside the record.
☐ Counsel should not introduce irrelevant matter.
☐ Counsel should not invoke the golden rule.

# TRIAL PREPARATION AND CASE MANAGEMENT

*"[Preparation] is the be-all of good trial work. Everything else—felicity of expression, improvisational brilliance—is a satellite around the sun. Thorough preparation is that sun."*

—**Louis Nizer**, quoted in *The New Lawyer's Wit and Wisdom: Quotations on the Legal Profession, in Brief* 269 (Bruce Nash & Allan Zullo eds., Kathryn Zullo comp., Running Press 2001)

*"It's in the preparation—in those dreary pedestrian virtues they taught you in seventh grade and you didn't believe. It's making the extra call and caring a lot."*

—**Diane Sawyer**, quoted in *The Book of Positive Quotations* 589 (Steve Deger & Leslie Ann Gibson eds., John Cook comp., 2d ed., Fairview Press 2007)

# I. INTRODUCTION

When called on, you rise, look the judge in the eye, and announce, "Ready for trial, Your Honor." Trial preparation—and indeed this book—is dedicated to ensuring that when you say you are ready, you truly are; that you have thoroughly prepared and are confident that you will prevail. Thorough preparation is the foundation for success in trial.

Getting to this state of readiness is challenging. Trial preparation is laborious. It means that the advocate has pursued a complete factual investigation, is organized, and has a command of the law and facts. Trial preparation encompasses a variety of activities, including fact investigation, legal research, informal and formal discovery, and motions' advocacy. These matters are discussed in depth in our *Pretrial Advocacy* book. Throughout this book we have examined trial preparation for every aspect of trial from jury selection through closing argument.

In this chapter we explore a critical part of trial preparation that overarches all the varied aspects of trial—organizing and managing your case information in an orderly manner—so that you understand the information you have and know how to retrieve it easily.

Specifically, we offer techniques and trial systems for organizing and managing the case, with an emphasis on electronic case management software.

# II. A MANAGEMENT SYSTEM

In trial, the management system should enable you to quickly locate, retrieve, and effectively display the information you want to show the jury. The system should facilitate how you perform each phase of trial from arguing motions, engaging in jury selection, making an opening statement on through to delivering closing argument. This chapter is devoted to management systems that will help you accomplish these goals, including a comprehensive trial preparation to-do list that lists everything that needs to be done throughout trial preparation.

Software is available to manage the information onslaught that can be part of your pretrial litigation. This software is designed to do the following tasks, among others:

- Receive and store the information in a database;
- Sort the information by categories, such as chronology, people, events, and issues;
- Search the database to locate and retrieve information;
- Facilitate case analysis by sorting and other analytical functions;
- Annotate documents and images in the database;
- Redact objectionable portions of a transcript;
- Manage transcripts; and
- Conduct a privilege review and produce discovery.

## Case Management and Trial Presentation Software

The following lists several case management and trial presentation software:

- **CaseMap** from CaseSoft—case management and analysis software (*http://www .casesoft.com*)
- **Visionary** from Visionary Legal Technologies—case management and trial presentation software (*http://www.visionarylegaltechnologies.com*)
- **PowerPoint** from Microsoft Corp.—trial presentation software (*http://www.office .microsoft.com*)
- **TrialDirector** from inData, Corp.—trial presentation software (*http://www .indatacorp.com*)

To truly grasp what this technology offers, you need to experience it. Most of the software mentioned offer a trial period to test the product and some offer Web seminars that walk you through the use of the software. The following overview of electronic management software provides a rudimentary guide about how the software operates and, more important, what this software can do for you in pretrial litigation and trial.

### Database

The lawyer, paralegal, and/or outside litigation support service, such as Litigation Abstract, Inc., or Visionary Legal Technologies, create the electronic management system's database. Documents and images, such as a photographic exhibit, are scanned into the system. Electronic documents, such as transcripts of depositions, e-mails, pleadings, and other electronic information, are coded, numbered, and also loaded into the system. Initially, this information may be entered into a database, such as Microsoft's Access, and later imported into case management software such as CaseMap.

### Search and Retrieval

A feature common to case management software is the ability to search for, locate, and retrieve what is needed from a mass of information. Using words, topics, or phrases, the software rapidly locates the sought information. For example, if you are planning to depose a witness, you can search for the witness's name in all the database information including prior testimony, inner-office memoranda, e-mails, correspondence, and so on.

### Case Analysis

Electronic case management software provides a case organization and analysis tool, somewhat like the fact-development diagram discussed earlier in this chapter. However, the electronic tool is more efficient and more effective.

CaseMap is an example of what computer technology can do for case organization and analysis. CaseMap provides a spreadsheet that links the essentials of a case: facts, objects (people, places), issues, questions (things the lawyer is searching for), and legal research. As the case is developed, new information, such as a new witness's name, is added to the spreadsheet. The program also has a thinking tool that permits the user to evaluate the information (a positive rating for a witness). The software links the spreadsheet's information so that with a double click all information relating to a particular person can be called up. CaseMap also exports information to TimeMap, a software program that creates timelines of events.

During case preparation, you can annotate and flag information for later retrieval. For example, Summation has a feature that allows the user to highlight, like a yellow highlighter, "Hotfacts" that can be called up later from the database. Another example of how the software can aid in analysis is Summation's transcript digest feature by which the lawyer highlights portions of the deposition transcript, types in desired annotations, and transfers the highlighted and annotated transcript excerpts to a digest for retrieval.

### Hosting the Database

Electronic case management allows the database to be accessed over the Internet. Therefore, for instance, multiple law firms working on a products liability case could share information online. Or an expert could review case information online.

### Discovery

With electronic management software such as Concordance, the lawyer can do a privilege review, redact where necessary, and then produce discovery. The software provides production numbers and tracks production of discovery. (Bates numbers, production numbers that are hand-stamped onto documents, generally have been replaced by electronic technology tools serving the same purpose.)

### Pretrial, Trial, and Settlement Presentations

For trial, alternative dispute resolution, or settlement conferences, the images and documents stored in the electronic management software may need to be transferred to trial presentation software—TrialDirector, Sanction, Visionary, TrialPro, or PowerPoint. This presentation software is used to display the images, such as photographs, documents, or portions of a deposition transcript, to the opposing side (for negotiation purposes) or to the fact finder. See Chapter 8, The Visual Trial and Today's Technology, which is devoted to visuals and the use of presentation software.

## III.  TRIAL SYSTEM

You need to be organized before trial. Eventually you will settle on a trial organizational system that works best for you. It may be primarily electronic in nature or it may be paper based, using trial notebooks, accordion files, file drawers, or some combination of these systems. Whatever trial system you adopt, to be effective, it must be orderly and enable you to store information easily and to retrieve it quickly. The following is a checklist for your trial system, whether it is electronic or paper based. If you adopt the trial notebooks approach, you could use the dividers in a three-ring binder notebook for trial subdivisions. With folders kept in an expanding file, you could label the tabs on the folders with the subdivision labels. If using an electronic system, the subdivisions could serve as folder labels on your computer.

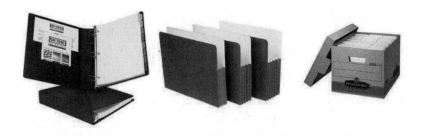

## Trial System Subdivisions

Consider these subdivisions for your trial system, whether it is electronic or paper based:

- Journal;
- Thinking;
- Case Summary Sheet;
- Motions, Orders, Stipulations, and Trial Brief;
- Jury Selection;
- Opening Statement;
- Witnesses;
- Direct Examination;
- Cross-Examination;
- Exhibits and Trial Visuals;
- Jury Instructions;
- Closing Argument;
- Pleadings;
- Discovery; and
- To-Do List.

Which trial system you adopt depends on your comfort level with the system. Some trial lawyers are comfortable with an electronic management system (others are not). Like so many trial lawyers, you probably will arrive at a system after trial and error with different methods.

### Journal

Your organizational system should include a chronological case journal of significant things that you do regarding the case. For example: "5/23/XX—

Received telephone call from plaintiff's counsel, Alfred Riggio, and scheduled a meeting on 6/28/XX at his office." However it is stored, electronically or on paper, it should be recorded with the case file, not just in a daily planner. The journal can come in handy in recalling dates and sometimes help you prove an event took place. For example, the judge might inquire into whether you conferred with opposing counsel before bringing a motion.

### Thinking File

You're commuting to work, and flash, you get an insight for your closing argument. Brilliant. In the middle of the night, you get the idea for that case theme that you have been searching for. Again, brilliant. A day or a week later, and you are struggling to remember those brilliant thoughts. Brilliant and forgotten because they were not written down.

At the outset of any case, open electronic and/or paper files for your thoughts. Then, record your brainstorms as they come to you. The notes will prove invaluable later as you plan to perform the particular pretrial or trial activity. Normally, at the outset of any case, as with any new endeavor, the mind will offer a wealth of thoughts, and those fresh ideas are some of the best. In particular, you should create thinking files on these topics:

- Case theories and themes,
- Settlement,
- Demonstrative evidence,
- Jury selection,
- Opening statement,
- Cross-examination, and
- Closing argument.

The computer is a particularly useful place to record your thoughts. As you open a case, just create an "Ideas" folder (or whatever label you wish to give the folder) and within this folder create subfolders labeled along the lines of the topics listed above. If the idea comes to you when you are at the computer, just type it in. Or, if you are away from the computer and do not use or have access to a PDA when the idea comes to you, scribble notes on whatever is available and then enter it in the computer at the next available opportunity.

### Case Summary Sheet

One more tool for your use: the Case Summary Sheet. We suggest that the basic information about the case be reduced to one piece of paper that is readily accessible during pretrial and trial. A lawyer will, in the press of a heavy caseload, eventually discover that moment when vital information slips away from the mind, such as the location of the collision or the client's name. The Case Summary Chart gives the trial lawyer a safety net.

```
┌─────────────────────────────────────────────────────────────────┐
│                        CASE SUMMARY                               │
│                                                                   │
│  CASE CAPTION:                                                    │
│  CLIENT'S NAME:                                                   │
│  OTHER PARTIES' NAME:                                             │
│  CLAIM(S) WITH DATE(S):                                           │
│  TIME(S) AND LOCATION(S):                                         │
│                                                                   │
│  THUMBNAIL CASE DESCRIPTION:                                      │
│                                                                   │
└─────────────────────────────────────────────────────────────────┘
```

### Motions, Orders, Trial Brief, Stipulations, and Pocket Briefs

*Motions, Orders, Trial Brief, and Stipulations*

If the motion has been served and filed, the trial system will contain a copy of the motion and an order if it has been ruled on. Each motion and order will be separately tabbed by subject, "Motion in limine—Bifurcation." Likewise, stipulations can be filed under a separate subdivision.

*Pocket Briefs*

A pocket brief (so-called because you figuratively keep it in your pocket until needed), is a brief on an evidentiary issue that may come up during trial that has not been served or filed. It is best to keep a pocket brief in a file so that when the time comes you can hand it to the court and opposing counsel. In the file, you will have the original that the court clerk can file, as well as copies to serve on opposing counsel and to provide the judge.

*Argument Notes*

We also prefer the technique of reducing motion arguments to outline notes and then placing those notes on the inside of a manila folder. This allows you to not only maintain eye contact with the judge and not read your argument but also appear professional and organized.

### Jury Selection

When it comes to organization, jury selection is particularly demanding if the trial lawyer is actively involved in the questioning. You do not want paper or other obstacles to your communication with prospective jurors, and yet you need to work with and manage paper.

*Jury Binder*

We prefer a separate jury selection binder that can be used for trial. The contents of the binder could include, among other things: law relevant to jury selection (statutes and court rules on challenges for cause and peremptory challenges); your agenda for jury selection; jury selection notes or questions grouped by subject areas to be asked during jury selection; good juror and bad juror profiles; list of witnesses with names, addresses, and occupations. You would include a Jury Seating Chart and a Challenges Chart, see Chapter 4, pages 74 and 75, respectively.

### Opening Statement and Closing Argument

The subparts of these two segments of trial can be organized in a similar fashion. Create one subdivision for opening statement and another for closing argument, and then create the following subsections for each.

#### *Preparing Opening and Closing*

Although some believe that trial lawyers should not write their opening statements or closing arguments because they then will tend to read instead of speak them, we disagree. Among the reasons for writing opening and closing is that the process will force the trial lawyer to select persuasive language and to carefully structure the opening and closing. Both are speeches, and speeches should be meticulously drafted. The subdivisions for opening would contain the written opening and, even more important, the brief outline with keywords that the lawyer can remove from the file or notebook and use during the opening or closing. Having only the outline during opening or closing prevents the trial lawyer from reading. Ideally, in fact, trial counsel will never look at a note but speak directly to jurors throughout his opening and closing.

### Witnesses
#### *Witness Lists*

This trial system subdivision should contain a witness list with all contact information for each witness, including name, home and business addresses, and phone numbers; relatives or other people who can be contacted to locate the witness if necessary; and an indication that the witness has been subpoenaed. Also, you should create another witness list without contact information on it. The one with contact information is most useful if it is alphabetical so you can easily locate the witness. Make the list into a document with the case caption and the title, such as "Plaintiff's List of Witnesses." This list can be provided to the judge and opposing counsel. The judge can read the list to the prospective jurors and inquire if any of them recognize the witnesses.

#### *Order of Witnesses*

While the witness list with contact information and the one given to the judge can have any order you wish, you must develop an order-of-witness list in which you will call witnesses. The most common way to arrange the order of your witnesses for your case-in-chief is to start with a strong witness and end with a strong witness and bury the weaker ones in the middle, keeping in mind the desire to present as coherent a narrative as possible.

#### *Direct Examination Outline or Questions*

We suggest writing the questions you intend to ask on direct examination. Later, you can outline, list bullet points, or keep writing the questions. Important questions, such as a question to elicit an expert's opinion, should be written out even by experienced trial lawyers. If you have written the full question, the challenge is to deliver it naturally so the direct is like an unscripted conversation. A method for preparing notes is to draw a line down the center of a page of lined paper and write the questions on the left side for direct or cross-examination. During direct, you can use the right side to jot notes of significant answers. Put notations in the margins to indicate the legal authority supporting admission of the evidence if there is any question about it. Also, in appropriate places in your notes, indicate the exhibits you wish to introduce or use to illustrate the points you need to present.

Direct examination notes can be filed in a computer, a notebook, or a folder or another storage place that can be in hand as you question the witness. We prefer to put them in a folder with fasteners (those two metal strips that stick out at the top) that go through holes at the top of the paper. You can put your questions or outline on the right side of the file and on the left side put the witness's prior statements, checklist of essential facts, and an exhibits' list for that witness. This folder is easier to work with than a bulky notebook, and you can flip the pages over the top of the folder as you finish a page.

### Prior Statements and Depositions

Depositions and witness prior statements can be stored in notebooks and/or in a computer. Either way, they must be easily accessible and retrievable if need be. Computer software enables the user to quickly locate and retrieve necessary documents. If the trial lawyer is not using computer software, prior statements can be indexed with keywords and phrases so that the lawyer can access the pertinent part of the deposition or statement when needed. Page references can be noted in the margin of the direct examination questions or outline.

### Cross-Examination Outline or Questions

The methods for storing notes for cross-examination questions are the same as those for direct examination, but the format differs. Write the title for the argument you will make at the end of the case ("Witness Is Biased"). Number each page relating to that subject. When you start a new topic, start with a new page one. Next, draw a line down the middle of the page. On the left side, write short statements of fact. The right column is available to write references to the file (such as a statement in witness's deposition or e-mail) in case the witness does not provide the desired answer and you need to promptly access your proof. Also, the right column can be used to record and highlight the witness's notable answers.

### Exhibits and Trial Visuals
#### Exhibit List

An exhibit list is the place where you keep track of action taken with your and the other side's exhibits. An exhibit list contains information about exhibits offered and the disposition of them. Were they admitted? Denied? Why? While this list can be stored in a file, notebook, or computer, we prefer an exhibit file with fasteners at the top because it is handy and can be easily carried around in the courtroom when working with exhibits.

#### The Exhibits

How you manage an exhibit naturally depends on the nature of the exhibit. The trial lawyer can store exhibits such as documents and photographs separately or in the same folder as the first witness who will sponsor the exhibits. For example, photographs could be filed in the witness's file or in a pocket in the trial notebook in the subsection for that witness. A large chart would just be brought to court. If the exhibit is a voluminous set of documents, it could be placed in a notebook with copies for opposing counsel and the judge. Electronically stored information can be easily accessed with a computer and displayed with a projector or on a monitor. As a backup in case there is a computer glitch, have the images printed on letter-size paper so it can be shown to the jurors. The printouts can be stored in the notebook or file folder. In a criminal case, prior to trial much of the prosecution's evidence is maintained in the evidence room of the investigating law enforcement agency.

### Jury Instructions
#### Proposed Jury Instructions

A file folder is a suitable place for your proposed set of jury instructions until they are served and presented to the judge. You can keep a copy of yours and the other side's set of proposed instructions either in a notebook or file folder. The jury instructions chart, as well as supportive legal authority for your proposed instructions, can be kept in either a file or your trial notebook.

### Pleadings

You will also have a subdivision for pleadings that can be located as with the other subdivisions either electronically, in file folders, or in notebooks. The pleadings—such as complaint, answer, amended pleadings, and so on—are also tabbed for easy retrieval.

### Discovery

Discovery can be organized just as the pleadings are with subdividers in either notebooks, computer folders, or file folders. We suggest subdividers for initial disclosures, interrogatories, and responses; requests for production and responses; and requests for admissions and responses.

### To-Do List

So that you do not neglect to do an essential task, have a to-do list for your case. As you complete the tasks, you can check them off. It is also important that you give due dates to the items on your list. For example: "Set deposition of Myrna Kostich by 5/19/XX."

Your to-do list generally will include two types of deadlines: self-imposed deadlines and those imposed by others, such as a judge's deadline for submission of a trial brief. When faced with an imposed drop-dead due date (judge-imposed deadlines are normally firm), you should schedule a due date far enough in advance of the final date so that if unforeseen events occur, as they will (your computer with no backup crashes), you can still make the deadline.

With experience, you will create a stock to-do list with time periods assigned for accomplishing each task. It is a good practice to set a finishing-touches date for the case and note it in your calendar. A finishing-touches date is set far enough out from trial that you still have time to complete any necessary task before trial. A month out from trial generally is a good length of time, but you may need to adjust the finishing-touches date for such factors as the complexity of the case. On the given finishing-touches date, review your to-do list and take stock of what needs to be done. Then, make plans with new completion dates to complete trial preparation. Ask other experienced lawyers in your jurisdiction if they have such a to-do list and whether you can adapt it to your use. This stock to-do list should be augmented for each new case.

---

### Comprehensive To-Do List

- **Journal**—record activities
- **Thinking notes**—note ideas for opening, closing, etc.
- **Case Summary** Sheet
- Develop **case theory and themes**
  - Draft tentative closing argument
  - Conduct a case assessment
  - Draft a trial plan outline
- **Motions**
  - Prepare motions in limine to exclude and admit evidence
  - Prepare responses to motions
- **Review the files** and if needed:
  - Amend pleadings
  - Update discovery

*continued* ▶

- **Scout the court** to determine courtroom practices, preferences, and layout
- **Witnesses** for trial
  - **Subpoena** witnesses—pay statutory witness fees and costs
  - **Keep in touch** and tell them when they will be called
- Prepare a **trial system**—electronic case management, trial notebook, and/or file folders
- **Objections**
  - Plan to make objections and have an objections list for trial
  - Anticipate and plan to meet objections
- Seek and, where appropriate, enter into **stipulations and other agreements**, such as premarking exhibits with the other side
- **Court dates**
  - Check scheduled court dates
  - Set necessary hearings
  - Move to continue if needed
- **Jury selection** preparation
  - Jury consultant
  - Jury selection binder
  - Jury seating chart
  - Jury challenges chart
  - Jury selection agenda
  - Good and bad juror profiles
  - Prepare jury selection questions
  - Juror questionnaire
  - Learn about jury pool
- Prepare **opening statement**
- Prepare **direct examinations**
  - Select witnesses to call
  - Witness preparation
  - Order of witnesses
- Prepare **cross-examinations**
- Draft and organize proposed **jury instructions**
- **Exhibits and trial visuals**
  - Gather and organize real, documentary, and demonstrative evidence
  - Consultant
  - Arrange for equipment, such as document camera, monitors, LCD projector, screen, and so on
  - Exhibits list
  - Premark exhibits
  - Backup plan for computer presentation
  - Create trial visuals for all phases of trial
  - Research evidentiary foundations and prepare pocket briefs where needed
  - Arrange with the court to display visuals such as computer slideshow or to set up a document camera
- Prepare **closing argument**
- **Prepare yourself** (mentally and so on)

# Index